THE FIRST STONES

THE FIRST STONES

PENYWYRLOD, GWERNVALE AND THE BLACK MOUNTAINS NEOLITHIC LONG CAIRNS OF SOUTH-EAST WALES

Edited by

WILLIAM BRITNELL AND ALASDAIR WHITTLE

With contributions by
Alistair J. Barclay, William Britnell, Astrid Caseldine, Lucy J.E. Cramp, Seren Griffiths, Adrian Humpage, Daniel Lewis, Samantha Neil, Charlotte O'Brien, Michael Richards, Anne Roseveare, Martin Roseveare, Elizabeth A. Walker, Alasdair Whittle, Isabel L. Wiltshire and Michael P. Wysocki

OXBOW | books
Oxford & Philadelphia

Published in the United Kingdom in 2022 by
OXBOW BOOKS
The Old Music Hall, 106–108 Cowley Road, Oxford, OX4 1JE

and in the United States by
OXBOW BOOKS
1950 Lawrence Road, Havertown, PA 19083

Paperback Edition: ISBN 978-1-78925-739-7
Digital Edition: ISBN 978-1-78925-740-3 (epub)

A CIP record for this book is available from the British Library

Library of Congress Control Number: 2022944598

Printed in the United Kingdom by Short Run Press

For a complete list of Oxbow titles, please contact:

UNITED KINGDOM
Oxbow Books
Telephone (01865) 241249
Email: oxbow@oxbowbooks.com
www.oxbowbooks.com

UNITED STATES OF AMERICA
Oxbow Books
Telephone (610) 853-9131, Fax (610) 853-9146
Email: queries@casemateacademic.com
www.casemateacademic.com/oxbow

Oxbow Books is part of the Casemate Group

Front cover: Penywyrlod long cairn and Mynydd Troed from the NW during excavation in 2016. © Future Aerial Innovations.
Back cover: Blocked entrance to Penywyrlod Chamber NE I and section through Penywyrlod Chamber NE II.

Contents

Preface

William Britnell

It is now over two centuries since the first recorded examination of one of the Black Mountains Neolithic tombs, by the eminent antiquary Sir Richard Colt Hoare and his coterie of friends at Gwernvale in 1804. To Colt Hoare, the burning question about the visible chamber at Gwernvale was a simple one: 'is it sepulchral or altaral?'. And it is also already nearly 40 years since the appearance of *Gwernvale and Penywyrlod: two Neolithic long cairns in the Black Mountains of Brecknock*, published in 1984 and presenting excavations at the former by Hubert Savory and at the latter by myself. Even since that time, the questions we have asked of these sites have expanded enormously, bolstered in recent decades by a wide variety of new analytical techniques.

The present volume attempts to summarise some of the new information and ideas that have come to light about these two Severn-Cotswold (or Cotswold-Severn) tombs and others in this small yet distinctive cluster of sites in south-east Wales, following fresh fieldwork and the opportunity for further analysis and interpretation.

The *Gwernvale and Penywyrlod* volume (now available digitally at https://doi.org/10.5284/1091095) was perhaps the first publication about megalithic sites in Wales to make use of radiocarbon dating but, even so, only a handful of determinations were available at that time. We now have over 50 dates for the Black Mountains tombs alone, which with the application of Bayesian modelling hint at dynamic processes within the early Neolithic, which we can begin to track on a century-by-century basis; the sequence potentially encompasses distinctive early foundations on new ground (possibly evidenced at Penywyrlod) and later ones overlying previously occupied sites (as at Gwernvale), arguably to maintain established tradition. Other studies, involving isotopic and lipid analyses and more rigorous analysis of human and plant remains bring us closer to an awareness of the upbringing, diet and lifeways of the communities that constructed them.

Many questions still remain, however, not least the relationship of the tombs to settlement and other types of contemporary sites such as those found in advance of the construction of the South Wales Gas Pipeline and those emerging within the neighbouring Dorstone Hill complex to the east.

Of the 15 or so sites known within the Black Mountains group one has been entirely lost and excavations at one scale or another have been undertaken at 10 others, emphasising the necessity of conservation and the fine tuning of future research in order not to jeopardise this diminishing resource.

Acknowledgements

Thanks are due to all the colleagues who have generously given their time to contribute to this volume, whose publication is grant-aided by Cadw – the historic environment service of the Welsh Government – and by the Marc Fitch Fund. The Cambrian Archaeological Association, which published the 1984 report, generously funded some of the new radiocarbon dates from Gwernvale, the remainder of which were funded privately. The analysis of human bone assemblages reported in Chapter 6 was originally funded by The Leverhulme Trust in a project led by Alasdair Whittle.

The excavations at Penywyrlod in 2015–16 were carried out for the Clwyd-Powys Archaeological Trust on behalf of Cadw. Finds and archives have been deposited with the National Museum Wales. Grateful thanks are due to the following for their help and assistance during the project: Mr Elwyn Griffiths and Mrs Elizabeth Griffiths, of Penywyrlodd, Talgarth, and to Mr Williams, tenant farmer, and Mr John Evans and Mrs Anne Evans. Will Davies, Paul Hughes, Paul Cascarini, and Alan Cornish of Cadw; Bill Stebbing and colleagues of Scan to Plan, and Dave Bush of Future Aerial Innovations; Pat Ruddock, Mann Williams; Mike Williams and colleagues of Taliesin Conservation; Martin Roseveare and colleagues of Archaeophysica (now TigerGeo); Steve Burrow and Jana Horák, of Amgueddfa Cymru – National Museum Wales; Charlotte O'Brien and colleagues of Archaeological Services, Durham University; geologist Adrian Humpage; and Jenny Britnell, Nigel Jones and colleagues of the Clwyd-Powys Archaeological Trust.

Invaluable information and advice during the production of this volume have kindly been provided by the following, in no particular order: Vicki Cummings, Colin Richards, Frances Lynch Llewellyn, Jane Kenney, Lesley McFadyen, Keith Ray, Julian Thomas, Richard Bradley, Timothy Darvill, Alison Sheridan, Tom Booth and Caroline Wilkinson. We are grateful to Richard Bradley, Vicki Cummings, Tim Darvill, Chris Scarre, Alison Sheridan and Julian Thomas for constructive criticism of earlier drafts of various parts of the volume.

Finally, Julie Gardiner and colleagues at Oxbow are to be thanked for their patience in waiting for the final delivery of text and illustrations for this volume.

Except where otherwise acknowledged, photographs in this volume are from the archives of the Clwyd-Powys Archaeological Trust and line drawings are by Bill Britnell.

List of figures

List of tables

Summary

The First Stones brings together the results of recent research on the Neolithic long cairns lying in the shadow of the Black Mountains in south-east Wales, focusing upon Penywyrlod and Gwernvale, the two best known tombs within the group, previously excavated in the 1970s.

Important results lie in both new site detail and reassessment of the wider context. Small-scale excavation, geophysical survey and geological assessment took place at Penywyrlod in 2015–16, in advance of much-needed conservation by Cadw. This and subsequent analyses and interpretation have given important new perspectives and significant further information about the distinctive external and internal architecture of the monument, and about its place in the sequence of regional development. The largest of the Welsh long cairns, around 50m long, the Penywyrlod construction probably had several chambers and an imposing dummy entrance. Chambers probably varied. The three investigated ones were quite small; they were sealed off by well-built external walling, but had probably been entered on several occasions. Another unexcavated chamber may have been much bigger, and survey suggests the existence of other chambers. Human remains had been placed in varying quantities and conditions into two of the investigated chambers, and a detailed report on those remains is presented. Radiocarbon dates suggest pre-cairn activity in the late 39th or early 38th century cal BC, part of the Neolithisation of the region probably from the 39th century cal BC onwards, and part of the wider Neolithisation in western Britain in the 40th and 39th centuries cal BC, probably principally driven by the arrival of new populations from abroad but potentially involving some involvement of the indigenous people. The imposing Penywyrlod long cairn was probably built quite early in this regional process of change, the substantial and impressive construction arguably representing land-taking and the incorporation of disparate social groupings across a relatively sparsely occupied landscape (as suggested by the results of other projects including the South Wales Gas Pipeline). The stone used for the external walling of the cairn probably comes from the local hill, Mynydd Troed, which overlooks the monument, and there is thus an intriguing relationship between cairn and landscape, seen also in other tombs in the Black Mountains group. Radiocarbon dates suggest extended and probably episodic use of the chambers for the deposition of human remains.

In turn, the research at Penywyrlod opened the opportunity to reassess the pre-monument sequence at Gwernvale and complete various investigations of its finds and features, with re-examination of both Mesolithic and Neolithic occupations, including a timber structure and midden, lithic and pottery assemblages, and cereal and other plant remains, and with a further programme of radiocarbon dating. Again, Neolithic activity at Gwernvale probably goes back to the 39th century cal BC, helping to define the character of pre-monumental activity in the region. The succession from house and midden to tomb is compared with the very similar but much earlier situations at Ascott-under-Wychwood and Hazleton North in the Cotswolds, raising intriguing questions of shared memory. The construction of the Gwernvale long cairn itself, slightly shorter and narrower than Penywyrlod but still a carefully built and impressive monument, is probably no earlier than the 36th or 35th century cal BC, so that by this date a traditional form of architecture as well as associations and memories were perhaps used to reinforce land-keeping and claims to place.

Radiocarbon dating and chronological modelling also included results and fresh date estimates for two other, much shorter, local long cairns, Pipton and Ty Isaf. These were probably built after Penywyrlod but before Gwernvale. The details of their architecture and layout help to underscore a sense of locally distinctive practice, and these monuments can be seen as part of a process of infill and consolidation of settlement at a regional scale. The human remains from Pipton and Ty Isaf are also reported in detail (with a review of the evidence for diet, trauma and lifestyles of the populations represented), collectively perhaps representing smaller social units than at Penywyrlod. That investigation has been reinforced by dietary isotopic analyses of human samples including from Penywyrlod and Ty Isaf (and three other early Neolithic tombs in the wider region). Further analyses of strontium and oxygen isotopes for lifetime mobility, principally using samples from Penywyrlod and Ty Isaf, may suggest a wider-ranging and more mobile early population and perhaps a more settled existence subsequently. Lipid analyses of pottery from the pre-cairn contexts at Gwernvale show that the sampled vessels were used predominantly for the processing of dairy products. In these varying ways, Penywyrlod, Gwernvale and other Black Mountains long cairns can be given both a settlement context and an economic setting, enhanced now by the study of the cereal and other plant remains from Gwernvale.

The First Stones makes a significant contribution to the study of tomb building, treatment of the dead, place making, the relationship of monuments to landscape, local and regional identities, connections and affiliations across southern Britain and the adjacent continent, and Neolithisation in western Britain. Viewed within the context of tombs within the Cotswold-Severn tradition as a whole, and of differences to the dolmen tradition found principally to the west, this volume leads to an appreciation of the local and regional distinctiveness of architecture and mortuary practice exhibited by the tombs in this area of south-east Wales, emerging as part of the intake and development of a significant inland area in the early centuries of the Neolithic.

1

Penywyrlod and Gwernvale Neolithic long cairns: context and history

Alasdair Whittle

Introduction

Excavations by Hubert Savory in 1972 at the then newly discovered long cairn at Penywyrlod, Talgarth, Powys, in south-east Wales (SO 151 316), showed that it is a large, stone-built trapezoidal cairn, over 50m in length, with at least four lateral chambers, and a forecourt and orthostatic portal structure at the broader end, characteristic of the Black Mountains group of Neolithic Severn-Cotswold tombs to which it belongs (Savory 1984; Fig. 1.1). Recent recording and small-scale excavations in advance of conservation work by Cadw at the monument have provided not only a wealth of significant new details about the monument but also an opportunity to review the considerable body of new information that has come to light about this major monument since the excavations in 1972.

This reassessment has been extended to include further consideration of selected aspects of the closely related monument at Gwernvale, Crickhowell, Powys (SO 211 192), another trapezoidal cairn a little under 50m in length, overlying both Mesolithic and Neolithic finds and features, and with three lateral chambers, a forecourt and an orthostatic portal structure at its broader, eastern end, which was fully excavated in 1977–78 (Britnell 1984b; Fig. 1.2).

The new work also prompts, by way of introduction, a brief but critical review of how constructions of this kind have been treated in the extensive literature that has built up over a century and more of research. In essence, that literature has tended, perhaps inevitably, to generalise about monuments of this kind, following the dominant models of the day. In so doing, it has also tended to make these creations a very familiar and taken for granted part of the Neolithic way of life in this part of Britain. The suggested reconstruction of the physical appearance of the person whose skull was found in Chamber NE II at Penywyrlod

Fig. 1.1. High-level view of the Penywyrlod long cairn in 1973 following the excavations in the previous year, showing the remains of the portal structure in the foreground. The tomb was first discovered in 1972 following the extraction of stone from the NE end of the mound. © Crown copyright: Royal Commission on the Ancient and Historical Monuments of Wales.

Fig. 1.2. A 50m stretch of the former A40 and underlying turnpike road was taken up by hand at Gwernvale in 1977, after road realignment, to reveal the northern side of the long cairn and one of a number of previously unknown chambers. The one known chamber, visible in front of the lorry, was originally covered by a capstone (described as 'a huge tablet of unhewn rock') that was removed when the site was first investigated by a party of gentlemen including Sir Richard Colt Hoare in 1804.

could be seen as an emblem of this, presenting as it does 'an unexpectedly sensitive face', which would not be out of place in a modern context (Burrow 2006, 35; 2010; Wilkinson 2010; Fig. 1.3). So beyond detailing new information about these two highly significant monuments, this report also seeks to restore and highlight what is distinctive about the context, construction and use of Penywyrlod and Gwernvale in particular, and of the Black Mountains group as a whole, seen as part of dynamic process and history rather than a static distribution, as well as to underline the remaining major gaps in our understanding of these monuments.

Dominant models: a critical review

Before 1984

An extensive literature has built up on Severn-Cotswold – or Cotswold-Severn – monuments (Fig. 1.4) over a century and more of research, going as far back as John Thurnam in the later 19th century; no less a figure than Sir Richard Colt Hoare was involved in investigations at Gwernvale in the very early nineteenth century (Briggs 1984). Successive phases of research, involving both fieldwork and assessment, have been very well documented at intervals, for example by Glyn Daniel (1950) and Tim Darvill (2004), and we have no intention of listing once again all the field activity and discussion involved. It is useful, however, to reflect on how the literature has tended to operate, as this affects how individual monuments or smaller groups of monuments come to be regarded. The variation of terminology noted above – Severn-Cotswold (Daniel 1950, 52; Savory 1984) or Cotswold-Severn (Corcoran 1969; Darvill 2004) – might seem trivial, but in fact reveals still relevant questions about generalisation and the distinctiveness of human agency.

For the purposes of reflection here, we can break recurrent themes for discussion down into five closely related aspects: the typology of monuments; their possible sources and origins; constructional detail; depositional detail, especially of human remains; and overall characterisation of the role, meaning and significance of these monuments. By the time of the 1984 reports on Penywyrlod and Gwernvale (Britnell 1984b; Savory 1984), there were well established and significant debates about all of these.

Fig. 1.3. Above: Images showing the stages involved in reconstructing the facial appearance of the skull from Penywyrlod Chamber NE II by Caroline Wilkinson for an exhibition at St Fagans National Museum of History (© Caroline Wilkinson). Below: Elwyn Griffiths, finder of the skull, visiting the exhibition (© National Museum of Wales).

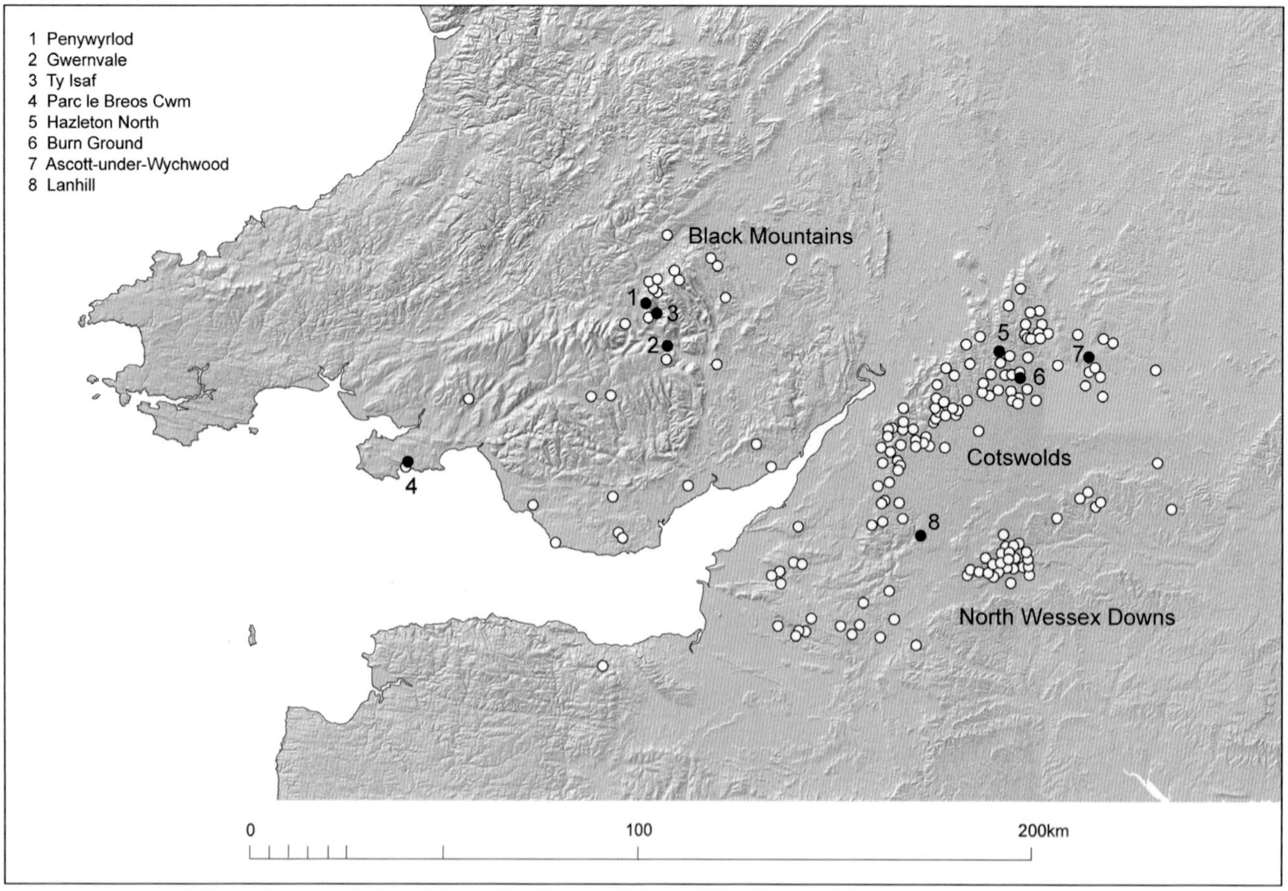

Fig. 1.4. Long barrows and long cairns within the Severn-Cotswold region (after Darvill 2004) with numbered sites mentioned in Chapter 1.

In this pre-1984 phase of research, typology and origins were both important topics. The former formed a thread started by Crawford (1925), continued among others by Daniel in papers in the 1930s (including Daniel 1939; 1941) and in his 1950 book, further elaborated by Grimes (1960) in his discussion of Burn Ground in the Cotswolds, and rounded off by Corcoran (1969; 1972). Though noting shrewdly 'some remarkable blank spaces on the map' including in Wales (Daniel 1950, 27), Daniel (1950, 95) identified five major groupings of megalithic chamber tombs, as he called them, in Britain, including the Severn-Cotswold group. Though he drew attention to the distinctive distribution of the Black Mountains 'sub-group' (Daniel 1950, 65; Fig. 1.5), he was thereby among the many scholars ready to work with generalised and widely shared characteristics. The Black Mountains sub-group itself is presented throughout his book as a unitary phenomenon, typically enough for most discussions of its kind: a point we will examine critically below. Daniel (1950, 67–70) followed Thurnam and Crawford in making a broad distinction between simple terminal chambers, transepted terminal chambers and lateral chambers, and he supported (*contra* Piggott 1937) Crawford's view of a sequence from constructions with terminal chambers to ones with lateral chambers, on the grounds that the former were more widespread including near coasts, while the latter were generally inland; the dummy portals in lateral chambered monuments implied the pre-existence of terminally chambered constructions; and continental parallels could be cited for terminally chambered examples but not for lateral chambered ones (Daniel 1950, 155). Among terminal chambers, transepted examples were seen as definitely the earliest, as already argued by Crawford and Childe (Daniel 1950, 157).

Daniel (1950, 158–9) also explored the typological similarities of monuments on the adjacent continent, including in the Retz group of western France, in the Morbihan, the lower Loire and the Vendée, with its transepted terminal chambers. It is worth quoting directly:

> It seems likely that the origin of the Severn-Cotswold group lies in a colonization of the shores of the Bristol Channel by people of the Retz group coming from the Loire area of western France (Daniel 1950, 158).

It was further suggested that six specific monuments, including Parc le Breos Cwm on the Gower, 'represent the first settlement of the Retz folk in southern Britain' (Daniel 1950, 159). This notion developed his earlier observations of close similarities in transepted chamber layouts (Daniel 1939,

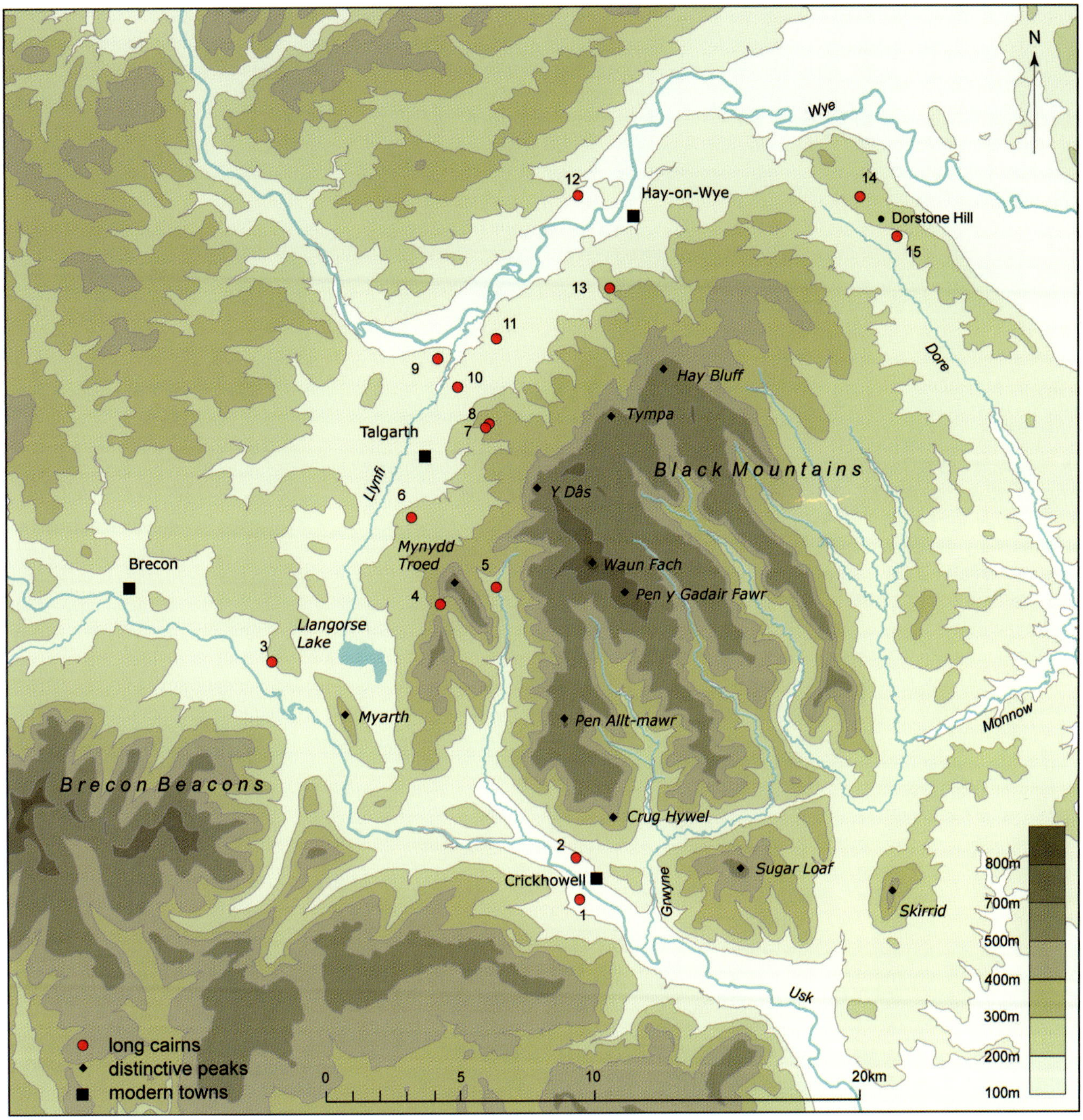

Fig. 1.5. Long cairns in the Black Mountains group: 1 Carn Goch; 2 Gwernvale; 3 Ty Illtyd; 4 Mynydd Troed; 5 Ty Isaf; 6 Penywyrlod (Talgarth); 7 Ffostyll South; 8 Ffostyll North; 9 Pipton; 10 Croesllechau; 11 Little Lodge; 12 Court Farm; 13 Penywyrlod (Llanigon); 14 Arthur's Stone; 15 Cross Lodge Farm.

163; 1941). The idea of a specific Pornic-Notgrove group was subsequently suggested and woven into a narrative of close descent and connections by Stuart Piggott (1962; see also Laporte and Tinévez 2004). That is discussed further in Chapter 12.

This kind of perspective was cast aside in many quarters from the late 1960s and 1970s onwards, with the preference in processual archaeology and subsequently for indigenist explanation and rejection of the 'invasion hypothesis'. But it is also to be found in an essay of Hubert Savory (1980a, 207), with its views of 'at least a leaven of immigrants' at the start of the Neolithic, and of common roots in western France for the two Severn-Cotswold sub-groups (Savory 1980a, 219), further detail for which was elaborated in the full discussion of Penywyrlod (Savory 1984, 30–2). Given the recent development of aDNA analysis and results demonstrating the arrival of new people at the start of the British Neolithic (Olalde *et al.* 2018; Brace *et al.* 2019), it is important to note again this older model of movement. That said, these older interpretations nearly always imply, without explicitly exploring the process further, that a given monument would represent first-generation activity by new arrivals, which in turn makes enormous assumptions about chronological development, as we shall see.

Pre-1984 discussion also gave plenty of attention to constructional details and to deposition and burial rites. There is no need to rehearse all the detail. One telling example is the debate about the external appearance of long cairns, prompted by arguments put forward by Grimes (1960) with reference to Burn Ground for the deliberate placement of extra-revetment material. How external walling was finished and treated is an important theme in the current report, and potentially an important element in forming a view of the character of monuments in the Black Mountains. It is also worth noting the thoughtful analysis by Daniel (1950, 98–115), on the basis of the then available evidence, of the processes involved in the deposition of human remains. His overall preference for successive deposition, with plenty of variation (Daniel 1950, 112), probably fits a majority of cases, including at monuments not yet excavated in 1950, but the sample of available Black Mountains deposits was so small that their potentially distinctive character was not brought out in this generalising account.

Looking back, it is perhaps odd to see so little curiosity in much of the earlier literature about the possible meaning or role of these monuments. Jacquetta Hawkes (1934, 26) and Gordon Childe (1939, 209; Darvill 2004, 35) had aired the possibility of their being the expression or symptom of the spread of a religious idea, carried by 'megalithic missionaries' (Scarre 2018, 169) but this idea appears to have gradually receded. More often, these constructions were taken simply as tombs, and discussion focused on their origins, scale, mortuary processes and development. For Keiller and Piggott (1938), contemplating Lanhill in the Cotswolds, this was a family tomb. Daniel (1950; see also Daniel 1958) used the term 'tomb' throughout his survey, and included discussion of ritual and symbolism, but signally without explicit further attention to wider meanings or roles. That soft characterisation changed radically in the 1970s with processualist ideas of territorial markers and legitimators of social position among small-scale tribal or segmentary societies, in a social evolutionary perspective (Renfrew 1973; 1976; see extensive comment by Barrett 2021). By the early 1980s, Tim Darvill (1982, 91) was writing confidently that 'the need to build tombs arose as the need to signal ownership of territory to others, and group solidarity to the builders themselves, increased'.

1984 and up to the present

In that shifting context, the main themes chosen for discussion in the 1984 report were quite varied, but within certain limits. Hubert Savory (1984, 29–35) ranged across several important aspects of the cairn architecture, but also addressed 'the place of Penywyrlod in the Severn-Cotswold group' and gave the greatest space to further, detailed and knowledgeable ruminations on the continental background. Bill Britnell (1984b) reflected on aspects of the pre-cairn sequence and the form and development of the cairn and its architecture. His conclusions were understandably cautious, but he suggested (Britnell 1984b, 149) that 'the repeated entry made to some of the chambers was presumably for the deposition, inspection, or removal or human remains'. He also noted (Britnell 1984b, 150) the effort involved in closing the monument, and took that to imply 'that the tomb held or retained symbolic functions irrespective of those concerned with burial, and possibly to be associated with territoriality'.

We do not intend to list and discuss the post-1984 literature exhaustively, but there have been several important further strands, which serve to set the scene for ongoing interpretation of Penywyrlod and Gwernvale. In his publication of the complete excavation of Hazleton long cairn in the Cotswolds, the late Alan Saville (1990, 253) was inclined to dismiss as 'generally less informative' the smaller-scale excavations of long cairns, citing Penywyrlod specifically, and to favour the use of more fully excavated monuments, Gwernvale included. He deliberately now turned his back on speculation about architectural influences or derivations, and European origins (Saville 1990, 256). Instead, he focused very much on Hazleton in its own right, seeing it as a single creation in plain sight, unadorned by either deliberate 'extra-revetment' material or deliberate blocking (Saville 1990, 256–7). For him, this was a probably short-lived monument, possibly built for use by all members of a small community, one of a series of 'small, essentially self-contained, local groups…not completely self-sufficient, not self-perpetuating without exogamous interchange' (Saville 1990, 266). Suggesting other roles besides burial and noting models of territorial markers and ancestor cults (citing Chapman 1981), he debated whether constructions such as Hazleton could have been the work of incoming colonists establishing territorial rights or of established communities 'perhaps under pressure in a situation of land or resource competition and population growth' (Saville 1990, 266). In his view, there was no clear pre-monument Neolithic in the Cotswolds, and he argued that monument construction ended when territorial identity had been established (Saville 1990, 267).

Bob Chapman (1981; see also Chapman and Randsborg 1981), as part of the social interpretation of monuments now dominant in processualist approaches, had already referred to the Saxe-Goldstein hypothesis 8, which postulated, in essence, a link between formal disposal areas, scarce resources and the existence of corporate descent groups. That was critically reviewed by Ian Morris (1991; cf. Parker Pearson 1999) and found to be often but not universally true.

Another, even wider-ranging review found, however, that the dominant processualist preference for social interpretations of mortuary practices was not fully supported by the comparative ethnographic evidence, which suggested broadly that 'philosophical-religious beliefs' were as likely to determine and structure mortuary activity as aspects of social organisation (Carr 1995).

From that perspective, Christopher Tilley's book (1994), *A phenomenology of landscape*, was extremely innovative in concentrating on the experience of monument builders and users. Though using the term 'small-scale societies' (Tilley 1994, ch. 2), and thus with one eye on the social context, the general argument was centred on the 'symbolic, ancestral and temporal significance of the landscape' (Tilley 1994, 67) (Fig. 1.6). One of three important case studies used the Black Mountains group (Tilley 1994, ch. 4). The successive deposition and subsequent rearrangement of ancestral remains were noted, as well as possible evidence for 'feasting cycles' in the form of animal bone depositions in chambers and forecourts (Tilley 1994, 142). The case study concluded that here there were distinctive, often monumental and quite massive monuments, 'designed to make an indelible and permanent impact on the landscape' (Tilley 1994, 142). 'The monuments draw out and emphasize important features of the landscape: the axes of the river valleys and prominent spurs, paths of movement and prominent landmarks whose ancestral significance had already been established during the Mesolithic' (Tilley 1994, 142). There are strong hints of a sacred landscape and a 'sacred ritual space' in the domain of monument chambers (Tilley 1994, 136, 140), the placement of the bones of the ancestral dead sedimenting them 'into the land' (Tilley 1994, 140).

It is also worth reflecting on what is not covered by Tilley. Individual sites are of course cited and discussed, but what appears to matter is the group as a whole, embracing too an inner or central core group of monuments, which includes Penywyrlod (Tilley 1994, 134). There is no further or wider discussion of the times and places in which this all took place, with no specific reference to the outside, beyond a general contrast to the preceding case study of south-west Wales, or to chronology or the duration of use, nor any further discussion of the social setting in which this striking activity took place.

This significant statement provoked further comment, insight and refinement. Vicki Cummings and colleagues (Cummings *et al.* 2002) made further shrewd observations

Fig. 1.6. Aerial view of Mynydd Troed and the northern escarpment of the Black Mountains from the NW. The Penywyrlod monument, which lies just out of view in the foreground, appears to be orientated towards the distinctive outline of the hill. © Clwyd-Powys Archaeological Trust.

of the landscape settings of the Black Mountains group, emphasising especially an apparent asymmetry or sidedness, created or enabled by the positioning of the monuments' long axes, which opened views out on to or up to contrasting aspects of the surrounding landscape. This seems to have been distinctive within the repertoire of the wider landscape settings of related monuments in Wales as a whole (summarised in Cummings and Whittle 2004). Perhaps some of the detail in this approach and in that of Tilley can be questioned, but the critiques in question (*e.g.* Fleming 1999; 2005) have served in our view unduly to dampen this promising line of enquiry into the then less familiar ground of symbolism and experience. A more pertinent reflection could now be that the challenge of combining social dimensions and what Carr (1995) called philosophical-religious beliefs, and integrating both into specific historical narratives, remains to be met in detail.

That is well illustrated by otherwise powerful characterisations of monument building and use by both Frances Lynch (2000) and Tim Darvill (2004). Frances Lynch recognised that the deposition of human bone in the 'great stone tombs' of western Europe might have been only part of their 'religious role' (F. Lynch 2000, 63, 64), and allowed for wider dimensions to be considered; monuments have been interpreted as 'the product of anxiety about continued fertility of land, animals and human groups arising from the shift to an active responsibility for food production' (F. Lynch 2000, 63). But there is also consideration of monuments as a 'symbol of desired permanence to the community, a visible link with the ancestors and a guarantor of legitimacy' (F. Lynch 2000, 64) and of their social role, 'great communal projects' but perhaps ones steered by figures of authority, using religion and ritual knowledge, in a conservative 'system of control which did not need force because fear of the displeasure of the gods and ancestors would be a more effective restraint' (F. Lynch 2000, 77, 78). The Breconshire tombs were underlined as a clear regional variant, and 'though each is distinct, their very eccentricity is a unifying factor' (F. Lynch 2000, 69). That is an important insight, but the sense of the architectural and depositional particular is never fully linked with the wide-ranging general interpretations noted above, to give an integrated, detailed and local narrative.

Fig. 1.7. On-site discussions at Gwernvale in 1976: (left to right) W.F. Grimes (excavator of Ty Isaf), Bill Britnell, Dai Morgan Evans, Don Benson (excavator of Ascott-under-Wychwood), and Chris Musson. Chamber 1 is visible to the left with the road wall beyond, viewed before the course of the A40 was moved to the south of the monument. Other visits by excavators of megaliths were made by Frances Lynch, Gabriel Cooney, Richard Atkinson and Stuart Piggott (following lunch at the Walnut Tree, Llanddewi Ysgyryd) and Alan Saville, actively planning the Hazleton campaign, which began in 1979.

Likewise, the authoritative and comprehensive survey by Tim Darvill (2004, 11, 44) of the whole gamut of Cotswold-Severn long cairns set out to provide an overtly social perspective, while recognising the diversity of particular though inter-linked communities. Possible chronological patterns were clearly articulated on a scale of centuries, through informal inspection of radiocarbon dates and associated material culture, really for the first time in the whole literature up to that point; principal development from *c.* 3800 cal BC onwards was proposed (Darvill 2004, 66), with suggested possible earlier forms of monument perhaps preceding that horizon, including rotundas. A mass of detail is considered, to which this introduction can hardly do credit, but beyond that there is a clear vision of context and social role, with some but less attention also given to accompanying worldviews. Context is discussed in terms of 'pressures connected with identity and ownership that required bold statements to be affixed to the landscape' (Darvill 2004, 79). The resulting monumental constructions are seen as 'put together by small-scale autonomous groups' (Darvill 2004, 89), in 'a pattern of numerous widely distributed, small-scale, biologically viable communities, each with their own long barrow serving in part at least as a family vault' (Darvill 2004, 165). An unusually explicit and full list of possible associations and connotations is given, which is worth quoting in full:

> …key aspects of life and death: creation myths; views of the world and the place of people in it; accepted patterns of social order; community identity; age and gender structures; the passage of time; cycles of life; the origins of the cosmos; and perhaps some apparatus to cope with the end of the world as they knew it (Darvill 2004, 132).

Nonetheless, though these dimensions are raised as valid questions, the main emphasis remains on social perspectives. Nor does the synthetic and selective format allow sufficient space for the distinctiveness of practices in the Black Mountains group to be underlined (in contrast to the treatment in F. Lynch 2000), or the possibility of a distinctive local setting and sequence to be explored. In the end, a rather general account and model win out, understandably enough in the light of the very wide scope of the synthesis.

Shortly after this major synthesis, the application of formal chronological modelling in a Bayesian framework enabled much more precise estimates of timing, duration and tempo to be achieved, first for a small sample of long barrows and cairns, but including Hazleton and Ascott-under-Wychwood in the Cotswolds (Bayliss and Whittle 2007; Benson and Whittle 2007), and subsequently for a much bigger sample of causewayed enclosures across southern Britain as a whole, along with provisional modelling of the wider early Neolithic context (Whittle *et al.* 2011). That work indicated that the first Neolithic activity – 'things and practices', as *Gathering Time* put it – was probably time-progressive, first appearing in the south-east in the 41st century cal BC and spreading at first gradually but then in accelerating fashion to the west and north, such that the first activity in the Cotswolds was estimated to belong probably to the 40th century cal BC, and in south Wales probably to the end of the 38th century cal BC (Whittle *et al.* 2011, fig. 14.54). Formal modelling also suggested that long cairns and barrows probably began to be constructed and used in the 38th century cal BC. Earlier constructions are few and far between, but probably including Coldrum in Kent (Wysocki *et al.* 2013); the position of other candidates including rotundas in the Cotswolds and the 'banana barrow' at Crickley Hill remains uncertain.

Modelled estimates suggest recurrently a duration of primary use in the order of probably one to two generations, though Ascott-under-Wychwood was probably in primary use for three to five generations. Causewayed enclosures were probably introduced from east to west across southern Britain from the late 38th century cal BC onwards. Despite recent discoveries, their distribution in southern Wales has so far appeared much less dense than in many parts of southern England (Whittle *et al.* 2011, ch. 11; 2022), though the new finding of an enclosure with a single segmented ditch at Dorstone Hill, Herefordshire (Ray and Thomas 2018; Overton *et al.* 2022) brings a further example, and now within the eastern shadow of the Black Mountains. Some enclosures across southern Britain show spans of primary use of up to three centuries, but others were much more short-lived; the phenomenon as a whole, in terms of new constructions, was also probably relatively short-lived, enclosures in their turn starting to be replaced by cursus monuments from the 36th century cal BC onwards. The sequence thus provisionally modelled (and revised in Whittle *et al.* 2022) appears to indicate an accelerating tempo of change overall (Whittle *et al.* 2011, 833–47). The dating available for Black Mountains monuments, including Penywyrlod and Gwernvale, modelled by Seren Griffiths in Chapter 4 (and see Whittle *et al.* 2011, ch. 11), fits well enough into this now more specifically defined context, though it is still imprecise at the local level.

Subsequent accounts have been informed by that more precise chronology (J. Thomas 2013; Cummings 2017; Ray and Thomas 2018; Harris 2021). Julian Thomas (2013, 322) proposed that timber halls 'brought into being a bounded human group who claimed affiliation to the community and the building, corporate ownership of a body of wealth, and probably real or fictive descent from a group of ancestors', and argued that tombs were closely aligned to halls in terms of affiliation and memory; he further importantly asserted (J. Thomas 2013, 329) that barrows and megalithic tombs were not the territorial markers of *existing* social groups but commemorated their *founding*. (The evidence for successive depositions and openings and closings of chambers is not discussed.) Underlying this view is once more a general social interpretation, on the lines that 'corporate wealth and shared identity now needed to be passed between generations, and the existence of durable architectural spaces and shared collective traditions, transmissible histories, and social memories made this possible' (J. Thomas 2013, 352). Individual monuments from the Black Mountains are discussed in some detail, including Gwernvale (J. Thomas 2013, 240–2), but not the regional group as a whole.

Vicki Cummings (2017, 89–90) envisaged special social circumstances leading to the construction and use of many monuments, at moments of conflict or social negotiation, producing short bursts of activity (followed by periods of inactivity). More explicitly than many other authors, she has made reference to possible beliefs in the separation of the spirit from the body and in an afterlife, which would have required rituals of separation (Cummings 2017, 94). Megalithic monuments served as places to engage with the dead, either founders or ancestors (Cummings 2017, 108–9). There is specific reference to the Black Mountains practice of assembling bodies from the parts of multiple persons (Cummings 2017, 106), but again no room is found for detailed discussion of the group or its sequence as a whole.

In a wide review, Keith Ray and Julian Thomas (2018, 113, 342) have proposed the existence in the early Neolithic of 'invested lineages', representative of a new kind of community, 'entities capable of owning and disposing of wealth', and have repeated the arguments for new communities at some barrows and tombs 'being brought into being through the creation of a group of founding ancestors to whom the living group could claim filiation' (Ray and Thomas 2018, 220). A contrast is explicitly drawn between the size of the groups involved at tombs and the much larger social scale of an enclosure such as Hambledon Hill (Ray and Thomas 2018; cf. Shennan 2018, 101–2). Individual monuments including Penywyrlod, Gwernvale and Ty Isaf are cited, along with the newly excavated enclosure at Dorstone, but the Black Mountains group of long cairns is not considered as such. Neither Penywyrlod nor Gwernvale, nor the Black

Fig. 1.8. On-site discussions at Penywyrlod in 2015: Jenny Britnell meeting (left to right) John and Ann Evans and Elwyn and Elizabeth Griffiths, who were all involved in the discovery and reporting of the monument in the 1970s. Other visitors that year included Alasdair Whittle, and Keith Ray and Julian Thomas during their excavations at Dorstone and prior to the start of their excavations at Arthur's Stone in 2021.

Mountains group, are specifically mentioned by Oliver Harris (2021), but his book highlights changing approaches to the interpretation of human and other kinds of agency, through discussion of bodies and architecture in particular; we will come back to these themes in the discussion presented in Chapter 12.

Finally, new aDNA analysis has recently been published of a large sample of the people deposited within the Hazleton long cairn (Fowler *et al.* 2021). This strongly indicates the existence of a patriline or male-dominated descent group, probably over five generations, in a 37th-century cal BC context in the Cotswolds. The implications of this for our understanding of Penywyrlod and Gwernvale will be followed in Chapter 12. It should be noted that insufficient aDNA was preserved in the human bone of monuments in the Black Mountains group for any comparable analysis to take place (Thomas Booth, *pers. comm.*, 2021).

Trends and gaps

The review given above serves to show, even in its deliberately brief form, how interpretive approaches and ideas have waxed and waned. We could note first the way in which the idea of monument-building incomers has largely fallen by the wayside in the more recent literature, though the recent aDNA research demonstrates the reality of substantial new population at the start of the Neolithic in Britain (Olalde *et al.* 2018; Brace *et al.* 2019). That probability in turn has to be accommodated within the newly available more precise chronology for the emergence, region by region, of new Neolithic practices across southern Britain and beyond. There has been a tendency for social interpretations – many of them in themselves attractive and plausible – to dominate discussion, with less emphasis on what Christopher Carr (1995) called philosophical-religious beliefs. There has been an understandable tendency, given both the wealth of information built up from well over a century of research, to generalise about this kind of monument building, at a variety of scales: that of Cotswold-Severn or Severn-Cotswold tombs as a whole (the terminological niggle revealing a more fundamental uncertainty about scale); that of Wales as a whole; and of the Black Mountains group as a whole. The distinctiveness of the Black Mountains distribution and practices has long been recognised, but over and over again the group has been treated as a ready-formed whole. So after presenting the new information about Penywyrlod and Gwernvale specifically, made possible by recent fieldwork, observations and analyses, we will come back in the Discussion to the further perspectives that open up when we give even more attention to distinctive local agency in a distinctive regional context and temporal setting, including varying scenarios for the unfolding of the Black Mountains regional sequence.

2

Penywyrlod Neolithic long cairn revisited

William Britnell, with contributions by Adrian Humpage, Martin Roseveare, Anne Roseveare, Daniel Lewis and Charlotte O'Brien

Introduction

As already set out in Chapter 1, the long cairn at Penywyrlod, Talgarth, Powys, in south-east Wales, is a large, stone-built trapezoidal cairn, over 50m in length, with at least four lateral chambers, and a forecourt and orthostatic portal structure at the broader end, characteristic of the distinctive Black Mountains cluster of Neolithic Severn-Cotswold tombs (Savory 1984). Adding to the knowledge gained by the excavations of Hubert Savory, further details of the monument came to light as a result of recording and key-hole excavation led by the author in 2015–16, in advance of important conservation work by Cadw, described more fully in an appendix to this volume. In turn, this process has enabled renewed interrogation and reinterpretation of many aspects of the monument, in the light of the considerable body of research that has been undertaken on Severn-Cotswold tombs since the original publication. This chapter presents these findings, which are further discussed in Chapter 12.

The cairn is orientated approximately NW–SE. It lies at an elevation of 255m on a promontory of land that rises towards the SE in the direction of the prominent summit of Mynydd Troed (Figs 2.1–2.3). It has extensive views over the north escarpment of the Black Mountains to the E and SE, the Wye valley to the N, the Llynfi valley to the W, and has more distant views of the Brecon Beacons to the SW.

The name of the cairn, Penywyrlod (pronounced 'Pen-er-whirl-odd'), is taken from the name of Penywyrlodd Farm on whose land it lies, which has the Welsh meaning 'top of the meadow'. It is sometimes referred to as Penywyrlod (Talgarth) after the nearest village, to distinguish it from a second long cairn of the same name in the Black Mountains area, referred to as Penywyrlod (Llanigon), after the name of a village about 11km to the NE.

It is important to stress from the outset that on the available evidence Penywyrlod was constructed and used from early in the local monument sequence, probably in the 38th century cal BC. Radiocarbon dates are given in this chapter and modelled by Seren Griffiths in Chapter 4. That chronological position and the character of many distinctive features noted below set up the motif of the 'first stones', to be discussed through this chapter and the following one on Gwernvale, and further in Chapter 12. Whether Penywyrlod was the earliest construction of its kind in the area is of course unknown, and how its date compares to that of timber constructions at Dorstone, Herefordshire, for example, immediately to the E of the Black Mountains (Ray and Thomas 2018; 2020; Overton *et al.* 2021), is noted below and discussed further in Chapters 4 and 12.

Summary of excavations and recording in the 1970s

The excavations in 1972 were undertaken in the same year as the discovery of the long cairn as a consequence of stone extraction (Figs 2.4–2.6; Savory 1973; 1984, 13). Only limited areas of the monument were examined, including the inner side of the portal structure, part of the SW hornwork of the forecourt, the partially destroyed Chamber NE I, the partially disturbed Chamber NE II, the passage of Chamber NE III, and part of the NW tail (Fig. 2.7). The capstone and supporting uprights of a fourth chamber, called the 'Main Chamber', were identified in the quarried face of the cairn. Inner and outer drystone revetment walls characteristic of Severn-Cotswold tombs were identified in a number of places. A cross-wall was subsequently recorded in 1974 following a fall of cairn material at the rear of Chamber NE II (Fig. 2.27, bottom right). A reasonably intact assemblage of human and animal skeletal remains was recovered from

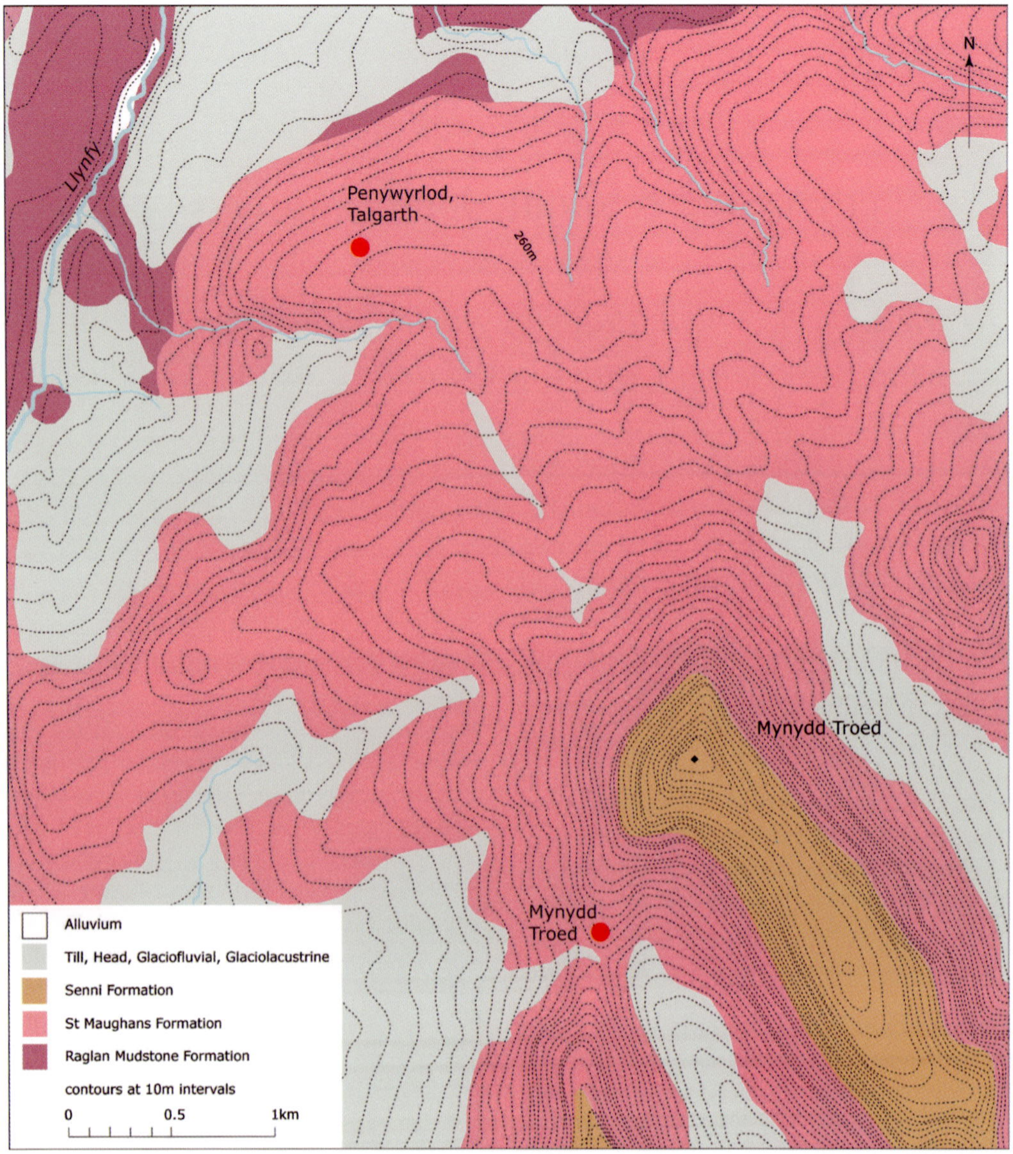

Fig. 2.1. Penywyrlod: the location of the long cairn in relation to topography, bedrock and superficial geology (simplified from British Geological Survey 1:50,000 map sheet 214, Talgarth). The Senni Formation, St Maughans Formation and Raglan Formation form part of the Mudstone Formation and Lower Old Red Sandstone stratification.

Chamber NE II and a partial sample of skeletal material was recovered from Chamber NE III, but only slight remains (described as 'a few small scraps of bone, including a human molar tooth') were found within Chamber NE I. A small cist containing human remains was found to have been inserted into the NE hornwork. A single radiocarbon date (HAR-674) was obtained from a mixture of human skeletal material from Chamber NE II (see Table 4.1 for details of this and subsequent dates from the site). Finds included a possible microlith from buried soil below the cairn, sherds of pottery below cairn collapse outside Chamber NE III (some probably belonging to a hemispherical bowl) and also sherds of pottery and two stone discs near the tail of the cairn (Savory 1984, 24–8). The tip of a leaf-shaped flint arrowhead was found in Chamber NE II (Savory 1984, fig. 10, no. 1).

Subsequent studies of the site and its finds

The site has been included in a number of studies since the original publication, notably concerning its landscape context (Tilley 1994; Nash 1997; Cummings and Whittle 2004), reassessments of the human (Wysocki and Whittle 2000; Schulting and Wysocki 2005) and animal remains (Thomas and McFadyen 2010), additional radiocarbon dating (presented summarily in Bayliss *et al.* 2011a), and isotopic analysis of human remains (Neil *et al.* 2017; 2020). As noted in Chapter 1 (see Fig. 1.3), facial reconstruction of a complete skull from Chamber NE II has been attempted

Fig. 2.2. Penywyrlod: the long cairn from the air from the NW during excavation in 2016, with Mynydd Troed in the background. © Future Aerial Innovations.

Fig. 2.3. Penywyrlod: the long cairn from the NW in 2015, with Mynydd Troed in the distance.

Fig. 2.4. Penywyrlod: aerial view from the NE in 2003, clearly showing the impact of stone extraction in the 1970s. © Crown copyright: Royal Commission on the Ancient and Historical Monuments of Wales.

Fig. 2.5. Penywyrlod: entrance to Chamber NE III during excavation in 1972, viewed from the N (scale divisions in feet).

Fig. 2.6. Penywyrlod: NW terminal of the long cairn during excavation in 1972, viewed from the N (scale divisions in feet).

(Burrow 2006, 35; 2010; Wilkinson 2010; Redknap 2002, 42). A perforated animal bone from the entrance passage of Chamber NE III, considered to be a possible musical instrument (Megaw 1984), has been cited in a number of publications (Burrow 2003, 81; Darvill 2004, 136; Wyatt 2009, 12) but there is continuing uncertainty about whether or not it was deliberately fashioned; a replica made as part of the Festival of British Archaeology in 2009 evidently proved difficult to play (Burrow 2009). More recent analysis of the sherds of pottery found outside the entrance to Chamber NE III suggests that they belong to two vessels (Peterson 2003, 140); one, a rim sherd probably from a hemispherical bowl (Savory 1984, fig. 10, no. 7) is made of clay which includes fragments of laminar shell from a coastal source, while the other is made of clay which includes locally available stone and grog.

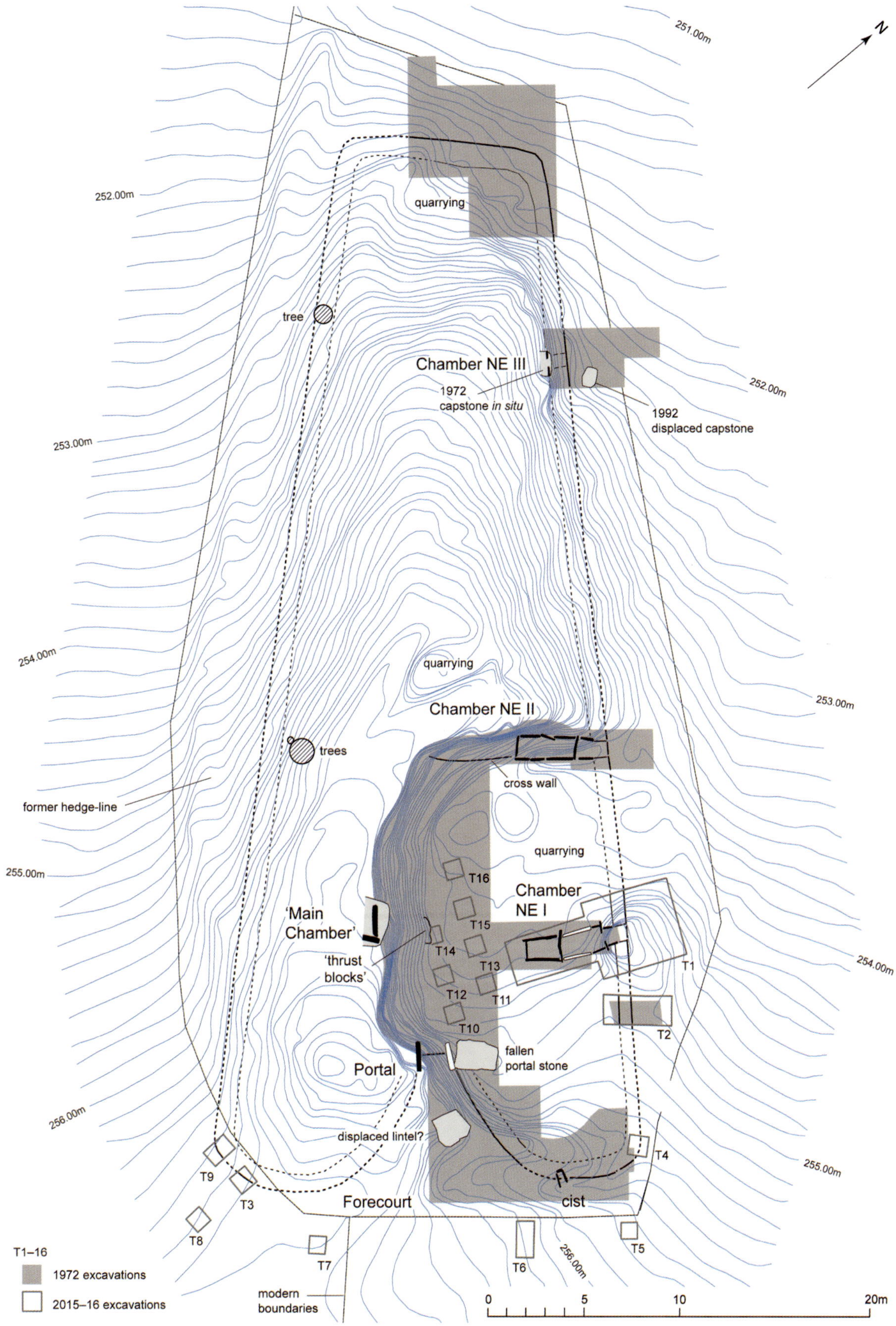

Fig. 2.7. Penywyrlod: revised plan of the long cairn based on Hubert Savory's published plan (1984), topographical survey in 1991 (Britnell 1992), and the excavations in 2015–16 reported upon here.

More recent survey work at Penywyrlod

The revised plan of the long cairn in Figure 2.7 is based on the published plan of Savory's excavations, an EDM survey of the monument in 1991 (Britnell 1992), geophysical survey in 2015 (Roseveare and Roseveare 2015) and the excavations in 2015–16 reported below. A number of other surveys have been undertaken that are not reported here, including geophysical and terrestrial laser scanning of the monument by TerraDat UK Ltd in 2010 (TerraDat 2010), terrestrial laser scanning and complementary multi-angled rectified photography of the exposed faces of the long cairn by the Royal Commission on the Ancient and Historical Monuments of Wales in 2013, and terrestrial and aerial laser scanning by Scale to Plan in 2016.

Geophysical survey of the long cairn and its environs

Martin Roseveare, Anne Roseveare and Daniel Lewis

Geophysical survey of the western half of the long cairn and its environs was undertaken by Archaeophysica (now TigerGeo) in conjunction with the recent excavation and conservation work.

Geophysical survey of the western half of the long cairn in 2014, involving electrical resistance tomography (ERT), with probe spacing at 0.5m intervals along lines 1.0m apart (Fig. 2.8; Roseveare and Roseveare 2015). This revealed a distinctive pattern of regular and slightly curving banding to either side of the long axis (Figs 2.9–2.10), which hints at the presence of two or three additional lateral chambers and associated structural units within the cairn. High resistivity regions mark air-filled voids and/or areas of uniform stone such as orthostats and lintels, each of which are associated with ribs of lower resistivity (though still much more resistive than the mound matrix), which possibly represent cross-walls.

The positions of the anomalies are likely to be reasonably accurate but the suggested dimensions of possible features are only indicative (Fig. 2.10). Anomalies 7 and 12 are almost adjacent on the N side of the long cairn but determining whether they are physically linked is beyond the resolution of the model. They correspond with Chamber NE III recorded in 1972 and suggest that this chamber

Fig. 2.8. Penywyrlod: electrical resistance tomography (ERT) of the NW end of the long cairn in 2014. Photograph: Rob Fry, Archaeophysica (now TigerGeo).

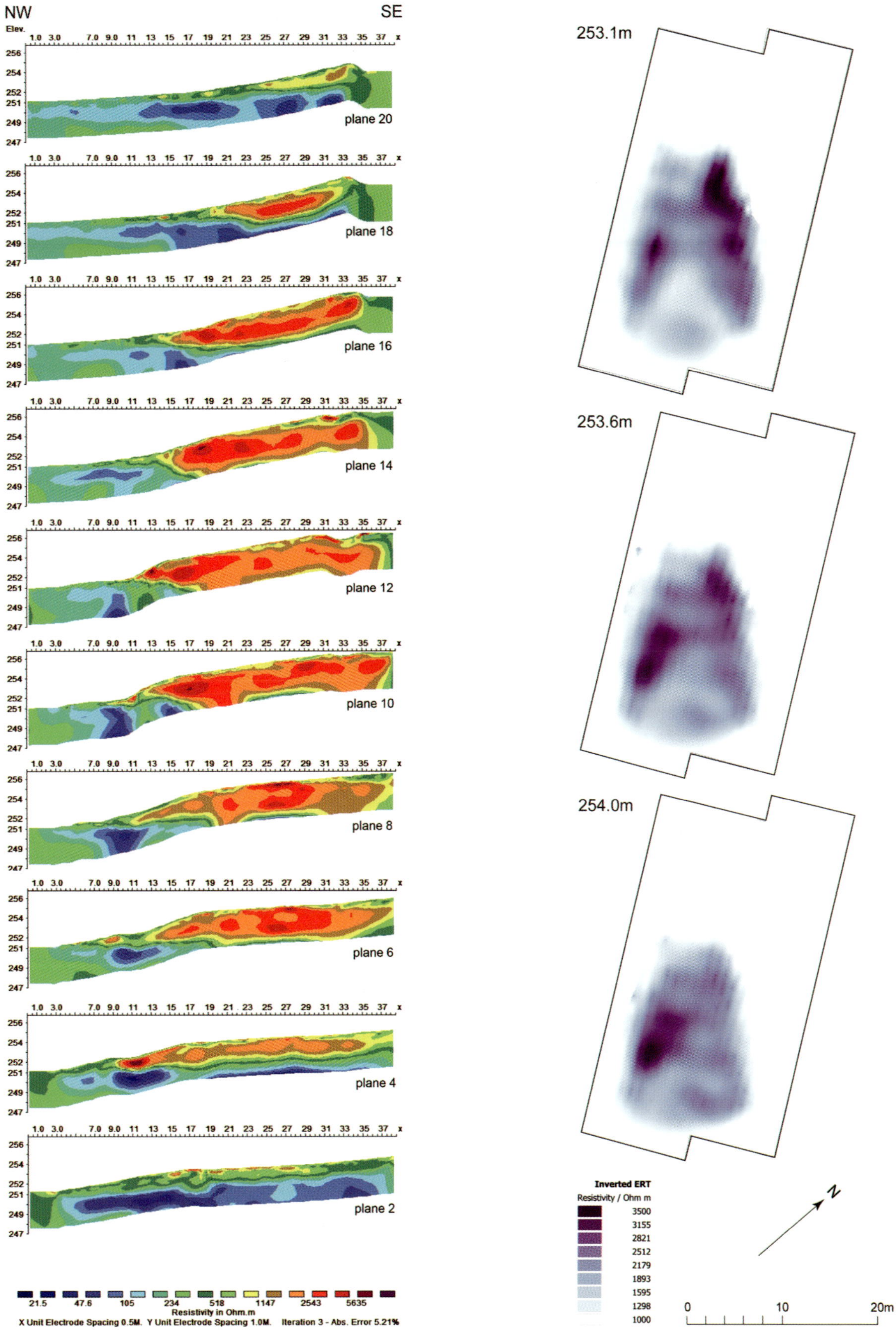

Fig. 2.9. Penywyrlod: results of electrical resistance tomography (ERT) of the NW end of the long cairn in 2014 by Archaeophysica (now TigerGeo). Left: selected vertical slices. Right: selected horizontal slices (see location on Fig. 2.10).

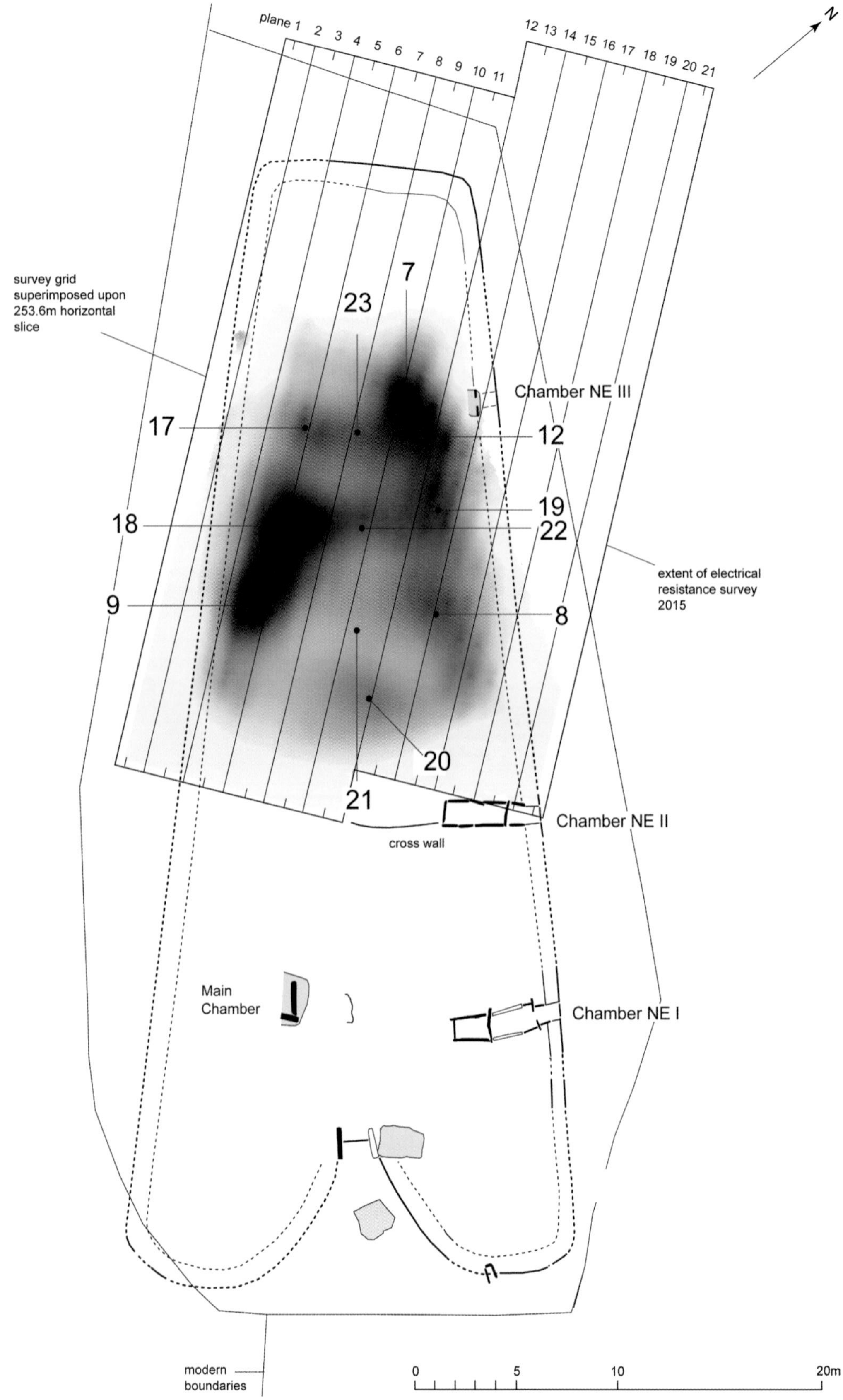

Fig. 2.10. Penywyrlod: interpretation of the geophysical survey of the NW end of the long cairn based on results of electrical resistance tomography (ERT) in 2014 by Archaeophysica (now TigerGeo).

might be L- or T-shaped like those known at Gwernvale, Pipton and Ty Isaf in the Black Mountains (see Fig. 2.30). The anomalies are between about 2.3–3.7m wide and up to 1.8m high and extend up to 6.2m from the side of the cairn. The lower resistance anomalies 23 and 17, which run across the mound from anomaly 12 are up to 1.2m wide and no more than 0.6m high and may represent a slightly curving cross-wall like that recorded in 1972 from the rear of Chamber NE II (Fig. 2.27, bottom right).

A similar pattern is represented by anomalies 18/22/19 and 9/21/8, which form bands running across the mound to the SE. The high resistance anomalies 18 and 9 on the S side of the mound are respectively 2.0m and 3.2m wide, 4.2m and 5.8m long, and 1.6m and 1.7m high and appear to represent additional chambers. Anomaly 19 on the N side of the mound seems to be about 2.5m wide and about 1.2m high. It is more poorly defined but may represent a chamber paired with the apparent chamber represented by anomaly 18, like the paired Chambers 2 and 3 at Gwernvale and Chambers I and II at Ty Isaf. Alternatively, it may represent a continuation of anomaly 22, which appears to represent a cross-wall like anomaly 23. Anomaly 8 is less distinct than some of the other examples and has a height of no greater than 0.6m and looks less like a chamber than a continuation of the high resistivity band-like structure 21, which together seem likely to represent a further cross-wall paired with 9. Anomaly 20 is about 0.6m high and 1.5m wide. It is less obvious than some of the others and may represent a cross-wall running halfway across the cairn from its N side.

A number of anomalies were detected below or to the sides of the mound whose interpretation is more speculative, but which might represent ancient infilled quarrying on the SW, W and NW sides of the mound (Roseveare and Roseveare 2015, 8; not shown on plan here).

In summary, the ERT survey has successfully revealed that the mound is not homogenous and that it contains discrete regions that may be regarded as voided, even if the stratigraphic detail is unclear due to the technical limitations of ERT and the specifics of the electrode array that was used. The presence of moisture between the stones of the mound has been critical and the same survey undertaken after a prolonged dry spell would probably be less successful. The monument has proved beneficial in displaying the utility of ERT for investigating stone mounds and further ERT survey may well produce more information at this site.

A magnetometer survey of an area of approximately 8ha in the fields to either side of the long cairn was undertaken in 2015 (Roseveare and Lewis 2015). Magnetic contrast is quite low and although the survey did not identify any previously unknown elements of the long cairn or features directly related to it, some buried structures have been identified that are thought to be associated with the existing agricultural landscape and some others preceding it (Figs 2.11–2.12).

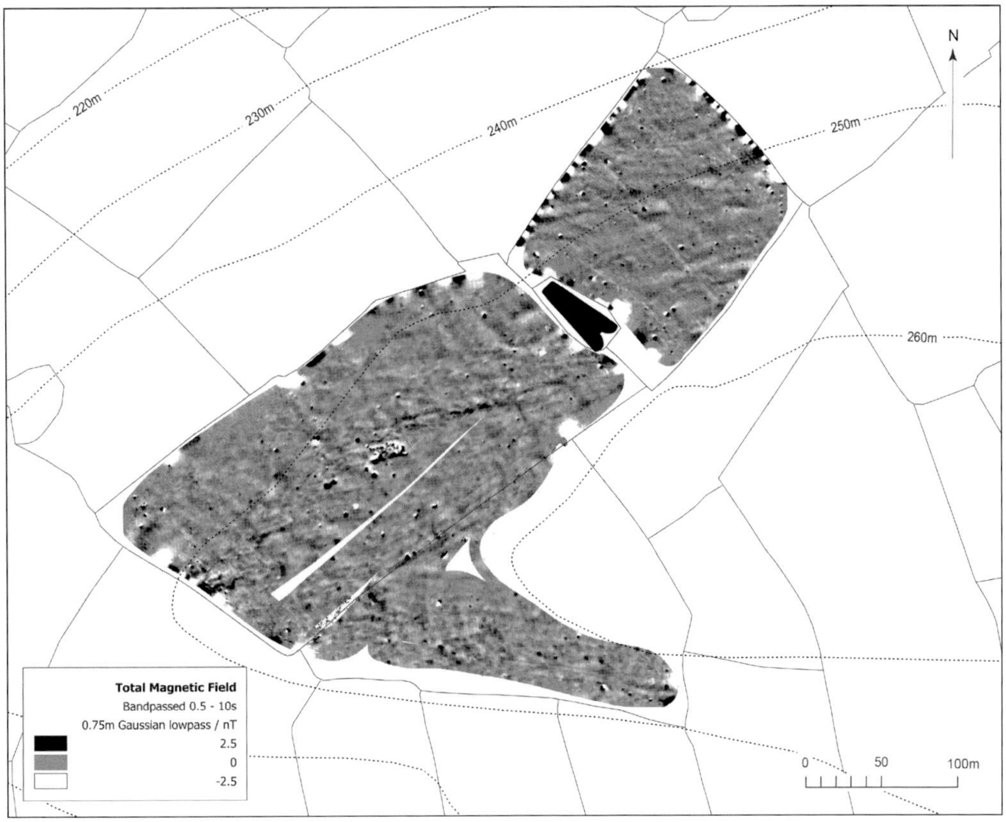

Fig. 2.11. Penywyrlod: geophysical survey of the environs of the long cairn in 2015 by Archaeophysica (now TigerGeo).

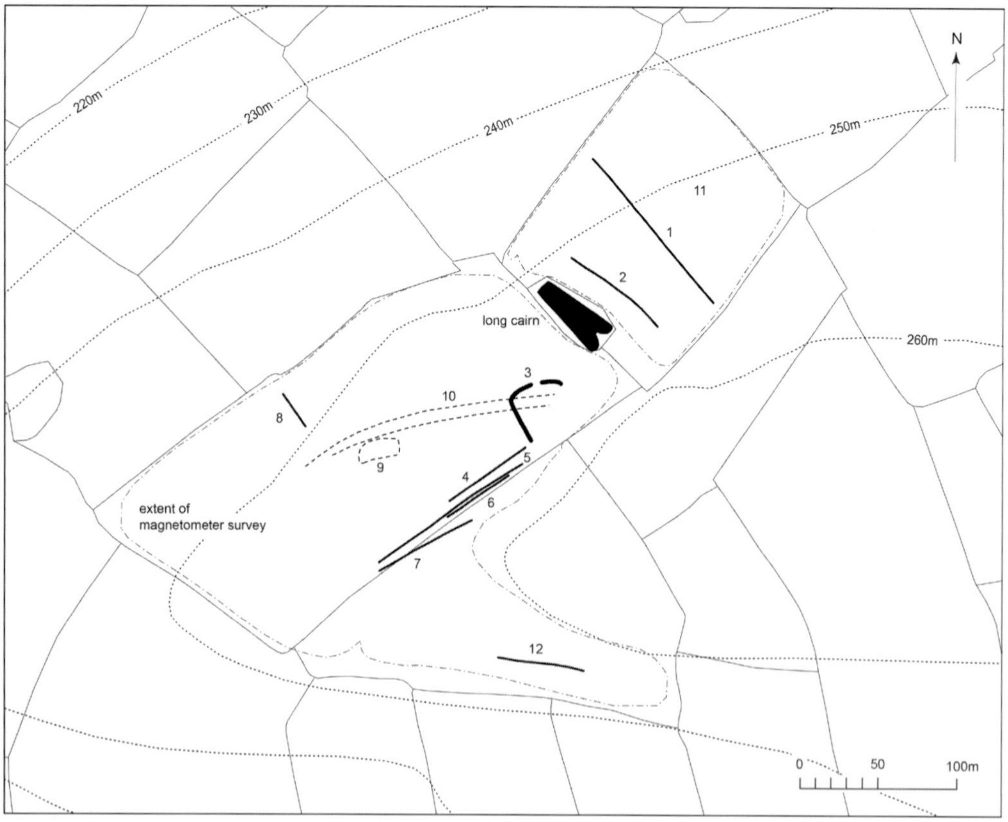

Fig. 2.12. Penywyrlod: interpretation of the geophysical survey of the environs of the long cairn (see text for key to numbered anomalies).

There is a significant amount of geological character in the data. In general the geological component of the surface magnetic field is fairly uniform (as for example at anomaly 11) but punctuated throughout by small and normally discrete enhanced intensity anomalies. These seem likely to originate in variations in soil depth or the possible presence of glacial erratics. There are several weak ENE–WSW trends that reflect the bedding of the rock, which may be augmented by outcrop quarrying, possibly indicating the source of material used to build the long cairn. Anomaly 10 (Fig. 2.12), a high magnetic anomaly extending for between 40–200m to the S of the long cairn and corresponding to a bed of harder sandstone, may suggest the sites of linear quarries, which it is speculatively conjectured might represent firesetting. Firesetting is known in Neolithic contexts elsewhere in Wales (Timberlake 1990; Edmonds 1999, 44) but as yet there is no evidence from stones observed *in situ* within the long cairn that firesetting was employed as a quarrying technique, though blackened stones have been identified in a pit below the cairn (see below). Anomaly 3 represents a small, undated, sub-rectangular ditched enclosure about 35m across with a possible entrance to the NW about 30m to the SE of the long cairn. This is undated but appears to pre-date the modern field system.

Linear anomalies 1–2 and 4–8 are interpreted as representing trackways or former field banks or boundaries. Anomaly 9 represents a former, partially infilled quarry.

Building materials

Adrian Humpage

Fieldwork was undertaken in 2016 to investigate the types and possible source of materials used to build the long cairn while exposed stonework still remained visible, before the commencement of conservation work (see Humpage 2016). A careful selection of building materials on the basis of structural properties and decorative properties is evident. Large, flat slabs were needed for the portal structure and the walls and roofs of the side chambers; smaller and more readily handled blocks were needed for the bulk of the cairn material; and more thinly-bedded slabs for building the outer revetment. The siting of the long cairn in relation to suitable, accessible building resources seems highly significant since these were mostly all readily accessible within relatively close proximity either by bedrock quarrying or as surface glacial erratic material. A few hundred metres to the N, W and S and the bedrock would either have been dominated by less competent (softer or more fragmented) mudstones or hidden by superficial deposits of glacial till. A few hundred metres to the E and there would probably have been fewer, less accessible bedrock exposures. The only stone used in the construction that appears to have been brought from greater distance is the distinctive, fine-grained, fissile, greenish-grey sandstone used for the outer revetment walls. The source is unknown, though it might conceivably be derived from the

Senni Formation, which outcrops on the higher elevation slopes of the prominent hill of Mynydd Troed, 2.5km or more to the SE.

In more detail, the site is underlain by Silurian to early Devonian rocks, which regionally dip gently towards the S to SSE at approximately five degrees (Barclay and Wilby 2003; BGS 2004). The oldest rocks are the mudstones and thin interbedded sandstones of the Raglan Mudstone Formation of Late Silurian age. These rocks form the lower slopes and floor of the Llynfi valley below an elevation of 190m OD. The mudstones are typically red to purplish-red in colour and often mottled. Sandstones are typically less than 0.3m thick, although occasional beds exceed a metre in thickness. Locally, calcrete nodules are present. Overlying the Raglan Mudstone, and directly underlying the long cairn, is the Lower Devonian-age St Maughans Formation, up to 350m in stratigraphic thickness, which comprises repeated successions of sandstones, siltstones and mudstones and some conglomerates. The sandstones are generally fine- to medium-grained and range in colour from red-brown to purple and grey-green. The conglomerates are up to a metre thick, mottled purple, red-brown and green and consist of calcrete, siltstone and sandstone clasts in a fine-grained matrix. Overlying the St Maughans Formation and capping the top of Mynydd Troed to the SE of the long cairn is the Senni Formation, of which only the stratigraphical lowest 140m is preserved on the hilltop. These rocks are mainly very fine- to medium-grained sandstones, which are variably purplish, grey-green and green in colour, interbedded with red-brown mudstones and siltstones, though coarser, more pebbly sandstones appear at higher stratigraphic levels.

The area of the Llynfi valley and northern and western flanks of the Black Mountains were glaciated during the last (Late Devensian) Ice Age and a veneer of till was deposited by the ice across the landscape. Glacial till consists of a heterogeneous mixture of clay, silt sand, gravel and boulders varying widely in size and shape (a diamicton), transported by the ice but largely derived from the local, upstream, underlying bedrock. During the archaeological excavations in 2015–16 the residual till deposits have been identified by sub-rounded or rounded clasts in the subsoil. Post-ice retreat mass movement processes, such as periglacial solifluction on a slope of this gradient, would have been able to largely remove any veneer of glacigenic sediments and attenuate thicknesses elsewhere, the reworked material being redeposited as Head on the lower valley slopes and in valleys, before the climate ameliorated and vegetation became established at the onset of the Holocene (present-day) warm period, approximately 11,650 years ago.

The outcrop pattern in the vicinity of the long cairn clearly shows a sequence of discrete and arcuate outcrops of harder sandstone, which are visible in the field (Fig. 2.13).

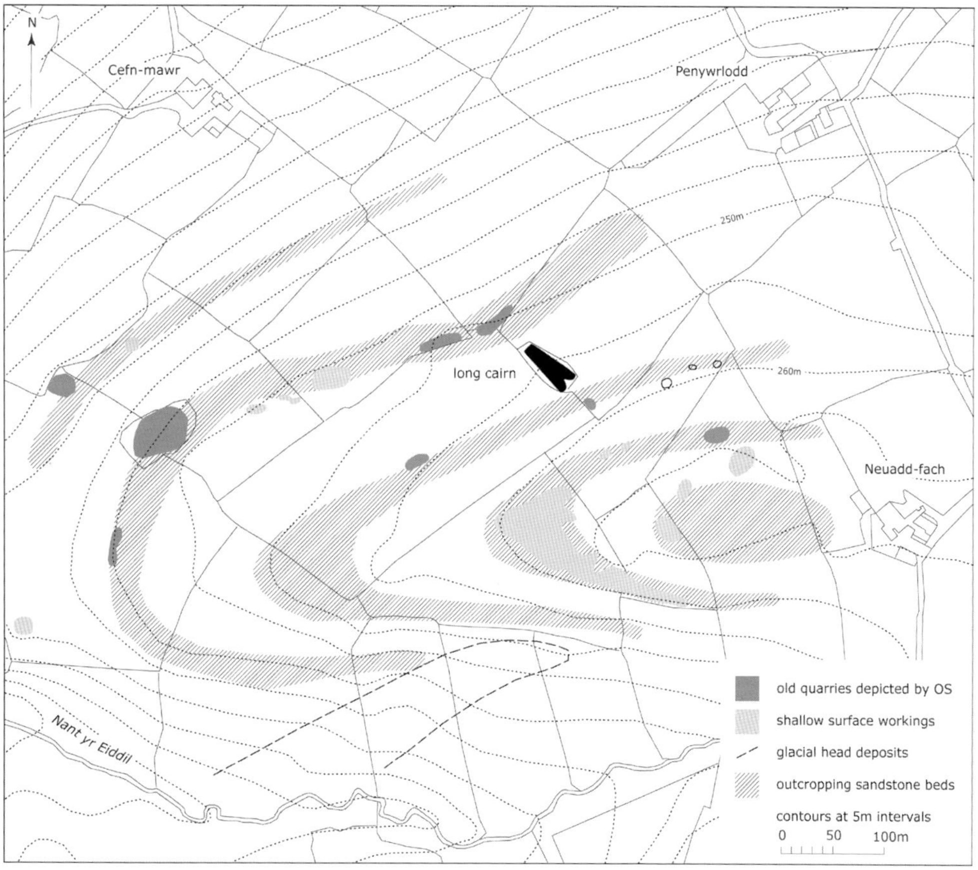

Fig. 2.13. Penywyrlod: rock exposures and surface quarries in the vicinity of the long cairn.

The long axis of the long cairn lies across the hillslope between two of these sandstone beds. One bed outcrops downhill from the long cairn and three others outcrop higher on the hillslope above the monument. Depressions between the feature-forming sandstone beds indicate softer mudstone, siltstone or less competent thin sandstone beds, such as the sandstone bed identified in various places beneath the cairn during the archaeological excavations in 2015–16 and the inferred sandstone bed of geophysical anomaly 10 (Fig. 2.12).

Inner cairn

The bulk of the inner cairn is composed of greyish-brown to purplish-brown, fine- to medium-grained angular to sub-rounded sandstone clasts (Fig. 2.14b) derived from the St Maughans Formation, which underlies the site. The material is generally in blocks up 0.7m across and 0.1m thick but the massive capstone of the 'Main Chamber' is composed of a slab of similar, weathered material (Fig. 2.14a). The wide selection of clasts within the fill suggests multiple origins. Some of the clasts may be of glacial origin, and were probably lying scattered across the surface of the hillside prior to the construction of the cairn. The more common angular clasts are likely to have been quarried to provide additional material, and the field survey has indicated a number of shallow pits along the slope and upslope from the monument that may have provided sources for this material.

Orthostats of Chamber NE I

A number of the fragmentary orthostats of Chamber NE I (*e.g.* 14, 15, ?23, ?26) are composed of rectilinear slabs of a reddish-brown thickly-bedded flaggy fine- to medium-grained sandstone, readily split along planar bedding plane surfaces into slabs up to 20–30mm thick (Fig. 2.14g). Weathering has caused splitting along the bedding planes. These sandstones are typical of the St Maughans Formation, which underlies the site. The field survey identified that the most likely source of these sandstone slabs was from a sandstone bed, which outcrops immediately downslope from the cairn. This sandstone forms a clearly defined feature that can be traced southwards into a more recent quarry (at SO 1470 3150) where similar slabs of sandstone are visible as quarry waste.

Portal orthostats

The two massive portal orthostats, both *c.* 2.2m tall, 1.5m wide and 0.35m thick, comprise locally derived greyish-red, flaggy medium-grained sandstone but of two distinctive facies. The fallen, northern, orthostat is of a distinctive ripple-bedded facies and weathering has picked out the bedding pattern (Fig. 2.14h). The fallen outer capstone of Chamber NE III is composed of similar ripple-bedded sandstone (Fig. 2.14e). The southern vertical orthostat, which remains *in situ*, is a similar greyish-red flaggy medium-grained sandstone although the bedding is planar and does not exhibit the distinctive ripple pattern (Fig. 2.14c). The source location of the orthostats has not been precisely determined during the detailed geological survey. The ripple-bedded sandstone may have a source from an outcropping sandstone bed on a local hilltop approximately 200m SE of the cairn. However, the dimensions of these boulders may suggest that they are glacially transported erratics, but probably only transported a relatively short distance from their origin, and may have lain on the land surface adjacent to the site at the time of construction of the long cairn.

Portal lintel

The lintel is a red to reddish-grey massive medium- to coarse-grained conglomerate containing numerous small rounded clasts up to 20mm in diameter, many of quartz, typical of the intraformational conglomerates of the St Maughans Formation (Fig. 2.14d). The probable lintel of the portal structure is formed of a slab of this material. No outcrop of the conglomerate was located, but the dimensions of this slab may suggest that it was a glacially transported erratic, possibly only transported a relatively short distance from its origin and possibly again derived from the land surface adjacent to the site at the time of construction of the long cairn. Other small rounded boulders of similar material, up to *c.* 0.5m across, were identified within the make-up of the inner cairn and are also to be seen in local field boundaries and are almost certainly glacially transported.

Outer revetment walling

The outer revetment walls of the long cairn and some of the orthostats of at least Chamber NE I (*e.g.* nos 10, 11, 24, 25) are largely composed of a distinctive pale greenish-grey to olive, thinly-bedded, fissile, fine-grained sandstone (Fig. 2.14f). Slabs used in the outer walls were typically up to 0.5m across and up to 80mm thick whilst orthostat 25 of Chamber NE I was *c.* 1.7m long and 100mm thick. However, these slabs consistently and readily split into thin slabs *c.* 10mm thick, with little apparent weathering. This material was probably quarried from an as yet unidentified outcrop some distance from the site. This lithology may be derived from the Senni Formation, which outcrops on the higher elevation slopes of Mynydd Troed, 2.5km or more to the SE, its colour being more indicative of this formation than of the St Maughans Formation underlying the cairn and its immediate vicinity. The Senni Formation is also thought to be the source of the outer walling at Gwernvale (Britnell 1984, 57).

In addition to recent quarrying activity in the area, field survey has identified possible historic shallow surface quarries in the vicinity of the long cairn (Fig. 2.13) some of which might represent contemporary stone quarries like those identified in close proximity to Hazleton North, Gloucestershire (Saville 1990, 23–31) and Ascott-under-Wychwood, Oxfordshire (Benson and Whittle 2007, 123–7).

Fig. 2.14. Penywyrlod: building materials. a) Thick greyish-brown, fine to medium-grained sandstone slab forming the capstone of the 'Main Chamber'. b) Greyish-brown to purplish-brown, fine to medium-grained sandstone visible in the section of inner cairn of the long cairn just to the SW of the portal structure. Most of the material is angular and appears to be quarried but the inner cairn includes some weathered, sub-rounded material that appears to be derived from a surface exposure or from glacially derived material. c) Greyish-red, flaggy medium-grained sandstone used for the still-standing orthostat of the portal structure. d) Red to reddish-grey mottled greenish-grey and white conglomerate used for the supposed fallen lintel of the portal structure. e) Ripple-bedded, greyish-red, flaggy medium-grained sandstone used for the fallen orthostat of the portal structure. f) Fissile greenish-grey fine-grained sandstone used for the outer revetment wall of the long cairn. g) Reddish-brown, planar, bedded flaggy sandstone used for orthostat 10 of Chamber NE I. h) Ripple-bedded, greyish-red, flaggy medium-grained sandstone used for the fallen outer capstone of Chamber NE III.

Recent excavations at Penywyrlod

The excavations described here were undertaken in 2015–16 in advance of conservation work and although limited in scope they provide important new information about the form and use of the monument and in particular evidence of the manner in which the chambers were accessed (Britnell 2015a; 2015b; 2016).

Re-excavation of Chamber NE I

Chamber and passage

Savory's trenches overlying and close to Chamber NE I (trenches 1–2) were reopened, the larger trench being extended to the N to examine the outer end of the passage, the passage entrance, outer revetment wall and an area of collapsed cairn material and buried soil beyond the margins of the cairn, which had formerly been inaccessible beneath a large ash tree (Fig. 2.15, top). Stone extraction in the 1970s had worked round the tree, preserving an almost isolated hump of relatively well-preserved deposits about 5m across and 1m high.

The chamber was accessed from the S side of the long cairn by a passage (Fig. 2.16). As previously noted most of the orthostats forming the walls and inner part of the entrance passage of the chamber had either been broken off or removed by stone extraction prior to excavation in 1972 (Fig. 2.17). All the exposed stones of the chamber were left *in situ*. Without the destructive removal of the shattered orthostats it would be difficult in some instances to tell whether they represent one or more than one stone, a difficulty compounded by the fact that orthostats may have been wedged by vertical stones that have also shattered.

The chamber was divided into two compartments separated by a shattered dividing slab or slabs (23) between the two (Figs 2.15, bottom and 2.16). The inner, S compartment (19), defined by shattered orthostats 23–26 and by paving slabs 21, is rectangular and approximately 1.6m long, 0.95m wide at its S end and 1.1m wide at the N end. Savory had considered orthostat 23 to be a single stone but there are hints from the colour and orientation of the shattered base of the stone, like the similarly shattered orthostat 24 forming the SW side of the S compartment, that they might represent more than a single orthostat, possibly in addition to any wedging stones.

As Savory concluded in the 1984 report, it is uncertain whether orthostat(s) 23 between the two compartments originally rose to the roof of the chamber and whether the inner compartment might in effect have been a closed cist, as was suggested in the case of the 'sealing slab' between the passage and chamber of Chamber NE II (Fig. 2.27, bottom left).

The outer, N compartment of Chamber NE I is defined by orthostat(s) 23 at the S end, with a possible sill on its NE side, by stonehole slots 16 and 17 on the E and W, by orthostat 30 at the NE corner, by orthostats 14 and 15 on the N, and by paving slabs 22. It is rectangular, 2.15m long by 1.15–1.17m wide. The entrance gap between orthostats 14 and 15 is only about 0.44m wide. Two of the large slabs lying across the outer end of the N compartment and interpreted as 'collapsed corbel stones?' in the 1984 report (Savory 1984, fig. 5) were lifted and found to have been split from the same

Fig. 2.15. Penywylod Chamber NE I: Top: Remains of the chamber viewed from the SW during excavation in 1972. The ash tree overlying the entrance passage prevented the excavation of the chamber entrance in the 1970s. Scale divisions in feet (after Savory 1984, pl. 6c. Photograph: Newport Museum and Art Gallery). Bottom: Fractured stones representing one or more orthostats on the division between the two compartments of the chamber, viewed from the SW during re-excavation in 2015. Scale 0.5m.

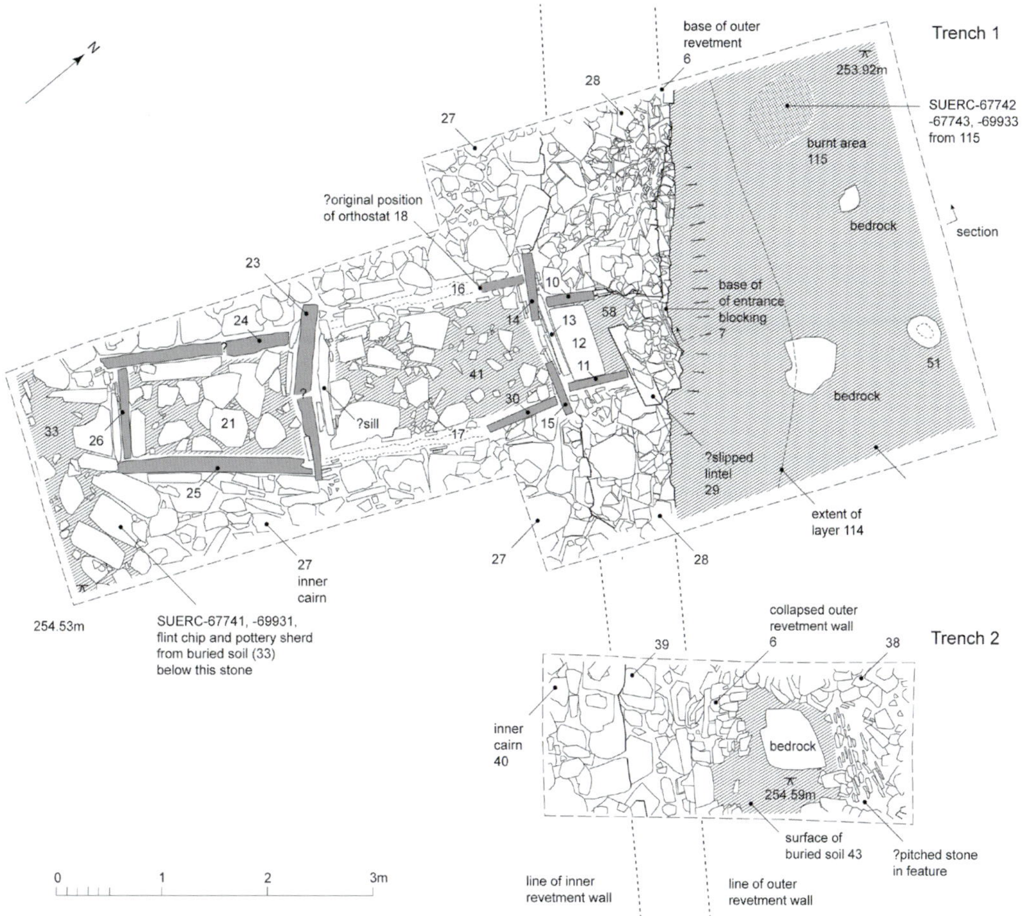

Fig. 2.16. Penywyrlod Chamber NE I: plan of the remains of the chamber in 2015–16, showing in situ *blocking in the entrance passage, the outer revetment wall and the buried ground surface outside the cairn.*

Fig. 2.17. Penywyrlod Chamber NE I: view from the SW during excavation in 2015. Scale 2m.

stone that is now considered to represent a fallen orthostat (18), 1.13m tall, originally standing at the NW corner of the chamber. Stonehole slot 16 in which it stood was 80–100mm deep, which suggests that the chamber would have had a minimum internal height of about 1m but which may have been heightened by corbelling. This is comparable to the suggested minimum heights of Chambers NE II and NE III.

Surviving deposits inside the chamber had been very largely excavated in 1972, apart from a small area below fallen orthostat 18, which sealed small areas of stone rubble 35 and underlying soil layer 45, which included charcoal fragments. The only human remains within the chamber in 1972 were 'a few small scraps of bone, including a human molar tooth' from the paving inside the inner compartment (Savory 1984, 18, 36). Savory considered that 'any human remains the compartments may have contained originally had been almost entirely removed by the farmer, who, however, claimed not to have noticed such remains'. However, the shattered stump of orthostat 25 on the S side of the inner compartment of Chamber NE II still stood to a height of about 0.25m above the floor of the chamber, which is probably not dissimilar to the thickness of the skeletal deposits recorded in Chamber NE II (Savory 1984, pl. 7b). This suggests that the inner chamber of Chamber NE I may have been largely devoid of human remains when the monument was abandoned. This is consistent with the absence of any human remains below fallen orthostat 18 at the NW corner of the outer compartment when this was lifted in 2015–16.

The entrance passage is about 0.8m wide and up to 1.2m long and met the outer revetment wall at a slight angle. It is defined by orthostats 10 and 11 at the inner end and by short stretches of drystone walling at the outer end. The height of orthostat 11 above the surface of the buried soil suggests that the inner end of the passage was originally at least about 1m high. At the inner end of the passage are threshold slab 12 and sill stone 13, both of which appear to be more symbolic than structural.

The inner end of the entrance passage was re-excavated down to the surface of a buried soil (58). The inner passage had been disturbed by machine prior to excavation in 1972 but the space behind the blocking wall between orthostats 10–11 is said to have been filled with 'a dark earth which contained nothing of archaeological interest and was probably of recent origin' (Savory 1984, 17). This suggests that the entrance passage behind the blocking wall had originally been empty and most probably roofed.

One unusually wide sandstone slab (29), 0.84m long, 0.16–0.17m wide and *c.* 70mm thick, partly resting against the outer face of orthostat 11, appeared to have slipped out of position on the outer wall-face and might represent a lintel above the passage entrance (Figs 2.19, 2.21; see suggested original position on Fig. 2.31). The absence of other slabs of comparable dimensions here and within collapsed cairn material suggests that the entrance passage may have largely been roofed by corbelling rather than capstones. Without complete excavation it is difficult to be certain but it appears that the floor of the passage and the chamber had been artificially lowered by up to about 50mm either during the course of construction or as a result of wear.

Inner cairn and inner revetment wall

Up to two to three layers of the inner cairn (27, 40) survived within the excavated area, standing to a height of between 0.05–0.3m. It was composed of large and irregular, quarried blocks of stone up to 0.7m across and included a mixture of greyish, reddish and brownish sandstone and paler yellowish-brown mudstone, distinct from the composition of the outer revetment wall. The basal stones lay directly on the buried soil and had been neatly placed against the base of the orthostats of Chamber NE I. The outer face of the inner cairn forms a coarse inner revetment wall, which loosely corresponds with orthostats 14 and 15, which mark the chamber entrance.

Passage entrance blocking

The passage entrance to Chamber NE I was marked by a break in the outer revetment wall about 0.6m across (Figs 2.18–2.19). A blocking wall (7) across the outer end of the

Fig. 2.18. Penywyrlod Chamber NE I: Top: View of the chamber entrance from the outside during excavation in 2016, showing the inserted blocking wall and short stretches of the outer revetment wall of the long cairn to either side. Bottom: The inserted blocking wall from the inside, with the possible slipped lintel (arrowed) resting against one of the orthostats in the inner passage. Scales 0.5m.

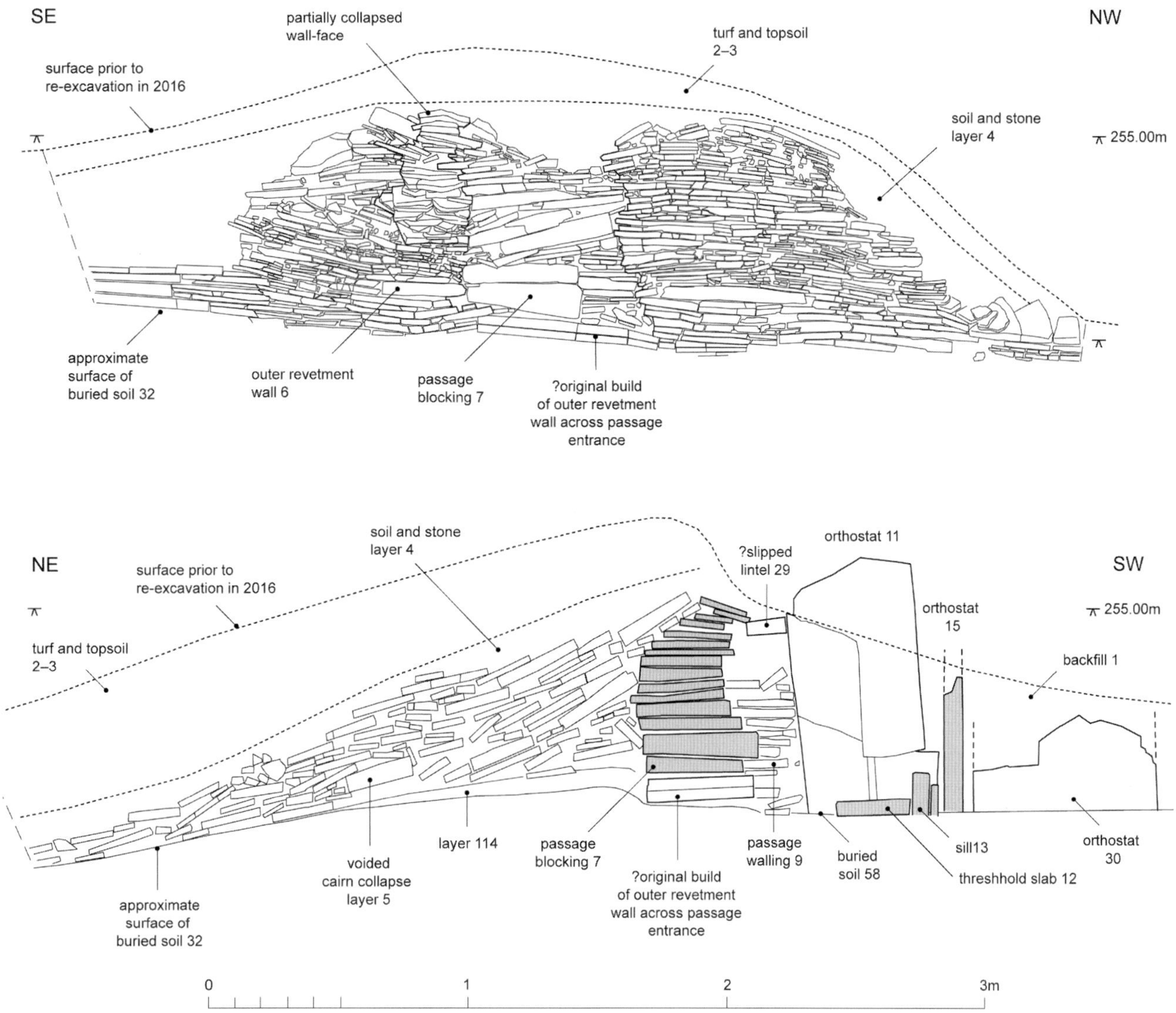

Fig. 2.19. Penywyrlod Chamber NE I: Top: Elevation of outer revetment wall and passage blocking. Bottom: Section through passage blocking and cairn collapse outside the passage entrance.

passage butted roughly up against the ends of the outer revetment wall to either side and was clearly a later insertion. It comprises up to 12–15 courses of stone slabs, surviving to a height of about 0.7m. The blocking wall is up to 0.45m thick at its base and narrows to about 0.3m towards the top. It is made of sandstone slabs between 20–120mm thick and up to about 0.45m across. Few if any of the stones in the blocking wall appear to span the entire width of the entrance passage and shorter and thinner stones generally fill the gaps to one or other side of larger slabs. The entrance blocking was left *in situ*, but a number of stones on the E side of the entrance protrude awkwardly across the end of the passage and suggest that the outer revetment wall may originally have been built continuously across the passage entrance and subsequently roughly broken through in order to gain access to the chamber, before being blocked up again. A large basal slab that had fractured into several pieces appears to represent the original build of the outer wall-face still *in situ* below the blocking.

Outer revetment wall and passage entrance

The outer revetment wall (28, 39) near the entrance to Chamber NE I is about 0.8–1.0m thick and as elsewhere butts against the inner revetment wall. It survives to a height of about 0.85m for a short distance to either side of the entrance passage (Fig. 2.20) but judging from the volume of collapsed material outside the cairn seems likely to have originally stood to a height of at least 1m at this point. Further from the entrance the walling had evidently largely collapsed in antiquity down to the lowest courses. Beyond this the upper

Fig. 2.20. Penywyrlod Chamber NE I: view from the N during excavation in 2016, with the inserted blocking wall, part of the outer revetment wall in the foreground and the remains of the chamber beyond. Scale 0.5m.

levels of the collapse had been quarried away in the 1970s. The walling is composed of thin slabs of greenish-grey, fissile sandstone. Slabs are up to 0.5m across and between 15–50mm thick and had often been laid with their long axes along the wall. The stone is fairly friable and although many stones had split it seems likely that up to about 20 courses survive. The base of the outer revetment wall lay directly on the buried soil below and extending beyond the edge of the cairn, having become slightly impressed into the surface of this layer by about 50mm due to worm action and the weight of stone overlying it.

Cairn collapse

Outside the outer revetment wall there was a substantial wedge of loose, pitched stone (5, 38), below modern turf and topsoil (2, 3). The layer was up to 0.85m thick and thinned about 3m away from the outer revetment wall (Figs 2.19, 2.21–2.22). It was largely composed of thinnish slabs similar to the outer revetment wall though it included one or two larger, thicker slabs up to 0.5m across and 0.15m thick more characteristic of the inner cairn. The stone deposit was surprisingly voided, especially towards the bottom, though an upper layer (4), about 0.15m thick, had an earth matrix. Stones within the deposit were mostly pitched downwards away from the outer cairn wall. It had the appearance of a natural scree and had clearly resulted from the partial toppling and collapse of the outer revetment wall.

Tree roots and the voided nature of the collapsed stone have evidently made it susceptible to intrusion since stone extraction in the 1970s and probably even prior to this. The deposit contained unburnt hazel nutshells and colonies of recent land snails (including *Discus rotundatus*), which

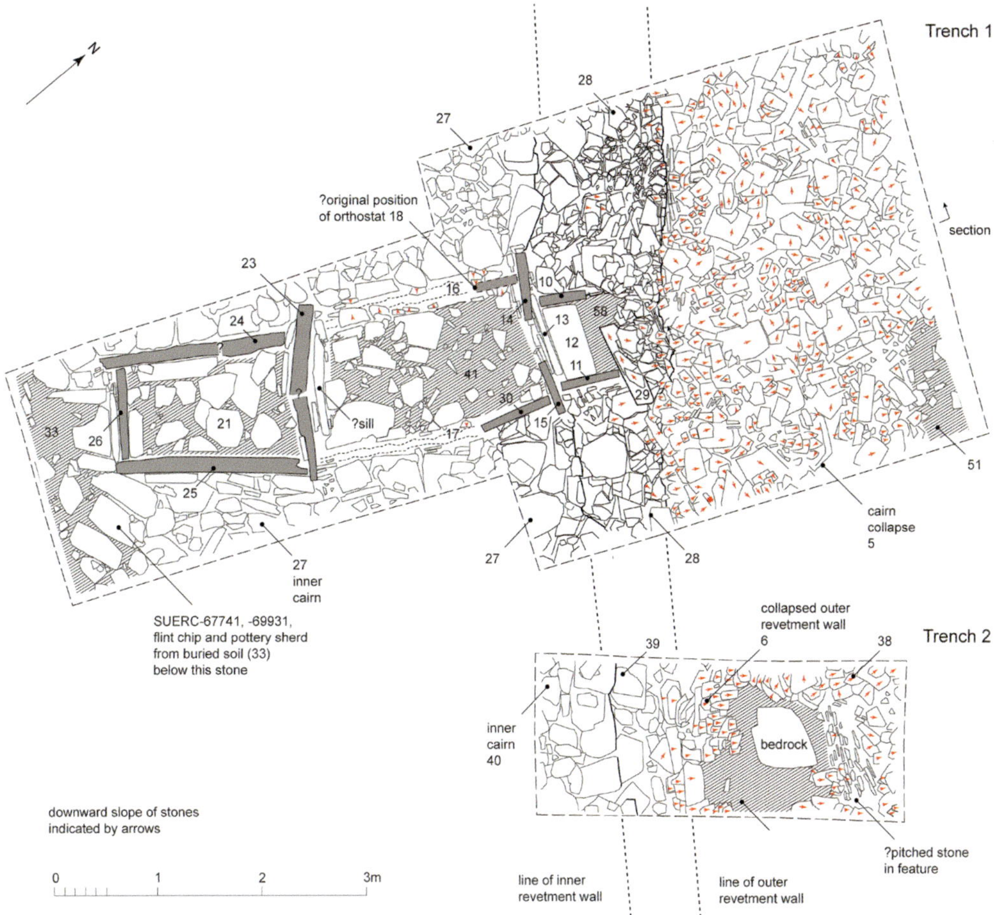

Fig. 2.21. Penywyrlod Chamber NE I: plan of the chamber in 2015, showing the collapsed cairn material lying against the outer end of the entrance passage and the outer revetment wall sealing the buried ground surface outside the long cairn.

Fig. 2.22. Penywyrlod Chamber NE I: section through collapsed cairn outside passage entrance, excavated in 2016, viewed from the NW. Scale 1m.

clearly calls into question the dating of a similar deposit of snail shells recorded in the 1972 excavations and the suggestion that they might indicate that the long cairn was built in a wooded environment (Luff *et al.* 1984, 39; Caseldine 1990, 52). The intrusion of modern material into and below this layer is confirmed by a modern radiocarbon date (SUERC-69934; Table 4.1) obtained from burnt twigs on the surface of the layer buried (114) immediately below the cairn collapse.

Buried surfaces below cairn collapse

Sealed immediately below the collapsed cairn material and extending for about 0.5–1m from the base of the outer revetment wall was a distinctive layer (114, see Figs 2.16 and 2.19) up to about 0.1m thick, composed of reddish-brown soil containing thin slabs and chips of stone, generally 30–100mm across, similar to those in the outer revetment wall. This overlay the surface of buried soil (32, 43) and butted up against the basal courses of the outer revetment wall and passage blocking in the entrance passage and probably represents a construction and/or weathering deposit contemporary with the long cairn.

A burnt area 115 (Fig. 2.16), 0.7 by 0.5m across, about 1m from the outer revetment wall of the cairn, was represented by a patch of dark reddish-brown silty loam identified at a level equivalent to the surface of the buried soil immediately below collapsed cairn material. The deposit contained a concentration of charcoal flecks, grey ashy material and small flecks of reddened stone, and extended to the full depth of the buried soil (32), here only about 40mm thick down to the surface of the buried subsoil (59). The burnt area produced a small quantity of charred plant remains including four wheat grains, a fragment of wheat chaff and Maloideae (hawthorn, apple and whitebeams) stemwood charcoal and a few small fragments of hazel (see report by Charlotte O'Brien below). Three AMS dates were obtained from this material (SUERC-67742, -67743, -69933; Table 4.1).

Buried soil and bedrock exposures

Underlying the long cairn and the collapsed stonework outside it was a layer of buried soil composed of fairly stone-free dark reddish-brown silty loam (33). This was largely unexcavated in order not to undermine the foundations of the outer revetment wall. Small test pits showed that the layer was between 40–120mm thick down to the surface of a more compact subsoil and/or bedrock. Following the natural pre-cairn ground surface, the surface of the layer sloped down by between 0.1–0.2m to the N, away from the outer revetment wall of the long cairn and by about 0.2m down from E to W across the width of the trench.

The buried soil (33) was sampled below a stone assumed to represent the base of the original cairn in trench 1 (see location on Fig. 2.16). Charred plant remains were not abundant but include hazel and oak charcoal (see report by Charlotte O'Brien below). Radiocarbon dates have been obtained from the hazel charcoal; SUERC-67741 from the surface of the buried soil immediately below the stone, and SUERC-69931 from the upper 0–55mm of the buried soil (see Table 4.1).

The surface of the buried soil in trenches T1–2 was broken by several exposures of bedrock or glacial erratics. One of these exposures, only a metre from the entrance to Chamber NE I, protruded up to 0.15m above the surface of the buried soil and suggests that the long cairn was built on an uneven surface across which protruding bedrock or glacial erratics are likely to have been exposed.

The excavation of trench 2, adjacent to Chamber NE I, was limited to the surface of deposits exposed in 1972 (Figs 2.16, 2.21). An area of pitched stone extending below the surface of the buried soil (43) towards the NE end of the trench remained unexcavated but appeared to resemble the so-called 'buttress pit' revealed in 1972 close to the tail of the cairn (Savory 1984, 24 and fig. 9). Both these features would now seem more likely to represent stoneholes resulting from the removal of larger erratic boulders lying beyond the margins of the long cairn during its construction.

Test-pits around the NE and SW hornworks

Seven small test-pits were dug to define the line of the outer revetment wall and the extent of collapsed stonework around the NE and SW hornworks (Fig. 2.7, T3–9). No trace of the outer revetment wall survived in trench 4. The partially collapsed outer revetment wall of the SW hornwork was found in trenches 3 and 9. The base of the wall was not identified but it was seen to still survive to a height of at least 0.35m (Fig. 2.23). A thin scatter of stonework that had collapsed from the outer revetment wall of the cairn was found in trench 8 but none survived in trenches 5–7. The spread of collapsed cairn material outside the SW hornwork suggests that the outer revetment wall at the outer ends of the forecourt had probably been no higher than recorded along the side of the cairn near the entrance to Chamber NE I, which is assumed to have originally stood to a height of about 1m.

Test-pits below cairn

Seven trial trenches (Figs 2.7, 2.24, T10–16) were excavated in the disturbed area beneath the cairn between Chamber NE III and the 'Main Chamber' to test for evidence of earlier activity and to recover palaeoenvironmental evidence and dating material. An intermittent scattering of stone, generally in a single layer 0.1–0.2m thick, represented the residual base of cairn material or more recent stone accumulation. Buried topsoil (33, 108) is represented by a layer of dark reddish-brown silt clay loam, 0.02–0.28m thick, which may have been truncated in places during stone removal in the

Fig. 2.23. Penywyrlod: test pits T9 and T3, locating the outer face of the SW hornwork in 2015. Top right: E section of T9. Bottom left: T9, viewed from the S (face of outer revetment wall arrowed). Bottom right: T3, viewed from the S (face of outer revetment wall arrowed). Scale 0.5m.

1970. Subsoil is a dark reddish-brown silt clay with occasional rounded sandstone pebbles probably derived from glacial drift. The fissured bedrock surface, consisting of dusky red to dark reddish-brown, fine-grained sandstone, lay within 0.05–0.3m of the surface of the buried soil. Charred plant macrofossils in samples of buried soils in the area below the cairn were not abundant but included a hazel nutshell fragment, a vetch seed and fragments of hazel charcoal from trenches 14–15 (see report by Charlotte O'Brien below). Radiocarbon date SUERC-69932 (see Table 4.1) has been obtained from hazel charcoal below stones assumed to represent the base of the original cairn in trench 15.

The only feature that was identified was pit 97 in the SE corner of trench 12 and possibly sealed by remnant basal cairn material (Fig. 2.24). The pit was over 0.62m across and about 0.22m deep from the buried surface, with rounded sides and bottom. Its fill consisted of dark reddish-brown silty loam (96) and a reasonably densely packed deposit of stone (98), which included small rounded sandstone pebbles (similar to those identified in the buried soil) and some larger angular blocks of sandstone up to 0.4m long, though there was no evidence that it represents a structural feature. Some of the angular pieces had blackened and shiny surfaces as though caused by heat.

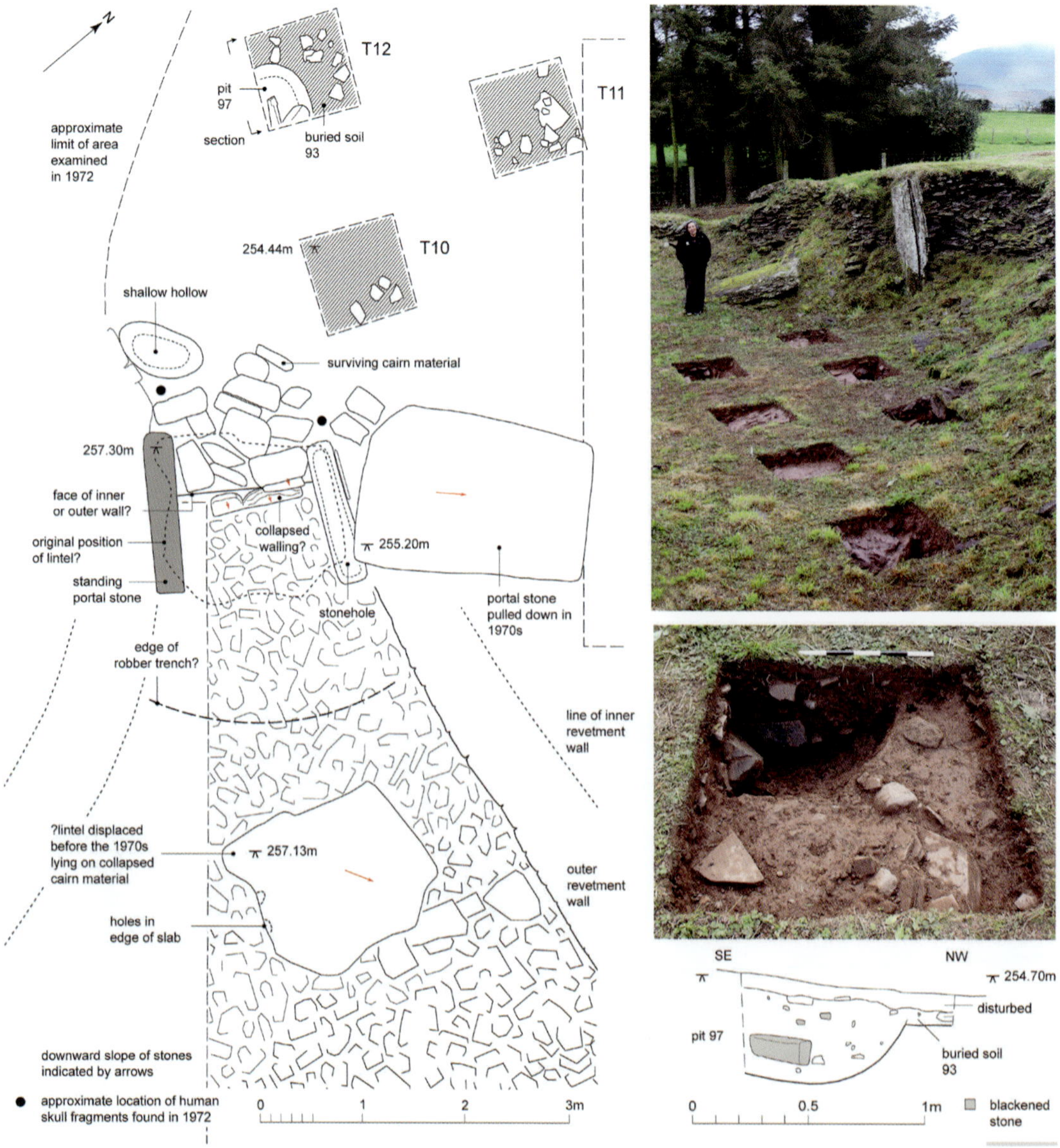

Fig. 2.24. Penywyrlod: portal structure. Left: Test pits T10–12 below the cairn in 2015, shown in relation to a reinterpretation of the portal structure recorded in 1972 (plan after Savory 1984, fig. 8, with spot heights and relabelling added). Top right: Test pits T10–16 in area below the cairn, excavated in 2015, with the remains of the portal structure beyond and Mynydd Troed in the distance. Bottom right: Sections of pit 97 in test pit T12, viewed from the NE (photographic scale 0.5m).

(Samples of stone were kindly examined by Dr Jana Horák of the National Museum of Wales using X-ray diffraction (XRD) and infrared spectroscopy (FTIR) analysis but these failed to provide any helpful information.) The absence of charcoal or other evidence of burning and the fact that some of the angular stones from different parts of the pit join together suggest that the burning occurred elsewhere. The burnt sandstone fragments appear to be from a bedrock surface that has been fractured by heat and might, speculatively, represent stone quarried by means of firesetting as tentatively suggested by geophysical survey to the SW of the long cairn (see above).

Finds

The only artefacts that were recovered were a single small sherd of early Neolithic pottery and a small flint chip from the buried soil (33) below basal cairn material in Trench 1, just to the S of Chamber NE I (location shown on Fig. 2.16).

Plant remains

Charlotte O'Brien

An assessment was undertaken on a limited programme of sampling during excavation, which is summarised here (for fuller report including methodology, see O'Brien 2016). The objective of the scheme of works was to assess the plant macrofossil, charcoal and pollen evidence within samples in order to establish their potential to provide information about the pre-cairn environment, land use and activity and to identify material suitable for radiocarbon dating.

Seven bulk samples and three small charcoal samples were submitted from the following Neolithic contexts: the buried soil below the cairn in trenches 1, 14, 15 (contexts 33, 105, 108); from the soil layer outside the cairn and below cairn collapse (context 32); from a soil layer within Chamber NE I (context 45); and from a burnt area outside the cairn and sealed by cairn collapse (context 115).

The results are summarised in Table 2.1. A small hazel nutshell fragment and vetch seed and hazel and oak charcoal were identified from the buried soil below the cairn (contexts 33, 105, 108). Oak charcoal was identified from the soil layer buried by collapsed cairn material outside the long cairn and from within Chamber NE I (contexts 32, 45). Poorly preserved cereal remains hazel and Maloideae charcoal were identified in the burnt area (115) outside the cairn. The wheat grains were heavily pitted and fragmented and could not be positively identified to species, although one of them had a high, v-shaped dorsal ridge suggestive of emmer wheat, a crop that was widely cultivated in Britain during the Neolithic and Bronze Age periods (Greig 1991; Caseldine 2004). The chaff fragment was a damaged spikelet fork, which could not be differentiated between spelt or emmer wheat. Maloideae (which includes hawthorn, apple and whitebeams), identified from the burnt area (115) outside the cairn, was largely stemwood, in good condition. Although members of the Maloideae group are difficult to separate, the anatomical properties most closely resembled those of hawthorn. The occurrence of hazel nutshell in buried soil reflects the importance of gathered wild foods in the early prehistoric period. The small charcoal assemblages indicate that the local woodland resource included oak, hazel, and Maloideae cf. hawthorn.

Samples were also submitted from the voided matrix of the collapsed cairn material from outside the cairn (5) and lying loose on the surface of the construction and/or weathering layer (114). Despite their black appearance, hand-recovered hazelnuts from context 5 (samples 24, 26, 27) were uncharred and the presence of small mammal holes suggests they probably represent a recent animal cache. Indeterminate charred plant material, resembling epidermis/thin bark, was recorded in context 5 as were a few remains of the land snail *Discus rotundatus* (Müller). This common snail is typical of woodland but also inhabits a range of moist sheltered places (Kerney and Cameron 1979) and is possibly also intrusive in this context. Three moderate-sized fragments of charred ash stemwood (*Fraxinus* sp.) in good condition were identified in a charcoal sample from the surface of 114 (sample 29) immediately below collapsed cairn material 5, which radiocarbon dating (see below) has shown to be modern (SUERC-69934; Table 4.1).

Table 2.1. Penywyrlod: charred plant remains and charcoal from Neolithic contexts.

Trench	1	14	15	1	1	1
Context	33	105	108	32	45	115
Sample(s)	4,6,7	23	18	15	1	28
Volume processed (l)	8	8	–	9	6	8
Charred plant remains						
Triticum sp. (wheat), grain	–	–	–	–	–	4[3]
Triticum dicoccum/spelta (emmer/ spelt wheat), spikelet fork	–	–	–	–	–	1
Corylus avellana (hazel), nutshell frag.	–	1	–	–	–	–
Vicia sp. (vetches)	–	1	–	–	–	–
tuber/rhizome	–	–	–	–	+	–
Charcoal (+ present)						
Corylus avellana (hazel)	+[1]	–	+[2]	–	–	+[4]
Maloideae (hawthorn, apple, whitebeams)	–	–	–	–	–	+[5]
Quercus sp. (oak)	+	–	–	+	+	–

Key: + = present; radiocarbon dates (see Table 4.1): 1. SUERC-67741, -69931; 2. SUERC-69932; 3. SUERC-67742; 4. SUERC-69933; 5. SUERC-67743

Radiocarbon dating

Fourteen radiocarbon dates are currently available from Penywyrlod. One (HAR-674) is from a bulked sample of human bone from several individuals from Chamber NE II, obtained in the 1970s (Savory 1984, 29). Six of the dates, from human skeletal remains in Chambers NE II–III (OxA-16494, -16525, -16526, -16527, -16569, -16608) are derived from an earlier unpublished dating programme undertaken by Alasdair Whittle and Michael Wysocki (Whittle *et al.* 2011, 546). One date (SUERC-63414), from a human tooth from Chamber NE II, was obtained as part of a programme of isotope analysis (Neil *et al.* 2017, 9). Six of the dates (SUERC-67741, -67742, -67743, -69931, -69932, -69933) are for charred plant remains or charcoal samples from the soil layer earlier than or potentially contemporary with the long cairn excavated in 2015–16 and reported upon here.

Further details of contexts, samples and dating are given in Table 4.1. Bayesian modelling of the available radiocarbon dates and the suggested phasing of various periods of activity at Penywyrlod are presented by Seren Griffiths in Chapter 4 in the context of dates from the Black Mountains monuments as a whole, and of the wider early Neolithic setting beyond.

The Penywyrlod long cairn revisited

Recent survey and excavation at Penywyrlod provide an opportunity to look again at its form, the use of materials employed in its construction, the manner in which the monument was used, its siting and symbolism, and eventual abandonment and decay. A particular focus in the review presented here is the attempt to relate the physical evidence for how the monument was used to the reassessments of skeletal remains and dating presented in subsequent chapters. Our discussion of these and many other aspects runs on into Chapter 12.

Pre-cairn activity activity

Prior to construction the land surface upon which the monument was built appears to have been fairly uneven and strewn with glacial erratics represented by the so-called 'marker blocks' and 'thrust blocks' recorded in 1972 (Savory 1984, 16, 23, 34). Similar stone was probably collected from the surrounding area for the construction of the monument and is also represented by more recent field clearance to be seen in adjacent field banks.

Slight evidence of pre-cairn activity recorded in 1972 included as Savory noted a possible microlith, a hollow containing some charcoal, and fragments of human skull found near the portal structure (Fig. 2.24; Luff *et al.* 1984, 36; Savory 1984, 22). The presence of human skull fragments in pre-cairn contexts near the forecourt area at Gwernvale and elsewhere is also mentioned in Chapter 3. Further evidence of pre-cairn activity is indicated by a shallow pit (97) with blackened stones found in trench 12 in 2015 (Fig. 2.24) and by a small sherd of pottery and a flint chip in the buried soil below the cairn in trench 1 (Fig. 2.16), but as yet there is no clear evidence at Penywyrlod of the kind of intensive pre-cairn activity represented by middens and timber structures at Gwernvale, Ascott-under-Wychwood and Hazleton North (see Chapter 3).

Siting

Various factors have been considered to have influenced the siting of Severn-Cotswold tombs, including places where there were woodland clearings, places that had already gained some significance within the landscape and were possibly associated with earlier domestic or ritual activity, or topographical settings that commanded significant views (cf. Darvill 2004, 92–6). The convergence of geology and topography appears to have been most significant at Penywyrlod. As noted above, stone suitable for the construction of the monument becomes less readily available a few hundred metres to the N, W and S. The combination of materials used at Penywyrlod and other long cairns in the Black Mountains area may have referenced or included tokens drawn from the wider landscape (cf. Cummings and Whittle 2004, 77; Darvill 2010, 6). A conscious or subconscious symbolic relationship between monument and mountain is suggested by the outer walling and blocked chamber entrances at Penywyrlod, which have the appearance of replicating the jointed and finely bedded strata visible in outcrops on Mynydd Troed from which the building stone appears to have been obtained (Fig. 12.6). The eventual erosion of the outer wall face would also in time match the scree slopes that lie below these outcrops. A parallel can perhaps be drawn with the passage entrances on the sides of the long trapezoidal monument at Prissé-la-Charrière, Deux-Sèvres, in western France, which it is argued were built as a continuation of the natural bedrock, in a manner suggesting the 'marking out of the passage entrances as the access to the subterranean world' (Laporte *et al.* 2002, 810). A similar argument might be advanced at Hazleton North, for example, where the quarries were dug close to the sides of the monument and to within only a metre of the entrance to the south chamber (Saville 1990, fig. 35). At Hazleton this was assumed to have been for practical convenience (Saville 1990, 241) but it must have had a marked visual impact upon the monument. This, together with the constricted entrance to lateral chambers in Severn-Cotswold tombs, may have resonance with contemporary early Neolithic cave burials in south Wales and elsewhere (*e.g.* Schulting *et al.* 2013).

The site chosen at Penywyrlod was to all intents and purposes a fresh location, an indication of novelty – more speculatively, an opportunity to engage with the first stones – points to which we will return in Chapter 12, as well as contrasting with the differing context at Gwernvale seen in the next chapter.

Form

The form of the monument, with its forecourt at the broader end and lateral chambers (Fig. 2.25), is generally similar to the other more fully excavated Black Mountains monuments at Ty Isaf, Pipton and Gwernvale. It has been suggested that some of the local constructions, such as Ffostyll South, Ty Illtyd and Penywyrlod (Llanigon), may have been terminally chambered but in the absence of detailed excavation this remains uncertain. The most closely similar Severn-Cotswold tombs, however, are probably Rodmarton in Gloucestershire (Saville 1989) and Luckington in Wiltshire (Corcoran 1970), which have stone portal structures at the broader end and simple box-like chambers with entrance passages spaced out along the sides of the mound.

Wider comparisons of this kind are significant as potential clues to affiliation and connectivity, but both here and further in Chapter 12 the aim is to put distinctive practice beginning probably in the 38th century cal BC in the first place into local context, in order to move away from the tendency identified in Chapter 1 to provide generalised and atemporal accounts of Severn-Cotswold monuments.

The monument is still relatively well preserved, despite the damage caused in the 1970s. Revised estimates of the form and dimensions of the long cairn can be given, combining details in Savory (1984) with more recent ground survey and electrical resistance tomography (ERT). This was a creation of considerable and impressive size, another point to which we will return in Chapter 12. The trapezoidal long cairn is now estimated to be about 53m long, narrowing from 22m wide at the broader end at the SE to 11m at the tail at the NW. It is similar in length but slightly broader than Ascott-under-Wychwood (*c.* 49m), Hazleton North (*c.* 53–56m), Belas Knap (53m) and Wayland's Smithy II (54m) (Saville 1990, table 96), which all lie within the upper size range of Severn-Cotswold tombs (Darvill 2004, fig. 38). Penywyrlod is the largest long cairn known in the Black Mountains cluster. The partially excavated long cairn at Little Lodge may have been of comparable size (RCHAMW 1997, 52) but, otherwise, only the lengths of Ty Isaf (27m+), Pipton (32m) and Gwernvale (45m+) are known with any degree of certainty. It is interesting to note

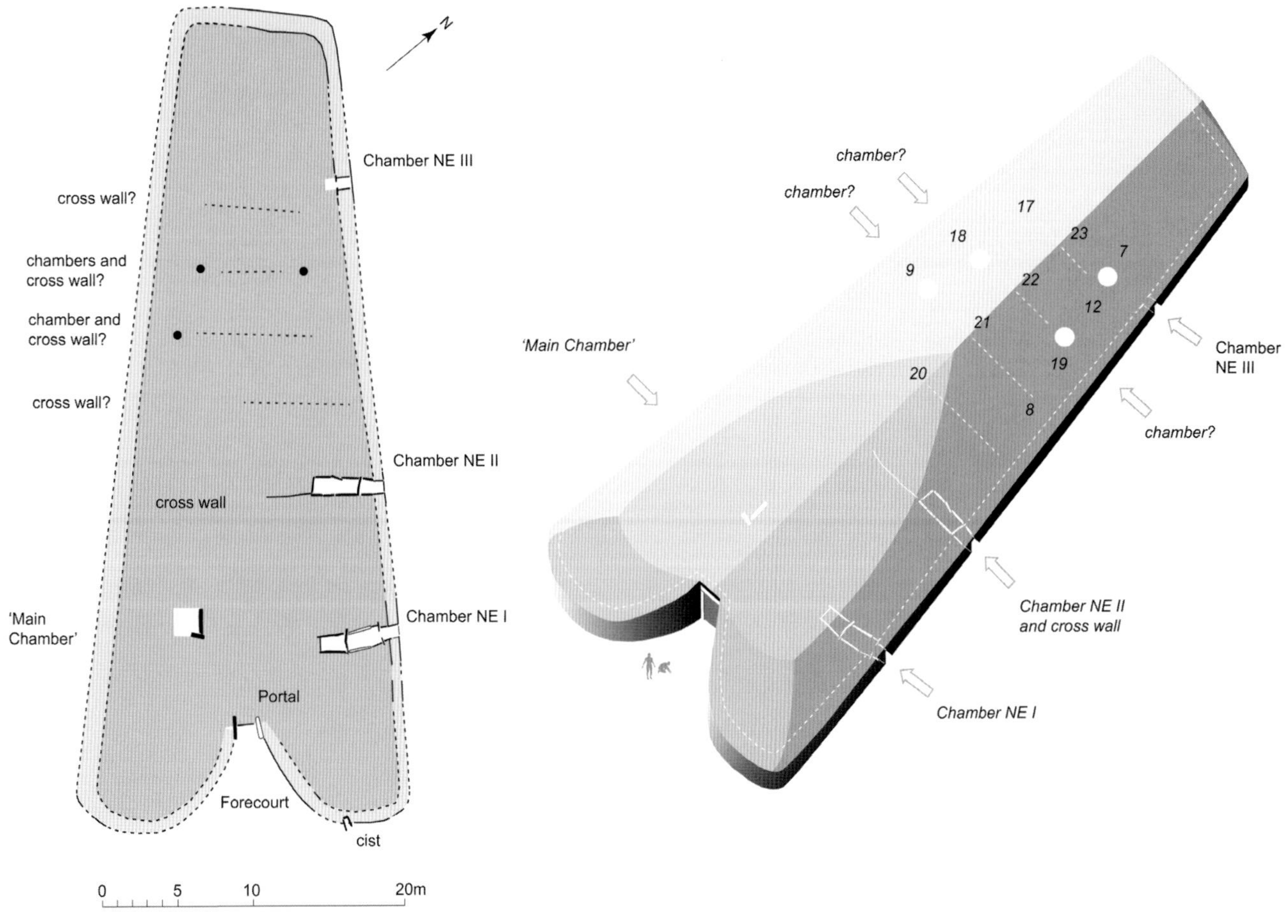

Fig. 2.25. Penywyrlod: conjectural reconstruction based on excavation and ground and ERT geophysical survey, indicating location of numbered geophysical anomalies (see Fig. 2.10). Note that no allowance is made in the sections for variations in the underlying buried land surface, which slopes uphill by about 4m from NW to SE and up to about 1m from SW to NE.

that the maximum widths of these more fully excavated long cairns in the Black Mountains are more closely similar than their lengths.

The monument was built on sloping ground that is about 5m higher at the broader end to the SE than the tail end at the NW and probably about 1m higher on the NE side than on the SW. The build-up of cairn material appears to be about 2.5m high near the portal structure, increasing to about 3m near Chamber NE II and then gradually diminishing to about 0.8m towards the tail, though due to the underlying slope the surface of the long cairn is highest close to the portal. Like other trapezoidal long barrows in Atlantic Europe the narrowing and lowering of the structure towards the tail creates a false perspective that may have been consciously employed to exaggerate the monument's length (cf. Laporte *et al.* 2002, 80).

A number of other long cairns in the Black Mountains area, such as Gwernvale, Mynydd Troed and Ffostyll South, occupy similar but less dramatically sloping sites. Although this does not appear to be typical of Severn-Cotswold tombs as a whole, sloping sites are a noted characteristic of dolmens (portal tombs) (F. Lynch 1972, 70; Ó Nualláin 1983, 86). Carnedd Hengwm South, a long chambered cairn with both Severn-Cotswold and dolmen affinities in NW Wales (F. Lynch 1969, fig. 47; Cummings and Whittle 2004, 132), occupies a markedly sloping site similar to that at Penywyrlod.

The tail of the cairn is ridged in cross-section and rises quite steeply to a point about midway along its length. Beyond this point its surface rises less steeply and becomes less ridged, giving the impression that it flattened out once its height matched that of the portal structure.

Inner and outer revetment walls have been identified in a number of the excavated trenches. The inner revetment, like the body of the cairn, is more roughly built of more locally sourced material. The outer revetment, characteristically of Severn-Cotswold tombs, is more neatly constructed, in this instance with specially selected stone brought from some distance away. Again, we will come back in Chapter 12 to the significance of bringing material from a prominent local hill to build the outer wrapping of the monument. The width of the outer revetment is between 0.8–1.5m thick, with variations in width, as at Hazleton North (Saville 1990, fig. 227) and elsewhere, evidently smoothing out irregularities that had crept in during the construction of the inner body of the cairn. Its outer face seems intended to have been vertical, though this had buckled outwards or inwards as a result of subsequent settlement and collapse.

Forecourt and portal

The Penywyrlod forecourt is about 7m long and narrows from about 11m at the outer edge of the horns to 1.5m in width at the point it meets the two othostats of the portal structure. One of the stones remained *in situ* and one had collapsed as a result of stone extraction in the 1970s (Figs 2.24 and 2.26, left). The fallen portal stone is 2.25m long, 1.5m wide and 0.28m thick. Its stonehole was 0.2m deep and the stone had therefore stood to a height of 2m above ground level. The standing orthostat is up to 1.7m wide, 0.38m thick and stands to a height of over 2.1m. The uprights appear to have originally supported a massive lintel represented by the adjacent slab 1.78 by 1.65m across and 0.2m thick, which lay towards the top of a mass of stone in the forecourt. (The dimensions of some of the portal stones are slightly larger than previously recorded in Savory (1984, 22).) The height of the portal structure including the lintel was probably not dissimilar to that at Pipton, where two contiguous orthostats appear to have stood to a height of 2.2m (Fig. 2.30; Savory 1956, 32–3). This was an impressively monumental feature in its own right, and one which must have carried significant connotations, evoking both similarity and difference compared to other monuments to the west and east.

The original build between the uprights of the portal structure was only partially exposed in the 1970s. Savory considered that there had been a sill 1m high between the verticals, formed of 'small vertical slabs standing two deep' (Savory 1984, figs 7–8 and pl. 2c, where the photographic scale is in feet). Photographic evidence (Fig. 2.26, right), however, suggests that the 'vertical slabs' are better interpreted as two to three courses of collapsed drystone walling between the orthostats, resting on three to four courses of *in situ* walling set back from the outer edges of the portal stones. It is uncertain whether this stonework corresponds to either the inner or outer revetment walls that envelop the cairn elsewhere, though it is perhaps more robust than the outer walling elsewhere.

A similar portal structure to that suggested at Penywyrlod, formed of orthostats with walling in between, is known at West Tump, Gloucestershire (Witts 1880–81, pl. xxvi; Darvill 2004, fig. 49C). As at Penywyrlod, the pairs of orthostats at West Tump and at Rodmarton are aligned upon the long axis of the cairn, the othostats at West Tump being about 1.6m high and those at Rodmarton being 2.6m high. The lintel slab above an H-shaped portal structure at Belas Knap (Darvill 2004, fig. 49), with portal stones up to about 1.8m high, is the only instance in a laterally chambered Severn-Cotswold tomb where a lintel stone is known to have survived *in situ*, though even the one now in place is a modern restoration (Hemp 1929, 262). If the large slab found leaning against the orthostats at Rodmarton was a fallen lintel (Darvill 2004, 115), like the one assumed to have been displaced at Penywyrlod, then it would have to have fallen at an early stage, while the forecourt remained open. There was no evidence of a lintel slab at West Tump, but a sketchy elevation in the 19th-century excavation report suggests that the outer revetment walling in the forecourt originally rose to the same height or possibly even extended above the uprights of the portal (Witts 1880–81, pl. xxvi). As noted above, it seems likely that the outer walling in the forecourt at Penywyrlod may likewise have risen up

Fig. 2.26. Penywyrlod: views of the portal structure recorded in 1972. Left: The standing and fallen portal stones, viewed from the NE (after Savory 1984, pl. 2b). The scale in the foreground (divisions in feet) lies along the line of the remains of the outer revetment wall on the NE side of the forecourt. Arrowed (top left) is the division between the two deposits in the forecourt noted by Savory. In this report the stones to the left of the arrow are reinterpreted as collapsed cairn material and the stones to the right as the infill of possible later robbing of unknown date against the portal structure. Right: To the left is the base of the fallen portal stone and stonehole (scale divisions in feet), viewed from the NW (after Savory 1984, pl. 2c). The sloping stones to the right form the surviving infill between the two portal stones. These were interpreted by Savory as a sill but in this report are reinterpreted as 2–3 courses of collapsed walling between the two portal stones.

to match the height of the portal structure. Cairn material to the SW of the portal survived to about the same height as the top standing orthostat but it can only be conjectured whether the upper surface of the supposed lintel stone was hidden by overlying cairn material, as suggested in the case at Belas Knap (Corcoran 1969, fig. 18), or whether the outer revetment rose above it, as hinted at by the evidence from West Tump.

The affinities of the portal structure at Penywyrlod and its relationship with the mass of stone recorded in the forecourt are considered further in sections on the symbolism and decay of the monument below, and we pick them up further in Chapter 12.

Chambers and entrance passages

Penywyrlod contains at least four chambers – the so-called 'Main Chamber' and Chambers NE I–III. Geophysical anomalies hint at the possibility of three additional chambers within the long cairn on one or other side of the cairn (Figs 2.10, 2.25), perhaps supporting Savory's speculation, based on the spacing of the known chambers, that the monument might contain as many as six or eight chambers (Savory 1984, 29). As will be seen from the chronology presented by Seren Griffiths in Chapter 4, this number of lateral chambers would prove over time to be quite exceptional in Severn-Cotswold long cairns; from a probably early date in construction sequences, Penywyrlod was distinctive (with the possible exception of Gwernvale) in having at least three lateral chambers entered from one side of the long cairn. Of the other more fully excavated long cairns in the Black Mountains area, Gwernvale has four chambers, Ty Isaf has three (including one with two transepts) and Pipton has two (including one with two transepts) (Fig. 2.30). Of the long cairns in Gloucestershire and Wiltshire the maximum number of lateral chambers appears to be four, at Belas Knap, Luckington and Lugbury (Corcoran 1969, 292 and figs 18, 20).

In contrast to the size of the Penywyrlod long cairn and the monumentality of its portal structure, what lay within seems quite small and restrained, but is also surprisingly diverse: an observation again with potentially significant implications. Chambers NE I–II were simple rectangular, box-like structures whose dimensions are characteristic of lateral chambers within other Severn-Cotswold tombs.

Chamber NE I was about 4.2m by 1.4m externally; it extended up to 5.1m from the edge of the cairn and was divided into two compartments. The inner compartment was about 1.6m long and 1m wide internally and may, like Chamber NE II, have been sealed by one or more cross slabs. The outer compartment, 2.15m long and 1.15m wide internally, probably had an internal height of at least 1m and an entrance gap only 0.44m wide. The entrance passage was up to 1.2m long and about 0.8m wide.

Chamber NE II was 2.9m long and 0.9–1m wide and internally probably up to about 1.2m high and extended up to 4.75m from the edge of the cairn (Fig. 2.27). Between the chamber and the entrance passage, which was about 1.8m long and 0.7m wide, was a fragmentary slab that Savory called a 'sealing slab' (see Fig. 2.27, bottom left and Fig. 2.28).

The plan of Chamber NE III is uncertain, but geophysical survey suggests that it may have an L- or T-shape (Fig. 2.10). The chamber appears to have been less than 1m high internally with an entrance gap only about 0.38m wide and 0.6m high. The passage was about 1.2m long and 0.7m wide (see Fig. 2.29, bottom).

The plan of the so-called 'Main Chamber' is again uncertain, though it appears to be 1.5m wide and possibly 1.5m high internally (Fig. 2.29, top right). It extends for up to about 7m from the outer edge of the cairn to

Fig. 2.27. Penywyrlod Chamber NE II during excavation in 1972. Top left: View from the NE with outer revetment in foreground (after Savory 1984, pl. 7A). Top right: Entrance passage and passage blocking, viewed from the SW (after Savory 1984, fig. 26b). Bottom left: Fractured 'sealing slab' between entrance passage and chamber, viewed from the SE (after Savory 1984, pl. 8a). Bottom right: Cross-wall viewed from NE with end slab of chamber at bottom right (after Savory 1984, pl. 8d). Scale divisions in feet.

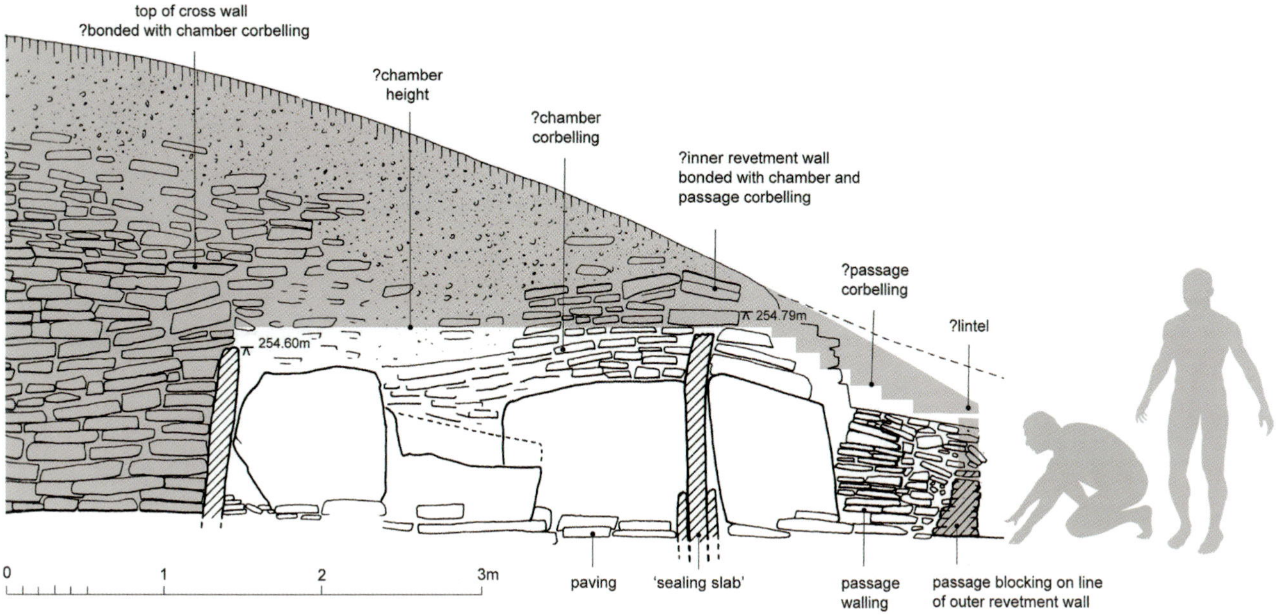

Fig. 2.28. Penywyrlod: Above: Section through Chamber NE II, recorded in 1972 and 1974, viewed from the SE (after Savory 1984, fig. 7, with spot heights, relabelling and shading added). Below: The same section photographed in October 2013.

the SW and like Chamber NE III its capstone (whose surface lies at about 256.2m) is covered by about 1m of cairn material. The 'Main Chamber' is larger than Chamber NE I but the difference in size appears no greater than that between the paired Chambers I–II at Ty Isaf, for example, which suggests it may also have been paired with Chamber NE I, in the sense of having been set out symmetrically from opposite sides of the cairn. Other possible pairings at Penywyrlod are suggested by geophysical anomalies (Fig. 2.10). Other chambers that are clearly paired in long cairns in the Black Mountains area are Gwernvale Chambers 2–3 and Ty Isaf Chambers I–II (Fig. 2.30). Paired lateral chambers are familiar in Severn-Cotswold tombs elsewhere, as at Belas Knap and Luckington, and may share a similarity with the symmetrical pairing of cells within the chambers of terminally chambered long cairns, as at Hetty Peglar's Tump and Parc le Breos Cwm (Corcoran 1969, fig. 13). At both Hazleton North and Ascott-under-Wychwood the pairing of lateral chambers entered from opposite sides of the monument was clearly a key element in the bilateral symmetry of both monuments (Saville 1990, 243; Benson and Whittle 2007, 93).

It is possible but by no means certain that the chambers may have diminished in height along the length of the cairn (cf. Tilley 1994, 119).

Fig. 2.29. Penywyrlod: Top left: Standing portal stone and 'Main Chamber' (to the right), viewed from the NW during excavations in 1972 (after Savory 1984, pl. 5c). Top right: 'Main Chamber' viewed from the NE (after Savory 1984, fig. 5d). Bottom: Chamber NE III, viewed from NE during excavation in 1972 (after Savory 1984, pl. 9b). Scale divisions in feet.

The 'Main Chamber' and at least the outermost part of Penywyrlod Chamber NE III were roofed by capstones but there was no surviving evidence that this was the case with Chambers NE I–II. Savory recorded circumstantial evidence that Chamber NE II had been roofed by one or more capstones (Savory 1984, 19) though in the case of Chamber NE II it seems likely that the chamber was roofed with corbelling or corbelling capped with stones, possibly in the manner of a barrel vault. Coursed stonework above the orthostats on the NW side of the chamber (Fig. 2.28) clearly leaves no space for a capstone of the same width as the chamber. Corbelling is widely recorded in Severn-Cotswold tombs elsewhere and is thought to have been likely in the case of the two chambers at Hazleton North (Saville 1990, 246).

The question of how the chambers at Penywyrlod were accessed and the possibility that the passages leading to the

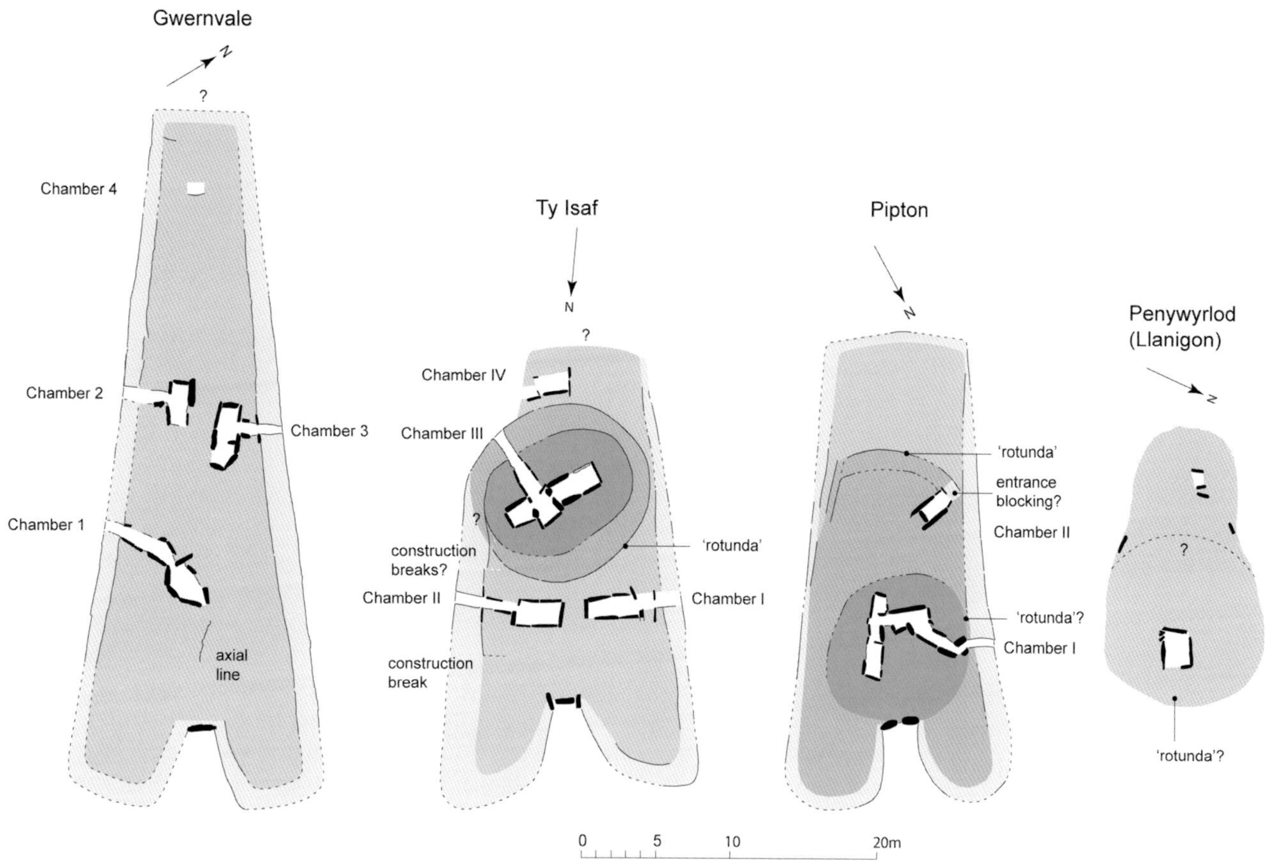

Fig. 2.30. Comparative plans of selected Black Mountains long cairns, showing hypothetical phasing of the Ty Isaf, Pipton and Penywyrlod (Llanigon) tombs. For alternative interpretations of the phasing of Ty Isaf, see Corcoran (1972, fig. 3), Darvill (2004, fig. 26), and Burrow (2006, 79). For alternative interpretations of the phasing of Pipton, see Darvill (2004, fig. 39). The plan of Penywyrlod (Llanigon) is based on the plan in Vulliamy 1922 with interpretation after Corcoran (1972, fig. 3, cf. Darvill 2004, fig. 23).

chambers from the side of the long cairn may also have been corbelled is discussed below.

Construction and sequence

A battered and slightly curving internal cross-wall, 1.3m high, was identified butting up against the end slab of Chamber NE II in 1974 (Figs 2.7, 2.25, 2.27 bottom right). Recent geophysical survey suggests the possibility of four more slightly curving lateral cross-walls up to about 0.6m high towards the tail of the cairn, spaced at intervals of 4–5m (Figs 2.10, 2.25). The cross-wall found in 1974 butts up against the orthostat at the SW corner of Chamber NE II and is battered to the NW, which shows that the chamber was built in advance of the cairn to the SE of the chamber (Savory 1984, 24). Geophysical evidence suggests a similar structural relationship between other chambers and cross-walls towards the tail of the long cairn (Figs 2.10, 2.25), which implies a clear link between the chambers and the structural divisions within the cairn.

Similar evidence of internal walling has been identified at other Severn-Cotswold tombs, such as Poles Wood South, Randwick, Burn Ground, Ascott-under-Wychwood and Hazleton North in the Cotswold region and at Tinkinswood in south-east Wales (Fig. 12.10; see also Darvill 2004, fig. 40), which are interpreted as cellular units representing stages in a more or less continuous process of construction (cf. Grimes 1960, 66; Saville 1990, 47; Darvill 2004, 117–8; Benson and Whittle 2007, 96–102). Cellular construction is otherwise unrecorded in the Black Mountains long cairns but may be represented by offsets and construction breaks in the line of the inner revetment wall at Ty Isaf (Fig. 2.30; Grimes 1939, pl. xiii, 4). A short and slightly wavering axial line was identified at Gwernvale between the NE corner of Chamber 1 and a natural monolith recognised at the base of the cairn at Gwernvale (Fig. 3.2; Britnell 1984, 59). It has been argued that a more extensive pattern of axial and lateral divisions can be recognised in plan at Gwernvale, perhaps built in association with timber or wicker shuttering and set out with regard to the pre-cairn timber structure below the SE end of the monument (McFadyen 2003, 81–104 and figs 3.1–3.9), but this remains conjectural.

At Hazleton and Ascott the cellular units were set out in relation to a prominent axial line, which together with lateral offsets are seen as a means of achieving, by stages, the final and predetermined trapezoidal plan of the monuments. At Hazleton the cellular divisions are defined solely by stone walling and at Ascott by a combination of timber posts and walling – the timber element at Ascott recalling the wooden posts and hurdling, which mark out the cellular divisions identified in earthen long barrows such as South Street and Beckhampton Road, Wiltshire (Ashbee *et al.* 1979). The lateral chambers at both Hazleton and Ascott were possibly built at an early stage and accommodated within cellular divisions, though in both instances it has been argued that the infilling of the bays containing the chambers (and therefore possibly the roofing of the chambers themselves) may only have been undertaken at an advanced stage of construction (Saville 1990, 227; Benson and Whittle 2007, fig. 4.73). There is uncertainty, however, about whether the chambers were fully functional before the completion of the monument.

The sequence of construction at Penywyrlod is quite distinct to that at Hazleton and Ascott. The way in which the cross-wall at Penywyrlod butts up against the end of Chamber NE II and the apparent relationships of other cross-walls and chambers suggests that single or paired back-to-back chambers and blocks of the inner cairn were built up at the same time. Other differences can be identified at Penywyrlod and in other long cairns in the Black Mountains area, which may also reflect different techniques or sequences of construction. The cross-wall at Penywyrlod has only been traced to about halfway across the mound but there is no indication in the ERT geophysical data (Fig. 2.10) of the kind of axial line that is evident at Hazleton and Ascott. Axial symmetry is so far unrecorded in long cairns in the Black Mountains area and in some instances would seem to be precluded at Ty Isaf, Pipton and Gwernvale (Fig. 2.30) by chambers that appear defiantly asymmetrical, being set at an angle to the sides of the long mounds and crossing the central axis. The large, angled chamber at Arthur's Stone, Dorstone (Hemp 1935), might have a similar relationship to the mound, the recent discovery of drystone walling here (Headland Archaeology 2011) seemingly confirming its structural affinities with other Severn-Cotswold tombs.

Other kinds of internal walling in the Black Mountains long cairns are represented by the so-called 'rotundas' at Ty Isaf and Pipton (which Savory compared to the curving cross wall at Penywyrlod) (Fig. 2.30; Savory 1984, 24), and are discussed in Chapter 12.

Building materials

The selection of materials used in the construction of the Penywyrlod long cairn (see above) displays an intimate knowledge of local resources. Choices may to some extent have been pragmatic and based upon the structural qualities of materials and their ready availability locally but the colour, texture and variety of some of the materials that were chosen appear to reflect distinctive aesthetic or spiritual concerns (cf. Darvill 2010, 7–8). For a start, we can note the use of reddish slabs for the construction of Chamber NE I and the selection of a distinctive slab of variegated conglomerate for the portal lintel. Such choices and selections would in time be repeated elsewhere in other monuments (cf. Cummings 2012, 40–1).

Much of the core of the Penywyrlod cairn was probably extracted from near-surface exposures of sandstone and surface stone including glacial erratics, which would have been scattered across the land surface and sourced from fairly close by. It has been noted above that Savory's 'thrust blocks' adjacent to the 'Main Chamber' (Fig. 2.7; Savory 1984, pl. 5b) might represent surface material of this kind, left more or less *in situ* below the long cairn. Large stones in the glacial till below the Gwernvale long cairn would similarly have been visible in the pre-existing land surface (Fig. 3.4). Geophysical anomalies in the environs of the Penywyrlod long cairn might also represent buried glacial erratics or potentially also holes resulting from their removal. As noted above, the so-called 'buttress pit', close to the tail of the cairn (Savory 1984, 24 and fig. 9) and a possible similar pit with pitched stone at the NW end of trench 2 close to Chamber NE I may both represent stoneholes created by the removal of erratic boulders. The large capstone above the 'Main Chamber' and the large slab that probably formed a lintel above the portal are both composed of highly weathered material, which seems likely to represent glacial erratics. The manner in which such slabs were removed from the ground and put in place – and indeed even their symbolic meaning – may not have differed significantly from the raised stones 'that float to the sky' associated with the dolmen tradition (Cummings and Whittle 2004, 72–8; Whittle 2004; Cummings and Richards 2021). Similarities and differences of this kind are followed further in Chapter 12.

As yet there is no clear evidence at Penywyrlod of the kind of stone quarries found next to Hazleton North and Ascott-under-Wychwood, though the possibility that some of the building material was also obtained from nearby is suggested by visible traces of surface quarries and geophysical anomalies in neighbouring fields, as described above. This evidence has not been explored in the field, however, though it seems likely that at least some of the orthostats of the chambers and the uprights of the portal structure were obtained from local sources or quarries.

The distinctive sandstone slabs used for cladding the outer face of the long cairn were almost certainly obtained from a greater distance, probably from outcrops of the Senni Formation on higher ground, 2.5km or more to the SE, in the direction of Mynydd Troed. Similar stone, likewise obtained from the beds of the Senni Formation, was selected for the outer revetment at Gwernvale (Britnell 1984b, 57). This rock is highly fissile and well suited to drystone walling but it also has a distinctive greenish hue, which differentiates it from the browns, reds and purples of the rock types occurring more locally. Both source and colour could therefore have been powerful signals of the assembly of difference and contrast.

The use of finer-grained stone for the outer revetment walls of long cairns can be found elsewhere, including both Hazleton and Ascott (Worssam 1990, 228–31; Roe 2007a, 80–1). The selection of material brought from some distance away is also paralleled elsewhere in Severn-Cotswold tombs. Some of the materials used in the architectural elements of Hazleton North, Stoney Littleton and West Kennet and other long barrows in the Avebury area, for example, were brought from distances of up to 6km, 8km and 32km away respectively (Darvill 2010, 7). We will discuss such practices further in Chapter 12, to help in the assessment of the distinctiveness of what went on at Penywyrlod.

Access and deposition

The question of how the chambered areas at Penywyrlod may have functioned can now be reassessed in the light of the new evidence obtained from the recording of the entrance passage to Chamber NE I. This is not only of interest in its own right but also has implications for how and when skeletal remains (see Chapter 6) were deposited, the timescale over which these depositions were made, and the dating of the monument as a whole.

Chamber NE I

It is possible, though by no means certain, that the inner compartment of Chamber NE I was a closed cist that became inaccessible upon completion of the monument. The passage and outer compartment of Chamber NE I appear to have been accessed during the period in which the long cairn remained in use. The recent exposure of the outer face of the revetment wall outside the entrance to Chamber NE I suggests the following sequence: (1) outer revetment wall built across the outer end of the entrance passage, as part of the original build; (2) the walling across the entrance passage removed to gain access to the passage, leaving the lowest courses in place; and (3) rebuilding of the outer revetment wall on one or more occasions. A possible lintel stone has been identified that may have been placed above the passage entrance and flush with the outer face of the outer revetment wall (Fig. 2.31), as suggested in the hypothetical reconstruction of the passage entrances at Hazleton North (Fig. 2.32). The facts that the blocking wall appears to have been free-standing, that the possible lintel was the only stone of these dimensions identified during excavation, and that it appears to have fallen inwards, as though into a void, suggest that the entrance passage may have been corbelled with smaller stones, as also suggested in Chamber NE II (see below). The height of the chamber compartments is unknown but the entrance passage was probably a minimum of 1m high, which is the height of orthostat 11 at the inner end of the passage. These were low, cramped spaces.

Human remains have only been found within the inner compartment but these are merely scraps representing an uncertain number of individuals. None of the fragments are dated. Savory had suggested that any human remains within the chamber would have been removed when the chamber was largely destroyed in 1972 during the process of stone extraction. However, as noted above, it seems possible that both compartments were largely devoid of human remains when the monument was abandoned.

Empty or essentially empty chambers are known elsewhere in Severn-Cotswold tombs though the reasons for this are poorly understood (cf. Darvill 2004, 142; Whittle *et al.* 2007a, 134). Within the long cairns in the Black Mountains area, for example, only small quantities of human remains were recovered from Gwernvale Chambers 1–2 and none at all from Chamber 3, though it is uncertain to what extent this may have been the result of later disturbance (Britnell 1984b, 149). Slight human remains were found in the south transept and passage of Pipton Chamber I but none at all in the north transept (Savory 1956, 22). Human remains were present in the passage and central compartment of Ty Isaf Chamber III but were very sparse in both its E and W transepts, though as in the case of Gwernvale it is uncertain to what extent this might reflect later disturbance or conditions of preservation (see Chapter 6). The fact that the outer compartment and passage of Penywyrlod Chamber NE I may have been largely devoid of human remains despite evidence that the passage entrance was unblocked suggests that either any depositions that had been made were subsequently meticulously removed or perhaps that entry was made to the passage and outer compartment of the chamber for some other spiritual purpose.

Chamber NE II

The passage and chamber of Chamber NE II appear to share many similar features with Chamber NE I. Savory considered that the outer revetment wall had been built 'without interruption', creating what he termed a 'dummy' entrance. He noted, however, that the upper portion of the wall across the entrance passage was made up of 'several courses of poorly built dry-stone walling which seem to represent a late stage of development of the 'dummy' entrance passage, after it had already been partially blocked' (Savory 1984, 19–20). This, and the presence of thin vertical slabs between the upper courses of the wall across the entrance and the outer revetment wall to the SE (Fig. 2.27, top right; see also Savory 1984, fig. 6), suggest that like Chamber NE I the outer revetment having originally been built across the passage entrance was then partly removed to gain access to the passage, and then rebuilt. Again, there is no evidence of the timescale over which these events took place or whether they were repeated.

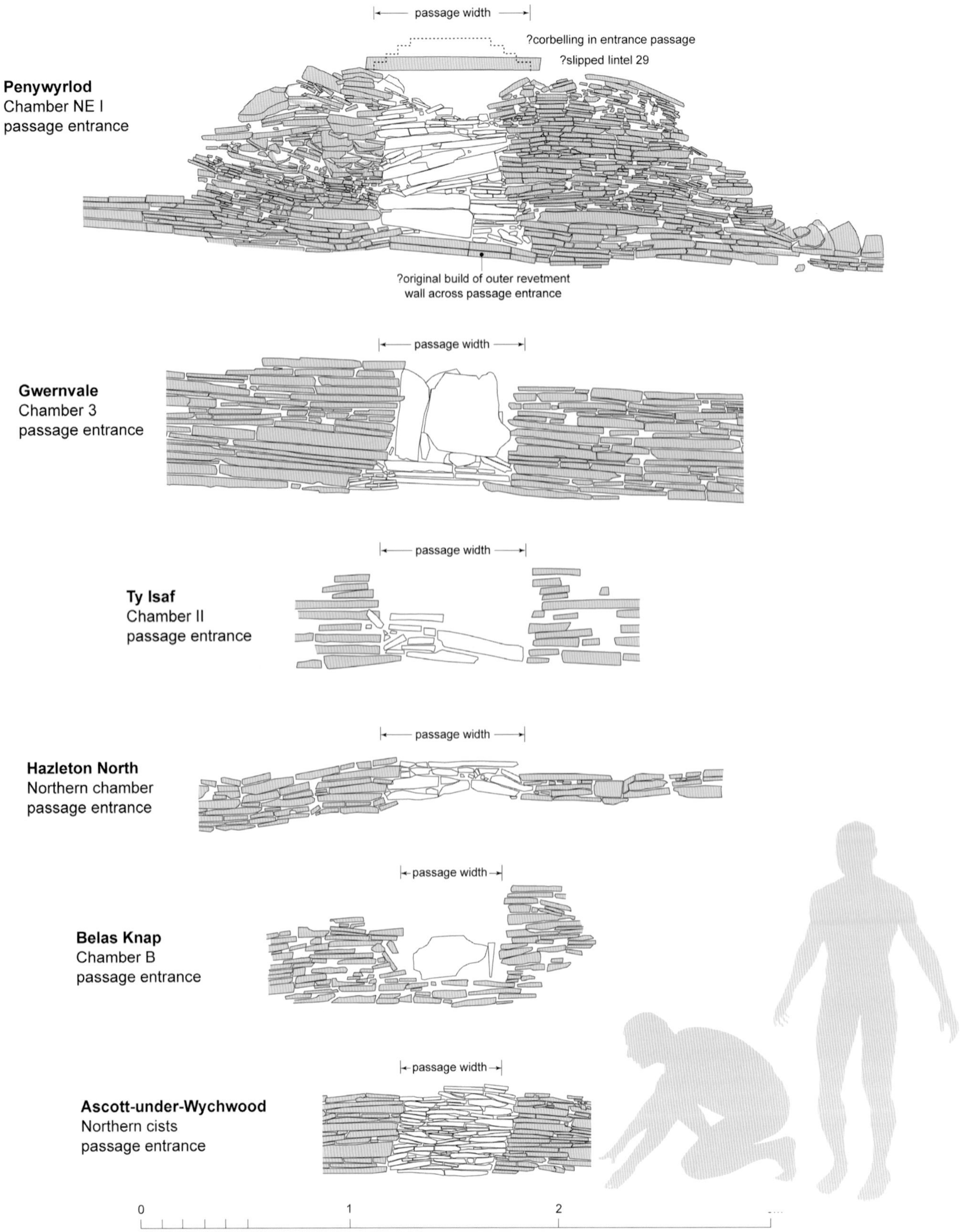

Fig. 2.31. Comparative passage entrance blocking (unshaded) on the face of outer walls (shaded) at Penywyrlod (this report; see Figs 2.18–2.19); Gwernvale (after Britnell 1984b, figs 16, 26; see also this volume Fig. 3.9); Ty Isaf (sketched from Grimes 1939, pl. xiv, 3); Belas Knap (sketched from Hemp 1929, fig. 13); Hazleton North (after Saville 1990, figs 66, 80); Ascott-under-Wychwood (sketched from Benson and Whittle 2007, fig. 4.5 and pl. 4.8). See Figs 2.16–2.19 for location of possible slipped lintel 29 at Penywyrlod.

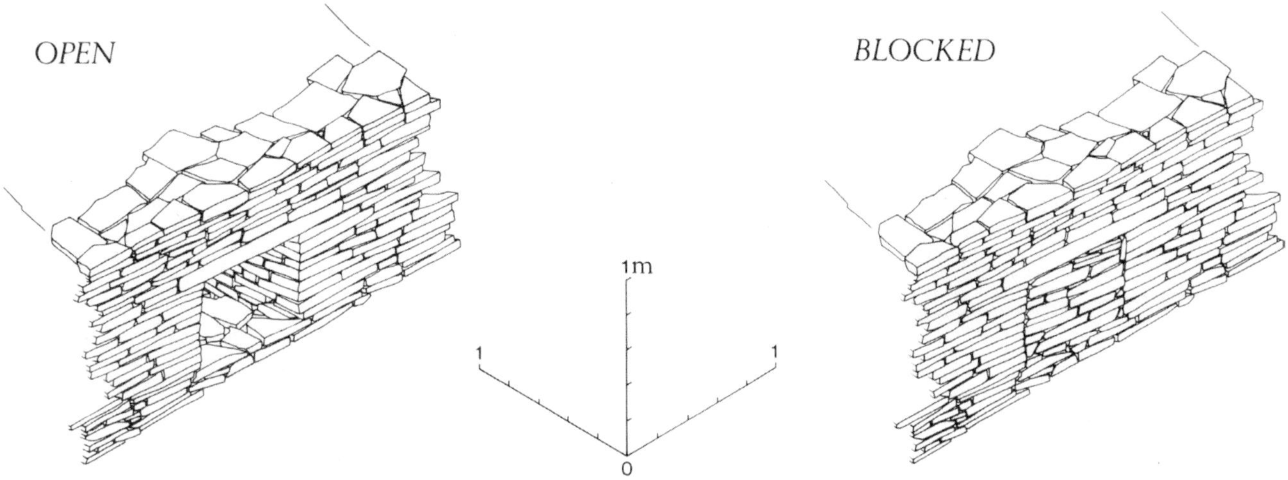

Fig. 2.32. Reconstruction of the entrance and blocking of the passage to the north chamber at Hazleton North (after Saville 1990, fig. 232).

The only certain skeletal remains from the passage are of domesticated and wild animals. These comprised the mandible of a young fox cub, two rib fragments and third phalanx, cannon bone and long-bone fragment of a calf, and two cannon bones from forelegs, right innominate and tibia of a sheep (Luff *et al.* 1984, 39), none of which were considered to be intrusive (Savory 1984, 38). None are dated. Envisaging the chamber passage as being non-functional, Savory (1984, 20, 35) considered that these animal remains belonged to the period of its construction and represented 'offerings' after the single deposition of the human remains in the chamber, but they might alternatively be associated with the subsequent opening and closing of the passage entrance. This is suggested by the presence of 'two more fragments of [animal] bone…found on top of the bottom four courses of well-built walling forming part of the outer revetment wall opposite the entrance passage', immediately below what is reinterpreted as the rebuilding of the blocking wall.

Stonework on the line of the inner revetment wall juts out above the top of the orthostat lining the inner end of the entrance passage on the NW side (Fig. 2.28). This, together with long rectangular blocks found within the passage (Savory 1984, fig. 6, left) suggested that the inner passage, probably like the chamber itself, had been roofed with corbelling at a height of up to about 1.2m. Savory noted that the outer revetment near the chamber entrance survived to a height of only about 0.35m but the volume of collapsed material outside the cairn and the height of the walling in the outer passage suggest that it had probably been at least about 0.7m high here originally. An unusually large slab about 1m by 0.6m across, found towards the base of the collapse immediately outside the passage entrance, specifically mentioned by Savory (1984, 24 and pl. 7c), may have been similar to the suggested lintel above the passage entrance to Chamber NE I. The section drawing shown in Figure 2.28 suggests that if the entrance passage had been corbelled then it must have risen quite sharply from the outer revetment wall towards the chamber entrance.

Mixed, disarticulated human remains of a minimum of six individuals were found in Chamber NE II together with one bone from a horse/pony (see Chapter 6). Only two fragments of human bone were found within the passage but in a disturbed superficial deposit, which suggested that they were intrusive (Savory 1984, 19).

As noted by Savory, the fragmentary 'sealing slab' at the NE end of Chamber NE II appears to create a closed cist, which was integral to the original structure (Fig. 2.27, top left and bottom left, and Fig. 2.28) – seemingly being held by stonework on the sides, gripped by sills at the base and overridden by corbelling at the top. In Savory's interpretation the 'sealing slab' must have been put in place during the construction of the monument, its apparent immovability suggested to him that the human remains within the chamber had been brought from elsewhere and deposited as a single act (Savory 1984, 19–20, 35).

The question of how and when the human remains were deposited in the chamber has implications for the date of construction of the monument as a whole. Bayesian modelling of the five radiocarbon dates that have now been obtained from human remains within the chamber (see Chapter 4) suggests that they belong to people who had died over a period of between *170–490 years* (*95% probability*), or *305–435 years* (*66% probability*; *duration_NE_II*). If the chamber had indeed been closed then it implies that the human remains within the chamber included ancestral material and were deposited on a single occasion prior to the completion of the monument (as envisaged by Savory) or that the chamber had been free-standing and been accessible from either above or for a significant period of time prior to completion of the long cairn (though for reasons given above this seems unlikely). In either case the monument would be later than the radiocarbon modelling suggests.

The only other solution to this 'locked room mystery' is to assume that there had been some less obvious means of entering the chamber, which it is worthwhile examining in some detail since it might also have implications for the possibly virtually empty inner compartment of Chamber NE I.

Although the 'sealing slab' has every appearance of having been fixed in position when the monument was constructed there is perhaps some possibility that it had once been moveable, like the 'blocking slabs' identified between passages and chambers in both the north and south chambers at Hazleton (Saville 1990, 69–72, 251 and fig. 84). Saville compared these to slabs recorded at Rodmarton and Tinkinswood and questioned whether the 'sealing slab' in Penywyrlod Chamber NE II might 'have originally been a blocking slab, fixed in place once that part of the chambered area had been abandoned' (Saville 1990, 259). The apparent immovability of the 'sealing slab' undoubtedly led to Savory's interpretation of the entrance passage as being non-functional, though as noted above, there are suggestions that this *had* probably been entered on one or more occasions after the completion of the cairn.

If the 'sealing slab' had been permanently fixed (which might only be confirmed by further excavation), there are several other ways in which the chamber might possibly have been entered following completion of the monument. The upper, SE corner of the 'sealing slab' was missing and assumed to have been destroyed when the site was disturbed during stone extraction in the 1970s. If the slab had originally been incomplete then there might have been a triangular gap up to about 0.6m across beginning at a height of about 0.3m above the 'sills' to either side of the 'sealing slab', through which entry could be made to the chamber above ground level, perhaps in the manner of the 'porthole entrances' known elsewhere in Severn-Cotswold tombs (Clifford and Daniel 1940, 149–65; Corcoran 1969, 94–5). Constricted openings of this kind were sometimes created by shaping stones (cf. an example from western France illustrated in Fig. 12.11), though in other instances a constricted opening was made by the juxtaposition of angled stones, as at Luckington Chamber A (Corcoran 1970, fig. IIb) and the western compartment of Ty Isaf Chamber III (Grimes 1939, 129 and pl. xv, 2). Alternatively, it is possible that there had been an irregular porthole-like entrance formed of roughly fractured slabs like the entrance to a chamber on the NW side of the Lanhill long barrow (Keiller and Piggott 1938, 125 and fig. 2), though here again there is uncertainty whether the stones were fractured at some more recent date.

A second possibility is that the chamber remained accessible from the surface of the cairn. As noted above, it seems likely that the roof of the chamber was corbelled and then capped with stones that were smaller than the chamber itself and perhaps reaching to within 0.5m of the modern surface of the cairn (see Fig. 2.28). Entry from above has been suggested in the case of Pipton Chamber II (Savory 1956, 42) and the paired cists at Ascott-under-Wychwood (Benson and Whittle 2007, 139), though in the case of Pipton it is suggested above that the chamber may have been accessible via an entrance passage at least during an early phase.

Another possibility is that human remains might have been deposited above the 'sealing slab', from within the passage. Though not explicitly acknowledging the potential ambiguity of a closed chamber approached by a 'dummy' entrance passage, Savory (1984, 32) did leave open the possibility that disarticulated human remains may in effect have been posted through a 'narrow gap which may or may not have been filled with smaller stones' between the top of the 'sealing slab' and the corbelling and cover slabs above the chamber and passage, though he suggested that such a gap would have been too narrow to permit human entry. It is assumed that the principal way in which articulated remains were deposited in the cists at Ascott-under-Wychwood was by removing the roofing. The insertion of some disarticulated remains through gaps between the tops of the orthostats and the roofing was also raised as a possibility, though not in this instance from a position within the passage (Whittle *et al.* 2007, 150).

There are therefore several competing possibilities, but overall a distinctive set of practices is indicated, a further point to return to in wider discussion in Chapter 12.

The only find associated with Penywyrlod Chamber NE II was a fragmentary arrowhead from the floor of the chamber (Savory 1984, fig. 10, no. 3). Like that identified more recently from Chamber NE III (see Chapter 6), this might have been deposited with human skeletal material.

Chamber NE III

Although the form of Chamber NE III is uncertain it clearly had an entrance passage similar to Chambers NE I–II, with an open chamber entrance similar to the outer compartment of Chamber NE I. The outer element of the chamber at least was roofed by a relatively small capstone (since fallen), 1.2m by 0.18m across and 0.18m thick. In this instance the mixed disarticulated remains of a minimum of seven individuals were found in the passage as well as in different levels in the largely unexamined chamber (see Chapter 6). Animal remains from the entrance passage comprised a tibia, four cannon bones from fore and hind limbs of red deer and a pig molar tooth (Luff *et al.* 1984, 38).

Like Chambers NE I–II, the outer end of the passage was blocked by walling in line with the outer face of the outer revetment wall, which survived here to a height of about 0.3m. Though Savory considered that it was more or less at the height it was built, it seems likely (based on the reinterpretation of the external walling elsewhere) that it was originally up to twice this height. Having assumed that the outer margins of the cairn were originally much lower, Savory (1984, 20) suggested that the passage may have been roofed with a capstone 'which could have been raised to gain access to the chamber', but no evidence of capstones has survived. It now seems more likely as suggested in the case of Chambers NE I–II that the passage may have been roofed with corbelling and slabs.

The surviving 'seven or eight courses' of walling across the outer end of the passage to Chamber NE III appear to be unbroken (Fig. 2.29, bottom) though Savory (1984, 20) noted that 'the upper two or three courses' projected 'somewhat irregularly, as though they were of a separate build'. In addition, like Chamber NE II, it was also noted that bones (whether human or animal is not stated) were found 'intermingled with small blocking slabs as in the dummy entrance passage of Chamber NE II'. There is therefore the possibility, as shown in Chamber NE I and inferred in Chamber NE II, that at least the upper walling across the entrance passage along the line of the outer revetment wall had been removed to gain entry to the passage and chamber for activities involving the handling of skeletal material. As elsewhere there may have been no necessity to remove all of such blocking walls down to ground level in order to gain entry to passages and chambers. Passage entrances appear to have been amongst the parts of the structure most vulnerable to later disturbance and in similar instances elsewhere, where only a few courses of walling survive, evidence of whether entry had been made might therefore not be apparent.

The only finds within Chamber NE III were a flint knife (Savory 1984, fig. 10, no 3) found in the lower blocking material in the outer end of the passage and a perforated bone considered to be a possible musical instrument found in the passage (ibid. no. 6). The tip of an arrowhead found embedded in a human rib bone appears to have also come from this chamber (see Chapter 6).

Almost identical evidence for the blocking and unblocking of passage entrances has been recorded at Hazelton North and Belas Knap (see Fig. 2.31) and probably also at Lanhill (Keiller and Piggott 125). Hemp (1929, 268) suggested that the passage of Chamber B at Belas Knap had been roofed entirely in corbelling. The upper levels of the passages had not survived at Hazleton but Saville considered that roofing entirely in corbelling was unlikely at Hazleton since this may have been too fragile. Instead, he suggested that they had probably been roofed with corbelling capped with roofing slabs at a height of about 0.5m and with a lintel on the line of the outer revetment wall (Saville 1990, 248; Fig. 2.32). The critical evidence in support of this interpretation comes from Luckington Chamber A where lintel stones still *in situ* above the passage entrances on the line of the outer revetment wall were blocked with walling below (Corcoran 1970, 42 and pl. IIa). A similar but possible fallen lintel stone was also found outside Luckington Chamber D (Corcoran 1970, 48 and fig. 5). The passage of Luckington Chamber A, like Gwernvale Chamber 3, appears to have been similarly blocked with stone (Corcoran 1970, 42).

The survival of the lintel stone at Luckington Chamber A suggests that the location of the chamber entrances would have been evident rather than being hidden and it also shows that entry to the entrance passage was severely constricted. The space below the lintel was evidently only about 0.4m high and 0.75m wide and would only be accessible to an adult shuffling along on their stomach. At Luckington Chamber A and at Lanhill there are suggestions that the height of the passages gradually rose from the passage entrance towards the chamber entrances (Corcoran 1970, 42) and presumably matched a rise in the surface of the overlying mound. This also seems likely in the case of the passages of Penywyrlod Chambers NE I–III.

An alternative means of accessing the chamber passages has been suggested in the case of the lateral chambers at Rodmarton, which would have involved climbing over the outer revetment wall and descending into the entrance passages (either unroofed or with removable roofing) by means of steps (Clifford and Daniel 1940, pl. x, lower; Darvill 2004, fig. 44). The steps are very much an oddity within Severn-Cotswold tombs, however, and although they have generally been assumed to be original (rather than rebuilding following excavations in the 1860s), this has yet to be confirmed by an examination of the outer face of the long cairn opposite the chamber entrances. Grimes suggested (1960, 93–4), subsequent to the publication of the original excavation report, that outer passages at Ty Isaf had been unroofed and had been accessed in a similar manner to that suggested by Clifford and Daniel at Rodmarton, via a 'shallow shaft' entered from the surface of the cairn behind the outer cairn wall. This interpretation, however, was based upon the assumption that 'extra revetment' material outside the cairn formed part of the original structure of the monument, though this is now generally considered to represent later collapse.

At first sight, the structure and sequence of construction and usage of the lateral passages at Ascott-under-Wychwood appear to have been quite different but reinterpretation of the published evidence suggests that these may have followed the recurrent pattern recorded at the other laterally chambered Severn-Cotswold tombs mentioned above. The back-to-back pairs of cists at Ascott were both approached by passages, which, as in similar instances elsewhere, are divided into an outer passage between the outer revetment wall and an inner revetement wall and an inner passage between the inner revetment wall and the cists themselves. The entrance to the northern passage entrance had been blocked along the line of the outer revetment wall, in a similar manner to Penywyrlod Chamber NE I and elsewhere (Fig. 2.31), though here it is suggested that the blocking may have been inserted shortly after the construction of the outer revetment wall, as a more or less single continuous act (Benson and Whittle 2007, 121). It is also implied that the inner revetment wall had been built continuously across the passage but had been subsequently partly opened up by the removal of some of the upper courses of stone (Benson and Whittle 2007, 121). There appears be no compelling evidence that the inner revetment wall *had* originally been constructed across the northern passage at Ascott, however. The blocking wall across the northern passage entrance does not appear to have been free-standing, like the blocking walls across the entrances to Penywyrlod Chambers NE I–III for example, but seems to closely parallel the stone deposits, noted above, which blocked the outer passages to chambers at Gwernvale and Luckington. In the case of Gwernvale Chamber 3 the passage blocking extended between the outer face of the outer revetment wall and ended in a stack of horizontally laid slabs on the line of the inner revetment wall (Fig. 2.33, top; Britnell 1984, 83 and fig. 23, iii, c). There was no surviving evidence of roofing of the passages at Ascott though there are hints of corbelling on the E side of the northern passage (Benson and Whittle 2007, fig. 4.55).

A sequence of activity involving the opening and closing of the passages at Ascott is suggested by the presence of human remains at the inner ends of both passages, the intermixture of slabs of stone of a similar kind to that of the outer revetment wall amongst the human remains in the northern passage, and by the presence of fragments of human or animal bone below the stone blocking the outer entrance and the stone that is reinterpreted as passage blocking. Neither the northern or southern passages appear to have given access to the cists themselves, however, which as in the original interpretation of Penywyrlod Chamber NE II must either have been closed deposits that were sealed when the monument was completed or remained accessible from above or by some other means, and which similarly led to the interpretation of the passages as being non-functional. There was no surviving evidence of how the chambers were roofed, though there is a suggestion of corbelling on the eastern side of the northern pair of cists, represented by blocks of stone partly overriding the orthostats (Benson and Whittle 2007, 128 and fig. 4.6). The cist orthostats at Ascott stood to a height of no more than 0.4–0.5m. If the roofing of the chambers had been carried up by corbelling to a similar height as that suggested at Penywyrlod, this would have left ample room for the cists to be accessed via the passages. By way of comparison, the corbelled roofs of the rounded chambers at Saltway Barn, Ablington and Cow Common in the Cotswold-Severn group, constructed wholly of corbelling, rose to heights of up to about 1.4m (cf. Grimes 1960, fig. 13).

In summary, the question of why, when and how each of the three excavated chambers at Penywyrlod were accessed raises a considerable range of possibilities, each of which can be paralleled in laterally chambered Cotswold-Severn tombs elsewhere. Penywyrlod Chamber NE I had an outer compartment accessible via the passage entered from the outside of the long cairn. An inner compartment of this chamber and the whole of Chamber NE II may only have been accessible before completion of the cairn and sealed when the monument was completed, or remained accessible from above, or may have been accessible by means of a 'porthole entrance' via the entrance passages, or by somehow moving the 'sealing slab'. Chamber NE III appears to have remained open and accessible via an entrance passage. One of the few recurrent activities recognisably affecting the structure itself was the opening and closing of passage entrances. This suggests that the three principal zones of the chambered areas – entrances, passages and chambers (cf. Darvill 2004, 109 and fig. 45) – may each have had its own particular significance in terms of procedure, ritual or metaphor to the builders of long cairns.

Whatever the correct interpretation of the details might be, the themes and contrasts continue of outer skin or wrapping, internal low chambers and quite small spaces, and probably repeated acts of entry and re-arrangement. These are followed up in Chapter 12.

'Main Chamber'

Savory's so-called 'Main Chamber' (Fig. 2.29, top right) remains unexcavated. Its form is uncertain but it is assumed to have been accessed from the SW side of the long cairn. Savory (1984, 16) noted that it was possible to see that 'the interior was evenly filled with earth covered with a thin layer of sandstone chips to within a few inches of the under surface of the capstone throughout in a manner which suggested deliberated filling at some time', though this remains conjectural. There is some evidence of animal burrowing in the surface of the long cairn near the chamber which may in the past have resulted in soil being carried down into it.

Activity elsewhere around the margins of the monument

Other evidence of activity around the cairn at Penywyrlod is slight. Sherds of a round-bottomed bowl were found on the surface of the buried soil immediately outside Chamber NE III and other sherds and two stone discs were found close to the tail end of the cairn (Savory 1984, fig. 10), though it is uncertain whether these finds derived from pre-cairn activity or activity contemporary with the use of the cairn. An area of burning that included cereal grain outside the entrance to Chamber NE I (Fig. 2.16) might pre-date or be contemporary with the construction of the cairn. A pit close to the tail of the cairn (the so-called 'buttress pit'), considered by Savory to have had a structural function (Savory 1984, 23 and fig. 9), now seems more likely to have been a quarry pit or stone-removal hole contemporary with the construction of the monument.

Closure, abandonment and decay

It is now widely accepted that upon completion the outer revetment walls of Severn-Cotswold tombs were exposed to view and that stone found beyond the outer wall – previously considered to be deliberately placed 'extra-revetment material' – largely represents the natural collapse of the original structure (cf. Saville 1990, 126–33). As at Hazleton North, the volume of this outer material varies significantly around the perimeter of Penywyrlod (Savory 1984, 24), with comparatively little beyond the SE hornwork and the N corner but extending up to 2–3m beyond the outer revetment walls outside Chambers NE I and NE II (Fig. 2.21).

The mass of stone recorded by Savory within the forecourt at Penywyrlod might simply represent the collapse of the higher walling here, within a confined space, but there remains the possibility, as suggested at some other Severn-Cotswold tombs, that the forecourt may have been deliberately blocked with stone, as an act of closure or as part of a process of monument 'antiquation' (cf. Darvill 2004, 181–2; J. Thomas 1988, 553–5). Savory suggested that the Penywyrlod forecourt may have been deliberately infilled in two stages, firstly by a 'a large heap of horizontally placed stones' towards the outer end of the forecourt and secondly by a deposit immediately next to the portal composed of 'many small slabs tilted downwards' (Savory 1984, 22). Photographic evidence suggests, however, that the inner deposit might be reinterpreted as a filled-in robber trench dug up against the outer face of the portal structure (Fig. 2.26, left), presumably after the removal of the lintel and after the forecourt had become filled with stone. The dating of such disturbance is unknown though it might represent an otherwise antiquarian investigation. Savory interpreted holes in the side of the suggested lintel (Savory 1984, fig. 8) as an attempt to split the stone by explosives, but this remains speculative. They might alternatively represent the weathering out of conglomeric pebbles. As noted above, it now seems more likely that the stones between the two uprights of the portal structure represent the remains of either an inner or outer revetment wall, the surviving upper courses of which had slipped forward. If this was the case then the walling is likely to have fallen into an empty space but it remains uncertain whether this might have occurred before the forecourt became filled with stone or following disturbance during the digging of the suggested robber trench.

Access to the chambers or passages would have remained possible until they were eventually hidden by the collapse of the external walling and the entrance passages. The drystone walling enveloping the monument appears to have been inherently unstable and some deterioration may have begun quite quickly after construction. There is some suggestion at Ascott-under-Wychwood that stones may have been placed against the outer revetment wall to arrest further decay (Benson and Whittle 2007, 355), but generally there is little evidence at Severn-Cotswold tombs that repairs were undertaken, giving the impression that the first builds of these monuments were the overriding concern (cf. Bradley 1993, 98). Indeed, one can wonder whether the outer walling was envisaged as a some kind of sacrificial outer skin, which through natural processes would contribute to an archaising effect yet leave the core of the monument and its hidden chambers intact (cf. Britnell 1984b, 150; Darvill 2004, 125). Parallels might even be drawn with the act of burning down the façades and revetments of earthen long barrows (Whittle 1988, 185; Bradley 2019, 61–2).

The differential rate of collapse around the monument might have some significance. As noted at other laterally chambered long cairns, as for example in the case of Gwernvale Chamber 3 (Fig. 2.33, bottom), the wall face immediately next to the entrance to Penywyrlod Chamber NE I remained standing after stretches of walling further away had collapsed down to foundation level. This is probably to be explained by assuming that the structure of the entrance passages and the chambers would have lessened the effects of lateral pressure, which caused the collapse of the outer walling elsewhere. This might have enabled access to chambers to have been maintained for a time

Fig. 2.33. Details of outer walling at Gwernvale shown for comparison with Penywyrlod Chambers NE I–III. Top: Gwernvale Chamber 3 and entrance passage. Below: Outer walling just to the E of the entrance passage to Gwernvale Chamber 3.

after the collapse of the outer face of the monument had begun elsewhere. Stone deposits immediately outside the entrance passages at Gwernvale were interpreted as deliberate external blocking structures (Fig. 2.33, top; Britnell 1984b, 150), though in retrospect they might possibly be reinterpreted as representing the collapse of stonework from corbelled passages after the external revetment walls had already begun to deteriorate to either side.

It seems likely that Penywyrlod Chambers NE I–III and their passages may have been essentially voided when the monument went out of use. Savory describes the unexcavated 'Main Chamber' as having been 'evenly filled with earth covered with a thin layer of sandstone chips to within a few inches of the surface of the capstone throughout' (Savory 1984, 16). He compared this to a thick layer of earth found within Pipton Chamber I (Savory 1956, 23) and suggested in both instances that this was evidence of deliberate infilling. At Penywyrlod at least there is evidence of recent animal burrowing in the vicinity of the 'Main Chamber' and in the absence of excavation it must remain uncertain whether the filling was deliberate.

There is little explicit evidence of later activity at Penywyrlod apart from the insertion of an undated cist in the NE hornwork following the partial collapse of the outer revetment wall, which, as noted above, contained the partial remains of several individuals (see Chapter 6; Savory 1984, 22–3; and Fig. 2.7). The cist was formed of thin vertical slabs and was paved and covered with small slabs. A parallel might be drawn with the four unusual crouched inhumations recorded within the southern revetment wall at West Tump (Witts 1881, 204–5). In the case of one of the burials, the wall is said to have 'showed signs of having been displaced', which might, as at Penywyrlod, suggest partial collapse of the outer revetment wall. In addition, 'two upright stones were placed to hold up the rubble above the skull, and below the skeleton were placed flat stones'. This burial at West Tump is undated but the three others that appear to lie in similar positions have been dated to between 3640–3370 cal BC, which is roughly contemporary with skeletal remains of one of the individuals within the one known lateral chamber at West Tump (Smith and Brickley 2006, 340–3).

3

Gwernvale Neolithic long cairn reconsidered

William Britnell

Introduction

The Gwernvale long cairn (SO 211 192), just to the west of Crickhowell, Powys, is orientated approximately NW–SE and lies at an elevation of 78m OD on a morainic ridge of glacial till, which forms a short, low promontory overlooking the northern edge of the floodplain of the river Usk (G. Williams 1968; Humpage 1992; Thomas and Humpage 2007). Situated at the northern end of the ridge where it abuts the foot of the south-facing valley side, the long cairn has extensive views of the Usk valley to the W, S and E and the southern side of the Black Mountains to the N (Fig. 3.1).

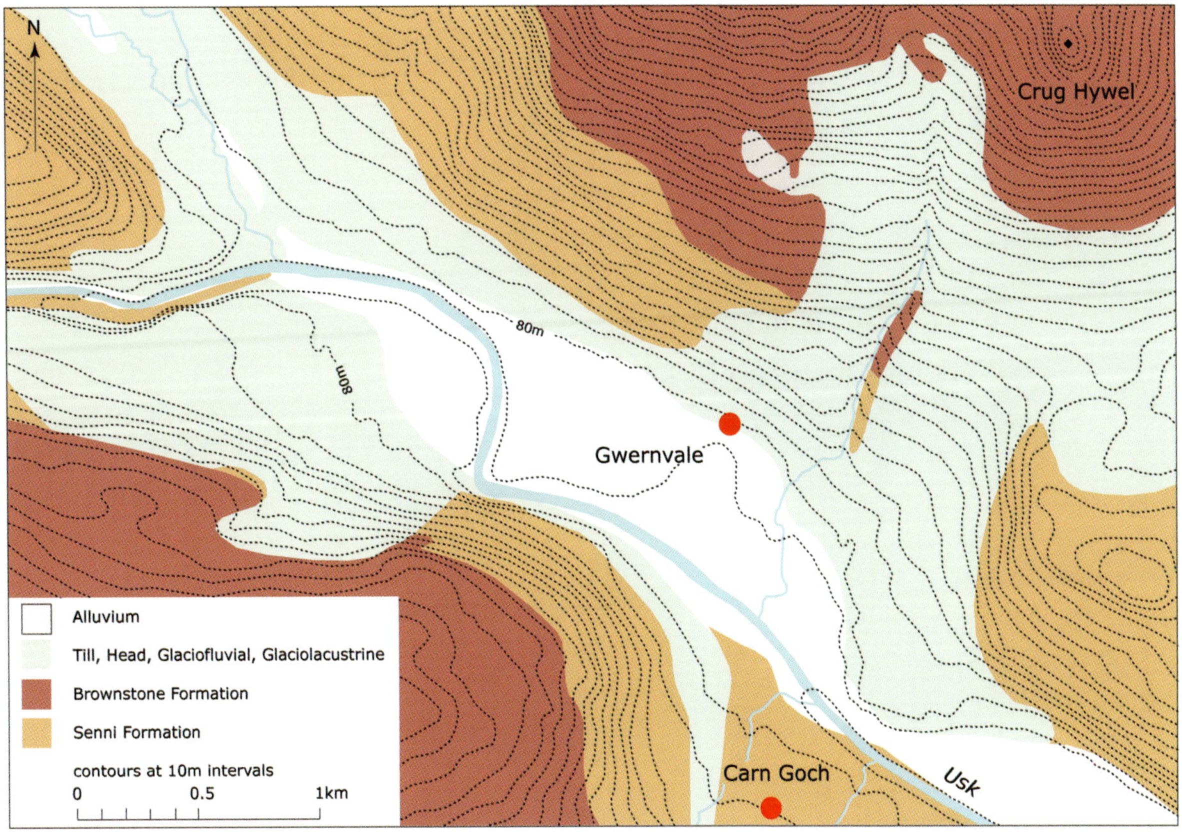

Fig. 3.1. Gwernvale: location of the long cairn shown in relation to topography, bedrock and superficial geology (simplified from British Geological Survey 1:50,000 map sheet 232, Abergavenny).

Rescue excavations in 1977–78, in advance of road improvements, revealed that the known chamber (Chamber 1) lay within a trapezoidal cairn, a little under 50m in length, with three certain lateral chambers and a possible fourth, and with a forecourt and an orthostatic portal structure at its broader, eastern end (Britnell 1984b; Fig. 3.2). Excavation below a restricted area of the cairn provided evidence of pre-cairn Mesolithic and early Neolithic activity, the latter associated with one or more timber structures below the eastern end.

In the original report on the excavations at Gwernvale in 1977–78, it was only possible to include a preliminary assessment of the palaeo-environmental evidence from the site (Britnell 1984b, 96, 141). The recent analysis of the charred plant remains and charcoal from the site by Astrid Caseldine, presented in Chapter 5, has also provided the opportunity for additional radiocarbon dating and for the reassessment of early Neolithic pre-cairn activity at Gwernvale presented in this chapter; in it, I link that to the local context and sequence, and draw parallels with the evidence published more recently from the Severn-Cotswold tombs at Hazleton North and Ascott-under-Wychwood and early Neolithic middens in the Thames Valley. Bayesian modelling of the radiocarbon dates from Gwernvale and other long cairns in the Black Mountains group by Seren Griffiths is presented in Chapter 4. Reassessment of the lithics and ceramic finds from Gwernvale, in the light of more recent

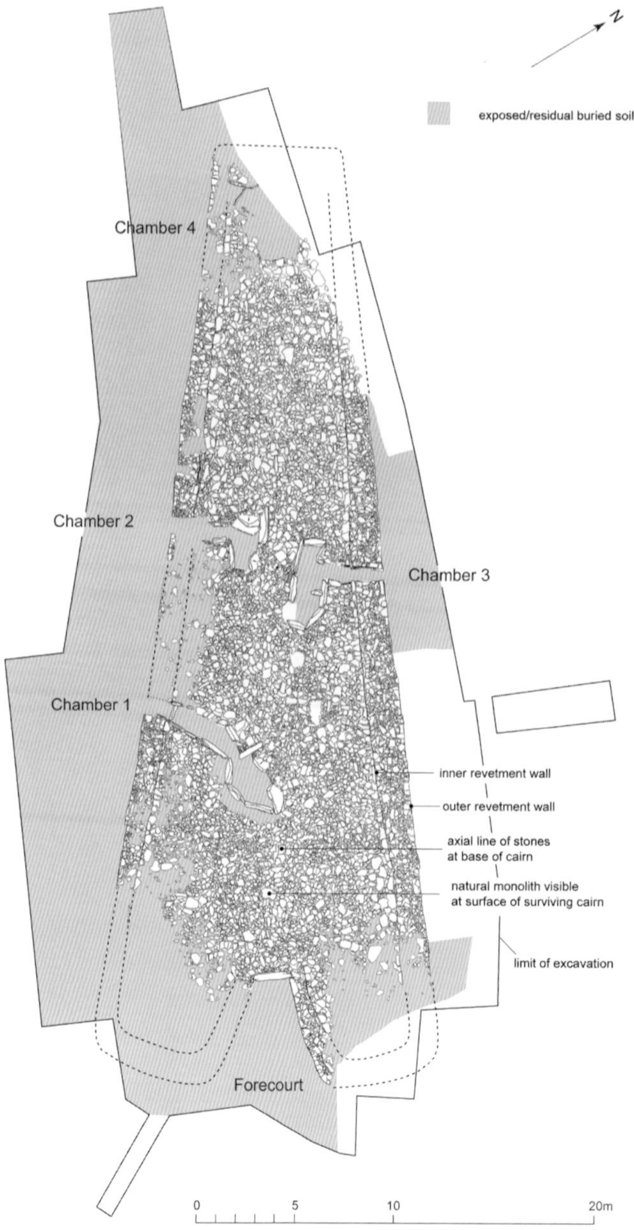

Fig. 3.2. Gwernvale: plan of the 1977–78 excavations showing the surviving elements of the long cairn (after Britnell 1984b).

research, is presented respectively by Elizabeth Walker in Chapter 9 and by Alistair Barclay in Chapter 10, while Chapter 11 provides analysis of organic residues in the pottery by Isabel Wiltshire and Lucy Cramp.

Gwernvale is further integrated into wider discussion of the local and broader context and sequence in Chapter 12. It offers a series of contrasts to the situation at Penywyrlod set out in the previous chapter. Whereas Penywyrlod was argued in the previous chapter to be a fresh location, Gwernvale was a place with a long history, including Mesolithic activity. Its pre-cairn early Neolithic use may span from the 39th to the 36th or 35th centuries cal BC, as set out below and in Chapter 4, and on that basis the monument itself is probably no older than the 35th century cal BC. This significant difference in date compared to Penywyrlod should be emphasised from the outset. Once again, it is important to try to relate the site in the first place to the developing local context, but the wider connections become if anything more significant as time goes on, and the transition from occupation to monument seen at Gwernvale – in contrast to the situation at Penywyrlod – can be mirrored widely elsewhere. The account in this chapter attempts to draw out such trends and contrasts, which we try to unpick further in Chapter 12.

Summary of excavations in 1977–78

Areas examined

Due to the selective nature of the excavations only parts of the deposits underlying the long cairn were excavated though not all of these were still sealed by extant cairn material (Fig. 3.3). These included the area below the N and S horns to either side of the forecourt, an area below the south-eastern side of the cairn, an area below the western end of the cairn, and an area between the forecourt and Chamber 1. Areas were also investigated beyond the northern and southern sides of the cairn, within the chambers and within the forecourt, which potentially include material earlier than, contemporary with, or later than the construction of the cairn.

Buried soils and natural boulders

Excavation revealed that the ground surface below the long cairn sloped gently by about a metre from E–W with its highest point below the area later occupied by the forecourt. The buried soil profile, freely drained brown earth (pH range 6.8–7.4), showed considerable evidence of human disturbance (Keeley 1978; 1980). The buried topsoil horizon was reddish-brown and relatively stone-free, up to about 0.13m thick with no clear indication of a buried turf line. The exposed ground surface below the cairn was deeply indented due to the sinkage of the basal layers of the cairn into the buried soil (Fig. 3.4).

A cluster of natural weathered boulders of Devonian sandstone punctuated the buried soil below the eastern end of the cairn (Fig. 3.3), at least some of which would have been visible in the surface of the ridge from early times and which are probably locally derived glacial erratics (Adrian Humpage, *pers. comm.*). It is perhaps significant that a flint burin of probable Mesolithic date was found jammed into a crevice in the top of a particularly prominent, natural and weathered sandstone boulder, 0.7m high (Fig. 3.4, termed 'natural monolith' in the original publication). This stone appears to form a focus for pre-cairn activity and subsequently fell along the axis of the long cairn and equidistant between the forecourt and Chamber 1.

The buried soil (30) excavated below the cairn had an average depth of 130mm. The assemblage of charred plant remains in samples from soils and features within the forecourt and in Chambers 2 and 3 might pre-date the long cairn or belong to the period of its abandonment between the 31st to 28th centuries cal BC. An upper, darker, layer of soil in the forecourt (95) was between 60–100mm thick. This was originally assumed to have accumulated during the life of the long cairn but it might alternatively represent an occupation layer within the timber structure pre-dating the long cairn. It included earlier lithic material, however, which implies that plant remains from it might include material that is either earlier or contemporary with the use of the long cairn. A lower layer (202), up to about 70mm thick, was continuous with the buried soil (30) sealed below the long cairn. Material from this context is assumed to be essentially of pre-cairn origin but might include plant remains contemporary with the use of the forecourt.

Pre-cairn Mesolithic activity

The focus in this chapter is on the evidence for early Neolithic activity prior to the construction of the long cairn but brief mention should be made of earlier lithic material at the site (see distribution on Fig. 3.5). In the original report (Healey and Green 1984), material of Upper Palaeolithic, early Mesolithic and particularly late Mesolithic date was identified but the presence of Upper Palaeolithic finds is questioned in the recent review of the material by Elizabeth Walker in Chapter 9. (Although a distinction between Late Mesolithic (*c.* 7000–5000 cal BC) and a Final Mesolithic (the 5th millennium) has been made (Conneller 2022), this report follows a simpler distinction between early and late Mesolithic.) The remaining Mesolithic evidence, as well as subsequent early Neolithic pre-cairn activity, underline the very different situation compared to that of Penywyrlod (set out in Chapter 2), and the elaboration of a long-enduring place is followed further in Chapter 12.

Recent studies of lithic scatters elsewhere in Wales have suggested that major river valleys such as the Usk were corridors for early hunter-gatherers moving seasonally between over-wintering bases near the coast and summer hunting grounds in the hinterland during the Upper Palaeolithic and Mesolithic periods (E. Walker 2015, 122–3; David and Painter 2014, 88) and it is probably in this context that

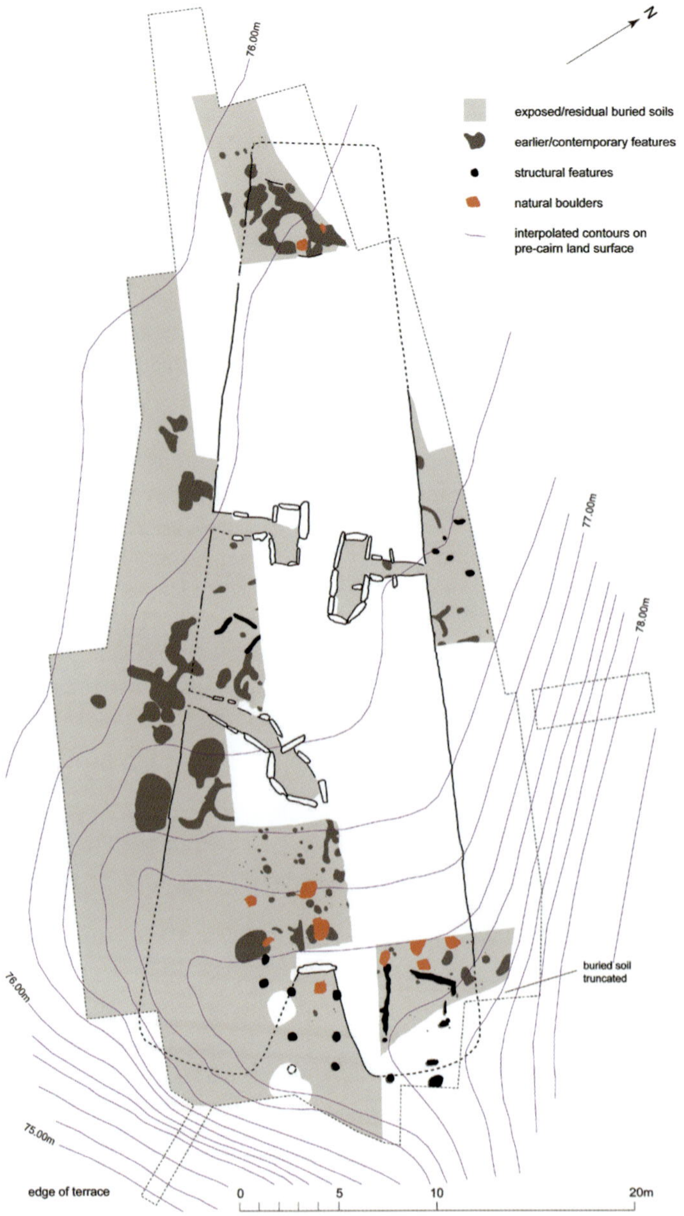

Fig. 3.3. Gwernvale: plan of the 1977–78 excavations showing extent of the buried soil revealed during excavation (contours on the surface of the buried soil at 0.2m intervals), sandstone boulders in the underlying glacial till, and features identified below and adjacent to the long cairn (after Britnell 1984b).

open-air and presumably temporarily occupied sites such as that at Gwernvale are to be viewed.

The Mesolithic lithic material that occurs in buried soil horizons below the cairn and as residual finds in Neolithic features together accounts for about 60% of the diagnostic lithic assemblage from the site (Healey and Green 1984, 129). The distribution of diagnostic Mesolithic material overlaps with that of diagnostic pre-cairn Neolithic material but is spread more widely (Healey and Green 1984, fig. 58) and possibly relates more to the edge of the terrace as much as the focal point suggested by the 'natural monolith' mentioned above. The only certain Mesolithic feature is a hearth whose dating is mentioned in the section on radiocarbon dating below, which appears to lie outside the area of lithic scatters. The nature of the relationship between late Mesolithic and early Neolithic lithic industries at the site is not considered further here, but we will return to the contribution of Mesolithic activity to the creation of a sense of place both below and in Chapter 12.

Pre-cairn Neolithic activity

Early Neolithic activity below the cairn is represented by structural features, finds scatters, several pits and a cluster of fairly amorphous hollows and gullies. As noted above,

Fig. 3.4. Gwernvale: buried soil (30) and the 'natural monolith', viewed from the SE during the course of excavation in 1978. This and a cluster of other weathered Devonian sandstone boulders of probable glacial erratic origin protruded from the underlying glacial till. The 'natural monolith' stood to a height of 0.7m above the surface of the buried soil. Scale 1m.

the soil profile below the cairn appeared to have been considerably disturbed, with no distinct turf line and with finds of different dates scattered randomly throughout the buried topsoil. Ploughing would have been impractical due to the presence of boulders of varying size protruding from the subsoil. Cultivation by digging would have been possible but no evidence of this was found. As already stressed, the monument at Gwernvale appears to have been a late construction, both in the local context and in terms of wider Severn-Cotswold practice, and this pre-cairn evidence offers significant insight into the conditions in which monumental practice was performed late in its tradition.

Structural evidence associated with early Neolithic pre-cairn activity is focused on a grouping of postholes and bedding-trenches below the eastern end of the long-cairn and in the area of the forecourt (Figs 3.3, 3.6–3.7). The original report left open the question of whether this might represent two separate structures or a single structure, parts of which were still visible when the long cairn was constructed. This evidence is re-examined in greater detail below, in the light of the increasing numbers of early Neolithic structures that have now been found in Britain and Ireland as well as the timber structures found below the Hazleton North and Ascott-under-Wychwood long cairns. A single structure is now proposed, the significance of which is noted below and further in Chapter 12.

Wet-sieving of soils in a restricted area of the buried soil below the cairn will no doubt have skewed the distribution of early Neolithic finds recovered from the buried soil and other pre-cairn contexts (Figs 3.5, 3.8), though this seems likely to have accentuated a real concentration between the area subsequently occupied by the forecourt and Chamber 1 of the long cairn. Confirmation of this is suggested by the overall occurence of Mesolithic lithics, whose distribution spreads more widely than the area sieved (Fig. 3.5), as well as by the low incidence of finds from sample areas sieved on the NW side of the cairn. In the light of evidence published more recently from Hazleton North (Saville 1990, 14–16) and Ascott-under-Wychwood (Benson and Whittle 2007, 34–50), it is now convenient in looking at the associated plant remains to use the term 'midden' in the sense in which it is used at these two other sites – to describe a concentration of material remains within buried soil horizons. Further discussion of the midden in the context of the pre-cairn timber structure is presented below.

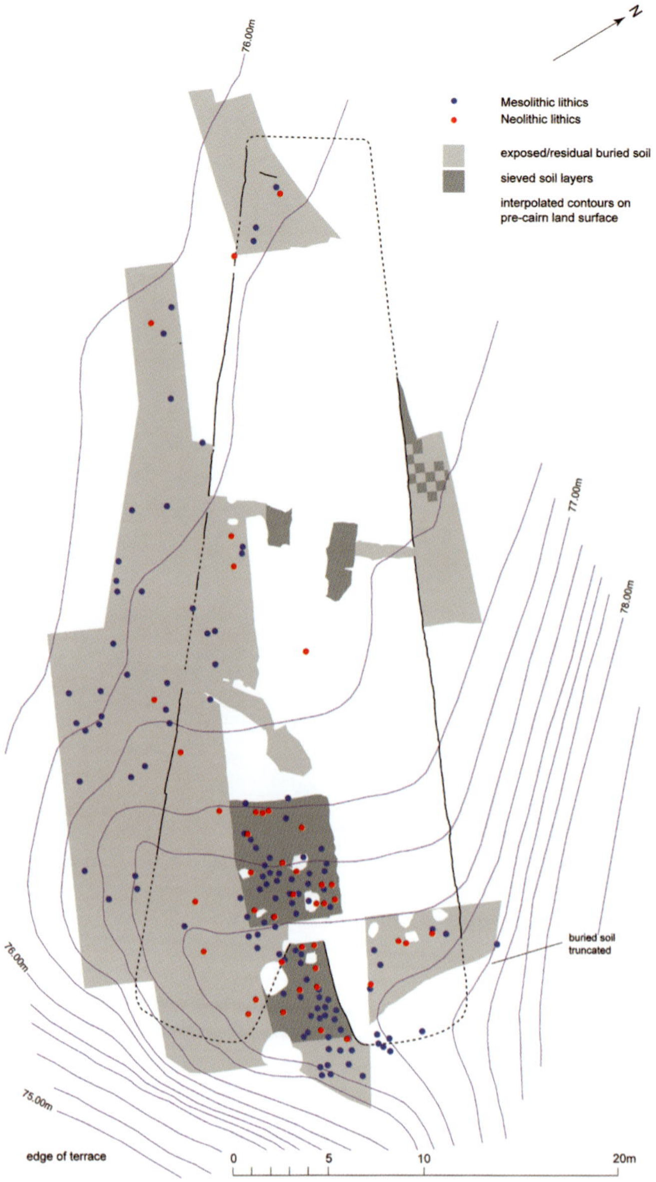

Fig. 3.5. Gwenvale: distribution of diagnostic Mesolithic and Neolithic lithic types from the 1977–78 excavations (after Healey and Green 1984).

In the original report it was suggested that some of the Neolithic finds within features belonging to the pre-cairn timber structure might have been residual from earlier phases of activity at the site (Britnell 1984b, 52), but other possibilities are considered below.

Construction, use and abandonment of the Neolithic long cairn

Final periods of Neolithic activity are represented by the construction and use of the long cairn (Fig. 3.2), followed by the eventual decay and abandonment of the structure. Dates are given below and modelled in Chapter 4, with further discussion in Chapter 12.

Though the view from the site at ground level is today obscured by trees, the monument affords a view of and connection to the distinctive local hill called Crug Hywel (Table Mountain), 2km to the NE (Fig. 12.5, no. 6). The monument at Carn Goch, under 2km to the S, has a similar view of Crug Hywel (Cummings and Whittle 2004, fig. 7.9).

As at Penywyrlod a careful selection of building materials is evident, the outer cladding of the long cairn being built of quarried sandstone (Britnell 1984b, 55–7) probably obtained from quarries at least 100m uphill and 300m away and probably, again as at Penywyrlod, from outcrops of the Senni Formation. The rock type is highly fissile and was no doubt selected for its suitability for drystone walling

Fig. 3.6. Gwernvale: postholes and bedding-trenches of the pre-cairn timber structure in the forecourt and beneath the N hornwork of the long cairn, recorded during the 1977–78 excavations.

Fig. 3.7. Gwernvale: posthole 211 of the pre-cairn timber structure, overlain by the outer revetment wall in the forecourt. The packing stones define the original position of the post in the posthole, suggesting that at least the stump of the post was still visible when the long cairn was under construction.

though its distinctive greenish colour may well also have had considerable significance (cf. Darvill 2010, 7–8). The continuation of the probable practice of asserting in architectural form affinity with potentially ancestral hills is further discussed in Chapter 12.

In the process of transformation from house to monument, a long trapezoidal cairn with three or four lateral chambers was created. The three or four chambers were each provided with a passageway leading to the sides of the cairn. We will deal with this multiplication contrasting with an apparently unified underlying house in Chapter 12. Likewise, the possible symbolic dimensions of the portal structure at the broader end of the cairn, evoking perhaps notions of entrances and access to other worlds, are followed in Chapter 12.

The chamber entrances at Gwernvale, as at Penywyrlod and other laterally chambered long cairns in the Severn-Cotswold tradition, are the only parts of the structure that show explicit evidence of deliberate alteration, involving the repeated blocking and unblocking of the chamber entrances, which again places an emphasis on the potential symbolic significance of doors to the world of the dead (Figs 3.9–3.10). Relatively few human remains survived in the chambers at Gwernvale, however, which therefore places limitations on the interpretation of how the chambers were employed. Evidence of other contemporary and later activity near the monument, pre-dating the marked stages of its decay, is limited to a clustering of ceramics and of pits principally outside the entrances to Chambers 2 and 3 (Britnell 1984b, 88–9).

The original report, strongly influenced by the ideas advocated by excavators such as W.F. Grimes and H.N. Savory at long cairns of the Severn-Cotswold tradition elsewhere, interpreted the external stonework surrounding the original monument (of which only the lowest layers survived) as having been due at least in part to a deliberate process of closure and concealment (Britnell 1984, 150). In the light of more recent work on better-preserved deposits at Penywyrlod and at Hazleton North in particular (Saville 1990, 127–33), it is now better to regard the external stone deposits, even those within the forecourt, as simply the result of natural decay, without human intervention. The concentration of distinctive slabs of white quartzitic sandstone in the collapsed material in the forecourt at Gwernvale (Britnell 1984b, 57, fig. 15) now implies that this distinctive stone was used for parts of the forecourt walling and as suggested for other sites this type of stone may have had some special meaning (Darvill 2002; 2010, 10). The concentrations of large, pitched slabs immediately outside the entrances to Chambers 2 and 3 interpreted as external blocking structures (Britnell 1984b, fig. 20, iv and fig. 23, v), might likewise, in retrospect, represent the collapse of passage roofing (see the discussion of the question of 'access and deposition' in Chapter 2). This continuing aspect of local tradition is also discussed further below.

Subsequent studies of the site and its finds

As in the case of the Penywyrlod long cairn, the site has been included in a number of studies since the original publication, notably concerning its landscape context (Tilley 1994; Nash 1997; Cummings and Whittle 2004). Other studies have considered issues relating to the sequence of construction (McFadyen 2003) and the ceramic fabrics from the site (Peterson 1999; 2003).

Radiocarbon dating

Four conventional radiocarbon dates (CAR-113, -114, -116, -118) were obtained from bulk charcoal samples from stratified contexts from the 1977–78 excavations (Dresser 1984). More recently, 11 AMS dates (SUERC-75856, -75857, -75858, -75859, -76330, -85560, -85561, -85562, -85563,

Fig. 3.8. Gwernvale: distribution of selected Neolithic pre-cairn vessels from the 1977–78 excavations (after Britnell 1984b).

-85599, -85600) have been obtained from plant remains from the 1977–78 excavations from pre-cairn contexts. Details of contexts, samples and dating are given in Table 4.1 and the on-site distribution of samples from which the dates were obtained is shown in Figure 3.21.

Two of the dates are Mesolithic and consistent with the evidence for pre-cairn late Mesolithic activity though neither is directly associated with artefacts. One of these dates (CAR-118) is from a hearth below the cairn and the other (SUERC-85563) from an area of buried soil below the cairn.

Eleven of the dates are from pre-cairn Neolithic contexts. Three are from carbonised cereal grain (SUERC-75856, -75858, -76330) from the wall-lines of the pre-cairn timber structure; one is from carbonised grain (SUERC-75859) from a burnt area immediately next to one of the wall-lines; one is from carbonised grain (SUERC-55857) from an irregular gully just to the W of the timber structure; one (CAR-113) is from a pit to the W of the structure; two are from carbonised grain from the buried soil below the cairn (SUERC-85562, -85599); one is from a carbonised hazelnut shell from the buried soil below the cairn (SUERC-85600); one is from carbonised cereal grain from the lower soil layer in the forecourt (SUERC-85560); and one is from carbonised cereal grain from the upper soil layer within the forecourt (SUERC-85561).

Fig. 3.9. Gwernvale: stone blocking in the outer entrance to Chamber 3, excavated in 1978.

Fig. 3.10. Gwernvale: entrance passage to Chamber 3 with the lowest courses of blocking still in place along the line of the outer revetment wall.

Two other dates (CAR-114, CAR-116) are from bulk charcoal samples from two pits (58, 47) outside the SW side of the cairn, associated with Peterborough Ware (Britnell 1984, fig. 41, no. 26), indicating continuing activity prior to its final abandonment.

Bayesian modelling of the available dates by Seren Griffiths and the suggested phasing of various periods of activity at Gwernvale are presented in Chapter 4.

Re-assessment of the pre-cairn Neolithic activity at Gwernvale

The study of the charred plant remains from pre-cairn contexts below the Gwernvale Severn-Cotswold long cairn has acted as a spur to re-evaluate the evidence for early Neolithic activity below the long cairn, first published in 1984. Further impetus has been provided by the publication of excavations of the similar long cairns at Hazleton North (Saville 1990) and Ascott-under-Wychwood (Benson and Whittle 2007), both of which show evidence of pre-cairn activity, by the more recent discovery of early Neolithic timber buildings in Britain and Ireland (*e.g.* Smyth 2014) and by the recent excavation of a number of early Neolithic middens, especially those at Dorney (Eton College Rowing Course) in the Thames Valley (Allen *et al.* 2013). The following discussion reviews the evidence for what can perhaps now more confidently be interpreted as an early Neolithic house and associated midden subsequently buried beneath the Gwernvale long cairn. Alongside wider comparisons to elsewhere, it is important to keep local context and development very much in mind.

Whether the presence of Mesolithic lithic material, as at both Hazleton North and Ascott-under-Wychwood, indicates any special significance for the site's location in earlier times is unclear, given the paucity of evidence, nor is there any clear indication either from microlith styles or radiocarbon dates (see Chapters 9 and 4 respectively) of the gap between late Mesolithic and early Neolithic activity, though this could have been considerable. It is unclear whether there was deliberate and conscious continuity of place, or whether a favourable location was simply re-used. It is above all the long pre-cairn early Neolithic use of the site that reinforces the sense of place that may have been one of the pre-conditions for the construction of a late monument, but there is no need to exclude the possibility of longer memories still, especially since just such a situation can be found elsewhere.

House

The timber features found below the E end of the cairn can be reassessed in the light of the larger number of early Neolithic houses that are now known in southern Britain, though these more recent discoveries tend to broaden rather than narrow the range of possible interpretations in terms of social significance and function. There is a potential play between local context and wider connections, with broader connectivity becoming even more significant as traditions developed. That is another theme followed in Chapter 12.

The circumstances of excavation resulted in the recovery of only a partial plan of the structure. Buried soils and features at the NE had been truncated by road building in the 19th century AD (Britnell 1984b, 93–4). Parts of the northern and central areas of the structure remained concealed below *in situ* cairn material. The area covered by the part of the SE end of the structure, already exposed by the destruction of much of the south horn, could only be superficially examined due to urgent road safety concerns following the construction of the new road in 1978 before the existence of the timber features was known. A probable posthole and fragment of wall-line at the S corner represented by a cluster of stones and a line of upright packing stones not shown on the original published plan but evident in archive plans (drawings 35 and 50), mean that the size of the overall structure can now be estimated with reasonable confidence to have been 9.7m by 5.5m.

The original publication of excavations at Gwernvale left open the question of whether the timber features identified below the eastern end of the cairn belonged to one structure or two. A definitive interpretation of the evidence was made difficult by the fact that the NE end of the structure, which was essentially of bedding-trench construction, had clearly been overlain by the long cairn, whereas the SW end was of posthole construction and appeared to have been still visible as free-standing posts when the monument was built. The apparent arrangement of six free-standing posts within the forecourt appeared similar to structures (Fig. 3.11) variously interpreted as exposure platforms, porches, or avenues associated with an early Neolithic mortuary structure at Wayland's Smithy (Whittle 1991), earthen long barrows at Fussell's Lodge (Ashbee 1966) and Kilham (Manby 1976) and with the long cairn at Street House (Vyner 1984).

In the light of evidence published more recently from a number of early Neolithic house sites the balance of probability now swings in favour of interpreting the structural features found below the long cairn at Gwernvale as belonging to a single house, elements of which were still visible when the long cairn was constructed. Other possibilities are considered below in the discussion of the sequence from house to monument, where parallels are drawn with the structural sequences between pre-cairn timber structures and the construction of the chambered long cairns at Hazleton North (Saville 1990) and Ascott-under-Wychwood (Benson and Whittle 2007). The timber settings at Wayland's Smithy, Fussell's Lodge, Kilham, and Street House may have had a different but related symbolic significance, a question returned to below in the discussion of the sequence from house to monument.

The clearest indication that the Gwernvale features represent a single structure, comes from its size, which falls comfortably within the range of Irish early Neolithic houses (Fig. 3.12; Smyth 2014, fig. 3.6). The presumed Gwernvale house has a suggested floor area of about 53m^2, slightly smaller than north Welsh houses at Llandygai (Llandegai) (Lynch and Musson 2001) and Parc Bryn Cegin, Llandygai (Kenney 2008) but significantly smaller than the house at

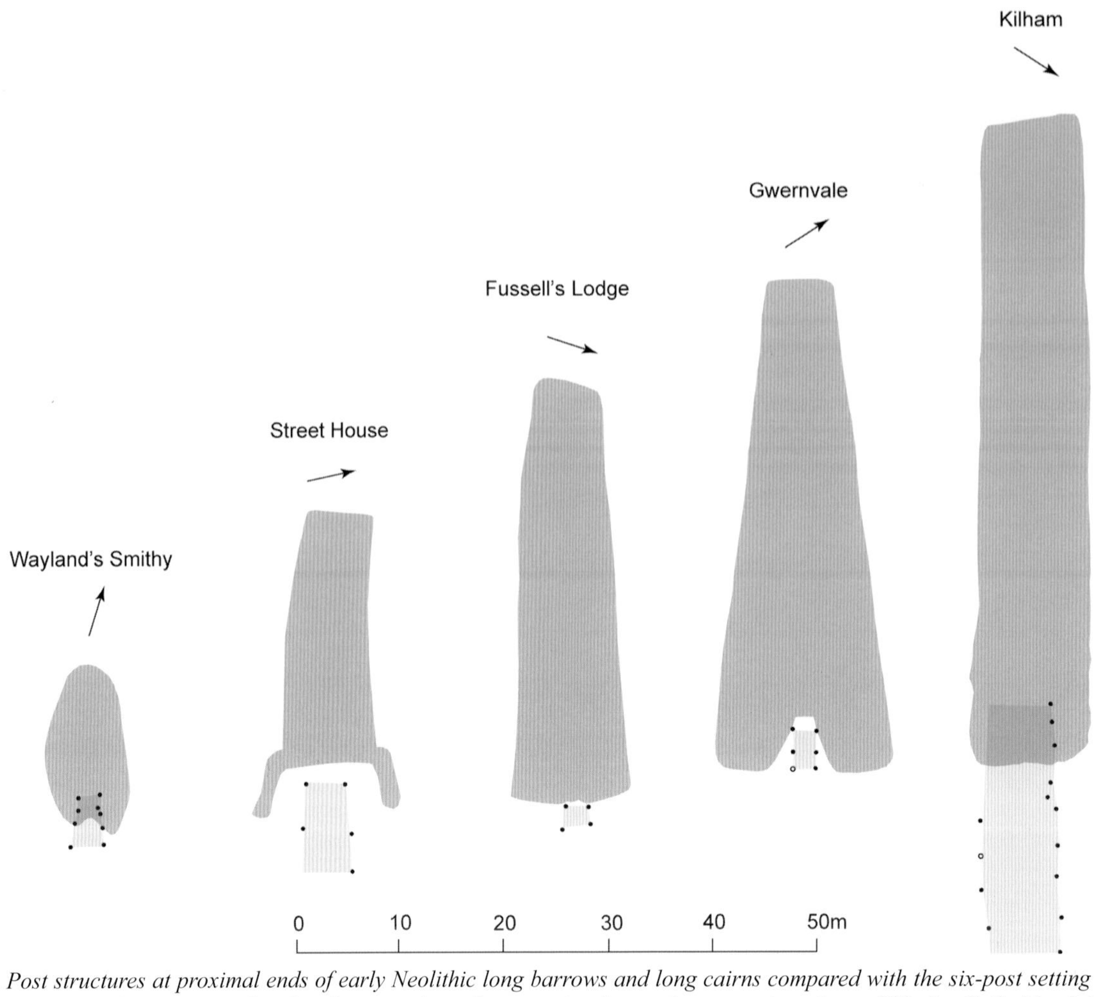

Fig. 3.11. Post structures at proximal ends of early Neolithic long barrows and long cairns compared with the six-post setting within the forecourt at Gwernvale, now considered to form one bay of a pre-cairn house. Interpretative plans of Wayland's Smithy (after Whittle 1991), Street House (after Vyner 1984), Fussell's Lodge (Ashbee 1966), and Kilham (after Manby 1976).

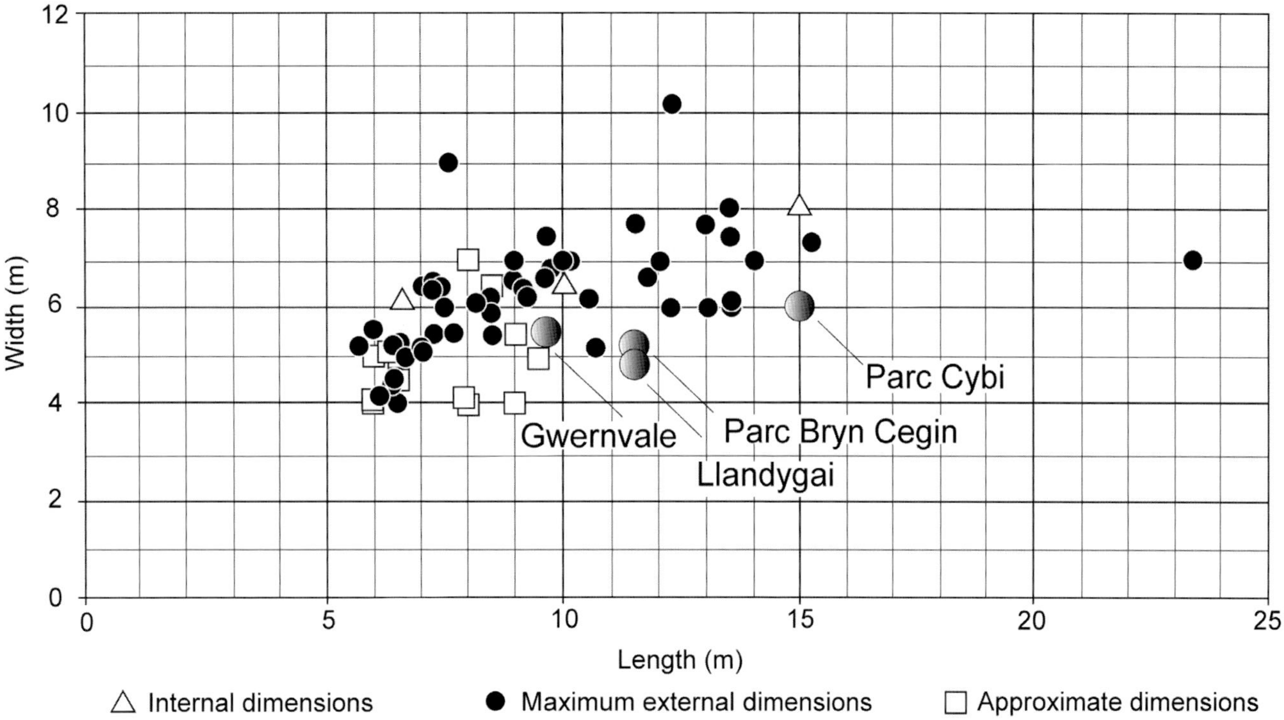

Fig. 3.12. Dimensions of some early Neolithic houses in Wales compared with those of similar Irish structures (after Smyth 2014).

Parc Cybi, though there is the possibility that the original building at Parc Cybi may have been extended by about 4.5m (Kenney 2021, 47–50) (Fig. 3.13). The aisled form of these houses in north-west Wales and their close similarity of orientation and size all suggest a distinctive regional sub-style (Kenney 2021, 47). These appear quite distinct, however, from the cluster of early Neolithic timber structures recently found at Llanfaethlu, also on Anglesey (Rees and Jones 2016; 2017), which may emphasise the existence of a range of contemporary settlement forms.

The use of individual posts and bedding-trenches for either planks or wattle panels are both characteristic of early Neolithic houses and there is now clearer evidence to show that these different construction techniques were often used in different parts of the same house, possibly denoting different functions in different parts of the structure (Smyth 2014, 36). At Gwernvale, the posts set in individual postholes were up to 0.18m in diameter and the possible planks or panels set in the bedding-trenches were up to 88mm thick (Britnell 1984b, 51–2).

A spread of charcoal on the surface of the buried soil and a streak of charcoally soil in the adjacent bedding-trench (Figs 3.14–15, context 249) might indicate that part of the structure had burnt down (Britnell 1984b, 52). Many of the Irish houses that were not subsequently monumentalised show evidence of burning (Smyth 2014, 62) though, as possibly the case at Gwernvale, this was sometimes restricted to just one part of building (Smyth 2014, 64). On the basis of the evidence of Irish houses (Smyth 2014, 52), the lack of evidence for a hearth inside the building is not unexpected. Likewise, no definite contemporary internal hearths were identified at White Horse Stone (Garwood 2011, 71) or Parc Cybi (Kenney 2021, 50), for example.

A small amount of charcoal from structural features associated with the timber structure below the E end of the long cairn was identified (see Chapter 5). Taxa from the two bedding-trenches 133 (133B, 133D) and 229 and from post-settings identified within bedding-trench 133 (133A, 133C, 133E, 133G) include oak, ash, hazel, blackthorn, Maloideae-type (crab apple, rowan, whitebeam, hawthorn) and elm (see location of sampled features in Fig. 5.4). Charcoal from other individual postholes (208A, 208B, 209A, 209B, 211A, 211B – samples A being from the post-packing and samples B being from the post-pipe in each instance) and possible postholes (205, 206) comprise oak, hazel and Maloideae-type as well as alder and cherry. The charcoal assemblage from charcoal spread 249 next to the NW side of the structure is similar and includes Maloideae-type, hazel, ash and oak.

Like the cereal grains and many of the other finds found in a number of the features belonging to the timber structure, the processes by which this charcoal came to be deposited in these features is unclear (Britnell 1984b, 52). As mentioned above, there are hints that parts of the structure may have burnt down and it is possible that the dominance of oak charcoal in postholes 133E and 205 might relate to former posts. Oak is thought to have been commonly used for the main structural components of early Neolithic buildings, as suggested for Parc Cybi (Kenney 2021, 44–5), Parc

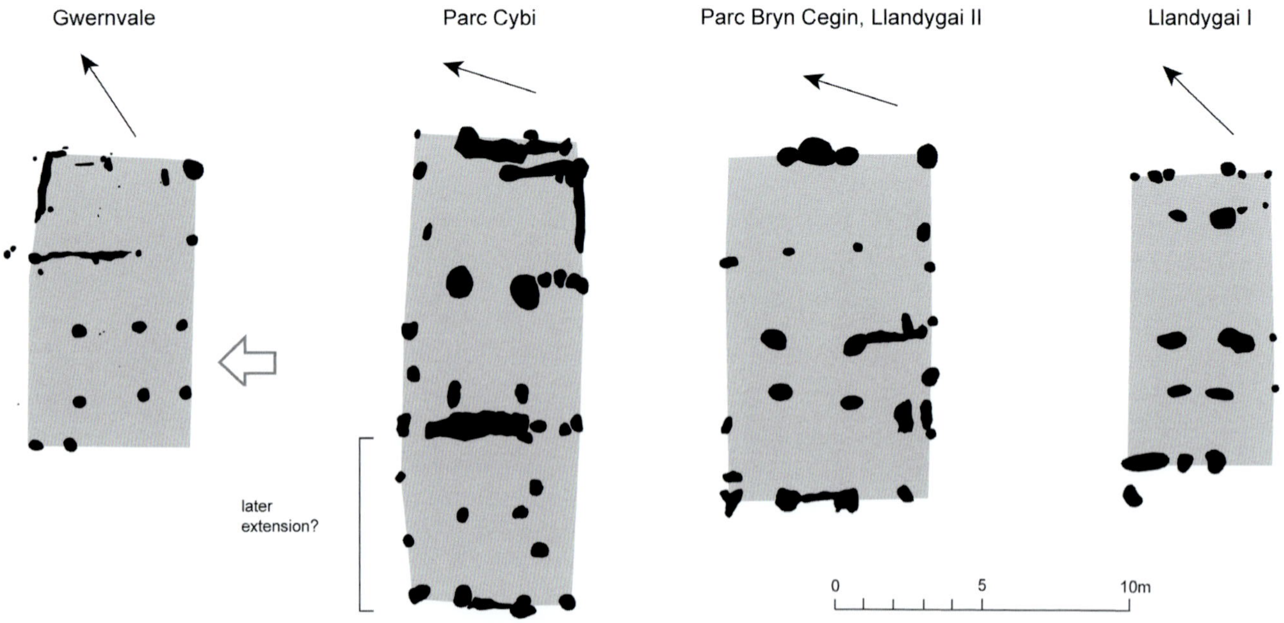

Fig. 3.13. Comparative plans of some early Neolithic timber houses in Wales, showing suggested position of door at Gwernvale. Interpretative plans of Parc Cybi (after Kenney 2021), Parc Bryn Cegin, Llandygai (after Kenney 2008), and Llandygai (after Lynch and Musson 2001).

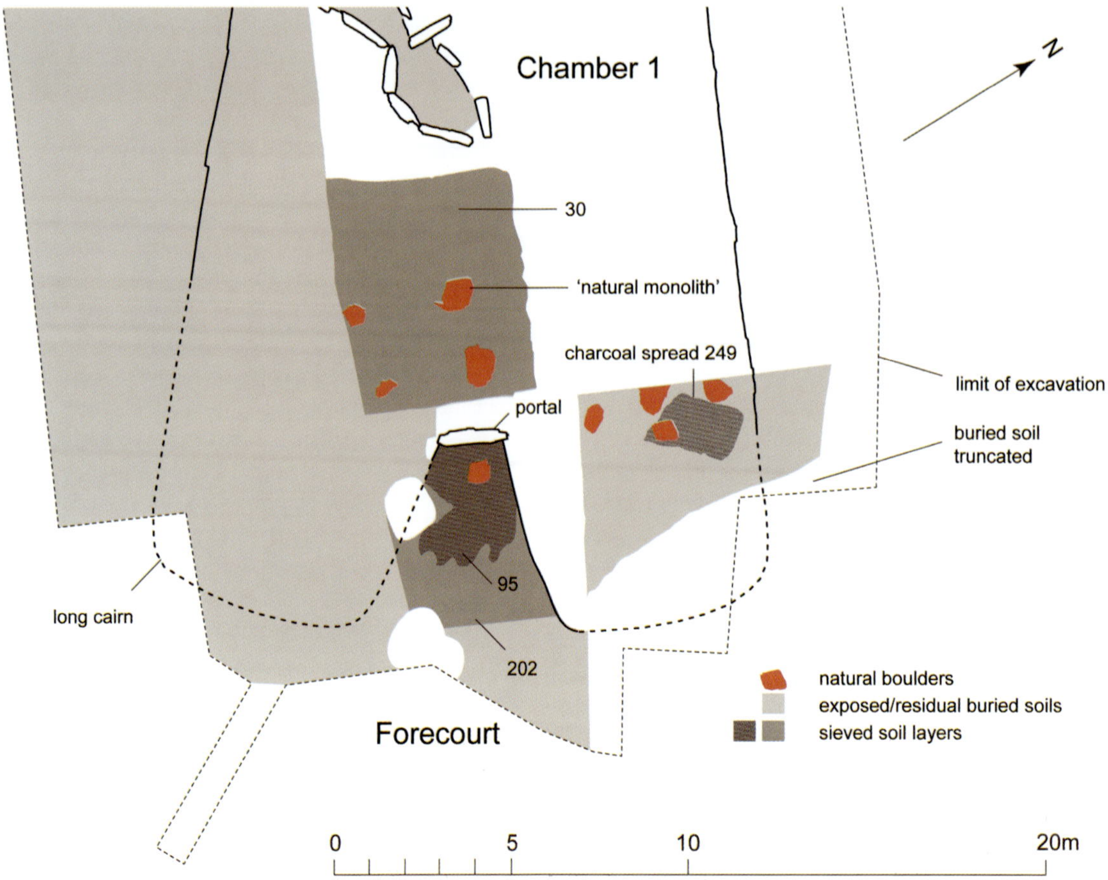

Fig. 3.14. Gwernvale: extent of sieved layers below the E end of the long cairn and in the forecourt area.

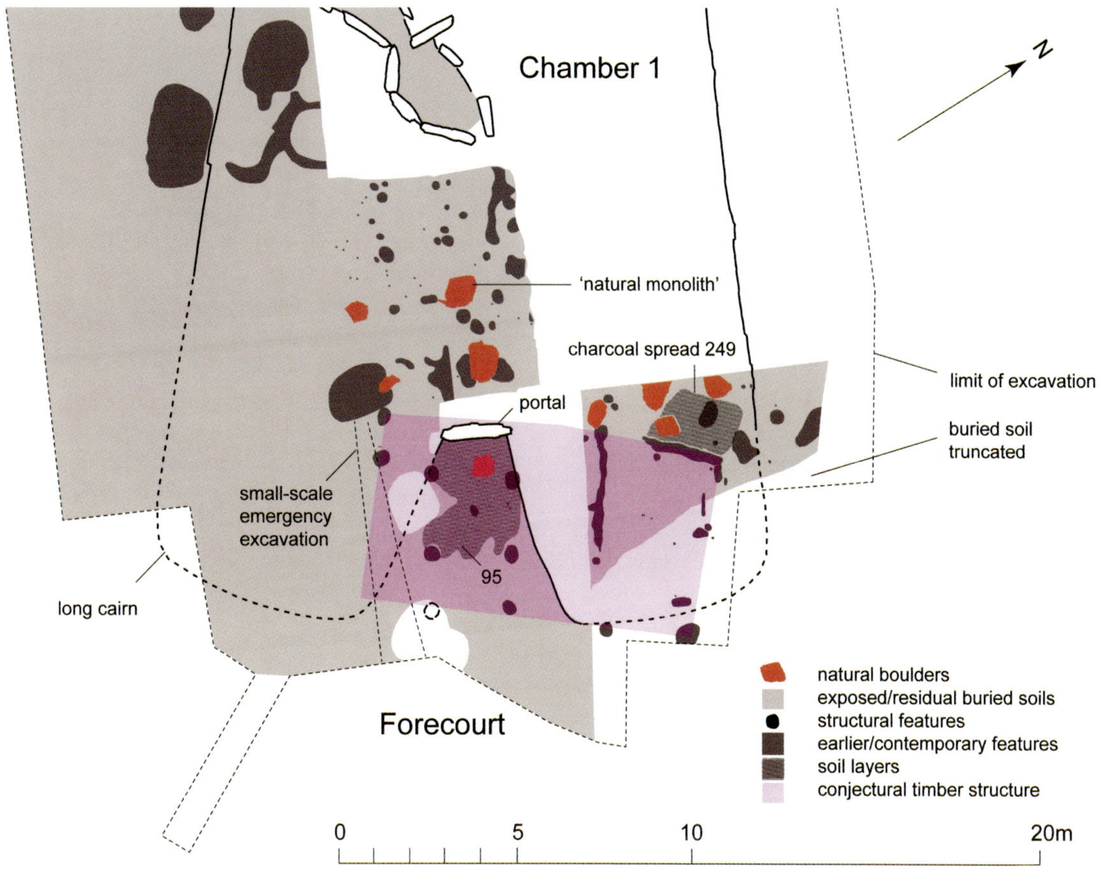

Fig. 3.15. Gwernvale: pre-cairn features and natural boulders below the E end of the long cairn and in the forecourt area.

Bryn Cegin (Kenney 2008, 25–6) and many Irish buildings (Smyth 2014, 34). Roundwood of other more slender species is also often represented, which it has sometimes been suggested might represent wattling or other fixtures and fittings within the building (Smyth 2014, 34), up to 12 different species being represented in the structural features of the three houses at Corbally, Co. Kildare (Purcell 2002, 71). The presence of blackthorn and hawthorn at Gwernvale seems less suited to wattling, and although it has been suggested at Corbally that thornier species such as these may have been used in external walling to keep animals away (Purcell 2002, 71; Smyth 2014, 34), this is not entirely convincing. It therefore seems more likely that at Gwernvale at least some of the roundwood charcoal is more likely to represent either earlier scrub clearance or wood that had been gathered for fuel. In view of the evidence for Mesolithic activity at Gwernvale, however, there is the strong likelihood that at least some of the assemblage of charcoal from features belonging to the timber structure represents residual material of much earlier date.

The house occupies the highest local point of the terrace upon which it is sited (Fig. 3.3), the land surface dropping down sharply to the S and SE by 10m or so to the floodplain of the Usk and rising steeply to the summit of the Black Mountains to the N and NE. The focus of the midden associated with the house, discussed below, appears to lie just a few metres to the W of the house. The sitings of early Neolithic buildings in southern Britain are very variable but are still relatively few and far between and may be uncharacteristic. The siting of the greater number of known Irish houses is not dissimilar to Gwernvale. They tend to be located in lowland regions, sometimes on the crests or sides of spurs, close to rivers, and often overlying evidence of earlier activity, and are often orientated with the long-axis NE–SW (Smyth 2014, 22).

There is no evidence for structural elements of the Gwernvale building having been replaced or refurbished and the structure is therefore considered to be of a single period. The taphonomy of the dated samples and the length of time the structure remained in use are both open to question but the house falls within the general date-range of other similar timber structures in Britain and Ireland (Whittle *et al.* 2011, 840–3).

Midden

As noted above, as in the case of the middens identified below the long cairns at Hazleton and Ascott-under-Wychwood, the term 'midden' is used in the sense of a concentration of material remains within buried soil below the long cairn at Gwernvale. As noted above, the soil profile within the area of the midden had been considerably disturbed and there was no clear evidence of vertical stratification and finds occurring throughout the buried topsoil. The broad range of finds, considered below, came from the topsoil below the cairn, on average about 0.13m deep, and extending downwards into a series of fairly amorphous hollows and gullies between 0.05–0.25m deep in the surface of the underlying subsoil, some of which might have resulted from the removal of stones or the grubbing up of roots some time before the construction of the cairn. Pits had been dug to either side of a large 'natural monolith', for example, as though in an attempt to remove it.

The range of finds in the Gwernvale, Hazleton North and Ascott-under-Wychwood middens is similar, including pottery, lithics and animal bone (see below). Some of these features produced Mesolithic flintwork but there are only rare instances in which this is not associated with diagnostic Neolithic lithics or ceramics and it therefore seems likely that the Mesolithic material is very largely residual and the great majority of identified features are of Neolithic date.

Unlike at Hazleton North and Ascott-under-Wychwood, the restricted area excavated below the cairn at Gwernvale did not permit the identification of colour changes in soil accompanying the finds concentration, though it was noted that the soil at this point below the cairn was distinctly darker. The full extent of the midden is uncertain, due to the selective nature of the excavations, and its boundaries are to some extent artificially defined by the limits of the area that were wet-sieved, though as noted above sieving is considered to have had the effect of accentuating a real concentration of material remains in this area. The midden occupied an area just to the W of the suggested Neolithic house and seems likely to have occupied an area perhaps 11m × 8m, roughly centred upon the natural monolith described above (Figs 3.4 and 3.14). The middens at Hazleton and Ascott-under-Wychwood were of a similar size, being respectively about 10m × 9m and 14m × 11m across (Saville 1990, 14–16; Benson and Whittle 2007, 34–50). By way of comparison, the larger early Neolithic surface midden at Dorney was 12.5m × 4.5m and the smaller ones up to 3m across (Allen *et al*. 2013, 92–8) (see Fig. 3.22).

Features within the midden area include two better defined oval pits (68, 170) up to 1.5m × 2m across and 0.29m and 0.58m deep, both of which produced early Neolithic pottery and lithics, and a scatter of stakeholes (Fig. 3.15). Pit 68 appeared to have been deliberately refilled with a sequence of layers introduced from the E side and with an upper charcoally fill suggesting burning *in situ* or the disposal of material burnt elsewhere, the upper and lower layers containing sherds of a Carinated Bowl (Britnell 1984b, fig. 39, no. 13). No other possible hearths were identified. The function of two irregular gullies (149, 167), between 0.15–0.21m deep, is unexplained but they may have been associated with the drainage of surface water. The latter contained sherds of a Carinated Bowl (Britnell 1984b, fig. 39, no. 12). A pit and areas of *in situ* burning are evident within the Ascott-under-Wychwood midden (Benson and Whittle 2007, 34–5) but there is no similar evidence from Hazleton North.

As in the case of the pre-cairn middens at Hazleton and Ascott-under-Wychwood, the condition and fragmentation of some of the finds from the midden area at Gwernvale (notably the animal bone, pottery and stone artefacts) suggest the disposal and subsequent weathering due to exposure or disturbance of domestic rubbish generated elsewhere, though not necessarily at any great distance (Saville 1990, 240–1; Benson and Whittle 2007, 34). Notwithstanding the potentially broader significance of middens as focal points within the early Neolithic landscape (Pollard 2005, 109–11; Whittle and Benson 2007, 345; Ray and Thomas 2018, 185), the clear implication at Gwernvale is that the midden is associated with and derived from the occupation of the adjacent house. This relationship is best exemplified by a number of the ceramic vessels, sherds of which have been found both within the midden and in structural features belonging to the house.

Evidence of associations between early Neolithic houses and surface middens is, however, scarce elsewhere. None are recorded at the house sites at Parc Bryn Cegin, Parc Cybi, Llanfaethlu, Lismore Fields, and White Horse Stone, for example, and the nearest deposits to the house at Yarnton thought to represent a midden are 500m away (Hey *et al.* 2016, 29 and fig. 2.5). Furthermore, the early Neolithic middens such as those at Hazleton North, Ascott-under-Wychwood and Dorney are thought to be unassociated with houses. It is uncertain to what extent this might be due to subsequent erosion of land surfaces, though phosphate analysis at Horton suggests the former presence of a midden (Chaffey and Brook 2010). The early Neolithic houses at Clegyr Boia are associated with a midden, 7m × 2m, containing flintwork, animal bone, charcoal and pottery, including joining sherds from the midden and houses, but this was preserved within a rock-cut hollow about 30m away (A. Williams 1953, 29 and fig. 2). Evidence for such kinds of association between surface middens and houses is only likely to be found in instances such as this, where structural remains and contemporary land surfaces are preserved beneath later deposits, in this instance the long cairn. Where contemporary land surfaces have not survived it is probable that surviving evidence for the disposal of domestic rubbish will, like this, be largely confined to the adjacent pits.

The interpretation of isolated surface middens has varied. Those at Dorney have been interpreted as temporary domestic occupation sites within a palaeochannel, possibly continuing from Mesolithic practice, representing a cyclical pattern of seasonal movement by a local group between midden sites. This is based on various strands of evidence, partly on the absence of structural evidence and partly on the basis that the quantities of finds, though large, are not sufficiently large for the likely period of use (Allen *et al.* 2013, 497–501). At Hazleton North the midden was interpreted as evidence for the settlement of a farming group living somewhere in the surrounding area (Saville 1990, 240–1). At Ascott-under-Wychwood the question was left open as to whether it might represent a small sedentary or more mobile group, the emphasis, as mirrored at Hazleton North and Gwernvale, being upon it having a significance as a persistent place within the landscape, transcending the Mesolithic-Neolithic boundary and culminating in the building of a long cairn (Whittle 2007a, 344–8). The presence of a house at Gwernvale presents a different pattern, but similarities in the sequences at these three sites and the question of whether the timber structures below Hazleton North and Ascott-under-Wychwood might represent houses or representations of houses is discussed below in the context of the transition from house and midden to monument at Gwernvale.

The Bayesian model for radiocarbon dates from pre-cairn contexts presented in Chapter 4 estimates that the pre-cairn Neolithic activity at Gwernvale first occurred in *3975–3710 cal BC* (*95% probability*), probably in *3890–3790 cal BC* (*62% probability* or *3740–3720 cal BC 5% probability*; *start_Gwernvale_pre_cairn*; Fig. 4.4) and continued for a period of *120–420 years* (*91% probability*, or *190–325 years 68% probability*, *span_Gwernvale_premonument_neolithic*).

Finds associated with the house and midden

This section presents a brief synopsis of the early Neolithic finds from pre-cairn contexts, essentially being those associated with the midden and house. Apart from the analysis of plant remains in Chapter 5 this is largely based upon the evidence presented in the original publication though some additional detail has been added from the site archive. Parallels are mostly made with assemblages from a number of early Neolithic house sites and middens elsewhere in southern Britain, principally from a taphonomic point of view.

The finds attributed to the midden are from a heavily bioturbated layer of buried topsoil below the cairn, extending into a series of irregular hollows in the underlying subsoil. There was no observed stratification and the deposit contained residual Mesolithic material. Finds associated with the house are largely from structural features, which again contain some residual Mesolithic material. The relatively unabraded condition of some of the pottery from the packing of some of the timber features suggests the deposition of contemporary material but it seems possible that the structural features might contain residual finds from the topsoil or from the period of use of the house, or from a period of decay preceding the construction of the long cairn. An association between the midden and the house is suggested by the fact that they share sherds of a number of the same vessels but there is no clear evidence of whether they share beginning and end dates.

Pottery (see distribution in Fig. 3.16)

Fragments of up to 17 carinated and hemispherical vessels were identified from pre-cairn contexts, of which 14 are associated with the area of the pre-cairn midden and the timber structure (see Chapter 10). Significantly, non-joining sherds attributed to six vessels at Gwernvale came from the midden area and from structural elements of the pre-cairn timber structure (Britnell 1984b, vessels 1, 3, 9–11, 13). Larger and less abraded sherds of a Plain Bowl (vessel 1) came from the packing of one of the bedding-trenches (229) of the timber structure, which suggested that they belonged to a period not far removed from the erection of the structure (Britnell 1984b, 97). Sherds of other vessels came from post-pipes, suggesting the movement of material following the decay of the building.

Sherds of pottery are a frequent occurrence in structural features of early Neolithic houses in Britain and Ireland, including north Welsh sites such as Llandygai, Parc Bryn Cegin and Parc Cybi (Lynch and Musson 2008, 34; Kenney 2008, 22–3; 2021, 40–3). Similar associations are known from the house sites at Lismore Fields (Garton 1991, 13) but little pottery was found at White Horse Stone (Garwood 2011, 69) and none at all at Yarnton (Hey *et al.* 2016, 466).

The presence of ceramics in structural features in early Neolithic houses has sometimes been interpreted as purposeful foundation deposits (*e.g.* Smyth 2014, 56–9). The fragmentary nature of the pottery found in structural features at Gwernvale, like that of lithics and stone artefacts, is (depending upon the context) interpreted as the inadvertent inclusion of material discarded prior to construction, during the use of or following the demise of the structure.

Comparable numbers of about 25 vessels were found in association with the pre-cairn midden at Hazleton North (Smith and Darvill 1990, 141) and about 17 with the pre-cairn midden at Ascott-under-Wychwood (Benson and Whittle 2007, 34). The low average sherd size, low ratios of sherds per vessel and the state of the pottery sherds in the middens at Gwernvale, Hazleton North and at the Dorney have been taken to indicate the deposition of vessels that had been broken elsewhere (Barclay 2013, 130–1).

Lithics (see distribution in Fig. 3.17)

The pre-cairn activity at Gwernvale, like at Hazleton and Ascott-under-Wychwood, involved the deposition of significant quantities of lithic material, though in each case the assemblages contain a significant component of Mesolithic lithic material, which likewise makes it difficult to isolate the Neolithic component except for distinctive forms. The main diagnostic types present at Gwernvale are polished

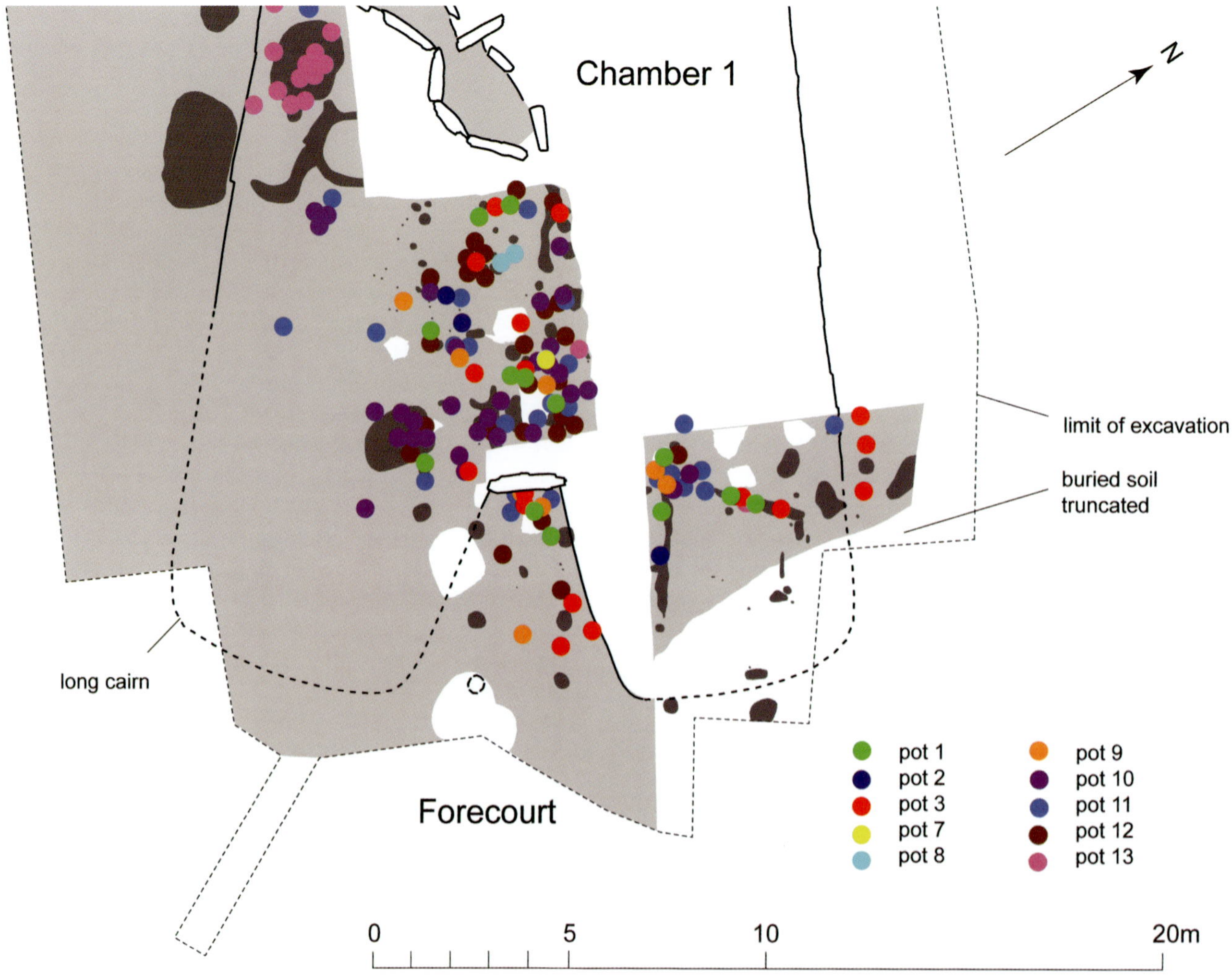

Fig. 3.16. Gwernvale: distribution of selected Neolithic pottery sherds below the E end of the long cairn and in the forecourt area (after Britnell 1984b).

axe fragments, leaf-shaped arrowheads, probably knives and edge-dressed flakes and a proportion of the scrapers and awls (Healey and Green 1984). Twenty leaf-shaped arrowheads came from pre-cairn contexts, of which 11 came from the area of the midden and two from the bedding-trench 229 of the timber structure and one from bedding-trench 133. The three arrowheads from structural features were all highly fragmented and seem unlikely to represent foundation deposits. Also from the midden at Gwernvale were three fragments of polished stone axes and four knives or edge-dressed flakes. Other lithic finds from structural features belonging to the timber structure were two undiagnostic scrapers and a Mesolithic microlith and truncated blade from bedding-trench 133.

The pre-cairn assemblage was considered by Healey and Green (1984, 131) not atypical of a Neolithic settlement, the relatively high proportion of tools possibly being explained by the scarcity of raw materials. In comparing the Hazleton and Gwernvale assemblages, Saville (1990, 175) noted the higher proportion of leaf-shaped arrowheads and scrapers at Gwernvale, but also remarked on the importance of broken axeheads at both sites used as blanks for further flaking. The early Neolithic midden at Dorney likewise contained leaf-shaped arrowheads and reworked polished axe fragments in addition to a wide range of other implement types evoking settlement activity (Anderson-Whymark 2013).

Structural features of the early Neolithic house at Parc Cybi contained a polished stone axe fragment and a flake of Graig Lwyd stone and other lithic waste (Kenney *et al.* 2011, 14) and lithic waste was found within postholes of the Llandygai house (Lynch and Musson 2001, 29). A large leaf-shaped arrowhead from the posthole packing of the early Neolithic house at Parc Bryn Cegin was similarly fragmentary but considered to have possibly been a deliberate deposition (Kenney 2008, 25). Similar assemblages of lithic artefacts and waste have also been found at Irish

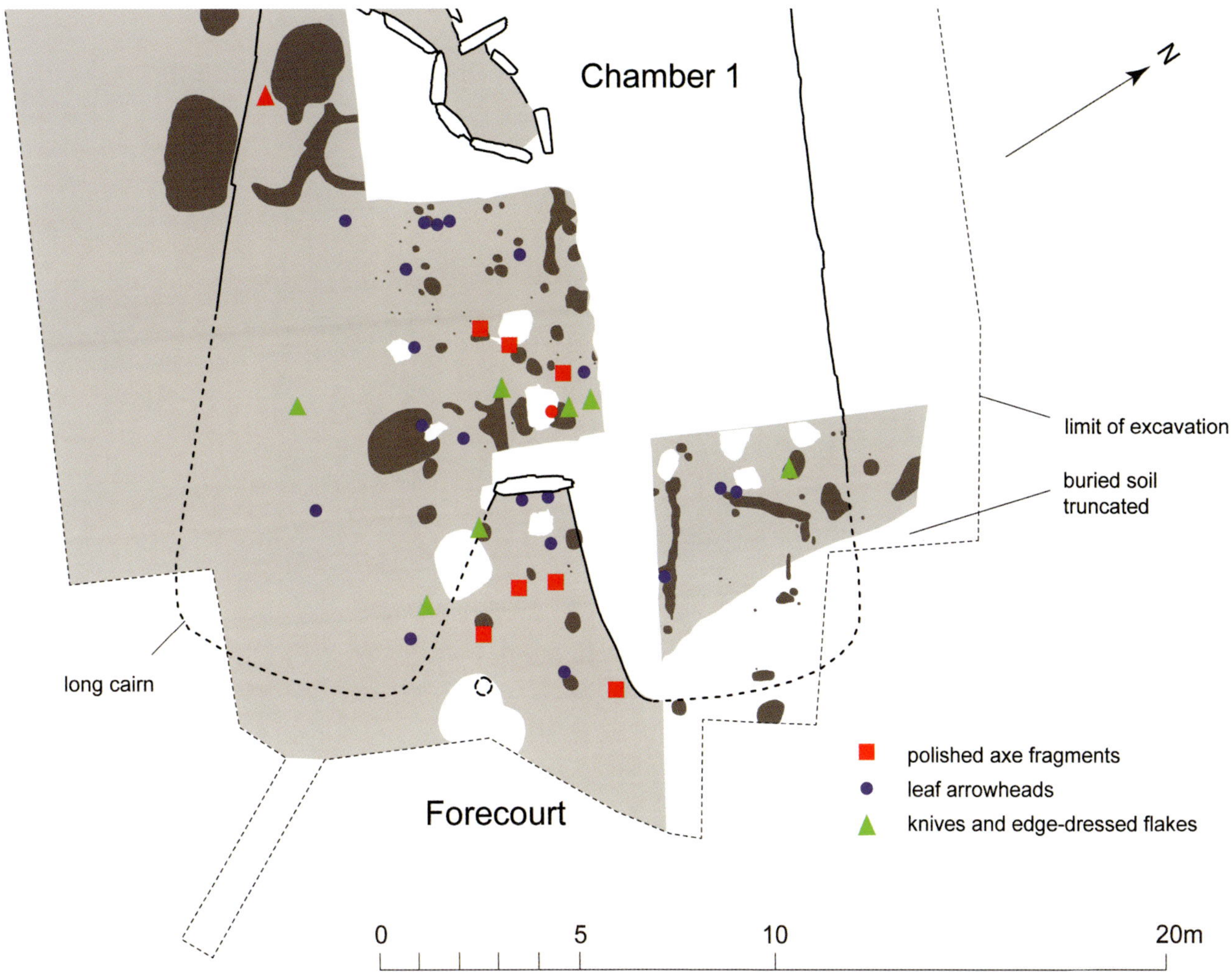

Fig. 3.17. Gwernvale: distribution of diagnostic Neolithic lithic implement types below the E end of the long cairn and in the forecourt area (after Healey and Green 1984).

house sites and have likewise sometimes been considered to be purposeful (Smyth 2014, 58–9).

An axe-polishing or sharpening stone from the long cairn is considered to represent re-sharpening of axes derived from some distance from the site rather than indicating the primary manufacture or completion of axes. The stone came from the basal layers of the cairn, only a metre or so from the portal stone, and is thought to have probably been residual from pre-cairn activity. As noted by Healey and Green (1984, 132), finds of this kind have only rarely been found or recognised on domestic sites such as Ehenside Tarn (Bunch and Fell 1949, 14), and there is possible evidence for axe manufacture at a number of Irish house sites (Smyth 2014, 52). Larger stones used for axe-sharpening are also known from the West Kennet long barrow (Piggott 1962, 19–21) and a quern from the pavement of the early mortuary structure at Wayland's Smithy was possibly later used for axe polishing (Whittle 1991, 87), which may have been derived from earlier occupation at the site.

Stone artefacts (see distribution in Fig. 3.18)

A range of activities, including food processing and axe polishing or sharpening, is implied by the presence of utilised stones from pre-cairn contexts. Fragments of five utilised stones classed as querns or rubbing stones were found in pre-cairn contexts, of which one from the area of the midden and four, including three classed as quern or rubbing stone fragments and one classed as a polishing stone, acted as packing stones in or close to various elements (133E, 207, 229) of the pre-cairn timber structure (Britnell 1984b, 132–5). Four other utilised stones came from the fully excavated portion of the long cairn itself – one classed as a quern, a fragment of polishing stone and an axe-polishing or sharpening stone from the make-up of the cairn in the area between the forecourt and Chamber 1, and one classed as a quern from the make-up of the cairn from the area between Chamber 1 and 2. The utilised stones recovered from the make-up of the cairn were larger and more complete than those directly associated with the pre-cairn structure and

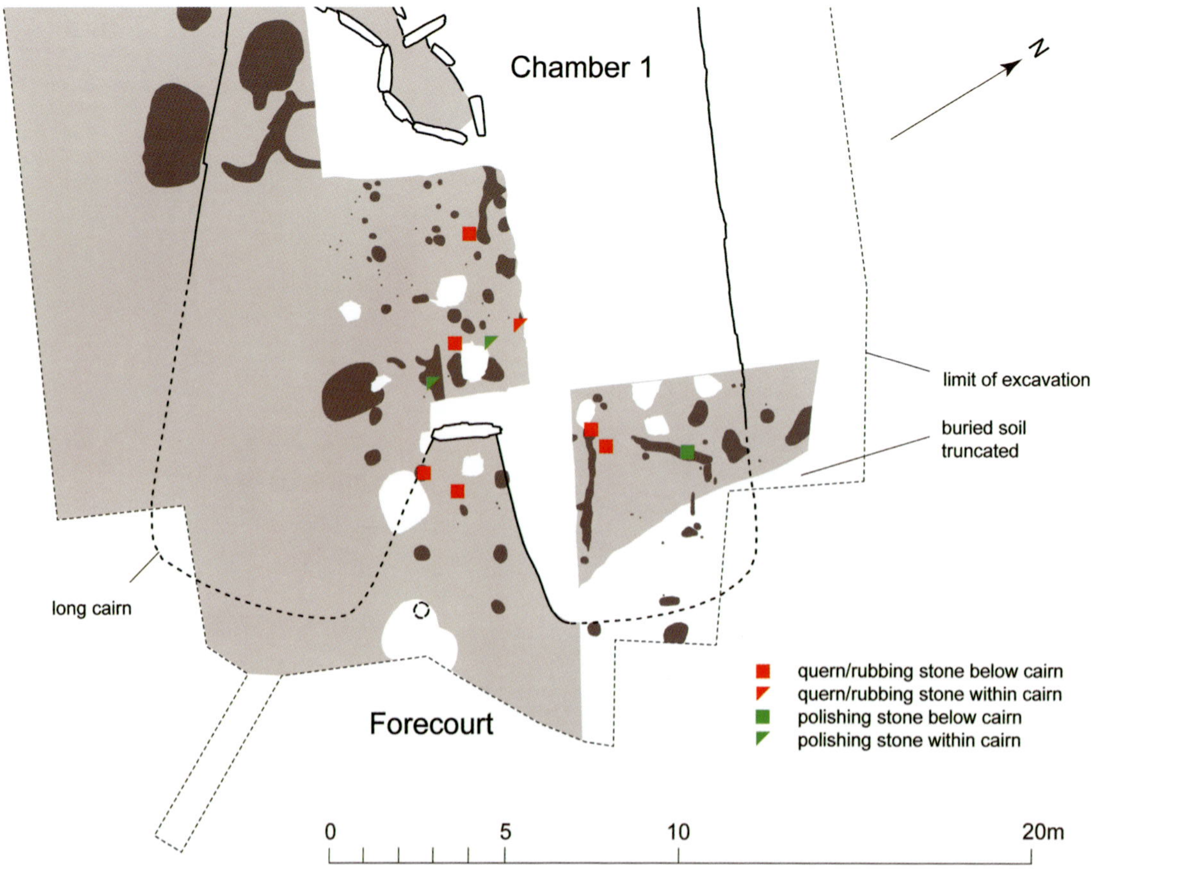

Fig. 3.18. Gwernvale: distribution of stone artefacts below the E end of the long cairn and in the forecourt area (after Britnell 1984b).

came mostly from the E end of the cairn. This is significant in that it suggests that the utilised stone within the cairn had been collected from the ground surface in the area of the pre-cairn structure. The relative size and more fragmentary nature of the utilised stones acting as packing stones within features belonging to the pre-cairn structure suggest that they may have been deliberately broken up for this purpose.

The occurrence of querns, rubbing stones and polishing stones within the make-up of a number of other long cairns or from underlying deposits appears to be fairly common. Querns were incorporated within both the primary mortuary structure and the secondary cairn at Wayland's Smithy, which were possibly derived from earlier occupation at the site (Whittle 1991, 87, 92). A fragmentary quern was found within make-up of the Burn Ground long cairn (Grimes 1960, 75) but in this instance there is no recorded evidence of earlier activity. At Ascott-under-Wychwood a fragmentary quern was found built into the inner wall-face of the cairn and a further fragment was found in a stone setting or posthole adjacent to one of the pre-cairn timber structures (Roe 2007b, 315). Numerous fragments of querns or small rubbing stones were found within the pre-cairn midden at Hazleton North, the dispersal pattern of the finds suggesting that at least two querns had been deliberately broken up elsewhere, possibly for reuse, and subsequently redeposited in the midden (Saville 1990, 177–8). Two of the smaller early Neolithic middens at Dorney likewise contained small fragments of burnt querns, and a fragment of an axe-polishing stone came from an overlying layer (Roe 2013, 178–9).

Querns and rubbing stones have been found in direct association with a number of early Neolithic timber buildings, particularly in Ireland (Smyth 2014, 52). At Tullahedy, as at Gwernvale, fragments of querns and rubbing stones were incorporated in structural features of one house and a quern appeared to have been deliberately placed inside another house (Smyth 2014, 79). A rubbing stone possibly used for axe polishing had been similarly reused as a packing stone of one of the postholes of the Neolithic house at Llandygai (Lynch and Musson 2001, 29, 123). A pit associated with one of the buildings at Ballygalley contained an inverted quern (Simpson 1996, 124) and a possibly later pit inside the building at Parc Cybi likewise contained an inverted quern (Kenney *et al.* 2011, 19). Polishing stones were reused as packing stones of one or possibly two of the postholes of the Llandygai Neolithic house though the precise function of the stones is uncertain (Lynch and Musson 2001, 29).

Animal and human remains (see distribution in Fig. 3.19)

The surviving animal remains from pre-cairn contexts came from the soil and from a number of features sealed below the cairn, largely in the area of the suggested midden. Because of the mildly acidic soil conditions the surviving fragments were largely of tooth enamel, the species represented being *Bos* (cattle), *Ovis* (sheep/goat) and *Sus* (pig). The cattle and pig fragments are generally too small to determine whether they all came from domestic animals. A single tooth of *Cervus* (deer) came from the base of the cairn but might properly be attributed to the surface of the underlying buried soil (O'Connor 1984, 153).

The quantity of material from Gwernvale is too small for detailed analysis but compares with the bigger assemblages from the midden deposits below the Hazleton North and Ascott-under-Wychwood long cairns. The relative proportions of identified fragments of cattle, sheep/goat, pig and deer remains at Gwernvale are not dissimilar to those from the pre-cairn midden at Ascott-under-Wychwood (Mulville and Grigson 2007), though a lesser proportion of cattle remains and higher proportions of sheep and pig remains are represented in material from the midden below the Hazleton North long cairn (Levitan 1990). The animal bone assemblage at Hazleton indicated slaughter and consumption of animal products close to the site of deposition, suggestive of domestic activity (Levitan 1990, 203) though the evidence for this at Ascott-under-Wychwood is less explicit (Mulville and Grigson 2007, 252). Evidence for 'ritual feasting' prior to the construction of any of these sites is perhaps unlikely (cf. Thomas and McFadyen 2010, 108) but the higher proportion of wild species in the pre-cairn midden at Ascott-under-Wychwood is considered less typical of domestic assemblages (Mulville and Grigson 2007, 253).

The components of the bone assemblage from the pre-cairn midden at Gwernvale have no doubt been skewed by the acidic soil conditions. Even so, it is interesting to note that the animal bone from the pre-cairn midden at Hazleton was highly fragmented and contained a high proportion of loose teeth (Levitan 1990, 200), and also that the assemblage from the early Neolithic Dorney midden was relatively poorly preserved and contained a high proportion of teeth (G. Jones 2013, 184) and in all these instances may indicate weathering due to exposure subsequent to deposition.

Three small fragments of human skull were recovered from a posthole and slot belonging to the pre-cairn timber structure below the long cairn at Gwernvale (see Fig. 3.19)

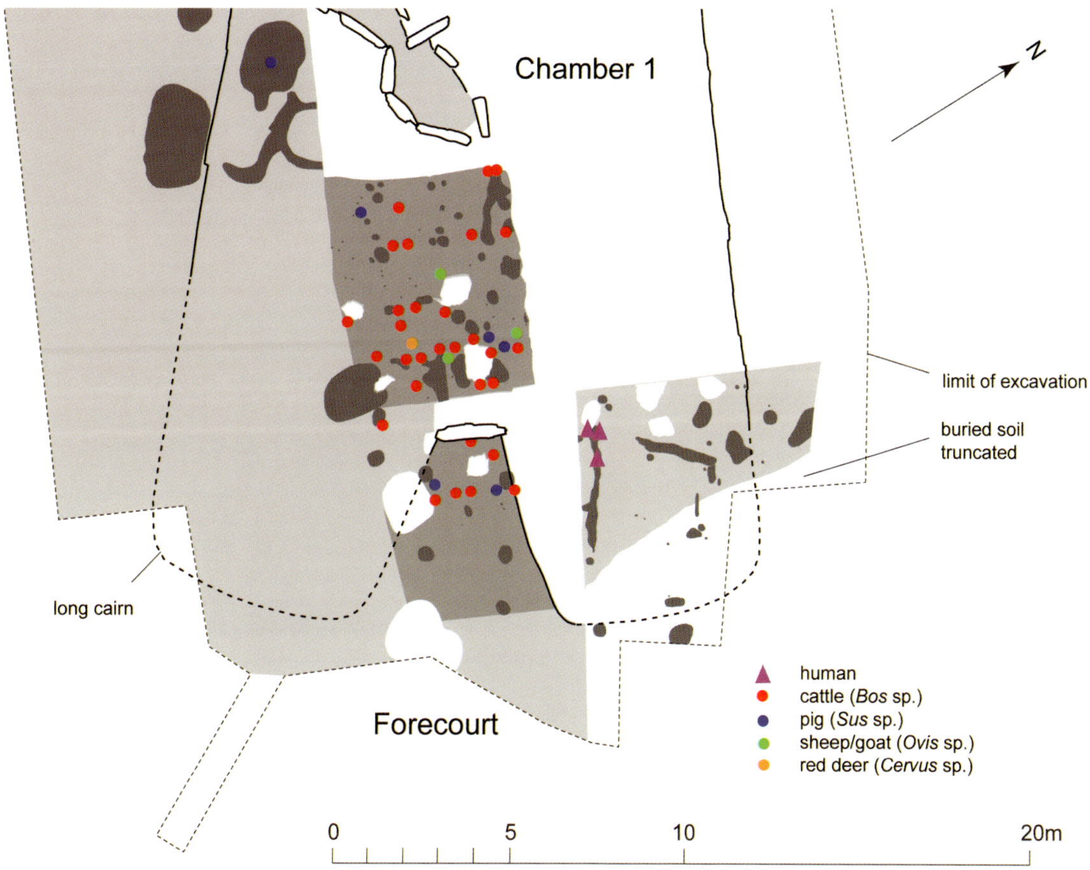

Fig. 3.19. Gwernvale: distribution of human and animal bone below the E end of the long cairn and in the forecourt area (after Britnell 1984b).

(O'Connor 1984, 153) but the significance of these finds is unclear; we will discuss them again in Chapter 12. Human remains are not infrequent in non-funerary early Neolithic contexts. Both burnt and unburnt human remains including skull fragments were found in structural features belonging to the early Neolithic building at Yarnton, for example (Hey *et al.* 2016, 58). There it was suggested that these could have been totemic items (Hey *et al.* 2016, 468; cf. Saville 1990, 253).

Human skeletal remains are also known from a number of other sites that were subsequently monumentalised, including Ballyglass, Co. Mayo (Smyth 2020, 150), Sale's Lot (Smith and Brickley 2009, appendix tables 14–15), Millbarrow (Whittle 1994, 16) and Hazleton North (Saville 1990, 197 and figs 20 and 195). The preferred model of the chronological sequence at Hazleton, where some pre-cairn human skull fragments have been dated, suggests that the human remains belong to a discrete phase of activity followed by a gap prior to the construction of the monument, though we cannot rule out the possibility that pre-cairn activity and monument construction represent a continuous phase of activity (Meadows *et al.* 2007, 56–6).

A fragment of human skull was also found below the cairn at Penywyrlod, close to the stonehole of one of the portal orthostats (Savory 1984, 22), and might have been contemporary with the construction of the monument. It seems significant, however, that as at Penywyrlod, the only human remains found in pre-cairn contexts at Gwernvale and Hazleton, were exclusively cranial fragments that came from below the broader ends of the long cairns, close to the subsequent forecourt areas, suggesting that human skulls or skull fragments played some role in the founding, setting out and orientation of these long cairns.

Plant remains (see distribution in Fig. 3.20)

Charred cereal grains and hazelnut shells are known from the area of the midden and from structural features belonging to the timber building (see Chapter 5). The only dated hazelnut shells at Gwernvale are of Mesolithic date but a high proportion are assumed to have derived from pre-cairn early Neolithic activity. Charred cereal grains and hazelnut shells have frequently been found in structural contexts associated with early Neolithic buildings in Britain, as for example at Parc Bryn Cegin (Kenney 2008, 25–6) and Lismore Fields (Garton 1991, 13) and hazelnut shells were again found in

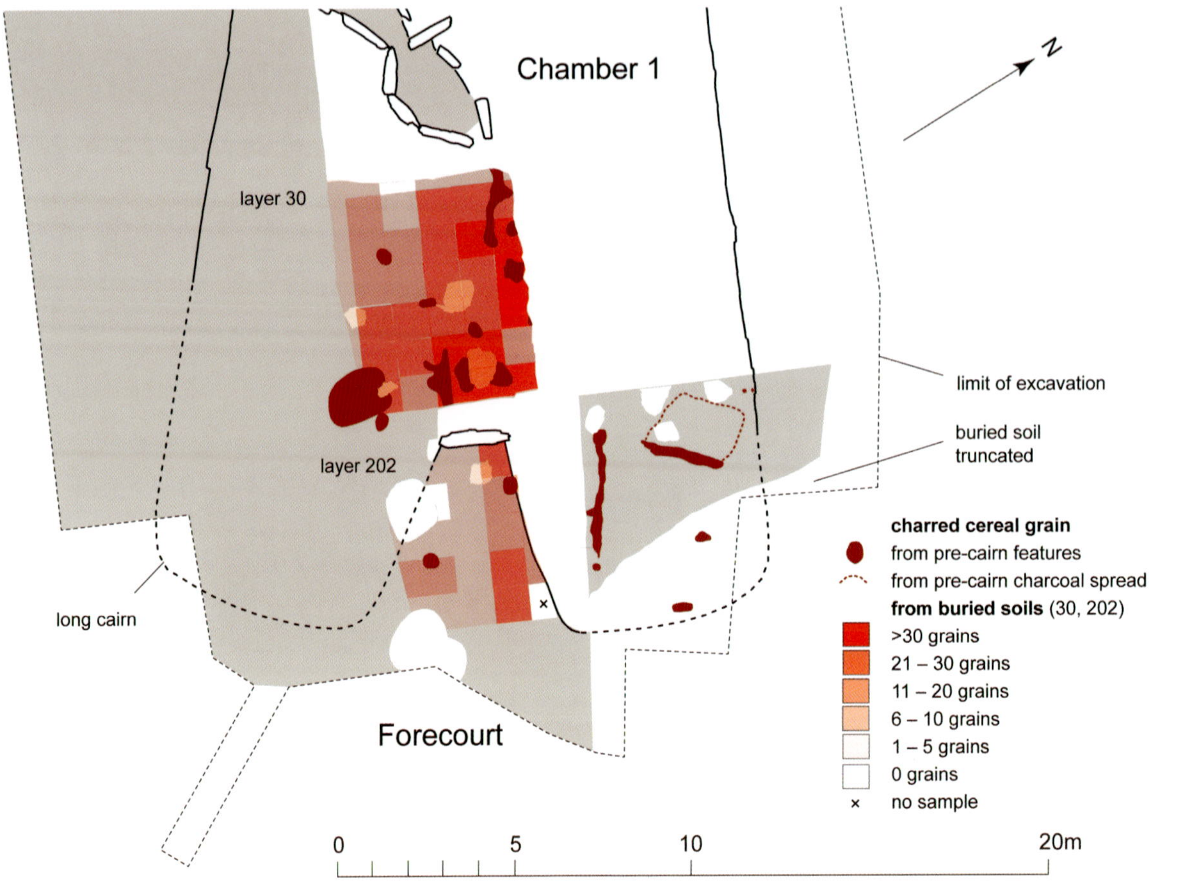

Fig. 3.20. Gwernvale: distribution of charred cereal remains below the E end of the long cairn and in the forecourt area (see Chapter 5 for further detail).

structural features at Parc Cybi (Kenney *et al.* 2011, 14). Cereals are particularly well represented at Irish house sites and are sometimes accompanied by evidence of food preparation and consumption as suggested by the presence of querns (Smyth 2014, 52). At Ballygalley (Simpson 1996, 129) as at Gwernvale, the general absence of evidence for grain processing implies either that processing was undertaken elsewhere in the vicinity or that only processed grain was brought to the site. Early Neolithic timber structures have been specifically associated with cereal cultivation and storage (Whittle 2003, 41), though cereal grain is not an invariable occurrence and was absent from other early Neolithic house sites, such as Yarnbury (Gibson 2017) and Yarnton (Hey *et al.* 2016).

The explanation for the presence of charred cereal grain and hazelnut shells within structural features at Gwernvale is open to debate. Some might represent residual material and some might represent material that made its way into structural features after the decay of timbers they contained. At Ballygalley the grain found with the wall-slots is said to have been more fragmentary than samples from elsewhere and on this basis Simpson argued (1996, 127–9) that this might be the result of trampling and brushing of floor waste.

The use of wet-sieving and flotation techniques similar to those employed at Gwernvale resulted in the recovery of similarly scanty charred cereals and hazelnut fragments within the pre-cairn midden at Hazleton North (Straker 1990), though similar data are lacking for the pre-cairn midden at Ascott-under-Wychwood. Charred grain and hazelnut shells appear again in relatively low quantities within the early Neolithic midden at Dorney (M. Robinson 2013, 200–1).

Cereals are associated with both the midden and house at Gwernvale. As further evidence accumulates for cereal cultivation and use in the early Neolithic, it is clearer that practice varied considerably and that single models of use and significance (cf. J. Thomas 1999, 24–5) are probably unhelpful. There are, for example, house sites such as Yarnton where grain is absent (Barclay 2007, 338), and there are midden sites such as Dorney where there are cereal remains but not apparently houses. Once again, this thread is picked up in Chapter 12.

Review of pre-cairn activity at Gwernvale

There appear to be reasonable grounds for assuming that the midden and house below the monument were a dwelling at which a wide range of customary domestic activities were taking place but, as discussed below, it may have had or acquired ceremonial or ritual significance as or after occupation ceased.

It remains uncertain whether the house necessarily belongs to the earliest phase of pre-cairn early Neolithic activity at Gwernvale, and depends upon an interpretation of how and when associated finds and dated radiocarbon samples arrived in the contexts in which they were found. There is also a possibility that the house was associated with other timber buildings or ancillary structures that have not been clearly identified or that existed in unexcavated or adjacent areas of the site.

The association between midden and house at some period (Fig. 3.21) is suggested by the distribution of sherds of six Plain Bowl or Carinated Bowl vessels (Britnell 1984, pots 1, 3, 9–11, 13), assuming that these are not all residual in structural features of the house. This leaves sherds of 11 other vessels from pre-cairn contexts, of which five are represented in the midden area, two are poorly stratified within the area of the house (pots 4, 5) and four others (pots 6, 15–17) were largely found elsewhere on the site. Radiocarbon dating and the distribution of ceramics would therefore at least not rule out the possibility that the midden had begun to form before the construction of the house or that there were a number of discontinuous periods of pre-cairn activity. There is reasonable evidence, however, discussed below, to suggest that the remains of the house were still visible when the long cairn was built, which suggests that it belonged to the latest phase of pre-cairn activity.

As noted above, the Bayesian model for radiocarbon dates from pre-cairn contexts presented in Chapter 4 estimates that the pre-cairn Neolithic activity at Gwernvale first occurred in *3975–3710 cal BC* (*95% probability*), probably in *3890–3790 cal BC* (*62% probability*, or *3740–3720 cal BC 5% probability*; *start_Gwernvale_pre_cairn*; Fig. 4.4) and continued for a period of *120–420 years* (*91% probability*, or *190–325 years 68% probability*, *span_Gwernvale_premonument_neolithic*).

However, since the date of construction of the overlying long cairn is not closely dated it is possible that the phase of pre-cairn activity was actually shorter.

Of other Welsh Neolithic houses that at Parc Cybi was probably in use for *30–75 years* (*68% probability*), ending in probably *3645–3625 cal BC* (*68% probability*), and that at Parc Bryn Cegin was probably in use for *40–110 years* (*68% probability*), ending probably in *3670–3620 cal BC* (*68% probability*) (Kenney 2021, 46). A longer period of continuous use has been proposed at White Horse Stone structure, which it is argued may have been in use for a period of *c.* 300–350 years, ending in *3745–3635 cal BC* (*68% probability*; *abandon WHS*) (Garwood 2011, 73; Whittle *et al.* 2011, 380). This is more compatible with the modelled period of pre-cairn activity at Gwernvale, but likewise seems longer than might be expected from the nature of the structural remains. Dates for the Llanfaethlu settlement (Rees and Jones 2016; 2017) will be available in due course (Catherine Rees, *pers. comm.*)

The pre-cairn sequence of timber structure and associated midden at Gwernvale appears to be closely mirrored at Ascott-under-Wychwood and Hazleton North (Fig. 3.22) and

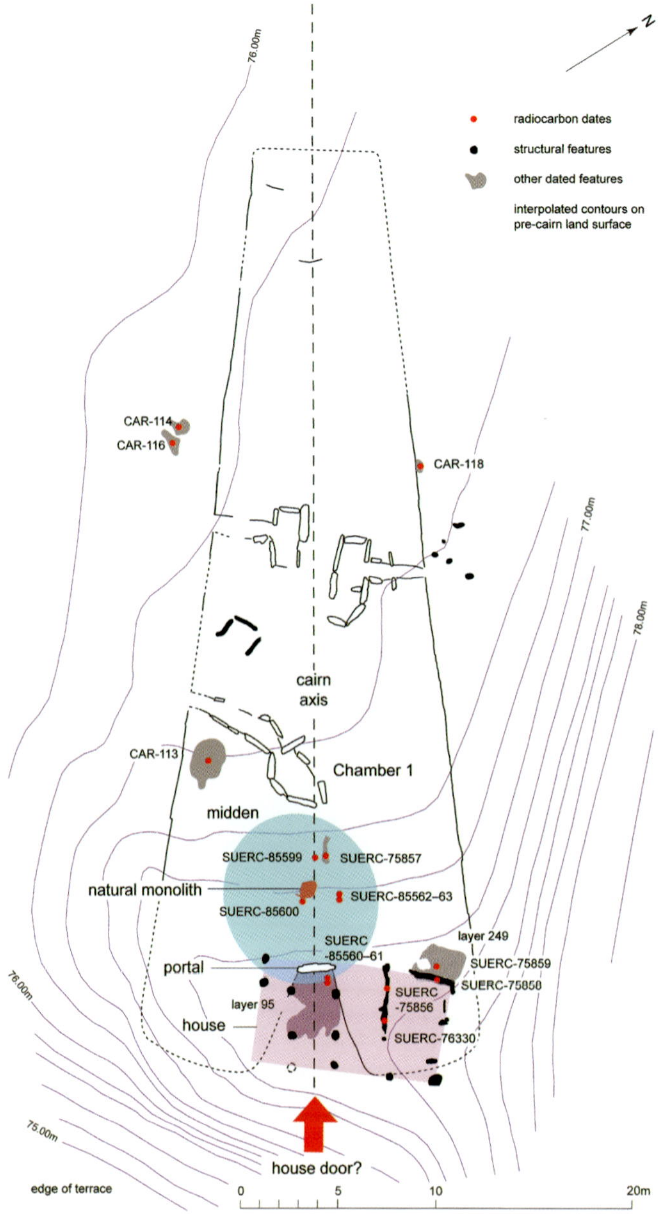

Fig. 3.21. Gwernvale: hypothetical extents of pre-cairn house and midden in relation to the long axis of the long cairn, the forecourt portal and the 'natural monolith' beneath the cairn.

potentially elsewhere beneath other Severn-Cotswold tombs. Whereas the creation of Penywyrlod involved fresh location and the performance of novel ideas, the transformation seen in the Gwernvale sequence may have relied on much wider connections and more broadly shared ideas to reinforce the efficacy of a late monument construction. The pre-cairn early Neolithic activity at Ascott appears to represent several discrete episodes taking place over a period of one to two centuries before the construction of the primary barrow in *3760–3700 cal BC* (*95% probability*; *primary construction*) (Benson and Whittle 2007, 232) whilst the pre-cairn activity at Hazleton appears to have lasted for between *40–180 years* (*68% probability*; *duration of pre-cairn phase*), ending in *3880–3660 cal BC* (*95% probability*; *end of pre-cairn phase*) (Meadows *et al.* 2007, 51).

By way of comparison the early Neolithic middens at Dorney (Fig. 3.22), which were not subsequently monumentalised, were in use for a period of between 100–170 years from the late 39th century BC (Allen *et al.* 2013, 243). On analogy with the interpretation of the early Neolithic midden at Dorney (Allen *et al.* 2013, 497–501), it is possible that the middens at Gwernvale, Hazleton North and Ascott-under-Wychwood each began to form through repeated visits on a seasonal cycle by small groups with no permanent settlement focus and that only at Gwernvale did a more permanent house become established.

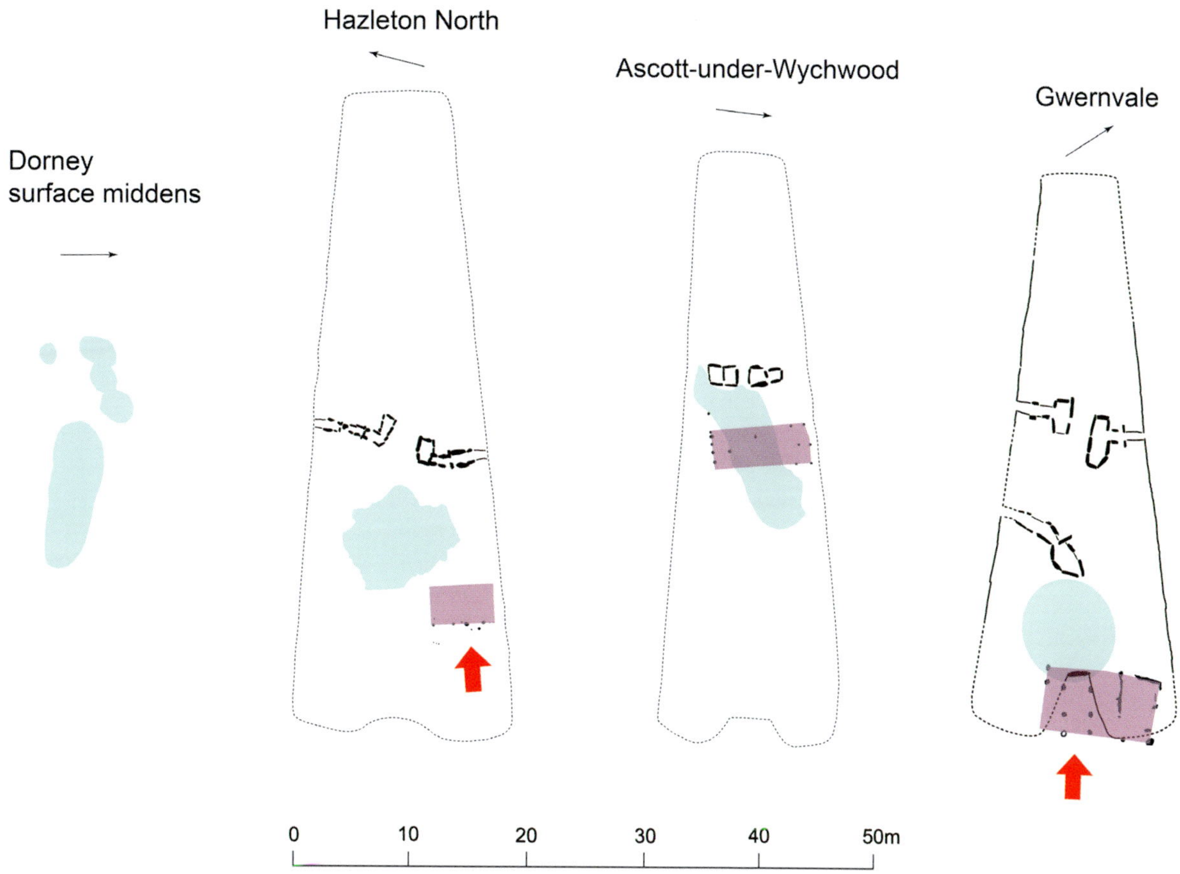

Fig. 3.22. Comparative plans of early Neolithic middens associated with timber structures and long cairns with an unmonumentalised midden at Dorney for comparison. The suggested positions of doors or entrances through the timber structures at Hazleton and Gwernvale are indicated by red arrows. Interpretative plans of Dorney (Eton Rowing Course) (after Allen et al. *2013), Hazleton North (after Saville 1990), and Ascott-under-Wychwood (after Benson and Whittle 2007).*

The mixing of finds in the soil profile in the area of the midden at Gwernvale shows that the buried soil had been considerably disturbed prior to the construction of the long cairn. It has been suggested elsewhere that middens might have improved soil fertility and could have been deliberately cultivated (Guttman 2005; Whittle 2007b, 345; Allen *et al.* 2013, 497). At Hazleton there appears to have been an episode of cultivation, possibly within small plots, in the period between the accumulation of the midden and the construction of the cairn (Macphail 1990, 225; Saville 1990, 240; see also comments in Chapter 5, this volume). There is no explicit evidence of this at Gwernvale apart from a disturbed soil profile, though cultivation may have been hindered by the presence of large boulders set firmly in the subsoil. If cultivation had taken place, the suggestion that at least some structural elements of the earlier timber structure were still visible when the monument was built suggests that the house site itself may have remained undisturbed.

The timber house at Gwernvale, like the timber structures at Hazleton North and Ascott-under-Wychwood, occupied a reasonably distinct yet undramatic place within the landscape. The Gwernvale midden, which seems to have focused upon a natural boulder, lay at the highest local point on the edge of a terrace overlooking the floodplain of the river Usk. Hazleton North occupied a high point on the edge of a slope, with ground dropping away to one side. Ascott-under-Wychwood occupied a bluff by a brook, above a valley. A similar pattern is shown by Irish houses, which show a tendency to be sited on gently sloping ground or on the summits of low ridges (Smyth 2014, 22). The Parc Cybi house similarly was built on a slight plateau (Kenney 2021, 32) and the Yarnton house on a slight gravel island on the Thames floodplain (Hey *et al.* 2016, 51). As noted in the case of other early Neolithic houses, the potential novelty and longevity of the Gwernvale structure suggest that it would have had a striking presence in the landscape (Garwood 2011, 84).

The siting of other comparable structures can be quite variable, however. The house at Parc Bryn Cegin, for example, lies along a slope (Kenney 2008, 14) whilst of the adjacent structures at White Horse Stone and Pilgrim's Way, the former lies up and down a quite marked slope whilst the latter lies along the slope (Garwood 2011, fig. 3.4). If parts of houses were used to stall domestic animals at certain times of the year, as suggested at Yarnton (Hey *et al.* 2016, 58) – which might also account for the use of more use of more robust plank walling in certain parts of some buildings – this might provide an explanation of why some houses, like more recent 'byre-house' longhouses, occupied markedly sloping sites for reasons of both drainage and status (Suggett 2005, 181).

The long-axis of the Gwernvale building is roughly NE–SW, and corresponds to that of a number of other early Neolithic timber buildings in Wales (Fig. 3.13). Various explanations have been offered for orientation of early Neolithic longhouses in central and western Europe, including an alignment upon an 'ancestral homeland' (Bradley 2001), a 'land of the sun' (Whittle 2011), the passage of the sun (Vondrovský 2018), or upon other celestial events as suggested at White Horse Stone, Yarnton, Lismore Fields (Garwood 2011, 84–5) and Parc Cybi (Kenney 2021, 52–3).

These arguments have to some extent depended upon the assumed location of an entrance within the gable end of the building, along its long axis, though in the case of many British early Neolithic buildings the positions of doors are often ambiguous or uncertain. As noted above, the juxtaposition of house and long cairn at Gwernvale implies a passageway through the long side of the house, which would significantly point along the Usk valley as well as being orientated, in common with many later prehistoric houses in Wales and elsewhere (cf. Burrow 2020, 79), in the direction of the rising sun in the E and SE.

Similar issues about orientation arise in relation to the Black Mountains long cairns themselves, which it has been suggested lie along river valleys or point towards prominent hills (Tilley 1994, 125; Cummings and Whittle 2004, 61). Although in the case of Gwernvale the orientation of house and long cairn eastwards along the valley seems the most meaningful, it may, however, be significant that the long axis (40° E of OS grid north) of the Gwernvale house points directly towards the prominent hilltop of Crug Hywel to the NE (Fig. 12.5, no. 6).

There are clear implications from the sequences at Gwernvale, Hazleton North and Ascott-under-Wychwood that the siting of earlier timber structures may have in some instances determined the siting and orientation of long cairns. Both these issues are followed further in Chapter 12.

Because of the nature of the excavation at Gwernvale, it is unknown whether the house was accompanied by other buildings or ancillary structures but important new information about the interrelationships between houses and monuments is emerging, again, from a number of large infrastructure projects. Visual relationships between pairs of houses are suggested at White Horse Stone, Llandygai and Lismore Fields (Garwood 2011, 84–5). At Parc Cybi it is argued that the house is orientated upon an earlier monument at Trefignath (Kenney 2020; 2021, 52–3). The phasing and dating of Trefignath are debatable, however, and it is not inconceivable that this sequence might be reversed and that the monument was orientated upon or related to an earlier house. Here, it may be significant that traces of an earlier timber structure may pre-date the monument (C. Smith 1987, 11). The relative proximity of the pair of houses at White Horse Stone and Pilgrim's Way to the megalithic chamber at Kit's Coty House has been noted, though they are not directly aligned upon it (Garwood 2011, 86).

Transition from midden and house to long cairn

The tradition of building long barrows or long cairns over earlier occupation sites is a widely recognised phenomenon across early Neolithic Europe and has been taken to express the concept of long cairns as ancestral houses (*e.g.* Hodder 1994; Bradley 1998, 44–8). The potential significance of the sequence at Gwernvale in terms of social dynamics during the early Neolithic in the Black Mountains area is further discussed in Chapter 12.

As noted in the original report, the outer revetment walls of the long cairn overlie the two north-eastern postholes of a setting of six now considered to form part of the earlier house. The relationship is so precise (Fig. 3.7) that it appears that the posts or at least the bases of the posts were still standing when the wall was built. Indeed, the juxtaposition of post-pipes and wall-face appears so exact that it seems unlikely that the posts could not have held external cladding, at least at ground level. In addition, assuming that the walling within the forecourt may have been of some height – up to 2.5m is suggested in the case of Penywyrlod (see Chapter 2) and at Hazleton (cf. Saville 1990, 260) – this also appears to rule out the presence of overhanging roof eaves, which further implies that the structure was by this stage unroofed.

A conscious and deliberate association between house and monument is implied by the fact that the long axis of the long cairn aligns precisely with the setting of six posts. A relationship with these particular posts might be explained either by the differential survival of different parts of the house. As noted above, there was slight though inconclusive evidence that the NE end of the house had burnt down. Evidence of this kind has been found at many Irish early Neolithic houses and those elsewhere. This is sometimes confined to parts of the structure and has been variously interpreted as accidental, hostile action or ritual destruction following abandonment (cf. Smyth 2014, 69–70). Otherwise, the different methods of construction of the two ends of the house – with stouter posts at the SW end and with lighter posts and possibly planking or wattle wall panels at the NE end – may have resulted in different rates of natural decay (cf. Noble 2017, 126–7).

Alternatively, the inferred intentional association may have been with a particular element of the earlier house and more specifically with a doorway or at least the memory of a doorway. Irish houses show evidence of both side and gable entrances, often towards a corner of the building, and some show evidence for entrances on opposite sides of the building (Smyth 2014, 27). There are uncertainties about the positions of doors within the comparable Welsh structures (Fig. 3.13) and although it is generally assumed that these were at one or both of the gable ends in the aisled structures at Parc Bryn Cegin and Parc Cybi there are again possibilities that doors were located in the long sides (Kenney 2008, 19; 2021, 50). The buildings at Llanfaethlu are also to be noted (Rees and Jones 2016; 2017). There is no explicit evidence for the position of a door at Gwernvale but the apparent relationship with the midden suggests there could have been at least one door on the W side of the building, paralleling the concentrations of artefacts that have been found close to entrances of some Irish houses (Smyth 2014, 32). The juxtaposition of the probable setting of six posts and the subsequent forecourt and portal structure of the long cairn appears significant and suggests an explicit, presumably symbolic relationship between house and monument. This might in turn suggest that the post setting may have formed a broad corridor or cross-passage in this position with possibly a single shorter bay to the SW and two wider bays to the NE. Similar cross-passages might be recognised in early Neolithic houses at Lismore Fields and White Horse Stone, depending upon whether they are considered to be single period or not (Garwood 2011, 64–5; Barclay and Harris 2017).

The location of the so-called 'natural monolith' in the midden area outside the house and also on the long axis of the long cairn also seems significant and had the remains of the house become obscured it might have helped to preserve a memory of where a door to the building had once been. This boulder, together with other natural boulders in the subsoil, are superficially reminiscent of the cluster of sarsen boulders below the broader end of the South Street long barrow and which probably influenced its siting and layout (Ashbee *et al.* 1979, 261–2). In this instance the stones had been deliberately rolled into placed some time prior to the construction of the long barrow and might be interpreted as a shrine (Whittle 1993, 43). Re-examination of the large, weathered sandstone slabs along the axis of the long cairn at Penywyrlod, identified as 'thrust blocks' by Savory (1984, fig. 4), suggested that some of these might also be natural boulders occurring within glacial drift.

The interval of time between the end of pre-cairn activity and the construction of the Gwernvale long cairn is unknown. The preferred interpretation of the radiocarbon evidence at Ascott suggests that there may have been a gap of probably *more than 50 years* between the end of pre-cairn activity and the construction of the long cairn (Benson and Whittle 2007, 232). At Hazleton the interval between the pre-cairn early Neolithic timber structure and midden, during which cultivation took place, is estimated to have been *between 1 and 75 years* (*68% probability*; *cultivation*) (Meadows *et al.* 2007, 55). A gap of no more than a generation or so seems to be compatible with the evidence at Gwernvale, which suggests that at least the stumps of some of the posts of the timber house were still visible when the monument was built. In addition, packing stones within one of the postholes of the structure were directly overlain by the basal courses of the revetment wall (Fig. 3.7), which suggests that little or no soil accumulation had taken place. In turn this implies a relatively short interval between the abandonment of the building and the construction of the monument. There is more fragmentary evidence of a timber structure below the Severn-Cotswold tomb at Sale's Lot, which might represent a further rectangular building up to 6m × 4.5m with a central hearth (Darvill 1996, 104).

As noted above there are hints that at least parts of the Gwernvale structure may have burnt down after it went out of use (Britnell 1985, 52), which appears to parallel the fate of a number of other early Neolithic timber halls elsewhere in Britain that were not monumentalised (Barclay and Harris 2018), including those at Dorstone prior to the superimposition of long mounds (Ray and Thomas 2020, 110). In Wales it is perhaps to be paralleled by the burning down of the Llandygai house (Lynch and Musson 2001, 31) and even by the dismantling or partial dismantling of the Parc Bryn Cegin and Parc Cybi houses, possibly followed in the latter instance by feasting (Kenney 2021, 51–2).

Clear parallels can also be drawn between the process of monumentalisation at Gwernvale and what have been referred to as 'uncanny' similarities in the sequences at Hazleton North and Ascott-under-Wychwood (Whittle 2007a, 346). All three sites show evidence of Mesolithic activity. All three have early Neolithic middens composed of a wide range of domestic debris which lie directly below laterally chambered Severn-Cotswold long cairns. At all three, the middens lie below the proximal ends of the long cairns, between the areas subsequently occupied by the forecourt and burial chambers (Fig. 3.22). At all three, the pre-cairn middens were associated with timber structures, which had possibly fallen into disuse before the long cairns were built. The sequences at these three sites appear strikingly similar, but the timber structures at the three sites have been interpreted quite differently, and may be of varying date. At Gwernvale the structural features were originally interpreted as possibly being two buildings but it is now argued here that these might now be considered to belong to a single house that had become dilapidated by the time the cairn was built. We come back to wider implications in Chapter 12.

The pre-cairn structure at Hazleton is represented by a hearth and a line of stakeholes and postholes approximately 5.3m across, with the suggestion of an entrance towards one end (Saville 1990, 17–20). Some of the postholes may have been deliberately removed and it was considered that features that were identified might form just one side of a larger structure. Saville (1990, 240–1) argued that nothing of the superstructure would have been visible when the long cairn was built and that although it appeared to be more than coincidence that the centre of the midden lay directly below the central axis of the long cairn, no obvious explanation for this was forthcoming. The sequence has been reinterpreted on a number of occasions. Darvill (1996, 85–8) suggested that the features belonged to a ridge-roofed building and Whittle *et al.* (1999, 350–2) drew parallels with a structure below the outer bank of the Windmill Hill causewayed enclosure. More recently, stratigraphic evidence has been invoked to suggest that primary dumps of material were placed over the midden and probably against the rotting stumps of the timber structure (McFadyen 2007, 352).

The structural evidence below the long cairn at Ascott-under-Wychwood was interpreted somewhat equivocally as two smaller timber structures around and then over which the midden was constructed, though the possibility that it might represent a single large structure was not entirely ruled out (Benson and Whittle 2007, 27–34). There has been more recent support for its interpretation as a single large building about 8.25m × 3.5m across with a central hearth (cf. Hey and Robinson 2011, 231).

This orientation of timber structures at right-angles to the axis of the monument is also shared by the more substantial timber structure at Nutbane, burnt down before the construction of the long barrows (Morgan 1959, 31). This clearly differentiates these structures from the timber settings at Wayland's Smithy (Whittle 1991), Fussell's Lodge (Ashbee 1966; Wysocki *et al.* 2007), Kilham (Manby 1970), and Street House (Vyner 1984), where timber structures have an orientation along the axis of the monument and in each case serve to extend the linearity of the timber mortuary structures that they contain. There is no suggestion that these particular timber settings were actual houses, and they may possibly simply have been symbolic representations of passageways. This raises the question of whether all the structures at Gwernvale, Hazleton North and Ascott-under-Wychwood were necessarily houses or whether the timber settings at Hazleton North possibly were simply a representation of a house facade and doorway and those at Ascott-under-Wychwood merely a representation of the gable ends of a building. The evident longevity of their use and subsequent decay in the absence of explicit ritual or funerary activity, however, suggests that they could be regarded as domestic dwellings.

On the basis of the evidence from Gwernvale, Hazleton North and Ascott-under-Wychwood, three of the more extensively excavated long cairns in the Severn-Cotswold group, it seems likely that the superimposition of monuments on top of earlier houses is likely to have happened fairly frequently. Recent reassessment of the sequence from timber house and the court tomb at Ballyglass, Co. Mayo (Smyth 2020), reveals a number of telling similarities with the evidence from Gwernvale, which illustrate even more widespread traditions that are independent of monumental forms. The Ballyglass house, dated to 3950–3650 cal BC at 95% confidence, is similar in size and constructional techniques to the Gwernvale house, which to all intents and purposes appears to have functioned in the same way as many other early Neolithic Irish houses. Parts of the structure may have been demolished or burnt down but, critically, the physical remains of the structure were still visible when the tomb was built, one of the chambers abutting posts at one end of the house and part of the outer kerb placed along the line of one of the outer walls. The house, tomb and chambers at Ballyglass follow a similar though not identical alignment, unlike Gwernvale where the house is set at right-angles to the cairn.

A further characteristic that links Gwernvale, Hazleton North and Ascott-under-Wychwood is that the pre-cairn timber structures are set at right-angles to the axis of the long cairns that they underlie (Fig. 3.22). If the setting of six posts had formed a cross passage, as suggested above, the spatial arrangement and orientation of house and midden may have consciously been set out in relation to the 'outside world' looking SE down the valley and an 'inner world' looking inwards to the midden, in a similar manner to the Amazonian longhouse described by Christine Hugh-Jones (1996, 189). This linear arrangement appears to be taken up in the design of the forecourt and chambered areas of the subsequent long cairn, which further suggests a trajectory from the land of the living to the land of the dead.

Further consideration of the orientation of house and long cairn at Gwernvale and their significance in terms of worldviews, land use, economy and social organisation in the Black Mountains region is given in Chapter 12.

4

A chronology of the Black Mountains tombs and their place in the early Neolithic of south Wales and the Marches

Seren Griffiths

Aims

New radiocarbon results were produced for this project on samples from the Black Mountains burial monuments of Penywyrlod (Talgarth), Gwernvale, Ty Isaf and Pipton, and the first aim of this chapter is to produce a chronology for them. The second aim is to compare the chronology of these sites with other comparable or relevant monuments in south Wales and the Marches; and as part of this process, new results on radiocarbon measurements from Tinkinswood in the Vale of Glamorgan are reported here for the first time. The third aim of the chapter is to update models for the chronology of early Neolithic activity in south Wales and the Marches, taking in a wide range of other kinds of site including evidence for occupation, so that the place of the Black Mountains monuments can be set in a wider temporal context. Even wider questions about the development of monuments and of processes of Neolithisation are debated in the concluding discussion, in Chapter 12.

Methods

The radiocarbon results presented here for the long cairns have accumulated over a long period of time and by varying means. These results are detailed in Table 4.1. They include those produced in the 1970s by the Cardiff Radiocarbon Laboratory and a single additional result produced by AWE Harwell for Penywyrlod. Further dates for Penywyrlod and Ty Isaf (already published in Whittle *et al.* 2011) were obtained during a project examining their human remains around the turn of the 21st century, as set out in Chapter 6. To these were then added those made in 2017 and 2019 for this research project by the Oxford and Glasgow laboratories. Additional results from Penywyrlod resulted from small-scale excavation in advance of conservation work, as set out in Chapter 2, while results from Gwernvale came from the programme of analysis of plant remains and re-evaluation of the pre-cairn activity, as set out in Chapters 3 and 5. Finally, more dates were obtained from Penywyrlod and Ty Isaf resulting from a programme of isotope analysis published in Neil *et al.* (2017), as summarised in Chapter 7.

Results from the wider context of Neolithic sites and material culture in Wales are drawn from the published literature, including recently produced developer-led work such as the South Wales Gas Pipeline project (Darvill *et al.* 2020), as well as work in preparation on the early Neolithic activity at Dorstone, Herefordshire (Ray *et al.* 2022). Citations for the sources of results included in this analysis, and the radiocarbon methods used to produce them, are given in Table 4.2. Sites mentioned in the text are shown in Fig. 4.1.

Measurements from the scientific dating work undertaken for this project were produced on samples that had robust associations between the 'archaeological event of interest' and the 'dated event' (Waterbolk 1971; Griffiths 2022). Samples were selected in order to explore the taphonomies of individual ecofacts, and to explore processes of deposit formation. Each of the different monuments had different sampling considerations arising from their unique preservation histories and the ways in which these sites had been excavated. As a result, the chronologies for each site include scientific dating evidence that emphasises different aspects of their histories. For example, the pre-monument activity at Gwernvale is much more robustly sampled than the rest of the earlier Neolithic activity at this site, and the use of the Pipton site is more fully represented than at other burial sites with new data discussed here, though there still remain aspects of the chronology of Pipton that are unclear given the available radiocarbon results.

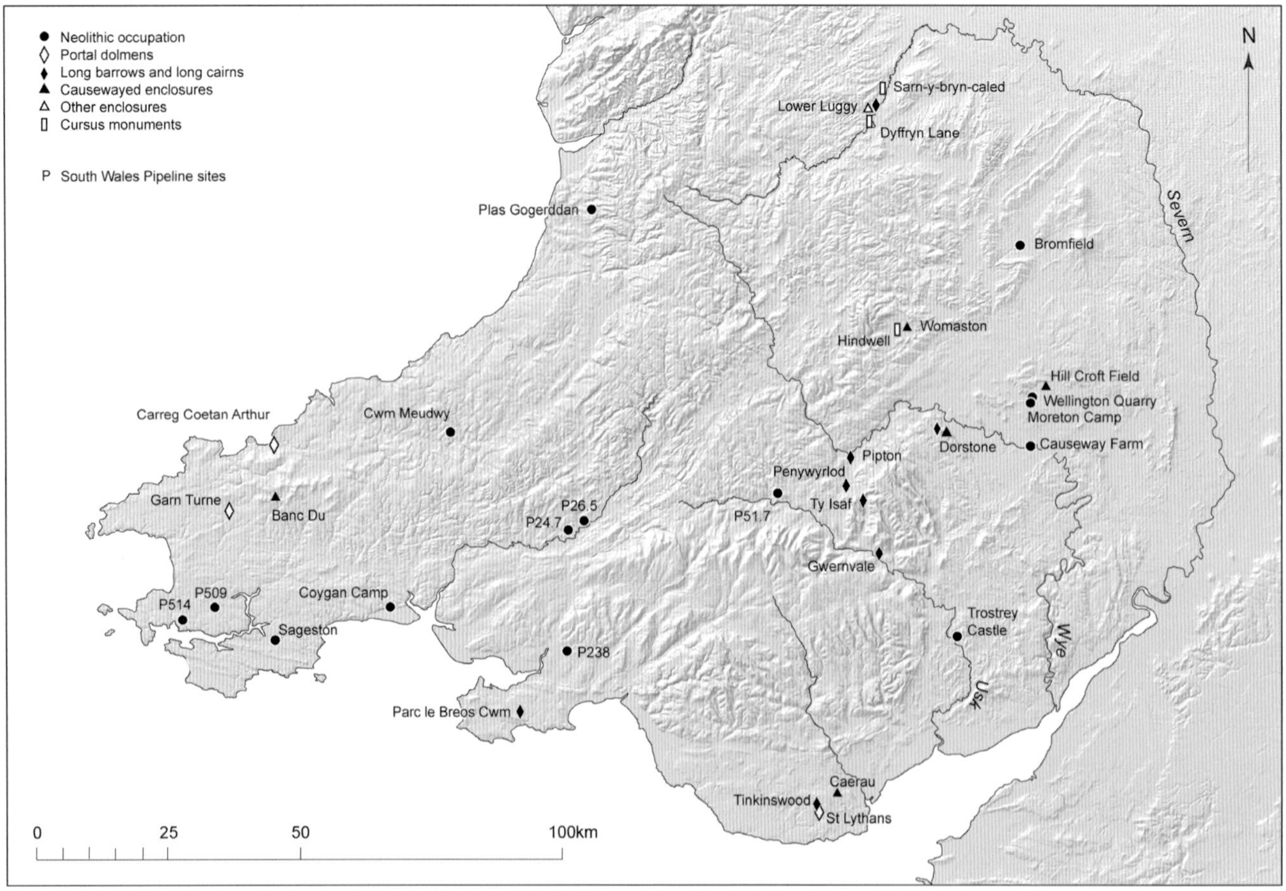

Fig. 4.1. Map of sites in south Wales and the Marches mentioned in Chapter 4.

Results from the recent scientific dating of the Black Mountains long cairns, and the wider Neolithic context from south Wales, have been analysed in Bayesian statistical models (Buck *et al.* 1991; 1992; 1996; Bronk Ramsey 2009; and references therein), using the program OxCal (Bronk Ramsey 1995; 2009), both to calibrate radiocarbon measurements and to interrogate groups of data in the light of archaeological 'prior beliefs' within Bayesian statistical models. This modelling produces formal, probabilistic outputs, which can be more precise than the calibrated radiocarbon ages. We use models below that make use of both highly 'informative' prior beliefs (such as the relative ages of different deposits suggested by site stratigraphy) as well as more 'uninformative' prior beliefs (such as the relationships suggested by archaeological phases of activity; cf. Bayliss *et al.* 2007c).

All the results of the Bayesian analysis presented here have been produced through models constructed using OxCal v4.3 (Bronk Ramsey 2009), and the calibration data of IntCal20 (Reimer *et al.* 2020). We illustrate the models applied here in the figures below, where the large square brackets and OxCal Chronological Query Language 2 keywords illustrate the treatment of the data. For each of the long cairns, site-specific models have been produced that reflect the archaeological prior beliefs from site phasing and site stratigraphy. The modelling choices for each long cairn are discussed below.

For the wider Neolithic of south Wales and the Marches, we have created site-specific chronological models where there is stratigraphic prior information, or more than four measurements from an archaeological phase of activity. We have included the posterior estimates from the burial monuments analysed as part of this project and the other regional data in a 'currency model' for the south Wales Neolithic.

Where a site only saw activity in the early Neolithic, all the results are included in the currency model. Where sites are multi-phase, only the early Neolithic results (associated with characteristic early Neolithic activity as defined below and in Griffiths 2021) are incorporated into the currency model. This approach allows us to identify results that may be unusual in terms of the currency model for the region as a whole, and to identify trends in practices. This approach has been very important in identifying some of the important conclusions discussed below.

The publications that provide the basis for our modelling choices for each result are indicated in the text and Table 4.2. The date ranges quoted below in italics are the posterior density estimates derived from these Bayesian models.

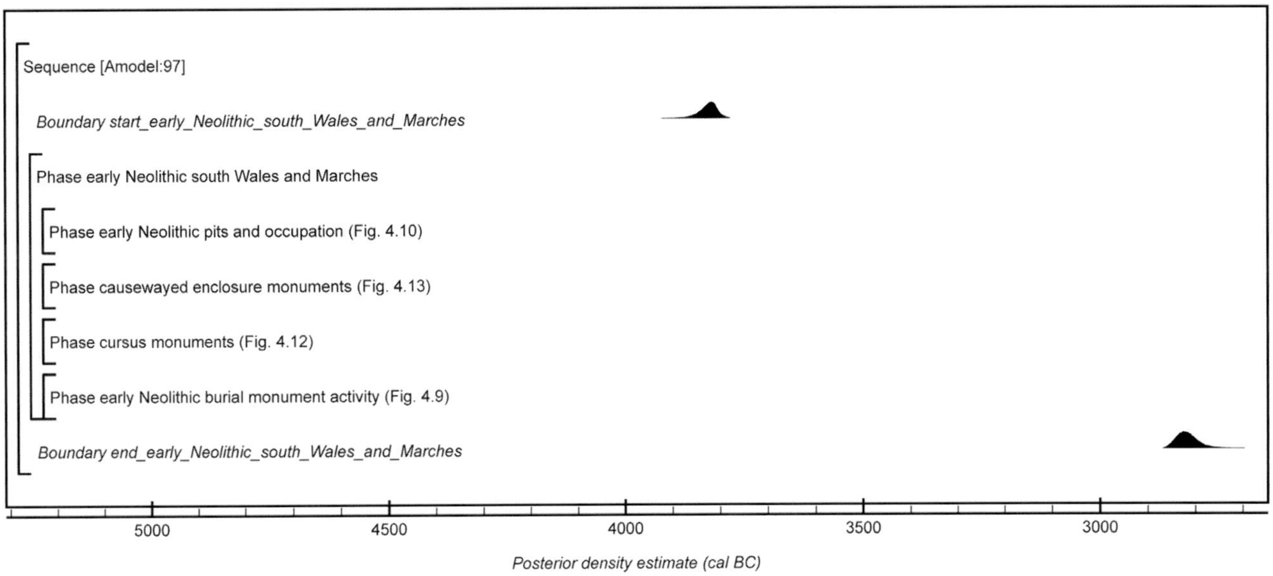

Fig. 4.2. Overall structure of the chronological model for early Neolithic activity in south Wales and the Welsh Marches. The component sections of the model are shown in detail in Figs 4.9, 4.10, 4.11. The large square brackets and the OxCal CQL2 commands in this and subsequent components define the model.

They are quoted at 95% probability, unless otherwise stated. The reporting follows criteria outlined in Millard (2014) and Bayliss (2015).

The overall model structure is shown in Fig. 4.2, with relevant segments for different types of early Neolithic activity detailed below, following the site-specific models for the burial monuments from the Black Mountains group, which form the focus of this study.

Since the emphasis is on modelled estimates, calibrated ranges for individual dates are not given in the tables.

Results

Penywyrlod (Talgarth)

Penywyrlod model construction

Fifteen radiocarbon measurements were produced over the history of investigation into Penywyrlod as set out above. Potential samples for radiocarbon measurements were available from three classes of deposits from the chambered cairn. These deposits were: from the buried soils that pre-dated the construction of the monument; from deposits in the chambers and passages associated with the use of the monument; and from deposits outside the footprint of the cairn that had been sealed by collapsed cairn material at some point in the past (Table 4.1). It was not possible to establish a relative chronological relationship between the deposits sealed by the cairn collapse and those recovered from within the cairn; measurements underlying the tumble could be associated with the monument use, or pre- or post-date use of the monument. These issues are discussed in Chapter 2.

Prior to this project, a single radiocarbon measurement (HAR-674) existed, which had been produced on a bulked sample of broken small human bones recovered from within Chamber NE II. Several measurements were obtained on samples from the buried soil under the monument, and from the deposits sealed by the cairn collapse. These multiple measurements were produced to explore the taphonomy of samples because none of these individual archaeological contexts were relatively rich in charred plant remains. In order to investigate the potential for residual or intrusive material, and in order to explore the relationships between the 'dated events' and the 'archaeological events of interest' (Griffiths forthcoming), we therefore obtained multiple measurements on ecofacts from these deposits. It was hoped that consistent results would provide assurance that the measurements were all closely associated with the 'archaeological events of interest', in this case, the formation of the pre-cairn deposits and the formation of the deposits underlying the cairn collapse.

From one of the buried soils below the inner cairn (context 33), two statistically inconsistent measurements were produced (SUERC-67741; -69931; $T'=22.0$, $T'5\%=3.8$; $\nu=1$; at the 5% significance level; Ward and Wilson 1978) on two separate single entities of *Corylus avellana* charcoal. Another result (SUERC-69932) was also produced from another deposit (context 108) pre-dating the monument. Of these results, SUERC-69931 is later than some of the results on human skeletal remains deposited within the monument, which are stratigraphically later than the context from which the sample for SUERC-69931 was recovered. SUERC-69931 is presented in the model described here as an 'outlier', which may represent intrusive material introduced to the pre-cairn deposits as a result of subsequent activity.

Eight measurements were produced on samples from within the monument and associated with its use.

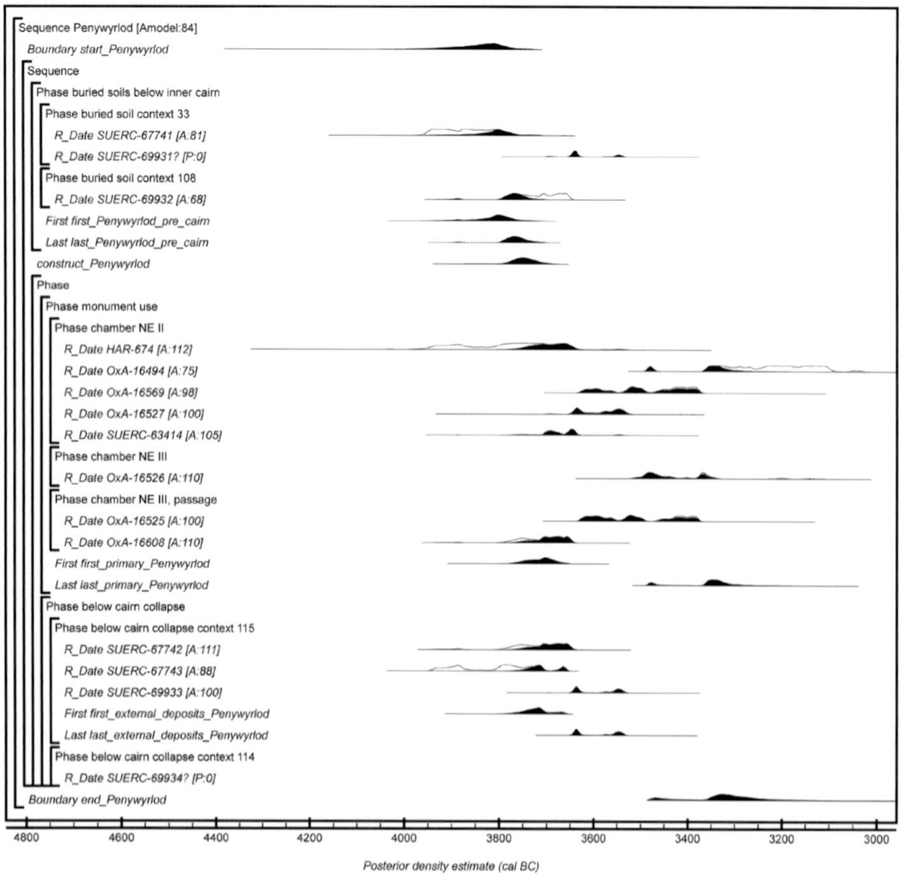

Fig. 4.3. Probability distributions for radiocarbon measurements from the Penywyrlod monument. The large square brackets and the OxCal CQL2 commands define the model.

These measurements (HAR-674, OxA-16494, -16569, -16525, -16526, -16527, -16608 and SUERC-63414) were all produced on samples of human bone or teeth. With the exception of HAR-674, the measurements were all produced on single-entity samples. Five measurements were produced on bone from the NE II chamber, one from the NE III chamber, and two from the NE III passage (Table 4.1). A re-analysis of the human remains from Penywyrlod by Mick Wysocki is given in Chapter 6 (see Figs 6.1 and 6.2 for the location of human remains retrieved from the site).

The original report had argued that Chamber NE II was in effect a closed cist, sealed when the monument was built, though it now seems possible that both the chamber and passage remained accessible (see Chapter 2; Savory 1984, 19). The chamber and passage of Chamber NE III appear to have remained accessible during the use of the tomb. Both chambers and their contents had been disturbed in advance of excavation, and the results have been modelled as if they derive from archaeological phases of activity without any additional stratigraphic relationships.

From under the cairn collapse, three results (SUERC-67742, -67743, and -69933) were produced on single-entity samples of different types of charred plant remains from context 115, an area of burning, including a *Triticum* sp. grain (SUERC-67742). These results were not statistically consistent (T'=16.8, T'5%=3.8; ν=2; at the 5% significance level; Ward and Wilson 1978), demonstrating that deposit formation outside the cairn could include ecofacts of a range of different ages, possibly including residual pre-cairn material. Another measurement (SUERC-69934) from context 114, underlying the cairn collapse, returned a recent radiocarbon result, and has not been included as an active likelihood in the analysis presented here.

Penywyrlod: results and discussion

The model for these results as applied in Fig. 4.3 has good overall agreement (A_{model} =84%). We estimate that Neolithic activity began at Penywyrlod in *3990–3730 cal BC (95% probability)*, probably in *3900–3780 cal BC* (*68% probability*; *start_Penywyrlod*; Fig. 4.3). Pre-cairn activity as presented here went on for between *1–130 years* (*95% probability*), but most probably could have occurred over a couple of generations, of between *1–60 years* (*68% probability*; *duration_Penywyrlod_pre_cairn*; parameter not shown).

An estimate for the date of construction of the monument can be produced because of the stratigraphic sequence available. This is that the cairn was constructed in *3815–3680 cal BC (95% probability)*, probably in the 38th century cal BC in *3775–3720 cal BC (68% probability; construct_Penywyrlod*; Fig. 4.3). People who died over a period of *190–505 years (95% probability)* or *320–445 years (68% probability; span_primary_Penywyrlod*; parameter not shown) were buried at the site. The last dated event associated with the use of the cairn for burial occurred in *3375–3200 cal BC (78% probability*, or *3495–3415 cal BC 18% probability)*, most probably in *3365–3305 cal BC (60% probability*, or *3485–3465 cal BC 9% probability; last_primary_Penywyrlod*; Fig. 4.3).

The radiocarbon results from samples from NE II demonstrate that people whose remains were buried in this chamber died over a considerable period of time, of between *170–490 years (95% probability)*, or *305–435 years (66% probability*, or *210–220 years 2% probability; duration_NE_II*; parameter not shown).

The first dated event associated with the prehistoric activity around the cairn and sealed by its collapse probably occurred in *3775–3655 cal BC (95% probability)*, most probably in the later 38th century cal BC (*3760–3700 cal BC; 68% probability; first_external_deposits_Penywyrlod*; Fig. 4.3). The activity represented by radiocarbon dated material from context 115 went on for some *25–220 years (95% probability*, or *70–140 years 40% probability*, or *150–195 years 28% probability; span_pre_cairn_collapse_Penywyrlod*; parameter not shown). Excluding the measurement (SUERC-69934) that returned a recent result, the latest radiocarbon determination means that activity at Penywyrlod is estimated to have ended in *3370–3145 cal BC (78% probability*, or *3485–3380 cal BC 18% probability;* or *3360–3245 cal BC 62% probability*, or *3475–3450 cal BC 6% probability; end_Penywyrlod*; Fig. 4.3). Excluding the recent result, the total duration of activity associated with the use of the monument as a place of burial over *255–635 years (95% probability)*, most probably over *410–575 years (67% probability; span_Penywyrlod*; parameter not shown).

Recent work by Neil *et al.* (2017) identified that the individual from which radiocarbon measurement SUERC-63414 was made had atypical strontium stable isotope values, which they suggest indicates that this individual obtained their childhood diet from outside England and Wales. While the individual measured by SUERC-63414 does represent an early *burial* in both the site history and southern Wales more widely (see discussion below), the presence of the pre-cairn activity at Penywyrlod demonstrates that this individual may not represent the very earliest Neolithic activity either at the site or in Wales or indeed Britain more generally.

In the currency model discussed below, the posterior density estimates associated with the use of the monument and the estimates associated with pre-cairn occupation are used to further explore the context of this monument in terms of early Neolithic activity in Wales and the Marches.

Gwernvale

Gwernvale model construction

Fifteen results exist from Gwernvale (Table 4.1), including those produced at the Cardiff Laboratory after the original 1970s excavation (Britnell and Savory 1984) and those from the recent re-assessment, as set out in Chapters 3 and 5, produced at the Glasgow SUERC Laboratory. Of these, the majority were produced on samples that derived from the pre-cairn deposits. They include results from a timber structure (SUERC-75856, -75858 and -76330), pre-cairn pit F68 associated with Neolithic pottery (CAR-116), pit 308 below the western end of the monument (CAR-118), a possible gully (SUERC-75857), and a charcoal-rich spread (SUERC-75859). One of these measurements (CAR-118) was produced on mixed charcoal from pit F308 and produced a 6th millennium result. It has been included as a *terminus post quem* in the model presented below to reflect the potential for an inbuilt 'old wood' offset, and to reflect its stratigraphic association with the construction of the monument. The results CAR-113, CAR-114 and CAR-116 may include charcoal with in-built 'old wood' offsets. The results have therefore been presented using the formal charcoal outlier analysis function within OxCal (Dee and Bronk Ramsey 2014).

Samples from two sequences of buried soils were used to produce radiocarbon measurements. This included two samples from a stratigraphic sequence recovered from under what became the cairn forecourt (SUERC-85560, -85561).

Four results were produced on samples recovered from the buried soil (layer 30) below the cairn, excavated in a sequence of spits. SUERC-85562 and SUERC-85563 were produced on samples from the same upper spit ('spit B') from within this buried soil. These measurements produced significantly different radiocarbon age estimates, with SUERC-85563 producing an 8th millennium cal BC age range. This result has been presented below as an outlier, with uncertain association with any activity associated with the use of the monument. This result probably represents redeposited material. The other results included a measurement (SUERC-85600) on a sample from the lowest spit in this sequence. Another result (SUERC-85599) was produced from the fourth lowest spit. The results are modelled to represent this stratigraphic sequence.

Two further results (CAR-114, -116) were produced on samples of mixed charcoal from pits (F58, F47) that were located below the cairn body collapse, and which contained later Neolithic Peterborough Ware. On the basis of the position of these features in plan, and the fact that they contained Peterborough Ware, the pits were believed to represent activity that took place later than the initial construction and use of the monument, and have been modelled to post-date the other activity. Because these results were associated with the use of Peterborough Ware, these

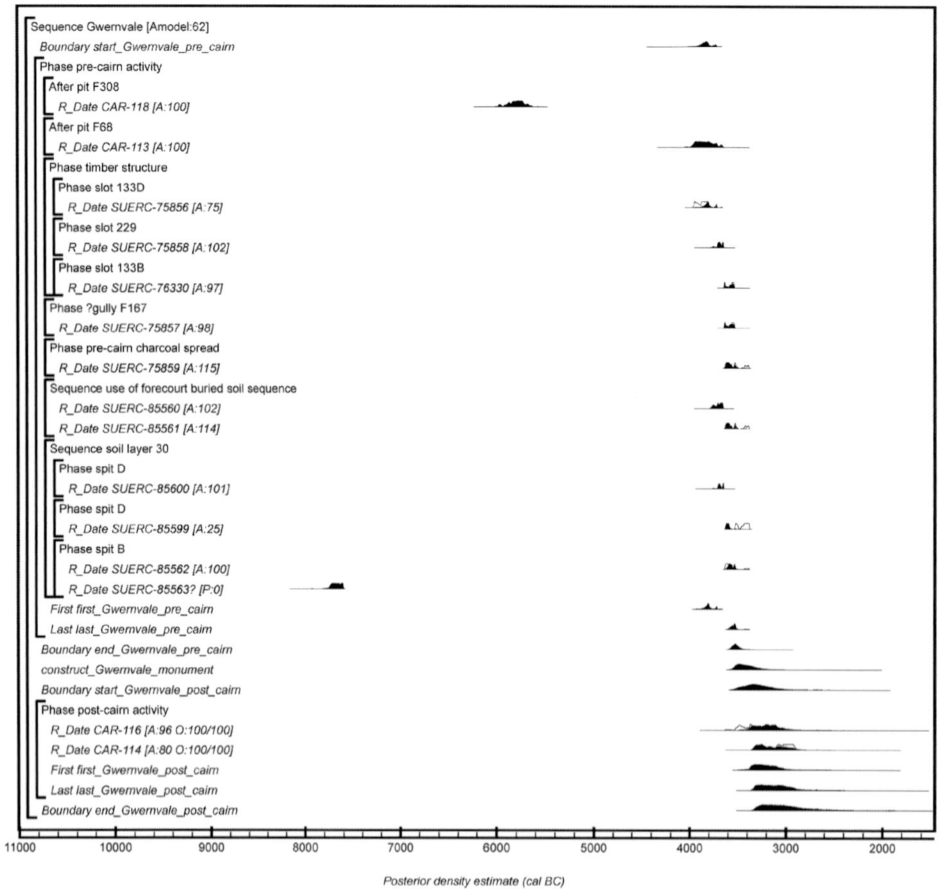

Fig. 4.4. Probability distributions for radiocarbon measurements from the Gwernvale monument. The large square brackets and the OxCal CQL2 commands define the model.

posterior density estimates have not been included in the currency model for the early Neolithic of south Wales and the Welsh Marches (see discussion below).

Gwernvale: results and discussion

The site-specific Gwernvale results have good overall agreement (A_{model}=62) with the model shown in Figure 4.4. The model estimates that the pre-cairn Neolithic activity at Gwernvale first occurred in *3975–3710 cal BC* (*95% probability*), probably in *3890–3790 cal BC* (*60% probability* or *3745–3715 cal BC 8% probability*; *start_Gwernvale_pre_cairn*; Fig. 4.4). The pre-cairn Neolithic activity went on here for between *120–420 years* (*95% probability*, *span_Gwernvale_premonument_neolithic;* parameter not shown). This long estimate for the pre-monument activity may be in part because we have no direct estimates for the use of the monument with which to constrain the pre-monument phase.

We have suggested in the model shown in Figure 4.4 that the Gwernvale monument was probably constructed before the use of the Peterborough Ware pits at the site. This provides us with the estimate for construction of the monument in *3570–3070 cal BC* (*95% probability*; or *3530–3300 cal BC 68% probability*; *construct_Gwernvale_monument*; Fig. 4.4).

The Peterborough Ware-associated activity is estimated to have first begun in *3475–2770 cal BC (95% probability*), probably in *3350–3020 cal BC* (*68% probability*; *first_Gwernvale_post_cairn*; Fig. 4.4). The last dated event associated with this activity is estimated to have occurred in *3320–2545 cal BC* (*95% probability*), probably in *3270–2880 cal BC* (*68% probability; last_Gwernvale_post_cairn*; Fig. 4.4).

From the available results, it is estimated that there may have been a considerable interval between the last dated event associated with the pre-cairn activity (*last_Gwernvale_pre_cairn*; Fig. 4.4), and the first dated event associated with the post-cairn activity (*first_Gwernvale_post_cairn*; Fig. 4.4). This interval is estimated to have been between *55–775 years* (*95% probability*), probably between *190–520 years* (*68% probability*; *interval_Gwernvale*; not shown in figures). In this interval, the cairn must have been in use, and so these estimates provide some indication of the potential duration of activity. As we noted above, the absence of results for the use of this monument makes it difficult to provide more precise estimates for the duration of use, but the presence of cereals and the complexity of pre-cairn activity emphasise the significance of this site (see discussion below, and Chapter 3).

A more precise estimate of the date of construction of the monument is suggested by the apparent relationship between pre-cairn activity and the monument. In the review of the pre-cairn activity at Gwernvale given in Chapter 3 it is argued that, as at Hazleton and Ascott-under-Wychwood, pre-cairn activity took the form of one or more timber structures and a midden. In the case of Gwernvale, it is now argued that the timber structure was a house and belonged to the last phase of pre-cairn activity. The potentially long period of pre-cairn activity suggested by associated radiocarbon dates might suggest that the midden came into existence before the construction of the building. As noted above, a number of dates have been obtained from the timber structure but some or all of these might be from residual material incorporated in features belonging to the structure when it was built and can therefore only provide *termini post quos* for its construction. The juxtaposition of the portal and the walls of the forecourt and some of the posts (with a use-life of say 15–30 years) belonging to the pre-cairn timber structure imply that at least the stumps of some of the posts, which were to about 0.18m in diameter, were still visible when the tomb was built. Similar relationships between pre-existing timber structures which are followed by the superimposition of Cotswold-Severn burial monuments are also notably found at Hazleton and Ascott-under-Wychwood. These are discussed further in Chapter 12.

Because of the long history of use of this site, including in the later Neolithic, only the estimates associated with the early Neolithic pre-cairn occupation and the estimate for construction of the monument itself have been included in the currency model discussed below.

Pipton

Pipton model construction

Six radiocarbon measurements (Table 4.1) exist, of which five are from samples of human bone from various locations within the long cairn, including from Chamber I and its south annexe, and Chamber II (see Figs 6.4 and 6.5). A single cattle horncore recovered from the forecourt provided the sixth sample. As in the case of Chamber NE II at Penywyrlod, Chamber II at Pipton appears to take the form of a closed cist (Savory 1956, 41–3) but the samples do not have a stratigraphic relationship with each other, and so all the samples have been modelled as representing an archaeological phase of activity associated with the cairn use.

Pipton results and discussion

The Pipton results and model have good overall agreement (A_{model}=108). From these results, the start of use of the cairn for burial is estimated to have occurred in *3940–3635 cal BC (95% probability)*, most probably in *3760–3650 cal BC (68% probability*; *start_Pipton*; Fig. 4.5). The end of this phase of activity occurred in *3495–3165 cal BC (95% probability)*, most probably in *3470–3325 cal BC (68% probability*; *end_Pipton*; Fig. 4.5). People buried at the site

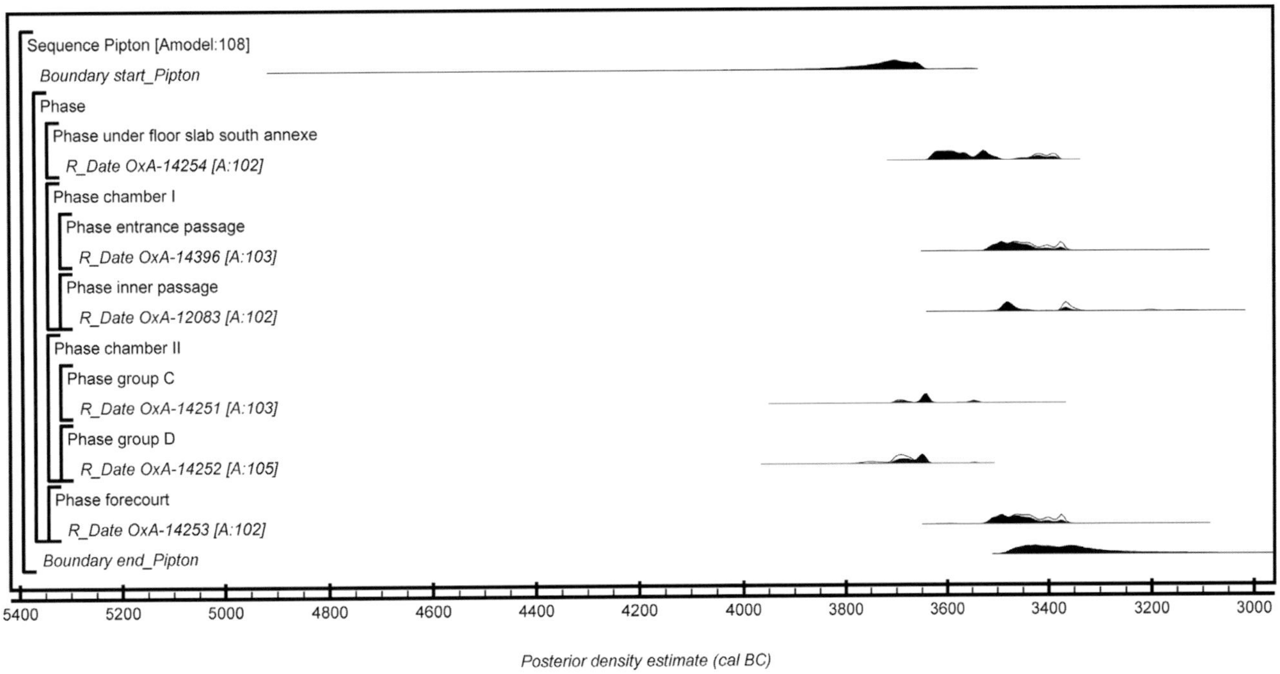

Fig. 4.5. Probability distributions for radiocarbon measurements from the Pipton monument. The large square brackets and the OxCal CQL2 commands define the model.

died over a period of *150–365 years* (*95% probability*), most probably *180–305 years* (*68% probability*; *span_Pipton*; parameter not shown).

Because the monument appears to represent undisturbed early Neolithic activity, all these results have been included as active likelihoods in the currency model which is discussed below.

Ty Isaf

Ty Isaf model construction

Seventeen results were produced on samples from Ty Isaf (Table 4.1). Sixteen of these results were produced on human skeletal remains that were recovered from the monument (see Fig. 6.6). Two of these measurements (OxA-14395, -14249) were statistically consistent replicates on the same sample (T′=0.0; T′ 5%=3.8; ν=1; at the 5% significance level; Ward and Wilson 1978). The remaining measurement (SUERC-57788) was produced on a cattle tooth. Four of the measurements (SUERC-57794, -57796, -57795 and -57790) on human remains were produced on samples that were only recorded as 'undocumented', so could originate from any part of the monument. Of the remaining measurements, three came from a lower level within the central compartment of Chamber III or the 'rotunda' (OxA-12055, -14248 and -14393), with OxA-14250 coming from an upper level within this context. OxA-14249 and its replicate -14395 together with OxA-14394 came from the rotunda passage. Four measurements were associated with Chamber I (SUERC-57785, -57787, -57784 and -57788), while another two measurements were associated with Chamber II (SUERC-57789 and -57786).

The phasing of Ty Isaf Chamber III, as presented by Grimes (1939) in the original excavation report is somewhat ambiguous, though his preferred interpretation was that the 'rotunda' represented part of the original construction. More recent commentators, on analogy with a number of other long cairns in the Cotswolds, have tended to see it as an earlier, free-standing structure (*e.g.* Darvill 2004, 68–9). We have taken a neutral view of the relative construction sequence of the monument here, and modelled the results as part of a single phase of activity. We discuss the implications of the chronology in terms of this interpretation further below.

Ty Isaf results and discussion

The results from Ty Isaf have good overall agreement (A_{model}=97), and the start of burial activity at the site is estimated in *3970–3520 cal BC* (*95% probability*), most probably in *3740–3560 cal BC* (*68% probability*; *start_Ty_Isaf*; Fig. 4.6). The radiocarbon results from the site represent a considerable period of activity, with burial occurring at the site for over *1695–2000 years* (*95% probability*), most probably over *1825–1965 years* (*68% probability*; *span_Ty_Isaf*; parameter not shown). The last dated activity represented at the site occurred in *1860–1335 cal BC* (*95% probability*), probably in *1735–1515 cal BC* (*68% probability*; *end_Ty_Isaf*; Fig. 4.6).

The first dated events associated with burials from Chamber I, Chamber II and Chamber III/the 'rotunda' are all broadly of the same age (Fig. 4.7); certainly, no clear chronological patterning in the age of the deaths of the people interred in these separate sections of the monument appears. The first dated event associated with the use of Chamber I occurs in *3530–3370 cal BC* (*95% probability*), probably in *3515–3460 cal BC* (*68% probability*; *first_chamber_I*; Fig. 4.6). The first dated event associated with Chamber II occurs in *3520–3365 cal BC* (*95% probability*; or in *3470–3420 cal BC 34% probability*, or *3515–3485 cal BC 18% probability*, or *3410–3370 cal BC 17% probability; first_chamber_II*; Fig. 4.6). The first dated event from Chamber III/the 'rotunda' occurred in *3520–3365 cal BC* (*95% probability*; or *3510–3425 cal BC* (*61% probability*, or *3385–3370 cal BC 8% probability*; *first_rotunda_Ty_Isaf*; Fig. 4.6).

After this early activity, all elements of the monument saw the interment of human skeletal remains from people who died much later. This is apparent in the inclusion of the skeletal remains that provided the sample for SUERC-57788 (*2635–2465 cal BC 93% probability*; or *2540–2475 cal BC 44% probability,* or *2585–2550 cal BC 18% probability,* or *2620–2605 cal BC 7% probability*; *SUERC-57788*; Fig. 4.6) from the western compartment of Chamber I, and the deposition of the material measured by SUERC-57789 in *1775–1610 cal BC* (*84% probability* or *1875–1840 cal BC 11% probability;* or *1745–1640 cal BC 62% probability* or *1865–1850 cal BC 6% probability*; *SUERC-57789*; Fig. 4.6), which was recovered outside Chamber II. It should be noted that the locations of the samples for both these measurements could represent activity associated with the use of the site *after* the primary use of these two lateral chambers. These parts of the monument may not, therefore, have seen continuous use over the *775–1050 years* (*95% probability*; *duration_chamber_I*; parameter not shown) represented by results from Chamber I, or the *1535–1890 years* (*95% probability*; *duration_chamber_II*; parameter not shown) represented by results from Chamber II.

Results from Chamber III or the 'rotunda' represent a similarly long duration of activity, occurring over *630–1000 years* (*95% probability*; *span_rotunda_Ty_Isaf*; parameter not shown). Chamber III equally may indicate episodic activity at the site after the primary use for burial; one of the three results from the lower level within this structure (OxA-14248) is significantly later than the other results (OxA-12055 and -14393) from this level. These results could be consistent with disturbance to the lower, earlier deposits by later activity in Chamber III.

Three of the four measurements on samples of 'undocumented' origin from the site relate to the earliest activity

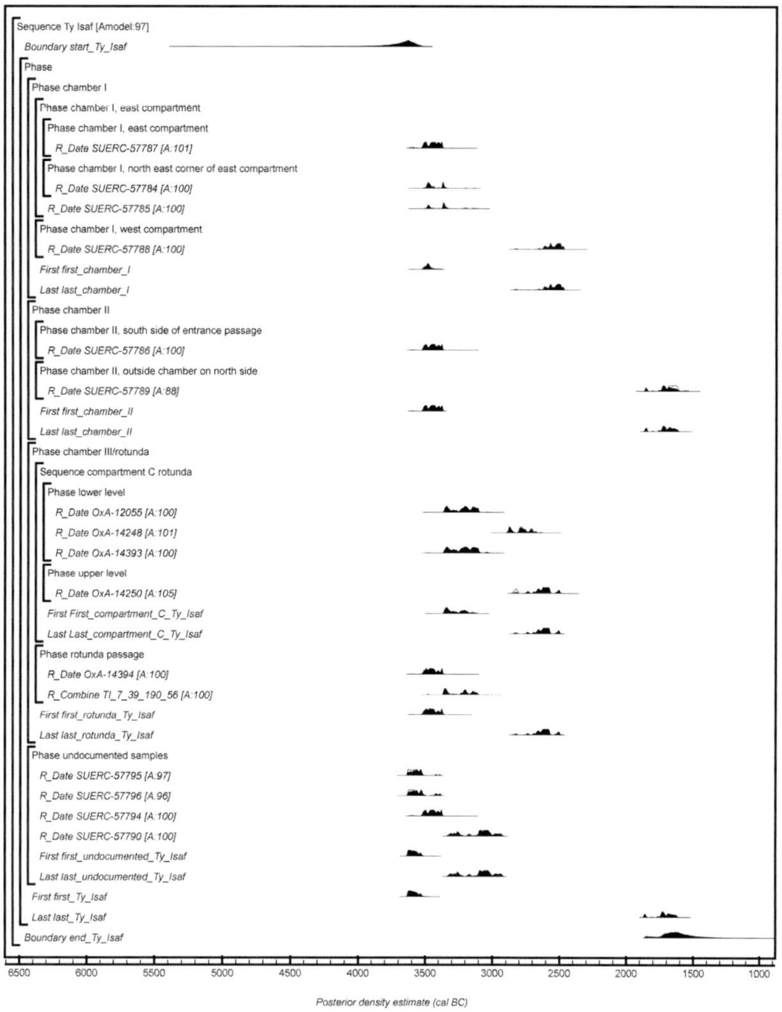

Fig. 4.6. Probability distributions for radiocarbon measurements from the Ty Isaf monument. The large square brackets and the OxCal CQL2 commands define the model.

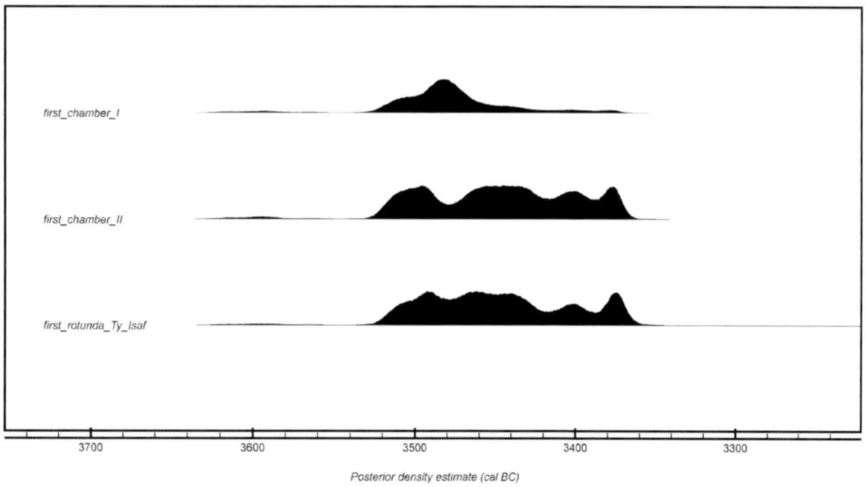

Fig. 4.7. Parameters estimating the first dated events associated with the use of different parts of the Ty Isaf monument. They are calculated as shown in Fig. 4.6.

associated with the monument, while the other (SUERC-57790) is later.

Because of the longevity of activity at this site, and the uncertainty over which results are associated with diagnostic early 'Neolithic' practices, only the estimate for the start of Neolithic activity at the monument is included in the currency model discussed below. The long phase of activity associated with individuals buried at the monument suggests that there could be a more complex history of use of the site, but the chronology of the burials does not currently suggest a sequential of history of construction or use of different elements of the structure. It may be that architecturally early elements were reused at the same time as other elements of the structure. Critically, the available results cannot be used to estimate the age of construction of different elements, an important limitation in our current understanding of this important site.

The Black Mountains tombs within the wider south Wales and Marches context, and beyond

Tombs, cairns and dolmens

There are considerable differences in our understandings of when burial monuments were constructed across the region, and the nature of their subsequent use. The Penywyrlod burial monument was probably constructed in the 38th century cal BC, with burial activity at Pipton beginning most probably in the second half the of the 38th or first half of the 37th centuries cal BC. The chronology for Ty Isaf is less precisely defined, but probably post-dates the beginning of both of these monuments, with the beginning of burial activity here in the late 38th, 37th or early 36th centuries cal BC (Fig. 4.6). This said, it is difficult in the current state of information to suggest a definitive order of appearance. While there is a case for seeing Penywyrlod as the earliest dated construction so far, shortly followed by Pipton and Ty Isaf, perhaps in sequence, these monuments could also be seen as different types of burial structure being built at the same time.

In contrast, our estimate for the construction of Gwernvale is significantly later and much less precise, estimating that this monument was constructed in the second half of the 4th millennium. In part, this late estimate may derive from the nature of the radiocarbon dates available from Gwernvale; we do not have any demonstrably accurate results associated with the construction or use of this monument. This estimate for the construction event is defined between the pre-cairn activity, and the post-cairn results. It may be that Gwernvale was constructed towards the earlier end of this estimate.

The wider picture

Turning to other activity, since the analyses on the timing of the early Neolithic in south Wales and the Marches completed in 2011 (Griffiths 2011; Whittle *et al.* 2011), radiocarbon results from a number of other research- and developer-led projects have become available, most notably including the South Wales Gas Pipeline (Darvill *et al.* 2020). In order to contextualise the results from the Black Mountains long cairns, here we present both already published and recently available data. Table 4.2 details the sites and the sources for the radiocarbon results and modelling considerations. Those analyses had demonstrated that the earliest activity associated with long cairn construction and use in Wales followed much of the rest of the country in first appearing in the 39th to 37th centuries cal BC (Griffiths 2011, 849; Whittle *et al.* 2011, 543, 551).

Given this relatively imprecise chronology for Neolithic activity in Wales and the Marches generally, the aim of the scientific dating and modelling presented here is to establish the possible sequences of construction, set against the development of other Neolithic activity. How the trajectory of monument construction differed in Wales from other parts of Britain, and the evidence for distinct cultural choices as part of this activity, are discussed further in Chapter 12.

Results included in this analysis are from sites with evidence for occupation or pits that contain diagnostically early Neolithic things (such as characteristic early pottery forms, including Carinated Bowls, and Plain Bowls, but not including Peterborough Ware; polished stone axeheads, leaf-shaped arrowheads, and domesticated plants and animals (excluding dogs and horses) are also here associated with early Neolithic activity), and from causewayed and other enclosures and cursus monuments. Much of the interpretation of these results follows that given in Whittle *et al.* (2011) and Griffiths (2011); the chronological modelling of these results, however, has been developed specifically for this project, to ensure that we are exploring only the early Neolithic activity at burial monuments that are sometimes sites of complex, multi-phase activity.

The structure of the currency model for results associated with this activity is shown in Figure 4.9. Constituent elements for the different site-specific models are shown below. This model has been constructed so that the stratigraphic prior information is applied to site-specific elements as discussed below. However, only results are included that are associated with diagnostic early Neolithic activity in the currency model. This is in order to ensure that we are accurately estimating the start of the regional Neolithic. If we simply included all results from the burial monuments (including later activity), our resultant currency model would likely estimate the start of the Neolithic as inaccurately early, as 'boundary' parameters are calculated to reflect the distribution of calibrated data within an unordered uniform 'phase' model (Bronk Ramsey 2009 and references); this is the case for Penywyrlod, Ty Isaf and Gwernvale, but it is also the case for Parc le Breos Cwm where there are radiocarbon results from a wide range of activity. Our site-specific model for Parc le Breos Cwm is shown in Figure 4.8; we include posterior density estimates for the use of this Neolithic monument in Figure 4.8. This model adapts that shown in Whittle *et al.* (2011, 544) with new information to reflect the belief that material identified as coming from the 'passage' of this monument actually comes from the nearby site of Cat Hole Cave, and the material was misidentified in the museum stores (Wysocki *et al.* in press). It is also to be noted that one of the probable Cat Hole samples (PC15) has been redated, and an older date obtained with ultrafiltration (OxA-14430). The samples from the chambered tomb were produced prior to the issue with ultrafiltration incorporating exogamous carbon as part of the pretreatment process; these results should therefore be accurate (Wysocki *et al.* in press).

In our currency model, we have grouped activity associated with occupation, burial, causewayed enclosures and cursus monuments together for analytical purposes. We have used this approach to estimate the timing of key events associated with specific sites, as well as for the timing of different types of practices. The approaches to modelling these legacy data follow those outlined above for the new results from this project.

For Dorstone, Penywyrlod, Gwernvale and Ty Isaf, we included posteriors associated with different types of early Neolithic activity at these sites in the relevant part of the model. So, for example, we differentiate between pre-burial monument occupation and *use* of the burial monument. The results from Dorstone derive from the recently completed analysis (Ray *et al.* 2022) of recent seasons' work.

The early Neolithic of south Wales and the Marches

The currency model for data from south Wales and the Marches shown in Figure 4.2 has good agreement (A_{model}=97). From this model we estimate that the first appearance of Neolithic material culture and practices appeared in this region in *3880–3790 cal BC* (*95% probability*), most probably in *3845–3805 cal BC* (*68% probability*; *start_early_Neolithic_south_Wales_and_Marches*; Fig. 4.2).

We can summarise this regional picture in terms of the centuries in which different types of activity most probably took place. It is *91% probable* that the start of early Neolithic activity in south Wales and the Marches occurred in the 39th century cal BC. Pit digging and other occupation evidence associated with diagnostic early Neolithic material culture most probably (*98% probable*) occurred in the century between 3850 cal BC and 3750 cal BC, with this type of activity probably beginning in *3855–3780 cal BC* (*95% probability*), and most probably in *3830–3795 cal BC* (*68% probability; first_south_Wales_and_Marches_Neolithic_pits_and_occupation;* Fig. 4.10). Pit-digging, occupation and non-monumental presence in the landscape appear to be the earliest Neolithic evidence identified in this part of Wales. It is *91% probable* that the first dated event associated with the use of Neolithic pit sites or other occupation evidence (*first_south_Wales_and_Marches_Neolithic_pits_and_occupation*) occurred before the first dated event associated with the construction or use of burial monuments (*first_south_Wales_and_Marches_Neolithic_burial_monument*) in this part of the world. It is also *98% probable* that the first dated event associated with the use of Neolithic pit sites or other occupation evidence (*first_south_Wales_and_Marches_Neolithic_pits_and_occupation*) occurred before the first dated event associated with the construction of causewayed enclosures (*first_south_Wales_and_Marches_causewayed_enclosure*) (Fig. 4.13).

The first evidence for burial monuments occurred in *3830–3740 cal BC* (*95% probability*; or *3800–3760 cal BC 68% probability*; *first_south_Wales_and_Marches_Neolithic_burial_monument*; Fig. 4.9). In terms of centuries, it is most probable (*94% probable*) that the 100 years between 3850 and 3750 cal BC saw the first evidence for burial monuments. The first estimate associated with the use of causewayed enclosures places this activity in *3810–3645 cal BC* (*95% probability*), most probably in *3755–3665 cal BC* (*68% probability*; *first_south_Wales_and_Marches_causewayed_enclosure*; Fig. 4.13). The first evidence for causewayed enclosures in this part of the world is less precisely defined, but it is *78% probable* that the first activity associated with these monuments occurred in the 100 years between 3750 cal BC and 3650 cal BC.

Burial monuments in south Wales and the Marches

To the dated early Neolithic Black Mountains burial activity, we can add the first use of the burial monuments at Tinkinswood and Parc le Breos Cwm, from the Vale of Glamorgan and the Gower peninsula respectively. Tinkinswood is closely linked to the Cotswold-Severn monument repertoire, but is remarkable for the huge capstone that roofs the single chamber (Ward 1915; 1916; Cummings and Whittle 2004; Thompson 2019). Parc le Breos Cwm is also allied to the Severn-Cotswold architectural repertoire, with its wedge-shaped plan, encircling forecourt, and five chambers, arranged in two transepted pairs, either side of a central passage (Whittle and Wysocki 1998). The original dates for Tinkinswood referred to in previous publications (*e.g.* Cummings and Whittle 2004; Whittle *et al.* 2011; Thompson 2019) should now be replaced by the corrected values given here, following corrections made by the Oxford laboratory (Bronk Ramsey *et al.* 2004).

Our currency model estimates the first use of Tinkinswood in *3815–3655 cal BC* (*95% probability*), probably in *3765–3680 cal BC* (*68% probability*; *start_Tinkinswood*; Fig. 4.9), and the first Neolithic burial at Parc le Breos Cwm occurred in *3730–3525 cal BC* (*95% probability*), probably in *3660–3540 cal BC* (*68% probability*; *first_Parc_le_Breos*; Fig. 4.8). The first activity associated

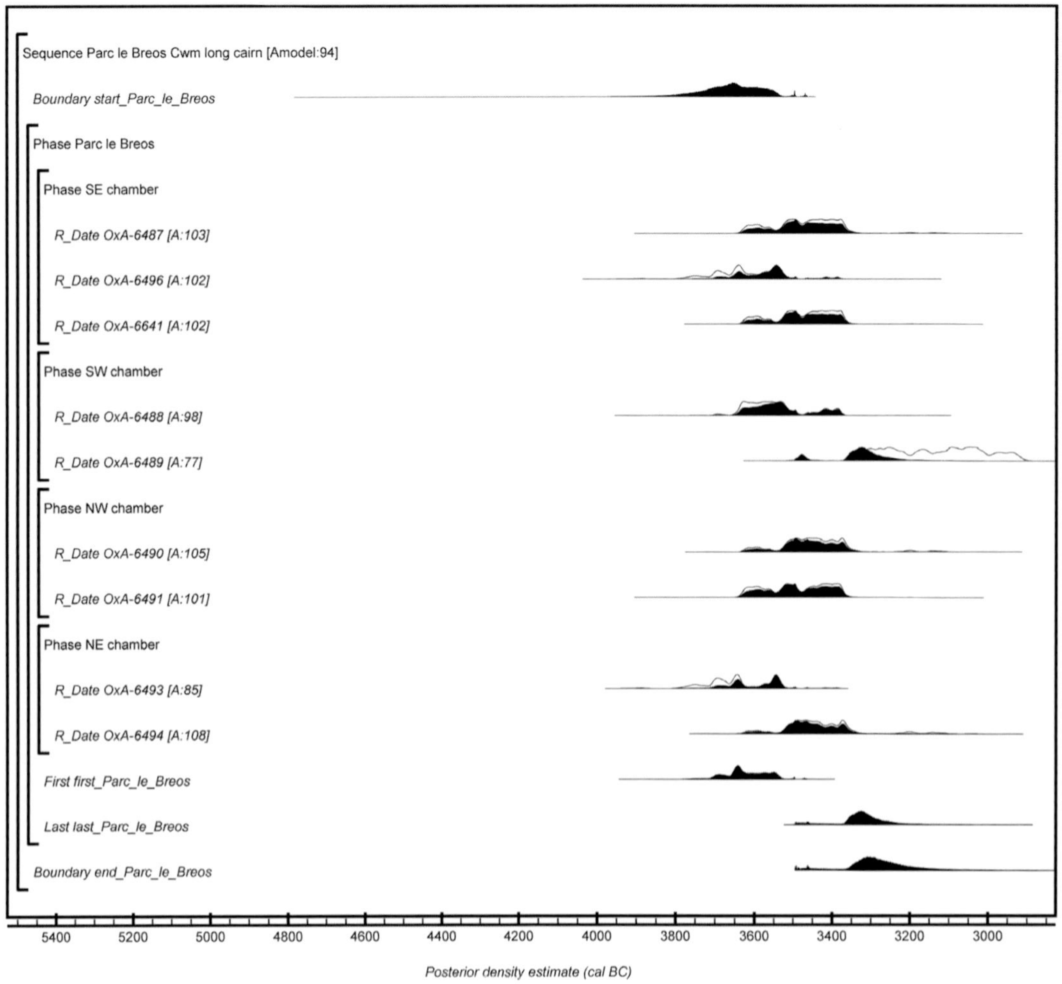

Fig. 4.8. Probability distributions for radiocarbon measurements from the Parc le Breos Cwm monument. This makes use of new information about the association of measurements from Cat Hole Cave, as described in the text. The large square brackets and the OxCal CQL2 commands define the model.

with the use of Tinkinswood (*start_Tinkinswood*) probably occurred in the hundred years between 3750 and 3650 cal BC; with the first Neolithic burials at Parc le Breos Cwm (*first_Parc_le_Breos*) most probably occurring in the 37th century cal BC. With what we currently know, it is plausible that Tinkinswood, near the coast, and Penywyrlod, inland, appeared at much the same sort of time, and the significance of their similarities and differences is discussed further in Chapter 12.

In the other direction, inland to the north-east, we estimate the first use of the Lower Luggy burial cairn in *3700–3520 cal BC (95% probability)*, probably in *3645–3545 cal BC (68% probability*; *first_Lower_Luggy_cairn*; Fig. 4.9). At Lower Luggy (Gibson 2000), we see a different style of monument. Here, a long cairn had been constructed from earth and stone, and defined by a ditch. Parts of the ditch held a wooden palisade, which had been burnt. As a long monument constructed with timber and earthen elements, Lower Luggy fits into a well-recognised style of early Neolithic monument, which is often associated with the deposition of human remains, though none were found here probably due to the limited scale of the excavations, nor was any other characteristic early Neolithic material culture.

The wider chronology of Severn-Cotswold architecture, including models for monuments in the Cotswolds themselves, is discussed in Chapter 12.

Looking further to the south-west of Wales, 'Severn-Cotswold' monuments are not found west of the Gower (Corcoran 1969; F. Lynch 2000; Cummings and Whittle 2004; Darvill 2004), though monuments with elements strongly evocative of dolmen architecture are found east of the Gower, as also discussed further in Chapter 12. Instead, portal dolmens predominate (Cummings and Richards 2014; 2021), a distribution that continues into Ireland. Few portal dolmens anywhere have yet been well dated (Cummings and Richards 2021), and producing accurate chronologies for dolmens in general may present more difficulties than producing robust chronologies for

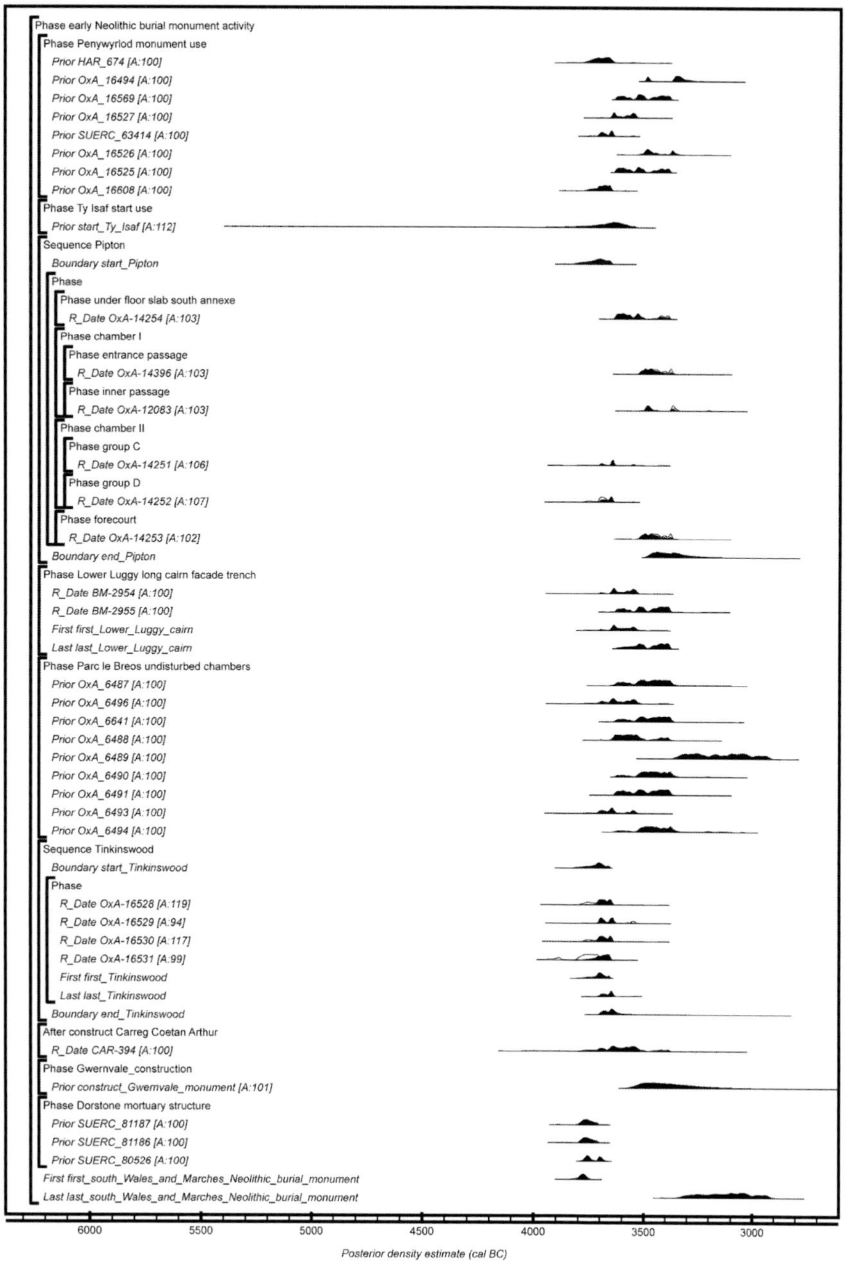

Fig. 4.9. Probability distributions associated with early Neolithic burial monuments in south Wales and the Marches. The overall structure for the model for early Neolithic activity in south Wales and the Welsh Marches is shown in Fig. 4.2, and the other components that feature in this model are shown in Figs 4.10 and 4.11. Posteriors from Figs 4.3, 4.4, 4.6, 4.7 and 4.8, and from Ray et al. *(2022) are also included in this model.*

other types of Neolithic monuments. In south-west Wales, only one sample (CAR-394) produced from Carreg Coetan Arthur (CAR-394) appears to be robustly associated with Neolithic activity (Whittle *et al.* 2011, chapter 10; S. Rees 2012). The nature of the sample means that this result should provide an imprecise *terminus post quem* for the erection of one of the orthostats in *3795–3385 cal BC* (*95% probability*), probably in *3695–3515 cal BC* (*68% probability*; *CAR-394*; Fig. 4.9).

At Garn Turne, Pembrokeshire (Cummings and Richards 2014; 2021, chapter 5), a sequence of radiocarbon dates from the pit underlying a failed dolmen indicates activity from the 38th or 37th century cal BC. There was, however, considerable later disturbance in the 3rd millennium cal BC, and activity in the 1st millennium cal BC. This wide-ranging chronological evidence means it is difficult to characterise the nature of the earlier 4th millennium activity, and we have not included these results in our currency model for early

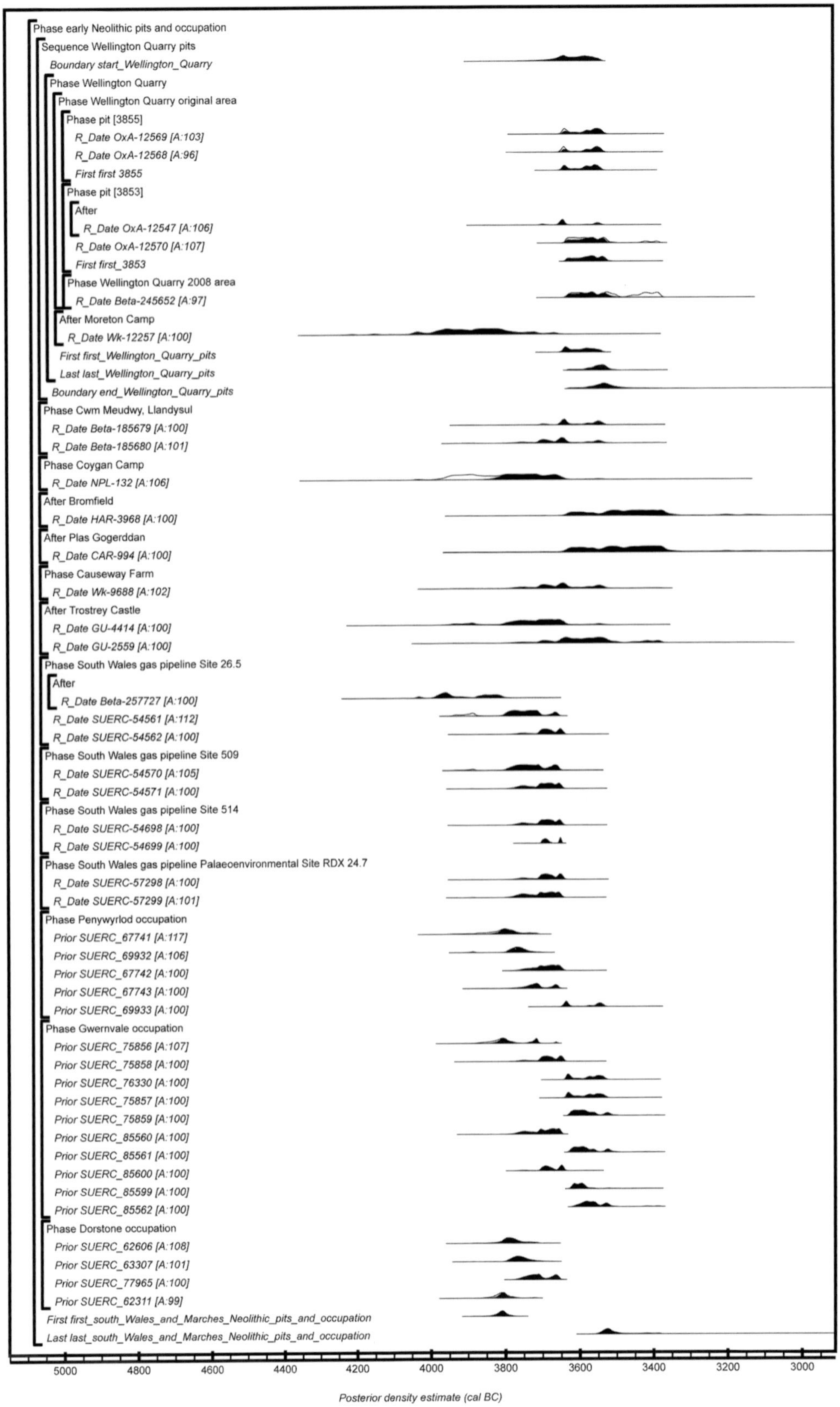

Fig. 4.10. Probability distributions associated with early Neolithic pits and other occupation evidence from south Wales and the Marches. The overall structure for the model for early Neolithic activity in south Wales and the Welsh Marches is shown in Fig. 4.2, and the other components that feature in this model are shown in Figs 4.12, 4.13 and 4.15. Posteriors from Figs 4.3 and 4.4, and from Ray et al. *(2022) are also included in this model.*

Neolithic activity in south Wales. Further afield, in western Ireland, the published results from Poulnabrone, on the Burren in Co. Clare, indicate that that construction probably dates from *c*. 3800 cal BC (A. Lynch 2014; Schulting 2014). The important wider implication from Poulnabrone is that this very different architecture was probably in existence by the time Penywyrlod, Pipton and Ty Isaf came to be constructed.

It is worth noting in passing the debate about whether these structures were originally covered by any mound material (cf. Scarre 2016). If these structures were not covered with a mound, their relatively open natures may have contributed to sites that were subject to revisiting and disturbance of deposits over many years. Indeed, the very mixed nature of age ranges associated with the Poulnabrone monument may mean that at least some of the remains were subject to secondary burial rites, and removed from some other initial burial location, in early prehistory. We can see this, for example, in the later radiocarbon results (*e.g.* OxA-1906, UBA-22179, UBA-18809, UBA-18820, UBA-18817, UBA-18818, UBA-18819, UBA-18811 and OxA-26716; Schulting 2014). Unfortunately, this kind of scenario makes providing demonstrably accurate chronologies for the *construction* of these kinds of monuments difficult. Here we revisit old discussions about the association of any chronometric measurement with an archaeological event of interest (Waterbolk 1971; Griffiths 2022). Where human remains are recovered, such as at Poulnabrone, we can at least provide well-understood estimates for the age of the human skeletal remains. In other cases, where the potential for residual material exists, as well as the potential for the ebb and flow of material culture and ecofacts, our understanding of the chronology of construction of dolmens remains unclear.

Pit deposits and other occupation evidence in south Wales and the Marches

Relatively few results on short-life samples associated with Neolithic pit deposits or occupation evidence have been produced from south Wales and the Marches. Radiocarbon measurements on this type of activity are only slightly better represented than activity associated with causewayed enclosures, presented below. Aside from the evidence for pre-cairn activity at Gwernvale and Penywyrlod, the work at Wellington Quarry (Jackson and Miller 2011) and results from the South Wales Gas Pipeline (Darvill *et al.* 2020) account for a disproportionate number of the measurements produced from pits or other occupation evidence on short-life samples. Measurements on short-life samples robustly associated with early Neolithic occupation – rather than monuments – are still a research priority in Wales as a whole.

Excluding the many results produced on materials that may have inbuilt 'old wood' offsets (and are presented in the model as *termini post quos*), the earliest activity associated with pit deposits and occupation may be represented at Coygan Camp (*3830–3560 cal BC 95% probability*; *NPL-132*; Fig. 4.10) and by sites excavated as part of the South Wales Gas Pipeline that indicate activity most probably in the 38th century cal BC. The pit deposits at these sites all contain Carinated Bowl pottery. Several of them also contain domesticated plant or animal remains, as at Coygan Camp, and the South Wales Gas Pipeline site 26.5 and site RDX 24.7. Evidence for potential continuity with Mesolithic practices in this part of the world includes the presence of lithics from pit 265639 from site 26.5, which are also characteristic of late Mesolithic/early Neolithic blade-based reduction strategies.

Deposits in pits are well known from the Mesolithic as well as from the Neolithic, as are deposits of material culture in other negative features, especially tree-throw bowls. Allen and Gardiner (2002), and more recently Blinkhorn (2012), have emphasised that pit deposits in England and Ireland were quotidian parts of Mesolithic life. Beyond this, Pollard (2017) has recently summarised the evidence for 'monumental' pit structures, in terms of both the scale of these features, and the role of some in holding timbers. In Ireland, the famous pit at Hermitage seemed to represent an even more specialised series of practices, probably representing a burial. Here the deposit included a Mesolithic axe, and human bones produced an age estimate that placed it early in the Mesolithic culture history sequence (Collins 2009; Little *et al.* 2017). There are continuities here in Neolithic practices. Blinkhorn and Little (2018, 413) recently emphasised that many Mesolithic pit deposits are concerned with the 'correct' treatment of materials, while Chatterton (2006) noted that 'Mesolithic' pit deposits included some very 'Neolithic' trends, such as the structured deposition of lithics.

From this perspective, there remains a case for seeing some kind of continuity in this regard between Mesolithic and Neolithic practices. It may be relevant that the earliest types of 'Neolithic' sites that we see in south Wales and the Marches are identified as pit or other occupation sites, some preceding monuments, rather than the monuments themselves. Wider questions to do with Neolithisation are discussed further in Chapter 12.

Pre-cairn activity, cereals and occupation evidence

Taking as our point of departure the pre-cairn activity at both Gwernvale and Penywyrlod, it is notable that at both these sites pre-cairn activity has a similar age range, with activity probably in the second half of the 39th or early 38th centuries cal BC. At both sites charred plant remains were preserved in deposits that were then buried by the long cairns. The pre-cairn activity at Gwernvale includes structural evidence for a timber structure, pits, gullies, stakeholes and what are now interpreted as midden deposits (see Chapter 3).

At Penywyrlod, the buried soil deposits have less certain evidence for structural activity. What is interesting is that at both these sites, the pre-cairn evidence is amongst the earliest Neolithic activity for the region as a whole. The unusually large scale of the Penywyrlod monument and the earliness of the pre-monument activity would seem to mark out the location as a focus of significance. Comparisons with the situations at Ascott-under-Wychwood and Hazleton, and middens elsewhere in southern Britain, are followed in Chapter 12.

At Gwernvale, important evidence for early activity includes early and late Mesolithic assemblages, but the reassessment by Elizabeth Walker in Chapter 9 brings into question the presence of Upper Palaeolithic material identified in the original excavation report. The radiocarbon dates CAR-118 and SUERC-85563 could be associated with this activity. However, this cannot be determined given the nature of the sample for CAR-118 (the potential for old wood) and the apparent redeposition of the sample for SUERC-85563 (in contexts with early Neolithic evidence). Gwernvale could therefore represent a location with natural affordances that attracted people to these locations over considerable periods of time, both in the 8th and 6th millennia cal BC (Barton *et al.* 1995), but also in terms of the considerable evidence we have for pre-monumental early Neolithic occupation at the site.

It is also perhaps significant that the earliest pre-cairn results from Gwernvale include those produced on domesticated cereal remains. SUERC-75856 has good individual agreement in its current position in the model; however, it could also resolve on an earlier part of the calibration curve (in the 39th century cal BC); this measurement could represent much earlier cereal presence at this site that is under-sampled. A radiocarbon measurement on a cereal remain was also produced in this study from Penywyrlod (SUERC-67742).

Significant quantities of domesticated cereals have been recently recovered from the early Neolithic house structures at Llanfaethlu excavated by C.R. Archaeology on Anglesey (Catherine Rees, *pers. comm*., 2020). It seems probable that the house structures at Llanfaethlu are older than that at Gwernvale – structures and occupation seem to be older than monuments in this part of the world – and that therefore the Llanfaethlu cereals will prove to be older than those at Gwernvale.

While the number of cereals and radiocarbon results from Llanfaethlu outnumbers those from the Black Mountains monuments, the Gwernvale data make a significant contribution to our understandings of the importance of domestic plant resources in pre-monument contexts in south Wales. Currently, this result is earlier than any other results on cereals from Wales (Griffiths 2018).

We can compare these results with those other direct measurements on cereals that exist from Britain and Ireland (Griffiths 2018; cf. Treasure *et al.* 2019; Fig. 4.11). There are notably very few direct radiocarbon measurements produced on cereals from Wales in comparison with direct dates on cereal remains from other parts of Britain and Ireland. As we can see, there is scant but important evidence for nationally early cereals at sites along the west cost of Britain – at Penhale Round, Holbeck Park (H. Evans 2018) and Gwernvale – that could be as early as the earliest Neolithic in Britain, in the south-east of England, for example at White Horse Stone (Whittle *et al.* 2011).

The limited number of radiocarbon measurements on cereal remains from Wales reflects a history of investigation with a tendency to produce radiocarbon measurements associated with the construction of monuments in research excavations, combined with relatively low levels of developer-led archaeology in Wales in comparison to other areas of the UK. Major infrastructure projects like the South Wales Gas Pipeline (Darvill *et al.* 2020), the A55 project on Anglesey (Cuttler *et al.* 2012), the Wylfa power station works and the A487 Caernarfon to Bontnewydd bypass (Fraser Brown, *pers. comm*., 2020) are making significant impacts on our understandings of non-monumental earlier Neolithic activity. The results presented here suggest that non-monumental Neolithic activity in this part of the world probably pre-dates evidence from monuments across Wales as a whole – not just in the cases where burial monuments seal earlier occupation evidence.

Other monuments in south Wales and the Marches

We have only included one result from a cursus monument from south Wales and the Marches in the model presented here. The estimate from Sarn-y-bryn-caled suggests that this monument could have been in use in *3815–3630 cal BC* (*95% probability*; *OxA-3997*; Fig. 4.12). This single result may be better thought of as a *terminus post quem* for infilling in the absence of any other scientific dating measurements from the site. Other results are available from south Wales and the Marches from the Dyffryn Lane cursus monument, and the Hindwell cursus monument (Britnell and Jones 2018). The results from the Dyffryn Lane monument comprise three measurements on hazel nutshells and charcoal from three different secondary fills of the ditches. These are all of very different ages, and even the two 4th millennium results are of statistically significantly different ages (Beta-263746, 4800±40 BP; SUERC-26897, 5060±35 BP; $T'=23.8$; $T'5\%=3.8$, $\nu=1$, at the 5% significance interval; Ward and Wilson 1978). These results may indicate mixing or disturbance to the fills of the feature. The later of these results, Beta-263746, may provide a *terminus post quem* for the formation of the secondary fill of the ditch in 3650–3515 cal BC (95% confidence).

Five results exist from the Hindwell monument, from the primary and secondary fills of the northern and southern ditches. These also suggest potentially complex deposit

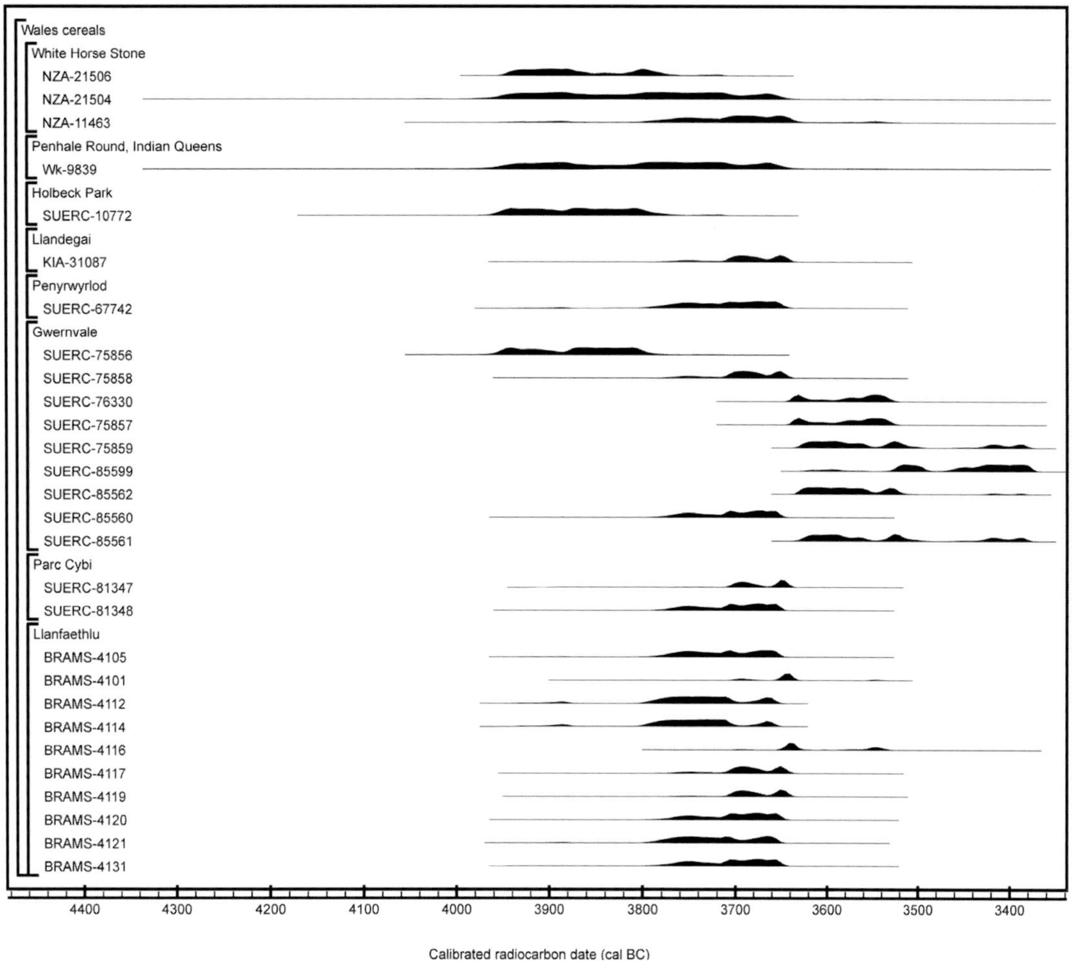

Fig. 4.11. Calibrated radiocarbon results on cereals from Wales and selected sites from the west coast of England, and from the early Neolithic site in south-east England, White Horse Stone (see Griffiths 2021 and Whittle et al. *2011 for measurement details).*

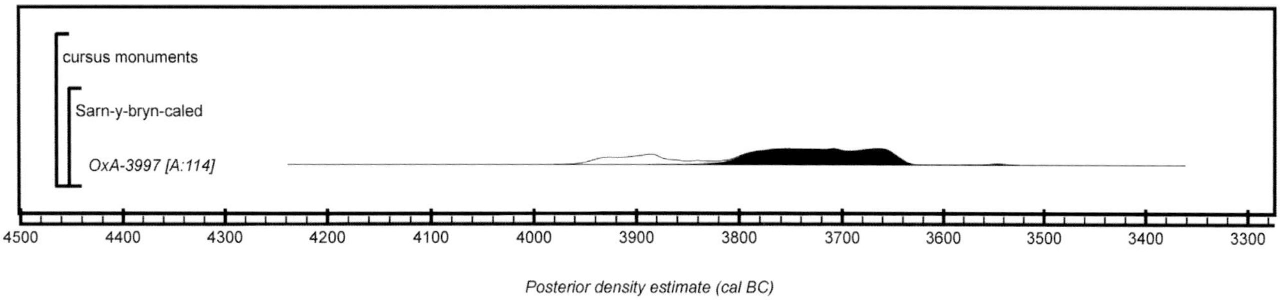

Fig. 4.12. Probability distributions associated with a cursus monument from south Wales and the Marches. The overall structure for the model for early Neolithic activity in south Wales and the Welsh Marches is shown in Fig. 4.2, and the other components that feature in this model are shown in Figs 4.10, 4.13 and 4.15.

formation, with both sequences producing results on short-life ecofacts from the primary fills that are younger than the results produced on short-life ecofacts from the secondary fills. To further complicate matters, the results from the primary fills are statistically inconsistent (SUERC-34209, 4955±40 BP; SUERC-24619, 4815±53 BP; T'=7.0; T'5%=3.8; at the 5% significance interval; ν=1, Ward and Wilson 1978). The latest result from the primary fills, SUERC-24619, may provide a *terminus post quem* for the infilling of the monument in 3700–3380 cal BC (95% confidence). However, at both Hindwell and Dyffryn Lane cursus monuments the chronological data could indicate more complex histories of activity, perhaps including redeposition of deposits from middens or other sources. A similar scenario may be apparent in terms of the causewayed enclosure sequences that we discuss below.

Outside the study area of this research, a single, much later result (GrN-26828, 4080±35 BP, 2860–2490 cal BC, 95% confidence) was produced on oak charcoal from the Llandygai Site C cursus (Lynch and Musson 2001). This result may provide a *terminus post quem* for the infilling of the feature.

Given the limited number of radiocarbon results, the range of age estimates that they have produced, and the indications of complex infilling of these monuments, establishing accurate chronologies for cursus monuments in Wales should be a research priority.

The recently produced radiocarbon results from the Dorstone Hill causewayed enclosure may represent the earliest of these monuments in south Wales and the Marches. An estimate for the first dated event associated with this monument indicates activity in *3770–3645 cal BC* (*95% probability*; or *3730–3655 cal BC 68% probability*; *first Dorstone enclosure*; Fig. 4.13). The three radiocarbon measurements from the enclosure fill sequence are internally consistent with their stratigraphic relationships; however, there is the potential that some or all of these results may be residual or redeposited. While there are a limited number of samples from this site, its chronology therefore cannot be regarded as robust as the best-dated causewayed enclosure in this part of the world – Caerau – the results from Dorstone have important implications for other causewayed enclosures in south Wales and the Marches.

At the Hill Croft Field enclosure, four results in the lowest deposit in the fill sequence (context 30) were statistically inconsistent (OxA-16022, -15867, GrA-31963, -32095; T'=16.3; T'5%=7.8; ν=3 at the 5% significance level; Ward and Wilson 1978). Whittle *et al.* (2011, 523) regarded these results (on disarticulated bone and charcoal samples) as representing redeposited material associated with unspecified earlier Neolithic activity in the area. We have modified this approach in the currency model shown here (following the rationale given in Griffiths 2011, 281), but there are other important alternative ways of thinking about these results. We have rerun these results in an alternative model for Hill Croft Field (Fig. 4.14). This makes use of the general outlier model (Bronk Ramsey 2009) using the notation `Outlier_Model("General",T(5),U(0,4),"t");`. In this model we have given every result a probability (0.05) that they represent an outlier. The revised model shown in Figure 4.14 therefore allows us to estimate the first dated event associated with the early use of the site in *3795–3650 cal BC* (*95% probability*; or *3760–3675 cal BC 68% probability*; *revised_build_Hill_Croft*; Fig. 4.14). It is also apparent in Fig. 4.14 that the three earlier results (OxA-150867, GrA-32095, -31963) from this deposit are statistically consistent (T'=1.9, T'5%=6.0, ν=2; at the 5% significance level; Ward and Wilson 1978). The latest result (OxA-16022) was on a single fragment of *Prunus* sp. charcoal, while the older measurements were produced on a cow femur, a human femur and another sample of short-life charcoal. It seems most plausible, therefore, that the earlier three statistically consistent measurements on samples including large osseous elements are accurate age estimates for the deposition of this material in the ditch, and a good estimate for the construction of the monument as a whole.

The revised estimate for the first activity at Hill Croft is important because it is very similar to the estimate for the first activity from the Dorstone enclosure (Fig. 4.13), with the first activity at Hill Croft probably occurring in the 38th or 37th centuries cal BC, and the activity at Dorstone possibly slightly later in the 37th century cal BC. Both of these important sites would benefit from additional radiocarbon measurements from early in their sequences; given the poor preservation conditions at Dorstone for osseous samples, this seems unlikely for that site.

Of the enclosure sites with radiocarbon results, Banc Du and Lower Luggy have similar estimates for earliest activity (Fig. 4.15). At Banc Du activity associated with the causewayed enclosure first took place in *3810–3415 cal BC* (*95% probability*), probably in *3730–3515 cal BC* (*68% probability*; *start_Banc_Du*; Fig. 4.13). Activity at the Lower Luggy enclosure probably occurred in *3635–3405 cal BC* (*95% probability*), probably in *3615–3490 cal BC* (*68% probability*; *first_Lower_Luggy_enclosure*; Fig. 4.13). Caerau and Womaston both appear to be built later, with activity at Womaston estimated to have occurred in *3625–3420 cal BC* (*95% probability*), probably in *3610–3460 cal BC* (*68% probability*; *first_Womaston_enclosure*; Fig. 4.13), and Caerau appears to have been constructed in *3555–3390 cal BC* (*95% probability*), probably in *3510–3405 cal BC* (*68% probability; start_Caerau*; Fig. 4.13). Many of these causewayed enclosure sites do not have very robust chronologies, and additional measurements should be a research priority in south Wales and the Marches.

It is important to note, however, that while we have estimates above for the construction of causewayed enclosure monuments, many of the sites discussed here have evidence of earlier Neolithic activity *prior* to the construction of the enclosures. We can see this in the range of radiocarbon ages produced from discrete deposits in causewayed enclosure ditch fills – as we discussed above for Hill Croft. Whichever model of the Hill Croft data is applied – and the alternative one discussed above seems preferable – material was collected, curated or stored prior to deposition in the enclosure ditch; the skeletal remains were disarticulated.

We can also see this especially at Caerau (Davis and Sharples 2017; Griffiths 2019) where several of the ditch circuits feature already old materials that are not in agreement with their position in the stratigraphic sequence.

At Womaston, there may be evidence that one of the samples is redeposited; Beta-254592 may be slightly too

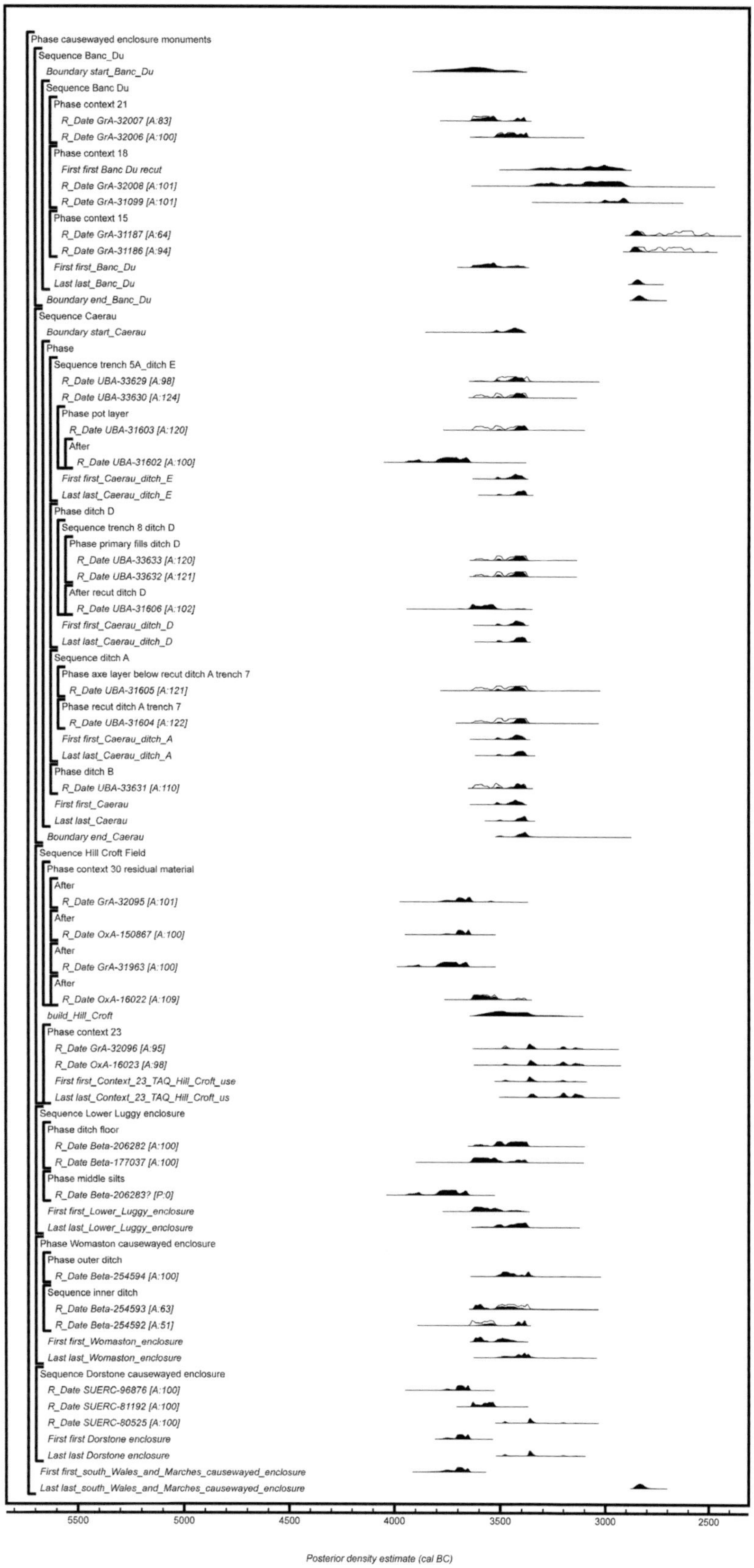

Fig. 4.13. Probability distributions associated with early Neolithic causewayed enclosure monuments in south Wales and the Marches. The overall structure for the model for early Neolithic activity in south Wales and the Welsh Marches is shown in Fig. 4.2, and the other components that feature in this model are shown in Figs 4.10, 4.12 and 4.13. Data from Ray et al. *(2022) are also included in this model.*

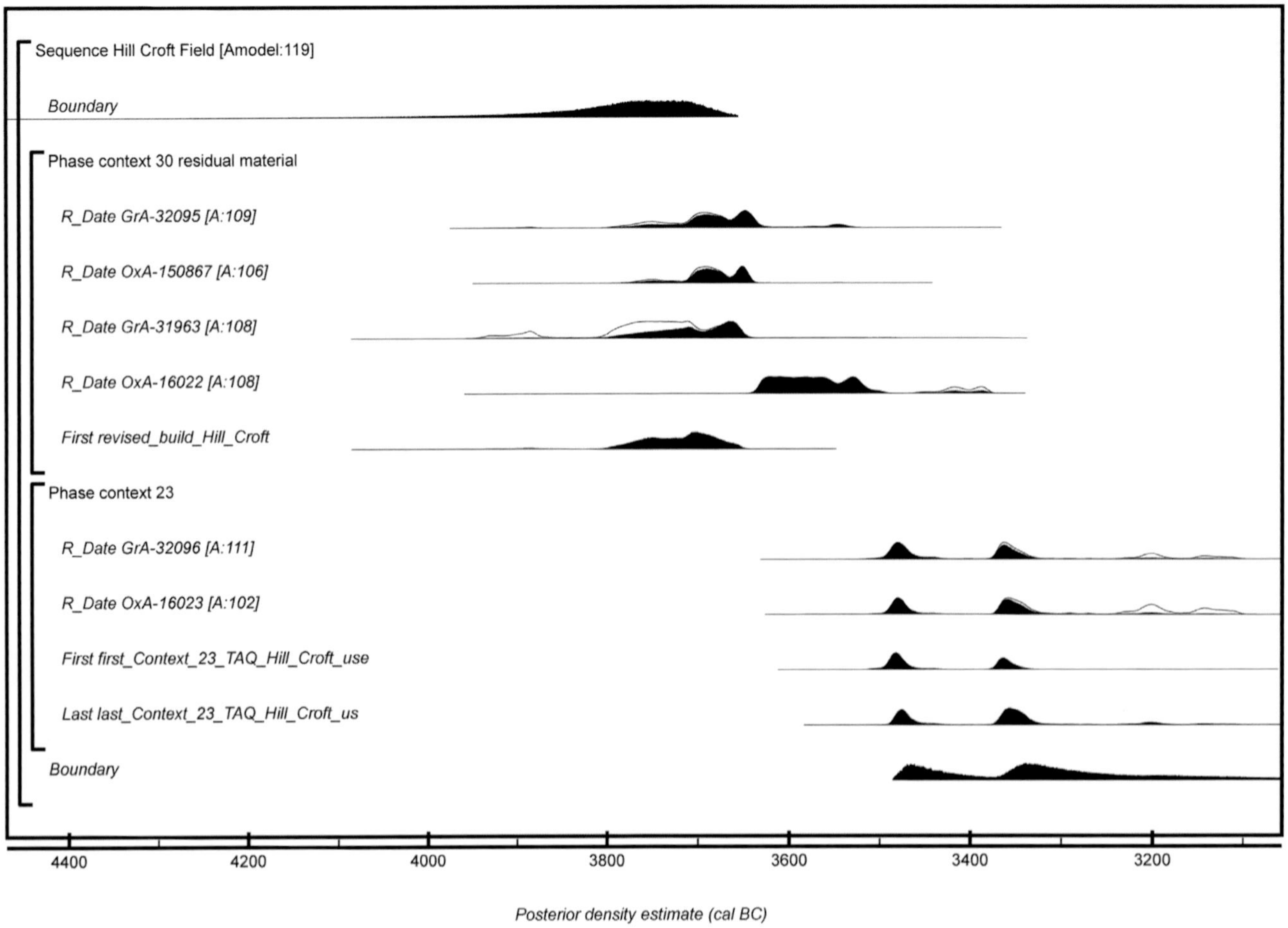

Fig. 4.14. An alternative model for the results associated with Hill Croft enclosure. The large square brackets and the OxCal CQL2 commands define the model.

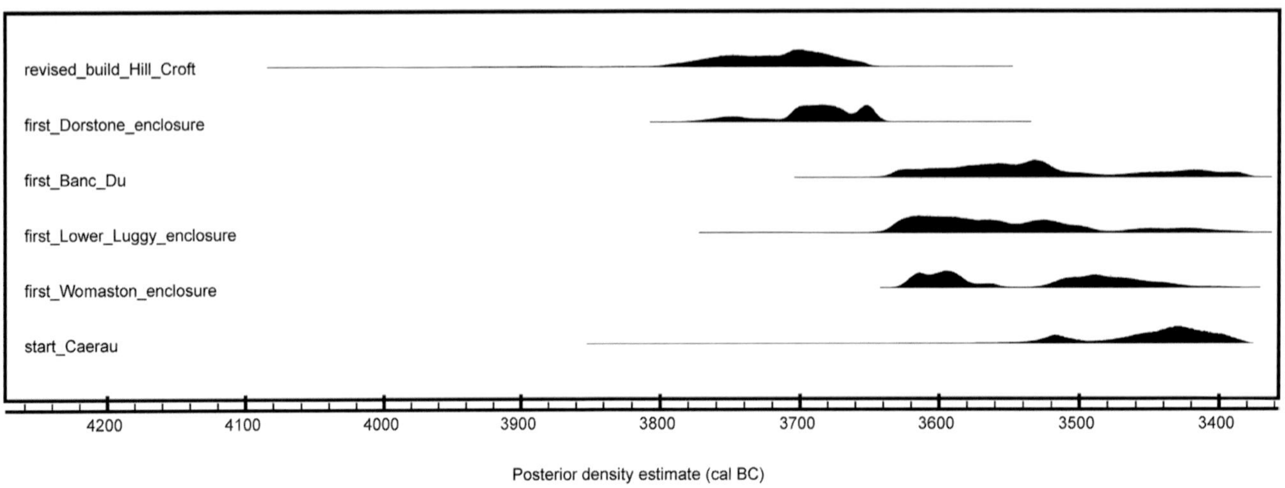

Fig. 4.15. Key probability distributions associated with early Neolithic causewayed and other enclosure monuments in southern England and south Wales and the Marches. The parameters for our study region are calculated as shown in Fig. 4.11, except the parameter from Hill Croft which is calculated in the alternative model shown in Fig. 4.12.

old for its position in the fill sequence. At Lower Luggy, a result from the middle silts (Beta-206283) is too old for its position in the stratigraphic sequence, and has been presented as an outlier in the currency model because of this.

It is evident that enclosures were a significantly later feature in south Wales and the Marches than tombs, long cairns and portal dolmens, but that prior to all monuments we have evidence for occupation and pit deposits – the structures at Llanfaethlu on Anglesey are likely to be amongst this suite of pre-monumental early Neolithic presence. Monuments in the Neolithic of south Wales and the Marches were distinctly different from both latest Mesolithic activity in this area (which might show continuity with early Neolithic practices) and the earliest Neolithic practices.

Conclusions

This research has identified distinct regional trends in the nature of early Neolithic practices, and in the timing of the appearance of early Neolithic material culture and sites in south Wales and the Marches.

We can begin to build up a regional picture of early Neolithic practices in south Wales and the Marches. In this part of the world, and possibly in Wales more widely, settlement sites and occupation precede burial monuments. Neolithic pit deposits and other occupation pre-date the appearance of burial monuments and causewayed enclosures in south Wales and the Marches. The earliest Neolithic evidence from south Wales for occupation and pit deposits has considerable continuity with practices using Mesolithic material culture, and on sites that were important in the very late 5th millennium. Domestic cereals and other forms of portable material culture probably pre-date monuments in this part of the world. Early domesticated cereals may have been introduced along the western coast of Britain prior to other parts of Britain. Because cereal remains are found in pits and tree-throw bowls that show continuity with Mesolithic practices it may be that cereals were first adopted by people who were engaged in lifestyles that were otherwise 'Mesolithic'.

In south Wales and the Marches, the real disjuncture in the archaeological record occurs after the first evidence for the earliest Neolithic, only in the subsequent creation of burial monuments. So, the earliest activity at sites like Penywyrlod and Gwernvale that come to be memorialised with Severn-Cotswold long cairns, is actually the pre-cairn activity. At both these sites, as at other Cotswold-Severn locations, the first Neolithic activity is associated with portable material culture, not monuments.

In terms of Cotswold-Severn burial monuments, the earliest examples in the Black Mountains cluster are probably constructed at Penywyrlod, followed by Pipton, and possibly Ty Isaf. The date for the monumental construction at Gwernvale is poorly defined, because of the phases of activity that produced samples for radiocarbon measurement, but this site appears to have been built later. Beyond the Black Mountains, the Dorstone mounds may be amongst the earliest burial monuments (Ray *et al.* 2022), perhaps followed by Tinkinswood – at a similar time to the Penywyrlod monument – and then Parc le Breos Cwm. The activity at the Lower Luggy burial cairn for which we have evidence also fits into this slightly later phase of burial monument. At the moment, producing robust chronologies for the use of portal dolmens, such as those at Carreg Coetan Arthur and Garn Turne, represents a challenge.

What marks many of these burial monument sites out is the extended period of use, so identifying which of these results were associated with specific material culture signatures can be challenging. In many cases, in contrast to the rapid tempos of construction and use that we see at some Neolithic burial monuments, these places had significance beyond their immediate use and cultural affiliations. The evidence from some sites such as Gwernvale, and to a lesser extent Penywyrlod, demonstrates that these places may have offered affordances to people beyond those understood within a specific cultural worldview. In some cases, the extended use and limited prior information result in imprecise estimates for the start of burial activity at these sites.

Several of the causewayed enclosures from south Wales and the Marches probably appear later than other such monuments in southern Britain, for example at Caerau and Womaston. However, reconsideration of the taphonomy of material from Hill Croft Field and the new evidence from Dorstone could suggest that some of these sites were as early as causewayed enclosures in other parts of Britain. At sites like Hill Croft Field, the collection and deposition of materials that were recognised as 'already old' could again emphasise that the earliest Neolithic activities occurred prior to the construction of monuments. These qualities may have been part of the aesthetics of deposition, concerns that appear to be mirrored in pit deposits in south Wales and other parts of Britain.

Table 4.1. Radiocarbon results from the Black Mountains group of Cotswold-Severn tombs.

Laboratory number	*Sample reference*	*Material*	*Context*	*Radiocarbon age BP*	*$\delta^{13}C$ (‰)*
Penywyrlod (Talgarth), Powys					
HAR-674		Bulked sample of broken small *Homo sapiens* bones	Chamber NE II	4970±80	−21.5
SUERC-67741	Sample 6	*Corylus avellana* (hazel) fragment	Trench 1, context 33, buried soil below inner cairn	5062±36	−27.4
SUERC-69931	Sample 4	*Corylus avellana* (hazel) fragment	Trench 1, context 33, buried soil below inner cairn. Included as an outlier in the model presented here, see text	4849±28	−27.5
SUERC-69932	Sample 18	*Corylus avellana* sp. (hazel) fragment	Trench 15, context 108, buried soil below inner cairn	4948±28	−26.2
SUERC-69933	Sample 28	*Corylus avellana* sp. (hazel) fragment	Trench 1, context 115, burnt area outside long cairn	4831±28	−25.0
SUERC-69934	Sample 29	*Fraxinus* sp. (ash) fragment	Trench 1, context 114, surface of buried soil below cairn collapse: intrusive. Included as an outlier in the model presented here, see main text	96±29	−25.8
SUERC-63414	74.23H/9.2.3/P23	*Homo sapiens* adult, L M_2	Chamber NE II, NE end of NW side	4888±37	−20.6
OxA-16494	P2/74.23M/95/ NEII.Z.3	*Homo sapiens* left femur	Chamber NE II	4512±40	−21.15
OxA-16569	P7/74.23M/95/ NEII.Y.2	*Homo sapiens* left femur	Chamber NE II	4713±38	−20.39
OxA-16527	P6/74.23H/9.14/ NEII.X.1	*Homo sapiens* left femur	Chamber NE II	4823±39	−19.83
OxA-16526	P5/74.23H/9.7/ NEIII.C	*Homo sapiens* left femur	Chamber NE III	4611±39	−20.06
OxA-16525	P3/74.23H/9.1/ NEIII.P.6	*Homo sapiens* left humerus	Chamber NE III, passage	4726±39	−19.77
OxA-16608	P1/74.23M/95	*Homo sapiens* left humerus	Chamber NE III, passage	4937±34	−21.05
SUERC-67743	Sample 28	Maloideae stemwood fragment	Trench 1, context 115, burnt area outside long cairn	5007±34	−26.0
SUERC-67742	Sample 28	*Triticum* sp. single grain	Trench 1, context 115, burnt area outside long cairn	4942±38	−22.4

(Continued)

Table 4.1. (Continued)

Laboratory number	*Sample reference*	*Material*	*Context*	*Radiocarbon age BP*	*δ*^{13}*C (‰)*
Gwernvale					
SUERC-85563	GV78 30/25/B2	*Corylus* sp. nutshell	From pre-cairn buried soil layer 30 – 1m^2 sample area 25, spit B (the second of 5 spits A–E in this area) – the same area and spit as a dated *Triticum* cereal grain SUERC-85562). As noted above, the buried soil profile had evidently been disturbed since there is Neolithic pottery from spits A–D and diagnostic Mesolithic lithics from spits A and B. The sample (which turns out to be later Mesolithic) was submitted on the basis that there might be Mesolithic hazelnut shells in these samples. Included as an outlier in the model presented here, see main text	8701±24	−27.0
SUERC-85600	GV78 30/27/D2	*Corylus* sp. nutshell	From pre-cairn soil layer 30 – 1m^2 sample area 27, spit D (of 5 spits A–E in this area). It was one of the few datable samples from a spit with diagnostic Mesolithic material (a microlith) and without diagnostic Neolithic material (there are lithics also from spits A–C and E, mostly undiagnostic but including stone axe fragment and flake from spit B, and Neolithic pottery from spits A–B). The sample was submitted on the basis that it might provide a Mesolithic date and if so indicate whether there might be remnant stratification in the buried soil. The result is in fact Neolithic and perhaps confirms other suggestions that the buried soil profile is thoroughly disturbed	4904±24	−24.5
CAR-113		Mixed charcoal	From pit F68 sealed below long cairn	5050±75	−26.0
CAR-114		Mixed charcoal	From pit F58 adjacent to pit, with Peterborough pottery, below cairn collapse and assumed to represent later activity adjacent to the long cairn. Presented using the OxCal charcoal outlier model, see main text	4390±70	−26.4
CAR-116		Mixed charcoal	From pit F47 below area of long cairn and assumed to be contemporary with other pre-cairn Neolithic activity. Presented using the OxCal charcoal outlier model, see main text	4590±70	−25.3
CAR-118		Mixed charcoal	From pit F308 below cairn, pre-cairn pit assumed to be contemporary with lithic evidence of later Mesolithic activity. Included as a *terminus post quem* in the model presented here. See discussion above	6900±80	−26.4
SUERC-75856	GV78 133D	*Triticum* cf. *dicoccum* cereal grain	From slot 133D assumed to form part of pre-cairn Neolithic timber structure, but it might either represent remnant material in soil profile or activity contemporary with the structure	5074±28	−25.0 (assumed)
SUERC-75857	GV78 167	*Triticum* cf. *dicoccum* cereal grain	From non-structural feature (?gully) F167 below the cairn and assumed to be contemporary with pre-cairn Neolithic activity	4799±26	−24.5
SUERC-76330	GV78 133B	*Triticum* cf. *dicoccum* cereal grain	From slot 133B assumed to form part of pre-cairn Neolithic timber structure, but it might either represent remnant material in soil profile or activity contemporary with the structure	4803±24	−25.0 (assumed)

(Continued)

Table 4.1. Radiocarbon results from the Black Mountains group of Cotswold-Severn tombs. (Continued)

Laboratory number	*Sample reference*	*Material*	*Context*	*Radiocarbon age BP*	*δ¹³C (‰)*
SUERC-75859	GV78 249	*Triticum* sp. (cf. *dicoccum/spelta*) cereal grain	From burnt area adjacent to slot 133, which is assumed to form part of pre-cairn Neolithic timber structure, but it might either represent remnant material in soil profile or activity contemporary with the structure	4742±27	−24.9
SUERC-75858	GV78 299A	*Triticum* sp. cereal grain	From slot 229 assumed to form part of pre-cairn Neolithic timber structure, but it might either represent remnant material in soil profile or activity contemporarywith the structure	4913±30	−24.7
SUERC-85560	GV78 202/3/B	*Triticum* sp. cereal grain	From lower soil layer 202 in forecourt – 1m² sample area 3, spit B (the lower of spits A–B) – stratigraphically below SUERC-85561 sample), assumed to be same as buried soil 30 below the cairn and assumed and contemporary with pre-cairn Neolithic activity. Taken to confirm contemporaneity with midden and/or timber structure. The sample area falls inside the assumed extent of the timber structure	4943±24	−25.4
SUERC-85561	GV78 95/3/15	*Triticum* sp. cereal grain	From upper, darker, soil layer 95 in forecourt – 1m² sample area 3 stratigraphically above SUERC-85560. The original publication assumed that layer 95 had accumulated within the forecourt and was therefore contemporary with the 'use' of the long cairn. It was anticipated that the date would show whether or not the grain in this layer was contemporary with those from the midden area (SUERC-85562, -85599 -85600). The stratigraphic sequence from layer 202 to 95 is reliable, but layer 95 contains sherds of pottery that appear to belong to one or more pre-cairn vessels (pots 1, 3, 11, 12): there is therefore the possibility that the layer contains residual material from pre-cairn activity contemporary with the midden and/or the pre-cairn timber structure. The layer falls inside the assumed extent of the timber structure and might conceivably be reinterpreted as representing activity within the structure	4738±24	−23.9
SUERC-85562	GV78 30/25/B1	*Triticum* sp. cereal grain	From pre-cairn buried soil layer 30 – 1m² sample area 25, spit B (the second of 5 spits A–E in this area). The buried soil profile had evidently been disturbed since there is Neolithic pottery from spits A–D and diagnostic Mesolithic lithics from spits A and B. There were relatively frequent (undated) *Rubus* sp. (*e.g.* blackberry) seeds in this layer, which it was felt might indicate there was a period of abandonment before renewed agricultural activity. It was also anticipated that dating the cereal would also allow comparison with the date from 1m² area 27 spit D (SUERC-855600). The dated hazelnut shell SUERC-85563 is from the same area and spit	4759±24	−22.2

(Continued)

Table 4.1. (Continued)

Laboratory number	Sample reference	Material	Context	Radiocarbon age BP	$\delta^{13}C$ (‰)
SUERC-85599	GV78 30/14/D1	*Triticum* sp. cereal grain	From pre-cairn buried soil layer 30 – 1m² sample area 14, spit D (the lowest of 4 spits A–D in this area) from which came a fragment of quern/rubbing stone. The sample is one of the few datable cereal grains from this lowest spit of the buried soil	4702±24	−24.4
GU45416	GV 211/B/1st	*Triticum* sp. grain	Failed due to insufficient carbon	–	–
Pipton					
OxA-14253	P20/99.5 H/21	Cattle horncore	Forecourt	4658±33	−21.3
OxA-12083	P15/99.5 H/11	*Homo sapiens* adult right mandible	Inner passage of Chamber I	4601±33	−20.3
OxA-14396	P14/99.5 H/12	*Homo sapiens* left ulna	Entrance passage of Chamber I	4653±34	−18.7
OxA-14251	P19/99.5 H/4[2]	*Homo sapiens* right femur	Group C, Chamber II	4866±32	−20.4
OxA-14252	P18/99.5 H/2	*Homo sapiens* right femur	Group D, Chamber II	4906±33	−20.6
OxA-14254	P21/99.5 H/19	*Homo sapiens* skull fragment	Under floor slab, in S annex of Chamber I	4742±34	−20.5
Ty Isaf					
SUERC-57788	39.190/cow	Cattle, tooth, PM_3 cervix	Chamber I, W compartment	4039±30	−22.9
OxA-12055	9/39.190/315	*Homo sapiens* adult cranium, ?female	Central compartment of Chamber III (rotunda), lower level	4529±31	−20.4
OxA-14394	TI 5/39.190/54	*Homo sapiens* adult right humerus	Passage of Chamber III (rotunda) (17.9)	4658±32	−18.9
OxA-14249	TI 7/39.190/56	*Homo sapiens* adult right humerus. Replicate of OxA-14395	Passage of Chamber III (rotunda) (17.9)	4545±50	−20.6
SUERC-57785	39.190/148a	*Homo sapiens* adult tooth, L M_2	Chamber I, E compartment	4594±30	−21.2
SUERC-57787	39.190/148b	*Homo sapiens* adult tooth, L M_2	Chamber I, E compartment	4680±30	−21.0
SUERC-57786	39.190/310	*Homo sapiens* adult tooth, L M_2	Chamber II, S side of entrance passage	4672±31	−20.7
SUERC-57794	39.190/201	*Homo sapiens* adult tooth, L M_2	Undocumented	4672±31	−20.6
SUERC-57795	39.190/317	*Homo sapiens* adult tooth, L M_2	Undocumented	4772±30	−20.7

(Continued)

Table 4.1. Radiocarbon results from the Black Mountains group of Cotswold-Severn tombs. (Continued)

Laboratory number	Sample reference	Material	Context	Radiocarbon age BP	$\delta^{13}C$ (‰)
SUERC-57790	39.190/59	*Homo sapiens* adult tooth, L M_2	Undocumented	4430±33	−20.6
SUERC-57796	39.190/312	*Homo sapiens* adult tooth, L M_3	Undocumented	4755±31	−20.8
SUERC-57789	39.190/324	*Homo sapiens* child (3–4 years) tooth, L DM_2	Chamber II, outside chamber on N side	3309±32	−20.7
OxA-14250	TI 9/39.190/200	*Homo sapiens* cranium	Central compartment of Chamber III (rotunda), upper level	4082±30	−20.8
OxA-14248	TI 1/39.190/316.1	*Homo sapiens* cranium (Individual a)	Central compartment of Chamber III (rotunda), lower level	4202±31	−20.5
OxA-14393	TI 2/39.190/316.2	*Homo sapiens* cranium (Individual b)	Central compartment of Chamber III (rotunda), lower level	4523±35	−18.9
SUERC-57784	39.190/58	*Homo sapiens* subadult (>12 years) tooth, L M_2	Chamber I, NE corner of E compartment	4616±30	−20.9
OxA-14395		Replicate of OxA-14249	Replicate of OxA-14249. T′=0.0; T′ 5%=3.8; df=1 (Ward and Wilson 1978)	4552±35	−19.5

Table 4.2. Radiocarbon results from early Neolithic sites and material culture from the Marches and south Wales. The list includes selected 4th millennium results which are not robustly associated with early Neolithic activity for the reasons stated.

Laboratory number	Sample reference	Material	Context	Radiocarbon age BP	$\delta^{13}C$ (‰)
NEOLITHIC OCCUPATION					
Wellington Quarry, Marden, Herefordshire, original permitted area					
OxA-12570	3852/1	Charred hazelnut shell	Pit 3852. One of a group of pits containing Neolithic Bowl pottery, struck flint, stone artefacts, animal bone and charred cereals (Bapty 2007; Jackson and Miller 2011)	4762±31	−22.8
OxA-12547	3852/2	Single charred wheat grain	From the same context as OxA-12570. The result is too old for this context when compared with the measurement OxA-12570, this result has therefore been presented as a *terminus post quem* for this context as outlined in Griffiths (2011, 270)	4850±31	−24.5
OxA-12568	3854/1	Charred hazelnut shell	Pit 3854. One of a group of pits containing Neolithic Bowl pottery, struck flint, stone artefacts, animal bone and charred cereals (Bapty 2007)	4823±32	−23.5
OxA-12569	3854/2	Single charred wheat grain	From the same context as OxA-12568	4810±33	−23.5

(Continued)

Table 4.2. (Continued)

Laboratory number	*Sample reference*	*Material*	*Context*	*Radiocarbon age BP*	*$\delta^{13}C$ (‰)*
Wellington Quarry, Marden, Herefordshire, Moreton Camp extension					
Wk-12257		Single fragment of wood charcoal	Single pit identified during evaluation, containing a reworked fragment of a ground stone axe, a small assemblage of struck flint and a sherd of quartz-tempered pottery (Bapty 2007; Jackson and Miller 2011). The result could include an inbuilt 'old wood' offset and so has been included as a *terminus post quem* as outlined in Griffiths (2011, 271)	5100±79	–
Wellington Quarry, Marden, Herefordshire, new area, 2008					
Beta-245652		Charred hazelnut fragment	Single pit containing plain Neolithic Bowl pottery (Robin Jackson, *pers. comm.*; Griffiths 2011)	4730±40	–
Cwm Meudwy, Llandysul, Ceredigion					
Beta-185679		*Corylus avellana* charcoal	Pit 50. Small, shallow pit with sherds of at least five Bowls, including two with everted decorated rims (Murphy 2003; Caseldine and Griffiths 2005; Murphy and Evans 2007)	4840±40	–
Beta-185680		*Corylus avellana* charcoal	Pit 113. Pit with sherds of two Bowls, one shouldered (Murphy 2003; Caseldine and Griffiths 2005; Murphy and Evans 2007)	4870±50	–
Beta-185678		*Alnus glutinosa* charcoal	Pit 142. Small isolated pit with very charcoal-rich fill but no pottery, to south-west of later prehistoric palisade enclosure, on settlement where most of pottery assessed as early Neolithic (Murphy 2003; Caseldine and Griffiths 2005; Murphy and Evans 2007). Not included in the model as not demonstrably associated with diagnostic early Neolithic material culture	4800±40	–
Beta-189116		*Prunus* sp. charcoal	Posthole 64. Flanking NE entrance of sub-trapezoid palisade enclosure, undoubtedly measured on redeposited sample because other entrance postholes of same enclosure yielded dates in 2nd millennium cal BC and 1st millennium cal AD (Murphy 2003; Caseldine and Griffiths 2005; Murphy and Evans 2007). Not included in the model as not demonstrably associated with diagnostic early Neolithic material culture	5080±40	–
Coygan Camp, Carmarthenshire					
NPL-132		Charred hazelnut shells	Pit CXIX (3). Isolated pit containing sherds of a single heavy-rimmed plain Bowl, struck flint, animal bone, charcoal (Wainwright 1967, 14–20, figs 3, 6)	5000±95	–25.0

(Continued)

Table 4.2. Radiocarbon results from early Neolithic sites and material culture from the Marches and south Wales. The list includes selected 4th millennium results which are not robustly associated with early Neolithic activity for the reasons stated. (Continued)

Laboratory number	*Sample reference*	*Material*	*Context*	*Radiocarbon age BP*	*$\delta^{13}C$ (‰)*
Bromfield, Shropshire					
HAR-3968	S163	Bulked charcoal sample	F247. From base of one of two Neolithic pits, overlain by sherds of 3 or 4 bowls, one heavy-rimmed and one with simple linear decoration on the rim. Also present were charred hazelnut shells, and small amounts of charred cereals and struck flint (Stanford 1982, 282–7). The result could include an inbuilt 'old wood' offset and so has been included as a *terminus post quem* as outlined in Griffiths (2011, 280)	4680±80	−26.9
Plas Gogerddan, Ceredigion					
CAR-994		Unidentified charcoal	Pit 206, containing charred emmer wheat, barley, chaff, apple pips and fragments, hazelnut shells. No artefacts (Murphy 1992, 7, 24–6). The result may provide a *terminus post quem* for the assemblage, and has been included in the model presented here to reflect this	4700±80	–
Causeway Farm, Herefordshire					
Wk-9688	Sample <3>	Unidentified charcoal	Context (6001) from pit (6000/6001). Pit contained 40% charred inclusions including hazel nutshell, emmer, wheat grains, an emmer spikelet, apple pips, part of an apple fruit body, and weed seeds (Monckton 2001). Within the fill were 34 sherds of early Neolithic pottery (defined by Gibson (2001) as 'no sign of a well-defined carination, but the fabric and rim suggest an open shouldered bowl'), two flint blades and two waste flakes. The pottery was hand-formed, quartz-tempered, with organic inclusions and a grass- or vegetable-wiped finish	4868±60	−25.9±0.2
A477 Sageston-Redberth bypass, Pembrokeshire					
Wk-10153	SR01-026	'small charcoal sample', of *Corylus avellana*	Context 026. Secondary fill of linear pit 025 on W end of 'settlement of early to late Neolithic date' covering 100m of easement and extending to either side of it (Page 2001; 2002; Gale 2002). Not included in the model as not demonstrably associated with diagnostic early Neolithic material culture	4656±67	–
Wk-10156	SR01-517	'small charcoal sample', of *Corylus avellana*	Context 517. Spread of burnt material on E end of 'settlement of early to late Neolithic date' covering 100m of easement and extending to either side of it (Page 2001; 2002; Gale 2002). Not included in the model as not demonstrably associated with diagnostic early Neolithic material culture	4553±62	–
Wk-10158	SR01-537	'small charcoal sample', of *Corylus avellana*	Context 537. Fill of posthole 536 in posthole row 552 on W end of 'settlement of early to late Neolithic date' covering 100m of easement and extending to either side of it (Page 2001; 2002; Gale 2002). Not included in the model as not demonstrably associated with diagnostic early Neolithic material culture	4965±57	–

(Continued)

Table 4.2. (Continued)

Laboratory number	*Sample reference*	*Material*	*Context*	*Radiocarbon age BP*	$\delta^{13}C$ *(‰)*
Wk-10159	SR01-554	'small charcoal sample', of *Corylus avellana*	Context 554. Fill of posthole 553, one of a pair W of row 552, on W end of 'settlement of early to late Neolithic date' covering 100m of easement and extending to either side of it (Page 2001; 2002; Gale 2002). Not included in the model as not demonstrably associated with diagnostic early Neolithic material culture	4791±57	–
Trostrey Castle, Monmouthshire					
Beta-169094	C476	Charcoal	Base of post 0.40m in diameter, rotted *in situ*. One of three large postholes S of ovoid stone mound (Mein 2002). Not included in the model as not demonstrably associated with diagnostic early Neolithic material culture	5050±50	–
Beta-173357	C532	Charcoal. Undated remainder mainly scrubby and short-lived, identified by Rowena Gale	Pyre 3 (Mein 2002, 107–8; 2003, 67). Not included in the model as not demonstrably associated with diagnostic early Neolithic material culture	4800±90	–
GU-4414	C278	Charcoal	Pyre 1. Later series of firings in linear hearth seen as pyre and including pottery described as Grimston Ware (Mein 1996, 65; 2003, 67). The result may provide a *terminus post quem* for the assemblage, and has been included in the model presented here to reflect this	4930±70	–
GU-2559	C91	Charcoal	Hearth in flint-working area including leaf arrowheads (Mein 1994, 50; 1996, 65). The result may provide a *terminus post quem* for the assemblage, and has been included in the model presented here to reflect this	4820±80	–
GU-2624	Charcoal		From a firepit (Mein 1992, 11) Not included in the model as not demonstrably associated with diagnostic early Neolithic material culture	5340±60	–
South Wales Gas Pipeline Site 26.5, Land west of Cwmifor, Carmarthenshire					
Beta-257727		*Corylus avellana* nut shell	Single fill of pit 265639 which contained 13 lithics including two diagnostically late Mesolithic/early Neolithic flints, pottery representing three early Neolithic vessels, a small assemblage of burnt bone and emmer/spelt grain	5130±40	–
SUERC-54561		*Corylus* sp. charcoal	The earlier of the results (Beta-257727) may represent residual material, and has been included in the model using the 'After' function. The other two results are statistically consistent (T'3.5; T'5%=3.8; df=1; Ward and Wilson 1978).	4989±30	−25.8

(Continued)

Table 4.2. Radiocarbon results from early Neolithic sites and material culture from the Marches and south Wales. The list includes selected 4th millennium results which are not robustly associated with early Neolithic activity for the reasons stated. (Continued)

Laboratory number	*Sample reference*	*Material*	*Context*	*Radiocarbon age BP*	*δ^{13}C (‰)*
SUERC-54562		*Corylus* sp. charcoal	This context contained sherds from a simple everted Carinated Bowl and possibly sherds from two 'developed' Carinated Bowls (Alex Gibson, *pers. comm.* 2014). The later results on hazel charcoal are consistent with estimates for the start of the Neolithic in south Wales (Griffiths 2011), and may provide accurate dates for the presence of early Neolithic Carinated Bowl on the site, in the 38th or 37th centuries cal BC. The earlier result suggests the potential that the site had more complex multi-phase activity. Because the cereal grains recovered from this deposit were not directly dated, it is unclear if these were part of any early Neolithic activity at the site, or were associated with later presence on the site	4910±30	−24.7
Beta-257726		*Corylus avellana* nut shell	Single fill of pit 265072. Not included in the model as not demonstrably associated with diagnostic early Neolithic material culture	7720±50	–
SUERC-54566		*Corylus* sp. charcoal	Spread of burnt material overlying tree-throw hole 265649. Context 265738, tree-throw 265737/265649. Not included in the model as not demonstrably associated with diagnostic early Neolithic material culture	4929±30	−25.2
SUERC-54567		*Corylus* sp. charcoal	Fill of tree-throw hole 265649. Not included in the model as not demonstrably associated with diagnostic early Neolithic material culture	3011±29	−26.4
SUERC-54568		*Corylus* sp. charcoal	Fill of tree-throw hole 265649. Not included in the model as not demonstrably associated with diagnostic early Neolithic material culture	2988±29	−24.9
South Wales Gas Pipeline Site 509, Land West of Middle Bastleford, Pembrokeshire					
SUERC-54570		*Corylus avellana* nut shell	Fill 255105 of pit containing sherds of early Neolithic 'Developed' Carinated bowl (Alex Gibson, *pers. comm.* 2014)	4968±30	−24.3
SUERC-54571		*Corylus sp.* charcoal	Fill 255105 of pit containing sherds of early Neolithic 'Developed' Carinated bowl (Alex Gibson, *pers. comm.* 2014)	4931±30	−25.2
South Wales Gas Pipeline Site 51.7, Land North-West of Pen-y-Crug, Powys					
SUERC-54691		Hazelnut shell	Fill 51.07.305 of pit. Not included in the model as not demonstrably associated with diagnostic early Neolithic material culture	4844±29	−22.8
Beta-253575		Hazelnut shell	Fill 51.07.305 of pit. Not included in the model as not demonstrably associated with diagnostic early Neolithic material culture	4630±40	–
SUERC-54692		Hazelnut shell	Fill 51.07.303 of pit. Not included in the model as not demonstrably associated with diagnostic early Neolithic material culture	4886±29	−24

(Continued)

Table 4.2. *(Continued)*

Laboratory number	*Sample reference*	*Material*	*Context*	*Radiocarbon age BP*	$\delta^{13}C$ *(‰)*
Beta-253576		?	Fill 51.07.318 of pit. Not included in the model as not demonstrably associated with diagnostic early Neolithic material culture	2330±40	–
Beta-253574		'Carbon sample'	Ring Ditch A fill 51.07.242. Not included in the model as not demonstrably associated with diagnostic early Neolithic material culture	4740±40	–
Beta-253573		A roundwood charcoal sample	Fill of posthole 51.07.152. Not included in the model as not demonstrably associated with diagnostic early Neolithic material culture	2370±40	–
South Wales Gas Pipeline Site 514, Land South-East of Upper Neeston, Pembrokeshire					
SUERC-54698		Hazel nutshell	Fill 511055 of enclosure ditch	4925±29	−28
SUERC-54699		Hazelnut shell	Fill 511069 of pit 511071. Charcoal rich, produced 34 early Neolithic 'developed' Carinated Bowl sherds along with charcoal fragments, possibly from oak, and *c.* 50 charred hazelnut shells. The same pit also contained unburnt and burnt flint micro-debitage indicative of flint knapping	4910±29	−24.1
South Wales Gas Pipeline Palaeoenvironmental Site RDX 24.7, Gurrey Cottage, Carmarthenshire					
SUERC-57298	2473000	Charred plant remains; hazelnut shell fragments ×3	247002 pit fill identified in palaeoenvironmental sampling by James Rackham. Produced a charred plant remains assemblage including hazelnut shell, apple/pear pip and flesh, and emmer/spelt grains	4913±30	−27.5
SUERC-57299	2473000	Charred plant remains; emmer wheat-type grains ×3		4939±30	−26.6
South Wales Gas Pipeline Palaeoenvironmental Site 238, Land South-West of Gelli-Wern-Isaf, Swansea					
SUERC-57303	238000	Charred plant remains; hazelnut shell fragments ×2	23002. Not included in the model as not demonstrably associated with diagnostic early Neolithic material culture	4734±30	−24.8
South Wales Gas Pipeline Palaeoenvironmental Site 22.4					
SUERC-57306	2243000	Charred plant remains; hazelnut shell fragments (multiple small fragments)	224003. Not included in the model as not demonstrably associated with diagnostic early Neolithic material culture	5069±30	−26.5
DOLMENS					
Carreg Coetan Arthur, Pembrokeshire					
CAR-391	Sample 1	Bulked charcoal sample	Old ground surface sealed beneath mound material (Dresser 1985, 381; S. Rees 2012). Not included within the currency model, because of uncertain association with diagnostic early Neolithic material culture	4560±80	−28.2

(Continued)

Table 4.2. Radiocarbon results from early Neolithic sites and material culture from the Marches and south Wales. The list includes selected 4th millennium results which are not robustly associated with early Neolithic activity for the reasons stated. (Continued)

Laboratory number	*Sample reference*	*Material*	*Context*	*Radiocarbon age BP*	*δ¹³C (‰)*
CAR-392	Sample 2	Bulked charcoal sample	F36. Area of burning sealed beneath stone kerb. Not included within the currency model, because of uncertain association with diagnostic early Neolithic material culture	4830±80	−27.8
CAR-393	Sample 3	Bulked charcoal sample	Within material of the mound. Not included within the currency model, because of uncertain association with diagnostic early Neolithic material culture	4470±80	−26.8
CAR-394	Sample 4	Bulked charcoal sample	F44. Socket of orthostat framing chamber. Used in the currency model as a *terminus post quem* for the construction of the dolmen its presence in the socket, and the potential for an inbuilt 'old wood offset'	4700±80	−27.6
LONG BARROWS AND LONG CAIRNS					
Lower Luggy long barrow, Powys					
BM-2954		Fast-grown *Quercus* sp. charcoal	Trench 1. Outer rings of partly charred post *c.* 0.10m in diameter, closely set in palisade trench along SE side of barrow and extracted from NE section of trench mid-way along its length (Gibson 2000, 6–11; 2003)	4830±45	−24.1
BM-2955		Fast-grown *Quercus* sp. charcoal	Trench 2. Outer rings of post *c.* 0.20m in diameter, burnt *in situ* near proximal end of palisade trench along SE side of barrow (Gibson 2000, 10–11; 2003)	4710±40	−23.8
Tinkinswood long cairn, Vale of Glamorgan					
OxA-16528	TI-2/TINK.FE.8	Right femur of adult woman	From the terminal chamber excavated by John Ward in 1914–15 (Thompson 2019, 39). Samples from separate adults selected by Michael Wysocki (see Wysocki and Whittle 2000)	4916±41	−19.8
OxA-16529	TI-3/TINK.FE.12	Right femur of adult man	From the terminal chamber excavated by John Ward in 1914–15 (Thompson 2019, 39). Samples from separate adults selected by Michael Wysocki (see Wysocki and Whittle 2000)	4859±39	−19.6
OxA-16530	TI-5/TINK.FE.9	Right femur of adult, sex indeterminate	From the terminal chamber excavated by John Ward in 1914–15 (Thompson 2019, 39). Samples from separate adults selected by Michael Wysocki (see Wysocki and Whittle 2000)	4907±39	−20.5
OxA-16531	TI-8/TINK.FE.6	Right femur of adult man	From the terminal chamber excavated by John Ward in 1914–15 (Thompson 2019, 39). Samples from separate adults selected by Michael Wysocki (see Wysocki and Whittle 2000)	4970±39	−20.0
Parc le Breos Cwm long cairn, Swansea					
OxA-6487	PC1	Human. Adult. L humerus	SE chamber (Whittle and Wysocki 1998)	4685±65	−21.2
OxA-6496	PC11	Human. L humerus	SE chamber (Whittle and Wysocki 1998)	4850±65	−21.5

(Continued)

Table 4.2. (Continued)

Laboratory number	*Sample reference*	*Material*	*Context*	*Radiocarbon age BP*	*$\delta^{13}C$ (‰)*
OxA-6641	PC2	Human. Adult. L humerus	SE chamber (Whittle and Wysocki 1998)	4690±55	−20.4
OxA-6488	PC3	Human. Adult. L humerus	SW chamber (Whittle and Wysocki 1998)	4780±60	−20.7
OxA-6489	PC4	Human. Adult. L humerus	SW chamber (Whittle and Wysocki 1998)	4445±60	−21.3
OxA-6493	PC8	Human. Adult. L humerus	NE chamber (Whittle and Wysocki 1998)	4875±55	−21.8
OxA-6494	PC9	Human. Adult. L humerus	NE chamber (Whittle and Wysocki 1998)	4645±60	−21.4
OxA-6490	PC5	Human. Adult. L humerus	NW chamber (Whittle and Wysocki 1998)	4660±60	−21.2
OxA-6491	PC6	Human. Adult. L humerus	NW chamber (Whittle and Wysocki 1998)	4710±60	−21.2
OxA-6495	PC10	Human. Subadult skull	Now thought likely to have come from Cat Hole Cave (Wysocki *et al.* in press)	3705±55	−21.4
OxA-6492	PC7	Human. L humerus	Now thought likely to have come from Cat Hole Cave (Wysocki *et al.* in press)	4805±55	−21.3
OxA-6497	PC12	Human. Occipital	Now thought likely to have come from Cat Hole Cave (Wysocki *et al.* in press)	3750±55	−21.6
OxA-6498	PC13	Animal bone, sheep or roe deer: sources differ	Now thought likely to have come from Cat Hole Cave (Wysocki *et al.* in press)	2315±50	−22
OxA-6499	PC14	Animal bone, dog skull or badger: sources differ	Now thought likely to have come from Cat Hole Cave (Wysocki *et al.* in press)	7665±65	−19.5
OxA-14430	PC15	Animal bone, large butchered ungulate	Now thought likely to have come from Cat Hole Cave (Wysocki *et al.* in press) This replaces OxA-6500; the new sample was treated with ultrafiltration	12395±70	−18.8
ENCLOSURES					
Hill Croft Field, Herefordshire					
GrA-32095	HC06 30/C	Single fragment *Corylus* sp. charcoal	Trench 1, feature 4, context 30. On base of ditch, in thin layer of silt sealed by apparent backfill, scattered in deposit of sherds, probably from one pot, and human and animal bone with numerous macroscopic snail shells clustered around bones. The results from context 30 may represent curated or stored material. These results are discussed fully in Griffiths (2011, 273), and are represented as *termini post quos* in order to provide an estimate for the construction of the causewayed enclosure monument	4895±40	−26.11

(Continued)

Table 4.2. Radiocarbon results from early Neolithic sites and material culture from the Marches and south Wales. The list includes selected 4th millennium results which are not robustly associated with early Neolithic activity for the reasons stated. (Continued)

Laboratory number	*Sample reference*	*Material*	*Context*	*Radiocarbon age BP*	*δ¹³C (‰)*
OxA-16022	HC06 30/A	Single fragment *Prunus* sp. charcoal	From the same context as GrA-32095	4762±37	−26.0
OxA-15867	HC06 30/B	Human. From robust R femur shaft fragment, weighing 114g	From the same context as GrA-32095	4911±29	−19.5
GrA-31963	HC06 30/D	Cattle. From distal R femur fragment weighing 173g	From the same context as GrA-32095	4970±40	−22.47
GrA-32096	HC06 23/A	Single fragment *Quercus* sp. sapwood charcoal	Trench 1, feature 4, context 23. Charcoal lens, not burnt *in situ*, above apparent backfill sealing context 30 and above subsequent silt	4585±35	−23.88
OxA-16023	HC06 23/B	Single fragment *Quercus* sp. sapwood charcoal	From the same context as GrA-32096	4568±35	−23.3
Womaston, Powys					
Beta-254592		*Corylus avellana* charcoal	Basal fill (32) of recut of inner ditch	4800±40	–
Beta-254593		*Corylus avellana* charcoal	Lower fill (45) of inner ditch	4660±40	–
Beta-254594		*Corylus avellana* charcoal	Fill (18) of feature cut into upper fill of outer ditch	4630±40	–
SUERC-26461		*Corylus avellana* charcoal	Fill of pit (38) within interior. Not associated with diagnostic Neolithic material culture and so not included in the model	2410±35	–
Caerau, Cardiff					
UBA-31602	CAER02	Single fragment *Corylus avellana* charcoal	Ditch E in Trench 5A, secondary fill (5106=5103) containing large sherds (Davis and Sharples 2017)	4970±52	–
UBA-31603	CAER03	Single fragment of *Prunus spinosa* charcoal	Terminus of Ditch E in Trench 5A, secondary fill (5112) containing large sherds	4719±47	–
UBA-33629	CAER07	Single fragment *Corylus avellana* charcoal	Ditch E in Trench 5A, primary fill (5135). This result is older than the other measurement (UBA-31603) on material from this layer. It has therefore been presented as a *terminus post quem* to reflect this. Further discussion is provided in Griffiths 2019	4657±43	–
UBA-33630	CAER08	Single fragment of *Prunus spinosa* charcoal	Ditch E in Trench 5A, sealing primary fill	4712±35	–

(Continued)

Table 4.2. (Continued)

Laboratory number	*Sample reference*	*Material*	*Context*	*Radiocarbon age BP*	$\delta^{13}C$ *(‰)*
UBA-31604	CAER04	Single fragment *Corylus avellana* charcoal	Ditch A in Trench 7, burnt layer in recut of ditch (7045)	4691±48	–
UBA-31605	CAER05	Single fragment of *Prunus spinosa* charcoal	Ditch A in Trench 7, secondary fill (7063) containing polished axe fragments below recut	4699±54	–
UBA-33631	CAER09	Single fragment of *Prunus spinosa* charcoal	Ditch B in Trench 7, fill (7152) sealing stone deposit	4725±32	–
UBA-31606	CAER06	Single fragment *Corylus avellana* charcoal	Ditch D in Trench 7, burnt layer in recut of ditch (7075). This result, from the fill of a recut, is older than the other measurements (UBA-33632 and -33633) from the fills of the initial cut. It has therefore been presented as a *terminus post quem* to reflect this. Further discussion is provided in Griffiths 2019	4802±47	–
UBA-33632	CAER10	Single fragment of Maloideae charcoal	Ditch D in Trench 8, primary fill in southern end of trench (8117)	4699±32	–
UBA-33633	CAER11	Single fragment of *Prunus spinosa* charcoal	Ditch D in Trench 8, primary fill of ditch segment (8074) joining north and south segments	4698±32	–
Banc Du, Pembrokeshire					
GrA-31187	BDE 05 ES <1> (b)	Single fragment Ericaceae charcoal	F1, Context 15. Upper of two layers rich in charred material (the lower being context 18) within a possible recut, stratified above context 18 (Whittle *et al.* 2011, chapter 10)	4085±35	−26.88
GrA-31186	BDE 05 ES <1> (a)	Single fragment Ericaceae charcoal	From the same context as GrA-31187	4120±35	−28.15
GrA-32008	BDE 05 ES <12> (c)	Single fragment Ericaceae charcoal	F1, Context 18. Lower of two layers rich in charred material (the upper being context 15) within a possible recut, stratified above context 21	4390±80	−26.62
GrA-31099	BDE 05 ES <12> (a)	Single fragment Ericaceae	From the same context as GrA-32008	4315±40	−26.32
GrA-32007	BDE 05 ES <14> (d)	Single fragment unidentified bark charcoal	F1, Context 21. Initial silt on floor of ditch, stratified below contexts 15 and 18	4775±40	−27.51
GrA-32006	BDE 05 ES <14> (c)	Single fragment *Quercus* sapwood charcoal	From the same context as GrA-32007	4665±35	−23.25
Lower Luggy enclosure, Powys					
Beta-177037		*Corylus* sp. twigs, charcoal	Charcoal deposit on ditch terminal floor (100SW) immediately below primary silts (Gibson 2006)	4760±50	–

(Continued)

Table 4.2. Radiocarbon results from early Neolithic sites and material culture from the Marches and south Wales. The list includes selected 4th millennium results which are not robustly associated with early Neolithic activity for the reasons stated. (Continued)

Laboratory number	*Sample reference*	*Material*	*Context*	*Radiocarbon age BP*	*$\delta^{13}C$ (‰)*
Beta-206282		*Corylus* sp. twigs, charcoal	From the same context as Beta-177037	4690±40	–
Beta-206283		*Corylus* sp. charcoal	Middle silts of ditch, redeposited (Gibson 2006). Included as outlier in model as too old for its position in the stratigraphic sequence	4980±40	–
CURSUS MONUMENT					
Sarn-y-bryn-caled cursus, Powys					
OxA-3997	SYBC 92:1	Fast-grown *Quercus* sp. charcoal	Patch of small charcoal fragment immediately above primary silt of east ditch (Gibson 1994)	4960±70	−25.2

5

The beginnings of agriculture in Wales: the evidence from Gwernvale

Astrid Caseldine

Introduction

There has been a marked increase in the amount of archaeobotanical data relating to the Neolithic period in Britain and Ireland in recent years, much of it as a result of developer-funded archaeology (McClatchie *et al.* 2014). This has led to further research into Neolithic farming practices as well as wild plant exploitation (Bogaard and Jones 2007; Jones and Rowley-Conwy 2007; Bishop *et al.* 2009; Pelling and Campbell 2013; McClatchie *et al.* 2014; 2016; Treasure *et al.* 2019; Rowley-Conwy *et al.* 2020). The analysis of archaeobotanical evidence from Gwernvale has provided an opportunity to add to the investigation of the development of agriculture and the collection of wild plant foodstuffs during the early Neolithic in Wales where archaeobotanical evidence from early Neolithic sites is still relatively scarce (Treasure *et al.* 2019), though excavations associated with some recent developer-funded projects (*e.g.* Kenney 2008; 2021; Barber *et al.* 2019; Darvill *et al.* 2020) have resulted in significant contributions.

An extensive sampling programme, rarely undertaken at that time, was implemented at the excavations at Gwernvale during the late 1970s by the director of the excavation, Bill Britnell, under the guidance of the late Professor Gordon Hillman, attached to the then Department of Botany, University College, Cardiff. The sampling programme resulted in a large number of samples but unfortunately, although

Fig. 5.1. Gwernvale: on-site bulk environmental sample processing in 1978 using an Ankara-type flotation tank.

initially identification of the charred plant remains was undertaken by Gordon Hillman in Cardiff and subsequently in the Institute of Archaeology, London, with the assistance of Lisa Moffett, circumstances prevented full analysis. The analysis of all the samples for charred plant remains has now been completed and forms the basis of this report. In addition, a small amount of wood charcoal has been identified from a limited number of samples.

Sampling

Samples were taken from features and buried soils below the E end of the long cairn and within the forecourt, features including possible tree-roots and irregular pits/hollows below the W end of the long cairn, features and buried soils on the NW side of the long cairn, and from soil layers within Chambers 2 and 3 (Figs 5.2–5.4).

The area of buried soil (30) beneath the cairn between the forecourt and Chamber 1 was excavated and the full volume of the soil profile sampled in 1m squares (including partial squares) in spits (A–D), depending on the depth, which varied between 0.10–0.20m (Fig. 5.3). Buried soil layers within the forecourt were sampled on a similar basis. A lower layer of buried soil (202) within the forecourt, which is thought to have been continuous with the buried soil below the cairn, was excavated in one or two spits (A–B). An upper, darker, soil layer (95) within the forecourt (sealed by later stone deposits)

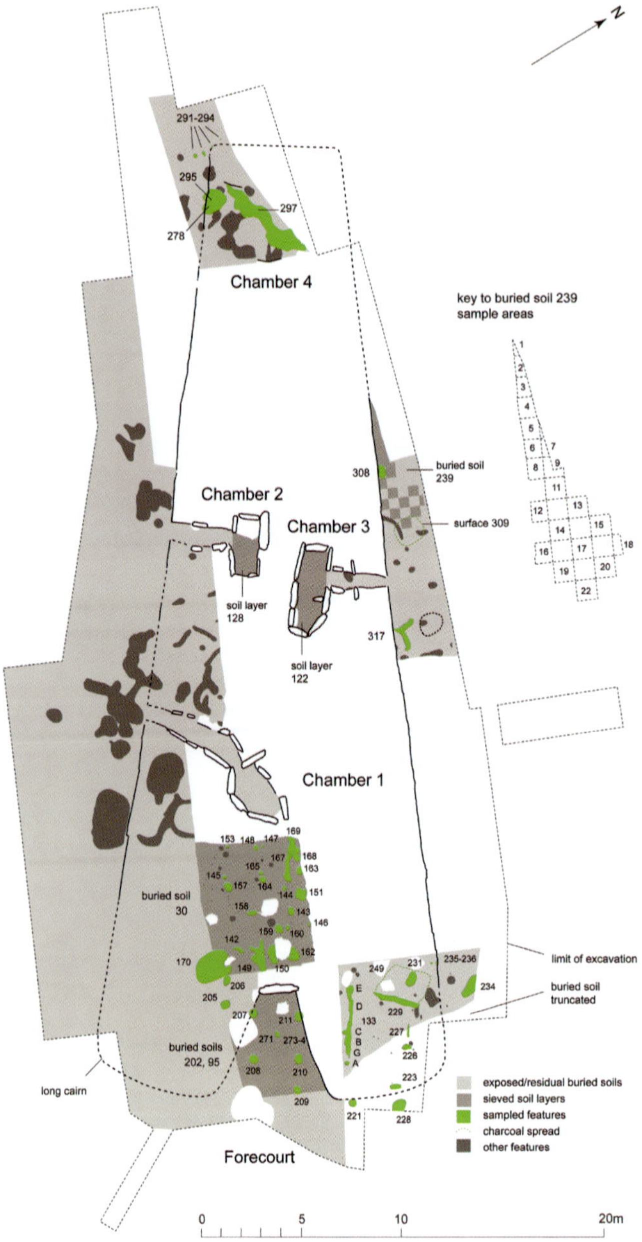

Fig. 5.2. Gwernvale: features and soil layers sampled for charred plant remains (see also Figs 5.3–5.4 for the E end of the long cairn).

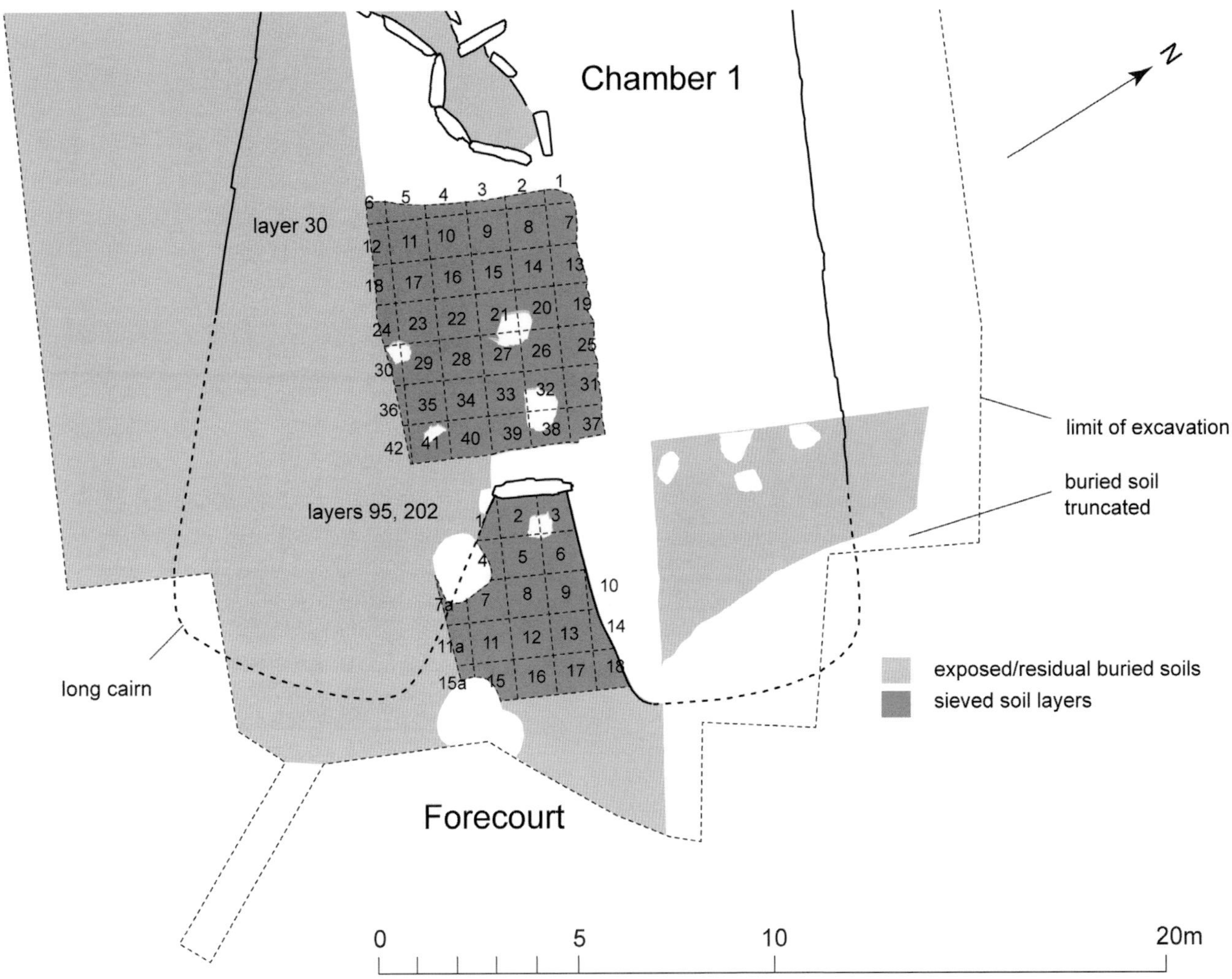

Fig. 5.3. Gwernvale: sampled areas of buried soils below the E end of the long cairn (30) and in the forecourt area (202, 95).

was excavated in a single spit. This layer had remained exposed during the construction and use of the cairn though it seems likely to include material belonging to phases of pre-cairn activity. For comparative purposes, an area of buried soil (239) on the NW side of the long cairn was selectively sampled in 0.5m² squares (Fig. 5.2). The soil layer, sealed by later cairn collapse, was considered to be continuous with the buried soil below the cairn. Selective samples were also taken from soil horizons within Chambers 2 (128) and 3 (122), again essentially considered to be continuous with the buried soil below the cairn.

The full volumes of selected pre-cairn features were sampled, including features associated with the pre-cairn timber structure below the E end of the long cairn (Fig. 5.3). For taphonomic purposes, where possible, the post-pipes and post-packing of postholes were sampled separately. On these grounds it is assumed that items from the post-pipes may post-date the structure and that items from the post-packing are more likely to be contemporary with or pre-date the structure.

The area of buried soil and the timber structure below the eastern end of the long cairn are reinterpreted in Chapter 3 as an early Neolithic timber house and associated midden deposit.

Methods

The majority of samples were processed on site using an Ankara-type flotation tank (Fig. 5.1). The flots were collected in 1mm and 250 micron sieves and the residues on a 1mm nylon mesh. After the initial flotation of the sample the residue was allowed to dry and re-floated. Contexts with small amounts of material were simply washed through a stack of sieves. A few samples were processed in the laboratory at the Department of Plant Sciences, University College, Cardiff, to check recovery efficiency.

Charred plant remains

The samples available for analysis were 1mm flot samples and hand-collected samples from the residues. The finer fraction flots were unavailable and it is assumed that these were examined earlier and considered not to contain any significant remains and therefore not retained.

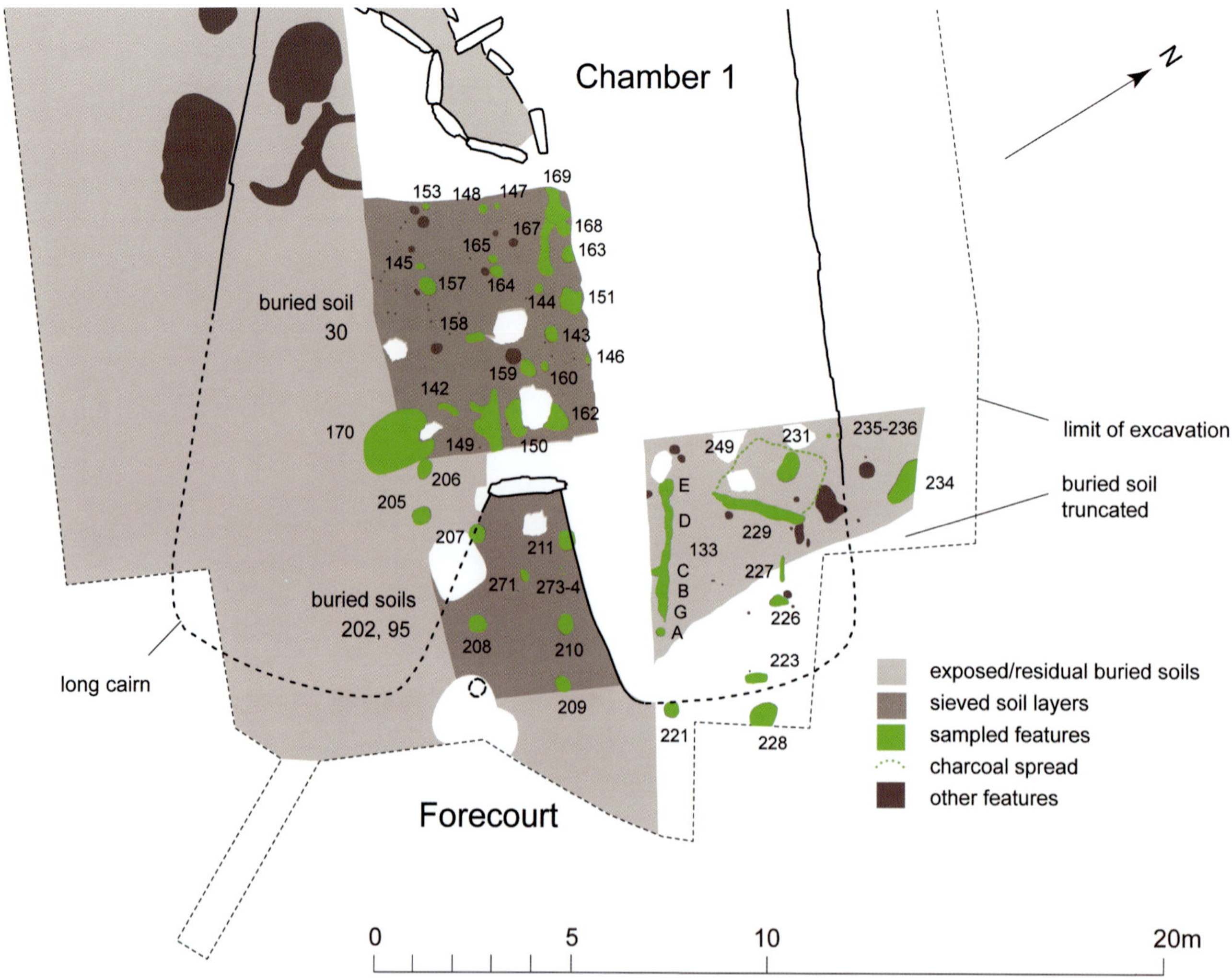

Fig. 5.4. Gwernvale: sampled features below E end of the long cairn and in the forecourt area.

Sorting and identification was undertaken using a Leica MZ16 stereo-microscope with magnification up to ×120. Remains were identified by comparison with modern reference material and descriptions and images in seed atlases (*e.g.* Berggren 1969; 1981; Schoch *et al.* 1988; Anderberg 1994; Cappers *et al.* 2006; Jacomet 2006; Neef *et al.* 2012). The results are presented in Tables 5.1–5.5 and Figures 5.5–5.9.

Charcoal

A small amount of charcoal was identified from selected contexts. The charcoal was randomly selected and fractured to produce transverse, transverse longitudinal and radial longitudinal sections to allow the wood anatomy to be examined using a Leica DMR microscope with incident light source and magnification up to ×200. Identification was by reference to images and descriptions of wood anatomy (*e.g.* Schweingruber 1978; Gale and Cutler 2000; Schoch *et al.* 2004). The results are presented in Table 5.6 and discussed within the main text as well as separately at the end.

Results

The assemblage as a whole is dominated by hazelnut shell fragments whilst cereal grain forms a small but significant element; weed seeds and other seeds occur in small amounts, and chaff and flax are scarce (Tables 5.1–5.5). A slightly higher percentage of cereal and a lower percentage of hazelnut shell occurs in the features. Weed seeds are slightly more frequent in buried soil 202 and soil layer 95, whilst other seeds, namely fruitstones, are more frequent in buried soil 30, and flax is present in buried soil 30 and possibly soil layer 95.

Wheat dominates the cereal assemblage, notably emmer wheat (*Triticum dicoccum*). Several of the emmer grains displayed characteristics typical of those from a single-grained, terminal spikelet, including a curved ventral face and somewhat rounded apex but one or two grains had a slightly more attenuated apex and were allocated to an einkorn/emmer (*T. monococcum*/*T. dicoccum*) category. However, the only spikelet forks, which were rare, were of emmer wheat, which tends to suggest the einkorn/emmer grains are more likely to be emmer. Other wheat grains were also assigned to broader categories, including one grain that had a slightly 'bullet'-shaped appearance and was assigned to wheat/rye (*Triticum*/*Secale cereale*) whilst others were assigned to emmer/spelt (*T. dicoccum*/*T. spelta*) and indeterminate wheat (*Triticum* sp.). Barley (*Hordeum vulgare*) occurred occasionally and included a few hulled grains but generally it was not possible to be certain whether the grain was hulled or naked, straight or twisted. A possible oat (*Avena* sp.) grain was also present. Much of the grain was poorly preserved and fragmented and assigned to an indeterminate cereal category. Total numbers of indeterminate grains were estimated based on whole and fragments of grains, the latter including smaller fragments as well as half grains and so on. Hazelnut shell fragments were weighed as well as counted.

Even though frequencies of charred plant remains are generally quite low, there is some variation in the spatial distribution, both horizontally and vertically, of charred plant remains at the site. The distribution of cereal and hazelnut shell is shown in Figures 5.5–5.9. The values used for the soil layers are based on actual counts for cereal and weights rather than number of fragments (the latter being particularly misleading where there is a high degree of fragmentation) for hazelnut shell rather than densities/litre as, unfortunately, the sample volumes processed were not recorded. However, the total volumes were roughly estimated for the whole of the grid squares, but not the individual spits, of buried soils 30 and 202 and soil layer 95, though the last is problematical as it included a later pit (see below), and the density of grain calculated (unpublished data). The estimated densities were low with average densities of 1–2 grains/litre and with the majority of sample squares with either less than 1 grain/litre or 1–2 grains/litre. The estimated grain density spatial distributions were largely in agreement with the spatial distributions based on the raw count data.

The low concentration of cereal is in keeping with results from many sites in Ireland (McClatchie 2014) and elsewhere in Britain, as well as Europe, where sites with

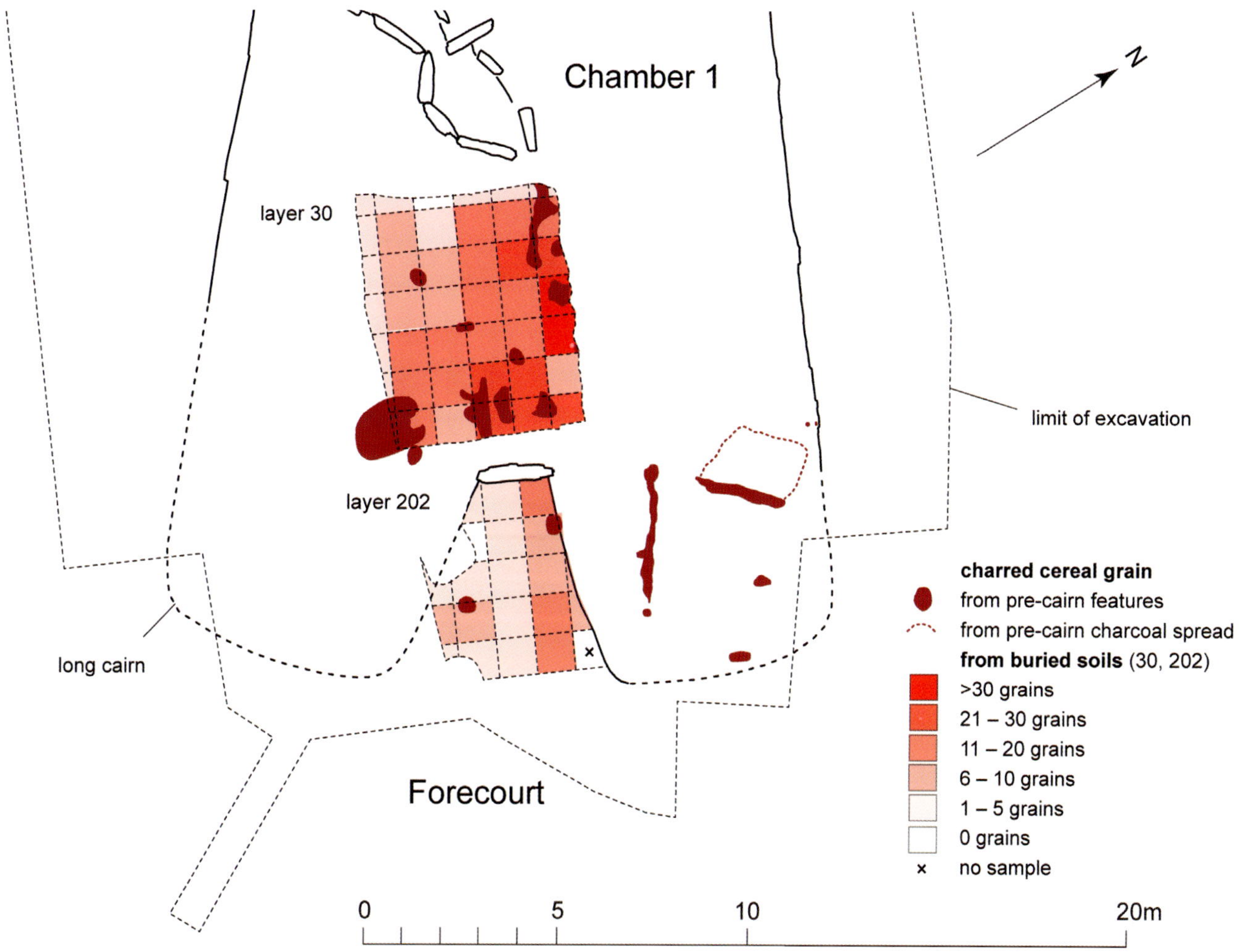

Fig. 5.5. Gwernvale: distribution of charred cereal grains in pre-cairn features, the buried soil below the long cairn (30) and in the lower soil layer (202) in the forecourt area.

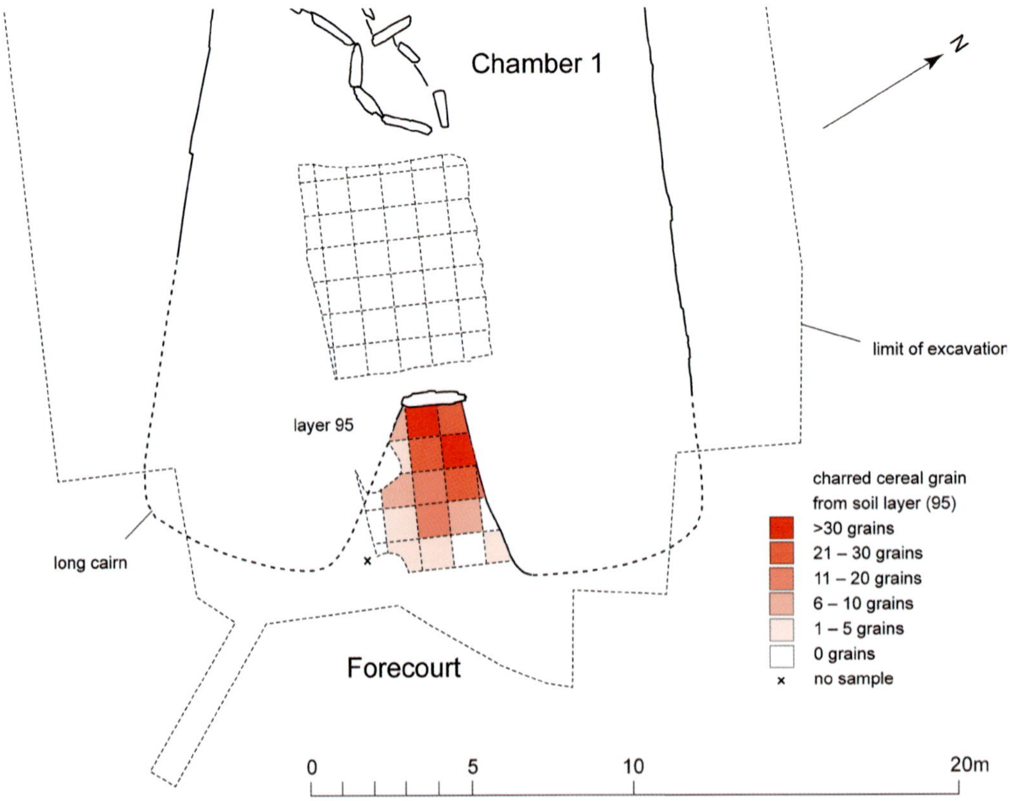

Fig. 5.6. Gwernvale: distribution of charred cereal grains in the upper soil layer (95) in the forecourt area.

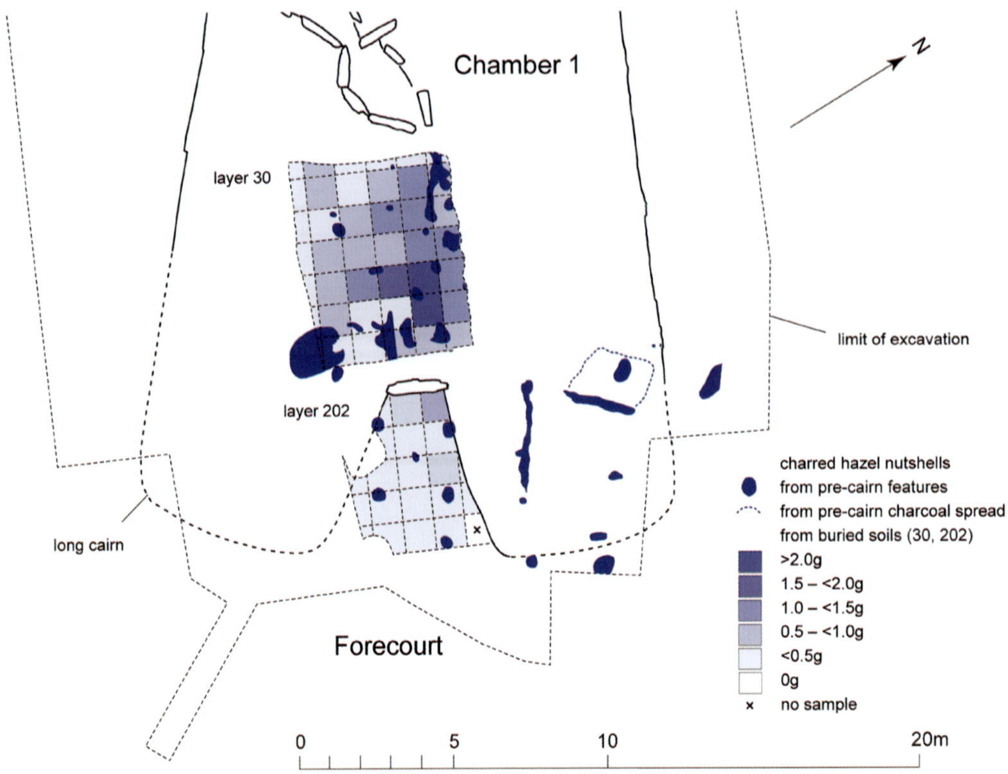

Fig. 5.7. Gwernvale: distribution of charred hazel nutshells in pre-cairn features, the buried soil below the long cairn (30) and in the lower soil layer (202) in the forecourt area.

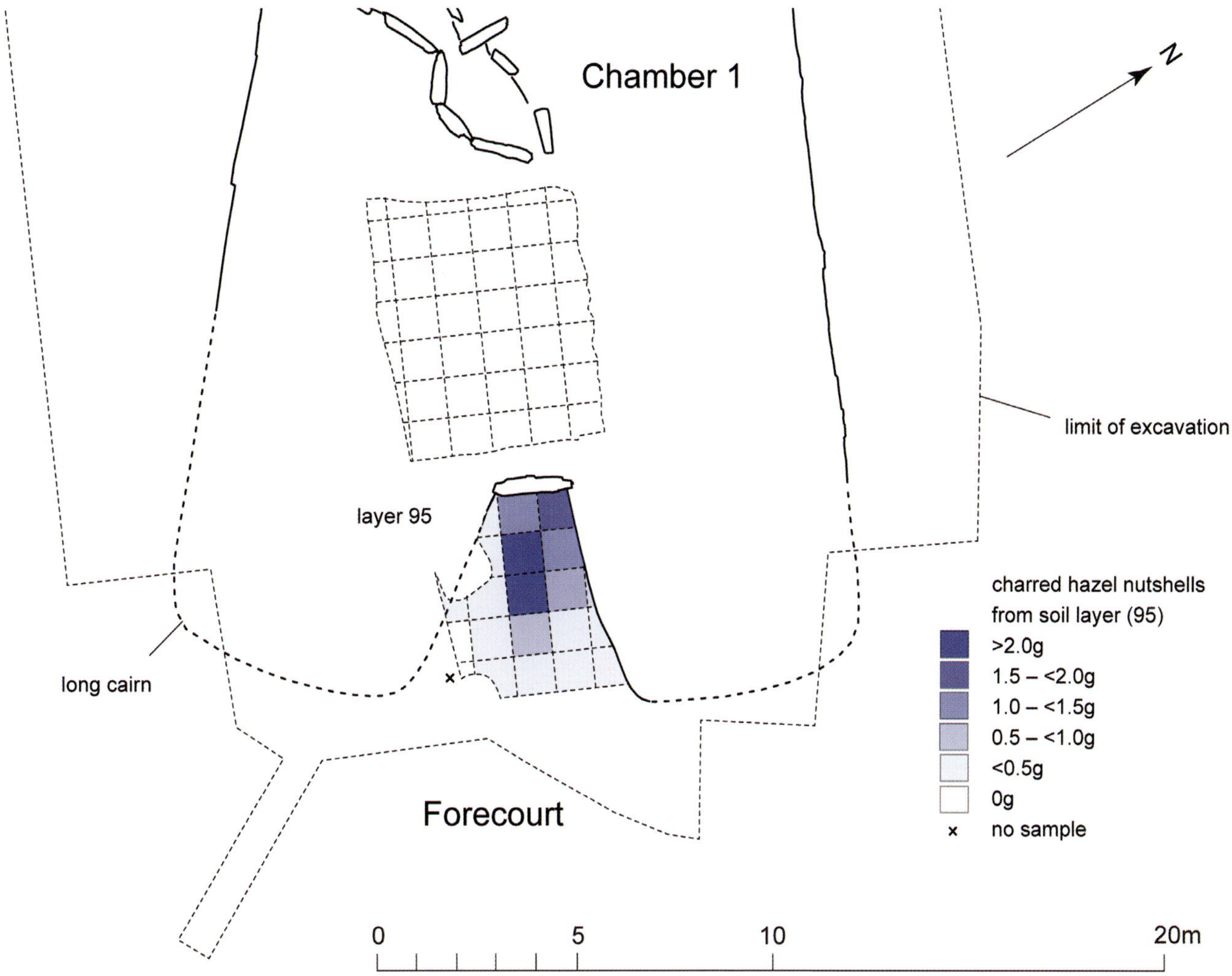

Fig. 5.8. Gwernvale: distribution of charred hazel nutshells in the upper soil layer (95) in the forecourt area (95).

large-scale sampling have resulted in an abundant number of low-density samples (Bogaard and Jones 2007). Although the Gwernvale cereal is scattered in relatively low amounts within the buried soils and soil layer, overall the assemblage as a whole comprises several hundred grains, supporting the case for extensive sampling strategies.

Posterior density estimates in this chapter are given at 95% probability unless otherwise stated (see Chapter 4).

Pre-cairn features

Samples from pre-cairn features included features associated with the house structure and midden below the E end of the cairn, below the W end of the cairn and to the NW of the cairn (Figs 5.2, 5.4, 5.5 and 5.7; Table 5.1).

Features associated with house

Originally some of the pre-cairn features were interpreted as a separate rectilinear timber structure whilst others were regarded as part of a separate six-post structure, though it was also acknowledged that the features could form part of the same structure (Britnell 1984b). It is now suggested that the latter view – that the features represent one larger house structure in which different construction techniques were used – is more likely (see Chapter 3).

Although none of the features associated with the structure contained large amounts of charred plant remains, there was some variation in the frequency and nature of the remains from different parts of the structure. Hence cereal remains from samples from the wall-line trenches (133B, 133D, 229) and associated postholes (133A, 133C, 133E, 133G) in the area below the N horn of the cairn were generally relatively rich in cereal grain, mainly wheat, including emmer wheat and emmer/spelt, as well as barley and indeterminate cereal, most of the latter fragmented, notably in wall-line trench 229. Hazelnut shell fragments were also present and comparatively frequent in samples 133B and 229 whilst other remains were scarce but included a seed of hairy vetch (*Vicia hirsuta*) and a grass (Poaceae) seed and grass culm/rhizome fragments. The pre-cairn activity began in *3920–3705 cal BC* (*95% probability*; *first_Gwernvale_pre_cairn*;

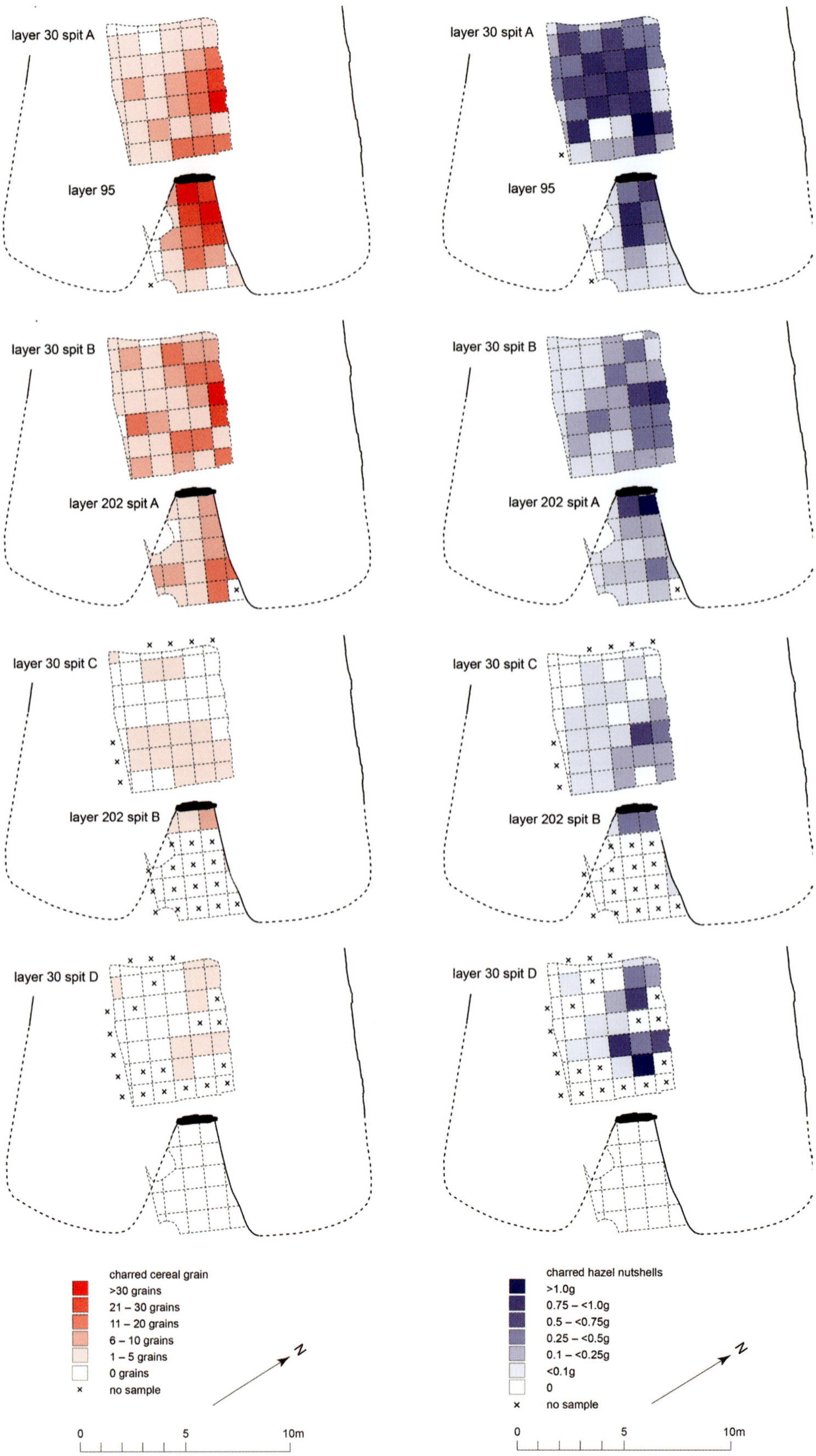

Fig. 5.9. Gwernvale: vertical distribution of charred cereal grains and charred hazel nutshells in various spits in the buried soil below the long cairn and in the forecourt area.

Fig. 4.4) and stopped in *3605–3495 cal BC* (*93% probability*; *last_Gwernvale_pre_cairn*; Fig. 4.4).

Elsewhere below the N horn of the cairn, in contrast, no charred seeds were retrieved from a slight gully (227), which may have formed part of a wall-line nor from another small gully (226A) though cereal grain, including emmer wheat, hazelnut shell and a fruitstone of raspberry/blackberry (*Rubus* sp.) were present in an adjacent possible posthole (226). A small amount of cereal, including emmer wheat, and hazelnut shell was recovered from another gully (223), whereas cereal was absent from two other possible postholes (221, 228) but hazelnut shell and a possible vetch (cf. *Vicia* sp.) seed and an immature seed capsule were present.

The remaining evidence was from postholes lying within the forecourt area, where posts were the main construction technique used. Cereal was absent from three postholes (207, 209, 210) but present in postholes 208 and 211 and included emmer wheat and indeterminate cereal. All five postholes contained hazelnut shell and other remains included possible wall barley (*Hordeum murinum*) type, cleavers (*Galium aparine*), knotgrass (*Polygonum* sp.), vetch and a cereal/grass culm node. In three instances (208B, 210B, 211B), plant remains were slightly more frequent in the post-pipes than the post-packing and are likely to have been deposited after the posts decayed, although they may be contemporary with the use of the building. This is consistent with the pottery evidence (see Chapter 3), which also suggests the movement of sherds after the building decayed. Two other possible postholes (205, 206) produced only a few remains, namely hazelnut shell fragments and wheat from 206 and only an indeterminate seed from 205. Other features in the area of the house in the forecourt area included a shallow scoop (271), which produced only a hazelnut shell fragment and two stakeholes (273–274), which failed to produce anything, apart from wood charcoal.

Charred plant remains from other features below the N horn of the cairn outside the house include hazelnut shell fragments and blackberry (*Rubus fruticosus* agg.) from pit 231 and nettle (*Urtica dioica*) from pit 234. Hazelnut shell was also recovered from burnt area 249 near to wall-line 229 and from stakeholes 235–236, as well as cereal grain, including emmer wheat from the burnt area. The posterior density estimate for the cereal grain from burnt area 249 indicates the presence of cereals at the site in *3635–3510 cal BC* (*95% probability*; *SUERC-75859*; Fig. 4.4).

Overall, there seems to be a slight difference in the distribution of charred plant remains within the structure. Although hazelnut shell fragments occurred throughout the building, there was more cereal from the features below the N horn of the cairn than elsewhere. This might be partly attributable to the nature of the features sampled in the former area, cereal being quite frequent from the wall-lines (133, 229), but all the postholes also produced cereal compared with only three of the eight postholes and possible postholes in the forecourt area of the structure. As noted in Chapter 3, soil profiles had been largely truncated in the area below the N horn of the cairn and consequently there was no opportunity to identify original floor levels in this area. Equally, cereal was absent from other possible postholes (221, 228) towards the NE end of the house, though was present in a gully. Weed seeds, although scarce, occurred more commonly in the postholes in the forecourt area and a quern fragment was also recovered from one of the postholes.

Features in the midden area

A number of other features underlay the cairn in the midden area, including gullies, pits and scoops. In general, the assemblages consisted of hazelnut shell fragments, small amounts of cereal, including emmer, and occasional other plant remains. Of the four gullies (142, 149, 167, 169), hazelnut shell and cereal grain were most plentiful in gully 167, which contained both grain and a spikelet fork of emmer wheat. The radiocarbon measurement from emmer wheat from this feature indicates its presence in *3640–3530 cal BC* (*95% probability*; *SUERC-75857*; Fig. 4.4). Other remains from the gullies included an immature seed capsule in 149.

The pit samples that produced the most remains, mainly hazelnut shell and cereal, were two pits, 150 and 162, either side of a large weathered boulder. Wheat, including emmer wheat, was present in both and possible barley in pit 162. Other remains included cleavers, docks (*Rumex* sp.), wild radish (*Raphanus raphanistrum*) from pit 150 and a fruitstone of raspberry/blackberry from pit 162. Plant remains from another pit (170), also associated with a boulder, included cereal, hazelnut shell, blackberry, possible bedstraw (*Galium* sp.) and buds, whereas no remains, apart from wood charcoal, were recovered from pit 160.

Charred plant remains from a number of scoops (143, 144, 145, 146, 147, 151, 157, 158, 159, 163, 168) were limited largely to hazelnut shell with occasional grains of cereal in some, including emmer wheat, as well as blackberry in scoop 157. Plant remains other than wood charcoal were absent in scoops 148 and 152/3. A measurement on unidentified bulk charcoal from oval pit 68, further to the west under the cairn, may provide a *terminus post quem* for this feature of *3480–2650 cal BC* (*CAR-113*; Fig. 4.4).

Features below W end of the cairn

Charred plant remains from irregular pits/hollows (278, 295, 297) and possible burnt tree roots (291–294) beneath the cairn at the western end comprised hazelnut shell and an immature seed capsule from irregular/pit/hollow (295) and a possible mustard/charlock (*Brassica*/*Sinapis* sp.) seed and possible vetch seed from irregular pit/hollow 278.

Features to NW side of the cairn

Hazelnut shell and indeterminate cereal were recovered from a stony surface (309) sealed below collapsed cairn material on the northern side of the cairn and either contemporary with the use of the cairn or earlier than it. An irregular gully (317) pre-dating the cairn produced only a few hazelnut shell fragments and only an indeterminate seed occurred in hearth 308.

Soil layers below and adjacent to the cairn

Midden (30) below long cairn

The midden is interpreted as an area of buried soil containing a concentration of occupation material rather than a distinct physical entity (see Chapter 3). As previously mentioned, the buried soil in this area was excavated in spits (A–D) and sampled accordingly (Figs 5.5–5.9; Table 5.2). Examination of the buried soils at the midden area indicated considerable evidence of human disturbance (Keeley 1978; 1980), which was also suggested by the distribution of the artefacts in this area (see Chapter 3). Samples from the different spits were examined separately to see if the plant assemblages from the different levels, as well as radiocarbon dates from selected plant remains, provided any evidence to indicate whether any residual stratification was discernible within the midden (though for economy of space the results from different spits are not presented in Table 5.2). Hazelnut shell, as well as cereal grain, was dated to ascertain if both Mesolithic and Neolithic hazelnut shell was present in the assemblages.

Hazelnut shell fragments dominated the assemblage from the midden buried soil (30) as a whole, followed by cereal and small amounts of weed seeds, fruitstones and flax seeds. Most of the cereal was indeterminate with the remainder largely wheat, including emmer, einkorn/emmer and emmer/spelt. Barley was also present whilst chaff, namely emmer spikelet forks, was very rare and weed seeds occurred occasionally.

Some variation in the spatial distribution of the remains, both vertically and horizontally, is evident, though the radiocarbon dates confirm that some remains are residual and that some mixing of remains in the soil profile had occurred. The largest amounts of cereal from the buried soil (30) as a whole occurred in squares 19 and 25 (Figs 5.3 and 5.5; Table 5.2) to the north of the 'natural monolith' (Fig. 3.4), though in both instances much of it was indeterminate cereal. Hazelnut shell was concentrated in squares 26 and 32 (Figs 5.3, 5.7), and to a lesser extent 27, between the 'natural monolith' and a large natural boulder. However, the area of excavation was limited and it is possible that excavation of a larger area would have produced different results.

At the lowest spit level, D, fewer squares were sampled and cereal grain, including emmer wheat, was scarce but hazelnut shell was relatively frequent in several squares, particularly square 32 followed by squares 14, 25 and 27 (Figs 5.3 and 5.9). Hazelnut shell from square 27 produced an estimate of *3715–3635 cal BC* (*94% probability*; *SUERC-85600*; Fig. 4.4), whilst an estimate of *3630–3555 cal BC* (*93% probability*; *SUERC-85599*; Fig. 4.4) was obtained from wheat from spit D from square 14, which tends to confirm disturbance and mixing of the buried soil.

Blackberry/raspberry occurred in several squares whilst other seeds were rare but included possible ribwort plantain (cf. *Plantago lanceolata*), possible mint (cf. *Mentha* sp.) and possible daisy family (cf. Asteraceae). Other remains included a thorn and a grass/cereal rhizome fragment. Overall, charred plant remains were most frequent in squares in the area of the 'natural monolith' and a large natural weathered boulder. Cereal, much of it indeterminate and again including emmer wheat, hazelnut shell, weed seeds and fruitstone were all scarce in spit C though hazelnut shell again tended to be more frequent in squares in the area around the 'natural monolith' and a large natural boulder, particularly square 26. Other remains included blackberry, equal-leaved knotgrass (*Polygonum arenastrum*), rose (*Rosa* sp.) and bedstraw (*Galium* sp.).

In contrast to the lower two levels there was a marked increase in the quantity of charred plant remains present in spit B, especially cereal, with the greatest quantities in squares 19 and 25, though most of this was indeterminate cereal and fragmented. Most of the identifiable cereal grain was wheat, including emmer, but barley, including hulled, as well as a spikelet fork of emmer wheat were present. Wheat from square 25 gave a date of *3625–3510 cal BC* (*95% probability*; *SUERC-85562*; Fig. 4.4). Hazelnut shell was also more abundant in square 19 and, to a lesser extent, square 20, whilst hazelnut shell from square 25 produced a calibrated radiocarbon date of 7770–7595 cal BC (95% confidence; SUERC-85563; Fig. 4.4), confirming that some of the hazelnut shell was residual and again that mixing of the buried soil had occurred. This result has been included as an outlier in the model presented in Chapter 4. Flax, possibly cultivated flax (*Linum* cf. *usitatissimum*), was also present at this level, whilst other plants, though scarce were also more common than in the lower spits. The most frequently occurring was blackberry/raspberry but other taxa included rose, cleavers, grass, deadly nightshade (*Atropa belladonna*), vetch, docks, small water-pepper (*Persicaria minor*), equal-leaved knotgrass, stitchworts (*Stellaria* sp.), common chickweed (*Stellaria media*), fat-hen (*Chenopodium album*), possible mint (cf. *Mentha* sp.), woundworts (*Stachys* sp.), possible hawthorn (cf. *Crataegus* sp.), possible violet (cf. *Viola* sp.), and grasses. Grass remains included a possible culm node and rhizome fragment whilst other remains included a tree leaf bud and immature seed capsules and indeterminate vesicular plant material.

Charred plant remains were also frequent in spit A. Cereal was again most abundant in squares 19 and 25 and again much of the grain was indeterminable and fragmented.

Essentially there was the same range of taxa with wheat dominating, notably emmer, and a few grains of barley including hulled. Flax was also present. The hazelnut shell was generally more frequent than in the previous spits, with larger quantities more widely distributed, most notably in squares 14, 16, 21, 26, 28, 32 and 35. There was a similar range of other plants to those in spit B with blackberry/raspberry the most frequent. Other taxa included docks, equal-leaved knotgrass, rose, mouse-ear (*Cerastium*) type, common chickweed, stitchworts, violets, vetches, deadnettle family (Lamiaceae), cleavers, bedstraw and grasses. Other remains included a catkin fragment, probably of hazel (*Corylus avellana*) as well as grass culm/rhizome fragments and immature seed capsules.

Lower soil layer (202) in forecourt

Charred plant remains were relatively scarce in the buried soil (202) in the forecourt area (Figs 5.5, 5.7 and 5.9; Table 5.3). Although it was dug in two spits, A and B, only five samples were from the lower level. Cereal, largely indeterminate but also including emmer wheat and hulled barley, occurred in four of the five sample squares and emmer wheat from square 3 was dated to *3770–3645 cal BC* (*95% probability*; *SUERC-85560*; Fig. 4.4). Hazelnut shell was present in all the squares and most frequent in squares 2 and 3. Other remains included a possible lesser celandine (*Ranunculus ficaria*) tuber, a possible fragment of acorn cupule and leaf bud.

In spit A there was a thin scatter of cereal across most of the area, mainly indeterminate or wheat dominated by emmer, as well as one or two grains of barley, a possible oat grain and a grain assigned to a wheat/rye (*Triticum*/*Secale cereale*) category. The greatest amounts of cereal, but still at a relatively low level, occurred in squares 14, 15 and 17. Hazelnut shell, as in spit B, was most frequent in squares 2 and 3, especially the last. Other charred plant remains were generally scarce but seeds of cleavers were present in a number of squares, whilst other taxa including raspberry/blackberry, buttercup (*Ranunculus* sp.), clustered dock/wood dock, small water pepper, common chickweed, ribwort plantain and grass occurred occasionally. Grass culm/rhizome fragments occurred in several squares, notably 15/15A.

Upper soil layer (95) in forecourt

Charred plant remains were more abundant from the upper soil layer (95) in the forecourt area compared with the buried soil (202) (Figs 5.6, 5.8 and 5.9; Table 5.4). Cereal was richest in squares 2, 3, 5, 6 and 9, whilst the greatest quantities of hazelnut shell occurred in squares 3, 5 and 8, especially the latter two. A later pit had been dug in the area of squares 8 and 12 and because of some uncertainties as to whether certain samples were from the pit or the soil layer the results have been combined from all the samples within each square. From the similarity of the assemblages, it is thought that the remains from the pit samples were largely residual material from the upper layer, though there is a possibility that there could be later material present and the results should be treated with caution. A radiocarbon date of *3635–3505 cal BC* (*95% probability*; *SUERC-85561*; Fig. 4.4) was obtained from emmer wheat from square 3, suggesting an early Neolithic date for soil layer 95, though the presence of later material cannot be totally ruled out. Much of the cereal in the richest samples was indeterminable and fragmented whilst the cereal determinable to genus or species was dominated by wheat, notably emmer wheat. Barley was rare and also present were two possible seeds of flax. Other seeds in the assemblage included buttercup, common chickweed, equal-leaved knotgrass, docks, vetches, raspberry/blackberry, greater plantain (*Plantago major*), possible dead-nettle family (cf. Lamiaceae), grasses and, most frequently, cleavers. Grass stems/rhizomes were also present as was the occasional thorn and indeterminate vesicular plant material.

Soil layer (239) on NW side of cairn

The buried soil on the north side of the cairn (Table 5.5) yielded only a small amount of hazelnut shell, a trace of indeterminate cereal, cereal/grass rhizomes and a possible culm node, a stitchwort seed and a raspberry/blackberry fruitstone, suggesting this area was on the periphery of the main activity.

Soil layers in Chambers 2–3

Very few remains were recovered from the soil horizons in the cairn chambers that were continuous with the buried soils elsewhere beneath the cairn (Table 5.5). Plant remains from soil 128 in Chamber 2 comprised a grain of barley and a small quantity of hazelnut shell fragments. Indeterminate cereal and a few hazelnut shell fragments were recovered from 122 in Chamber 3. The remains are probably contemporary with pre-cairn activity rather than with use of the chambers.

Discussion

Early Neolithic activity

The charred plant assemblage, comprising both cereal and wild plant foods, notably hazelnuts, is typical of early Neolithic assemblages from Wales and elsewhere in Great Britain and Ireland (Moffett *et al.* 1989; G. Jones 2000; M. Robinson 2000; Bishop *et al.* 2009; McClatchie 2014; 2016; Treasure *et al.* 2019; Rowley-Conwy *et al.* 2020), and suggests that the community at Gwernvale was engaged in the cultivation of cereal but also continued to gather wild plant foodstuffs. Of particular note is the emmer wheat grain date of *3885–3705 cal BC* (*93% probability*; *SUERC-75856*; Fig. 4.4) from wall-line trench 133D, which is earlier than any of the other cereal dates from Gwernvale and currently from other early Neolithic sites in Wales such as Parc Cybi (Kenney 2021), Parc Bryn Cegin (Kenney 2008) and sites associated with the South Wales Gas Pipeline (Darvill *et al.* 2020) (Fig. 5.10). Modelling of radiocarbon measurements produced directly on cereal and other domesticated plant remains from Britain and Ireland has suggested they mostly do not appear before the 38th century cal BC but this is dependent on the sample radiocarbon measurements representing the earliest appearance of cereals and, in addition, the shape of the calibration curve, which may also contribute to this impression (Griffiths 2018). A date of 3970–3770 cal BC (SUERC-10772) from Holbeck Park, Cumbria, similar to that from Gwernvale, may also be earlier than other direct early cereal measurements from Britain (Griffiths 2018; and see Chapter 4).

The dates from Gwernvale also suggest that pre-cairn occupation at Gwernvale occurred around the same time that the cairn at Penywyrlod was constructed and in use, whilst a small amount of wheat that was recovered from a burnt area below cairn collapse at Penywyrlod (see Chapter 2) provides further evidence for cereal cultivation in the region. Most of the evidence for activity from charred plant remains at Gwernvale is associated with the house structure and midden area at the east end of the long cairn. Only limited evidence, mainly hazelnut shell, occurred at the west end and on the northern side of the cairn while that from the chambers also probably relates to pre-cairn activity.

Plant remains associated with the pre-cairn house

In order for cereal or other plant remains to be preserved in a charred state, they have to come into contact with fire. Hence charred cereal assemblages are only likely to occur when a building storing grain has burnt down, when accidents during food preparation have occurred or when waste has been deliberately burnt. The remains may be *in situ* or redeposited, either deliberately or accidentally. The distribution, frequency and nature of the remains may therefore give some indication of activities at a site.

In the case of Gwernvale the relatively low concentration of cereal remains from within the building features suggest accidental charring and general waste from domestic fires incidentally becoming incorporated in deposits rather than grain storage. An early date of *3885–3705 cal BC* (*93% probability*; *SUERC-75856*; Fig. 4.4) for one of the cereal grains suggests some of the cereal grain may be residual and perhaps indicates the inclusion of earlier deposits in the wall-line (133). Slightly higher amounts of cereal, much of it

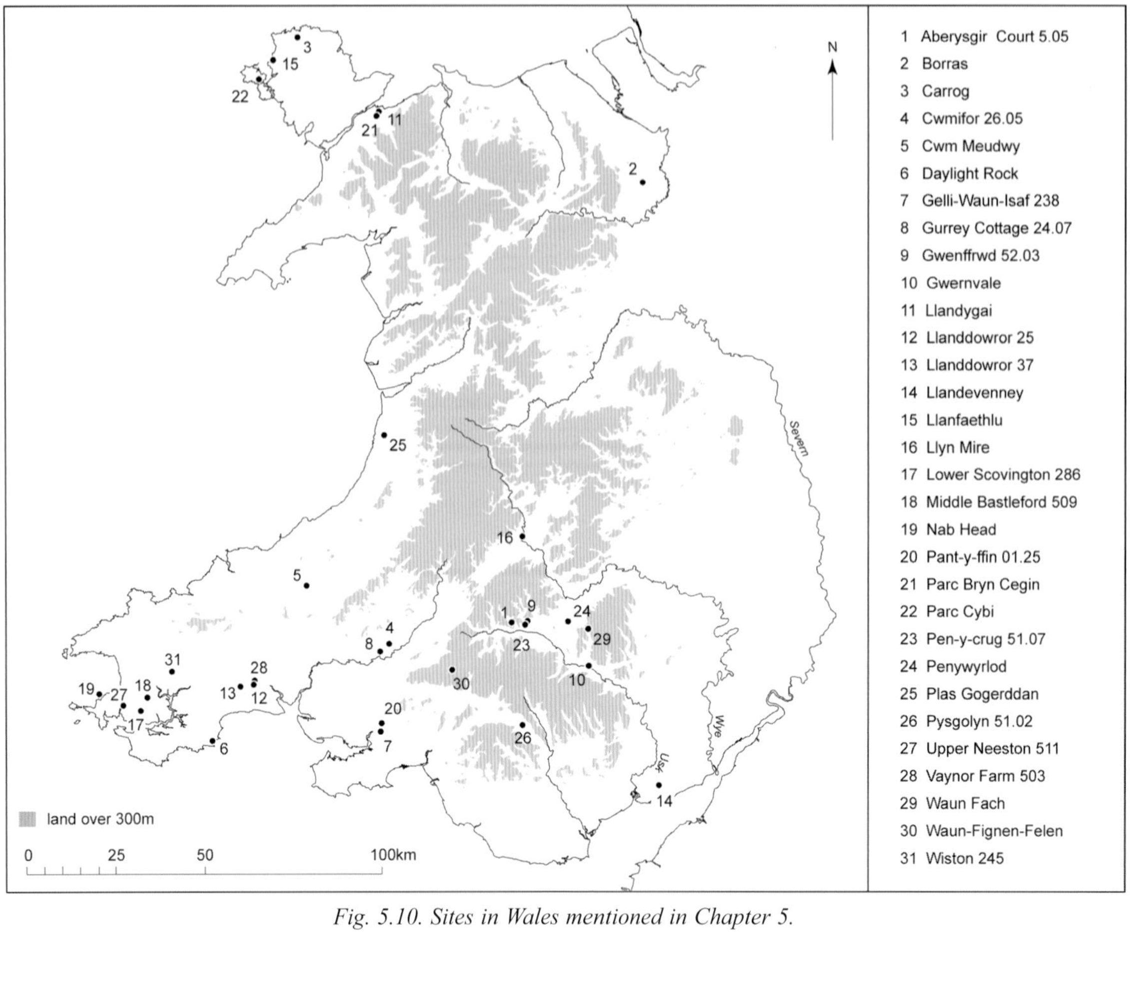

Fig. 5.10. Sites in Wales mentioned in Chapter 5.

fragmented, possibly reflecting trampling, from the wall-line trenches and associated postholes of the building compared with the other postholes might relate to cooking activity in that area, either within the building or nearby outside, but also might be at least partially related to the type of feature sampled. The low occurrence of cereal grain in general in the post-hole fills from Gwernvale is typical of that from many other Neolithic sites with buildings both in Britain and LBK sites in central Europe (Bogaard and Jones 2007).

The buried soils in the forecourt area and their relationship with the building structure are open to debate. Within the building in the forecourt area the frequency of remains in the lower soil layer 202 and upper soil layer 95 is also generally low, although higher in soil layer 95. Dates from buried soil 202B and soil layer 95 are comparable with those from the midden and house features, suggesting they are contemporary, but it is possible that soil layer 95 might represent a later soil accumulation contemporary with the forecourt. Furthermore, interpretation of the soils in this area is complicated by disturbance caused by the later building activity associated with the cairn and by a later pit in the forecourt area. The charred plant remains in soil layer 202 in the forecourt area could be contemporary with the building or even include earlier remains, as indicated in the midden area by the 8th millennium result (SUERC-85563) on hazelnut shell. Equally, the presence of oat and wheat/rye could be intrusive and reflect later activity. It is also possible that charred plant remains were either trampled into the soil as a result of activities either within the house or brought in from the adjacent midden area, either of which may account for the possible flax in soil layer 95. In the reinterpretation presented in Chapter 3 it is suggested that the position of the portal stone may mark the former position of where a door to the house giving access to the midden may have been and remains, particularly in the upper soil layer 95, tend to be more frequent in this area of the forecourt. The charred plant assemblage from the upper soil layer 95 may represent the upper level of the buried soil and a floor layer/occupation layer contemporary with the timber structure but it could also incorporate or represent later material associated with activity from around the time of tomb construction or even later. Although charred plant remains are more frequent towards the portal stone, to what extent this is a true reflection of the distribution of the remains is uncertain because of the limits of the excavation and the absence of samples from floor layers/buried soils in the area below the N horn of the cairn with which to draw comparisons or any firm conclusions with regard to activity areas within the house structure itself. The relatively high levels of poorly preserved indeterminate cereal may also reflect weathering and exposure as well as trampling activity associated either with the cairn construction or activity within the house.

The occurrence of cleavers in the soils in the forecourt area of the building, especially soil layer 95, may indicate the final stages of crop processing. Along with other weed seeds this may reflect waste from hearths, but cleavers and other weed seeds, as well as raspberry/blackberry fruitstones, grass rhizomes, a lesser celandine tuber and indeterminate vesicular plant material, could reflect burning of grassland and scrub growing locally prior to construction of the house or reflect burning after a period of abandonment prior to construction of the cairn, or both.

Although it is difficult to draw any firm conclusions with regard to activity areas within the house structure itself, fragments of quern stone in a posthole and from the surface of the soil layer in the posthole/forecourt area, and other quern fragments elsewhere at the site, including the midden buried soil, indicate food preparation (see Chapter 2 and Britnell 1984b, 132–5).

Comparison with cereals in other early Neolithic buildings

There are comparatively few early Neolithic houses or possible houses in Wales with charred plant remains with which to compare the evidence from Gwernvale. In north Wales only hazelnut shell was recorded from Llandygai (Lynch and Musson 2001) though the evidence from Parc Bryn Cegin, Llandygai (Kenney 2008), where an extensive sampling programme was also undertaken, although scarcer is not dissimilar to that from Gwernvale, namely large numbers of hazelnut shell fragments, low amounts of cereal, largely emmer wheat, and rare chaff and weed seeds. In contrast, although at Parc Cybi (Kenney 2021, 45) charred plant remains were also generally scarce, both abundant hazelnut shell and indeterminate charred cereal grains, along with fragments of chaff, including spikelet forks and glume bases, occurred in the upper part of a hearth and frequent hazelnut shell as well as indeterminate charred cereal grains and chaff occurred in a posthole. At Llanfaethlu, the first recorded multi-house settlement in Wales, hazelnuts and other seeds have been recovered (Rees and Jones 2015; 2017).

In south Wales three sites with possible house structures, associated with the South Wales Gas Pipeline, have also yielded charred plant remains. At Site 26.05 Cwmifor, Carmarthenshire (Hart 2014), where there was a possible structure, the postholes produced only low amounts of cereal whereas a group of pits were richer and produced emmer wheat and chaff as well a few grains of barley and abundant hazelnut shell reflecting domestic waste or possibly closure deposits. Similarly at Pen-y-Crug, Yscir, Powys (Site 51.07) (Hart and Leonard 2014), the density of hazelnut shell fragments and cereal grain from the postholes of the possible building was markedly lower than from the pits, whilst less than a kilometre to the north-east a large assemblage of cereal and hazelnut shell was recovered from another possible settlement, Gwenffrwd, Llandefaelog

(Site 52.03) (Brannlund 2014), where there were pits, postholes and gully.

Another site where postholes have tentatively been interpreted as possibly a small rectangular structure is Site 37 near Llanddowror on the St Clears to Red Roses Road Improvement route in Carmarthenshire (Barber *et al.* 2019). Postholes failed to produce any charred plant evidence, whereas again pits contained substantial amounts of midden waste and were interpreted as domestic waste, structured deposition or closure deposits (Cobain 2019).

Varying amounts of charred cereal grain and hazelnut fragments, largely the latter, as well as other remains have been recovered from a number of other sites with pits, whether interpreted as settlement or ceremonial sites, and include several connected with the South Wales Gas Pipeline including the pit cluster at Wiston, Pembrokeshire (Site 245) (Hart and Busby 2014) where remains have been interpreted as representing the later stages of food processing and food preparation. Other pipeline sites include Gelli-wern-Isaf, Mynydd Pysgodlyn, Swansea (Site 238) (Sausins 2013), Pant-y-ffin, Mynydd Pysgodlyn (Site 01.25) (Leonard 2014a), Pysgodlyn Farm, Yscir, Powys (Site 51.02) (Busby 2013) and Gurrey Cottage (Site 24.07) (Hart 2013), whilst elsewhere a pit at Plas Gogerddan, Ceredigion (Caseldine 1992), contained a noticeable amount of cereal as well other remains but shallow pits at Carrog, Anglesey (Caseldine *et al.* 2014), were dominated by hazelnut shell.

Evidence from pits at Gwernvale is generally scarce, the most being from two shallow pits (150, 162) either side of a natural boulder in the midden area. They were possibly dug during construction of the cairn in an attempt to remove the boulder and the charred plant remains are probably derived from the midden deposit below the cairn, which is quite rich in plant remains in this area, rather than deliberately deposited. Similarly, the plant remains from other features, such as scoops and gullies, in the midden area may be derived from the buried soil.

Elsewhere in Britain and Ireland there is charred plant remains evidence from a number of house sites but at others little or no evidence, for example at Yarnton where, though there was close to 100% flotation, no cereal was recovered (Hey *et al.* 2016). In contrast to the evidence from the building at Gwernvale there are several early Neolithic house sites where rich grain assemblages, mainly emmer, have been found, notably the timber hall at Balbridie in Scotland (Fairweather and Ralston 1993) where an exceptionally rich assemblage of cleaned grain was recovered but, as at Gwernvale, cereal processing by-products were lacking. However, at Lismore Fields, Buxton, whereas from one building the remains appeared to represent the remnants of fully processed emmer and grain storage, the dominance of glume bases in deposits in another building clearly indicated the processing of emmer and represented either dehusking activity or chaff storage (Jones and Bogaard 2017). Yet a third building yielded little evidence of charred plant remains and the three buildings clearly indicate different uses and a more extensive excavation at Gwernvale might have led to other buildings and different results.

Significant cereal assemblages have also been recorded from a few early Neolithic sites in Ireland including rectangular houses at Tankardstown South (Gowen and Tarbett 1989; 1990; Monk 1988; 2000), whilst concentrations of crop-processing waste in House 3 at Corbally suggested it may have had a specific function; cereal grain and crop processing waste in a particular area of House 5 and in the area outside might indicate an area of crop processing activity (Purcell 2002; Smyth 2014). At both Balleygalley and Tankardstown South fragmented grain from wall-slots and post-pit fills, respectively, has been interpreted as the result of trampling and brushing of floor surfaces (Simpson 1996; Monk 2000), and trampling may account for some of the fragmented cereal at Gwernvale.

Plant remains from the midden

The occurrence of charred plant remains, largely cereal grain and hazelnut shell fragments, along with other occupation material, in the midden buried soil suggests a distinct activity area during the early Neolithic, as well as at times during the Mesolithic. Although the concentration of plant remains is generally low, reflecting general waste from hearths, the greatest quantities of charred plant remains are broadly from the area around the 'natural monolith' and a natural weathered boulder (Figs 5.5 and 5.7), suggesting a focus of activity. Much of the cereal, as well as the hazelnut shell, is fragmented, perhaps a result of trampling. However, the area excavated was limited and larger, undiscovered, concentrations might occur elsewhere, though the low occurrence of charred plant remains, mainly hazelnut shell, in the buried soil on the northern side of the cairn and from features at the western end does emphasise the concentration of remains in the midden buried soil and in the soils in the house/forecourt area at the eastern end of the cairn.

Low amounts of charred plant remains in the lower levels and an increase in charred plant remains in the upper levels of the midden soil could indicate an expansion in activity associated with occupation of the house and a date of *3715–3635 cal BC* (*95% probability*; *SUERC-85600*; Fig. 4.4) was obtained from spit D whilst a date of *3625–3510 cal BC* (*95% probability*; *SUERC-85562*) was obtained from spit B. However, a date of *3630–3555 cal BC* (*93% probability*; *SUERC-85599*; Fig. 4.4) was also obtained from spit D suggesting mixing and that the vertical distribution largely reflects taphonomic processes. Nevertheless, a date of *3885–3705 cal BC* (*93% probability*; *SUERC-75856*; Fig. 4.4) from emmer grain from the structure does suggest an earlier low level of Neolithic activity at the site, whilst an 8th millennium date of 7770–7590 cal BC (95% confidence; SUERC-85563; Fig. 4.4) from hazelnut shell and lithics evidence indicate Mesolithic activity in the area of the midden prior to early Neolithic activity (see below).

The assemblage from the midden is dominated by hazelnut shell and cereal grain though flax is also present and low amounts of weed seeds occur including common chickweed, knotgrass, fat hen and cleavers, which are typical of cultivation as well as disturbed ground and waste tips; other taxa such as ribwort plantain and docks are commonly found in grassland, but most occur in a variety of habitats. Raspberry/blackberry (mainly blackberry) fruitstones are relatively frequent while seeds of rosehip occur occasionally and could indicate exploitation of scrub at the woodland edge for food or fuel. Indeterminate vesicular plant material is also present. The weed seeds also include deadly nightshade, which, as well as being a weed of cultivated ground, is very poisonous and also known for its hallucinogenic properties, which could mean its presence might indicate its use for ritual activity. However, it is also a scrub/woodland edge species and whilst the remains may represent waste material from hearths, many of the weed seeds, including deadly nightshade, docks and common chickweed, as well as rosehip seeds, raspberry/blackberry (mostly blackberry) fruitstones and grass culm/rhizome fragments could derive from plants growing at or near the site and reflect local burning, perhaps to clear the area after a period of abandonment prior to occupation in the early Neolithic or possibly prior to construction of the tomb. The same may apply to charred plant remains in the buried soil and overlying soil layer in the forecourt area (see above) but, as already mentioned, interpretation is further complicated in the latter area by the house structure and later pit. Further evidence for a period of abandonment and reversion to scrub at the site is also suggested by the presence of hawthorn type and blackthorn charcoal from features associated with the structure (see below).

In comparison to middens elsewhere, there is more charred plant material from the midden buried soil at Gwernvale than from the midden at the Eton Rowing Course, Dorney, where the midden was spread out over a wider area (M. Robinson 2013) but is similar to the more discrete area of midden beneath the barrow at Hazleton (Straker 1990). The assemblages from all three are, however, similar in that of the cereals emmer predominated. Chaff was absent at Dorney and, as at Gwernvale, scarce at Hazleton. The weed assemblage at Hazleton is similar to that at Gwernvale though there is more evidence of grasses, including onion couch grass, suggesting a period of grassland (Straker 1990, 217). Hazelnut shell was present at all three sites and at Dorney there was also evidence of sloe and hawthorn and at Gwernvale blackberry and rosehip and possible hawthorn, indicating scrub and woodland. The midden at Hazleton is dated probably to the 39th century cal BC, earlier than at Gwernvale, and the micromorphological and environmental evidence from the site indicates cultivation followed by a period of scrub development before construction of the tomb probably in the first half of the 37th century cal BC (Meadows *et al.* 2007). At Gwernvale the plant remains may suggest a period of reversion to scrub either prior to early Neolithic activity or possibly after occupation of the building but prior to construction of the tomb.

Crop processing activity

The cereal assemblage at Gwernvale is dominated by grain whilst chaff is rare. This is consistent with much of the evidence from other British Neolithic sites where chaff is scarce (Bogaard and Jones 2007), though there are exceptions such as The Stumble (Murphy 2012), Lismore Fields (Jones and Bogaard 2017), Hambledon Hill (Jones and Legge 2008) in England and Plas Gogerddan (Caseldine 1992) and sites on the St Clears to Red Roses Road Improvement route (Cobain 2019) in Wales. If hulled wheat grain was stored in spikelet form at the site then spikelet forks and glume bases might be expected to be present in significant amounts, so the scarcity of chaff in the cereal assemblage and relatively small numbers of weed seed may indicate that the cereal was fully processed away from the site, or at least not in the area excavated. However, there are several reasons why chaff may be under-represented on sites. Parching to help dehusking is not essential, which would reduce the likelihood of accidental charring (M. Robinson 2000; Bogaard and Jones 2007). Also, chaff is less likely to survive the burning process than the grain (Boardman and Jones 1990) and chaff, along with straw, may have been too valuable to waste and throw on to fires and may have been used as fodder (G. Campbell 2000; Stevens 2007). Elsewhere, for example at Lismore Fields, chaff-rich deposits in one building have been interpreted as representing dehusking activity or chaff storage and, along with high phosphate values, may indicate the use of cereal processing by-products as animal fodder (Jones and Bogaard 2017). Equally, the large grain assemblage in one building is interpreted as the storage of fully processed emmer, or grain stored as spikelets from which the glumes had largely been destroyed (Jones and Bogaard 2017). At Gwernvale, although there are only a few spikelet forks, it is possible that grain was stored as spikelets to help reduce spoilage (Hillman 1981), but likewise it could have been stored as clean grain. Clean grain would also have been easier to transport and this has implications for the exchange and movement of cereal (Stevens 2007), especially as Gwernvale may lie on a long-established routeway (Bell 2020, 117).

As well as chaff, weed seeds are also indicative of crop processing. Weed seeds are present in relatively low amounts at Gwernvale, in common with many other British and Irish early Neolithic assemblages, and whilst they may be a by-product of crop processing they may also be derived from plants growing at the site. The higher frequency of cleavers seeds in samples from the forecourt house area could indicate final hand-sorting of clean grain and waste from fires, but it is possibly more likely that the cleavers reflect burning of local vegetation (see above). The relatively low incidence of weed seeds might also be at least partially attributable to the harvesting methods; for example, ear-harvesting would avoid the harvesting of most weeds apart from climbing weeds such as black bindweed or cleavers (Kreuz and Schäfer 2011). It has also been suggested that slash-and-burn cultivation may account for the rarity of weed seeds (D. Robinson 2007; Rösch *et al.* 2014) but weeds similarly may be rare in plots for a few years following recent clearance of woodland where there is only very limited burning of cut vegetation (Halstead 2018).

Although evidence from the charred plant remains for crop processing at the site is slight, evidence for the grinding of cereal is provided by the presence of querns/quern fragments thought probably to relate to the pre-cairn phase (Britnell 1984b, 134–5; see also Chapter 3).

In contrast to Gwernvale, there is some evidence for crop processing by-products at other early Neolithic sites in Wales. As mentioned above, chaff has been recorded at Parc Cybi (Kenney 2021) and in notable amounts from a few early Neolithic sites in Wales including Plas Gogerddan (Caseldine 1992) and Site 37 near Llanddowror on the St Clears to Red Roses Road Improvement Scheme (Cobain 2019) where it has been recovered from pits. At the latter, wheat glume bases and spikelet forks and barley rachis have been interpreted as reflecting the parching and hummeling stages of crop processing, respectively, and along with other remains, representing midden waste.

Crop husbandry

The main cereal cultivated was wheat, especially emmer wheat, though there is some very tentative evidence that einkorn may have been present. Barley was also present, including hulled, but most of it was indeterminate. The possible oat is most likely to have been a wild weed rather than cultivated, or possibly contamination. In addition to cereal, another crop plant, flax, was also represented and may have been grown for its fibre or its oil or used as food.

In general emmer wheat is dominant and einkorn rare elsewhere in Wales (Treasure *et al.* 2019; Rackham 2020) and other parts of Britain and Ireland. Naked wheat grains are typically only a minor component and in many cases intrusive (Pelling and Campbell 2013; Pelling *et al.* 2015) but rivet/durum wheat has recently been identified from the early Neolithic site at Thanet Earth (Carruthers 2019). Barley, both naked and hulled, occurs frequently but is generally less important than emmer wheat during the early Neolithic, including early Neolithic rectangular structures in Scotland, though it is dominant at some early Neolithic Scottish sites before dominating in the Late Neolithic (Bishop *et al.* 2009).

Whilst flax has not been recorded from other Neolithic sites in Wales, it has been found on several Neolithic sites in Scotland, England and Ireland. In Scotland, significant numbers occurred at Balbridie and Lockerbie and it was present at Achnasavil (Bishop *et al.* 2009). Whereas the flax seeds at Gwernvale were largely from the midden area, at Balbridie most of the seeds were associated with the building (Fairweather and Ralston 1993) and at Lockerbie the remains were interpreted as either a store of flax seeds burnt during destruction of the building or charred during linseed oil processing (Hastie 2011, 23). In England a large quantity of flax seeds was also recovered from a posthole in Building 1 at Lismore Fields and also from Building 2 (Jones and Rowley-Conwy 2007; Jones and Bogaard 2017). Other Neolithic sites where it has been recorded include Windmill Hill, Wiltshire (Helbaek 1952), and The Stumble, Essex (Murphy 2012), as well as Thanet Earth (Carruthers 2019). In Ireland flax has been found on two Early Neolithic II sites (with an estimated date span of 3750–3600 cal BC) including Clowanstown 1, Co. Meath where it has been dated probably to the 39th–38th centuries, demonstrating that it was one of the earliest crops to be cultivated in Ireland (McClatchie *et al.* 2014) and also at Tullahedy in Co. Tipperary dated to the Middle Neolithic I (with an estimated date span of 3600–3400 cal BC) (McClatchie *et al.* 2016).

Information about the environmental conditions where the cereals and flax were grown and the harvesting techniques employed is limited as the weed seed assemblage from Gwernvale is relatively small, though more extensive than on many early Neolithic sites in Wales and elsewhere in Britain and Ireland. Indeed, in a review of Irish evidence only one weed genus/type was recorded from the majority of sites (McClatchie 2014). Nettle may indicate nitrogen enrichment from animal faeces whilst small water-pepper could indicate damp conditions, cleavers either loams or clay soils, ribwort plantain loams or sandy soils and wild radish acid soils. Wild radish could also indicate spring-sown cereals whereas cleavers is often associated with winter sown cereals and, as it is a climbing weed, it may indicate harvesting by uprooting.

Management practices

In recent years there has been much discussion about the nature of early Neolithic farming regimes and whether or not extensive cultivation, for example shifting cultivation, with larger areas of land and less often cropping and perhaps taking advantage of available clearings, or the cultivation of more permanent plots took place. It is argued that permanent plots would require intensive cultivation practices, including weeding and manuring, and involve a high labour input to maintain soil fertility and crop productivity (Bogaard 2005; G. Jones 2005). It has been suggested that small-scale 'garden' cultivation near to settlements along with modest numbers of animals would have resulted in sustainable plots (Stevens 2007). No archaeological evidence was found during the excavation for cultivation using an ard or for hand-digging with hoes or other tools, perhaps due to the limited excavation area (Britnell 1984b, 49). Equally the use of an ard was thought unlikely given the number of boulders present and hand-digging would have been difficult to identify if the midden buried soil had been cultivated. However, at the Neolithic farmstead at Knap of Howar, Orkney, it has been suggested that a spread of midden material may have been used for small-scale intensive cultivation (Ritchie 1983) and at other sites in Scotland geoarchaeological techniques have demonstrated cultivation of Neolithic midden material (Guttman 2005). Micromorphological evidence for cultivation of the soils and midden was also found at Hazleton North long cairn in Gloucestershire (Macphail 1990).

One approach to determining management practices is by analysis of the type of arable weeds present. It has been suggested using experimental research that the practice of shifting agriculture would result in the dominance of perennial weed taxa, especially woodland perennials, whereas more intensively managed long-lived cultivation plots would result in the dominance of annual taxa and plants indicative of disturbed ground (Bogaard and Jones 2007). The weed assemblage from Gwernvale is small with the greatest range from the midden buried soil, whilst the most commonly occurring weed across the site is cleavers, which was relatively frequent in the upper soil layer 95, though still in small numbers. Annual weeds include cleavers, equal-leaved knotgrass and wild radish, though there are also some perennial weeds such as ribwort plantain, docks and deadly nightshade. Interpretation of management practices from the weed taxa alone is inconclusive but the perennial weeds along with other woodland scrub species such as blackberry and cleavers, as discussed above, may suggest scrub clearance involving fire.

An alternative to using weed data to investigate the cultivation of cereal is the application of stable isotope analysis to cereal grains, in particular cereal nitrogen isotope ($\delta^{15}N$), which can be used to identify manuring (Treasure *et al.* 2019). Cereal $\delta^{15}N$ values largely reflect the soil they are grown in and the values can be elevated by practices such as manuring to improve its fertility. Manuring would enable productivity/yields to be maintained and suggest the presence of permanent plots. As part of a research project undertaken by Ed Treasure, cereal from Gwernvale, along with that from Cwm Meudwy (Caseldine and Griffiths 2006), Plas Gogerddan (Caseldine 1992) and Parc Bryn Cegin (Schmidl *et al.* 2008), was analysed (Treasure *et al.* 2019). Emmer wheat mean $\delta^{15}N$ values from Gwernvale suggested either no manuring or a low level of manuring and perhaps short-term manuring of 1–2 years. Mean $\delta^{15}N$ values for barley lay in the 'medium' intensity range, possibly indicating a moderate level of less intensive/shorter-term manuring (Bogaard *et al.* 2013), but these results are based on only two samples and the barley mean $\delta^{15}N$ values for all four sites from Wales suggested 'no manuring or low manuring'. Overall, the stable isotope evidence suggested that intensive manuring was not undertaken at Gwernvale, or at the other three sites, and suggested a less intensive cultivation regime on poor soils (Treasure *et al.* 2019) and is not inconsistent with the cereal evidence from Gwernvale, though the stable isotope evidence is limited and more needs to be done (Rowley-Conwy *et al.* 2020). Another possibility is that as flax is present and as this is a very demanding crop, which results in nutrient depletion in the soil, as well as being demanding in terms of weeding and hence time and labour, it is possible that any manure may have been preferentially used for this as it may have been viewed as a more valuable crop, that is assuming that flax was grown locally.

Unfortunately, evidence at Gwernvale for animal husbandry as part of the farming economy, and hence the extent to which manure was available, is restricted by the acid nature of the soils resulting in bone preservation being poor with only limited evidence for cattle, sheep/goat and pig from the midden buried soil 30 and soil layer 95 (O'Connor 1984, 153–4). Lipid analysis from early Neolithic vessels does, however, suggest they were largely used for the processing of dairy products (see analyses by Isabel Wiltshire and Lucy Cramp in Chapter 11), whilst the dietary isotope results from human bone from other chambered tombs in south Wales, including Penywyrlod, also indicate that animal protein, either from meat or milk, was an important part of the diet (see analyses by Michael Richards in Chapter 8).

Regional variability in farming practices has been proposed (Bishop 2009; McClatchie 2014; 2016) and the evidence from Gwernvale contrasts with that from Lismore Fields, for example, where the cereal grain nitrogen isotope results suggest medium to high levels of manuring and the integration of crop cultivation and animal husbandry and a highly sustained mixed farming regime (Bogaard *et al.* 2013; Jones and Bogaard 2017). At Stepleton Neolithic causewayed enclosure at Hambledon Hill lower $\delta^{15}N$ values suggest a moderate level of manuring, either less intensive or shorter-term than at Lismore Fields (Bogaard *et al.* 2013.) Here, as at Lismore Fields, both sites have large cereal assemblages compared with Gwernvale. The results from Gwernvale, possibly suggesting cultivation in low-intensity regimes on poor soils, also contrast with the model of widespread, systematic and intensive manuring at other European Early Neolithic sites (Bogaard 2013; Treasure *et al.* 2019) and with the argument for an intensive and integrated garden cultivation system in Britain (Rowley-Conwy *et al.* 2020).

Pre-cairn activity with low-intensity cereal cultivation, even if not continuous, is probably of considerable duration (see Chapter 4), before construction of the cairn probably in *3570–3070 cal BC* (*95% probability*; or *3530–3300 cal*

BC 68% probability; *construct_Gwernvale_monument*; Fig. 4.4). The end of cereal cultivation at Gwernvale broadly coincides with a suggested shift away from cereal production to a slightly more pastoral-based society around 3600 cal BC, which was later followed by a further decline in arable cultivation around 2900 cal BC, based on summed radiocarbon probability distributions from cereal grain (Stevens and Fuller 2012; 2015), though their use as a proxy for the changing importance of arable cultivation through time has been criticised (Bishop 2015a; 2015b). The putative decline in cereal after around 3600 cal BC and into the Middle Neolithic is also linked to a deterioration in climatic conditions and increasing exploitation of wild foods and mobility in southern Britain, though cereal, namely barley, which is more tolerant of cooler and wetter conditions, increased in the Scottish Isles and in Scotland and northern England barley persisted while wheat declined (Stevens and Fuller 2015).

There is no cereal grain at Gwernvale dated to the Middle and Late Neolithic, although the possibility of later cereal at the site cannot be totally ruled out. Nonetheless, the evidence from elsewhere in Wales does suggest a decline in arable cultivation as cereal is recorded on fewer sites and occurs in smaller quantities during these periods (Treasure *et al.* 2019), though one exception is a large grain assemblage from a Late Neolithic pit at Capel Eithin, Anglesey (D. Williams 1999), although the grain itself is undated. However, the decline may also to some extent reflect a research and taphonomic bias as well as a sample bias. In Wales, apart from wood charcoal, radiocarbon dates have largely been obtained from hazelnut shell rather than cereal grain for the Middle and Late Neolithic and more dates from cereal grain need to be obtained to assess the importance of arable cultivation during these periods and to determine whether the cereal is intrusive or contemporary. The decline in cereal in Wales is consistent with the evidence for a decrease in cereal in the later Neolithic from much of Britain and Ireland (Moffett *et al.* 1989; Pelling and Campbell 2013; McClatchie *et al.* 2016), although there are exceptions to this (Treasure *et al.* 2019), suggesting local and regional diversity.

The exploitation of wild plant resources

There is some evidence for the exploitation of wild plant foods, notably hazelnuts, which were present in almost every sample at Gwernvale. These would have provided a useful supplement to the diet, particularly in the event of a poor harvest. The relative importance of hazelnuts and other wild plant foods in comparison to cereals in the Neolithic economy has been widely debated (Entwhistle and Grant 1989; Moffett *et al.* 1989; M. Robinson 2000); in particular, it has been argued that hazelnut shell is generally over-represented in archaeobotanical assemblages because of preferential survival. Hazelnut shell, being a waste product, is more likely to be discarded on to fires compared with cereal grain, which, as a food, is less likely to be (G. Jones 2000; Jones and Rowley-Conwy 2007). Furthermore, in comparison to cereal grain, hazelnut shell is more likely to survive the charring process over a greater range of temperatures making it more likely to be present in the archaeological record (Bishop 2019). In general, though it is likely that hazelnuts and other wild plants were a useful additional food source (McClatchie *et al.* 2014; 2016; Smyth *et al.* 2020), and their importance probably varied to some degree from site to site, it is suggested the Neolithic plant economy was probably based primarily on cereal agriculture (Rowley-Conwy *et al.* 2020, 412).

The widespread exploitation of hazelnuts in Wales at this time is demonstrated by their presence on virtually all early Neolithic sites from which charred plant remains have been retrieved, as is also the case in other parts of Britain and Ireland (Bishop 2009; McClatchie2014; 2016). Whilst on some sites hazelnut shell is scarce, on others hazelnut shell fragments are frequent or abundant including a number of sites in south Wales associated with the gas pipeline such as Upper Neeston (Site 511) (Barber and Hart 2014b), Lower Scoveston (Site 286) (Brannlund 2013), Pysgodlyn Farm (Site 51.02) (Busby 2013), Pen-y-Crug (Site 51.07) (Hart and Leonard 2014), Gurrey Cottage (Site 24.07) (Hart 2013), and Gelli-Wern-Isaf (Site 238) (Sausins 2013) as well as Site 37 near Llanddowror on the St Clears to Red Roses Road Improvement Scheme (Cobain 2019). Elsewhere in Wales hazelnut shell was frequent at Plas Gogerddan (Caseldine 1992) and abundant at Borras Quarry (Archaeological Services Durham University 2013) and also frequent at Carrog (Caseldine *et al.* 2014) and Parc Bryn Cegin (Kenney 2008) in north Wales.

The hazelnuts at Gwernvale may have been eaten raw, roasted before de-shelling or dried prior to storage. Although the charred hazelnut shell is probably largely discarded food waste, some could derive from branches collected as fuel or result from clearance activity. Raspberry/blackberry may have been gathered for food from woodland margins or scrub but the charred fruitstones may also reflect incidental inclusion with fuel or burning on or close to the site to clear vegetation, perhaps after a period of abandonment (see above), rather than accidental or deliberate waste from cooking activity. Rosehips and hawthorn berries may also have been collected for food, but again charred remains may indicate fuel or burning of scrub. Deliberate management practices would have favoured light-demanding species such as blackberry through opening up woodland (Colledge and Conolly 2014), whilst abandonment of land would also promote favourable habitats for scrub species. A fragment of acorn cupule may signify that acorns were also gathered, but again may reflect fuel collection. Acorns are rare from British sites, which may reflect a preservation bias (Treasure *et al.* 2019), or that they were not widely exploited for food

(Pelling and Campbell 2013). In addition, several weed taxa represented at the site could have been exploited for food, including docks, plantain, fat hen, nettle and cleavers, particularly if there was a poor harvest.

There is also some limited evidence from sites elsewhere in Wales for the exploitation of wild plants for food apart from hazelnuts, notably crab apple from Plas Gogerddan (Caseldine 1992) and Gurrey Cottage (Site 24.07) (Carruthers 2013) and Site 37 near Llanddowror on the St Clears to Red Roses Road Improvement Scheme (Cobain 2019), while cherry and blackthorn were recorded at Site 25 on the same route, again near Llanddowror. At Llandevenney, a wetland edge site at the Severn Estuary, abundant charred raspberry/blackberry fruitstones and other occasional charred seeds, including nettle and ribwort plantain, in a Neolithic plant assemblage from the upper occupation layer, indicate *in situ* burning and the promotion of scrub on the woodland edge (A. Brown 2007, 253).

Apart from providing a source of wild plant foodstuffs, woodland would have been exploited for timber and roundwood for building as well as other products and fuel. Charcoal identifications (see below) suggest the presence of woodland and scrub containing oak, ash, elm, alder, hazel, blackthorn, cherry and hawthorn type.

Radiocarbon dates from hazelnut shell and charcoal suggest exploitation and possibly manipulation of the local woodland had already commenced during the Mesolithic and continued into the early Neolithic. Given that some of the hazelnut shell dates to the Mesolithic, it is also possible that some of the other wild plant remains date to the Mesolithic and earlier burning activity.

Mesolithic exploitation of wild plant resources

The use of wild plant resources during the Mesolithic is widely recognised (Zvelebil 1994; Bishop *et al.* 2013; Warren *et al.* 2014). At Gwernvale, although the majority of charred plant remains probably date to the early Neolithic, the earliest evidence for the possible collection and use of plant resources comes from a fragment of hazelnut shell dated to the 8th millennium cal BC (SUERC-85563; Fig. 4.4), from the buried soil in the midden area. This is somewhat earlier than the 6th-millennium date (CAR-118; see Chapter 4) from wood charcoal from a hearth (308) on the northern side of the cairn and though no hazelnut shell was recovered from this feature it was present in the buried soil and other features in this area. The dates, together with the lithics (see Elizabeth Walker in Chapter 9), suggest intermittent activity at the site during the early and late Mesolithic. Elsewhere in south Wales, for example Waun-Fignen-Felen, occupation sites with earlier and later Mesolithic flints also indicate repeated use of the site as a 'persistent place' (Barton *et al.* 1995). Given the scatter of Mesolithic lithics at the site in the area of the midden and the forecourt area, it is not surprising that some of the hazelnut shell proved to be of this date and may account for the higher amounts of nutshell in some samples. Hazelnut shell was also recovered from features at the western end of the cairn, which might have been associated with woodland clearance, though this could equally be early Neolithic in date. It is also possible that some of the other charred wild plant remains, rather than being early Neolithic in date, could be Mesolithic, for example lesser celandine tuber, hawthorn, raspberry/blackberry, fat hen, vetches and docks, all of which could have been exploited for food.

Typically, charred plant assemblages dating to the Mesolithic in Wales are dominated by the ubiquitous hazelnut and include sites such as Nab Head (David 1990; David and Walker 2004) and Daylight Rock, Caldey (David and Walker 2004) and sites such as Parc Bryn Cegin, Llandygai (Kenney 2008), Parc Cybi (Kenney 2021) and Llanfaethlu (Rees and Jones 2015; 2017) in north Wales where there is evidence for Mesolithic activity prior to construction of early Neolithic rectangular buildings. Similarly in south Wales late Mesolithic hazelnut shell was recovered from a site near Cwmifor, Carmarthenshire (Site 26.05) where there was evidence for a possible early Neolithic structure (Hart 2014), whilst hazelnut shell provided early Mesolithic dates at Site 50.05, Aberyscir Court, Yscir (Leonard 2014b) and Site 503, Vaynor Farm, Llandddowror (Barber and Hart 2014a), where there was also evidence of early Neolithic activity. As at Gwernvale, these sites suggest that at least some areas previously exploited during the Mesolithic for their wild resources were later returned to during the early Neolithic by communities engaged in farming activity. At Gwernvale the activity over a long period of time may reflect a long-lasting routeway (Bell 2020, 117).

The evidence for the availability and exploitation of hazelnuts during the Mesolithic is in keeping with pollen records from the Black Mountains and Brecon area (*e.g.* M. Walker 1982; Chambers 1983; Walker *et al.* 1993; Pardoe 2019; Rackham 2020) as well as elsewhere in Wales (*e.g.* Walker *et al.* 2001; Dark 2007), which indicate that hazel was an important component of the woodland.

Charcoal results: the evidence for woodland and the use of wood

Charcoal identification was largely confined to samples associated with the pre-cairn house, and although the assemblage is small, give some indication of the species available for exploitation. A range of taxa were recorded from the samples from the features below the N horn of the cairn, both the posts (133A, 133C, 1333E 133G, 229) and the wall-lines (133B, 133D, 229), and included oak, ash, hazel, blackthorn, Maloideae type (crab apple, rowan, whitebeam, hawthorn) and elm. Charcoal from the post-packing and post-pipes of other postholes (208, 209, 211) and possible postholes (205, 206) also comprised oak, hazel, and hawthorn type as well as alder and cherry. The charcoal assemblage from charcoal spread 249 was similar and again included hawthorn type, hazel, ash and oak. The most frequently occurring taxa were oak and hawthorn type, followed by ash and hazel with elm, blackthorn, cherry and alder being rare.

Although no large fragments of charcoal occurred that might indicate *in situ* burning, dominance of oak in postholes 133E and particularly in possible posthole 205 might suggest oak posts, possibly charred during destruction of the building or that the bases were possibly charred to help prevent decay. The occurrence of other taxa such as hazel might indicate the use of more slender roundwood stems for wattling or other purposes. Similarly, a fragment of ash roundwood could indicate a similar use though ash is also suitable for timber, as is elm. Species such as hazel and ash would be more commonly used as wattle to support oak planks and the high frequency of hawthorn type is unusual if it was used for construction purposes. However, at the three houses at Corbally, Co. Kildare, the range of species is similar to that at Gwernvale and it is proposed that the occurrence of hawthorn type charcoal may indicate its use in external walling to keep animals outside the houses, though hazel wattle is considered to have been used to support planks and oak the main wood used for structural purposes (Purcell 2002, 45, 57, 67).

Elsewhere in Ireland, oak also appears to have been the main wood used in the construction of buildings (Smyth 2014, 34) and in England, for example at Yarnbury and Lismore Fields, oak was used for posts and hazel for infill panels (Challinor 2017, 199–201). Likewise in Wales, oak is regarded as the main timber used in construction of the Llandygai I building (Lynch and Musson 2001, 31), where large pieces of oak charcoal were recovered from posts, and at the nearby building at Parc Bryn Cegin (Kenney 2008, 25–6). At the latter, oak was generally dominant, along with some hazel, in the richer charcoal deposits associated with postholes and a post-trench. Pine was also recorded from a posthole and possible stakehole. Similarly, at Parc Cybi oak dominated the charcoal assemblages from most of the features in the building but hazel occurred in notable amounts and willow/poplar, alder and Rosaceae were also present (Kenney 2021, 44–5).

The mix of species in individual features and widespread occurrence of hawthorn type suggests, however, that at least some of the charcoal may represent the remains of wood collected for firewood and/or clearance activity rather than building purposes and, given the radiocarbon and lithics evidence for Mesolithic activity, may be residual. The assemblage suggests oak woodland including ash, elm, hazel, rowan hawthorn, whitebeam, crab apple in the area was exploited but the presence of hawthorn type as well as blackthorn and hazel possibly indicates the exploitation or clearance of scrub woodland after a period of abandonment and regeneration following late Mesolithic activity or, perhaps, an early phase of Neolithic activity, prior to construction of the building (see above). It is also evident that although Gwernvale lies close to the floodplain of the river Usk and it is likely that alder was growing nearby, it was not particularly exploited. There is insufficient evidence to say whether there had been any attempt at woodland management such as coppicing.

The assemblage from Gwernvale is similar to that from pre-cairn deposits at Penywyrlod which include oak, hazel and hawthorn type, the latter from a burnt area outside the cairn. It is also in keeping with other charcoal assemblages from Neolithic sites in Wales including those associated with the South Wales Gas Pipeline (Rackham 2020, 155) in which oak dominates the assemblages and hazel is relatively frequent but alder is relatively scarce and other species such as *Prunus* (probably mainly blackthorn), birch, ash, holly, holly, elm, lime and conifer were rare, but it differs in the relatively high frequency of hawthorn type. A single fragment of hawthorn type charcoal was recorded from an early Neolithic pit at Site 509 near Middle Bastleford, Rosemarket (Challinor 2015, 29), whilst a few fragments were identified from early Neolithic pits found along the route of the A477 St Clears to Red Roses Road Improvement Scheme, Carmarthenshire (Cobain 2019, 95–6). Cherry and blackthorn also occurred at the latter site. Rosaceae family pollen is generally rare in the pollen record so charcoal evidence is a useful additional indicator of these species in Mesolithic/early Neolithic woodland, and along with raspberry/blackberry fruitstones indicate woodland-edge environments around woodland clearings as well as colonisation by scrub of previously cleared land.

In the wider area, pollen evidence suggests that oak and hazel woodland continued to dominate but clearance activity is indicated in records from the Waun Fach plateau (Price 1981; Price and Moore 1984) and Llyn Mire where it is suggested there is evidence of early Neolithic cereal cultivation (Moore 1978).

Acknowledgements

I would like to thank Kate Griffiths for assistance with some of the sorting and Kate and Wendy Carruthers for helpful discussions about identifications. I am also grateful to Cotswold Archaeology, Clwyd-Powys Archaeological Trust and Gwynedd Archaeological Trust for access to unpublished data.

Table 5.1. Gwernvale: charred plant remains from pre-cairn features (features in area of pre-cairn house).

	Features in area of pre-cairn house										
Feature type	*posthole*	*wall-line*	*posthole*	*wall-line*	*posthole*	*posthole*	*?posthole*	*gully*	*?posthole*	*gully*	*wall-line/ gully*
Feature/sample no.	*133A*	*133B*	*133C*	*133D*	*133E*	*133G*	*221*	*223*	*226*	*226A*	*227*
Cereals											
Triticum dicoccum, emmer grain	–	–	–	–	–	–	–	1	–	–	–
T. cf. *dicoccum*	–	1*	–	2*	3	2	–	1	–	–	–
T. cf. *dicoccum*, emmer spikelet fork	–	–	–	–	–	–	–	–	–	–	–
T. dicoccum/spelta, emmer/spelt wheat grain	–	1	–	–	1	1	–	–	–	–	–
Triticum sp., indeterminate wheat grain	–	7	4	2	2	4	–	2	2	–	–
cf. *Triticum* sp.	1	–	–	–	–	–	–	1	–	–	–
Hordeum vulgare L., indeterminate barley grain	–	–	–	–	2	–	–	–	–	–	–
cf. *Hordeum* sp.	–	–	–	–	–	–	–	–	–	–	–
Cerealia indet. (estimated), indeterminate cereal grains	2	10	2	4	12	4	–	3	3	–	–
Cerealia indet., (whole, frags)	(3)	(2, 24)	(6)	(1, 9)	(29)	(14)	–	(11)	(1, 5)	–	–
Cerealia/Large Poaceae, cereal/ large grass culm node	–	–	–	–	–	–	–	–	–	–	–
Other Plants											
Urtica dioica L., common nettle **CDFWn**	–	–	–	–	–	–	–	–	–	–	–
Corylus avellana L., hazelnut shell fragments **HSW**	6	33	9	11	5	6	6	4	9	–	–
C. avellana L., wgt. gms	0.03	0.24	0.15	0.04	0.02	0.04	0.03	0.01	0.11	–	–
Polygonum sp., knotgrass **CDGo**	–	–	–	–	–	–	–	–	–	–	–
Rumex sp., docks **CDGHW**	–	–	–	–	–	–	–	–	–	–	–
cf. *Brassica/Sinapis* sp., charlock/mustard etc. **CD**	–	–	–	–	–	–	–	–	–	–	–
Raphanus raphanistrum L., wild radish fruit **CD**	–	–	–	–	–	–	–	–	–	–	–
Rubus fruticosus agg., blackberry **DGHSWo**	–	–	–	–	–	–	–	–	–	–	–
Rubus sp., raspberry/blackberry **DGHSWo**	–	–	–	–	–	–	–	–	1	–	–

(Continued)

Table 5.1. Gwernvale: charred plant remains from pre-cairn features (features in area of pre-cairn house). (Continued)

Feature type	*posthole*	*wall-line*	*posthole*	*wall-line*	*posthole*	*posthole*	*?posthole*	*gully*	*?posthole*	*gully*	*wall-line/ gully*
Feature/sample no.	*133A*	*133B*	*133C*	*133D*	*133E*	*133G*	*221*	*223*	*226*	*226A*	*227*
Vicia hirsuta (L.) Gray, hairy tare **DG**	–	1	–	–	–	–	–	–	–	–	–
Vicia sp., vetches **DGHSWo**	–	–	–	–	–	–	–	–	–	–	–
cf. *Vicia* sp.	–	–	–	–	–	–	–	–	–	–	–
Galium aparine L., cleavers **ACHSo**	–	–	–	–	–	–	–	–	–	–	–
cf. *Galium* sp., bedstraw **GHSWow**	–	–	–	–	–	–	–	–	–	–	–
cf. *Hordeum murinum* type, wall barley **DG**	–	–	–	–	–	–	–	–	–	–	–
Poaceae, grass family **G**	–	–	–	–	–	–	–	–	–	–	–
Poaceae, culm/rhizome frag.	–	–	–	–	–	–	–	–	–	–	–
Immature seed capsule	–	–	–	–	–	–	1	–	–	–	–
Bud	–	–	–	–	–	–	–	–	–	–	–
Vesicular plant material indet.	–	–	–	–	+	–	–	–	–	–	–
Wood charcoal	+	+	+	+	+	+	+	+	+	+	+
Indet.	–	–	–	–	–	–	–	–	–	–	–
Total number of items	9	53	15	19	25	17	7	12	15	0	0
Feature type	*?posthole*	*wall-line*	*wall-line*	*?posthole*	*?posthole*	*post-packing*	*post-pipe*	*post-packing*	*post-pipe*	*post-packing*	*post-pipe*
Feature/sample No.	*228*	*229*	*229A*	*205*	*206*	*207A*	*207B*	*208A*	*208B*	*209A*	*209B*
Cereals											
Triticum dicoccum, emmer grain	–	2	–	–	–	–	–	–	1	–	–
T. cf. *dicoccum*	–	4	–	–	–	–	–	–	–	–	–
T. cf. *dicoccum*, emmer spikelet fork	–	–	–	–	–	–	–	–	–	–	–
T. dicoccum/spelta, emmer/spelt wheat grain	–	1	–	–	–	–	–	–	–	–	–
Triticum sp., indeterminate wheat grain	–	10	3*	–	2	–	–	–	–	–	–
cf. *Triticum* sp.	–	–	–	–	–	–	–	–	–	–	–
Hordeum vulgare L., indeterminate barley grain	–	–	–	–	–	–	–	–	–	–	–

(Continued)

Table 5.1. (Continued)

Feature type	*?posthole*	*wall-line*	*wall-line*	*?posthole*	*?posthole*	*post-packing*	*post-pipe*	*post-packing*	*post-pipe*	*post-packing*	*post-pipe*
Feature/sample No.	*228*	*229*	*229A*	*205*	*206*	*207A*	*207B*	*208A*	*208B*	*209A*	*209B*
cf. *Hordeum* sp.	–	–	–	–	–	–	–	–	–	–	–
Cerealia indet. (estimated), indeterminate cereal grains	–	34	2	–	–	–	–	1	–	–	–
Cerealia indet., (whole, frags)	–	(2,116)	(2)	–	–	–	–	(1)	–	–	–
Cerealia/Large Poaceae, cereal/large grass culm node	–	1	–	–	–	1	–	–	–	–	–
Other Plants											
Urtica dioica L., common nettle **CDFWn**	–	–	–	–	–	–	–	–	–	–	–
Corylus avellana L., hazelnut shell fragments **HSW**	17	43	5	–	10	12	7	4	25	14	2
C. avellana L., wgt. gms	0.19	0.29	0.03	–	0.05	0.05	0.03	0.03	0.14	0.1	0.01
Polygonum sp., knotgrass **CDGo**	–	–	–	–	–	–	–	–	–	–	–
Rumex sp., docks **CDGHW**	–	–	–	–	–	–	–	–	–	–	–
cf. *Brassica/Sinapis* sp., charlock/mustard etc. **CD**	–	–	–	–	–	–	–	–	–	–	–
Raphanus raphanistrum L., wild radish fruit **CD**	–	–	–	–	–	–	–	–	–	–	–
Rubus fruticosus agg., blackberry **DGHSWo**	–	–	–	–	–	–	–	–	–	–	–
Rubus sp., raspberry/blackberry **DGHSWo**	–	–	–	–	–	–	–	–	–	–	–
Vicia hirsuta (L.) Gray, hairy tare **DG**	–	–	–	–	–	–	–	–	–	–	–
Vicia sp., vetches **DGHSWo**	–	–	–	–	–	–	–	–	1	–	–
cf. *Vicia* sp.	1	–	–	–	–	–	–	–	–	–	–
Galium aparine L., cleavers **ACHSo**	–	–	–	–	–	1	1	–	2	–	–
cf. *Galium* sp., bedstraw **GHSWow**	–	–	–	–	–	–	–	–	–	–	–
cf. *Hordeum murinum* type, wall barley **DG**	–	–	–	–	–	–	–	–	1	–	–
Poaceae, grass family **G**	–	1	–	–	–	–	–	–	–	–	–
Poaceae, culm/rhizome frag.	–	3	–	–	–	–	–	–	–	–	–

(Continued)

Table 5.1. *Gwernvale: charred plant remains from pre-cairn features (features in area of pre-cairn house). (Continued)*

Feature type	*?posthole*	*wall-line*	*wall-line*	*?posthole*	*?posthole*	*post-packing*	*post-pipe*	*post-packing*	*post-pipe*	*post-packing*	*post-pipe*
Feature/sample No.	*228*	*229*	*229A*	*205*	*206*	*207A*	*207B*	*208A*	*208B*	*209A*	*209B*
Immature seed capsule	–	–	–	–	–	–	–	–	–	–	–
Bud	–	–	–	–	–	–	–	–	–	–	–
Vesicular plant material indet.	–	–	–	–	+	+	+	+	+	+	+
Wood charcoal	+	+	+	+	+	+	+	+	+	+	+
Indet.	–	–	–	1	–	–	–	1	–	–	–
Total number of items	18	99	10	1	12	14	8	6	30	14	2
Feature type	*post-packing*	*post-pipe*	*post-packing*	*post-pipe*	*pit*	*pit*	*stake-holes*	*charcoal spread*	*small scoop*	*stake-holes*	*gully*
Feature/sample no.	*210A*	*210B*	*211A*	*211B*	*231*	*234*	*235–236*	*249*	*271*	*273–274*	*142*
Cereals											
Triticum dicoccum, emmer grain	–	–	2	–	–	–	–	–	–	–	–
T. cf. *dicoccum*	–	–	–	1	–	–	–	1*	–	–	–
T. cf. *dicoccum*, emmer spikelet fork	–	–	–	–	–	–	–	–	–	–	–
T. dicoccum/spelta, emmer/spelt wheat grain	–	–	–	–	–	–	–	1*	–	–	–
Triticum sp., indeterminate wheat grain	–	–	1	3	–	–	1	–	–	–	–
cf. *Triticum* sp.	–	–	–	–	–	–	–	–	–	–	–
Hordeum vulgare L., indeterminate barley grain	–	–	–	–	–	–	–	–	–	–	–
cf. *Hordeum* sp.	–	–	–	–	–	–	–	–	–	–	–
Cerealia indet. (estimated), indeterminate cereal grains	–	–	1	2	–	–	1	2	–	–	–
Cerealia indet., (whole, frags)	–	–	(2)	(3)	–	–	(1)	(5)	–	–	–
Cerealia/Large Poaceae, cereal/large grass culm node	–	–	–	–	–	–	–	–	–	–	–
Other Plants											
Urtica dioica L., common nettle **CDFWn**	–	–	–	–	–	1	–	–	–	–	–
Corylus avellana L., hazelnut shell fragments **HSW**	–	9	1	26	11	6	6	10	1	–	1
C. avellana L., wgt. gms	–	0.04	0.01	0.22	0.14	0.03	0.04	0.06	0.005	–	0.005

(*Continued*)

Table 5.1. (Continued)

Feature type	*post-packing*	*post-pipe*	*post-packing*	*post-pipe*	*pit*	*pit*	*stake-holes*	*charcoal spread*	*small scoop*	*stake-holes*	*gully*
Feature/sample no.	*210A*	*210B*	*211A*	*211B*	*231*	*234*	*235–236*	*249*	*271*	*273–274*	*142*
Polygonum sp., knotgrass **CDGo**	–	–	1	–	–	–	–	–	–	–	–
Rumex sp., docks **CDGHW**	–	–	–	–	–	–	–	–	–	–	–
cf. *Brassica/Sinapis* sp., charlock/mustard etc. **CD**	–	–	–	–	–	–	–	–	–	–	–
Raphanus raphanistrum L., wild radish fruit **CD**	–	–	–	–	–	–	–	–	–	–	–
Rubus fruticosus agg., blackberry **DGHSWo**	–	–	–	–	1	–	–	–	–	–	–
Rubus sp., raspberry/blackberry **DGHSWo**	–	–	–	–	–	–	–	–	–	–	–
Vicia hirsuta (L.) Gray, hairy tare **DG**	–	–	–	–	–	–	–	–	–	–	–
Vicia sp., vetches **DGHSWo**	–	–	–	–	–	–	–	–	–	–	–
cf. *Vicia* sp.	–	–	–	–	–	–	–	–	–	–	–
Galium aparine L., cleavers **ACHSo**	–	–	–	–	–	–	–	–	–	–	–
cf. *Galium* sp., bedstraw **GHSWow**	–	–	–	–	–	–	–	–	–	–	–
cf. *Hordeum murinum* type, wall barley **DG**	–	–	–	–	–	–	–	–	–	–	–
Poaceae, grass family **G**	–	–	–	–	–	–	–	–	–	–	–
Poaceae, culm/rhizome frag.	–	–	–	–	–	–	–	–	–	–	–
Immature seed capsule	–	–	–	–	–	–	–	–	–	–	–
Bud	–	–	–	–	–	–	–	–	–	–	–
Vesicular plant material indet.	–	–	–	+	–	–	–	–	+	–	–
Wood charcoal	+	+	+	+	+	+	+	+	+	+	+
Indet.	–	–	–	–	–	–	–	–	–	–	–
Total number of items	0	9	6	32	12	7	8	14	1	0	1
Feature type	*scoop*	*scoop*	*scoop*	*scoop*	*scoop*	*scoop*	*gully*	*pit*	*scoop*	*scoop*	*scoop*
Feature/sample no.	*143*	*144*	*145*	*146*	*147*	*148*	*149*	*150*	*151*	*152–153*	*157*
Cereals											
Triticum dicoccum, emmer grain	–	–	–	–	–	–	–	1	–	–	–
T. cf. *dicoccum*	–	–	–	1	–	–	–	1	–	–	–

(Continued)

Table 5.1. Gwernvale: charred plant remains from pre-cairn features (features in area of pre-cairn midden). (Continued)

Feature type	*scoop*	*scoop*	*scoop*	*scoop*	*scoop*	*scoop*	*gully*	*pit*	*scoop*	*scoop*	*scoop*
Feature/sample no.	*143*	*144*	*145*	*146*	*147*	*148*	*149*	*150*	*151*	*152–153*	*157*
T. cf. *dicoccum*, emmer spikelet fork	–	–	–	–	–	–	–	–	–	–	–
T. dicoccum/spelta, emmer/spelt wheat grain	–	–	–	–	–	–	–	–	–	–	–
Triticum sp., indeterminate wheat grain	–	–	–	–	–	–	–	1	–	–	1
cf. *Triticum* sp.	–	–	–	–	–	–	–	–	–	–	–
Hordeum vulgare L., indeterminate barley grain	–	–	–	–	–	–	–	–	–	–	–
cf. *Hordeum* sp.	–	–	–	–	–	–	–	–	–	–	–
Cerealia indet. (estimated), indeterminate cereal grains	–	–	–	–	–	–	1	–	1	–	–
Cerealia indet., (whole, frags)	–	–	–	–	–	–	(1)	–	(4)	–	–
Cerealia/Large Poaceae, cereal/ large grass culm node	–	–	–	–	–	–	–	–	–	–	–
Other Plants											
Urtica dioica L., common nettle **CDFWn**	–	–	–	–	–	–	–	–	–	–	–
Corylus avellana L., hazelnut shell fragments **HSW**	41	13	1	2	6	–	8	34	52	–	1
C. avellana L., wgt. gms	0.14	0.03	0.01	0.01	0.02	–	0.03	0.28	0.31	–	0.005
Polygonum sp., knotgrass **CDGo**	–	–	–	–	–	–	–	–	–	–	–
Rumex sp., docks **CDGHW**	–	–	–	–	–	–	–	1	–	–	–
cf. *Brassica/Sinapis* sp., charlock/mustard etc. **CD**	–	–	–	–	–	–	–	–	–	–	–
Raphanus raphanistrum L., wild radish fruit **CD**	–	–	–	–	–	–	–	1	–	–	–
Rubus fruticosus agg., blackberry **DGHSWo**	–	–	–	–	–	–	–	–	–	–	4
Rubus sp., raspberry/blackberry **DGHSWo**	–	–	–	–	–	–	–	–	–	–	–
Vicia hirsuta (L.) Gray, hairy tare **DG**	–	–	–	–	–	–	–	–	–	–	–
Vicia sp., vetches **DGHSWo**	–	–	–	–	–	–	–	–	–	–	–
cf. *Vicia* sp.	–	–	–	–	–	–	–	–	–	–	–

(Continued)

Table 5.1. (Continued)

Feature type	*scoop*	*scoop*	*scoop*	*scoop*	*scoop*	*scoop*	*gully*	*pit*	*scoop*	*scoop*	*scoop*
Feature/sample no.	*143*	*144*	*145*	*146*	*147*	*148*	*149*	*150*	*151*	*152–153*	*157*
Galium aparine L., cleavers **ACHSo**	–	–	–	–	–	–	–	1	–	–	–
cf. *Galium* sp., bedstraw **GHSWow**	–	–	–	–	–	–	–	–	–	–	–
cf. *Hordeum murinum* type, wall barley **DG**	–	–	–	–	–	–	–	–	–	–	–
Poaceae, grass family **G**	–	–	–	–	–	–	–	–	–	–	–
Poaceae,culm/rhizome frag.	–	–	–	–	–	–	–	–	–	–	–
Immature seed capsule	–	–	–	–	–	–	1	–	–	–	–
Bud	–	–	–	–	–	–	–	–	–	–	–
Vesicular plant material indet.	+	–	–	–	–	–	–	–	–	–	–
Wood charcoal	+	+	+	+	+	+	+	+	+	+	+
Indet.	–	–	–	–	–	–	–	–	–	–	–
Total number of items	41	13	1	3	6	0	10	40	53	0	6
Feature type	*scoop*	*scoop*	*pit*	*pit*	*scoop*	*scoop*	*scoop*	*gully*	*scoop*	*gully*	*pit*
Feature/sample no.	*158*	*159*	*160*	*162*	*163*	*164*	*165*	*167*	*168*	*169*	*170*
Cereals											
Triticum dicoccum, emmer grain	1	–	–	–	–	–	–	–	–	–	–
T. cf. *dicoccum*	–	–	–	6	–	–	–	2*	–	–	–
T. cf. *dicoccum*, emmer spikelet fork	–	–	–	–	–	–	–	1	–	–	–
T. dicoccum/spelta, emmer/spelt wheat grain	–	–	–	–	–	–	–	–	–	–	–
Triticum sp., indeterminate wheat grain	–	–	–	4	–	–	–	3	–	–	1
cf. *Triticum* sp.	–	–	–	–	–	–	–	–	–	–	–
Hordeum vulgare L., indeterminate barley grain	–	–	–	–	–	–	–	–	–	–	–
cf. *Hordeum* sp.	–	–	–	1	–	–	–	–	–	–	–
Cerealia indet. (estimated), indeterminate cereal grains	–	1	–	7	2	–	–	4	–	2	2
Cerealia indet., (whole, frags)	–	(1)	–	(1, 14)	(4)	–	–	(1, 9)	–	(3)	(4)
Cerealia/Large Poaceae, cereal/large grass culm node	–	–	–	–	–	–	–	–	–	–	–

(Continued)

Table 5.1. Gwernvale: charred plant remains from pre-cairn features (features in area of pre-cairn midden). (Continued)

Feature type	*scoop*	*scoop*	*pit*	*pit*	*scoop*	*scoop*	*scoop*	*gully*	*scoop*	*gully*	*pit*
Feature/sample no.	*158*	*159*	*160*	*162*	*163*	*164*	*165*	*167*	*168*	*169*	*170*
Other Plants											
Urtica dioica L., common nettle **CDFWn**	–	–	–	–	–	–	–	–	–	–	–
Corylus avellana L., hazelnut shell fragments **HSW**	3	7	–	79	62	1	1	37	24	1	10
C. avellana L., wgt. gms	0.01	0.03	–	0.57	0.27	0.01	0.01	0.25	0.19	0.005	0.03
Polygonum sp., knotgrass **CDGo**	–	–	–	–	–	–	–	–	–	–	–
Rumex sp., docks **CDGHW**	–	–	–	–	–	–	–	–	–	–	–
cf. *Brassica/Sinapis* sp., charlock/mustard etc. **CD**	–	–	–	–	–	–	–	–	–	–	–
Raphanus raphanistrum L., wild radish fruit **CD**	–	–	–	–	–	–	–	–	–	–	–
Rubus fruticosus agg., blackberry **DGHSWo**	–	–	–	–	–	–	–	–	–	–	1
Rubus sp., raspberry/blackberry **DGHSWo**	–	–	–	1	–	–	–	–	–	–	–
Vicia hirsuta (L.) Gray, hairy tare **DG**	–	–	–	–	–	–	–	–	–	–	–
Vicia sp., vetches **DGHSWo**	–	–	–	–	–	–	–	–	–	–	–
cf. *Vicia* sp.	–	–	–	–	–	–	–	–	–	–	–
Galium aparine L., cleavers **ACHSo**	–	–	–	–	–	–	–	–	–	–	–
cf. *Galium* sp., bedstraw **GHSWow**	–	–	–	–	–	–	–	–	–	–	1
cf. *Hordeum murinum* type, wall barley **DG**	–	–	–	–	–	–	–	–	–	–	–
Poaceae, grass family **G**	–	–	–	–	–	–	–	–	–	–	–
Poaceae, culm/rhizome frag.	–	–	–	–	–	–	–	–	–	1	–
Immature seed capsule	–	–	–	–	–	–	–	–	–	–	–
Bud	–	–	–	–	–	–	–	–	–	–	2
Vesicular plant material indet.	–	–	–	+	+	+	–	–	–	+	+
Wood charcoal	+	+	+	+	+	+	+	+	+	+	+
Indet.	–	–	–	–	–	–	–	–	–	–	–
Total number of items	4	8	0	98	64	1	1	47	24	4	17

(Continued)

Table 5.1. Gwernvale: charred plant remains from pre-cairn features (features below W end and in area to NW of long cairn). (Continued)

Feature type	*irreg. pit/ hollow*	*burnt tree roots*	*irreg. pit/ hollow*	*irreg. pit/ hollow*	*hearth*	*stone surface*	*irreg. gully*
Feature/sample no.	*278*	*291–4*	*295*	*297*	*308*	*309*	*317*
Cereals							
Triticum dicoccum, emmer grain	–	–	–	–	–	–	–
T. cf. *dicoccum*	–	–	–	–	–	–	–
T. cf. dicoccum, emmer spikelet fork	–	–	–	–	–	–	–
T. dicoccum/spelta, emmer/spelt wheat grain	–	–	–	–	–	–	–
Triticum sp., indeterminate wheat grain	–	–	–	–	–	–	–
cf. *Triticum* sp.	–	–	–	–	–	–	–
Hordeum vulgare L., indeterminate barley grain	–	–	–	–	–	–	–
cf. *Hordeum* sp.	–	–	–	–	–	–	–
Cerealia indet. (estimated), indeterminate cereal grains	–	–	–	–	–	1	–
Cerealia indet., (whole, frags)	–	–	–	–	–	(1)	
Cerealia/Large Poaceae, cereal/ large grass culm node	–	–	–	–	–	–	–
Other Plants							
Urtica dioica L., common nettle **CDFWn**	–	–	–	–	–	–	–
Corylus avellana L., hazelnut shell fragments **HSW**	20	1	1	3	–	7	4
C. avellana L., wgt. gms	0.13	0.01	0.06	0.02	–	0.06	0.05
Polygonum sp., knotgrass **CDGo**	–	–	–	–	–	–	–
Rumex sp., docks **CDGHW**	–	–	–	–	–	–	–
cf. *Brassica/Sinapis* sp., charlock/mustard etc. **CD**	1	–	–	–	–	–	–
Raphanus raphanistrum L., wild radish fruit **CD**	–	–	–	–	–	–	–
Rubus fruticosus agg., blackberry **DGHSWo**	–	–	–	–	–	–	–
Rubus sp., raspberry/blackberry **DGHSWo**	–	–	–	–	–	–	–

(Continued)

Table 5.1. Gwernvale: charred plant remains from pre-cairn features (features below W end and in area to NW of long cairn). (Continued)

Feature type	*irreg. pit/ hollow*	*burnt tree roots*	*irreg. pit/ hollow*	*irreg. pit/ hollow*	*hearth*	*stone surface*	*irreg. gully*
Feature/sample no.	*278*	*291–4*	*295*	*297*	*308*	*309*	*317*
Vicia hirsuta (L.) Gray, hairy tare **DG**	–	–	–	–	–	–	–
Vicia sp., vetches **DGHSWo**	–	–	–	–	–	–	–
cf. *Vicia* sp.	1	–	–	–	–	–	–
Galium aparine L., cleavers **ACHSo**	–	–	–	–	–	–	–
cf. *Galium* sp., bedstraw **GHSWow**	–	–	–	–	–	–	–
cf. *Hordeum murinum* type, wall barley **DG**	–	–	–	–	–	–	–
Poaceae, grass family **G**	–	–	–	–	–	–	–
Poaceae, culm/rhizome frag.	–	–	–	–	–	–	–
Immature seed capsule	–	–	1	–	–	–	–
Bud	–	–	–	–	–	–	–
Vesicular plant material indet.	+	–	–	–	–	–	–
Wood charcoal	+	+	+	+	+	+	+
Indet.	–	–		–	1	–	–
Total number of items	22	1	2	3	1	8	4

Key: * = radiocarbon dated; + = present. Habitat preference: **A** = arable; **C** = cultivated; **D** = disturbed; **G** = grassland; **H** = hedgerows; **S** = scrub; **W** = woodland; **n** = nutrient rich; **o** = open; **w** = wet, damp.

Table 5.2. Gwernvale: charred plant remains from the buried soil (30) in area of pre-cairn midden.

Sample square	*1*	*2*	*3*	*4*	*5*	*6*	*7*	*8*	*9*	*10*	*11*	*12*	*13*	*14*
Cereals														
T. monococcum/T. dicoccum, einkorn/emmer wheat grain	–	–	–	–	–	–	–	–	–	–	1	–	–	–
Triticum dicoccum, emmer grain	–	–	1	–	–	–	–	1	1	–	–	–	2	–
T. dicoccum, spikelet fork	–	–	–	–	–	–	–	–	–	–	–	–	–	–
T. cf. *dicoccum*	–	1	1	–	–	–	2	4	1	1	–	–	3	6*
T. dicoccum/spelta, emmer/spelt grain	–	–	–	–	–	–	–	–	1	–	–	–	–	–
Triticum sp., indeterminate wheat grain	–	–	–	–	–	–	2	2	–	–	2	–	9	–
cf. *Triticum* sp.	–	–	–	–	–	1	–	–	1	–	2	–	1	4
Hordeum vulgare L., hulled barley grain	–	–	–	–	–	–	1	–	–	–	–	–	–	–
H. vulgare L., indeterminate barley grain	–	–	–	–	–	–	–	–	–	–	–	–	–	–
cf. *Hordeum* sp.	–	–	–	–	–	–	–	–	–	–	–	1	–	–
Cerealia indet. (estimated), indeterminate cereal grain	3	4	1	–	1	1	6	9	11	5	4	3	15	13
Cerealia indet., (whole, frags)	(6)	(10)	(3)	–	(1)	(4)	(18)	(1,22)	(16)	(14)	(1,10)	(6)	(2,45)	(47)
cf. *Cerealia*/Large Poaceae, cereal/large grass, culm node	–	–	–	–	–	–	–	–	–	–	–	–	–	–
Cerealia/Large Poaceae, cereal/large grass, culm base/rhizome	–	–	–	–	–	–	–	–	–	–	–	–	–	1
Other plants														
Ranunculus sp., buttercups **CGWo**	–	–	–	–	–	–	–	–	–	–	–	–	–	–
Corylus avellana L., hazelnut shell fragments **HSW**	32	33	29	14	57	21	99	156	58	64	110	6	65	184
C. avellana L., wgt. gms	0.315	0.43	0.34	0.06	0.52	0.14	0.715	1.05	0.81	0.495	0.64	0.105	0.59	1.49
cf. *C. avellana* L., hazel catkin frag.	–	–	–	–	–	–	–	–	–	–	–	–	–	–
Chenopodium cf. *album* L., fat hen **CDn**	–	–	–	–	–	–	–	–	–	–	–	–	–	–
Cerastium type, mouse–ears type **CDGo**	–	–	–	–	–	–	–	1	–	–	–	–	–	–
Stellaria media (L.) Villars, common chickweed **CDGno**	–	–	–	–	–	–	–	–	–	–	–	–	–	1
Stellaria sp., stitchworts **CDGHWo**	–	–	–	1	–	–	–	–	–	–	–	–	–	–
Persicaria minor (Hudson) Opiz, small water–pepper **Gw**	–	–	–	–	–	–	1	–	1	–	–	–	–	–
Polygonum arenastrum Boreau, equal–leaved knotgrass **CDGo**	–	–	1	–	–	–	–	–	–	–	1	–	–	–

(Continued)

Table 5.2. Gwernvale: charred plant remains from the buried soil (30) in area of pre-cairn midden. (Continued)

Sample square	*1*	*2*	*3*	*4*	*5*	*6*	*7*	*8*	*9*	*10*	*11*	*12*	*13*	*14*
Rumex conglomeratus/sanguineus, clustered dock/wood dock **DGHWw**	–	–	–	–	–	–	–	–	1	–	–	–	1	2
Rumex sp., docks **CDGHW**	–	–	–	–	–	–	–	1	–	–	–	–	–	–
Viola sp., violets **CDFGHSW**	–	–	–	–	–	–	–	–	–	–	–	–	–	–
cf. *Viola* sp.	–	–	–	–	–	–	–	–	–	–	–	–	–	–
Rubus fruticosus agg., blackberry **DGHSWo**	1	2	–	5	1	–	8	11	4	1	2	–	4	9
Rubus sp., raspberry/blackberry **DGHSWo**	–	–	–	–	–	–	3	4	1	–	–	–	–	2
Rubus/Rosa type, blackberry/rose type thorn	–	–	–	–	–	–	–	–	–	–	–	–	–	1
Rosa sp., roses **HSWo**	–	–	–	–	–	–	–	–	–	–	1	–	–	2
cf. *Crataegus* sp., hawthorns **HSW**	–	–	–	–	–	–	–	–	–	–	–	–	–	–
Linum cf. *usitatissimum* L., flax **C**	–	–	–	–	1	–	–	–	–	–	1	1	–	–
Linum sp.	–	–	–	–	–	–	–	–	–	–	–	–	–	–
cf. *Linum* sp.	–	–	–	–	–	–	–	–	–	–	1	–	–	1
Vicia sp., vetches **DGHSWo**	–	–	–	–	–	–	–	–	–	–	–	–	–	–
cf. *Vicia* sp.	–	–	–	–	–	–	–	–	–	–	–	–	–	–
Vicia/Lathyrus sp., vetches/peas,vetchlings **DGHSWo**	–	–	–	–	–	–	–	–	–	–	–	–	–	–
cf. *Vicia/Lathyrus* sp.	–	–	–	–	–	–	–	–	–	–	–	–	–	–
Atropa belladonna L., deadly nightshade **CD**	–	–	–	–	1	–	–	–	–	–	1	–	–	–
cf. *Plantago lanceolata* L., ribwort plantain **Dgo**	–	–	–	–	–	–	–	–	–	–	–	–	–	–
Stachys sp., woundworts **ADGoH**	–	–	–	–	–	–	–	–	–	–	–	–	–	–
cf. *Mentha* sp., mints **AGWow**	–	–	–	–	–	–	–	–	–	–	–	–	–	–
Lamiaceae, deadnettle family	–	–	–	–	–	–	–	1	–	–	–	–	–	–
Galium aparine L., cleavers **ACHSo**	–	–	–	–	–	–	1	–	1	–	–	–	–	–
Galium sp.(?immature), bedstraw **GHSWow**	–	–	–	–	–	–	–	–	–	–	–	–	–	–
cf. *Galium* sp.	–	–	–	–	–	–	–	–	–	–	–	–	–	–
cf. *Asteraceae* indet., daisy family	–	–	–	–	–	–	–	–	–	–	–	–	–	1
Poaceae, grasses **G**	–	–	–	–	–	–	–	1	–	–	–	–	–	–
Poaceae, culm/rhizome frags	–	–	–	–	–	–	–	–	–	–	1	–	–	–
Immature seed capsule	–	–	–	–	–	–	–	1	–	–	–	–	–	–
Stem – 7 ridges, frag.	–	–	–	–	–	–	–	–	–	–	–	–	–	–
Bud (tree)	–	–	–	–	–	–	–	–	–	–	–	–	–	–

(Continued)

Table 5.2. (Continued)

Sample square	*1*	*2*	*3*	*4*	*5*	*6*	*7*	*8*	*9*	*10*	*11*	*12*	*13*	*14*
Bud scar	–	–	–	–	–	–	–	–	–	–	–	–	–	–
Vesicular plant material indet.	–	+	+	+	+	+	+	+	–	+	+	+	+	+
Wood charcoal	+	+	+	+	+	+	+	+	+	+	+	+	+	+
Indet.	–	–	–	–	–	–	2	1	–	2	1	1	–	–
Total number of items	36	40	33	20	61	23	125	193	81	73	128	12	100	227
Sample square	*15*	*16*	*17*	*18*	*19*	*20*	*21*	*22*	*23*	*24*	*25*	*26*	*27*	*28*
Cereals														
T. monococcum/T. dicoccum, einkorn/emmer wheat grain	–	1	–	–	–	–	–	–	–	–	–	–	1	–
Triticum dicoccum, emmer grain	3	1	1	–	2	2	2	1	–	–	3	–	1	2
T. dicoccum, spikelet fork	–	–	–	–	–	–	–	–	1	–	–	–	–	–
T. cf. *dicoccum*	–	1	–	–	7	1	–	2	–	–	8*	1	2	3
T. dicoccum/spelta, emmer/spelt grain	–	–	–	–	1	–	–	–	–	–	–	–	–	–
Triticum sp., indeterminate wheat grain	3	–	2	1	10	4	2	–	2	–	4	4	2	2
cf. *Triticum* sp.	–	–	–	–	–	–	–	–	–	–	–	–	–	–
Hordeum vulgare L., hulled barley grain	–	–	–	1	–	–	–	–	–	–	–	–	–	–
H. vulgare L., indeterminate barley grain	–	–	–	–	–	1	–	–	–	–	–	–	–	–
cf. *Hordeum* sp.	–	–	–	–	–	–	–	–	1	–	–	1	–	–
Cerealia indet. (estimated), indeterminate cereal grain	7	6	4	1	39	12	8	5	5	2	32	10	8	5
Cerealia indet., (whole, frags)	(15)	(12)	(2,2)	(2)	(6,113)	(2,35)	(1,19)	(1,15)	(1,12)	(3)	(2,107)	(3,23)	(1,21)	(1,15)
cf. *Cerealia*/Large Poaceae, cereal/large grass, culm node	3	–	–	–	–	–	–	–	–	–	–	–	–	–
Cerealia/Large Poaceae, cereal/large grass, culm base/rhizome	1	–	–	–	–	–	–	–	–	–	–	–	–	–
Other plants														
Ranunculus sp., buttercups **CGWo**	–	–	–	–	–	–	–	–	–	–	–	–	–	–
Corylus avellana L., hazelnut shell fragments **HSW**	167	91	41	15	226	187	116	98	74	20	267*	339	266*	149
C. avellana L., wgt. gms	1.22	0.875	0.40	0.285	1.285	0.62	1.21	0.835	0.64	0.275	1.17	2.255	1.59	1.065
cf. *C. avellana* L., hazel catkin frag.	–	–	–	–	–	–	–	–	–	–	–	–	–	–
Chenopodium cf. *album* L., fat hen **CDn**	–	–	1	–	–	–	–	–	–	–	–	–	–	–
Cerastium type, mouse–ears type **CDGo**	–	–	–	–	–	–	–	–	–	–	–	–	–	–
Stellaria media (L.) Villars, common chickweed **CDGno**	–	–	–	–	–	–	–	–	1	–	–	–	–	–

(Continued)

Table 5.2. Gwernvale: charred plant remains from the buried soil (30) in area of pre-cairn midden. (Continued)

Sample square	*15*	*16*	*17*	*18*	*19*	*20*	*21*	*22*	*23*	*24*	*25*	*26*	*27*	*28*
Stellaria sp., stitchworts **CDGHWo**	–	–	–	–	–	–	–	–	–	–	–	–	–	–
Persicaria minor (Hudson) Opiz, small water–pepper **Gw**	–	–	–	–	–	–	–	–	–	–	–	–	–	–
Polygonum arenastrum Boreau, equal–leaved knotgrass **CDGo**	–	–	–	–	–	1	–	–	–	–	–	1	–	–
Rumex conglomeratus/sanguineus, clustered dock/wood dock **DGHWw**	–	–	–	–	–	–	–	–	14	–	–	–	5	3
Rumex sp., docks **CDGHW**	–	–	–	–	–	–	–	–	–	–	–	–	–	–
Viola sp., violets **CDFGHSW**	–	–	–	–	–	–	–	–	1	–	–	–	–	–
cf. *Viola* sp.	–	–	–	–	–	–	–	–	–	–	–	–	–	1
Rubus fruticosus agg., blackberry **DGHSWo**	5	3	–	–	13	12	–	1	1	–	5	3	–	2
Rubus sp., raspberry/blackberry **DGHSWo**	1	–	–	–	2	1	3	–	–	–	7	1	1	–
Rubus/Rosa type, blackberry/rose type thorn	–	–	–	–	–	–	–	–	–	–	–	–	–	–
Rosa sp., roses **HSWo**	–	–	–	–	–	1	1	–	1	1	3	1	–	–
cf. *Crataegus* sp., hawthorns **HSW**	–	–	1	–	–	–	–	1	–	–	–	–	–	–
Linum cf. *usitatissimum* L., flax **C**	–	–	–	–	–	–	1	–	1	–	–	–	–	–
Linum sp.	–	–	–	–	–	–	–	–	1	–	–	–	–	–
cf. *Linum* sp.	–	–	–	–	–	–	–	–	–	–	–	–	–	–
Vicia sp., vetches **DGHSWo**	–	–	–	–	–	–	1	–	–	–	–	–	–	–
cf. *Vicia* sp.	–	–	–	–	–	–	–	–	–	–	–	–	–	–
Vicia/Lathyrus sp., vetches/peas,vetchlings **DGHSWo**	–	–	–	–	–	–	–	–	–	–	–	–	–	1
cf. *Vicia/Lathyrus* sp.	–	–	–	–	–	–	–	–	–	–	–	–	–	1
Atropa belladonna L., deadly nightshade **CD**	–	–	1	–	–	–	–	1	–	–	–	–	–	–
cf. *Plantago lanceolata* L., ribwort plantain **Dgo**	–	–	–	–	–	–	1	–	–	–	–	–	–	–
Stachys sp., woundworts **ADGoH**	–	–	–	–	–	–	–	–	–	–	1	–	–	–
cf. *Mentha* sp., mints **AGWow**	–	–	–	–	–	–	–	–	–	–	–	–	–	2
Lamiaceae, deadnettle family	–	–	–	–	–	–	–	–	–	–	–	–	–	–
Galium aparine L., cleavers **ACHSo**	1	–	–	–	–	–	1	–	1	–	–	–	–	–
Galium sp.(?immature), bedstraw **GHSWow**	–	–	–	–	–	–	–	–	–	–	–	1	–	–
cf. *Galium* sp.	–	–	–	–	–	–	–	–	–	–	–	–	–	–
cf. *Asteraceae* indet., daisy family	–	–	–	–	–	–	–	–	–	–	–	–	–	–
Poaceae, grasses **G**	–	–	–	–	–	–	–	–	–	–	–	–	–	–

(Continued)

Table 5.2. (Continued)

Sample square	*15*	*16*	*17*	*18*	*19*	*20*	*21*	*22*	*23*	*24*	*25*	*26*	*27*	*28*
Poaceae, culm/rhizome frags	–	–	–	–	–	1	–	–	–	–	–	–	–	–
Immature seed capsule	–	–	–	–	–	–	–	–	–	–	–	–	–	–
Stem – 7 ridges, frag.	–	–	–	–	–	–	–	–	–	–	–	–	–	–
Bud (tree)	–	–	–	–	–	–	–	–	–	–	1	–	–	1
Bud scar	–	–	–	–	–	–	–	–	–	–	1	–	–	–
Vesicular plant material indet.	+	+	+	–	+	+	+	+	+	+	+	+	+	+
Wood charcoal	+	+	+	+	+	+	+	+	+	+	+	+	+	+
Indet.	–	–	–	–	–	1	–	–	–	–	2	–	–	–
Total number of items	191	103	51	18	300	224	136	109	104	23	334	362	286	172
Sample square	*29*	*30*	*31*	*32*	*33*	*34*	*35*	*36*	*37*	*38*	*39*	*40*	*41*	*42*
Cereals														
T. monococcum/T. dicoccum, einkorn/emmer wheat grain	–	–	–	–	–	–	–	–	–	–	–	–	–	–
Triticum dicoccum, emmer grain	1	1	2	3	7	–	1	1	3	–	3	–	1	–
T. dicoccum, spikelet fork	–	–	1	–	–	–	–	–	–	–	–	–	–	–
T. cf. *dicoccum*	1	–	–	2	2	–	1	–	5	3	1	2	3	–
T. dicoccum/spelta, emmer/spelt grain	1	–	–	1	–	–	–	–	–	1	1	1	1	–
Triticum sp., indeterminate wheat grain	4	–	–	4	4	5	1	–	3	4	7	2	2	–
cf. *Triticum* sp.	–	–	–	–	–	–	1	–	–	–	–	–	–	–
Hordeum vulgare L., hulled barley grain	–	–	–	–	–	–	–	–	–	–	–	–	1	–
H. vulgare L., indeterminate barley grain	–	–	–	–	–	–	–	–	1	–	–	–	–	–
cf. *Hordeum* sp.	–	–	–	–	–	–	–	–	1	1	–	–	–	–
Cerealia indet. (estimated), indeterminate cereal grain	9	–	4	9	8	8	7	1	12	10	11	3	3	–
Cerealia indet., (whole, frags)	(4,21)	–	(9)	(28)	(24)	(1,27)	(29)	(2)	(31)	(1,29)	(1,42)	(18)	(12)	–
cf. *Cerealia*/Large Poaceae, cereal/large grass, culm node	–	–	–	–	–	–	–	–	–	–	–	–	–	–
Cerealia/Large Poaceae, cereal/large grass, culm base/rhizome	–	–	–	–	–	–	–	–	–	–	–	–	–	–
Other plants														
Ranunculus sp., buttercups **CGWo**	–	–	–	–	–	–	–	–	1	–	–	–	–	–
Corylus avellana L., hazelnut shell fragments **HSW**	116	11	158	401	69	19	104	18	65	87	109	28	26	1
C. avellana L., wgt. gms	0.82	0.075	1.21	2.60	0.35	0.14	0.905	0.205	0.64	0.78	0.64	0.14	0.155	0.005

(Continued)

Table 5.2. Gwernvale: charred plant remains from the buried soil (30) in area of pre-cairn midden. (Continued)

Sample square	*29*	*30*	*31*	*32*	*33*	*34*	*35*	*36*	*37*	*38*	*39*	*40*	*41*	*42*
cf. *C. avellana* L., hazel catkin frag.	–	–	–	–	–	–	–	–	–	–	–	–	–	–
Chenopodium cf. *album* L., fat hen **CDn**	–	–	–	–	–	–	–	–	–	–	–	–	–	–
Cerastium type, mouse–ears type **CDGo**	–	–	–	–	–	–	–	–	–	–	–	–	–	–
Stellaria media (L.) Villars, common chickweed **CDGno**	–	–	–	–	–	–	–	–	–	–	–	–	–	–
Stellaria sp., stitchworts **CDGHWo**	–	–	–	–	–	–	–	–	–	1	–	–	–	–
Persicaria minor (Hudson) Opiz, small water–pepper **Gw**	–	–	–	–	–	–	–	–	–	–	–	–	–	–
Polygonum arenastrum Boreau, equal–leaved knotgrass **CDGo**	–	–	–	–	–	–	–	–	–	–	–	–	–	–
Rumex conglomeratus/sanguineus, clustered dock/wood dock **DGHWw**	5	1	–	–	–	–	–	–	–	–	–	–	–	–
Rumex sp., docks **CDGHW**	–	–	–	–	1	–	–	–	–	–	1	–	–	–
Viola sp., violets **CDFGHSW**	–	–	–	–	–	–	–	–	–	–	–	–	–	–
cf. *Viola* sp.	–	–	–	–	–	–	–	–	–	–	–	–	–	–
Rubus fruticosus agg., blackberry **DGHSWo**	3	–	4	3	2	1	3	–	–	6	2	1	1	–
Rubus sp., raspberry/blackberry **DGHSWo**	2	–	6	2	4	1	1	–	1	–	2	–	2	–
Rubus/Rosa type, blackberry/rose type thorn	–	–	–	–	–	–	–	–	–	–	–	–	–	–
Rosa sp., roses **HSWo**	–	–	1	–	–	–	–	–	–	–	–	–	–	–
cf. *Crataegus* sp., hawthorns **HSW**	–	–	–	–	–	–	–	–	–	–	–	–	–	–
Linum cf. *usitatissimum* L., flax **C**	–	–	–	–	–	–	–	–	–	–	–	–	–	–
Linum sp.	–	–	–	–	–	–	–	–	–	–	–	–	–	–
cf. *Linum* sp.	–	–	–	–	–	–	–	–	–	–	–	–	–	–
Vicia sp., vetches **DGHSWo**	–	–	–	–	–	–	–	–	–	–	–	–	–	–
cf. *Vicia* sp.	–	–	–	1	–	–	–	–	–	–	–	–	1	–
Vicia/Lathyrus sp., vetches/peas,vetchlings **DGHSWo**	–	–	–	–	–	–	–	–	–	–	–	–	–	–
cf. *Vicia/Lathyrus* sp.	–	–	–	–	–	–	–	–	–	–	–	–	–	–
Atropa belladonna L., deadly nightshade **CD**	–	–	–	–	–	–	–	–	–	–	–	–	–	–
cf. *Plantago lanceolata* L., ribwort plantain **Dgo**	–	–	–	–	–	–	–	–	–	–	–	–	–	–
Stachys sp., woundworts **ADGoH**	–	–	–	–	–	–	–	–	–	–	–	–	–	–
cf. *Mentha* sp., mints **AGWow**	–	–	–	–	–	–	–	–	–	–	–	–	–	–
Lamiaceae, deadnettle family	–	–	–	–	–	–	–	–	–	–	–	–	–	–
Galium aparine L., cleavers **ACHSo**	–	–	–	–	–	–	–	–	–	–	–	–	1	–

(Continued)

Table 5.2. (Continued)

Sample square	*29*	*30*	*31*	*32*	*33*	*34*	*35*	*36*	*37*	*38*	*39*	*40*	*41*	*42*
Galium sp.(?immature), bedstraw **GHSWow**	–	–	–	–	–	–	–	–	–	–	2	–	–	–
cf. *Galium* sp.	–	–	1	–	–	–	–	1	–	–	1	–	–	–
cf. *Asteraceae* indet., daisy family	–	–	–	–	–	–	–	–	–	–	–	–	–	–
Poaceae, grasses **G**	–	–	1	–	–	–	–	–	–	–	–	–	–	–
Poaceae, culm/rhizome frags	–	–	–	–	–	–	–	–	–	–	–	–	1	–
Immature seed capsule	1	–	–	–	1	–	–	–	–	–	–	–	2	–
Stem – 7 ridges, frag.	–	–	–	–	–	–	–	–	–	–	–	–	–	1
Bud (tree)	–	–	–	–	–	–	–	–	–	–	–	–	–	–
Bud scar	–	–	–	–	–	–	–	–	–	–	–	–	–	–
Vesicular plant material indet.	+	+	+	+	+	+	+	+	+	+	+	+	+	+
Wood charcoal	+	+	+	+	+	+	+	+	+	+	+	+	+	+
Indet.	2	1	2	–	–	–	–	–	–	1	–	–	–	–
Total number of items	145	14	180	426	98	34	119	21	92	114	140	37	45	2

Key: * = radiocarbon dated; + = present. Habitat preference: **A** = arable; **C** = cultivated; **D** = disturbed; **G** = grassland; **H** = hedgerows; **S** = scrub; **W** = woodland; **n** = nutrient rich; **o** = open; **w** = wet, damp.

Table 5.3. Gwernvale: charred plant remains from lower soil layer (202) in the forecourt area.

Sample square	*1*	*2*	*3*	*4*	*5*	*6*	*7–7A*	*8*	*9–10*	*11–11A*	*12*	*13*	*14*	*15—15A*	*16*	*17*
Cereals																
Triticum dicoccum, emmer grain	–	–	3*	–	–	1	–	–	2	2	–	2	2	–	–	4
T. cf. *dicoccum*	–	2	6	–	–	–	–	–	–	3	1	1	4	–	1	3
T. dicoccum/spelta, emmer/spelt grain	1	1	1	–	–	–	–	–	1	–	–	–	–	–	–	–
Triticum sp., indeterminate wheat grain	–	1	2	–	–	2	1	–	2	2	–	5	1	–	–	4
cf. *Triticum* sp.	–	–	–	–	–	–	–	–	–	1	–	–	–	–	–	1
Hordeum vulgare L., hulled barley grain	–	1	–	–	–	–	–	–	–	–	–	–	–	–	–	–
H. vulgare L., indeterminate barley grain	–	–	–	–	–	–	–	1	–	–	–	1	–	–	–	–
cf. *Triticum/Secale cereale*, wheat, rye grain	–	–	–	–	–	–	–	–	–	–	–	–	1	–	–	–
cf. *Avena* sp., oat grain	–	–	–	–	–	–	–	–	–	–	–	–	1	–	–	–
Cerealia indet. (estimated), indeterminate cereal grain	1	2	4	–	1	3	3	–	4	5	3	4	2	1	–	4

(Continued)

Table 5.3. Gwernvale: charred plant remains from lower soil layer (202) in the forecourt area. (Continued)

Sample square	*1*	*2*	*3*	*4*	*5*	*6*	*7–7A*	*8*	*9–10*	*11–11A*	*12*	*13*	*14*	*15—15A*	*16*	*17*
Cerealia indet., (whole, frags)	(3)	(4)	(11)	–	(1)	(5)	(1,6)	–	(1,4)	(8)	(5)	(7)	(6)	(1)	–	(6)
Other plants																
cf. *Ranunculus ficaria*, lesser celendine tuber **GdHW**	–	–	1	–	–	–	–	–	–	–	–	–	–	–	–	–
Ranunculus sp., buttercups **CGWo**	–	–	–	–	–	–	–	–	–	–	–	1	–	–	–	–
Quercus petraea/robur, oak – cupule frag. **W**	–	–	1	–	–	–	–	–	–	–	–	–	–	–	–	–
Corylus avellana L., hazelnut shell fragments **HSW**	19	89	201	5	9	26	9	3	37	40	34	67	20	2	2	12
C. avellana L., wgt. gms	0.13	0.71	1.32	0.03	0.1	0.13	0.07	0.01	0.25	0.36	0.24	0.48	0.16	0.02	0.05	0.13
Stellaria media (L.) Villars, common chickweed **CDGno**	–	–	1	–	–	–	–	–	–	–	–	–	–	–	–	–
Persicaria minor (Hudson) Opiz, small water-pepper **Gw**	–	–	–	–	–	–	–	–	–	–	–	1	–	–	1	–
Rumex conglomeratus/sanguineus, clustered dock/ wood dock **DGHWw**	–	–	–	–	–	–	–	–	–	1	–	–	–	–	–	–
Rubus fruticosus agg., blackberry **DGHSWo**	–	1	–	–	–	–	–	–	–	–	–	1	–	–	–	–
Rubus sp., raspberry/blackberry **DGHSWo**	–	–	–	–	–	–	–	–	–	–	–	–	–	–	–	–
Rubus/Rosa type, blackberry/rose type thorn	–	–	–	–	–	–	–	–	–	–	–	–	–	–	–	–
Plantago lanceolata L., ribwort plantain **DGo**	–	–	–	–	–	–	–	–	–	–	1	–	–	–	–	–
Galium aparine L., cleavers **ACHSo**	1	1	2	1	1	4	1	–	–	2	1	4	3	–	–	–
Poaceae, grasses **G**	–	–	–	1	–	–	–	–	–	–	–	–	–	–	–	–
Poaceae, culm/rhizome frags	1	–	–	–	–	–	1	–	–	1	–	–	–	16	1	2
Bud (tree)	1	–	–	–	1	–	–	–	–	–	–	–	–	–	–	–
Vesicular plant material indet.	+	+	–	+	+	–	+	–	+	+	–	–	–	+	+	–
Wood charcoal	+	+	+	+	+	+	+	+	+	+	+	+	+	+	+	+
Indet.	1	–	1	–	–	–	–	–	–	–	–	1	–	1	–	–
Total number of items	25	98	223	7	12	36	15	4	46	57	40	88	34	20	5	30

Key: * = radiocarbon dated; + = present. Habitat preference: **A** = arable; **C** = cultivated; **D** = disturbed; **G** = grassland; **H** = hedgerows; **S** = scrub; **W** = woodland; **n** = nutrient rich; **o** = open; **w** = wet, damp.

Table 5.4. Gwernvale: charred plant remains from upper soil layer (95) in the forecourt area.

Sample square	*1–2*	*3*	*4*	*5*	*6–6A*	*7–7A*	*8*	*9*	*10*	*11–11A*	*12*	*13*	*14*	*15*	*16*	*17*	*18*
Cereals																	
Triticum dicoccum, emmer grain	3	4*	–	3	4	–	2	3	–	–	–	–	–	1	–	–	–
T. cf. *dicoccum*	4	6	–	1	8	2	5	3	1	1	2	1	–	–	–	–	–
T. dicoccum/spelta, emmer/spelt grain	–	–	–	–	–	–	1	–	–	–	–	–	–	–	–	–	–
Triticum sp., indeterminate wheat grain	7	3	–	5	10	2	2	5	3	–	3	4	–	–	–	–	–
cf. *Triticum* sp.	–	–	–	–	–	–	–	–	–	1	–	1	–	–	–	–	–
Hordeum vulgare L., indeterminate barley grain	–	–	–	–	–	–	1	–	–	–	–	–	–	–	–	–	–
Cerealia indet. (estimated), indeterminate cereal grain	26	17	–	14	22	3	5	16	7	1	5	4	–	1	1	–	1
Cerealia indet., (whole, frags)	(10,52)	(2,36)	–	(2,34)	(3,49)	(1,5)	(1,8)	(3,37)	(2,19)	(2)	(10)	(1,7)	–	(1)	(1)	–	(1)
Other plants																	
Ranunculus sp., buttercups **CGWo**	–	–	–	–	1	–	–	–	–	–	–	–	–	–	–	–	–
Corylus avellana L., hazelnut shell fragments **HSW**	200	194	4	421	122	32	289	148	112	58	67	86	6	3	6	8	11
C. avellana L., wgt. gms	1.815	1.57	0.02	2.79	0.16	0.26	2.89	1.47	0.63	0.3	0.55	0.46	0.11	0.04	0.05	0.1	0.06
Stellaria media (L.) Villars, common chickweed **CDGno**	1	–	–	–	–	–	–	–	–	–	–	–	–	–	–	–	
Polygonum arenastrum Boreau, equal-leaved knotgrass **CDGo**	–	–	–	–	1	–	–	–	–	–	–	–	–	–	–	–	–
Rumex conglomeratus/sanguineus, clustered dock/wood dock **DGHWw**	–	–	–	–	1	–	–	1	–	1	–	–	–	–	–	–	–
Rubus sp., raspberry/blackberry **DGHSWo**	–	–	–	–	2	–	–	–	–	–	–	1	–	–	–	–	–
Rubus sp., thorn	–	–	–	–	–	–	–	–	–	–	–	–	–	–	1	–	–
cf. *Linum* sp.	1	–	–	–	–	–	–	–	1	–	–	–	–	–	–	–	–
Vicia sp., hairy tair **DG**	–	1	–	–	–	–	–	–	–	–	–	–	–	–	–	–	–
cf. *Vicia* sp.	–	–	–	1	–	–	–	–	–	–	–	–	–	–	–	–	–
Vicia/Lathyrus sp., vetches/peas, vetchlings **DGHSWo**	–	–	–	–	1	–	–	–	–	–	–	–	–	–	–	–	–
cf. Lamiaceae, deadnettles	1	–	–	–	–	–	–	–	–	–	–	–	–	–	–	–	–

(Continued)

Table 5.4. Gwernvale: charred plant remains from upper soil layer (95) in the forecourt area. (Continued)

Sample square	*1–2*	*3*	*4*	*5*	*6–6A*	*7–7A*	*8*	*9*	*10*	*11–11A*	*12*	*13*	*14*	*15*	*16*	*17*	*18*
Plantago major L., greater plantain **CDGo**	–	–	–	–	–	–	–	–	–	1	–	–	–	–	–	–	–
Galium aparine L., cleavers **ACHSo**	14	6	–	6	6	1	2	3	–	1	–	2	–	–	–	–	–
Large Poaceae, grasses **G**	–	–	–	–	–	–	–	1	–	–	1	–	–	–	–	–	–
Poaceae, culm/rhizome frags **G**	1	–	–	2	1	1	–	3	–	–	1	–	–	–	–	–	–
Vesicular plant material indet.	+	+	+	+	+	+	+	+	+	–	+	–	–	+	–	–	–
Wood charcoal	+	+	+	+	+	+	+	+	+	+	+	+	+	+	+	+	+
Indet.	1	1	–	1	1	–	–	–	–	–	–	–	–	–	–	–	–
Total number of items	259	232	4	454	180	41	307	183	124	64	79	99	6	5	8	8	12

Key: * = radiocarbon dated; + = present. Habitat preference: **A** = arable; **C** = cultivated; **D** = disturbed; **G** = grassland; **H** = hedgerows; **S** = scrub; **W** = woodland; **n** = nutrient rich; **o** =open; **w** = wet, damp.

Table 5.5. Gwernvale: charred plant remains from the soil layers within Chamber 2 (128), Chamber 3 (122) and the soil layer (239) to the NW of the long cairn.

	Chamber		*Soil layer 239 to NW of the long cairn**										
Sample square	*2*	*3*	*3*	*4*	*5*	*6*	*12*	*14*	*16*	*17*	*18*	*19*	*20*
Feature/sample no.	*128*	*122*											
Cereals													
Hordeum vulgare L., indeterminate barley grain	1	–	–	–	–	–	–	–	–	–	–	–	–
Cerealia indet. (estimated), indeterminate cereal grain	–	1	1	–	1	–	–	–	–	–	–	–	–
Cerealia indet., (whole, frags)	–	(2)	(1)	–	(1)	–	–	–	–	–	–	–	–
cf. *Cerealia*/Large Poaceae, cereal/large grass, culm node	–	–	–	–	1	–	–	–	–	–	–	–	–
Cerealia/Large Poaceae, cereal/large grass, culm base/rhizome	–	–	–	–	–	1	–	–	–	1	–	–	–
Other plants													
Corylus avellana L., hazelnut shell fragments **HSW**	20	6	1	3	5	4	1	2	1	3	1	10	1
C. avellana L., wgt. gms	0.12	0.05	0.01	0.02	0.04	0.03	0.01	0.04	0.01	0.02	0.01	0.06	0.01
Stellaria sp., stitchworts **CDGHWo**	–	–	–	1	–	–	–	–	–	–	–	–	–
Rubus sp., raspberry/blackberry **DGHSWo**	–	–	–	–	–	–	–	–	–	–	–	–	1
Vesicular plant material indet.	–	–	+	+	+	–	+	–	–	–	–	+	–
Wood charcoal	+	+	+	+	+	+	+	+	+	+	+	+	+
Total number of items	21	7	2	4	7	5	1	2	1	4	1	10	2

Key: * The only charred plant remains in other sampled squares are indeterminate vesicular plant material from squares 8–9 and wood charcoal from squares 1–2, 7, 11, 15, 22. + = present. Habitat preference: **C** = cultivated; **D** = disturbed; **G** = grassland; **H** = hedgerows; **S** = scrub; **W** = woodland; **n** = nutrient rich; **o** = open.

Table 5.6. Gwernvale: charcoal identifications from selected features associated with the pre-cairn timber structure.

Feature type	*post-hole*	*wall-line*	*post-hole*	*wall-line*	*post-hole*	*post-hole*	*?post-hole*	*?post-hole*	*post-pack-ing*	*post-pipe*	*post-packing*	*post-pipe*	*post-pack-ing*	*post-pipe*	*wall-line*	*charcoal spread*	
Feature/sample no.	*133A*	*133B*	*133C*	*133D*	*133E*	*133G*	*205*	*206*	*208A*	*208B*	*209A*	*209B*	*211A*	*211B*	*229*	*249*	*Total*
Ulmus spp., elm	–	–	–	1	–	–	–	–	–	–	–	–	–	–	–	–	1
Quercus spp., oak	3	1	1	3	7	–	19	2	–	1	3	3	3	1	1	1	49
Alnus glutinosa (L.) Gaertner, alder	–	–	–	–	–	–	–	–	–	–	–	–	–	2	–	–	2
Corylus avellana L., hazel	–	1	–	–	1	–	1	1	–	–	–	–	1	–	–	2	7
Prunus spinsosa L., blackthorn	–	–	–	–	–	–	–	–	–	–	–	–	–	–	1	–	1
Prunus spp., cherries	–	–	–	–	–	–	–	–	–	–	–	–	–	1	–	–	1
Maloideae type, crab apple, rowan, whitebeam, hawthorn	2	2	3	3	–	2	–	–	5	5	3	2	1	2	4	5	39
Fraxinus excelsior, ash	–	1	1	3	2	4	–	–	–	–	–	–	–	–	9	1	21
Total	5	5	5	10	10	6	20	3	5	6	6	5	5	6	15	9	121

6

Neolithic people of the Black Mountains: human remains from Penywyrlod, Pipton and Ty Isaf

Michael P. Wysocki

Introduction: historical background and technical notes

Human skeletal collections from Neolithic chambered tombs in SE Wales, held at the National Museum of Wales, were examined by this writer in 1998, as part of a Leverhulme-funded project directed by Alasdair Whittle, which reviewed archived skeletal remains from chambered tombs and long barrows in southern Britain. Following a preliminary account of the remains from the Black Mountains tombs of Penywyrlod, Pipton and Ty Isaf (Wysocki and Whittle 2000), the opportunity now arises to present a more detailed report of these mortuary deposits. This chapter has been prepared from the author's original notes, data and earlier drafts, reviewed and revised in 2019–22. The co-operation and support of Richard Brewer, Elizabeth Walker and Steve Burrows of the National Museum of Wales, Cardiff (NMW), who facilitated access to the collections, are gratefully acknowledged.

In general, analysis of skeletal remains and dentition here followed methods, protocols and guidelines set out in Buikstra and Ubelaker (1994), Steele and Bramblett (1988), T. White (1991), Bass (1992), Scheuer and Black (2000) and Hillson (1986; 1996). Age estimation based on dental attrition utilised Lovejoy (1985). Age estimates based on dental development follow AlQhatani *et al.* (2010). Sex assessment techniques used for fragmented and incomplete postcranial remains are summarised in Table 6.1. Taphonomic observations followed methods and principles presented in Lyman (1994) and Haglund and Sorg (1997; 2001); bone weathering analysis followed Behrensmeyer (1978) and fracture pattern analysis adopts the method of Villa and Mahieu (1991). Palaeopathological observations are based on Ortner (2003) and

Table 6.1. Sex assessment of fragmentary remains utilised in Chapter 6.

Element	*Method*	*Metric*	*Reference*
Scapula	Glenoid cavity length	GL	Bass (1992)
Humerus	Vertical head diameter	VHD	Stewart (1979); Dittrick and Suchey (1986)
	Epicondylar width	EW	Stroud (1993); Dittrick and Suchey (1986)
Radius	Max/min diameter radial head	DRH	Berrizbeitia (1989)
Femur	Mid-shaft circumference	CM	Black (1978); DiBennardo and Taylor (1979); Dittrick and Suchey (1986)
	Vertical head diameter	VHD	Steward (1979); Dittrick and Suchey (1986)
	Anteroposterior shaft diameter	APD	MacLaughlin and Bruce (1985); Dittrick and Suchey (1986)
Tibia	Circumference at nutrient foramen	CNF	Iscan and Miller-Shaivitz (1984)
	Biarticular breadth	BB	Holland (1991)
Calcaneus	discriminant function 1	DF1	Steele (1976)
Talus	discriminant function 2	DF2	Steele (1976)

Aufderheide and Rodriguez-Martin (1998). Recording of musculoskeletal stress markers (MSM) followed the method of Hawkey and Merbs (1995). Stature estimates used the formulae of Formicola and Franceschi (1996). Analysis of human cremated remains followed McKinley (2000). Animal bone identifications were courtesy of NMW staff.

Human remains from Penywyrlod

Background

Human and animal skeletal remains are recorded from several contexts (see Fig. 6.1, Table 6.2; Luff *et al.* 1984). The focus here is on the substantial disturbed assemblage from Chamber NE II and the partial assemblage from Chamber NE III and passage.

A short report on the human and animal remains was produced by Luff *et al.* (1984). In 2005 Caroline Wilkinson undertook a facial reconstruction of an almost complete skull from Chamber NE II (see below and Luff *et al.* 1984, 37), which is on display at the St Fagans National Museum of History, Cardiff (Fig. 1.3).

Eight radiocarbon dates are now available for human bones from Penywyrlod (see Chapter 4). Four specimens from Chamber NE II were dated. A bulked sample from Chamber NE II is dated to *3780–3625 cal BC* (*93% probability*; HAR-974; Fig. 4.3). Three single entity specimens from Chamber NE III and passage were also dated. The first use of the site for burial occurred in *3770–3655 cal BC* (*95% probable*; *first_primary_Penywyrlod*; Fig. 4.3), and the last individual died in *3490–3415 cal BC* (*95% probable*; *last_primary_Penywyrlod*; Fig. 4.3).

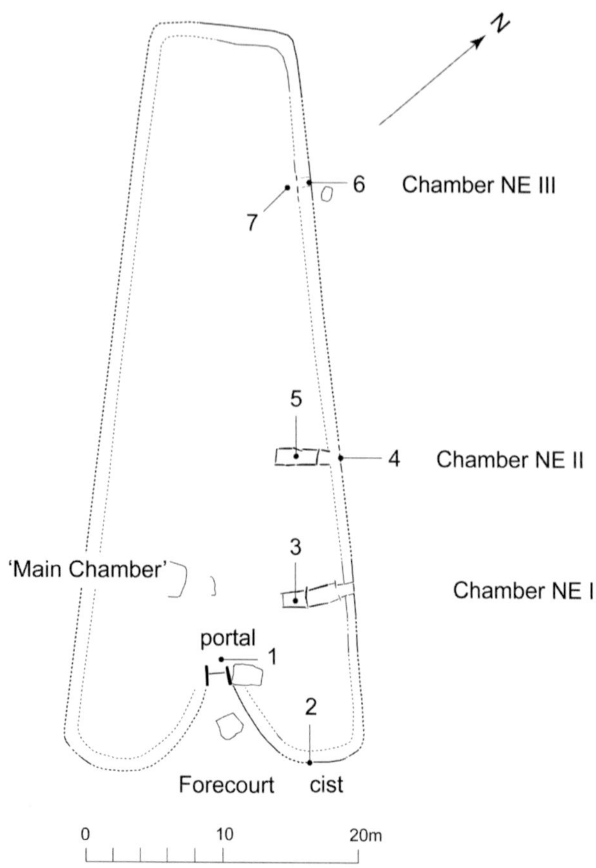

Fig. 6.1. Penywyrlod: contexts in which human and animal bone are recorded. See also Table 6.2.

Table 6.2. Penywyrlod: contexts from which human and animal bone are recorded.

Context	*Location description*
1	Socket of fallen portal orthostat
2	Cist adjoining forecourt
3	Chamber NE I – paving of inner chamber
4	Chamber NE II – entrance passage
5	Chamber NE II – chamber, subdivided into the following groups
	Group A: 'NE end of NW side'
	Group B: 'Against foot of second side slab from SW end, 5ft [1.5m] from end slab NW side'
	Group C: 'Wedged under leaning side slab'
	Group D: 'NW end SW end slab'
	Group E: 'Halfway along NE side; halfway along chamber on S side'
	Group F: 'NE end of SE side'
	Group G: 'Middle of floor 3ft [0.9m] from SW end'
	Group H: '3ft [0.9m] from W end of chamber S side under paving slab'
6	Chamber NE III – entrance passage
7	Chamber NE III – front part of chamber

Chamber NE II

The chamber (Figs 6.1–6.3) had been partially damaged and its contents disturbed upon discovery in the early 1970s. In the original report it was argued that when the tomb was built the chamber had been constructed as a closed cist, sealed at its NE end by a large slab with a 'dummy' passage leading to it from the side of the cairn (Savory 1984, 19). Based on evidence from the more recent excavation of Chamber NE I it is suggested that the passage to the chamber was probably opened on more than one occasion and that the chamber itself may have remained accessible by various means (see Chapter 2). There were no human remains in the Chamber NE II passage, and only a few fragmentary animal bones at various levels in the filling material (Savory 1984, 19).

Following removal of a top scatter of disturbed and recently broken human bones, evidently remnant groupings of disarticulated bones along the sides and in the corners of the chamber were recorded (Fig. 6.2, numbered in this chapter

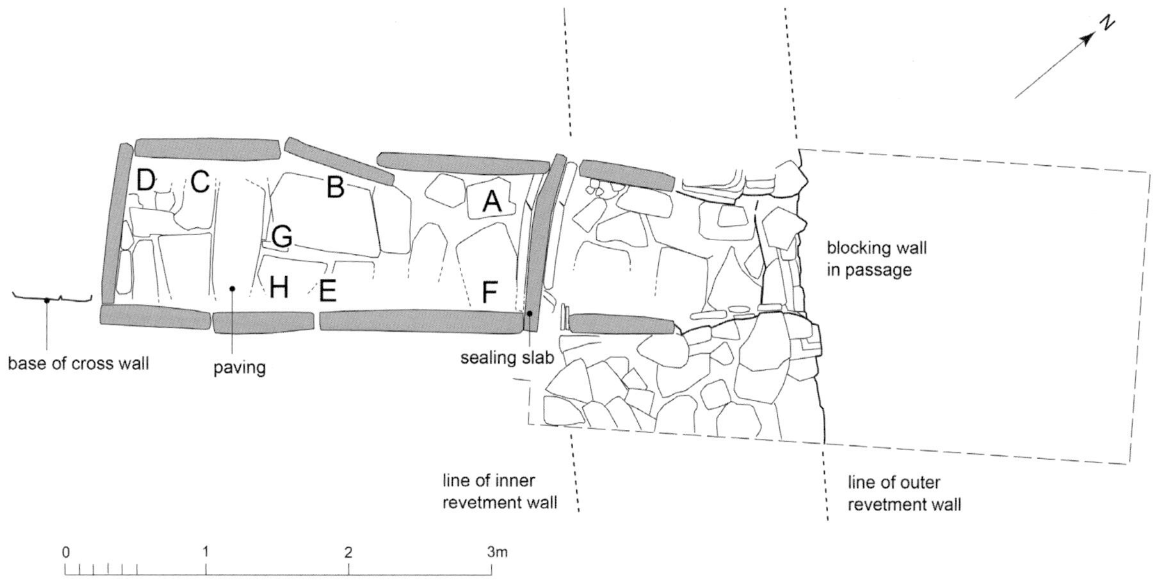

Fig. 6.2. Penywyrlod: plan of Chamber NE II (after Savory 1984, fig. 6 and Britnell 1992) showing bone groups. Note that the location of the bone groups has been amended from Wysocki and Whittle 2000, fig. 2.

as Groups A–H); it is worth repeating some of the original description from Hubert Savory (1984, 19; see also Fig. 6.3):

> The contents had naturally been badly disturbed, but it was clear that it had been an ossuary containing a considerable quantity of disarticulated bones. .... What could be seen *in situ* in June 1972 was clearly a charnel deposit with bones piled chiefly against the foot of the side walls, especially along the NW side and towards the SW end, usually lengthwise, as can be seen in the photograph, taken when the deposits had already been partially cleared, leaving only those which were certainly in their original position.

Luff *et al.* (1984, 36) reported that the remains of at least six adults were present, including three males and one female, while Savory (1984, 35) confidently interpreted the disarticulated bones in terms of 'reburial from some temporary resting place', and presumed that their deposition was 'a single act, followed by sealing and offerings of animal bones in the filling of the "dummy" entrance passage'.

Chamber NE III and passage

The entrance area of Chamber NE III and its short functional passage had also been exposed by quarrying, but it is not known if the passage deposits were significantly disturbed. Skeletal remains recovered from the passage were described as 'close to the top of the drystone walling of the SE side of the entrance passage, intermingled with small blocking slabs...and more were found mixed with blocking material lower down' (Savory 1984, 20). This contextual distinction was not preserved in archive and the relevant material is simply labelled 'Entrance Passage'.

Full recovery of the contents of Chamber NE III was beyond the scope of the 1972 rescue excavation and only those visible disarticulated bones from just inside the entrance were removed (Savory 1984, 20). Some were high up, close to the top of the SE chamber orthostat (labelled '*top scatter*') and the remainder lower down, in a loose

Fig. 6.3. Penywyrlod: skeletal remains in Chamber NE II during excavation in 1972, after partial clearance, viewed from the NE (after Savory 1984, pl. 7b). Scale divisions 1ft (0.3m).

stony filling (labelled '*material recovered from inside the entrance area*'). Luff *et al.* (1984, 37) reported that the human bones recovered from the passage represented at least two individuals; remains from the chamber entrance were estimated to be from seven people: five adults, an adolescent and a child. Following the analysis presented here, the 1984 results have been revised and adjusted slightly (see below).

Taphonomy

Present condition of the human skeletal remains

The remains were unordered at the time of re-examination in 1998. Fortunately, almost every bone and fragment had been labelled with its context as excavated and it was possible to reconstitute the original *in situ* piles and groupings using this information (Table 6.2). Two collections of human bones, fragmented and scattered during the disturbances, were recovered from the top of the deposit: a substantial main concentration and a smaller group from the SW end of the chamber (Savory 1984, 19). A few of these recently broken elements (with fresh, unpatinated transverse fractures) were found to conjoin with broken specimens from the *in situ* groupings listed below and have been relocated accordingly. Some 16 cranial and three postcranial fragments, unlabelled and unmarked, were taphonomically consistent with material from Chamber NE II and have been included in the disturbed fraction. Among these was a right-sided parietal with a healed depressed fracture, previously reported in Schulting and Wysocki (2005, 119, and see below).

Postmortem bone modifications in Chamber NE II

Despite recent (1970s) breakages, bones from Chamber NE II were in relatively good condition and 10 limb bones (including reconstructed recently broken ones) were intact or nearly intact. In contrast, cranial remains were, with one exception, largely fragmented and incomplete: one skull (previously reported in Luff *et al.* 1984, 37) was undamaged, but no other skulls could be reconstructed to anywhere near the same extent. The bones were 'clean': presenting lightly patinated surfaces with no evident soil staining.

Mammalian traces

A few bones displayed light rodent gnawing.

Fragmentation and bone survivorship

The great majority of broken limb bones displayed transverse, right-angled fractures (Table 6.3), typical of bones broken when in a dry, denatured state (Villa and Mahieu 1991; Knusel and Robb 2016; Scheirs *et al.* 2017); most displayed clean, granulated, unpatinated fracture surfaces with sharp, 'fresh' edges, these features almost certainly representing damage inflicted during the late 20th-century episodes of quarrying and disturbance. While a number of such recently fractured segments could be conjoined, others were left without their missing portions and it must be assumed that some fragmented and, possibly, intact specimens, were destroyed before the rescue excavation began.

Table 6.3. Penywyrlod: Chambers NE II and NE III, human bone weathering and fracture analysis.

	Chamber NE II		Chamber NE III	
	N	*% frequency*	*N*	*% frequency*
Weathering stage				
0	57	79.2	11	29.0
1	9	12.5	14	36.8
2	2	2.8	4	10.5
3	4	5.5	5	13.2
4	–	–	4	10.5
Total	72	100	38	100
Fracture morphology				
Transverse	24	85.7	17	70.8
V/Spiral	3	10.7	1	4.2
Intermediate	1	3.6	6	25.0
total	28	100	24	100
Fracture angles				
Right	26	92.8	16	69.6
Oblique	1	3.6	1	4.3
Right/oblique	1	3.6	6	26.1
Total	28	100	23	100

Curiously, except for the single complete skull, parts from the facial skeleton and even fragmentary remains from individual sphenoid bones were almost entirely missing. Although the quarrying episodes were likely responsible for destructive damage to cranial remains, it might be expected that some facial/sphenoidal fragments would be consequently scattered amongst the surviving material. The possibility remains that certain crania may have been to some extent damaged and incomplete when originally deposited in this chamber.

Vertebrae (cervical to lumbar) were poorly represented: only 27 specimens from an expected total for six individuals of 144 (18.75%). Small bones of the hand and wrist numbered 20 (6.2% of expected total) and foot bones, not including calcaneus and talus, totalled 27 (8.7% of expected total) (see Tables 6.4 and 6.12). Ribs were represented by only two fragments.

Weathering modifications

The material was largely unweathered (Table 6.3). Several limb fragments displayed localised patches of subaerial weathering modifications (stages 2 to 4: Behrensmeyer 1978), sometimes focused at one surface while the rest of the affected bone was unweathered (stage 0). These semi-weathered segments very probably represent bones left partially

Table 6.4. Penywyrlod: Chamber NE II, human bone survival frequencies based on MNI 6.

Bone/segment	*Number*	*% surviving*
Frontal R	6	100
Frontal L	5	83
Parietal R	5	83
Parietal L	3	50
Occiptal	5	83
Temporal R	2	33
Temporal L	2	33
Mandible R	6	100
Mandible L	5	83
Clavicle R	1	16
Clavicle L	1	16
Scapula R	5	83
Scapula L	5	83
Innominate R	4	66
Innominate L	6	100
Humerus R prox. end	4	66
prox. shaft	5	83
dist. shaft	3	50
dist. end	2	33
Humerus L prox end	4	66
prox. shaft.	5	83
dist. shaft	4	66
dist. end	2	33
Radius R prox. end	3	60
prox. shaft	3	50
dist. shaft	2	33
dist. end	1	60
Radius L prox. end	1	16
prox. shaft	1	16
dist. shaft	2	33
dist. end	1	16
Ulna R prox. end	4	66
prox. shaft	4	66
dist. shaft	4	66
dist. end	2	33
Ulna L prox. end	4	66
prox. shaft	4	66
dist. shaft	3	50
dist. end	2	33
Femur R prox. end	3	50
prox. shaft	6	100
dist. shaft	5	83
dist. end	4	66

(Continued)

Table 6.4. (Continued)

Bone/segment	*Number*	*% surviving*	
Femur L prox end	6	100	
prox. shaft	6	100	
dist. shaft	5	83	
dist. end	2	33	
Tibia R prox. end	3	50	
prox. shaft	2	33	
dist. shaft	1	16	
dist. end	1	16	
Tibia L proximal end	2	33	
prox. shaft	4	66	
dist. shaft	2	33	
dist. end	1	16	
Fibula R	3	50	
Fibula L	5	83	
Calceneus R	5	83	
Calcaneus L	2	33	
Talus R	6	100	
Talus L	3	50	
		Expected	
Hand	20	324	6.2
Foot	27	312	8.7
Vertebrae	27	144	18.7

exposed to the elements during the period between the 1970s disturbance and the beginning of Savory's excavation. The point is emphasised by two conjoining portions of left humerus, one part from *in situ* Group B, and one part from the disturbed top scatter. Both segments displayed recent transverse fracture surfaces and reconnected with perfect fit. The *in situ* fragment from Group B was unweathered (stage 0), while the fragment from the top scatter was weathered to stage 1 with multiple fine split-lines.

Biogeochemical erosion

Several bones displayed small, localised patches of black/dark-grey staining, with light to moderate surface erosion within the area of staining, representing biogeochemical processes of diagenesis. Fragments of cranial vault from Group A, identified as 'burnt skull' in the original report (Savory 1984, 19), were in fact not burnt, but heavily stained black; the surfaces of these fragments were covered in a fine crystallised coating, or dusting, representing destructive secondary remineralisation (Nielsen-Marsh *et al.* 2000; Kendall *et al.* 2018, 30–1). The affected material was relatively friable, but the fragments were found to conjoin with larger pieces of supra-occipital and temporal, largely unstained, from the same context. When reconstructed the resulting skull portion displayed an area of concentrated staining, dissipating marginally, with crystal remineralisation at the focus of fragmentation. The specimen is a remarkable 'snapshot' of the *in situ* process of differential destruction. It is possible that the skull portion was deposited in the corner of the chamber, the affected area perhaps resting against the NE end slab, with water, intermittently seeping down the side of the stone (as noted by Savory 1984, 19), creating a damp microenvironment and acting as a catalyst for destructive processes (Kendall *et al.* 2018). Given the otherwise good condition of the skeletal remains, however, it is judged unlikely that *in situ* erosion of skeletal material has been a major agency of destruction in this chamber.

Postmortem bone modifications in Chamber NE III and passage

The condition of the skeletal material from both these contexts is largely uniform, but of a different character to that found in Chamber NE II. Many fragments are soil-stained reddish-brown, although a few have a 'bleached' white appearance. Savory (1984, 22) commented that the bones from the chamber entrance area 'were in a good condition when they came from the higher levels' while those from the paved floor of the chamber 'were in a poor condition owing to damp', but the distinction was not evident in this examination. Unexfoliated bone surfaces display extensive, multiple, randomly orientated scratch-like linear abrasion marks, found all-over or concentrated on one or two surfaces. Most likely the result of one or more episodes of turbation (Fisher Jr. 1995, 34–5), these striations are patinated, and in some cases truncated at the margin of unexfoliated/exfoliated surfaces, indicating that they were extant before the onset of later-stage weathering changes. Savory (1984, 20) noted that the bones from the chamber entrance were in a loose stony filling and the presence of this debris could account for much of the surface modifications, while the bones from the passage were intermingled with blocking slabs (Savory 1984, 22).

Mammalian traces. More rodent-gnawed specimens are in evidence here than found in Chamber NE II, with patination of exposed cortical bone indicating 'old' gnawing. Mandible 1 from the Chamber entrance deposit (see below) displays unusual rodent gnawing at the left lateral surface, along the oblique line. The right coronoid process appears to have been gnawed away as well, with gnaw marks at the left anterior border of the ramus; gnawed surfaces are close or 'smooth' textured and are patinated to the same hue as surrounding unmodified bone. The appearance strongly suggests gnawing may have taken place while the bone was still in a 'fresh' state, although this could be a matter of several years *postmortem* (Klippel and Synstelien 2007; Wieberg and Wescot 2008).

Fragmentation. Fragmentation in this fraction is more intense than that in Chamber NE II. Fracture morphology is mostly transverse and right-angled (Table 6.3). Fracture surfaces, however, are almost invariably patinated and some present abraded fracture edges, indicating 'old' dry-bone breakages, not excavational or recent quarrying damage. The small (450g) assemblage of fragmented adult and immature material from the top scatter of the chamber entrance deposit shares no anatomical duplications with the material found lower down, has the same demographic profile (see below) and could be a (?disturbed) sub-fraction of those remains.

Weathering modifications. Several specimens are heavily weathered and exfoliated; less intense grades of subaerial weathering are evident in many other elements (Table 6.3).

Skeletal remains from Penywyrlod Chamber NE II

Disturbed: decontextualised material from the 'top scatter'

Adult human bones. **Skull**: almost complete adult male skull and matching mandible (see Luff *et al.* 1984, 37); almost complete right parietal; adult occipital; two almost complete adult mandibles; right half of adult mandible; left half adult mandible; portions of maxillae with dentition from three adults. **Axial**: portion of right clavicle; portion of right scapula; four cervical, five thoracic and one lumbar vertebrae; portions from five left and two right innominates. **Upper limbs**: three broken right humeri; portion of left humerus; right ulna; left radius; two metacarpals and seven small bones from hand. **Lower limbs**: two right femora (broken); two left femora (broken); right tibia (broken); two left tibiae (broken); right patella; six right tali; left talus; right calcaneus; left calcaneus; six metatarsals; and five small bones from foot.

Immature human bone. **Axial**: portion left innominate. **Lower limbs**: distal end right fibula.

Six individuals are represented by left innominates and right tali.

Sex assessment. The majority of metrically or morphologically assessable material is male (See Table 6.5). Elements assessed as female consist of only a left and right innominate portion.

Age estimation. Two fragments, a portion of adult-sized left male innominate with unfused ischium and the distal end of a right fibula that has not completely fused medially, represent a similar stage of skeletal development (*c.* 16–20 years). The remaining postcranial elements are all skeletally mature.

The complete male skull, reported on by Brothwell and O'Connor in Luff *et al.* (1984, 37), is estimated on dental wear to be of a young adult *c.* 20–25 years. A second

Table 6.5. Penywyrlod: Chamber NE II, metric sex assessments and stature assessments.

Group	Specimen	Metric*	Datum (mm**)	Stature estimate (cm)	Assessed sex	Notes
A	R scapula	GL	37.5		male	
A	L humerus	EW	59.6		?male	
		Length	305	161.3		
A	L femur	VHD	47.7		male	
		CM	93.7			
		APD	34.5			
		Length	441	164.5		
A	R femur	CM	81.0		female	Probable antimere of L femur,
		APD	27.0			Group G
B	L humerus	VHD	45.2		male	
		EW	60.9			
		Length	318	166.5		
C	L scapula	GL	36.5		indet.	
C	R humerus	VHD	45.2		male	
		EW	60.0			
		Length	319	166.9		
C	L humerus	EW	63.7		male	
C	R radius	DRH	24.2/22.8		male	
C	L ulna	Length	268			
C	L femur	VHD	44.2		?male	
C	L femur	CM	93.9		male	
D	R scapula	GL	37.5		male	
E	R ulna	Length	230		female	
F	R scapula	GL	36.2		indet.	
F	L scapula	GL	38.6		male	
F	R radius	DRH	21.4/20.0		indet.	
G	L scapula	GL	37.3		male	
G	R radius	DRH	23.4/22.1		male	
		Length	243	164.3		
G	R ulna	Length	264			
G	L ulna	Length	258			
G	R femur	CM	89.5		male	
		APD	32.4			
		Length	435	163.0		
G	R femur	VHD	47.5		male	
		CM	93.4			
		APD	33.8			
		Length	439	164.0		
G	L femur	VHD	38.8		female	Probable antimere of R femur,
		CM	80.3			Group A
		APD	27.5			

(Continued)

Table 6.5. Penywyrlod: Chamber NE II, metric sex assessments and stature assessments. (Continued)

Group	Specimen	Metric*	Datum (mm**)	Stature estimate (cm)	Assessed sex	Notes
		Length	388	147.3		
G	R tibia	CNF	98.8		male	
		BB	74.8			
		Length	354	162.2		
G	R tibia	BB	79.1		male	
G	L tibia	CNF	96.1		male	
		Length	354	162.2		
G	R calcaneus	DF1	32.6		indet.	
G	R calcaneus	DF1	34.3		male	
G	R calcaneus	DF1	32.0		indet.	
G	L talus	DF2	42.4		male	
S	R scapula	GL	39.6		male	
S	R humerus	VHD	45.9		male	
S	R humerus	VHD	45.5		male	
S	R humerus	VHD	46.1		male	
S	L humerus	VHD	45.2		male	
S	R femur	CM	83.0		male	
S	L femur	VHD	44.2		male	
		CM	87.9			
S	L femur	VHD	43.3		male	
		CM	92.6			
		APD	30.1			
S	R tibia	CNF	96.3		male	
S	L tibia	CNF	96.9		male	
S	L tibia	CNF	100.1		male	
S	L calcaneus	DF1	33.3		male	
S	R talus	DF2	40.2		male	
S	R talus	DF2	37.7		indet.	
S	R talus	DF2	38.7		indet	
S	R talus	DF2	42.2		male	
S	L talus	DF2	37.5		indet.	

Key: * see Table 6.1; ** except DF1, DF2; S = Disturbed top scatters; indet. = indeterminate; ? = probable

complete mandible is also from a male of similar age, possibly a little older (there is slightly heavier wear at M_1s and C). A third, almost complete, mandible is from a somewhat older individual with heavier dental wear than the previous two specimens (*c.* 30–35+ years). An additional fragment of right mandible bears only an extremely worn first molar stump with pulp chamber exposed, with *antemortem* loss of the first premolar. At face value the degree of attrition in the molar suggests an individual of advanced age, but tooth loss in this jaw means that wear in remaining teeth is likely to have been accelerated. A male left innominate portion is a pair with a right sided specimen from Group G; both display degenerative changes associated with advanced age (see below).

Group A

Adult human bone. **Skull**: portion of cranial vault (part frontal, left and right parietals); portion of cranial vault from second individual (right mastoid, supra-occipital with right temporal); 11 fragments of cranial vault; almost complete mandible. **Axial**: fragment each of left and right scapula; single thoracic vertebra; right innominate portion. **Upper**

limbs: complete left humerus (reconstructed with portion from top scatter), left humerus shaft; right ulna, broken distally. **Lower limbs**: left femur (intact) and right femur (broken proximally at trochanters); left talus.

Animal bone. Horse phalanx ('wild pony').

A permanent second molar from the almost complete mandible produced a date of *3750–3630 cal BC* (*92% probability*; *SUERC-63414*; Fig. 4.3; see Chapters 4 and 7).

The two skull portions are anatomically contiguous; both display male characteristics, and at first glance would appear to represent the same skull. Savory (1984, 19) refers to a single skull in this context. However, the two portions do not conjoin; respective anatomically contiguous lambdoid sutures are incompatible, and the two specimens are from different individuals, as are two left humeri and the left and right femora.

Sex assessment. With one exception, elements that could be sexed metrically or morphologically – cranial portions, right scapula, right innominate, intact left humerus, left femur – are male or probably male (Table 6.5). The right femur, however, is assessed female and is certainly the antimere of a left femur from the central deposit (see below, Group G); both these bones are of similar appearance, visually gracile and from a short-statured (*c*. 147.3cm) individual. Both exhibit striking, symmetrically located, florid enthesopathies along markedly hypertrophic *linea aspera* and elsewhere, both also have similar all-over colouration, displaying a distinctive grey hue, not seen in the other femora (see also section on pathology, below).

Age estimation. Dental attrition (stage D/E) in the complete mandible indicates a younger adult of *c*. 25 years.

Summary. A minimum of three adults are represented in Group A. Cranial remains are drawn from two probable males. A left femur is also male, but a right femur is from a female (and is a pair with a left femur from the central deposit).

A horse phalanx is the only animal bone to be recovered from this chamber.

Group B

Adult human bone. **Axial**: thoracic vertebra, complete left clavicle. **Upper limbs**: complete left humerus (distal ¼ conjoins with proximal ¾ from top scatter); metacarpal. **Lower limbs**: right patella, two metatarsals.

Immature human bone. **Skull**: basi-occipital fragment.

Age and sex. The basi-occipital is of near adult size but has only partially fused with the sphenoid indicating probable adolescent age, *c*. 11–18 years (Scheuer and Black 2000, 59, table 5.1). All the remaining material is skeletally mature and the humerus is male (Table 6.5).

Group C

Adult human bone. **Skull**: right maxillary fragment. **Axial**: left scapula; sternum fragment. **Upper limbs**: complete right humerus; left humerus broken at head; proximal ¾ right radius; right radius midshaft; complete left ulna; one metacarpal; two hand phalanges. **Lower limbs**: proximal portions of both a right and a left femur; right calcaneus; four metatarsals.

Immature human bone. **Axial**: fragment immature iliac crest.

Sex assessment. All parts that could be metrically assessed (scapula, left and right humeri, right radius, left ulna, left and right femora) are male or indeterminate (Table 6.5).

Age estimation. Apart from a small fragment of unfused iliac crest, all the remains are skeletally mature. Fusion of the iliac crest normally commences at around 17–20 years (Scheuer and Black, 2000, 372) and while the fragment itself is small, its dimensions suggest an adolescent to young adult age-range (*i.e.* not child or infant). A left-sided innominate fragment with unfused ischial epiphysis was found in the disturbed top scatter (see above) and could possibly represent the same individual, as could the basi-occipital fragment in Group B, noted above.

Summary. Except for two incomplete right radii there are no duplications in Group C. The pair of proximal femora segments are certainly from one person and display unusual morphology as does the right humerus (see pathology section below) which is also likely to belong to the same individual. In absolute terms the deposit consists of remains from a minimum of three people – an adult male, a second adult of indeterminate sex and an adolescent – but the indeterminate adult and immature individual are clearly represented by only one fragment each (right radius shaft, unfused iliac crest respectively).

A solitary adult male left femur portion, broken distally at the divergence of the *linea aspera*, is tagged 'from all the way along the floor along the NW side'. It is assumed that this was located towards the SW end of the chamber beyond Group C and close to Group D.

Group D

Adult human bone. **Skull**: two frontal bones (both reconstructed by Rosemary Luff); several adult cranial vault fragments; **Axial**: axis; two thoracic vertebrae; eight lumbar vertebrae; a portion each of right and left scapula; right clavicle. **Upper limbs**: two hand phalanges. **Lower limbs**: right distal fibula; left proximal fibula; five metatarsals; two phalanges.

Immature human bone. **Skull**: immature cranial vault fragment. **Lower limbs**: immature metatarsal.

Two adults are indicated by duplication of lumbar vertebrae and frontal bones.

Sex assessment. Based on supraorbital morphology, the two frontal fragments are from a male and female. The distal fibula fragment is robust and the right scapula is metrically male (Table 6.5).

Age estimation. Most of the material is skeletally mature. Two exceptions are a small, thin, cranial vault fragment from an immature individual, and a first metatarsal with unfused epiphysis from an adolescent, probably under *c.* 18 years (Scheuer and Black 2000, 466).

The anatomical composition of the assemblage is unusual, with an absence of large limb bones (humeri, radii, ulnae, femora or tibiae) and a preponderance of vertebrae – 11 specimens, 40.7%, of the total number of vertebrae recovered from the chamber. Surviving contextual information is not very precise and there are no plans of the skeletal deposits. A suspicion remains that Groups C and D together with the solitary left femur (above) could all be parts of an originally single grouping.

Group E

Adult human bone. **Axial**: complete adult sacrum. **Upper limbs**: one right and two left ulnae.

Sex assessment. The right ulna is visually gracile, displays florid spiculated enthesopathies at the *brachialis* insertion site and a distinctive grey hue, similar that that noted previously in the pair of enthesopathic female femora found in Groups A (above) and G (see below), and is almost certainly from the same individual. Neither of the two left ulnae appear to pair with the right. The sacrum is morphologically female.

Age estimation. All the material is skeletally mature.

Summary. The remains are from at least three adults: one female and two of indeterminate sex.

Group F

Adult human bone. **Skull**: a fragment each of occipital, left temporal and left frontal bones. **Axial**: a portion each from two right scapulae and one left scapula; one adult cervical vertebra; **Upper limbs**: left humerus shaft; right radius; distal fragment left radius. **Lower limbs**: two left fibulae; right patella; left calcaneus fragment.

Immature human bone. **Axial**: two immature cervical vertebra; three fragments immature sacrum (sacral vertebrae).

Sex assessment. The occipital fragment is robust, with rugged, characteristically male architecture. The left scapula is certainly male, the right radius is female (Table 6.5). The remaining limb bones are all visually robust.

Age estimation. At least two adults are represented by duplications of scapulae and fibulae. The adult cervical vertebra exhibits degenerative changes (see pathology section below) suggesting advanced age. Two cervical vertebrae with unfused superior and inferior annular rings and fragments of sacral vertebrae with unfused auricular surfaces are from one or more immature individuals, probably under *c.* 18 years (Scheuer and Black 2000, 210–13); there is no other material in this group that can be assigned to this age category.

Group G

Adult human bone. **Skull**: (1) large portion cranial vault (substantial fragment frontal bone, left parietal, superior half right parietal); (2) left occipital from second individual with portion of left parietal; fragment right posterio-lateral parietal, possibly from skull (2). **Axial**: left scapula; atlas, axis; thoracic vertebral body; 5th lumbar vertebra; two rib fragments; right innominate portion (complex pathology: 'weaver's bottom'). **Upper limbs**: complete right and left ulnae (pair); complete right radius. **Lower limbs**: complete left femur; two complete right femora; complete right and left tibiae (pair); proximal fragment each of right and left tibiae; right fibula; two left fibulae; left talus; two right calcanei.

Sex assessment. Sexually diagnostic features are not well enough preserved in the cranial remains to allow reliable sex assessment. The intact left femur is female and antimere of the damaged right femur from Group A (above, and Table 6.5). Apart from the right fibula, ribs, vertebrae and two of the right calcanei, which are all indeterminate, the postcranial material is male (Table 6.5). The innominate fragment displays a characteristically male, V-shaped, greater sciatic notch and absence of a pre-auricular sulcus. Many of the limb bones are complete and a number have tentatively been assigned to a single adult male: a right and left ulna, a right radius, a right femur, and right and left tibia. Two adult males are represented by right femora.

Age estimation. All the remains from this group are skeletally mature. A lumbar vertebra (L5), and the portion of right innominate both display sparse trabecular structure and other complex changes associated with older or advanced age (see pathology section below).

Summary. The disturbed assemblage contains skeletal remains from at least three adults, two males and a probable female. Some of the postcranial remains have been assigned to a single adult male while a duplicated right femur and calcaneus, left fibula and fragment of proximal tibia are from at least one other male. An innominate and 5th lumbar are from an aged individual and could represent the remains of a third adult male. A female is represented by only one left femur paired with a right femur from Group A.

Group H

Adult human bone. **Skull**: two small fragments of parietal; fragment of right mandible, conjoins with a solitary left mandible fragment labelled 'halfway along chamber on S side' (see below); left mandible fragment; loose permanent teeth, mandibular and maxillary. **Axial**: fragment sacrum. **Upper limbs**: left distal fibula end; metacarpal II; triquetral; proximal phalange hand. **Lower limbs**: metatarsal fragment, two distal phalanges and one proximal phalange foot.

Immature human bone. **Axial**: right clavicle fragment.

Two maxillary molars exhibit an unusual, *postmortem*, accretion over the crowns, similar to that encountered in the molar dentition from the largely complete skull recovered from the top scatter (cf. Brothwell in Luff *et al.* 1984, 37). As noted above, the right mandible fragment conjoins with a fragment of left mandible assigned to 'halfway along chamber on S side'. The conjoining fragments unite with perfect fit at the delicate labial and lingual incisor socket walls. A left lateral incisor and canine from the loose teeth assigned to Group H also belong to this 'stray' left mandibular element. Savory (1984, 19, 26) noted that these fragments, associated with a loose tip of a flint arrowhead, were from the floor of the chamber, underneath the uppermost floor slabs, which were two or three deep. He felt that the flint tip (and therefore presumably the bone fragments that accompanied it) was brought into the chamber at the same time as the other bone groups. There was no suggestion that these fragments represent an earlier 'ritual' or 'foundation' deposit.

Sex assessment. No reliable sex assessment obtains.

Age estimation. The right clavicle is small, slender, with unfused medial end and likely to be from an individual aged under *c.* 18 years (Scheuer and Black 2000, 251). Hand and foot bones all display fused epiphyses where observable. The distal fibula end is skeletally mature, fusion completing between 15 to 20 years across both sexes (Scheuer and Black 2000, 422, 425).

The conjoined mandible carries both 1st and 2nd left permanent molars and a 3rd molar crown in the initial stages of eruption. Dental development and relatively mild occlusal attrition in the molars indicate an age range of *c.* 17–25 years. The second left mandible fragment from Group H carries a permanent first molar only, but the remnant 2nd permanent molar root socket indicates this tooth was fully erupted. Occlusal wear in the M_1 is mild, indicating a second individual also aged *c.* 17–25 years.

Loose mandibular dentition consists of a set of possibly single-entity right mandibular permanent molars (M_1 to M_3). Dental wear stages are compatible with either of the mandibles. M_3 displays complete roots with open apices indicating a probable age under *c.* 25 years. Maxillary dentition consists of both permanent molar and anterior teeth with no duplications, again displaying moderate wear compatible with either set of mandibular teeth where observable (several specimens are exfoliated or eroded).

Summary. Dental remains are from two individuals, both late adolescents or young adults (*c.* 17–25 years); postcranial remains are not incompatible.

Penywyrlod Chamber NE II demographic summary

Based on consistent anatomical duplications (Table 6.5) and age and sex indicators, the bones recovered from NE II represent a minimum of six people (cf. Luff *et al.* 1984). Four individuals are young adults or older adolescents *c.* 17–25 years; one individual is somewhat older, around *c.* 30–35 years; one individual may be of advanced age; and five are here assessed as males and one as female. There are also a few skeletally immature fragments present. A small thin human skull fragment and an unfused metatarsal (both from Group D), and two cervical vertebrae with unfused annular rings and sacral fragments with unfused auricular surfaces (from Group F) could represent an adolescent perhaps under *c.* 16–18 years. Unfused fragments of innominate (Group C and top scatter) suggest a slightly older individual, as do a distal fibula (top scatter) and a basi-occipital (Group B) which display incomplete fusion. A fragment of small unfused clavicle (Group H) may be from an individual of similar age, probably under 18–20 years. It is not impossible, however, that all these immature remains represent a single individual and none of this material need be incompatible with one or more of the four older adolescents/young adults.

Skeletal remains from Chamber NE III

Passage

Adult human bone. **Skull**: conjoining fragments – frontal, parts of left and right parietals, parts of left and right temporals; left temporal fragment; portion basi-occipital. **Axial**: cervical vertebra; portion of right innominate, greater sciatic notch; four rib fragments. **Upper limbs**: distal end of left humerus; distal end of right humerus; left distal radius; hand phalange. **Lower limbs**: fragment of left proximal tibia shaft; left patella; right talus; fragment of right talus, gracile; right navicular; two metatarsal fragments; 1st medial phalange foot.

Immature human bone. **Axial**: rib fragment. **Upper limbs**: left proximal ulna.

Animal bones: tibia and four cannon bones of red deer.

Sex assessment and age estimation. The majority of cranial remains conjoin to form a portion of adult skull with masculine morphology and a persistent metopic suture. Two further cranial fragments appear to be from one or more additional adults: occipital condyles on a basi-occipital fragment display notably sparse trabecular structure, possibly indicating an older or aged individual. Postcranial fragments include a portion of adult right innominate with a wide greater sciatic notch and left distal humerus, both assessed to be from a female, and a right talus from a male (Table 6.6). A proximal portion of left ulna with unfused epiphysis and a rib fragment are skeletally immature, proportional size of the ulna suggesting an age range of *c.* 9–16 years (Scheuer and Black 2004, 287). All that can be said of the remaining material is that it is skeletally mature. The remains represent a minimum of three individuals: two adults, one of whom is female and an older child or younger adolescent (cf. Luff *et al.* 1984, 37).

Chamber NE III, top scatter

Adult human bone. **Skull**: 10 small fragments of vault; **Axial**: portion of right scapula; three rib fragments; two thoracic vertebrae; two lumbar vertebrae; fragment of left ilium; complete sacrum. **Upper limbs**: left proximal radius; a right and left metacarpal V. **Lower limbs**: left metatarsal II.

Immature human bone. **Skull**: two thin cranial vault fragments (young child/infant). **Axial**: fragment of scapula blade; portion each of left and right ilium (older child/ young adolescent); fragments of two unfused sacral vertebrae. **Lower limbs**: portion of right femur shaft (younger adolescent); distal end left femur (older adolescent); portion of left tibia (older adolescent); proximal left fibula (adolescent).

This diverse collection of adult and immature fragmentary remains represents a minimum of four or five individuals at different stages of skeletal development (Table 6.6) – adults, older and younger adolescents, a child or infant. The material is demographically consistent with material found lower down in the chamber entrance, with no anatomical duplications between the two groups, and probably represents a disturbed fraction of that deposit (see below).

Chamber NE III, material recovered from inside the entrance area

Adult human bone. **Skull**: 15 cranial fragments; maxillary arc; three mandibles, reconstructed. **Axial**: one atlas, one cervical, six thoracic, five lumbar vertebrae; two left scapular glenoid cavities; three left clavicle portions, two right clavicle portions, one robust; rib fragments; three right, one left, innominate fragments. **Upper limbs**: left humerus, proximal end, head damaged; two left humerus distal ends; right humerus, distal end fragment; left ulna proximal end; left ulna proximal ¼; right radius, distal ½; left radius distal ⅕; right metacarpal III, medial phalange hand. **Lower limbs**: Right femur, proximal end, head damaged; right femur distal ⅓, robust; left femur proximal end, head damaged; left femur shaft, proximal ¾; right tibia, distal ½; left tibia, distal ½; left tibia, robust; fibula shaft fragment; two right calcanei; right calcaneus, damaged, right calcaneus fragment; left calcaneus; left calcaneus fragment; one right talus; two right metatarsal I, II, V, one right metatarsal III, IV, left metatarsal III, six cuneiforms, two naviculars, two cuboids; unidentified fragments and splinters.

Immature human bone. **Skull**: 25 thin cranial vault fragments; three very thin cranial fragments (?infant); maxillary arc (infant); three mandibles, reconstructed (infant, 2 × adolescent). **Axial**: one each immature thoracic and cervical vertebra; three unfused sacral vertebrae; right clavicle portion; rib fragments; right and left immature ilium. **Upper limbs**: left humerus, distal ½, recently fused; fragment humeral diaphysis; left ulna broken distally, incomplete fusion proximally; left ulna proximal shaft fragment. **Lower limbs**: right femur, proximal ¼, head, trochanters unfused; left femur, proximal fragment, head trochanters unfused; one left, one right proximal femoral epiphysis fragment (not commensurate with proximal ends); right femur, distal ⅓ diaphysis; two fragments distal femoral epiphyses; splinter distal femur shaft, anterior surface; left tibia shaft fragment; right tibia proximal epiphysis fragment; left fibula diaphysis; right metatarsal I and II.

Age estimation. Mandibular fragments were reconstructed to form six mandibles (Mb1–Mb6, Table 6.7, see also pathology below).

Of the six individuals represented, two are full adults (Mb1, Mb3), one of whom is possibly of advanced age. A third individual (Mb2) is probably a near adult (*c.* 17–20 years). Two further adolescents (*c.* 15–18 years), one possibly a little older than the other, (Mb4, Mb5), and an infant (Mb6) complete the group. The mandibular dentition is matched by two maxillary specimens, one from an infant at the same stage of development as Mb6, and one from an adult exhibiting chronic *antemortem* tooth loss and probably a match with Mb3.

Postcranial material is not inconsistent with this assessment (Table 6.6). Two adults are indicated by duplicating proximal left ulnae and distal left humeri fragments (Mb1, Mb3). A further left proximal ulna and distal left humerus both display incomplete epiphyseal fusion, indicating adolescence (Mb4/Mb5; Scheuer and Black 2000, 283–5, 304–6). Unfused proximal and distal ends of the right femur are robust, of near-adult size and probably represent a later adolescent (Mb2). Both a tibia and fibula diaphysis are not as developed as the right femur and represent somewhat younger adolescence (Mb4/Mb5). There are no postcranial remains that can be assigned to the infant, but a few very thin skull fragments are consistent. A fibular diaphysis and fragments of unfused acetabulum appear to be from an older child not represented by dental remains.

Metric data (Table 6.6) suggest that at least two individuals over 18 years, represented by right calcanei, are male and one of the adolescents is female.

Table 6.6. Penywyrlod: Chamber NE III and Passage metric sex assessment and postcranial age estimation.

Context/ID no.	*Specimen*	*Metric**	*Datum***	*Assessed sex*	*Estimated age range*	*Notes*
Passage						
1	L humerus distal end	EW	52.1	female	adult	–
2	L ulna proximal ⅓	–	–	–	*c.* 9–16 y	–
3	R talus	DF2	40.5	male	adult	–
Chamber – upper scatter						
4	R scapula portion	GL	37.0	?male	adult	–
5	Portion L and R ilium	–	–	–	*c.* 9–14 y	Unfused acetabulum, proportions suggest older child or early adolescent
6	Fragment scapula	–	–	–	< *c.* 23 y	Unfused medial border
7	R femur diaphysis proximal ¾	CM APD	79.5 26.8	indet.	?*c.* 13–16 y	Head, greater trochanter unfused; possible match with 20 below
8	L femur distal diaphysis and metaphysis fragment	–	–	–	14–20 y	Fragments conjoin
9	L tibia, proximal ⅔	CNF	96.1	male	*c.* 15–19 y	Proximal epiphysis unfused
10	Left fibula, proximal ⅓	–	–	–	*c.* 12–18 y	Unfused, proportional size suggests adolescent
Chamber entrance						
11	L scapula glenoid cavity	GL	36.4	indet.	adult	–
12	L distal humerus end	EW	61.0	male	adult	–
13	L humerus distal end	EW	62.9	male	adult	–
14	L humerus distal half	EW	50.5	female	*c.* 15–18 y	Anterior fusion complete, deep posterior epiphyseal line
15	L ulna broken distally above articulation	–	–	–	*c.* 12–16 y	Fusion incomplete medially
16	R femur diaphysis proximal ¼	–	–	–	*c.* 14–18 y	Head, greater trochanter, unfused; robust
17	L femur diaphysis proximal fragment	–	–	–	*c.* 14–18 y	Head, greater trochanter, unfused
18	R femur diaphysis distal ⅓	–	–	–	*c.* 14–20 y	Robust
19	L femur shaft	CM	82.3	indet.	adult	–
20	L tibia, diaphysis, broken distally	–	–	–	*c.* 13–16 y	Incommensurate with 16 and 17 above
21	L fibula diaphysis	Length	255	–	*c.* 7–9 y	–
22	R calcaneus	DF1	33.7	male	adult	–
23	R calcaneus	DF1	33.5	male	adult	–
24	L calcaneus	DF1	32.4	indet.	adult	–

Key: * See Table 6.1; ** mm except DF1 and DF2; y = years; indet. = indeterminate; ? = probable

Table 6.7. Penywyrlod: Chamber NE III mandibles from entrance area.

ID no.	Specimen details	Dentition	Wear stage	Estimated age range	Morphology	Notes
Mb1	Reconstructed, condyles, R coronoid process missing	$\times M_2$ AM × × × × × × × × × × AM × ×	H	25–40+ y	indet.	*Perimortem* gnawing
Mb2	Reconstructed, L P_4 to C sockets damaged.	M_3 M_2 M_1 - - - × × × × × × × × M_1 M_2 M_3	B2	17–20 y	indet.	L and R M_3 erupting, R M_3 root ¾ complete, L M_3 compacted
Mb3	Intact, chronic tooth loss	Only R I_2 retained, L I_2, L C lost PM, remaining dentition lost AM	I+	45–55+ y	indet.	–
Mb4	Ascending rami/condyles broken	U M_2 M_1 × × × I_2 × I_2 × P_3 P_4 M_1 M_2 U	B2/C	16–18 y	masculine	M_3 crypts opening, crowns visible; P_3, P_4, M_2 root apices closed
Mb5	Reconstructed	U M_2 M_1 × × × × × × × × - - × M_1 × U	A/B1	15–17 y	indet.	M_3 roots ¼ complete
Mb6	Child	u m_1 × × × × × × m_1 u	–	15–22 m	indet.	m_2 early-stage eruption, root ½ complete, m_1 root complete apices open

Key: U = unerupted; AM = *antemortem* loss; × = *postmortem* loss; - = damaged; R = right; L = left; y = years; m = months. Wear stages after Lovejoy (1985). Developmental age after AlQahtani *et al.* (2010)

Chamber NE III and passage demographic summary

The entrance area of Chamber NE III held skeletal remains from a minimum of seven people: two adults, one near- or young adult, two adolescents, an infant and a child represented by two postcranial fragments only. There is some suggestion in the form of a small assemblage of fragmentary material from the upper fill of the chamber entrance with no evidence of recent breakages, that the contents of Chamber NE III may have been disturbed in the past. The sparse mixed deposit from the passage leading to the chamber consists of the remains of at least two adults, one of whom is female and one male, and an older child or younger adolescent. It is uncertain if these remains represent a deposit in their own right or spillage from any episode(s) of chamber disturbance.

Human remains from cist in SE horn of cairn

A child's skull, which was once apparently complete but is now broken into many pieces, was recovered together with a fragmented immature atlas vertebra (C1) and two immature rib fragments, an adult cranial fragment (left mastoid and external auditory meatus) and two loose permanent maxillary first molars. Both the child's maxillary permanent first incisor crowns are complete and show the first stage of root formation, permanent mandibular first molar crowns are complete but retained in crypts, and a permanent mandibular second molar crown is between ¼ and ½ complete; dental development is consistent with an age range of *c.* 4–6 years (AlQhatani *et al.* 2010). Occlusal wear on the adult molars suggests an age of *c.* 30–40 years.

O'Connor (in Luff *et al.* 1984, 38), noted no evidence of *perimortem* sharp force trauma to the C1. However, *perimortem* or *postmortem* decapitation need not necessarily damage C1, with related trauma often occurring from C2 to C5 (Harman *et al.* 1981; Saržinski 2009, table 11). The presence of C1 and the mandible could imply that the skull became detached from the child's body (by whatever means) and was placed in the cist while the atlas and mandible were still held in place by muscles and ligaments, though this could be a matter of several or more weeks *postmortem* (Cunningham *et al.* 2011, 192–3).

Palaeopathology and markers of occupational stress

Dentition

Caries and tooth loss. At least 13 adults or adolescents who might be expected to carry full or near- full permanent dentition are represented in the Penywyrlod skeletal remains from both chambers, equating to 416 potential individual tooth observations. The remains yielded only 108 teeth and 181 empty tooth sockets. Caries was observed in three teeth and there were 30 counts of *antemortem* tooth loss.

Four counts of *antemortem* tooth loss were noted from Chamber NE II. An adult (*c.* 25–35 years) mandible displayed an almost completely healed right first molar mesial root socket but an only partially healed distal socket with notable alveolar bone loss buccally, suggesting an infection or abscess in the socket possibly following loss of the tooth, likely extremely painful and potentially leading to sepsis. A right mandibular third molar from a small fragment, and both canines from an adult maxilla, complete the tally; bilateral loss of maxillary canines is unusual.

From the entrance area of Chamber NE III, mandible Mb1 displayed bilateral loss of first molars and recent loss of the left second premolar. The near edentulous Mb3 retained only its right lateral incisor, with left lateral incisor and left canine lost *postmortem* or possibly *perimortem*. Various stages of remodelling and closing of sockets in the jaw portray a history of progressive tooth loss, incomplete alveolar remodelling indicating loss of the left first premolar *c.* 6–12 months *antemortem*, and of the right first premolar and right canine *c.* 18–24 months *antemortem*. Remaining teeth, molars and premolars, had been lost considerably earlier in life: alveolar remodelling has resulted in a sharp bilateral lingual crest along the line of first and second molars, probably a response to long-term chewing with the toothless gums. Ramus height at the approximate bilateral sites of first and second molars was L: 14.5mm, R: 11.4mm, with bone loss to the level of the right mental foramen. This variance suggests primary loss of the right-sided mandibular molar dentition and/or preferential chewing along the right side of the mouth following tooth loss elsewhere. The matching maxilla had correspondingly retained right-sided canine, premolars and first molar, as well as the left second premolar, with all other teeth lost *antemortem*. Maxillary tooth loss appears to have been comparatively recent and rapid, accompanied by severe gum disease. The left lateral incisor had been lost first and the site had completely healed over. Remaining sockets were in various stages of remodelling. Chronic alveolar resorption was evident along the right side, with ⅔ of surviving lingual roots exposed.

Enamel hypoplasia. Hypoplastic teeth were noted in three mandibles and two maxillae from Chamber NE II and in mandible 4 from Chamber NE III; one loose tooth from beneath a paving slab in Chamber NE II was also affected. Details are given in Table 6.8.

Table 6.8. Penywyrlod: Chambers NE II and NE III, tooth enamel hypoplasia.

Side/element	*Context*	*Tooth*	*Details*
Mandible 4	NE III	R I_2	one band, mild
		R PM_3	one band, mild
		R M_2	one band, mild
Maxilla	NE II	L C	two bands, moderate
Maxilla	NE II	R M^3	one band, mild
		R M^2	one band, mild
Mandible	NE II	L C	one band, moderate
		R C	one band, moderate
		R PM_3	shallow pit
Mandible	NE II	R C	strong, deep band with surface irregularity
		R PM_3	one band, moderate
		R PM_4	one band, mild
Mandible	C.II	L C	one band, mild
		R C	one band, mild
Loose	beneath slab, NE II	R M_3	single band, moderate

Cranial skeleton

Mild pitting – porotic hyperostosis (PH) – of the cranium was noted on all relevant cranial vault observations from the Chamber NE II assemblage. At Penywyrlod PH typically occurs bilaterally along the sagittal plane of parietals and extends to the superior half of the occipital. Despite long and ongoing debate, aetiology remains uncertain (Brickley 2018). The condition has often been associated with iron-deficiency anaemia, particularly when coupled with similar lesions in the orbital vault – *cribra orbitalia* or CB (*e.g.* Angel 1966; Stuart-Macadam 1987), but recent studies take the view that different and separate forms of anaemia may be responsible for each of the two pathologies (Walker *et al.* 2009; Lahr and Rivera 2017), with PH linked to various causes of anaemias other than iron-deficiency, such as, for example, stress, viral and bacteriological infection and dietary/nutritional deficiencies including scurvy (Zuckerman *et al.* 2014; Brickley 2018).

Bilateral *cribra orbitalia* with accompanying PH at the crown was noted in only one specimen from Group D. It should, however, be stressed that there were few surviving orbital vault specimens available for observation.

A decontextualised, adult right parietal displayed an old, healed, oval-shaped depressed fracture (18mm by 12mm), probably caused by a non-fatal blow to the head from a pebble-sized projectile or blunt-tipped implement (previously reported in Schulting and Wysocki 2005, 119, table 2, fig. 20).

Porotic hyperostosis was notably absent in the conjoined skull portion from the passage to Chamber NE III (see above). This skull, however, displays a lesion on the posterior aspect of the left parietal. Roughly oval (9 by 13mm) and 5–6mm deep, exposing diploe, the lesion has sharp borders with marginal increased porosity. Internally the bipolar area is marked by a patch of porous reactive bone, suggesting some limited post-traumatic reaction following a wound to the side of the head.

Postcranial skeleton: Chamber NE II

Seven vertebrae exhibit mild arthritic changes in the form of slight to mild marginal osteophytes. Moderate Schmorl's nodes were noted in two thoracic bodies.

Nine vertebrae (two cervical, three thoracic, four lumbar, no duplicates) displayed notable degenerative changes and may possibly all represent the same individual. Trabecular structure in these vertebral bodies was sparse, the lumbar ½ displaying a crush-fractured profile, suggesting senile osteoporosis with partial collapse of the vertebral body. Strong to exuberant marginal osteophytes were accompanied by osteophytosis and spiculated exostosis at articulating and transverse processes. Thoracic and lumbar bodies displayed focal destruction at both superior and inferior surfaces: deep lesions with thin marginal non-porous remodelling. These changes share some similarity with vertebral reactions to brucellosis or tuberculosis but the vertebrae do not exhibit other associated diagnostic features, as described by Ortner (2003, 216–21).

Although differential diagnoses remain open, the degenerative changes in these vertebrae suggest relatively advanced age and are matched in a right innominate from Group G and a left innominate portion from the disturbed upper scatter. Both the innominates are light with very sparse trabecular structure, again indicative of senile osteoporosis, perhaps linked to a lengthy period of physical inactivity. Acetabular rims display mild osteophytic lipping with eburnation and porosity of the anterior segment. Muscle attachment sites are marked with rugacious enthesopathies and stress lesions. Acetabular notches display sparse, 'basket-work' woven remodelling, and the right specimen displays a small oval osteoma. Both ischial tuberosities bear exuberant exostosic and osteophytic outgrowths, orientated medially. These changes could reflect a degree of metabolic disorder in the body, but similar bilateral ischial osteitis has been termed 'weaver's bottom' and is considered to be a consequence of long periods of sitting on a hard surface (Capasso *et al.* 1999, 100).

Non-fusion of the left lamina in the first sacral vertebra is evident in the morphologically female sacrum from Group E; *spina bifida* of *occulta* type, this is an insignificant condition with no adverse consequences in life (Roberts and Manchester 1997).

Upper limbs, male: Chamber NE II. A healing wrist fracture is evident at the distal articular surface of a robust right radius (at the junction of the styloid process and lateral border of the articulating surface for the scaphoid), possibly the result of a fall. A right clavicle displays an irregular anterior surface with extension of the costoclavicular ligament insertion site to almost mid shaft which may indicate a well healed old fracture in this bone. A right-sided humerus (Group C) also displays unusual morphology with flattening at the surgical neck so that the intertubercular groove is effectively absent, the medial lip forming a ridge or border.

Upper and lower limbs: female, Chamber NE II. As noted, a pair of femora and a right ulna probably represent a solitary female individual. All three bones display florid enthesopathic formations at muscle attachment sites. These surface rugosities are of a different order to surface remodelling usually noted at MSM sites; more exuberant and without sharp edges or ridges, they resemble wax-drips on the surface of a candle. In both femora, these form an exuberant formation along the *linea aspera*, growth orientated superiomedially. Other muscle attachment sites on both bones are similarly affected. In the right ulna spiculated enthesopathies are located at the *brachialis* and *supinator* insertion sites. The new bone formations on these limbs are distinct from common MSM formations as categorised by Hawkey and Merbs (1995) and probably reflect a degree of metabolic disorder in the subject. Extraspinal enthesopathies of this kind, particularly in the proximal ulna and femora, are a widely recognised secondary characteristic of diffuse idiopathic skeletal hyperostosis (DISH), also known as Forestier's disease (Kacki *et al.* 2018, table 1). The disease primarily affects the spine, with gradual to complete fusion of vertebrae in the thoracic region. Various authorities argue that fusion of four contiguous vertebrae is necessary for a definite diagnosis of DISH (Resnick and Niwayama 1988; Roberts and Manchester 1997; Rogers and Waldron 2001) and the very few surviving vertebrae from Penywyrlod showed no evidence of fusion. However, strikingly similar patterns of extraspinal enthesopathic growth in the femora to those seen at Penywyrlod have been recorded by Kacki *et al.* (2018) in a skeleton with a definitive spinal diagnosis of DISH.

The specific cause of DISH is unknown and it has been suggested that the disorder 'may not represent a disease *per se* but rather a vulnerable state in which extensive ossification results from an exaggerated response of the body in some patients to stimuli that produce only modest new bone formation in others' (Resnick and Niwayama 1988, 1600). In archaeological literature the condition has been frequently associated with obesity and diabetes or a rich diet (meat, fat, wine) and lack of exercise in monastic and medieval groups (Rogers and Waldron 2001; Spencer 2009). Prehistoric instances are rare and it has been argued that in such cases genetic or metabolic factors which predispose individuals to be 'bone formers', combined with active lifestyles, may be responsible (Faccia *et al.* 2016). It is notable that all three specimens here exhibit a distinctive grey hue, not seen in other bones from Penywyrlod which may indicate specific differences in the bone chemistry of this individual. In present-day cases DISH is largely asymptomatic or causes mild pain and stiffness (Faccia *et al.* 2016, 76).

Both femora displayed additional features. The right specimen, missing its proximal end, displayed striated periosteal reaction along the medial midshaft. In addition, two irregular small lenticular lesions with regular marginal remodelling were evident on the medial midshaft. The left specimen exhibits marginal porosity at the head with eburnation and destructive marginal remodelling superiorly.

Flint arrowhead, probably from Chamber NE III or Passage

An unlabelled bag with some 40 adult and immature rib fragments was found packed with the material from Chamber NE III and Passage. Surface modifications (soil staining and scratch-like turbation marks) are consistent with the other skeletal remains from these contexts, in contrast to material from Chamber NE II, but the precise location is not known. A small sternal fragment was found to have a flint projectile tip embedded in its anterior surface (previously reported in Wysocki and Whittle 2000, 599–600, fig. 5). The visible broken section has a flattened discoidal shape and appears to be from a leaf-shaped arrowhead. Penetration is superficial; the tip does not project through the posterior surface of the rib. There is no evidence of osseous reaction around the traumatised area, indicating a *perimortem* injury. The rib fragment is gracile and from one of the central ribs from the ?left side. Sex assessment is not possible. The morphology of the sternal rib-end changes with age, but with considerable individual variation. The sternal end displays definite pit formation with a V to U (transitional) pit shape and no evidence of deterioration in the pit wall or rim. These observations suggest a younger rather than older adult age (Işcan *et al.* 1984; Molleson and Cox 1993).

Markers of musculoskeletal and occupational stress: Chamber NE II

Sample size, weathering, fragmentation and other modifications in material from Chamber NE III render it unsuitable for similar analysis.

Shoulders and upper arms. Marginal lipping, and in one case eburnation, of the glenoid fossa was evident in four scapulae, both left and right side. Two right scapulae also each exhibit an additional small porous lesion at the articulating surface. A left clavicle displays a stress lesion at the costoclavicular ligament insertion site, and a right clavicle exhibits porosity at the joint surface of the acromial facet. Both scapulae and clavicles exhibit strongly marked muscle attachments, notably at the infraglenoid tubercle of the scapula (origin site for long head of *triceps*). One right scapula displays a strong (S2) stress lesion along the upper border of the scapular spine (insertion site for middle fibres of the *trapezius*). Three out of four surviving male right proximal humeri display marginal porosity and lipping at the articulating surfaces of the head, one specimen exhibiting additional small porous lesions at the joint surface.

This latter specimen has a notably thin shaft cortex (mean cortical thickness at midshaft area = 4.3mm) and muscle insertion sites are strongly stress-marked, but with evident remodelling and smoothing out of sharp crests and ridges. These features in the shaft suggest disuse atrophy, though there is no evidence of injury to the limb. The bone may belong to an individual who had ceased to be engaged in once strenuous physical activity.

Male humeri also display strong bilateral expression of muscle insertion sites in the proximal humerus. Stress lesions at the *pectoralis major* insertion site were evident in three specimens (two left; one right). Lateral bowing with prominent *deltoid* tuberosity was noted in five out of nine observations.

These muscles are all utilised in the wide range of motions of the shoulder joint in many different planes. Typical actions that place stress on these muscles involve raising the arms, moving the arms in a horizontal plane away from the chest, moving the arm from the flexed position to the posteriorly extended position, rotating the arm laterally and drawing the arm from the abducted position down to the side and toward the midline of the body (Thompson and Floyd 1984). Relevant activities could involve throwing a stone or spear or using a sling, although a wide range of other possible activities can also place repeated stress on these muscles.

It is notable that severity of expression appears to be bilateral, insofar as surviving material allows for such observation. Frequent use of the bow may be one activity involving bilateral stress on the glenohumeral complex (A. Thomas 2014; Dorshorst 2019). A stress lesion at the insertion site for the middle fibres of the *trapezius* on a right scapula is notable. The middle fibres of the *trapezius* provide strong elevation, upward rotation and adduction (retraction) of the scapula (Thompson and Floyd 1984, 18), actions involved in pulling back and holding a bowstring, among a number of other possible activities.

The suite of features described above, both muscular and involving changes to the anatomical structure of shoulder-joint components, indicate activity regimes that place high levels of mechanical loading and stress at the glenohumeral joint. Comparison with other male mortuary groups from Welsh Neolithic sites is limited and perhaps nugatory because of the poor survival rate of relevant elements.

Lower limbs, male: Chamber NE II. Unsurprisingly, MSMs and other occupational markers in the lower limbs exhibit strong expression of muscles utilised in running or walking. Proximal femora generally display mild degenerative changes probably related to general wear and tear at the hip joint.

A pair of male femora from Group C display unusual morphology with flattening of the posterior surface of the proximal shaft to create an approximately square-shaped cross-section. In both specimens the *linea aspera* is sited laterally, forming a sharp lateral border. Both limb shafts are notably slender. Without a complete skeleton the factors responsible for these adaptations remain obscure.

Periosteal stria are evident medially in two right and two left tibial shafts, most likely reactions to knocks and bruises over the shins and lower leg. A further left shaft displayed strong reactive periosteal striations over all shaft surfaces. Three fibulae exhibited strong enthesopathic rugosity at the interosseous ligament attachment and one also displayed enthesopathies along its anterior and posterior borders and at the anterior talofibular ligament attachment, possibly resulting from a sprained ankle (Thompson and Floyd 1994, 132). Two right and one left calcaneus exhibit osteophytes at the Achilles tendon site which may reflect responses to long-distance walking or running and have been known to form in obese individuals (Capasso *et al.* 1999, 139).

Penywyrlod: commentary and overview

Chamber NE II

The damage to Chamber NE II and its contents means that we have lost full knowledge of the location or distribution of bones, of the integrity of groupings and of their contents or intra-group arrangements. The excavator, however, was confident that the chamber was a secondary burial ossuary, where bones from corpses that had become skeletonised elsewhere were placed in groups, along the sides of the chamber and in the centre, and the chamber sealed in a single act, though this is now questioned in the reinterpretation presented in Chapter 2. Certainly, radiocarbon dating evidence (see Chapter 4) indicates that the remains accumulated over a period of at least *170–490* years *(95% probability*; *duration_NE_II*; parameter not shown) before being sealed in Chamber NE II, sometime after in *3490–3415 cal BC* (*95% probable*; *last_primary_Penywyrlod*; Fig. 4.3). The process of accumulation could possibly have been over an even longer period, as not all individuals from Chamber NE II produced dates.

Discrete groups? Could the various groupings simply be artefacts of the 20th-century disturbance? While Savory may have to a certain extent been influenced by his experience at Pipton (see below), there is no reason to doubt that he was a skilled field archaeologist capable of distinguishing between rifled bones and those that had remained *in situ,* and that his recognition of remnant groupings is sound, even though the groups themselves were dissipated. Moreover, disarticulated and mixed human bones, placed or pushed into more or less uniformly orientated piles or groups, against the sides, in the centre and in the corners of rectangular chambers are a recurring trope in some chambered tombs in SE Wales – certainly also seen at Pipton (Savory 1956; see below), and possibly in the remnant deposits of Chambers I and II at Ty Isaf (Grimes 1939; see below), and further afield at Coldrum (Bennet 1913; Wysocki *et al.* 2013), with something similar being played out at Lanhill (Keiller and Piggott 1938) and in the bone groups at Fussell's Lodge (Ashbee 1966; Wysocki *et al.* 2007).

Secondary burial? If the remnant groups, which contain comingled remains from different individuals, are indeed *in situ* they can only be the result of rearrangements from a pool of already disarticulated bones, and this must also be the case with the bones from singular individuals dispersed among the *in situ* groups: elements assessed as female were found in Groups A, D, E, F and G (Table 6.9) as well as the rifled scatter, there were no anatomical duplicates and both femora and the ulna are certainly from the same individual.

Table 6.9. Penywyrlod: Chamber NE II, distribution of assessed female elements.

Bone Group	*Skeletal part*	*Assessment criteria*		*Notes*
Disturbed	Left innominate portion	Wide GSN, pre-auricular sulcus	female	Part iliac crest, acetabulum, ischium
	Right innominate portion	Wide GSN	?female	Acetabulum, ischium, portion ilium
A	R femur	CM: 81.0 mm APD 27.0 mm Length: 386 mm	female	Exuberant enthesopathies, grey hue
D	frontal	Subdued glabella, sharp supra-orbital margins	female	–
E	R ulna	Length: 240 mm	female	Spiculated enthesopathies, grey hue
G	L femur	VHD: 38.8 mm CM: 80.3 mm APD 27.5 mm Length 388 mm	female	Exuberant enthesopathies, grey hue

Key: GSN = greater sciatic notch; ? = probable

Skeletally immature remains were also dispersed among *in situ* Groups B, C, D, F and H, although it is uncertain if these are all from one person.

The relatively low counts of hand and foot bones, vertebrae (Tables 6.4 and 6.12), and particularly ribs, could be taken to support the view that already skeletonised or partly skeletonised remains were collected and brought from elsewhere, with many smaller and perhaps insignificant bones lost in transport and handling, left behind, or damaged during the period of accumulation. This argument is, however, compromised because of the disturbances, which must account for some, if not many, of these missing and incomplete bones. Nonetheless, it seems unlikely that the absence of almost 99% of ribs, with only two fragments recovered from an expected count of 144 complete bones is the result of rifling alone. Similarly, it is unlikely that rifling alone could account for the almost total absence of bones or fragments from the facial skeleton or sphenoid and as noted earlier some skulls could already have been damaged and incomplete when originally deposited in the chamber. Limited subaerial weathering and absence of mammalian carnivore scavenging modifications both argue against the notion that individuals were left exposed to the elements to decompose before their bones were brought to Chamber NE II or held elsewhere, while the absence of soiling or strong patination on the bones militates against their being buried and disinterred (cf. Wysocki *et al.* 2007, 68). The almost uniform colouration and condition of the bones suggest that they were all kept in, or brought from, one place rather than from different locations.

A single act? Savory's assertion that human remains were placed and sealed in Chamber NE II in a single act, while plausible enough in its own right and in line with earlier models of ossuaries (see Daniel 1950, for example), hinges on his interpretation of the structural evidence. Once that is challenged, however (see Chapter 2), the surviving skeletal evidence is not necessarily contradictory. It would still remain likely that already disarticulated bones were brought periodically to the chamber, where they became mixed and were rearranged, possibly to create more space for new arrivals, as seems to have happened in the NW chamber at the Lanhill long barrow (Keiller *et al.* 1938, fig. 2). There is a hint that this may be the case in the rather more coherent composition of the centrally placed remnant Group G, where several postcranial bones appear to be from the same individual, perhaps the last interment before final closure.

Reconnecting with the ancestors? Whether or not bones were collected from elsewhere or accumulated in the precincts of the cairn, what is evident is that the mixed skeletal remains of six or seven people were rearranged or redistributed in piles within Chamber NE II. Wysocki and Whittle (2000, 598–9) suggested that the more substantial groupings in the chamber consisted of cranial, axial and both upper and lower limb remains which appeared to be loose anatomical replications of the human skeleton, although the bones had been drawn from a number of different individuals. This seems to be the case in bone groups from three of the four corners of the chamber (here identified as A, F and C/D; Fig. 6.2). Could these configurations be more by accident than design – pushing aside individual or partial skeletons to make room for further deposits, as argued above? Two factors suggest intentionality – the rearrangements into distinct groups, although these are less clear-cut here than at Pipton (see below), and the apparent representation of a single skull in Group A, assembled from left- and right-side portions from two individuals. Again, frustratingly, without full knowledge of the actual contents of the groups and of the specific arrangements of those contents, some uncertainty remains.

Overview. We can have more confidence in other observations. The Chamber NE II mortuary assemblage is largely male and young adult or near-adult, there were certainly no children nor pre-pubescents and, intentionally or unintentionally, parts from no more than one female were dispersed among the various piles. It appears to have been an exclusive and ultimately inaccessible group, their resting place finally sealed to prevent further ingress or egress.

Chamber NE III

In contrast Chamber NE III contains the remains of adults, both young and old, males and females, older and younger youths and children. Again, we lack full knowledge of the contents and of the spatial and contextual relationships of the recovered bones to what lies within, but the impression here is of something more domestic, certainly more accessible, with a functional passage. The presence of children and infants gives pause for thought. Does it imply a difference in the 'quality of life' of the two mortuary groups, or different criteria for selection?

The taphonomic traces speak of different *postmortem* pathways. The bones are more weathered, soiled, scratched and abraded, perhaps already broken when deposited. These modifications could reflect some much earlier disturbances. On the other hand, Savory (1984, 22) noted that the bones from the chamber entrance were in a loose stony filling; perhaps both were introduced at the same time in a similar manner to the human skeletal remains mixed with secondary fill at West Kennet (Piggott 1962, 53; Bayliss *et al.* 2007, 93). The same may apply to the remains mixed with blocking material in the passage to Chamber NE III

One thing that both the Chamber NE II and Chamber NE III people appear to have in common are the consequences of inter-personal violence, from both ranged weapons or possibly hand-to-hand engagements. Of the former, the embedded flint arrowhead from Chamber NE III (or passage) is unequivocal; the loose flint arrowhead tip found in Chamber NE II (Group H) is less so, although it too is more than likely to have found its way into the chamber embedded in soft tissue, ligaments or bone as the result of an impact fracture (Titmus and Woods 1986; Smith *et al.* 2007). Possibly of the latter, although slingshots could instead have been involved, healed and healing head wounds attest that some may have lived to fight another day.

Human remains from Pipton

Background

The chambered cairn at Pipton was excavated in 1950 (Savory 1956). It has a transepted lateral chamber with functional passage (Chamber I), within a 'rotunda', and a second simple chamber also within a 'rotunda' (Chamber II), all set within a trapezoidal long cairn with a forecourt at the broader end (Figs 2.30 and 6.4). It is uncertain whether Chamber II was conceived as a sealed cist, similar in manner to Chamber NE II at Penywyrlod, or whether it was accessed before being sealed, via a gap on the NW side, or possibly from above (Savory 1956, 42). Savory (1956, 37–8) considered the tomb to have been built as a single act though later commentators have suggested multi-period construction (for example, Corcoran 1969, 86–7; Darvill 2004, 70).

Contexts from which human and animal bone were recorded are given in Table 6.10 and shown in Figs 6.4 and 6.5.

Table 6.10. Pipton: contexts from which human and animal remains are recorded (see also Fig. 6.4).

Context	*Location*	*Description*
Chamber I	1	Entrance passage, 5ft [1.5m] from entrance under tilted slab against south side of passage
	2	Entrance passage, 6ft [1.8m] from N corner against S orthostat
	3	Entrance passage, 6ft 6ins [2m] from N corner, underneath corner of S orthostat, partially overlain by portal sill stone
	4	Inner passage on floor against face of second orthostat going inwards on N. side, beneath collapsed roof slabs
	5	Under paving slab. Entrance passage 5ft [1.5m] from N corner, 8ins [0.2m] from S drystone wall, 4ft 2ins [1.3m] deep
	6	S annexe, beneath floor slab in NE corner
Chamber II	7	Groups A–G
	8	Under floor slabs

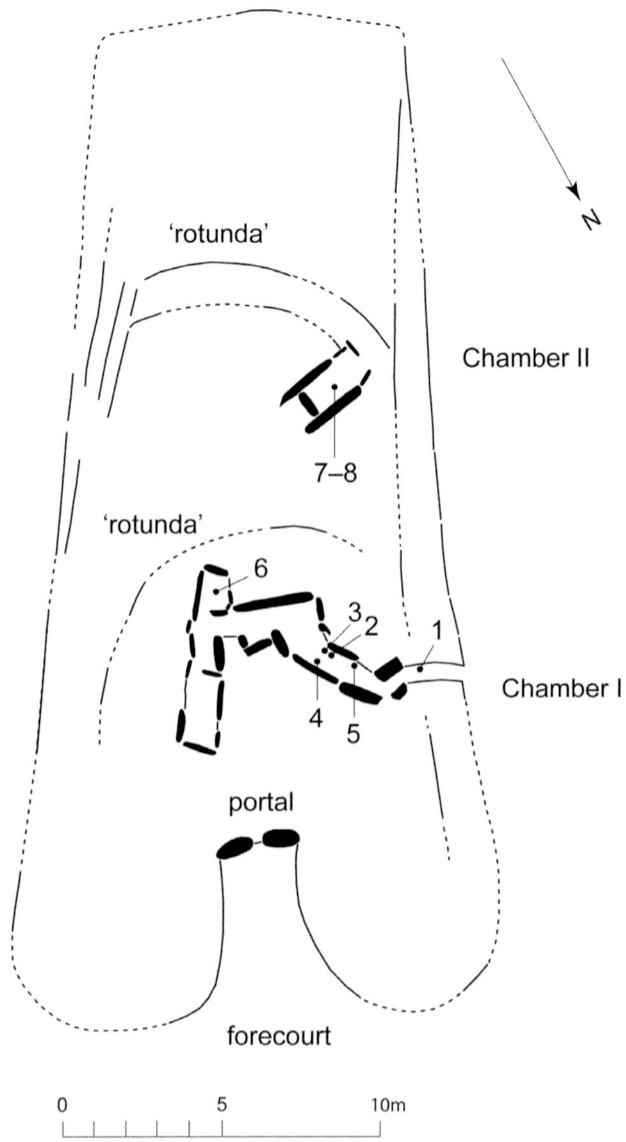

Fig. 6.4. Pipton: contexts in which human and animal bone are recorded (plan after Savory 1956, fig. 2). See also Table 6.10.

Six radiocarbon dates for human skeletal material and one cattle tooth are now available which show a significant span of use, as set out in Chapter 4.

Chamber I

Chamber I was found to contain only six small deposits of human remains overlain by a primary filling of dry reddish-brown sandy earth (Savory 1956, 22): five fragments under a tilted slab (Fig. 6.4, Context 1) and four other single bone fragments, one under a floor slab (Contexts 2–5), all within the vicinity of the entrance passage, interpreted by Savory as ritual deposits. A further small assemblage (Context 6), interpreted as a foundation deposit, was found under a floor slab in the south transept.

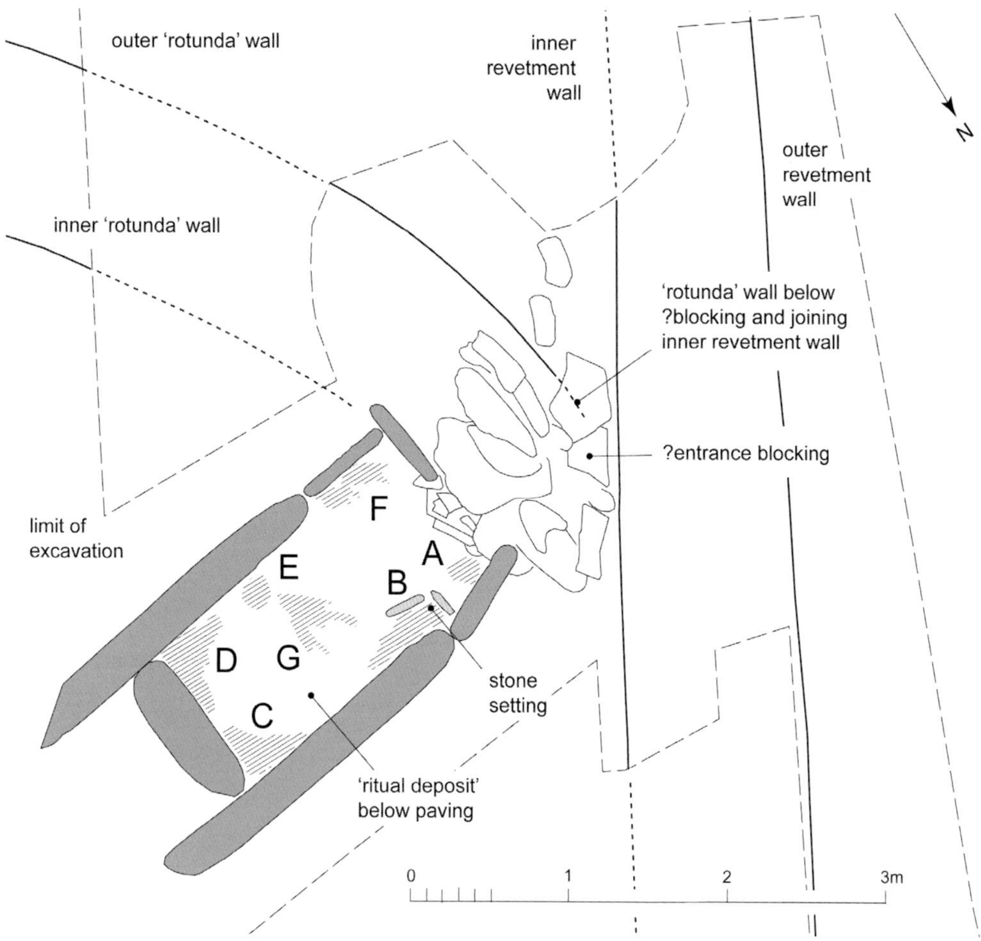

Fig. 6.5. Pipton: location of bone groups in Chamber II (after Savory 1956, fig. 3).

Chamber II

Chamber II contained a substantial amount of human skeletal material. Human bones were arranged in seven piles or groups (Fig. 6.5, numbered in this chapter as Groups A–G), along both the long sides of the chamber, in the corners and in the centre, with an additional 'foundation deposit' beneath a paving slab. Savory (1956, 26) noted some disturbance in the upper filling and disruption of the burial deposit in the centre of the chamber (Group G) but the rest of the groups appeared undisturbed and were overlain by a lower filling of brown earth said to be 6–9 inches (15–22cm) deep (Savory 1956, 26). One of the groups (B) was partly framed by a setting of upright stones. A one-page bone report (West 1956) estimated that the human remains from Chamber II represented a minimum of seven individuals.

Taphonomy

Present condition of the human skeletal remains

Except for Chamber II Group G, each discrete deposit was packaged in one or more plastic bags, accompanied by original, dated finds-labels giving contextual details. Individual bone fragments were ink-marked with chamber number and group. One unlabelled bag contained eight small cranial fragments, loose fragmentary teeth and five small postcranial fragments, all unmarked. Could this possibly represent Group G? Savory (1956, 26) considered this grouping to have been disturbed and noted 'the relatively crushed condition of the bones' but the original published plan (Savory 1956, fig. 3) shows Group G as a substantial collection of long bones. No details of this group, nor of Groups A and E, are given in West (1956).

The skeletal archive was tightly packed in several cardboard boxes. It had been re-packaged since excavation (some material having once been on display). Several long bone segments from Chamber II displayed unpatinated fresh fracture surfaces implying that some longer elements may have been broken during packing or re-packing. In most cases conjoins of these recent breakages were possible.

More seriously, much of the archive had been varnished without adequate prior cleaning of bone surfaces; soil had consequently smeared and mixed with the varnish, creating an opaque film. On some bones thick coats of muddied varnish had coalesced in crevices, cavities, between ridges, rendering bone surfaces and features unobservable. On some other bones the varnish had adhered to the overlying layer of soil, leaving some patches of the coating flaky and removable by soft brushing. Thick varnish had also been applied to dentition, making examination difficult or impossible. A number of varnished crown enamels had subsequently cracked, developing multiple vertical split-lines, or in some cases totally disintegrating. Observations of taphonomic modifications and pathology are consequently limited (Table 6.11).

Postmortem bone modifications: Chamber II

Where varnish could be cleaned off, bone surfaces, were consistently uniform in colour, with infrequent patches of mineral or fungal staining. Bone colour was generally a pale brown to deeper brown hue, corresponding with Savory's (1956, 26) description of the primary fill.

Mammalian traces. Rodent-type gnawing was evident in 14 fragments from 85 observations (16.5%), the majority occurring among Group B specimens (11 from 34 observations: 32%). Two specimens, a femur and tibia segment from Group B, displayed mammalian carnivore-type bi-polar tooth punctures.

Fragmentation and bone survivorship. Disregarding those damaged post-excavation, most skeletal elements were broken and incomplete, fracture morphology being consistent with fragmentation of dry bone (Table 6.11). Many fracture surfaces were patinated, with abraded fracture edges, indicating old breakages. Only one bone, a humerus from Chamber II Group B, presented intact. A femur and tibia from the same group, with old patinated dry bone fracture surfaces, probably already broken when placed in the chamber, were reconstructed during analysis. Other long bone segments with old dry bone fractures from Group B were also found to conjoin, forming incomplete shafts.

Table 6.11. Pipton: Chamber II, human bone weathering and fracture analysis.

	N	*% frequency*
Weathering stage		
0	37	59.7
1	21	33.9
2	3	4.8
3	–	–
4	1	1.6
Total	62	100
Fracture morphology	28	49.1
Transverse		
V/Spiral	7	12.3
Intermediate	22	38.6
Total	57	100
Fracture angles	42	80.8
Right		
Oblique	3	5.8
Right/oblique	7	134
Total	52	100

The intensity of fragmentation in Chamber II, however, was of a different order to that encountered in the human remains from Ty Isaf (see below) or Parc le Breos Cwm (Whittle and Wysocki 1998). Most surviving limb segments were relatively substantial (distal or proximal halves or thirds, two-thirds or three-quarters of shafts and so on). Proximal and distal epiphyses were frequently preserved, if only in part. However, small splinters and segments, amorphous chunks of trabecular bone and unidentifiable fragments, normally to be found in skeletal assemblages fragmented *in situ* (see, for example Ty Isaf, below), were largely absent. Equally notable was the total absence of any small bones from the hand or wrist. Small bones of the foot (excluding calcaneus and talus) were represented by only eight fragments, ribs by ten small fragments and vertebrae by only eight fragments (see Table 6.12).

Weathering modifications. Where observable, many elements showed no evidence of subaerial weathering (weathering stage 0), but about a third of the assemblage has been scored weathering stage 1 because of the presence of short longitudinal split-lines. These have a 'fresh' appearance and are not convincingly indicative of pre-excavation processes, more likely representing reaction to varnishing or other post-excavation agencies.

Skeletal remains from Chamber I

Context 1 (Entrance passage, 5ft [1.5m] from entrance under tilted slab against south side of passage)

Adult human bones. **Axial**: rib head fragment, two small rib shaft fragments. **Upper limbs**: proximal ⅔ left ulna.

Unidentified. Small splinter probably from a limb bone.

Context 2 (Entrance passage, 6ft [1.8m] from N corner against S orthostat)

Adult human bones. **Axial**: portion of right innominate, sex uncertain.

Context 3 (Entrance passage, 6ft 6ins [2m] from N corner, underneath corner of S orthostat, partially overlain by portal sill stone)

Adult human bones. **Upper limbs**: distal ⅓ right humerus, male.

Table 6.12. Comparative percentage frequencies of adult hand, foot and vertebral bones in selected southern British early Neolithic mortuary assemblages.

		HAND			FOOT			VERTEBRA		
Site	MNI	Ideal	Actual	%	Ideal	Actual	%	Ideal	Actual	%
Hazleton N: S chamber	14	756	350	46.3%	728	425	58.4%	–	–	–
N chamber	4	216	104	48.2%	208	117	56.2%	–	–	–
N entrance	3	162	124	76.5%	156	115	73.7%	–	–	–
Wayland's Smithy 1	13	702	209	29.8%	676	208	30.8%	312	191	61.2%
West Kennet	22	1188	198	16.6%	1144	238	20.8%	528	308	58.3%
Fussell's Lodge: group C–D	4	216	44	20.4%	208	47	22.5%	96	37	38.5%
group A–B	22	1188	63	5.3%	1144	75	6.5%	528	118	22.3%
Skendleby Giant's Hill 1	4	214	27	12.5%	208	51	24.5%	96	50	52.1%
Lanhill	7	378	46	12.2%	364	54	14.8%	168	79	47.0%
Penywyrlod: Chamber NE II	6	324	20	6.2%	312	27	8.7%	144	27	18.7%
Tinkinswood	17	918	51	5.5%	884	56	6.3%	408	37	9.1%
Ty Isaf	28	1512	20	1.3%	1456	85	5.8%	672	57	8.5%
Pipton Chamber II	10	540	0	0.0%	520	8	1.5%	240	8	3.3%

Hazleton North data from Saville (1990). All other sites: archived collections examined by MW 1998–2001

Context 4 (Inner passage on floor against face of second orthostat going inwards on N side, beneath collapsed roof slabs)

Adult human bones. **Skull**: fragment of right mandible with molar sockets M_1 to M_3.

Context 5 (Under paving slab. Entrance passage 5ft [1.5m] from N corner, 8ins [0.2m] from S drystone wall, 4ft 2ins [1.3m] deep)

Adult human bones. **Lower limbs**: Distal phalange of big toe.

Context 6 (Annexe [transept], beneath floor slab in NE corner)

Adult human bones. **Lower limbs**: proximal foot-phalange with fused epiphysis.

Immature human bones. **Skull**: eight small fragments of thin cranial vault; portion right petrous temporal, small, gracile; portion each of immature right and left mandible with dentition; pair of right first and second permanent mandibular molars; pair of left first and second permanent mandibular molars. **Upper limbs**: fragment of immature left humerus shaft; medial finger-phalange shaft. **Lower limbs**: fragment of immature left femoral midshaft. **Not identified**: 18 small limb shaft splinters.

This small deposit consists almost entirely of immature remains. Molar dentition in both mandible fragments is consistent with that of an older child, *c.* 7–9 years. Loose dentition consists of both a right and left permanent lower first molar with almost completed roots and open root apices, and right and left permanent lower second molar crowns, both near completion, representing a further child or children of a similar age. The foot phalange is from an older individual of at least *c.* 16 years.

Skeletal remains from Chamber II

Group A

Adult human bones. **Axial**: left iliac fossa fragment with portion acetabulum; left ischial tuberosity with portion acetabular notch and rim. **Lower limbs**: right calcaneus; right talus.

There is nothing in this small (120.2 g. total weight) assemblage to suggest that the remains are from more than one individual. Metric sexing of the calcaneus and talus indicates male sex (Table 6.13); the two bones articulate well and are from the same foot.

Group B

Adult human bones. **Skull**: fragments refitting to form *cranium 1* (reconstructed) – almost complete frontal with substantial portion right parietal, sphenoid, base of occipital, portions of right and left temporals with mastoids, maxilla carrying right-sided dentition PM^3 to M^3, right zygomatic arch; *cranium 2* (reconstructed) – left frontal, portions right and left parietals, left petrous temporal, portion occipital; *cranium 3* (reconstructed) – left frontal, left temporal, fragments left and right parietal, occipital; *unassigned* – small cranial vault fragments; almost complete mandible carrying

Table 6.13. Pipton: Chamber II metric sex assessment.

Group	*Specimen*	*Metric**	*Datum*	*Assessed sex*	*Notes*
A	R calcaneus	DF1	34.3	male	Articulates with R talus below
A	R talus	DF2	43.4	male	
B	L scapula fragment	GL	39.5 mm	male	
B	L humerus	VHD	44.5 mm	indet.	
		EW Length	59.1 mm 307 mm	indet.	
B	L femur	VHD	46.8 mm	male	Medial condyle damaged
		CM Length	87.4 mm 425 mm	male 1	
B	L femur proximal ⅔	VHD	45.5 mm	male	
		CM	90.9 mm	male 2	
		APD	30.0 mm	male	
B	L femur shaft, proximal ½	CM	84.1 mm	male 3	
B	L femur, proximal ½	CM	80.6mm	female	Femoral head damaged
		APD	25.3 mm	female	
B	L femur distal shaft	APD	30.4 mm	male	
B	R femur, broken distally	VHD	47.9 mm	male	
		CM	85.9 mm	male	
		APD	27.9 mm	indet.	
B	R femur distal shaft	CM	76.6 mm	female	
B	L tibia proximal ½	BB	75.1 mm	male	
		CNF	98.3 mm	male	
B	L tibia proximal ½	BB	74.1 mm	male	Epiphyseal line incompletely fused
		CNF	89.0 mm	indet.	
B	L tibia distal ⅔	CNF	89.3 mm	indet.	
B	R tibia	BB	74.2 mm	male	
		CNF Length	95.9 mm 347 mm	male	
B	R tibia distal ⅔	CNF	80.2 mm	female	Epiphyseal line well-marked
C	R humerus distal portion	EW	61.4 mm	male	
C	R femur proximal ⅓	VHD	44.8 mm	indet.	
		CM	85.7 mm	male	
D	L femur midshaft	CM	93.4 mm	male 4	
D	L femur midshaft	CM	84.5 mm	male 5	
D	R femur midshaft	CM	84.3 mm	male	
F	R femur shaft, proximal ½	CM	88.9 mm	male	
F	R femoral head	VHD	46.3 mm	indet.	
F	R tibia midshaft	CNF	99.3 mm	male	

Key: * See Table 6.1; indet. = indeterminate; 1, 2, 3, 4, 5 = single entities

all right and left molars; fragment of left mandible carrying M_1 and M_2 (M_3 lost *postmortem*). **Axial**: cervical body fragment; thoracic body fragment; three thoracic processes; sacrum fragment; three ribshaft fragments; left clavicle; acromial end left clavicle; fragment each from two left and one right scapula; three left and four right innominate fragments, two fragments ilium. **Upper limbs**: complete left humerus; fragment left distal humerus; distal ⅓ right humerus; right humerus shaft; humerus shaft fragment; left ulna proximal shaft portion, gracile; fragment left ulna head; proximal fragment each of two right ulnae; distal ½ left radius; left distal radius fragment; two unsided radius shaft fragments. **Lower limbs:** left femur, damaged medial condyle; left femur, proximal ⅔; left femur, proximal ½, head damaged; left femur shaft, proximal ½; left femur shaft, proximal ¼; left femur distal shaft fragment; left femur, distal end; right femur, broken distally above articulating end; right femur, proximal shaft segment, gracile; right femur, distal shaft segment, gracile; right femur, proximal shaft fragment; right femur distal end, lateral condyle damaged; fragment each right lateral and medial femoral condyles; two proximal ½s, left tibiae; left tibia, distal ⅔; left distal tibia fragment (talar facet); right tibia; right tibia distal ⅔; two fragments tibia shaft; left patella fragment; right calcaneus fragment.

Immature human bone. fragment right proximal ulnar epiphysis.

The majority (91%) of cranial fragments can be reconnected to form parts of three crania, two of which were partially complete at the time of excavation; remaining fragments probably also belong to these skulls but cannot be conjoined. Three individuals are represented by fragments of left and right innominates. Upper limbs represent at least two adults. At least three individuals are again indicated by tibiae. However, left femoral specimens are drawn from at least five individuals.

Sex assessment. Craniums 1 and 3 are morphologically male. Cranium 2 is morphologically female, thin-walled, with surviving sutures unfused. An almost complete, robust, mandible, carrying full sets of left and right molars, is morphologically male. The intact left humerus is metrically indeterminate, but comparatively robust. At least three males and one female are indicated by left proximal femora, while tibiae represent at least one male and one female (Table 6.13).

Age estimation. Light to moderate maxillary dental wear in Cranium 1 and the complete mandible (Lovejoy stage C/D), which are occlusally incompatible, indicates two adult males *c.* 18–24 years. Heavier dental wear in a fragment of left mandible indicates an older individual *c.* 25–35 years (stage E/F). An unfused proximal ulnar epiphysis fragment represents an adolescent or late adolescent; fusion patterns in the proximal ulna are very variable spanning an age range from *c.* 13 years to *c.* 19 years in males and females (Scheuer and Black 2000, 304–6). A fragment of gracile, thin-walled radius shaft may be from an individual of similar age. The proximal epiphyseal line in a left tibia segment (metric sex assessment inconclusive) is not completely fused indicating an age of *c.* 15–19 years (Scheuer and Black 2000, 408). A distal right tibia segment with fused epiphysis displays a distinct epiphyseal line indicating relatively recent fusion. This specimen is metrically female and the degree of metrical asymmetry between it and the left proximal segment above suggests that the two tibiae are from different individuals, although the age range is broadly similar: *c.* 15–18, possibly a little older. Two non-contiguous segments of gracile right femoral shaft may also be from this young female.

In summary, the majority of remains appear to be from no more than three people, two younger adult males under *c.* 25 years and a late adolescent or young adult female *c.* 15–18 years, but femoral specimens are from at least five individuals (three males, one female, one indeterminate) and a mandibular fragment is from a somewhat older adult.

Original finds labels and published photographs (Savory 1956) enable partial reconstruction of the stratigraphical composition of this group. Cranium 1 was the last item placed during the depositional sequence and can be clearly seen in a published photograph (Savory 1956, pl. VIII, no. 1) resting on top of the deposit, on a group of the more substantial long bones. Cranium 2 (young female) was found 'below first long bones', on a second group of long bones. The finds label also states cranium 2 was 'pierced by femur'. There is no further information, drawings nor photographs to clarify if this was an intentional manipulation or simple happenstance.

Group C

Adult human bones. **Skull**: adult occipital; right maxilla fragment with M^3; right maxilla fragment with M^1; right maxilla fragment with M^1, PM^4; left half mandible; fragment each of two left mandibles, fragment mental protuberance. **Axial**: fragment each left and right acetabula (left conjoins with innominate portion from Group F); fragment vertebral process; six small rib fragments. **Upper limbs**: distal portion right humerus; right ulna, proximal ½, robust; right ulna proximal shaft, gracile; left ulna shaft fragment, gracile; right radius shaft, robust. **Lower limbs**: right femur, proximal ⅓; right femur, proximal shaft, gracile; left femur, distal shaft segment, gracile; left femur proximal shaft segment, robust; small fragments femoral condyle; left tibia distal half, robust; left tibia, distal shaft fragment, gracile; three fragments proximal tibia shaft; distal ½ left fibula shaft.

Immature human bones. **Skull**: fragment thin occipital; fragment thin parietal.

The cranial vault is represented by three small fragments only, two fragments (occipital and parietal) are thin-walled and appear to be immature. The remaining cranial material is a mixture of maxillary and mandibular fragments which are drawn from at least four individuals but this is at odds with the postcranial remains which consistently indicate a minimum of two adults. Without anatomical siding and observation of duplicating root sockets, the mandibular fragments would not obviously appear to be from more than two people.

Sex assessment. A proximal right femur segment is metrically inconclusive, perhaps more likely to be male than female (Table 6.13). The rest of the postcranial material presents as a mixture of gracile and robust fragments.

Age estimation. Occlusal wear is evident in the surviving dentition but obscured by heavy layers of varnish. One of three left mandible fragments carries a third permanent molar, and the two others exhibit fully developed third molar root sockets indicating three individuals of at least *c.* 20 years. Mild wear (stage B1/B2) is visible on a mental protuberance fragment carrying incisors and canines only, but without the rest of the dentition this can only suggest a probable age range of 12–20 years.

Group D

Adult human bones. **Skull**: frontal fragment, left and right supraorbital border; two occipital portions, both with prominent external protuberance; four right petrous temporal portions, each with external acoustic meatus (EAM); left petrous temporal with EAM, robust; fragment each from two right mandibles; right maxilla fragment, several crown and root fragment from loose dentition. **Axial**: two thoracic vertebrae fragments; fragment right scapula; right acetabulum fragment; left innominate fragment, auricular surface; fragment of acetabular rim, conjoins with left acetabulum fragment from group F. **Upper limbs**: right humerus midshaft; right distal humerus shaft fragment; right distal humerus fragment, medial epicondyle; left ulna, proximal fragment. **Lower limbs**: two left femur midshafts; right femur midshaft; three fragments from left tibiae.

Immature human bone. **Skull**: frontal fragment with left and right supraorbital border: loose permanent canine. **Axial**: fragment right scapula, glenoid cavity.

Five petrous temporal fragments (external auditory meatus), four left and one right, are from at least four adults. The remaining adult cranial and postcranial fragments consistently represent a minimum of two individuals. Without careful siding the four left petrous temporal fragments could be taken to be from two people.

Sex assessment. All three femora (2L, 1R), two of which may be a pair, represent at least two adult males (Table 6.13). Two duplicated occipital fragments and a portion of adult frontal bone are morphologically male.

Age estimation. A thin, gracile frontal fragment appears to be from an immature individual, probably an older child or early adolescent. This is matched by an immature right scapula fragment with an unfused glenoid fossa also representing an older child or young adolescent under *c.* 14–15 years (Scheuer and Black 2000, 266) and possibly a solitary canine crown fragment with no occlusal wear or polishing. These three fragments are anomalous and there is nothing in the remaining postcranial material that can be assigned to this age category. Mandibular fragments and remaining dentition indicate only two individuals of indeterminate age.

Group E

Adult human bones. **Skull**: portion of right frontal/parietal (reconstructed); portion of left parietal (reconstructed); portion right temporal (reconstructed), several small fragments of cranial vault; fragment maxilla. **Axial**: two fragments from vertebral processes. **Lower limbs**: conjoining fragments forming segment of right proximal tibia shaft; unsided fibula shaft segment, fragment right talus; unsided metatarsal shaft fragment.

The deposit is largely composed of fragments of cranium, all probably from one skull, many of which conjoin to form three non-contiguous portions. Five tibial fragments also conjoin to form a segment of shaft. The remains appear gracile but none of the material is obviously skeletally immature and there are no anatomical duplications nor size differences to indicate more than one individual.

Group F

Adult human bones. **Skull**: portions of frontal, left and right parietals, occipital, left mastoid and styloid, fragment right mastoid, several cranial vault fragments, all probably from single entity; fragment occipital; several fragments cranial vault; fragment left parietal, immature; fragment mandibular ramus with condyle; six loose teeth. **Axial**: three fragmentary thoracic vertebrae; fragment right innominate; two conjoining left innominate fragments (conjoin with acetabular ridge fragment from Group C, above), fragment ischium. **Upper limbs**: right humerus shaft; distal ½ right humerus shaft, gracile; left humerus shaft. **Lower limbs**: proximal ½ right femur shaft; right femoral head; right tibia midshaft; right tibia, proximal shaft portion, gracile; right tibia, distal shaft portion, gracile; fragment proximal right tibia, posterior surface; fragment proximal condyle tibia, unsided; three fibula shaft segments.

Group F contains partial remains representing a minimum of two individuals. Bones or fragments from the forearms, hands, feet and ribs are entirely absent and the spinal column is represented by three fragmentary thoracic vertebrae

Sex assessment. Cranial material consists in large part of fragments attributable to an adult male skull. A portion of a right femur and a right tibia are also metrically male (Table 6.13) and a left and right humerus shaft are robust. A duplicate occipital fragment, a fragment of left parietal, a distal right humerus shaft, two segments of right tibia shaft and a fibula shaft are consistently gracile. Portions of left and right acetabulum are from two adult individuals, one smaller than the other.

Age estimation. Two third molar fragments and occlusal wear (stage D/E) where observable in three loose first and second permanent molars are indicative of a *c.* 20–30 years age range.

Chamber II: unlabelled bag (possibly group G)

Adult human bone. Six small fragments of cranial vault; two maxillary fragments; 13 heavily exfoliated and eroded tooth fragments; a fragment from the distal end of a left humerus; a patella; three fragmentary foot bones.

Context 8 (Chamber II: under floor slab)

Adult human bone. Cranial vault fragment; fragments of rib shaft; radius head fragment; metatarsal head fragment; metatarsal shaft fragment; proximal end proximal foot phalange; navicular fragment.

Unidentified. Seven splinters.

Pipton Chamber II demographic summary

The remains are mixed, fragmentary and incomplete, have suffered post-excavation damage and are analytically challenging. This examination found the most frequent anatomical duplication to occur in occipital remains, of which nine are adult or near-adult specimens and one is immature. At least eight adults or near-adults are also represented by duplicating portions of left and right proximal femur shafts and there are seven more immature fragments representing at least one older child or earlier adolescent. Other duplicating elements are listed in Table 6.14.

Morphological and metric sex assessment indicates that there are at least five males and at least one female (Table 6.13). Morphologically and metrically assessed female fragments occur in Group B (cranium, left femur, right femur, right tibia). There are also visually gracile possibly female or adolescent duplicating and non-duplicating fragments in Groups B, C, E and F. Immature fragments occur in Groups B, C and D.

The revised MNI estimate is ten individuals.

Palaeopathology and markers of occupational stress

Opaque varnishing and the incomplete character of individual bones meant that only limited observations of features were possible.

Dentition

The sample consists of a total tooth count of 33 specimens. No evidence of caries was noted. One example of AMTL (PM4) was recorded from a total of 68 observations. Malocclusion was noted in three examples. Enamel hypoplasia was absent in the Chamber II sample. A right canine from the immature mandible fragment in Context 6, Chamber I, displays moderate hypoplasia (one band and pitting).

Cranial skeleton

Light porotic hyperostosis (*cribra orbitalis*) is evident in the right orbital plate of the adult male frontal from Group F.

Postcranial skeleton

Axial skeleton. Slight osteophytes were noted on two thoracic body fragments from Group F.

Upper limbs. An adult male right humerus shaft from Group B displays a prominent swelling at the anterior surface immediately superior to the coronoid fossa with slight angulation. The condition suggests a well-healed transverse fracture between medial and lateral supracondylar ridges, just above the elbow joint.

Lower limbs. An adult left femur shaft segment from Group B is bowed medially. The feature may result from a healed fracture in this limb, or may be a consequence of trauma elsewhere in the leg or hip, or possibly relate to nutritional deficiency in earlier life.

Markers of musculoskeletal and occupational stress

Upper limb. Several humeri shafts display prominent deltoid tuberosities and mild to moderate lateral bowing. Both right and left bones are affected, as are both gracile and robust specimens. As detailed earlier (see above: Penywyrlod) lateral bowing and prominent deltoid tuberosities are both components of a suite of anatomical structures reflecting stress factors in the upper arm (Capasso *et al.* 1999, 63, 67–8, 83).

Lower limbs. Squatting facets were observed in four distal tibia fragments, both left and right, robust and gracile.

Pipton: commentary and overview

Chamber I

Savory (1956) interpreted the remains found beneath floor slabs (Contexts 5 and 6) as foundation deposits and the remaining material as ritual deposits possibly connected with the episode of red earth infilling. Finds labels (in archive) show that Context 6 (S annexe foundation deposit) was recovered over two days (30/09/50–2/10/50, a Saturday and Monday) and that there was some uncertainty over whether the floor slab was in fact paving or a fallen corbel. The deposits dispersed around the entrance passage (Contexts 1–4) were described as 'ritual deposits of fragmentary human bones, placed under tilted slabs at scattered points in the entrance passage' (Savory 1956, 13–14) but in fact only Context 1 was under a tilted slab, which could itself be a fallen corbel. It is possible that all the material in this chamber could represent residual remains, some left behind beneath fallen slabs, after an episode of clearance (perhaps itself instigated by partial collapse of the chamber roof).

Table 6.14. Pipton: Chamber II MNI estimates.

Total	*Element*	*Segment*	*Adult Male*	*Adult Female*	*Adult Indet.*	*Immature*
5	R frontal	–	3	–	1	1
7	L frontal	–	4	1	1	1
5	R parietal	–	3	1	1	–
6	L parietal	–	2	1	2	1
7	R temporal	–	1	–	6	–
5	L temporal	–	2	1	2	–
10	Occipital	–	5	1	3	1
3	R mandible	–	1	–	2	–
5	L mandible	–	2	–	3	–
3	R scapula	–	–	–	2	1
2	L scapula	–	1	–	1	–
0	R humerus	PE	–	–	-	–
3	R humerus	PS	–	–	3	–
7	R humerus	DS	–	–	7	–
3	R humerus	DE	–	–	3	–
1	L humerus	PE	–	–	1	–
2	L humerus	PS	–	–	2	–
2	L humerus	DS	–	–	2	–
2	L humerus	DE	–	–	2	–
2	R ulna	PE	–	–	1	1
4	R ulna	PS	–	–	4	–
0	R ulna	DS	–	–	–	–
0	R ulna	DE	–	–	–	–
3	L ulna	PE	–	–	3	–
3	L ulna	PS	–	–	3	–
0	L ulna	DS	–	–	–	–
0	L ulna	DE	–	–	–	–
2	R femur	PE	2	–	–	–
8	R femur	PS	4	–	4	–
5	R femur	DS	4	1	–	–
3	R femur	DE	–	–	3	–
3	L femur	PE	2	1	–	–
8	L femur	PS	5	1	2	–
6	L femur	DS	5	–	1	–
3	L femur	DE	1	–	2	–
2	R tibia	PE	1	–	1	–
5	R tibia	PS	2	1	2	–
4	R tibia	DS	2	1	1	–
2	R tibia	DE	1	1	–	–
2	L tibia	PE	2	–	–	–
2	L tibia	PS	2	–	–	–
2	L tibia	DS	–	–	2	–
2	L tibia	DE	–	–	2	–

Key: R = right; L = left; P = proximal; D = distal ; E = end; S = Shaft

Chamber II

Secondary burial? Savory (1956, 42) concluded that 'The confusion, fragmentation, and incompleteness of the bones at Pipton would be the natural result of transportation from the first resting place when already scarified [sic]' and the taphonomic evidence supports his interpretation. Conjoining fragments with old, patinated, dry bone fractures and the absence of small fragmentary material – the debitage and detritus of bone fragmentation – strongly imply two things. First, that breakage and fragmentation did not occur in Chamber II itself on any large scale and that a number of bones were already broken when brought to the chamber or were broken during transportation and redeposition. Secondly, that the bones were already old and mineralised, relatively brittle and dry, when transported. Furthermore, the total absence of bones of the hand, and notably low frequencies of other elements, such as ribs and vertebrae, cannot easily be explained away by the fact that these elements do not generally survive in high frequencies in Neolithic mortuary assemblages. Some *do* survive and their absence or virtual absence here is very likely to reflect the fact that these elements were never introduced in the first place (see Table 6.12). Equally, the recovery and preservation of both small bone fragments (including toe and finger bones) from beneath paving slabs in Chamber I, and minute traces of charcoal from various contexts (Hyde 1956), do not support the notion that any such small finds or fragments that might have existed in Chamber II were thrown away or not recovered, while the low frequency both of fungal staining and localised biochemical erosion on visible bone surfaces implies the absence of destructive damp micro-environments within the chamber.

Savory (1956, 43) speculated that the remains in Chamber II may have originally come from the empty Chamber I. However, none of the fragments from Chamber I could be refitted with any corresponding elements from Chamber II and three dates from Chamber I (OxA-14396 -12083, -14254) appear to be later than those from Chamber II (OxA-14251, -14252).

Discrete groups? Throughout his report, Savory (1956) emphasised that the skeletal remains were arranged in distinct piles, and the published plan, which is representational rather than schematic, shows that the spaces between the different groups of bones on the chamber floor were clear of dispersed or scattered material. The intentionally discrete nature of the deposits was emphasised in the case of Group B by a 'coffer-like' arrangement of two stone slabs, which contained and partially framed the group. Partial reconstruction of the stratigraphy of Group B – skull resting on long bones, resting on skull resting on long bones (see above) – also suggests a formal pattern of sequential deposition within this assemblage. Taken together these observations leave few grounds for arguing that the piles of bones are random artefacts of rearranging of bones to create new space.

A single act? Savory (1956, 42) was more open here to the possibility of sequential deposition from above, or possibly through the narrow gap in the NW corner of the chamber (Fig. 6.5), and there was some suggestion that the central Group G could be the articulated or partially articulated 'disturbed remains of a last burial still *in situ*' (Savory 1956, 42). Unfortunately, although the plan shows a substantial group of bones, nothing has survived (except for possibly a few scraps). Whether or not the bones were brought to the chamber sequentially or accumulated elsewhere over a period of time until one final interment, the end conception is of an exclusive closed chamber holding a limited number of individuals.

Reconnecting with the ancestors? An intention to represent or recreate the skeleton, as seems to be the case at Penywyrlod Chamber NE II, is evident in the broadly consistent composition of each of the four substantial bone groups (B, C, D, F). Each contains, in differing quantities, material representing the range of skeletal elements: skull, axial skeleton, upper limbs and lower limbs, although the arrangements are composites, elements drawn from different individuals whose bones are mixed with others. In Group C three of the four mandible fragments, an anterior segment (LC to RC) and two left body segments (M_3 to PM_3) might easily be mistaken as fragments of the same bone by someone with only limited anatomical knowledge. Equally, without purposeful examination and siding, the four right petrous temporal fragments from Group D may have been added to the assemblage in the belief that they represent only two individuals. In Group B, the sequence of structured deposition may also reflect a conscious decision to distinguish between specific entities. While bones from possibly singular individuals are dispersed among the groups (see above, Pipton Chamber II demographic summary), the composition of the assemblages does not suggest a denial of the individual. Rather, the character of the four substantial deposits suggests intentional acts concerned with maintaining the idea of the physical body and the representation of individuals whether known or mythical.

Overview. In common with Chamber NE II at Penywyrlod, the mortuary assemblage in Chamber II at Pipton is predominantly male and skeletally mature. There is no evidence to indicate the presence of young children or infants. Skeletally immature remains are very sparsely represented and dispersed and are possibly drawn from a single individual at around the age of puberty (and therefore perhaps already accepted into the world of adults). Metrically assessed female elements are also sparse and dispersed. Little age-diagnostic material has survived, but there is no evidence to suggest the presence of any individuals of advanced or great age. On the contrary, as far as the limited evidence allows the age profile appears to be predominantly younger adult or near-adult. The few loose and retained teeth display no more than moderate wear, unlikely to represent any individuals older than *c.* 30 years while surviving joint surfaces show no evidence of degenerative joint disease which might suggest the presence of adults of middle and later years (over *c.* 35 years).

Only minor disturbance within the chamber means that other themes are more clearly evident here than at Penywyrlod. The first of these is the spatial subdivision of the chamber and the consequent visual and contextual integrity of the mortuary deposits. This is most obvious in the case of group B, with its setting of two stone slabs. It remains open whether the setting is essentially pragmatic, constructed to contain and safeguard the human remains from spillage and cross-contamination or whether it is a focal device signalling reserved space or the presence of ancestral remains of particular distinction. Group B is also distinctive in that it contains the majority of remains (53%) from the entire chamber assemblage, many of the most substantial fragments and evidence of patterned assembly.

Two groups (A and E) are insubstantial. Are the bones in both these groups all that remains of, or all that can be found to represent, known individuals or supposed entities? Do these deposits reflect concerns with concepts of balance, symmetry and spatial harmony (so that something, anything, should occupy vacant space)? Or are the deposits texts of exclusion (all appropriate space is occupied, no more may be added to the chamber)?

Human remains from Ty Isaf

Background

Ty Isaf chambered cairn was excavated in the 1930s (Grimes 1939). It has opposed lateral chambers (Chamber I–II), a transepted chamber set within a 'rotunda' (Chamber III) and a ruinous fourth chamber towards the tail (Chamber IV), all set within a trapezoidal long cairn with a forecourt at the broader end (Figs 2.30, 6.6). Grimes (1939, 137–40) considered the possibility of multiple-period construction but came down in favour of a single episode. While later commentators have tended to assume a multi-period sequence (Corcoran 1969, 84–6; Darvill 2004, 58–60), as noted in Chapter 2 this issue may ultimately only be resolved by further excavation. The cairn had been disturbed and was in a semi-ruinous state at the time of excavation, though Grimes felt that some of the surviving bone assemblages had remained intact. His main focus was constructional and typological, however, and he may not have been present when some of the remains were exposed or excavated. Grimes (1939, 119) noted 'Our results were obtained with rather less than three weeks' digging by four men; and it is my duty to record the skill and intelligence of the workers'. Nonetheless, by present standards, recovery and recording of the skeletal remains are likely to have been wanting. A two-page bone report was produced by L.F. Cowley (1939). The contexts from which human and animal remains were recovered (numbered 1–21 in this chapter) are listed in Table 6.15 and shown on Figure 6.6.

Little subsequent study had been undertaken on the human and animal bone remains archived in the National Museum of Wales, though recent isotope analysis of a selection of teeth has been published (Neil *et al.* 2017; see also Chapter 7 and Chapter 8). Sixteen radiocarbon dates for human skeletal material and one cattle tooth are also now available which show a significant range in date (see Chapter 4; Whittle *et al.* 2011, 537; Neil *et al.* 2017, 7). Four dates on human skeletal material from Chamber I and a measurement on a cow tooth suggest Chamber I was in use between *3530–3370 cal BC (95% probability*; *first_chamber_I*; Fig. 4.6) and

Table 6.15. Ty Isaf: contexts from which human and animal bone are recorded (see also Fig. 6.6).

	Context	*Location description*
Chamber I	1	West compartment, SE corner (in angle of wall)
	2	West compartment, NW corner
	3	West compartment, dispersed material
	4	East compartment, NE corner
	5	East compartment, SE corner
	6	East compartment, dispersed deposits
	7	Entrance
Chamber II	8	Passage, just outside chamber on N side
	9	Passage, south side
	10	Chamber
Chamber III	11	Entrance to passage
	12	Upper layer in passage
	13	Lower layer in passage
	14	West compartment
	15	East compartment
	16	Central chamber, lower level
	17	Central chamber, upper level
Body of cairn	18	From various places among stones of the cairn/body of the cairn
Chamber IV	19	NW angle of chamber
	20	Near base of Bronze Age urn
Forecourt	21	From filling of false portal, amongst stones or on old surface
Decontextualised	22	Mandibles with no surviving locational details

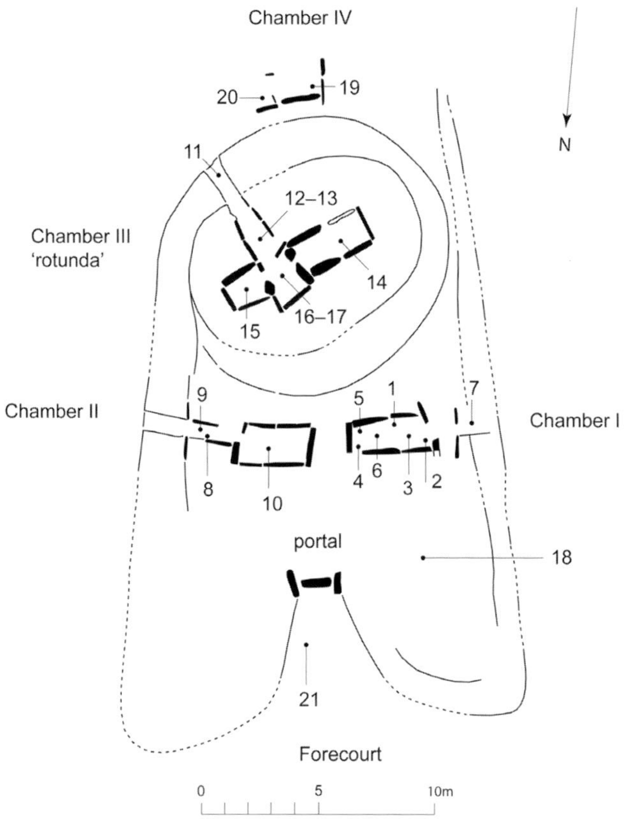

Fig. 6.6. Ty Isaf: contexts in which human and animal bone are recorded (plan after Grimes 1939, fig. 3). See also Table 6.15.

2665–2465 cal BC (95% probability; last_chamber_I; Fig. 4.6). A human bone from Chamber II is dated to 3630–3360 cal BC. Seven fragments of human bone from the passage and chamber of Chamber III date to between *c.* 3620–2490 cal BC. Three unprovenanced bones from the site are dated to between *c.* 3650–3360 cal BC. Post-Neolithic activity at the site is represented by a child's skeleton in the passage to Chamber II dated to 1670–1500 cal BC, several small sherds of Beaker from the upper filling of Chamber I and by the Bronze Age urn fragment and bone handle from Chamber IV, mentioned above (Grimes 1939, fig. 7).

Chamber I

Evidently undisturbed human remains were found beneath rubble which filled the ruined passage and bipartite chamber. Grimes' (1939, 126) account is sketchy but some of the human material was arranged in groups, 'consisting frequently of the cranium, lower jaw and one or two long bones carefully placed against the side-stones and sometimes pushed into angles and crevices, in places I do not think they could have reached by accidental means'. In the W compartment discrete bone groups were found in two corners, SE (Fig. 6.6, Context 1) and NW (Context 2), together with some charred and calcined fragments. Further human bones and a few cremated fragments were recovered from the W compartment but there are no details of their distribution (Context 3). In the E compartment groups of bones and small cremation deposits were found in the NE and SE corners (Contexts 4–5). More skeletal remains and cremated fragments were recovered from 'elsewhere in the same compartment' (Context 6). A few bone segments were also recovered from the chamber entrance (Context 7).

Chamber II

Here too, Grimes (1939, 127) considered the human remains, which included a comparatively substantial (328g) cremation deposit, to have survived undisturbed (Context 10), but he added 'the conditions made their examination a difficult and unsatisfactory business… the clay floor had a tenacious quality which made the removal of fragile bones and only less fragile potsherds tedious and difficult'. Human and animal bones and a few cremated fragments were also recovered from the passage (Contexts 8 and 9), but the account is cursory. For example, Context 8 (see below), described by Grimes only as 'much-broken long bones in positions suggesting articulation' is now known to be the substantial remains of a 3–4-year-old child (recently dated to the Bronze Age: Neil *et al.* 2017, 381, and see below).

Chamber III

Details are again limited, though Grimes (1939, 129) noted 'Bones were much broken and mostly in an advanced stage of disintegration'. Bones from the passage to Chamber III were recovered in two layers (Contexts 11–13). Both transepts (Contexts 14–15) yielded only very sparse remains, but the central compartment contained substantial skeletal deposits which are divided, in archive and in Cowley's (1939, 142) report, into an upper and lower layer (Contexts 16–17). These two layers are not mentioned in Grimes' account (1939, 129) but it is assumed here that they represent distinct stratified deposits rather than two arbitrary spits. Three fragments of cremated bone were found in the W transept and a few more (16 g) in the central compartment.

Chamber IV

The ruinous chamber contained the base of a Bronze Age urn and the bone handle of a metal dagger. Scattered cremated bone fragments were recovered from the NW angle (Context 19) and the charred shaft of a long bone from near the base of the urn (Context 20).

Other contexts

Scraps of human skeletal material were also recovered from 'various places' in the body of the cairn, and 'among stones high up in the central compartment' (Context 18).

A few cremated human bones were also recovered from the forecourt (Context 21).

Taphonomy

Present condition of the human skeletal remains

The entirety of the human and animal bone collected during Grimes's excavations is evidently preserved in archive and randomly packed in numbered boxes, labelled with contexts. Many larger fragments were marked with consecutive accession numbers (from 39.190/1 to 39.190/327) but most contexts also included considerable quantities of fragmented or comminuted unmarked remains which had never been washed or looked at (for example, in Context 3 some 200 identifiable fragments, weighing 1.56kg, labelled as 'indeterminate and undetermined bone fragments'). Unfortunately, the contextual integrity of the collection had been compromised. At some point between 1939 and 1970, over 140 substantial mandibular, maxillary and postcranial specimens had been removed from their original context-labelled containers and re-boxed with no contextual information. Many of these decontextualised specimens are numbered and runs of consecutive accession numbers *broadly* correspond to specific contexts as indicated by finds labels. For example, specimens numbered 39.190/1 to 39.190/53 are assigned to 'Rotunda chamber, central compartment, lower level' (Context 16, this chapter). While it should be possible to re-assign most of the decontextualised material on this basis, the numbering system is erratic; short runs of consecutive numbers assigned to other contexts occasionally interrupt longer runs, while some numbers are repeated on specimens from different contexts and none of the remains from Context 10 are numbered at all. In addition, groups of consecutively numbered decontextualised elements tend to appear at the ends and beginnings of assigned runs, so that it is not possible to be certain where, in the span of decontextualised numbers, one context finishes and another starts. Many hours were spent cross-checking assigned runs, unassigned runs, contexts and Cowley's (1939) report, and although some specimens had previously been catalogued by NMW staff as 'possibly' from one context or another, decontextualised material could not be relocated with certainty. Ty Isaf is not the only important archived assemblage known to have been examined by Cowley where significant quantities of material were left decontextualised and cannot now be reassigned (the late Stephen Aldhouse-Green, *pers. comm.*).

Postmortem bone modifications

Because of the highly fragmented and modified nature of the material only a preliminary taphonomic analysis was undertaken.

Just one bone, a humerus (39.190/271), was intact, although Cowley (1939) had reported three. Fracture morphology was very varied, fracture surfaces often weathered or eroded with varying degrees of patination. Only 27% of the 198 postcranial fragments suitable for subaerial weathering analysis were unmodified (stage 0), while over 30% were heavily weathered or eroded to stages 3 and 4 (Table 6.16); in many specimens the original bone surfaces have been almost completely destroyed.

Evidence of mammalian scavenging in the form of pits, punctures and rodent and non-rodent gnawing was noted in 59 of 563 human postcranial fragments examined (10.5%), most of these modifications occurring in material from Chamber I contexts. Two portions of gnawed fragmentary femur shaft from Context 1 conjoin to show an elliptical perforating trauma where the bone has been bitten through, suggesting that some mammalian scavenging took place *in situ*. A large ungulate limb shaft splinter from Context 16 also bears non-rodent gnaw marks.

It is more than likely that these bone modifications – fragmentation, weathering, mammalian scavenging – are as much a consequence of various episodes of incursion, disturbance, trampling and rifling, not least among which are the excavations themselves, as they are of any pre-interment or early post-interment processes.

Decontextualised skeletal remains

Human mandibles and maxillae

Forty-six fragmentary mandibular and maxillary specimens, removed from their original contexts, many with accession numbers, were packed in one box. Some have been tentatively re-assigned in the NMW catalogue based on accession number, and are listed as *possible* contexts in Table 6.17 and Table 6.18, but as noted above, most of these re-assignments remain uncertain and some are dubious. Most of the mandibular fragments are non-contiguous portions of left or right side and while some individual left and right portions can be shown to be from different individuals because of gross size differences or incommensurate dental wear, many cannot. In this analysis, a minimum number of 17 adults is obtained from anatomical duplications of left-sided mandibular fragments. It remains probable that more could be represented by non-contiguous fragments of right-sided mandibles. Cowley (1939) estimated the entire Ty Isaf human skeletal assemblage to represent 33 individuals (including four children) based on 'lower jaws' never specifying side nor segment,

Table 6.16. Ty Isaf: human bone weathering, all contexts.

Weathering stage	*N*	*% frequency*
0	54	27.3
1	47	23.7
2	34	17.2
3	35	17.7
4	28	14.1
Total	198	100

Table 6.17. Ty Isaf: decontextualised mandibles.

Accession no.	*Context*	*Specimen*	*Dentition*	*Wear stage*	*Estimated age range*	*Morphology*	*Notes (calibrated dates quoted at 95% confidence)*
39.190/58	Poss. 4	L mandible fragment	M_2 M_1 U P_3 U × ×	–	11–12 y	–	SUERC-57786: 3520–3340 cal BC
39.190/59	na	L mandible fragment	M_3 M_2 M_1 × × ×	G	35–40 y	masculine	SUERC-57790: 3330–2920 cal BC
39.190/60	na	L mandibular body and mental protuberance	M_1 (crown and alveolar region damaged pm)	–	–	feminine	–
39.190/90	Poss. 3	Mandible, broken at L and R vertical rami	× M_1 X P_3 C × × × × C × × M_1 × ×	H/I	40– 55 y	feminine	Possible match with maxilla 39.190/109 (Table 6.18)
39.190/92	Poss 3	L mandible fragment	M_3 M_2 M_1 P_4	I	45–55 y	robust	Same individual as 93, below?
39.190/93	na	R mandible broken at vertical ramus	I_2 I_1 I_1 I_2 C P_3 P_4 M_1 M_2 M_3	H/I	40–55 y	robust	–
39.190/106(i)	Poss. 9	R mandible fragment	Sockets only: P_4–M_3	–	adult	gracile	M_2 lost AM
39.190/106(ii)	Poss. 9	R mandible fragment	M_1 M_2 M_3	F	30–35 y		–
39.190/107(i)	Poss. 1	L condyle	–	–	–	–	TMJ disease
39.190/107(ii)	Poss. 1	L mandible fragment	AM × × × ×× M_1 ×	I ++	?50 y	feminine	R I_1 lost AM; M1 wear to pulp chamber
39.190/108	Poss. 1	Fragment mental protuberance	Sockets only: L I_2 – R I_2	–	–	–	–
39.190/125	Poss. 5	L mandible fragment	M_2	–	–	–	M_2 glued in, ? not from this mandible
39.190/143(i)	Poss. 4	R condyle and coronoid process	–	–	–	–	Eburnation condylar surface
39.190/143(ii)	Poss. 4	R condyle w portion coronoid process	Socket only: M_3	–	adult	–	M_3 impacted, socket horizontal
39.190/143(iii)	Poss. 4	L condyle w portion ramus	–	–	–	–	–
39.190/144(i)	Poss. 4	R mandible fragment	× × × × M_1 × M_3	F/H	30–45 y	–	Mild calculus. Two frags conjoin
39.190/144(ii)	Poss. 4	Mental protuberance	Sockets only: L I_1–R I_2	–	–	–	Not same person as 144(i), above
39.190/144(iii)	Poss. 4	L fragment w mental protuberance	Sockets only: L P_4 – RI_1	–	–	–	Different person to 144(i) and (ii), above
39.190/144(iv)	Poss. 4	R mandible fragment	M_3	F/G	30–40 y	–	–
39.190/148(a)	Poss. 6	L ramus and coronoid process	M_3 M_2 M_1 × × ×	E/F	24–35 y	feminine	Slight calculus M_2, M_3; SUERC-57785: 3500–3120 cal BC
39.190/148(b)	Poss. 6	L mandible fragment	M_3 M_2 M_1 ×	E/F	24–35 y	masculine	SUERC-57787: 3630–3370 cal BC
39.190/148(c)	Poss. 6	L ramus and mental protuberance	× M_2 M_1 × × × × × × × ×	H/I	40–55 y	feminine	–
39.190/182	Poss. 5	R portion, broken at L P_3	× × × × × × C × P_4 M_1 M_2 ×	C/D	18–24 y	–	–
39.190/183	Poss. 5	R fragment	M_3	H	40–45 y	–	–
39.190/184	Poss. 5	L condyle fragment	–	–	–	–	–

(Continued)

Table 6.17. *Ty Isaf: decontextualised mandibles. (Continued)*

Accession no.	*Context*	*Specimen*	*Dentition*	*Wear stage*	*Estimated age range*	*Morphology*	*Notes (calibrated dates quoted at 95% confidence)*
39.190/198	na	Immature mental protuberance w portion left ramus	Alveolar region damaged; L M_1 erupted, socket m1, crypt P_4	–	6–10 y	–	One of two specimens w No. 39.190/198; see 39.190/310, below
39.190/201	Poss. 17	Mandible, broken at coronoid processes	(L) M_3 M_2 M_1 P_4 × C AM AM (R) I_1* × × × P_4 M_1 M_2 ×	F/G	30–40 y	–	* I_1 root stump only; heavy oblique mesio-inferior wear at C; SUERC-57794: 3630–3360 cal BC
39.190/234	na	L mandible fragment	M_2 M_1 P_4	C/D	18–25 y	–	Eroded; *postmortem* damage
39.190/238	na	R mandible fragment	M_1 M_2 M_3	G/H	35–45 y	–	–
39.190/239	na	L mandible fragment	× × C I_2 I_1	E/F	24–35 y	masculine	–
39.190/310 + 39.190/198	see *notes*	2 Conjoining fragments forming dental arc	(L) M_3 M_2 M_1 × P_3 × × × (R) × × C P_3 P_4 M_1 M_2 M_3	G/H	35–45 y	–	310 unassigned; 198 possibly Context 9 (doubtful); SUERC-57786: 3630–3360 cal BC
39.190/311	na	L ramus fragment	M_3	F	30+ y	–	*Postmortem* damage
39.190/312	na	L mandible fragment	M_3 M_2 M_1 P_4	B2/C	16–22 y	–	SUERC 57719: 3640–3380 cal BC
39.190/313	na	R condyle and portion	Socket: M_3	–	adult	–	Slight eburnation, condyle
39.190/314	na	Immature mandible	U m_2 m_1 × × × × × m_1 m_2	–	12–18 m	–	Left m_1 roots not complete, m_2s erupting, unerupted M_1 crown cusp outline complete
39.190/318	na	R mandible fragment	M_2 M_3	D	22–25 y	–	M_3 complete
No number	na	L mandible fratment	M_2 M_1	C	18–22 y	–	–

Key: AM = lost *antemortem*; U = unerupted; × = lost *postmortem*; na = not assigned; Poss. = context unsecure; y = years; m = months. Dental age after AlQahtani *et al.* (2010). Dental wear age estimates after Lovejoy (1985).

Table 6.18. *Ty Isaf: decontextualised maxillae.*

Accession no.	*Location*	*Specimen*	*Dentition*	*Wear stage*	*Age range*	*Notes*
39.190/66	na	R palate/maxilla fragment	P^3 P^4 M^1 M^2	B1	15–17 y	Slight wear facet P^3, M^1 only, M^2 roots complete, apices open
39.190/94	na	L palatine fragment	M^3 × × × ×	–	18–22 y	M^3 root not quite complete
39.190/95	na	Fragment anterior palate	L I^1 R I^1 I^2 lost AM; sockets only L and R Cs to M^2s		Adult	Palatal suture fused
39.190/109	na	R maxilla w inferior orbit and zygomatic process	C P^3 P^4 M^1 M^2 M^3	F/G	30–40 y	Possible match with mandible 39.190/90 (Table 6.17)
39.190/145	Poss. 4	R maxilla/palate	× × × × × M^1 M^2	E/F	24–35 y	Palatine suture unfused. M^3 absent/unerupted
39.190/145b	Poss. 4	L maxilla/palate	× M^2 M^1 P^4 P^3 C I^2 I^1	?H+	40–50+ y	Damage to crowns wear observable in I^1 and P^3 only
39.190/316	na	Maxilla (2 specimens conjoin)	(L) M^3 M^2 M^1 P^4 P^3 × × × (R) I^1 I^2 C P^3 P^4 M^1 M^2 M^3	G	35–40+ y	Hypoplasia buccal dentition

Key: × = lost *postmortem*; na = not assigned; Poss. = context unsecure; y = years. Dental age after AlQahtani *et al.* (2010). Dental wear age estimates after Lovejoy (1985) and it seems likely that he considered many individual mandibular fragments (irrespective of side) to represent individual entities.

Four right and three left adult maxillae are also present as well as two complete maxillary arcs. One right maxillary arc (39.190/109) and a right mandible portion (39.190/90) exhibited good occlusal fit at molars and are likely a pair (Tables 6.17 and 6.18).

Stages of dental attrition were varied. A minimum of six individuals exhibited heavy wear (stages G to I), indicating adults probably over 30 years. Three of these individuals showed extreme wear (stage I), suggesting age over 40, possibly over 50 years. A further six individuals displayed light wear (stages C/D), indicating probable older adolescent/young adult age. The remaining five individuals displayed moderate wear (stages E/F), indicating probable age of between *c.* 20–30 years.

Human postcranial skeleton

Similarly unassigned postcranial remains consisted of 106 fragments and portions (Table 6.19). Right distal humeri are most frequently duplicated and come from at least six adults. Several adult specimens could be sexed metrically but only three males and one female could be unequivocally discriminated. Several immature fragments were also present.

Skeletal remains from Chamber I

Context 1 (West compartment, SE corner in angle of wall)

Adult human bones. **Skull**: Left side cranial vault (occipital, parietal, temporal, frontal); right side cranial vault; right temporal fragment; left zygomatic fragment; maxilla fragment; several small cranial vault fragments; left mandible fragment; loose M_3. **Axial**: two dens (axis); thoracic fragment; three vertebral processes; nine rib fragments; clavicle shaft fragment. **Upper limbs**: ulna shaft fragment. **Lower limbs**: tibia midshaft fragment; proximal tibia shaft fragment; right and left calcaneus fragment; left navicular, cuboid fragment; metatarsal shaft.

Immature human bones. **Skull**: small vault fragment, fragment left supraorbital border; loose teeth. **Upper limbs**: distal humerus fragment.

Animal bone. Pig tooth.

Unidentified. Four charred limb shaft fragments.

An almost complete left-sided adult cranial vault is accompanied by a substantial portion of right cranial vault. Both skull segments are of similar size and vault thickness but do not offer anatomically contiguous edges so cannot be conjoined. One cannot be sure that the two portions are from the same person. The left displays smooth architecture with an undeveloped external occipital protuberance and a neutral-sized mastoid process, all suggesting female sex. The right is heavily eroded. Two adults are represented by two dens (2nd cervical vertebra) fragments.

Age estimation. A left mandible fragment carrying M_1 and M_2 is from an individual of *c.* 30 years or more, based on dental wear (stage F). Wear in a loose M_3 is compatible.

A loose right PM^3 displays a ½ completed root indicating an older child (*c.* 9–11 years). An unerupted right M^2 crown is from an individual of similar age, as is a deciduous m_2 displaying medium wear and a degree of root resorption. A pair of deciduous i^1's display open apices and are likely to represent an infant or young child *c.* 18–30 months. Two immature cranial fragments appear to be from a young child. A fragment of immature humerus shaft cannot be aged with any precision but is likely to represent a child rather than young child or infant.

In summary, the deposit consists of two substantial portions of adult cranial vault and a few fragmentary adult postcranial remains. Two adults are indicated by a fragment each of axis vertebra, but in other respects the adult remains would appear to represent a single individual. Two immature skull fragments and two loose teeth are from an infant or young child, three further loose teeth and a fragment of distal humerus are from an older child.

Context 2 (West compartment, NW corner)

Adult bones. **Skull**: two left vault portions; basi-occipital fragment; four loose teeth. **Axial**: cervical body fragment; lumbar body fragment; six fragments vertebral processes; right clavicle (robust); right clavicle fragment (gracile); portions of two left scapulae; four ribshaft fragments. **Upper limbs**: humerus midshaft fragment; left proximal radius (gracile); left radius midshaft (robust); right distal radius fragment; metacarpal head fragment; medial phalange. **Lower limbs**: proximal half right femur shaft (gracile); distal end left femur; distal end left femur (robust); fragment trochanter; unsided femur midshaft fragment; left patella fragment; distal third right tibia (gracile); fragment proximal tibia shaft; tibia shaft fragment; fragment each right and left navicular; right metatarsal II; left metatarsal III; two metatarsal shafts; medial phalange foot.

Cremated human bone. Two limb bone splinters, one fragment ilium.

Unidentified. 26 bone fragments/splinters.

Sex assessment. One left-sided cranial vault is morphologically female. The second left cranial vault portion is rugged with strongly developed nuchal lines and greater vault thickness, and is probably male. Glenoid cavity lengths in two left scapulae indicate male and indeterminate (Table 6.20). Other fragmentary duplicating elements (right clavicles, distal left femora, left radii) are consistently dimorphic (robust and gracile).

Table 6.19. Ty Isaf: decontextualised postcranial specimens.

Accession no.	*Location*	*Specimen*	*Metric: datum*	*Morphology*	*Assessed sex*	*Estimated age*	*Notes*
39.190/67	Poss. 3	L humerus, distal end	EW: 59.9 mm	–	indet.	adult	–
39.190/68	Poss. 3	R humerus, distal shaft	–	–	–	adult	–
39.190/69	Poss. 3	L distal humerus fragment	–	gracile	–	adult	–
39.190/70	Poss. 3	L distal humerus fragment	–	–	–	adult	–
39.190/71	Poss. 3	L distal humerus fragment	–	gracile	–	adult	–
39.190/114	na	L calcaneus	DF1: 35.6	male	–	adult	–
39.190/116	na	Distal tibia fragment	–	–	–	adult	–
39.190/119	Poss. 5	R distal humerus fragment	–	gracile	–	adult	Gnawed
39.190/120	na	R clavicle shaft fragment	–	–	–	adult	–
39.190/121	na	R scapula fragment	GL:35.1 mm	–	indet.	adult	–
39.190/123	na	L patella	–	–	–	adult	Vastus notch, strong osteophytic growth
39.190/124	na	L distal radius fragment	–	–	–	adult	–
39.190/127	Poss. 5	R tibia midshaft	–	gracile	–	adult	–
39.190/128	na	Sacrum fragment	–	–	–	adult	–
39.190/230	na	L tibia shaft	–	gracile	–	adult	–
39.190/240	na	L proximal ¼ femur	–	robust	–	20–30 y	Femoral head damaged, epiphyseal line visible in exposed trabecular bone
39.190/241	na	L distal ¾ femur	–	–	–	adult	Not same individual as 39.190/240 (above)
39.190/242 + 39.190/246(i)	na	R femur	–	–	–	younger adolescent	Shaft and neck (242) + conjoining unfused femoral head (246(i)); damaged distally
39.190/244	na	R femur shaft	CM: 85.03 mm	–	male	adult	–
39.190/245 + 39.190/246(ii)	na	R femur shaft	–	–	–	adult	Two shaft fragments conjoin
39.190/246(iii)	na	R femur head and neck fragment	–	–	–	adult	–

(Continued)

Table 6.19. (Continued)

Accession no.	Location	Specimen	Metric: datum	Morphology	Assessed sex	Estimated age	Notes
39.190/247 + 39.190/253(i)	Poss. 5	L humerus	–	–	–	adult	Two fragments conjoin; proximal and distal ends damaged; lateral bowing
39.190/248	na	R humerus, distal ⅔	EW: 65.32 mm	–	male	adult	Lateral bowing
39.190/249	na	L tibia shaft	CNF: 100.9 mm	–	male	adult	–
39.190/251	na	Unsided tibia shaft fragment	–	–	–	adult	–
39.190/252	na	L tibia shaft	–	–	–	adolescent, *c.* 14–18 y	Unfused distal metaphysis
39.190/253(ii)	na	Femoral head fragment	–	–	–	adult	–
39.190/254	na	Femoral head fragment	–	–	–	adult	–
39.190/255	na	L proximal ulna fragment	–	–	–	adult	–
39.190/256	na	R proximal ulna fragment	–	–	–	adolescent, *c.* 14–16 y	Fusion incomplete posteriorly at proximal epiphysis
39.190/258	na	R radius, proximal portion	–	–	–	adult	–
39.190/259	na	R distal fibula fragment	–	–	–	adult	–
39.190/				–	–	adult	–
39.190/262	na	L calcaneus	DF1: 34.15	–	male	adult	Osteophytes at heel
39.190/264	na	L talus fragment	–	–	–	adult	–
39.190/265	na	Navicular fragment	–	–	–	adult	–
39.190/266	na	Scaphoid fragment	–	–	–	adult	–
39.190/267	na	Metatarsal fragment	–	–	–	adult	–
39.190/268	na	R metatarsal I, III, V and foot phalange	–	–	–	adult	–
39.190/270	na	R ilium portion	–	–	–	older child, under *c.* 14 y	Unfused iliac crest intact
39.190/271	na	R humerus	VHD: 46.4 mm EW: 59.3 mm Length: 32.1 cm	–	indet.	adult	intact
39.190/272	na	R humerus, distal ½	EW: 57.1 mm	–	female	adult	–

(Continued)

Table 6.19. Ty Isaf: decontextualised postcranial specimens. (Continued)

Accession no.	*Location*	*Specimen*	*Metric: datum*	*Morphology*	*Assessed sex*	*Estimated age*	*Notes*
39.190/273	na	R humerus distal ⅓	–	robust	–	adult	–
39.190/274	na	R humerus distal shaft fragment	–	–	–	adult	–
39.190/275	na	R humerus distal end	–	–	–	adult	–
39.190/276	na	L humerus, distal end	EW: 55.5 mm	–	female	adult	–
39.190/277	na	L humerus distal shaft	–	–	–	adult	–
39.190/278	na	L humerus distal fragment	–	–	–	adult	–
39.190/279	na	R humerus proximal ¼	–	–	–	adult	–
39.190/280	na	L humerus	–	–	–	adult	Damaged proximal and distal ends
39.190/281	na	5 × L proximal ulnae	–	1 × gracile		adult	5 individuals
39.190/282	na	4 × R proximal ulnae	–	–		adult	4 individuals
39.190/283	na	3 × R distal radius fragments	–	1 × robust, 2 × gracile		adult	3 individuals
39.190/284(i)	na	R radius proximal fragment	–	–		adult	–
39.190/284(ii)	na	L radius proximal fragment	–	–	–	adult	–
39.190/284(iii)	na	R radius proximal portion	–	–	–	adult	Possible pair with 39.190/285
39.190/285	na	L radius proximal portion	–	–	–	adult	Possible pair with 39.190/284(iii) adult
39.190/286	na	L tibia proximal shaft	CNF 88.4 mm	–	female	adult	–
39.190/287	na	R proximal tibia	–	robust	–	young adult, under *c.* 19 y	Unfused epiphysis
39.190/288(i)	na	L tibia distal end	–	–	–	adult	Squatting facet
39.190/288(ii)	na	Lumbar vertebra	–	–	–	adult	–
39.190/289	na	R tibia distal end	–	–	–	adult	Squatting facet
39.190/290	na	R tibia distal end	–	–	–	adult	2 pieces conjoin; squatting facet
39.190/291	na	2 × R distal fibula fragments	–	robust	–	adult	–
39.190/292	na	L distal fibula fragment	–	gracile	–	adult	–
39.190/293	na	R proximal femur shaft	–	–	–	adult	–

(Continued)

Table 6.19. (Continued)

Accession no.	*Location*	*Specimen*	*Metric: datum*	*Morphology*	*Assessed sex*	*Estimated age*	*Notes*
39.190/294	na	L proximal femur shaft	–	–	–	adult	–
39.190/296	na	L patella	–	–	–	adult	–
39.190/297	na	3 × acetabulum fragments	–	–	–	adult	–
39.190/298	na	Lumbar vertebra body frag. + 3 vertebral fragments	–	–	–	adult	–
39.190/299	na	R calcaneus	DF1: 33.74	–	male	adult	–
39.190/300	na	R calcaneus	DF1: 36.93	–	male	adult	–
39.190/301(i)	na	L calcaneus	DF1: 34.34	–	male	adult	–
39.190/301(ii)	na	R scapula fragment	–	–	–	older child, under *c.* 12–14 y	Unfused epiphyses
39.190/302	na	L calcaneus	–	gracile	–	adult	–
39.190/303	na	R talus	–	–	–	adult	–
39.190/304	na	R talus	–	–	–	adult	–
39.190/305	na	L talus	–	–	–	adult	–
39.190/306	na	R scapula fragment	GL: 40.7 mm	–	male	adult	–
39.190/308(i)	na	Two phalanges	–	–	–	adult	–
39.190/308(ii)	na	L and R metatarsal I	–	–	–	adult	Two individuals
No number	na	L femur shaft	–	gracile	–	–	–
No number	na	Femoral head fragment gracile	–	–	–	adult	–
No number	na	R distal femur segment	–	–	–	adult	Depressed articular surface at medial condyle
No number	na	L distal femur segment	–	–	–	adult	–
No number	na	Femoral head	VHD: 36.3 mm	–	female	adult	–
No number	na	Tibia shaft fragment	–	–	–	–	–

Key: indet. = indeterminate; y = years

Age estimation. A gracile left proximal radius fragment displays incomplete epiphyseal fusion. All remaining epiphyseal elements (proximal femur, distal tibiae, metatarsals) show complete fusion. Fusion in the proximal radius is usually complete by 14–16 years in females and males respectively but completion can be as late as 19 years (Scheuer and Black 2000, 295). Fusion of the proximal femur is usually complete by 12–16 years in females and 14–19 years in males, while the distal tibia is usually fully fused between 14–16 years in females and 15–18 years in males, with similar age ranges in metatarsals. The proximal radius fragment could represent an additional individual but is not necessarily age-incompatible with the other gracile and possibly female elements. Three loose teeth display medium wear consistent with adult age. An additional M_3 displays very heavy wear and may represent a mature or aged adult.

In summary, the deposit consists of human remains from at least two adults, a male and female. A gracile, not fully fused proximal radius could indicate a young adult or later adolescent age (under *c*. 19 years) for the female but may have come from a third, younger individual. Skull, axial skeleton, upper limbs and lower limbs are all represented in this group. Without anatomical siding and close observation, the selection of material might be taken to represent a single individual. Three human cremated fragments are completely calcined (surfaces and sections) and are likely to be from an adult or older adolescent.

Context 3 (West compartment)

Adult human bones. **Skull**: three small vault fragments; left zygomatic; left temporal fragment; maxilla fragment. **Axial**: 11 vertebral body fragments; four right clavicle shafts (two robust); two right glenoid cavities; right scapula spine, lateral border; fragment left glenoid cavity; left coracoid process; fragment sternum, 40 ribshaft fragments; fragment each from three left acetabula; two left ischia; left iliac crest; right auricular surface; right ischium; unsided acetabular fragment; pubis fragment; four fragments iliac crest. **Upper limbs**: portions of seven right distal humeri; right humeral midshaft fragment (robust); two left humeral midshafts, left distal shaft; two left proximal ulnae; left ulna midshaft (gracile); right proximal ulna end; ulna midshaft fragment; left radius midshaft; right proximal radius; right distal radius; three radius shaft fragments. **Lower limbs**: right proximal femur shaft (robust); right femur midshaft (robust); three right distal ends of femur; fragment left proximal femur and greater trochanter; unsided femoral fragments: shaft, greater trochanter, lesser trochanter, distal ends, head/neck; left and right patellae, two right proximal tibia fragments; right tibia midshaft; fragments from three left proximal tibiae; left midshaft tibia; left distal end tibia; two tibia midshaft fragments (gracile); unsided proximal end of tibia (recently fused); three fibula shaft fragments (one gracile, two robust); three right calcanei; left calcaneus; right talus; left talus; calcaneus fragment.

Immature human bones. **Skull**: two small vault fragments (young child/infant). **Axial**: unfused neural arch (young child/infant); unfused pubic symphysis (older child); fragment ilium (older child); seven rib fragments; fragments of scapula(e). **Upper limbs**: right proximal ulna shaft (young child/infant); left proximal ulna shaft (young child/infant); humerus shaft fragment (young child/infant); humerus shaft fragment (older child); right proximal ulna shaft fragment (older child); ulna shaft fragment (older child). **Lower limbs**: femur shaft fragment (young child/infant); right proximal tibia shaft fragment (young child/infant); right femur shaft fragment (older child); femur midshaft fragment (older child); fragment unfused proximal epiphysis of tibia (older child); tibia midshaft fragment (older child); fibula shaft fragment (older child).

Cremated bone. Four fragments cranial vault; proximal humerus shaft fragment; three fragments adult limb bones; two non-identified fragments.

Animal bone. Fox cub mandible; dog canine; ox premolar; fragments and splinters.

Cranial material is sparse (less than 16g total weight). At least seven adults are represented by duplications of right humeral fragments. Duplications of other postcranial remains are less frequent; four adults are represented by three right calcanei and a right talus which does not articulate with any of the calcanei, and three adults are indicated by duplications in fragments of left innominate, left humeri, right distal femora and right and left proximal tibiae.

Sex assessment. Metric sex assessment indicates the presence of at least two males (Table 6.20). Adult material presents as a mixture of robust, neutral, and gracile fragments. There are no duplications among the visibly gracile (possibly female) adult elements (right scapula fragment, distal right humerus, left humerus midshaft, left ulna midshaft, two fragments tibia midshaft).

Age estimation. No specific age estimates can be given for the adult remains. Based on comparative fragment size, immature remains represent both an older child and a young child or older infant. There are no anatomical duplicates within either age category while size differences between immature elements appear to be consistent.

Cremated remains. Fragments of burnt or cremated bone were found amongst each W compartment assemblage. Ten fragments (18.2g) were identified as human. Two shaft fragments are poorly combusted (all over black charring). The remaining eight fragments are thoroughly calcined (pure creamy white throughout). This range of colour variation is common in discrete prehistoric cremation assemblages (McKinley 2000). Poorly combusted fragments may represent individual bones which have become detached and buried under ash and pyre debris during the cremation, or, possibly, bones at the periphery of the pyre or from areas where oxygen circulation and intense combustion are impeded (McKinley 2000). One cannot say if the cremated material represents a dispersed assemblage culled from a single pyre event or separate deposits from more than one episode of burning or cremation.

West compartment demographic summary

Immature cranial fragments, loose dentition and a fragment of humerus shaft from Context 1 (SE corner) represent both an older child and a young child/infant. These age categories are compatible with the immature remains assigned to Context 3 and no anatomical duplications were found in the immature material from either context.

Both corner groups, Contexts 1 and 2 (NW and SE corners), contain substantial amounts of adult cranial material whereas only as a few small scraps were found among the remains from Context 3. At least three adults are represented by cranial remains from Contexts 1 and 2, but seven adults are represented by fragments of right distal humeri from Context 3. There were no humeral fragments in Context 1, and one fragment of unsided humerus midshaft in Context 2.

Metric sex assessment indicates the presence of at least two males in Context 3, while two females are indicated by a portion each of left cranial vault in Contexts 1 and 2. Much of the postcranial material was too fragmentary or too eroded to allow sex assessment, but both gracile and robust elements are present throughout.

Table 6.20. Ty Isaf: adults metric sex assessment.

Accession no.	*Context*	*Specimen*	*Metric: datum*	*Assessed sex*
39.190/102	2	L scapula fragment	GL: 40.7 mm	male
39.190/103	2	L scapula fragment	GL: 34.6 mm	indet.
No number	3	R scapula fragment	GL: 40.0 mm	male
39.190/84	3	R calcaneus	DF1: 39.7	male
39.190/86	3	R calcaneus	DF1: 34.8	male
39.190/87	3	L calcaneus	DF1: 37.5	male
39.190/88	3	L talus	DF2: 39.2	male
39.190/142	4	L scapula fragment	GL: 33.0 mm	female
39.190/136	4	L humerus, distal end	EW: 59.1 mm	female
39.190/137	4	L humerus, proximal end	VHD: 41.9 mm	female
39.190/176	5	L scapula fragment	GL: 35.5 mm	indet.
39.190/168	5	L humerus, distal end	EW: 57.9 mm	female
39.190/170	5	R humerus, distal end	EW: 56.9 mm	female
39.190/173	5	L femoral head	VHD: 41.7 mm	female
39.190/137	6	L humerus, proximal end	VHD: 43.0 mm	female
39.190/149	6	L humerus, distal end	EW: 61.6 mm	male
No number	6	R scapula fragment	GL: 40.5 mm	male
39.190/220	9	R humerus, proximal ⅓	VHD: 47.3 mm	male
39.190/57	12	L humerus head	VHD: 41.7 mm	female
39.190/55	12	L humerus, distal ½	EW: 49.0 mm	female
No number	13	R femur shaft	CM: 82.1 mm	male
39.190/212	13	R tibia midshaft	CNF: 94.4 mm	male
39.190/191	15	R femur distal, end missing	VHD: 44.3 mm CM: 80.6 mm	indet.
39.190/39	16	L scapula fragment	GL: 35.6 mm	indet.
39.190/2	16	R humerus, proximal ⅔	VHD: 45.7 mm	indet.
39.190/3	16	R humerus, distal ½	EW: 55.9 mm	female
39.190/4	16	L humerus head	VHD: 47.7 mm	male
39.190/21	16	R femur head	VHD: 47.3 mm	male
39.190/22	16	R femur head	VHD: 44.0 mm	indet.
39.190/23	16	L femur head	VHD: 44.3 mm	indet.
39.190/26	16	L femur head	VHD: 36.7 mm	female
39.190/10	16	R tibia shaft	CNF: 94.2 mm	male
39.190/203	17	R humerus, distal end	EW: 48.5 mm	female

Key: indet. = indeterminate

In total, the remains recovered from the West compartment of Chamber 1 represent a minimum of nine individuals: seven adults and two children, one younger, one older. Among the adults there are at least two males and two females. One individual is a young adult or older adolescent, probably no older than approximately 19 years. At least one adult is probably over 30 years.

Context 4 (East compartment, NE corner)

Adult human bone. **Skull:** seven vault fragments, six loose teeth. **Axial**: fragments of vertebral bodies and processes; right clavicle fragment; fragment each from two left scapulae; eight ribshaft fragments; right acetabulum fragment; right ilium fragment. **Upper limbs**: right distal humerus shaft (robust); left proximal humerus end; left distal end; two left humerus shaft fragments; three unsided humerus shaft fragments; left proximal ulna; left ulna midshaft; distal radius fragment; metacarpal fragment. **Lower limbs**: two right proximal femur shafts; distal end left femur; right proximal tibia fragment; right distal tibia fragment; right tibia midshaft; left proximal tibia fragment; two left fibula shafts (one robust, one gracile); right patella; calcaneus fragment; metatarsal I fragment; metatarsal shaft fragment.

Immature human bone. **Skull**: deciduous right m_2. **Axial**: vertebral body fragment. **Upper limbs**: right distal third humerus shaft; left proximal half ulna shaft; right proximal femur shaft; metatarsal shaft.

Cremated human bone (35g). **Skull**: fragment of cranial vault. **Axial**: portion of innominate with auricular surface. **Upper limbs**: radius shaft fragment. **Unidentified**: 15 fragments.

Cranial remains are sparse: seven small vault fragments and six loose teeth. At least two adults are represented by duplicated fragments of left scapulae, left humeri, right femora and left fibula.

Sex assessment. Metric sexing indicates the presence of at least one female (Table 6.20). Remaining adult postcranial elements are either robust or gracile.

Age estimation. Varying degrees of occlusal wear in the loose permanent dentition indicate two age ranges, B_1 (*c.* 16–20 years) and D (*c.* 20–24 years).

A child's deciduous molar is well-worn. Root tips have broken *postmortem*, but there is no evidence of advanced resorption, suggesting a probable age range of *c.* 7–10 years. Based on comparative size the immature postcranial fragments are from a child of broadly similar age.

Cremated bone has been efficiently incinerated and presents a creamy white colour throughout. The remains are gracile, but not obviously immature.

Summary. The human remains from this context are from a female adult, at least one more adult of undetermined sex and one child. One adult is probably under *c.* 20 years, the other somewhat older. The small quantity of cremated bones is unlikely to represent more than one person.

Context 5 (East compartment, SE corner)

Adult human bones. **Skull**: two right supraorbital borders (one robust, one gracile); left supraorbital border; left lateral portion frontal; right temporal; right petrous temporal fragment; left mastoid process (gracile); left zygomatic; 39 cranial vault fragments of varying thickness; maxilla fragment; two right mandible fragments. **Axial**: one atlas, thoracic, lumbar vertebra, two cervical vertebrae; 14 vertebral fragments; left scapula; left clavicle shaft; fragments from three left innominates. **Upper limbs**: left humerus shaft (robust); left distal humerus shaft; left distal humerus end; left proximal humerus end; two right humerus shaft; two right distal humerus ends; right distal humerus end, indeterminate; right proximal ulna (gracile); right distal ulna shaft; left proximal half ulna (robust); left proximal ulna shaft (gracile); two left distal ulna shaft fragments; two radius shaft fragments. **Lower limbs**: proximal half right femur shaft (robust); proximal third right femur shaft (gracile); right proximal femur shaft fragment; right distal femur; left femur head; left femur shaft; left femur head fragment; two fibula shafts; fragment right calcaneus; right talus.

Immature human bone. Worn m_2; immature clavicle shaft; fragments of immature innominate; left proximal femur shaft; right calcaneus.

Cremated human bone. 176.2g. **Skull**: 15 fragments of thin cranial vault displaying open sutures; gracile left zygomatic fragment with orbital border; damaged dentine crown with roots of a mandibular molar (?M_1). **Axial**: four rib fragments, a fragment of ilium with auricular surface, a vertebral body fragment. **Upper** and **lower limbs**: 36 shaft fragments from all limb bones (humerus, radius, ulna, femur, tibia and fibula); distal end of a metatarsal. **Unidentified**: about 30 fragments.

Animal bone. Sheep right calcaneus.

Generally, duplications and size differences suggest two adults, but at least one more adult is represented by a third fragment each of right distal humerus and left innominate. Cranial material consists of relatively few fragments, both gracile and robust, and represents a minimum of two individuals.

Sex assessment. Measurements from distal ends of left and right humeri and a left femur head indicate female sex (Table 6.20). Remaining postcranial material is dimorphic or neutral.

Age estimation. Immature remains include a worn deciduous 2nd mandibular molar, from a child of between 7–10 years. Remaining immature material appears to be of a similar age range. A small right calcaneus is in the earlier stages of epiphyseal fusion, normally seen at around 10–12 years (Scheuer and Black 2000, 460–1, fig. 11.60). As there can be considerable variation in the timing of deciduous tooth shedding, the calcaneus need not necessarily indicate another slightly older child.

Cremated remains. The cremation deposit is relatively substantial. The material is largely creamy white/buff throughout, including cortical sections. A few long bone fragments exhibit light to dark grey colouration on inner surfaces. The fragments are strongly warped and twisted. All indications are that this material has been deliberately cremated in a well-oxygenated pyre over an extended period. There are no obvious anatomical duplications or inconsistencies to suggest more than one individual is represented. Epiphyseal ends have not survived so even a broad age estimate is difficult. The material is generally gracile, but considerable warping and probably shrinkage have taken place. The remains are not obviously immature.

Summary. The SE corner deposit contains remains from at least three adults and a child. Only two adults are consistently indicated and a third individual is only indicated by two fragments. Four metrically sexed fragments are female, remaining adult fragments are visually dimorphic. The few immature fragments are consistent with a child of around 7–10, possibly 11, years. Cremated fragments represent a single adolescent or adult.

Context 6 (East compartment)

Adult human bones. **Skull**: Left petrous temporal fragment; 15 loose teeth. **Axial**: glenoid cavity of right scapula; four vertebral body fragments; left innominate fragment with greater sciatic notch. **Upper limbs**: left distal humerus (gracile); left distal humerus (robust); left proximal humerus; right and left proximal ulnae (robust and gracile); three metacarpal shaft fragments. **Lower limbs**: left tibia midshaft; right and left distal fibula fragments; left calcaneus fragment; right talus; fragment right talus; fragment each from two left tali; two metatarsal shaft fragments.

Immature human bone. Very thin skull fragment, deciduous canine, apex open; unerupted M_2 crown.

Cremated human bone. Three small skull fragments; I^1 root; distal humerus fragment.

Animal bone. Immature scapula fragment (?sheep); immature sheep maxilla fragment; pig's canine (charred); humerus tibia and mandible from mole.

This sparse collection of fragments and loose teeth represents at least two adults, a male and female (Table 6.20). A few molars and anterior teeth including a lower third molar display heavy uneven wear (stage G/H) and suggest older or aged adult age. In contrast, a left M_1 exhibits only slight occlusal wear facets (and both mesial and distal interproximal wear facets), indicating a later adolescent or young adult (stage B_1:16–20 years).

Immature material is from a young child of 2–4 years (deciduous canine) and a child of *c.* 7–10 years (unerupted second lower molar). A few scraps of cremated human bone are present.

East compartment demographic summary

Taking the E compartment deposits all together, duplications in right proximal femora, left distal humeri and left proximal ulnae all indicate a minimum of four adults. Metric sexing of distal humeri indicates at least two females and one male (Table 6.20). Cranial material is underrepresented throughout, most fragments coming from the SE corner. The central scatter yielded only one small adult cranial fragment.

Immature postcranial fragments and teeth consistent with an older child were found in both corner deposits (and one tooth from Context 6). There were no duplications or obvious size differences in these immature remains and they could all be from a single individual of *c.* 7–10 years. Additional immature fragments, a deciduous canine and scraps of thin cranial vault, from Context 6, are from a younger child or infant; there are more numerous immature fragmentary remains at a similar stage of development in the W compartment of Chamber 1.

This conclusion differs from Cowley (1939), who claimed that nine individuals were present, based on lower jaws. Even taking into consideration the 15 decontextualised mandibular fragments that might *possibly* come from Contexts 4, 5 and 6 (Table 6.17), a minimum of 4 adults is still indicated. This conclusion assumes that the deposits from this compartment represent the mixed, redistributed and/or scattered remains of four adults. An alternative view, that each context is a separate, self-contained interment, would give a minimum of seven adults, but there are no anatomical duplications, nor obvious age/sex/size differences to support such a view.

Context 7 (Entrance)

Adult human bones. **Upper limbs**: Four humerus shaft fragments, two conjoin. The remains are of three adult left humeri.

Skeletal remains from Chamber II

Context 8 (Passage, just outside chamber on N side)

Child skeleton. **Skull**: cranium, mandible, dentition. **Axial**: scapulae, vertebrae, sacrum fragments, pelves, ribs. **Upper limbs**: fragments of humerus shaft and proximal epiphysis; right ulna; fragments of metacarpals and phalanges. **Lower**

limbs: right proximal femur; both tibiae; fragments of metatarsals; right calcaneus.

Adult human remains. Loose upper second molar.

Cremated human bone. Ulna shaft fragment.

Animal bone. Four rib shafts (large ungulate).

Unidentified. Charred limb shaft fragment.

Age estimation. The child's skeleton is relatively complete and undamaged, the presence of the mandible and some ribs and hand and foot bones suggesting that the body was interred in a fleshed state. However, the left femur and left ulna are missing and the humeri are represented by a few splinters and a fragment of proximal epiphysis. Tooth punctures are evident on a few shafts and it appears that the corpse was subject to some scavenging by a small mammal. Limbs of the left side are missing, which could suggest that the body was laid on its right side.

Deciduous molars and some unerupted permanent crowns are retained. A loose maxillary permanent first incisor crown and permanent first molar crown are complete but roots have not yet developed, indicating an age of around 3–4 years (AlQahtani *et al.* 2010).

Associated with these remains were four large fragments of immature rib shafts from a large ungulate, a fragment of burnt human ulna shaft (calcined externally, inner surface/cortex grey), a second fragment of unidentified burnt limb shaft (charred black) and an unburned M^2 (wear stage F) representing an adult of possibly 30+ years. Human postcranial remains and fragments of burnt bone were also recovered from along the south side of the passage (see below, Context 9) and some of that material may have become incorporated with the child skeleton during excavation, or earlier. Some animal remains were also recovered from the south side of the passage – vertebrae of immature sheep/goat – but nothing that might be from a large ungulate.

Context 9 (Passage, south side)

Adult human bone. **Axial**: left scapula (acromion), left clavicle shaft; two vertebral fragments; left acetabulum. **Upper limbs**: proximal third right humerus; right humerus midshaft; two right distal humerus shafts (one gracile, one robust); proximal left humerus shaft (gracile); proximal right radius (robust); distal ulna shaft (gracile). **Lower limbs**: proximal half left femur (robust); a left lateral and a left medial femoral condyle (two individuals); right proximal femur shaft fragment; a right and left patella (two individuals); a fragment each of two left proximal tibia shafts; left and right distal tibia fragments (two individuals); four unsided tibia shaft fragments; left distal fibula fragment; three fibula shaft fragments (one robust); a left and right talus; fragment of left calcaneus; fragment each from two right calcanei; fragment each of navicular and cuneiform.

Cremated bone. Six long bone shaft fragments and one skull fragment (human/animal).

Animal bone. Vertebrae of immature sheep/goat; non-identified fragments.

A minimum of two adults is indicated by duplications of right humerus shafts, right calcanei and size differences. One is certainly male (Table 6.20). There are no cranial remains and the axial skeleton is represented by five fragments.

Context 10 (Chamber II)

Adult human bone. **Skull**: nine small fragments of cranial vault, hyoid. **Axial**: 15 vertebral fragments; fragment sacrum; left acromion; four small fragments scapula; fragment clavicle shaft; two rib fragments. **Upper limbs**: right humerus shaft (robust), right humerus distal end; two humerus shaft fragments; right and left ulna midshaft; right radius shaft; small fragments radius/ulna shaft. **Lower limbs**: left distal femur shaft fragment (robust); three femur shaft fragments; femur shaft splinters; two right distal tibia fragments (robust and gracile); three proximal tibia fragments; tibia shaft splinters; 16 hand/foot fragments; left patella; non-identified fragments.

Immature human bones. **Axial**: unfused sternebra; two fragments pelves. **Upper limbs**: two distal humerus shafts; radius shaft. **Lower limbs**: left femoral metaphysis; left unfused trochanter; right unfused trochanter, right distal femoral epiphysis; two fragments distal tibial metaphysis.

Cremated human bone. 328g cremated human bone.

Animal bone. Non-identified fragments.

Most of the adult material is of robust character. Two clearly dimorphic fragments of adult right distal tibia are from different individuals, but there are no other anatomical duplications of adult remains and in all other respects the remains appear to be of one individual. Immature fragments are all consistent with older child or earlier adolescent age, under 16 years (Scheuer and Black 2000, 393) and represent one individual.

The presence of an adult hyoid is notable as this bone is rarely recovered from Neolithic contexts (this is the only specimen in the entire NMW Neolithic archive). Situated in the larynx, the hyoid is frequently one of the first bones to fall away during decomposition (Dupras *et al.* 2011, 45). Its presence here could suggest that at least one individual was interred relatively shortly after death.

Cremated remains. The 328g of cremated human bone represents a relatively substantial deposit. On examination, the mixed material presented as two distinct categories. The first (A) consists of 93g of highly fragmented, gracile, cranial and postcranial fragments which have been efficiently fired; colour is white to light buff throughout including both surfaces and cortical sections. The material is clean with no patination or soiling and has the characteristic 'clinker'-like feel of bone incinerated at high temperatures in a modern crematorium. The second (B) consists of 235g heavily soiled and patinated material, containing larger, robust fragments which appear to be less well fired. Colour varies from patchy white, through light grey/blue grey/dark grey/charred black. Black charring is strongly evident in cranial fragments, in contrast to cranial material from category A. As noted previously, prehistoric cremated bone from a single firing can exhibit considerable variation in colour, but given the contrasts in bone colour, soil staining and texture here it is difficult to envisage that both categories are from the same cremation pyre. Group A represents an adult or older adolescent of indeterminate age and sex. Group B contains a skeletally mature sternal end of clavicle indicating an adult probably over *c.* 25 years.

Skeletal remains from Chamber III

Context 11 (Entrance to passage)

Adult human bone. **Skull**: loose permanent lower canine and first molar. **Upper limbs**: left distal humerus shaft fragment; small splinters of humerus shaft; fragment of ulna shaft; **Lower limbs**: proximal ½ right femur shaft (robust); three fragmentary splinters of tibia. **Unidentified**: some 40 fragmentary limb bone splinters.

Immature human bone. Fragment of cervical vertebra; fragment right distal humerus shaft.

Little can be gleaned from this collection of weathered long bone fragments and splinters. The femur fragment is robust; other elements appear to be relatively gracile. Based on comparative size, the two immature fragments represent an older child or younger adolescent rather than a young child or infant. There is nothing in this collection to counter the suspicion that it is a disturbed fraction of Context 12.

Context 12 (Passage)

Adult human bone. **Axial**: clavicle shaft fragment; fragment each of left and right scapula; fragment of two ankylosed cervical vertebrae; thoracic vertebra fragment; a few rib fragments; fragments of innominate. **Upper limbs**: left humeral head; fragment each of left and right humerus shaft, probably pair; left humerus shaft; left distal humerus shaft; right distal humerus shaft; unsided humeral mid-shaft fragment (robust); right proximal radius fragment; left radius shaft; four fragments unsided radius shaft; fragment each of left and right proximal ulna. **Lower limbs**: several small splinters and fragments of femoral and tibial shaft; fragment each of left and right fibula; calcaneus fragment.

Immature human bone. **Axial**: lumbar body; fragment of ilium. **Lower limbs**: unfused lesser trochanter; unfused tibial proximal epiphysis; metatarsal shaft.

Animal bone. Eight non-human rib fragments, one of which is charred (dark brown/black).

Unidentified. Numerous small splinters.

There are no cranial elements. Based on anatomical duplications of left and right humeri, the adult remains are from at least three individuals. Metric data from proximal and distal humeral fragments indicate at least one is female (Table 6.20). A fragment of unsided humerus midshaft is anomalously robust, and possibly represents a fourth adult. The immature remains are of a similar age range to those from Context 11. Grimes (1939, 129) stated that the bones from the passage 'appeared to be the remains of an articulated burial or burials'. The published photograph (Grimes 1939, pl. xv, 3) is hardly convincing, but does seem to show some disturbed limb bones in anatomically correct juxtaposition; unfortunately, such associations have not been preserved in archive. Grimes' following comment (1939, 129), that 'the bones themselves were broken beyond hope of much being learned from them' is, however, indubitable.

Taking both these passages (Contexts 11–12) together, a minimum of three adults is indicated, one of whom is female. An immature individual (probably under *c.* 16 years) is represented by nine fragments. Two more robust fragments could be from a fourth adult.

Context 13 (Passage, from bottom at S end among stones and clay, distinct from Contexts 11 and 12)

Adult human bone. **Upper limbs**: fragment each of right radius, right ulna, left ulna, **Lower limbs**: right femur midshaft; right tibia midshaft; right talus fragment; fragment each left talus and left calcaneus.

Immature human bone. **Axial:** lumbar vertebra body fragment. **Lower limbs**: unfused distal epiphysis, femur, unfused proximal epiphysis tibia.

Cremated bone. Thin cremated cranial vault fragment, ?animal/?human.

Unidentified. 36 small fragments and splinters.

The immature bones appear to be of older child/earlier adolescent age and could represent contamination or scatter from similarly aged remains in Contexts 11 and 12. The adult bones appear to be from a single individual; metric data from the femur and tibia indicate male sex (Table 6.20). Although this group is labelled as being distinct from Contexts 11 and 12, there are no anatomical duplications nor obvious size differences to confirm that these bones represent an additional passage interment.

Context 14 (West transept)

Adult human bone. **Upper limbs**: fragment unsided ulna shaft. **Lower limbs**: left proximal femur shaft segment; fragment each of unsided tibia and fibula shaft.

Cremated human bone. Three small fragments: femur shaft, poorly combusted (grey/brown-black); tibia shaft, white outer surface, grey/black cortex; cranial fragment, white to light grey.

Unidentified. Three long bone splinters.

These few scraps are probably residual.

Context 15 (East transept)

Adult human bone. **Skull**: reconstructed partial cranium (portion posterior frontal, right parietal, most of occipital); loose teeth: I^2, PM^1, two M_2, M_3. **Axial**: cervical vertebra; right clavicle shaft. **Upper limbs**: proximal ½ left ulna. **Lower limbs**: proximal ½ right femur, proximal end left tibia; fibula shaft fragment; metatarsal I.

Surviving cranial morphology and metric data from the femur and tibia are indeterminate. The remains are consistent with a single adult, except for two loose M_2s, displaying widely disproportionate wear (stages A and G).

Context 16 (Central compartment, lower level)

Adult human bone. **Skull**: (a) substantial portion cranial vault – frontal with left and right supraorbital borders, parietals, occipital; (b) reconstructed craniofacial portion – frontal, right orbit, maxilla with full dental arc, central and lateral incisors lost *postmortem*; (c, d) portion each of two frontals with left and right supraorbital borders; (e, f) two frontal fragments with portions right supraorbital borders; (g) fragment right medial supraorbital border; frontal fragment with left supraorbital border; left mastoid; fragments of six right petrous temporals; fragment occipital; several unsided cranial vault fragments; 14 loose teeth. **Axial**: 17 fragments from rib shafts; three left and one right clavicle shaft fragment; two left and one right scapula fragments, innominate fragment. **Upper limbs**: (i) proximal ⅔ right humerus; (ii) distal ½ right humerus; (iii) distal ¾ right humerus shaft; (iv) distal ½ right humerus shaft; (v) splinter distal right humerus shaft, anterior surface; (vi) right humerus mid-shaft fragment; distal ¾ left humerus; two left humerus shafts; distal left humerus shaft fragment; left humeral head; fragment distal humerus, trochlea; right proximal ulna segment; right proximal ulna shaft; two left proximal ulna segments; left proximal ulna head; four unsided ulna shaft fragments; right proximal radius segment; distal ½ right radius shaft; three left proximal radius segments; four unsided radius shaft fragments; two metacarpal fragments. **Lower limbs**: two right and two left femoral heads; right femoral head and neck fragment; fragment right greater trochanter; right proximal femur shaft fragment; fragment each three right distal femora; segment each two proximal left femora shafts; distal ½ left femur shaft; left femur distal shaft segment; left femur distal shaft fragment, posterior surface; right patella; distal ⅔ right tibia; segment right tibia shaft; seven unsided tibia shaft fragments, left proximal fibula segment; left distal fibula fragment; two unsided fibula shaft fragments; two right tali; two left tali; right calcaneus, fragment calcaneus; cuboid, right and left metatarsal I; right metatarsal II; two metatarsal fragments; two foot phalanges.

Immature human bone. **Skull**: frontal with left supraorbital border; lose maxillary first premolar, root ½ formed. **Axial**: fragment unfused sternebra. **Upper limbs**: (vii) shaft right humerus; (viii) distal shaft right humerus; left humerus shaft; radius shaft fragment.

Cremated bone (16g). Six cranial vault fragments and sixteen small postcranial fragments.

Animal bone. Limb shaft splinter, large ungulate; sheep/goat molar, sheep/goat tibia, vole maxilla.

At least nine individuals are represented: seven adults and two children. Duplications of frontal bones and supraorbital ridges (a to g, above) represent seven adults, while right-sided humerus fragments (i to viii, above) are from at least six adults and two immature individuals. Anatomical duplications in remaining postcranial elements are less abundant and the axial skeleton is sparsely represented.

Sex assessment. Cranial morphology indicates four males, one female, and two adults of indeterminate sex. Sparse postcranial metric data (Table 6.20) do not add to nor contradict this assessment and remaining adult postcranial remains present as both robust and gracile specimens.

Age estimation. The reconstructed male craniofacial portion (b, above) carries maxillary dentition with light to moderate dental wear suggesting younger adult age *c.* 20–25 years. Loose permanent teeth exhibit a wide range of dental attrition. An upper second molar with light dentine exposure is from a probable second younger adult. A left upper third molar and unsided upper first molar display extreme attrition, with exposure of secondary dentine, both teeth reduced to root stumps, suggesting age well over 40 years.

By relative size, the immature fragments appear to be from children (rather than younger children/infants). An upper first premolar with ½ complete root indicates a child of *c.* 9–11 years and the fragment of unfused sternebra is consistent with a similar age, or younger.

Cremated remains. Also present were 16g of cremated/charred bone consisting of cranial fragments and postcranial splinters, not identifiable to species.

Context 17 (Central chamber, upper level)

Adult human bone. **Skull**: partially reconstructed cranial vault; loose upper and lower third molar. **Axial**: left pubic symphysis; pelvic fragments. **Upper limbs**: right distal humerus. **Lower limbs**: 2 left metatarsal V, right metatarsal I, left phalange I.

Measurement of the distal humerus (Table 6.20) and morphology of the cranial vault both indicate female sex. All the material is skeletally mature. The cranium is from an adult additional to the seven represented by crania from the lower level. The right humerus fragment is likewise from an additional female to the one represented by a right humerus fragment from the lower level.

Central chamber summary

Altogether ten individuals are indicated by skeletal remains from both upper and lower levels in the central chamber: eight adults and two immature individuals, both probably children. At least two males and two females are present among the adults.

Immature material is very sparsely represented in the central compartment, including a fragment of frontal, three fragments of humerus and a single tooth. Scattered immature elements at a broadly similar stage of skeletal development are also present in the passage. Fragments of cremated bone are also dispersed in the central chamber, the W transept and the passage. Both examples could represent dispersal and cross-contamination during earlier disturbance, or during the excavation.

Context 18 (A – From various places among stones of the cairn/body of the cairn)

Adult human bone. **Skull**: fragment of inferior orbit; fragment of zygomatic arch; two cranial vault fragments; right mandible fragment; loose teeth **Axial**: vertebral fragments; clavicle shaft fragment; five rib fragments; iliac crest fragment **Upper limbs**: distal humerus fragment; ulna shaft fragment, gracile; three metacarpal shaft fragments **Lower limbs**: left distal tibia; right distal fibula fragment; fibula shaft fragment.

Immature human bone. **Skull**: right mandible fragment.

Context 18 (B – Amongst stones high up in central compartment)

Adult human bone. **Axial**: atlas fragment; iliac crest fragment. **Upper limbs**: two radius shaft fragments

Unidentified. Miscellaneous human and animal bone fragments including small mammal.

These cranial and postcranial fragments and loose teeth are drawn from both adult and immature individuals, but many are too small to be analytically viable. Smaller fragments are weathered to stage 3/4, while many of the larger fragments display localised patches of black staining and otherwise unmodified surfaces.

Adult remains. Duplicates of right distal fibulae are from three adults. Remaining identifiable human material consists of fragments of upper and lower limbs, both robust and gracile, and 21 small cranial vault fragments. A segment of right mandible carries an M_3 with mild wear suggesting a possible age of *c.* 25–35 years.

Immature remains. A fragment of immature right mandible carrying an unerupted M_1 crown and m_2 is from a young child of *c.* 3–5 years and a canine with ½ complete root represents an older child *c.* 7–9 years.

Skeletal remains from Chamber IV

Context 19 (NW angle of chamber)

Cremated human bone. The cremated material weighs 218g. 106.82g (49%) have been identified as skull. Unidentified postcranial fragments weighed 60g (27.6%). Most of the material is white to light buff. Seven small fragments of femoral midshaft are incompletely combusted, exhibiting mottled black/light brown/pale yellow colouration. Cranial vault fragments exhibit partial suture fusion indicating probable adult age. There are no anatomical duplications in the identified material nor obvious age differences to indicate more than one individual. Mean cranial vault thickness (Gejvall 1969; measurement 1a) of 3.8mm suggests female sex.

Context 20 (Near base of Bronze Age Urn)

A charred and very eroded/weathered fragment of adult femur. Charring appears as cloudy patches on the outer surface of the shaft and on a small area of fracture surface at one end, suggesting the bone was burned or exposed to heat when already broken.

Skeletal remains from the forecourt

Context 21 (Forecourt: filling of false portal, amongst stones or on old surface)

Cremated human bone (26.6 g). **Skull**: nine fragments thin cranial vault. **Upper limbs**: radius shaft fragment. **Lower limbs**: tibia shaft fragment. **Unidentified**: 14 fragments.

Animal bone. Three tooth fragments (*Bos*), a fragment of bird bone, three unidentified fragments.

The cremated material is notably gracile and possibly immature.

Estimate of minimum number of individuals (MNI)

The skeletally mature distal humerus is the most frequently duplicated element giving an absolute MNI of 26 individuals. Taking MNI estimates from each of the chambers and passages, however, at least 28 adults and later adolescents can be discriminated (Table 6.21), as well as eight skeletally immature individuals (including the Bronze Age child), giving a total MNI estimate of 37 individuals. Morphological and metric sex assessment indicates at least 9 males and six females. At least four, and quite possibly more, individuals are also represented by cremated remains.

Palaeopathology and markers of occupational stress

Dentition

Enamel hypoplasia was evident in four loose permanent teeth and an almost complete adult maxillary arc (39.190/316), with double bands evident in premolars and molars. A pair of deciduous i^1s (age at death 18–30 months) from Context 1 display strong hypoplastic bands and pitting on both labial surfaces at about ⅓ of the crown length from the incisive edge, which could reflect an episode of metabolic insult around the time of birth or earlier. Two mandibular specimens displayed strong alveolar loss at the M_1/M_2 site indicating periodontal disease. Two counts of caries were noted from a total tooth count (including loose teeth) of 182 permanent specimens. Seven counts of *antemortem* tooth loss (AMTL) were recorded from a total of 253 observations (AMTL frequency of 2.8%). However, six of the seven observations of AMTL were located at lateral or central incisors. The only observation of AMTL in the buccal dentition was of a right M^1 (1 out of 91 molar observations). *Antemortem* loss of incisors is seen in three specimens (Tables 6.17–18). One almost complete mandible (39.190/201) shows *antemortem* loss of left I_1 and left I_2; root sockets have completely healed over and the left canine is rotated through 90°, suggesting the teeth were lost some years before death. A loose right I^1 from Context 16 displays an occlusal notch or groove with trails both lingually and labially, possibly the consequence of processing or working twine or comparable material and similar activities might have led to incisor loss in the specimens noted here, although other factors, such as evulsion for cosmetic purposes, accidents or inter-personal violence cannot be ruled out (cf. Capasso *et al.* 1999, 150). Similar wear was not observed in the 27 remaining incisors, although strong oblique meso-distal wear of mandibular canines was noted in two cases, which again may reflect use of the mouth/teeth in processing or as a third hand (Capasso *et al.* 1999, 151).

Cranium

Cribra orbitalis was noted in two specimens: bilaterally in a frontal fragment from Context 16 (39.190/237), and in the left orbit (right n/a) of partially reconstructed cranial vault from Context 17.

Postcranial skeleton. Two examples of healed fractures were observed, both with exuberant exostosis: a distal tibia fragment from Context 18A and a distal fibula fragment from Context 16.

Table 6.21. Ty Isaf: MNI estimates and demographic summary.

	Sub-context	*Adults*	*Age ranges*	*Assessed sex*	*Immature*	*Age ranges*	*Notes*
Chamber I	W compartment	7	30+ y; *c.* 19 y	2 male 1 female	2	9–11 y; 18–30 m	–
	E compartment	4	16–20 y; 20–25 y; 30–40 y	2 female 1 male	2	7–10 y; 2–4 y	–
Chamber II	Passage	2	–	1 male	1	3–4 y	Bronze Age child
	Chamber	2	–	–	1	10–16 y	–
Chamber III	Passage	4	–	1 female 1 male	1	< 16 y	–
	W Transept	–	–	–	–	–	Residual fragments
	E Transept	1		–	–	–	–
	Central chamber, lower level	7	20–25 y × 2; 40 + y	4 male 1 female	2	*c.* 9–11 y	–
	Central chamber, upper level	1	–	female	–	–	–
Totals		28		9 male 6 female	9		

Key: y = years; m = months

Where observations were possible a few instances of degenerative changes in vertebrae, associated with age or general wear and tear were evident: six examples of osteophytic lipping, three examples of Schmorl's nodes and six examples of porotic exostosis with breakdown of trabecular structure. A fragment of two ankylosed cervical vertebrae was found among the material from Context 12.

Four calcanei exhibited osteophytes at the Achilles tendon insertion site, as seen at Pipton and Penywyrlod. Various markers associated with habitual squatting were also noted; six distal tibiae fragments carried squatting facets (White *et al.* 2012, 263), five out of eight surviving patellae exhibited a vastus notch (Messeri's Patella: Capasso *et al.* 1999, 121) and an osteochondritic imprint (Capasso *et al.* 1999, 111) was noted on one medial femoral condyle.

Ty Isaf: commentary and overview

Of the three monumental tombs under consideration here, Ty Isaf is perhaps the most intriguing, with its idiosyncratic, hybrid forms and evidence of multi-period use. From an osteoarchaeological perspective it is surely the most frustrating. Its wealth of potential data and information relating to biological anthropology, funerary rites, ancestors, social structures and habitual activities has been disturbed, broken, rifled, eroded, and muddled away and, in the absence of plans or detailed descriptions, only a few remarks by Grimes cast detailed light on the arrangements of human remains in the various chambers and passages. Nevertheless, as if peering at an old, fogged film or photograph, some impressions emerge.

Secondary burials and single acts?

The degree and intensity of *in situ* fragmentation, erosion and resultant destruction all combine to render these questions largely unapproachable within the limitations of this analysis. There is the suggestion, in the recovery of a hyoid from among the fragmentary remains of what appears to be a single adult in Chamber II (Context 10), that this individual may have been a primary, recently deceased interment, while the Bronze Age child was almost certainly placed in the passage outside Chamber II as a fleshed corpse, perhaps intentionally accompanied by ribs from an immature large ungulate.

The mixing of remains from different individuals among what appear to be composite representations of single skeletons in Contexts 1 and 2 implies re-arrangement of already disarticulated bones, as evidenced at Pipton and Penywyrlod. However, the functional passages in Chambers I, II and II and a wide range of radiocarbon dates, as set out in Chapter 4, all indicate repeated entry and re-entry up to the 2nd millennium cal BC, which means that such rearrangements could have taken place at any point within this timespan with bones that had long ago skeletonised and disarticulated entirely *in situ*.

Whether such repeated ingress was for the purpose of bringing in the recently deceased for primary interment, or piles of old bones from elsewhere, or in order to interact with and rearrange the remains of ancestors, or even to clear out chambers for re-use, or indeed for all these purposes, is hard to tell, though there are a few hints to suggest the latter activity may have played a role in the formation processes at Ty Isaf. Chamber II (Context 10) produced for the most part the fragmented remains of what appears to be a single adult skeleton, possibly interred as a fleshed corpse. It may seem unlikely to our ways of thinking that a chamber with functional passage was originally intended to contain the bones of just a single occupant. Also recovered were a few immature fragments and a portion of tibia from another individual. Could these extra bits be residual, left behind after a clearance of earlier remains, with the single skeleton a later interment? The W transept of Chamber III gave every appearance of having been emptied, leaving behind only fragments of bone, and we know that there were significantly later interments in the central compartment of Chamber III in the form of a female cranium from Context 17, dated to *2705–4790* (*87% probability*; *OxA-14250*; Fig. 4.6) and an indeterminate cranium from Context 16, dated to *2900–2840 cal BC* (*63% probability* or *2900–2840 cal BC 32% probability*; *OxA-14248*; Fig. 4.6), as well as the inclusion of a cattle tooth in the W compartment of Chamber I (*2665–2465 cal* BC; *95% probability*; *SUERC-57788*; Fig. 4.6). Unfortunately, a sample from a human humerus in Chamber II failed to produce a date. Something similar may have been played out in the E transept of Chamber III, but again a sample for radiocarbon dating failed.

Discrete groups and reconnecting with the ancestors?

As noted earlier, Grimes' (1939, 126) most salient observation concerning the mortuary remains in Chamber I is that 'bones were found mostly in groups consisting frequently of the cranium, lower jaw and one or two long bones carefully placed against the side-stones and sometimes pushed into angles and crevices, in places which I do not think they could have reached by accidental means'. Grimes here prefigures the circumstances later encountered by Savory at Pipton and Penywyrlod and it is hard to think of any other then-contemporary or earlier chambered tomb excavations that might have influenced his perceptions, with the exception of perhaps Lanhill (Keiller *et al.* 1938). This all lends his observation an air of authenticity, although, based on Cowley's (1939) report and the finds labelling in archive, we only know of four groupings in the chambers (Contexts 1, 2, 4 and 5). These all contain mixed remains from two or more adults and, with the exception of Context 2, a few immature fragments. Contexts 1 and 2 do resemble composites of single skeletons, as seen previously, whereas the selections of grouped bones in Contexts 4–5 appear to be more overtly representational of two individuals. There is no information about where or how the rest of the bones in Chamber I, nor those of Chamber II, were located. In his account of Chamber III, Grimes (1939, 129) states 'The finds and general conditions in Chamber III told the same story as those of the chambers already described … groups of bones as previously recorded were (with one exception) [the passage] the rule'. Again, there is no information about these groups; all we have are finds labels in archive and Cowley's (1939, 142) report indicating a sparse upper layer and substantial lower layer.

How do I bury thee? Let me count the ways

There is a clearer picture when we compare the mortuary populations at Ty Isaf with those from Penywyrlod Chamber NE II and Pipton Chamber II, although we may be effectively comparing apples with oranges. The Ty Isaf skeletal remains do not come from structures that might conform to Savory's (1956, 41) description of Chamber II at Pipton: 'little more than a large, closed cist'. They do, in contrast, appear to incorporate more or less equal numbers of males and females, with the selection of bones in the Chamber I groupings perhaps hinting at intentional pairing of male and female elements (there is, however, the risk of peering too long at murky pictures and seeing things that do not exist). Again, in contrast to the cist-like chambers at Pipton and Penywyrlod where the contents are dominated by the remains of young men, both Chambers I and III at Ty Isaf contain older, middle and younger adults, adolescents, children and infants. In this respect there is more in common with the remains from Penywyrlod Chamber III although the full extent of interments there is unknown.

While some of the human remains at Ty Isaf can only hint at varying practices – rearrangements and groupings of disarticulated bones, recently deceased fleshed interments – other variations stand out more clearly. Cremated remains are much more abundant throughout the various chambers than the 'few pieces indicating cremation' reported in Cowley (1939, 141). Willis (2021, 9, 23–32) has recently discussed the extent of known earlier Neolithic cremations in Britain but given the episodes of use and re-use at Ty Isaf, the deposits here could equally have been added in the Middle or later Neolithic (Willis 2021) or Bronze Age. The cremated material from Chamber IV, however, seems most likely to be unequivocally of Bronze Age origin. Also unequivocally Bronze Age, and perhaps one of the most striking images to be taken away from Ty Isaf, is the interment of a young child some 3–4 years of age in the passage just outside Chamber II. Barely given any regard by Grimes or Cowley, the delicate remains are sufficiently intact and well preserved to strongly suggest a fully fleshed corpse was placed here. In archive, the remains were bagged and labelled with context and accompanied by an adult molar, a few charred and calcined fragments and four substantial immature rib shaft segments from a large ungulate; one can only assume that all were found in association and the association was intentional. This may have been one of the last acts performed within Ty Isaf or within the passage to Chamber II. For us there are echoes too of earlier child/animal semiotic behaviours from a more distant past – a human infant's femur inserted into an ox humerus and an infant's cranium placed next to a cow's frontal bone at Windmill Hill (Whittle *et al.* 1999, 362).

Further implications

All this detail from the three individual sites covered here raises many questions. The individual accounts above have already dealt with a host of them: variation and difference between contexts and monuments; varying timespans, including issues of repeat visits and access to particular chambers and contexts; differing numbers and balances of age and sex; possibilities of direct deposition versus deposition following decay elsewhere; post-depositional disturbance; manipulation and re-arrangement of bones; and the use and re-use or rediscovery and reappropriation of monuments. The detail also raises questions of lifestyle and activities, including particular patterns of tooth loss resulting from not only diet but possibly from the preparation or processing of materials, adoption of postures such as squatting and even the possibility of obesity (cf. Wysocki and Whittle 2000), of inter-personal violence and martial skills.

There is of course enormous scope for comparison of all these features with other relevant assemblages elsewhere, particularly but not only within the Severn-Cotswold orbit. That would be rewarding, but is beyond the scope and length of this volume; this bone report is already long enough. What will make a useful contribution, however, and will also serve to underpin the overall arguments in this volume for distinctive regional practice in the Black Mountains and the beginnings of a discernibly more precise narrative for development there within the early Neolithic, is to weave the many themes raised in this chapter into as detailed and nuanced an account of the Black Mountains sequence as currently possible, in the wider discussion presented in Chapter 12.

7

‘Local’ or ‘non-local’? Interpreting isotope results from the Black Mountains long cairns

Samantha Neil

Introduction

This chapter reviews the isotope data from burial populations excavated from the Penywyrlod and Ty Isaf long cairns. Previous interpretation of the results from these sites, first published in Neil *et al.* (2017), is examined in the light of new biosphere $^{87}Sr/^{86}Sr$ mapping results (Johnson 2018; Johnson *et al.* 2022), new chronological modelling of radiocarbon dates from the region (set out in Chapter 4), further enamel $^{87}Sr/^{86}Sr$ isotope data and data recently obtained from other early Neolithic human populations buried in different regions of Britain.

Principles and procedures

Strontium ($^{87}Sr/^{86}Sr$) and oxygen ($\delta^{18}O$) analysis of tooth enamel was conducted on the assemblages from these sites between 2013–2016 as means to directly explore patterns of landscape use and mobility during the Neolithic in Wales. Use of strontium isotope analysis for geographic provenancing is well established, having been first employed in archaeology over 30 years ago (Ericson 1985). It is based on the principle that $^{87}Sr/^{86}Sr$ strontium isotope ratios vary geographically – variation that is primarily driven by the age and composition of underlying geology (Faure 1986; Dicken 2005; Faure and Mensing 2005).

Strontium has four naturally occurring isotopes (^{88}Sr, ^{87}Sr, ^{86}Sr and ^{84}Sr). Unlike the other isotopes of strontium ^{87}Sr is radiogenic, the product of the radioactive decay of another chemical element, rubidium-87 (^{87}Rb; Faure 1986, 117–18; Dicken 2005, 42–3; Faure and Mensing 2005, 76). $^{87}Sr/^{86}Sr$ varies geographically according to the age, initial Sr/Rb ratio and geological history of bedrock. Because ^{87}Sr gradually increases over geological timescales through the β-decay of ^{87}Rb, the highest most radiogenic $^{87}Sr/^{86}Sr$ values are often associated with older rocks with high concentrations of Rb bearing minerals (Faure 1986, 117–18; Dicken 2005, 42–3; Faure and Mensing 2005, 76). Strontium weathers out from rocks, into soils and ground waters where it becomes available to plants and enters the food chain (Capo *et al.* 1998, 202–3). Conventionally measured $^{87}Sr/^{86}Sr$ values do not vary significantly between trophic levels and as enamel does not remodel after formation, $^{87}Sr/^{86}Sr$ values within tooth enamel directly reflect the sources of dietary strontium to which individuals were exposed whilst their teeth were forming (Graustein 1989, 492; Montgomery 2002; 2010; Bentley 2006; Slovak and Paytan 2011, 743–4).

Sequentially mineralising adjacent second and third molar teeth were sampled from both Penywyrlod and Ty Isaf to compare isotope ratios in enamel that forms at successive stages of childhood. Strontium isotope ratios measured in archaeological tooth enamel are compared to mapped bioavailable values for plants and water to examine where an individual may have obtained their childhood diet (*e.g.* Evans *et al.* 2010; J.A. Evans 2018; Britton 2020). Both Penywyrlod and Ty Isaf are located on Lower Devonian St Maughans Formation (Chapter 2). Samples of modern plants were collected on bedrock lithology within a radius of 10 miles, approximately 16km, of both sites to study the locally bioavailable $^{87}Sr/^{86}Sr$ range (see Neil *et al.* 2017).

Whilst employing strontium isotope analysis, this study also undertook oxygen isotope analysis of enamel samples from each tooth. The ratio of $^{18}O/^{16}O$ (expressed as $\delta^{18}O$, as it is measured relative to standard reference materials) also varies geographically within water, influenced by factors such as latitude, altitude, temperature and distance from the coast (Mook 2005, 89–98; Gat 2010). Use of oxygen isotope analysis for geographic provenancing in archaeology is based on the premise that, whilst there is some contribution from respiratory oxygen and chemically bound oxygen in food, a significant component of the $\delta^{18}O$ values within mammalian bioapatite (tooth enamel and bone) derives from ingested fluids, which in turn reflect values in local drinking water (Longinelli 1984; Luz *et al.* 1984; Luz and Kolodny 1985; Levinson *et al.* 1987; Daux *et al.* 2008, 1146). It has been argued that differences in $\delta^{18}O_{phosphate}$ values of tooth enamel found in archaeological populations sampled from western Britain (mean 18.2‰±1.0‰, 2σ) and eastern Britain (mean 17.2±1.3‰, 2σ) reflect underlying variation in the isotope composition of local drinking water between these two regions (Evans *et al.* 2012, 759), as local groundwaters in western Britain are associated with higher $\delta^{18}O$ values than those in eastern Britain (Darling *et al.* 2003, 189–90). However, although the oxygen isotope values exhibited by human archaeological populations correlate with environmental factors, such as latitude, longitude and altitude, the oxygen isotope ranges found in populations buried in different regions of temperate Europe may overlap (Lightfoot and O'Connell 2016). $\delta^{18}O$ values found in populations buried in Britain can, for example, be similar to those recorded in adjacent mainland Europe (*e.g.* Brettell *et al.* 2012b, 127).

Whilst there is evidence that $\delta^{18}O$ values recorded in human populations vary with climate, another factor that must be considered when interpreting oxygen isotope results is the potential influence of culturally mediated behaviour on the oxygen isotope composition of ingested fluids. In contrast to conventionally measured $^{87}Sr/^{86}Sr$ values, which are not subject to significant change through biological, chemical or physical processes (see above), the isotope ratios of light elements such as oxygen can be subject to mass-dependent fractionation (variation in the isotope ratio) as a result of culturally mediated behaviour (Daux *et al.* 2008, 1144; Brettell *et al.* 2012a). The influence of human culinary activity, for example, boiling water or stewing foods, is therefore considered when evaluating the results of oxygen isotope analysis (Daux *et al.* 2008, 1144; Brettell *et al.* 2012a).

Breast feeding may also influence the oxygen isotope composition of enamel; breast milk has higher $\delta^{18}O$ value relative to fluids consumed by the mother (Roberts *et al.* 1988, 625). Teeth that form whilst an infant is being breast fed (*e.g.* deciduous molars or first molars) may therefore record higher $\delta^{18}O$ values than teeth that form later in childhood (Wright and Schwartz 1998, 14; Britton 2015, 8). Interpretation of values in enamel is therefore complicated by a number of different factors. In addition, a recent small-scale study of enamel from modern populations suggests that, when comparing samples taken from different third molars that belong to the same individual, oxygen isotope ratios can vary by up to ~2‰ (Plomp *et al.* 2020, 594). In contrast, $^{87}Sr/^{86}Sr$ values may only vary in the fourth decimal place (by up to 0.000192: Plomp *et al.* 2020, 594).

Oxygen isotope ratios may therefore be most useful for making broader-scale distinctions between, for example, values which can be associated with regions of cooler climate where lower values can be recorded (*e.g.* $\delta^{18}O_{phosphate}$ below approximately 15.5‰, or $\delta^{18}O_{carbonate}$ below approximately 24.5‰). Such regions include Scandinavia and the Alps and contrast strongly with values found in temperate locations (Müller *et al.* 2003; Chenery *et al.* 2014; Montgomery *et al.* 2014; Price and Naumann 2015).

There are two ionic forms of oxygen in tooth enamel that are suitable for oxygen isotope analysis: $\delta^{18}O_{carbonate}$ and $\delta^{18}O_{phosphate}$. The present study conducted analysis of the carbonate (CO_3^{2-}) fraction of enamel. To facilitate comparison of these results to data from other archaeological studies that sampled the phosphate (PO_4^{3-}) fraction (*e.g.* Evans *et al.* 2012; see below), conversion from $\delta^{18}O_{carbonate}$ to $\delta^{18}O_{phosphate}$ was undertaken, using the regression equation of Chenery *et al.* (2012, 310; $\delta^{18}O_{phosphate} = 1.0322 \times \delta^{18}O_{carbonate} - 9.6849$). In temperate climates, $\delta^{18}O$ values of the $\delta^{18}O_{phosphate}$ and $\delta^{18}O^{carbonate}$ fractions are considered to be well correlated and the error involved in calculating $\delta^{18}O_{phosphate}$ using this equation is considered to be low (0.28‰, 1σ; Chenery *et al.* 2012, 313).

The following section outlines in brief the methods used for strontium and oxygen isotope analysis; for a more detailed description of the techniques employed, see Neil *et al.* (2017). Strontium and oxygen isotope analysis was undertaken at the National Environmental Isotope Facility (NEIF, Keyworth, Nottingham, England), funded by NIGFSC grant IP-1290-0512. The external surface of the tooth was first mechanically cleaned, using tungsten carbide dental burrs to remove any adhering dirt and particulates. A chip of core enamel, approximately 20–30mg in weight, was taken from each tooth for strontium isotope analysis, and of approximately 10mg in weight for oxygen isotope analysis; these were excised using a flexible diamond-edged rotary saw. The exposed surfaces of each enamel chip were then again thoroughly abraded using dental burrs to ensure any adhering dentine was removed, as in contrast to tooth enamel, dentine is susceptible to diagenetic alteration (Montgomery 2002, 91). Once fully mineralised, tooth enamel is considered to be highly resistant to diagenesis and to retain *in vivo* $^{87}Sr/^{86}Sr$ values (Budd *et al.* 2000; Montgomery 2002, 330–3; 2010, 329; Trickett *et al.* 2003). However, following the recommendation of Montgomery (2002), none of the teeth sampled exhibited any evidence of caries; greater variation in the isotope ratio of carious enamel suggests that caries may alter the isotope composition of enamel (Plomp *et al.* 2020, 601). Analysis was conducted on bulk enamel. Isotope ratios are therefore considered to represent the weighted average of all the sources of dietary strontium to which the individual was exposed during tooth formation (Montgomery 2010, 333).

Permission to sample the assemblages from Penywyrlod and Ty Isaf was provided by the National Museum Wales, where the remains are stored. Contexts for remains are as given on labelling and documentation associated with the collections in the museum. Remains from both sites are disarticulated, fragmentary and commingled. Where cranial remains were incomplete, only teeth within fragments of left mandibular dentition were selected for sampling. This was to avoid the possibility of inadvertently sampling the same individual twice, for example by sampling loose teeth, or teeth in right mandibular and maxillary fragments that could potentially also belong to the same individual. The biological sex of sampled individuals cannot be determined with confidence using conventional osteological methods owing to the fragmentary nature of the assemblages and disarticulation of the cranial remains from other skeletal elements used for sex attribution. Facial reconstruction commissioned by the National Museum Wales for the purpose of gallery display suggests that one of the sampled individuals, 74.23H/9.23/P22, is male (Burrow 2010).

When considering the results of analysis below, it should be remembered that the assemblage from Penywyrlod represents a partial sample of what may be present. As discussed in Chapter 2, other chambers are known, or suspected, to exist within this monument. Very few remains were recovered during the excavation of Chamber NE I (Britnell and Savory 1984, 6; Savory 1984, 18; and see Chapter 2) and no dentition from this chamber was available that met the criteria for sampling specified above. Samples therefore only originate from two of the three excavated chambers (Chamber NE II and Chamber NE III). Of these two chambers, Chamber NE III has not been fully excavated. Remains originate from the passage only and represent a partial sample of what may be present (see Chapters 2 and 6).

Despite being located only 4km apart, Ty Isaf differs from Penywyrlod, being smaller, approximately 30m in length. Unlike Penywyrlod, it is a composite monument consisting of two distinct elements: a long cairn with two opposing lateral chambers (Chambers I and II) and a circular rotunda containing transepted Chamber III (Grimes 1939, 123–4; see Fig. 6.6). In contrast to Penywyrlod, the excavation of which benefited from use of more recent techniques, the Ty Isaf long cairn was excavated during the first half of the twentieth century and the context of the excavated remains is less precisely documented. Whilst the context of most specimens excavated from Ty Isaf is stated in paperwork associated with the collection, four specimens lacked documentation detailing their excavation context within the monument (those described as being of 'undocumented' context, see below, Fig. 7.1, and Neil *et al.* 2017). These specimens could have been excavated either from the rotunda or the lateral chambers. No dentition attributed to the rotunda monument at Ty Isaf was present in the assemblage that met the criteria for sampling specified above. To assist with understanding the chronology of Ty Isaf a programme of radiocarbon dating was also undertaken during the collection of samples for strontium and oxygen isotope analysis (see Neil *et al.* 2017, and Chapter 4).

Results

As described in Neil *et al.* (2017), samples of modern plants that were collected within a radius of 10 miles (approximately 16km) of Penywyrlod and Ty Isaf gave a range of strontium isotope ratios between 0.7097–0.7137 (mean 0.7107±0.001, 1σ, n=12; Neil *et al.* 2017, 381). Human individuals buried at Penywyrlod have strontium isotope ratios between 0.7132–0.7170 (mean 0.71486±0.0011 1σ, n=15; Fig. 7.1), with 12 of the 15 teeth that were sampled having strontium isotope ratios greater than 0.714. Of the three teeth with values lower than 0.714 from Penywyrlod, two are third molars that belong to individuals excavated from Chamber NE II; individual 74.23H/9.23/P22 has a value of 0.7139, which is just above the range found in locally sampled plants, and individual 74.23H/9.5.1/P27 has a value of 0.7133. However, both the individuals to whom these teeth belong also possess adjacent second molar teeth that have values higher than 0.714. The third tooth with a measured value lower than 0.714 is the deciduous second molar of a child aged approximately 2 years at death, excavated from Chamber NE III. Enamel from the tooth of this individual has the lowest value (0.7132) in the sampled population. All other sampled individuals have values higher than 0.714. These individuals include all others excavated from Chamber NE II, the passage of Chamber NE III and the deciduous second molar tooth of a child whose remains were recovered from an undated cist inserted into the outer revetment wall, after the partial collapse of the walling or insertion of blocking in the forecourt (Savory 1984, 22–3). Enamel samples from the second and third molars of one adult individual (74.23H/9.2.3/P23) from Penywyrlod gave particularly high $^{87}Sr/^{86}Sr$ values of 0.7170 and 0.7165 respectively (Fig. 7.1). This individual was excavated from Chamber NE II at Penywyrlod and has been radiocarbon dated to 4888±37 BP (3770–3540 cal BC, 95% confidence, SUERC-63414, calibrated using IntCal20, OxCal v.4.4.4; Neil *et al.* 2017).

The radiocarbon dating of remains from Ty Isaf revealed that one of the individuals in the group sampled from the monument, a child (39.190/324) aged approximately 3–4 years at death, dates to the Bronze Age (3309±32 BP, *1680–1500 cal BC, 95% confidence, SUERC-57789*, calibrated using IntCal20, OxCal v.4.4.4; Neil *et al.* 2017, and also see Chapter 4, this volume). This individual was excavated from the north side of the monument outside Chamber II. Enamel from the deciduous first and second molars of this individual gave $^{87}Sr/^{86}Sr$ values of 0.7141 and 0.7146. The remainder of the individuals who were

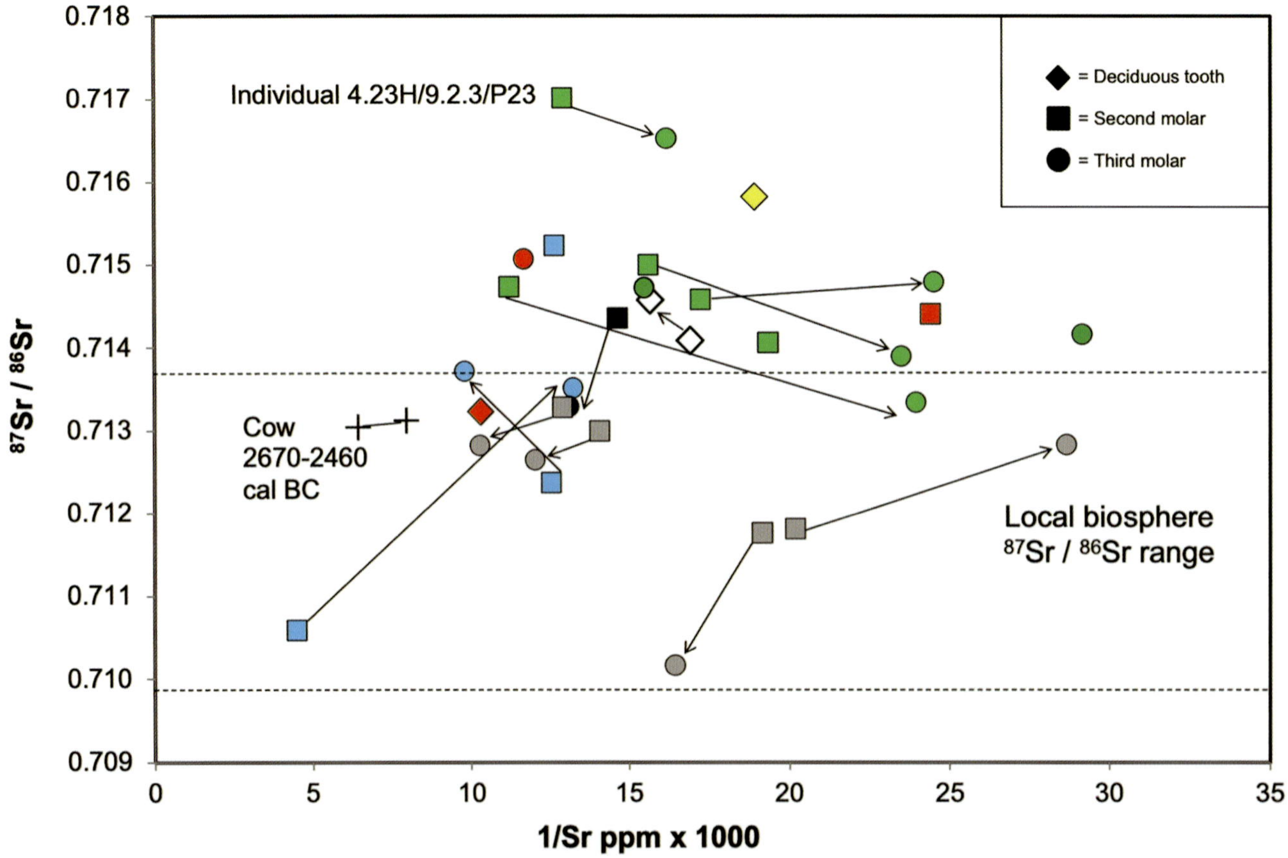

Fig. 7.1. Plot of strontium isotope ratio versus the inverse of concentration (1/Sr ppm × 1000) for human and cattle enamel from Penywrylod (Talgarth) long cairn and Ty Isaf, illustrating linked adjacent molar teeth that belong to the same individual. Symbols coloured according to the context to which each individual is attributed in documentation associated with the museum collections. Dashed lines delineate locally bioavailable $^{87}Sr/^{86}Sr$ values measured in modern plants growing within a radius of 10 miles (approximately 16km) of both sites. ***Green symbols*** *= individuals from Penywyrlod Chamber NE II.* ***Red symbols*** *= individuals from Penywyrlod Chamber NE III.* ***Yellow symbol*** *= child from Penywyrlod cist in forecourt.* ***Blue symbols*** *= human individuals attributed to Ty Isaf Chamber I. Black symbols = attributed to Ty Isaf Chamber II.* ***Grey symbols*** *= human individuals of unattributed context from Ty Isaf.* ***Crosses*** *= samples from the cusp and cervix of the third permanent premolar of a cow of later Neolithic date from Ty Isaf.* ***Open white symbols*** *= first and second deciduous premolars of a child of Bronze Age date from Ty Isaf. Tooth types are denoted by the key in the upper right of the diagram. Radiocarbon dates cited at 95% confidence, calibrated using IntCal20, OxCal v.4.4.4. 2σ errors for $^{87}Sr/^{86}Sr$ are within the symbol.*

sampled from Ty Isaf are radiocarbon dated to the mid 4th to early 3rd millennia cal BC. Enamel from the human individuals of Neolithic date gave a range of $^{87}Sr/^{86}Sr$ values between 0.7101–0.7152 (mean 0.71286±0.0013, 1σ, n=15), with only two individuals recording strontium isotope ratios higher than 0.7140: adult 39.190/310 excavated from Chamber II of the long cairn and sub-adult 39.190/58 from Chamber I, who have $^{87}Sr/^{86}Sr$ values of 0.7144 and 0.7152 respectively. A loose third permanent premolar of a cow excavated from the west compartment of Chamber I and dated to the late Neolithic (*4039±30 BP; 2670–2460 cal BC, 95% confidence, SUERC-57788*, calibrated as above) at Ty Isaf, was also sampled. Enamel sampled near to the cusp of the crown of this tooth gave an $^{87}Sr/^{86}Sr$ value of 0.7130, while that taken close to the cervix gave an $^{87}Sr/^{86}Sr$ value of 0.7131.

$\delta^{18}O_{carbonate}$ values of enamel from the second and third permanent molars of individuals of Neolithic date at Ty Isaf range between 25.4–27.7‰ (mean 26.7±0.6‰, 1σ, n=15).

There are no discernible trends in enamel oxygen isotope composition according to excavation context or radiocarbon date within this group. Enamel samples from the first and second deciduous molars of the child of Bronze Age date at Ty Isaf (39.190/324) both gave $\delta^{18}O_{carbonate}$ values of 27.2‰. Enamel from the second deciduous molars of two children buried at Penywyrlod (74.23H/9.18/P20 and 74.23H/9.7/P25) gave $\delta^{18}O_{carbonate}$ values of 28.2‰ and 27.5‰ respectively. $\delta^{18}O_{carbonate}$ values of enamel from the second and third permanent molars of the other individuals excavated from Penywyrlod ranged between 25.9–27.2‰ (mean 26.5±0.5‰, 1σ, n=13). This includes the adult individual (74.23H/9.2.3/P23) who has the highest strontium isotope ratio (0.7170) in the group and whose second and third permanent molar teeth gave $\delta^{18}O_{carbonate}$ values of 26.5‰ and 25‰ respectively.

Discussion

Having briefly outlined the principles and procedures of analysis and described the results, we now turn to the question of how they might be interpreted. Previous interpretation of the results (Neil *et al.* 2017) can be tested against new $^{87}Sr/^{86}Sr$ biosphere data and additional chronological evidence. The results can also be compared to further data from other Neolithic populations in England and Wales. As illustrated in Figure 7.1, despite being located only 4km apart, the two burial groups from Penywyrlod and Ty Isaf exhibit contrasting strontium isotope ratios. The majority of those buried at Ty Isaf have $^{87}Sr/^{86}Sr$ values that are lower than 0.714. In contrast, the majority of individuals who were excavated from Penywyrlod have strontium isotope ratios that exceed 0.714 and are higher than those measured in modern locally collected plants, which range between 0.7097–0.7137 (mean 0.7107±0.001, 1σ, n=12). This could suggest that those buried at Penywyrlod did not obtain their resources locally.

Biosphere values between 0.714–0.716 have been recorded just over 35 miles (56km) away in the Malvern Hills to the east of Penywyrlod and Ty Isaf, on lithology dated to the Late Precambrian (Chenery *et al.* 2010; Evans *et al.* 2010). A single sample of plants growing above the Precambrian bedrock in this area recorded a value of 0.71622 (Chenery *et al.* 2010, 155). However, further biosphere sampling in this area has recently been undertaken by Johnson (2018), which found that high values such as this are difficult to reproduce in the Malvern Hills and they do not represent the average for the area. The highest value that could be recorded by Johnson from plants growing on the Malvern Complex was 0.7135 (Johnson 2018, 86). This is perhaps because the Precambrian bedrock is limited to a very small area, with the Malvern Hills being only approximately *c.* 13km in length and surrounded by younger geology, the sedimentary formations of the Silurian to the west and the Triassic to the east. Current data suggest that overall the mean for the biosphere on the Precambrian Malvern Complex is only 0.7133 $^{87}Sr/^{86}Sr$±0.0031 (n=11, 2σ: Montgomery *et al.* 2006; Chenery *et al.* 2010; Johnson 2018; J.A. Evans 2019). However, as biosphere values between 0.714–0.716 have been recorded on the Malvern Hills complex, the possibility that individuals buried at Penywyrlod and Ty Isaf who have comparable values obtained their diet from this area cannot be ruled out.

Recent sampling has shown that plant $^{87}Sr/^{86}Sr$ values between 0.714–0.716 can also be recorded on small areas of Precambrian lithology that are located along the Welsh Borderland Fault system (Johnson 2018). One sample taken on Silurian bedrock close to the Stanner-Hanter complex, in the Welsh borderlands between New Radnor, Powys, and Kington, Herefordshire, recently recorded a plant $^{87}Sr/^{86}Sr$ value of 0.71613 (Johnson 2018, 127). The Stanner-Hanter complex, which is currently the oldest dated lithology found in southern Britain (Schofield *et al.* 2010; 2016) is located only approximately 16 miles (26km) to the NE of Penywyrlod and Ty Isaf. However, the exposures of Precambrian bedrock here, which form the Stanner Hill and Hanter Hill are very small, under 5km long. Overall the Sr-isotope biosphere around this area is also much lower, with values with plant samples taken on Precambrian inliers here giving an average value of $^{87}Sr/^{86}Sr$ 0.7123±0.001 (n=3, 2σ; Johnson 2018, 128). Slightly further to the NE, three further high plant values have been recorded in samples taken in an aureole around the base of another small area of Precambrian bedrock at Church Stretton, Shropshire, which is part of the Welsh Borderlands Fault System (samples CS L3 0.71524, CS L12 0.71536 and CS L2 0.71406; Johnson 2018, 111). However, here again it should be noted that other plant samples taken in this area have also recorded lower values and overall plant samples on the Precambrian Uriconian and Longmyndian gave a mean $^{87}Sr/^{86}Sr$ value of 0.7116±0.0003 (n=5, 2σ; Johnson 2018, 114).

The recent study by Johnson (2018; Johnson *et al.* 2022) also explored the potential role of environmental changes on bioavailable $^{87}Sr/^{86}Sr$ ranges, suggesting that deforestation could perhaps account for lowering the average bioavailable ranges on some types of lithology in southern Britain. Based on a small number of samples taken on Triassic lithology from trees growing in the ancient woodland of Sherwood Forest, Johnson proposes that local biosphere $^{87}Sr/^{86}Sr$ values could be elevated in heavily wooded conditions (Johnson 2018, 174–84, 228, 272). This may be a consequence of the build-up of leaf litter over time, increasing the pH of soils, in turn leading to decalcification and the removal of Ca-bearing minerals that have lower $^{87}Sr/^{86}Sr$ ratios from the underlying lithology. It is therefore suggested that plants in areas of ancient woodland may have higher strontium isotope ratios (Johnson 2018; Johnson *et al.* 2022). Heavily wooded conditions, where there has been sufficient time for accretion of leaf litter that forms the humus layer to change the pH of soils, may result in higher average biosphere values.

This may only affect plants growing on certain types of bedrock: it would have limited effect on lithology such as limestone or chalk, that are dominated by carbonate minerals (Johnson 2018; Johnson *et al.* 2022). This is illustrated by Warham (2011, 120), who showed that plants growing on areas of Clay-with-Flints in southern Britain, superficial deposits that result from *in situ* weathering and decalcification in areas of Cretaceous Chalk, have slightly elevated $^{87}Sr/^{86}Sr$ values (by approximately +0.0002–0.0018). Based on the recent results from Sherwood Forest, however,

Johnson (2018, 184) proposes that the effect may be greater on lithologies, such as siltstones and mudstones, from which carbonate minerals may be leached out over time; it is proposed that this could increase bioavailable $^{87}Sr/^{86}Sr$ values. Due to the age and composition of lithology in England and Wales, Johnson (2018, 174, 263) suggests that such environmental factors alone are not expected to lead to radiogenic $^{87}Sr/^{86}Sr$ values that surpass the current maximum values for England and Wales (see below). However, it may perhaps lead to greater local variability in local Sr-isotope biosphere ranges. Interpretation of human strontium isotope results should therefore consider the potential effect of changes in the local distribution of ancient woodland over time on local bioavailable $^{87}Sr/^{86}Sr$ values (Johnson 2018, 228–31; Johnson *et al.* 2022). For example, it could be hypothesised that individuals at Penywyrlod and Ty Isaf who have $^{87}Sr/^{86}Sr$ values between 0.714–0.716 may have exploited areas in the local region that had been more heavily wooded than those who exhibit lower $^{87}Sr/^{86}Sr$ values, close to 0.713. Johnson argues that, as Penywyrlod and Ty Isaf are situated on Lower Devonian sedimentary bedrock, deforestation during the Neolithic might potentially explain the overall differences in values between the groups (Johnson 2018, 229–31).

However, this suggestion assumes there to be a difference in chronology between the individuals buried at the two sites. It should be remembered that only one of the individuals sampled from Penywyrlod has been directly dated. Although as shown in Chapter 4 modelling suggests that although Penywyrlod was indeed constructed at an early date, probably in the 38th century cal BC in *3770–3710 cal BC* (*68% probability; construct_Penywyrlod*, or *3780–3680 cal BC, 95% probability*), it was also in use for a long time. The last dated event associated with the use of the cairn for burial occurred in *3490–3210 cal BC* (*95% probability*), most probably in *3470–3300 cal BC* (*68% probability*; *last_primary_Penywyrlod*; see Chapter 4). It is therefore possible that some of the undated individuals from this site on whom strontium isotope analysis has been conducted, might actually be contemporary with those from Ty Isaf where all the individuals sampled post-date 3670 cal BC. In addition to this, as noted by Johnson, the highest value of 0.7137 previously recorded in modern plants by Neil *et al.* (2017; sample S-Wales 42) and used to define the maximum of the local bioavailable range around these sites, was a single occurrence. The average plant $^{87}Sr/^{86}Sr$ value for the local area is much lower (0.7107±0.0010, n= 12, 1σ). Since the original publication of the results from Penywyrlod and Ty Isaf, further biosphere sampling has also been undertaken across southern Wales. One sample of plants, which was taken in a woodland setting on Silurian sedimentary bedrock that lies close to Penywyrlod and Ty Isaf at Hell's Mouth, north-west of Boughrood, Powys, Wales, gave a high value of 0.71550 (Evans *et al.* 2019, sample USK-04). However, this does not represent the average for the area, with further values recorded in plants in this area being comparable to those already published (Jane Evans, *pers. comm.*).

Contrasts in values between those buried at Penywyrlod and Ty Isaf are indicative of differences in the landscape and environments that were used by the two groups, with the majority of individuals from Penywyrlod having higher, more radiogenic values, than those at Ty Isaf. Values exhibited by individuals at both Penywyrlod and Ty Isaf do, however, rule out their having obtained the majority of their diet on areas of Limestone and Chalk lithology, which is, for example, present across large areas of south-central England and is associated with much less radiogenic values (Warham 2011; J.A. Evans 2018).

As things currently stand, local biosphere data suggest that the majority of the individuals sampled at Penywyrlod obtained their diet beyond the immediate environs of the site. However, how far away they could have obtained these values is open to question. The possibility that individuals buried at Penywyrlod who have $^{87}Sr/^{86}Sr$ values of 0.714 obtained their diet from just beyond the immediate environs of the site, for example the Welsh Borderlands or Malvern Hills, cannot be ruled out. However, larger areas of geology further afield also provide biosphere values of 0.714 or higher and could equally be considered as sources for such values; individuals buried in passage graves in north-western France, for example, have also recorded comparable values to those found at Penywyrlod, which will be published in due course.

One of the individuals sampled at Penywyrlod (74.23H/9.2.3/P23), excavated from Chamber NE II and directly dated to 4888±37 BP (3770–3540 cal BC, 95% confidence, SUERC-63414, calibrated using IntCal20, OxCal v.4.4.4), has a strontium isotope ratio that exceeds 0.717. Since the original publication of the results in Neil *et al.* (2017), there is still no available evidence to suggest this value is bioavailable locally. It is not currently possible to attribute this value to the region. This enamel $^{87}Sr/^{86}Sr$ value of 0.717 remains higher than all currently known modern biosphere $^{87}Sr/^{86}Sr$ values in Wales. Following detailed investigation of radiogenic biospheres in Britain, Johnson (2018, 266–7, 270) proposes the maximum bioavailable $^{87}Sr/^{86}Sr$ value in England and Wales to be 0.716. She suggests that whilst the 'woodland effect', described above, could potentially elevate locally bioavailable values on some types of lithology, this effect is not expected to exceed this proposed maximum value (Johnson 2018, 263). Values of 0.716 have so far been encountered in only two samples of plants, taken around the Stanner-Hanter Complex near the Welsh border and in the Malvern Hills as described above (sample SHC L6, $^{87}Sr/^{86}Sr$ 0.71613, Johnson 2018, 127, 270, and sample G-V-026, $^{87}Sr/^{86}Sr$ 0.71622; Chenery *et al.* 2010, 155). Values of 0.716 remain difficult to reproduce on some of the oldest lithology in England and Wales, which may be expected to be associated with the most radiogenic values (Johnson 2018).

In contrast to the European mainland, bedrock lithology in Britain of an age and composition capable of conferring highly radiogenic biosphere values is spatially very limited (Johnson 2018, 263). It should also be remembered that isotope ratios in bulk enamel represent the average of the dietary strontium to which people were exposed during the period of tooth mineralisation (Montgomery 2010, 333). To get a value of 0.717 would necessitate use of an area of landscape, of sufficient size from which the individual could have obtained the majority of their diet and that consistently gave bioavailable $^{87}Sr/^{86}Sr$ values equivalent to or greater than 0.717. In Britain, radiogenic values greater than 0.716 are known to be bioavailable in a limited number of areas. Values between 0.716–0.718 are recorded on Grampian terrain in Scotland, which is dominated by Precambrian lithology. Here the most radiogenic values have been recorded in a small aureole around the base of the Cairngorm mountains, from samples of plants taken within the Cairngorms National Park (Johnson 2018, 144–73). It has not been possible to replicate radiogenic values greater than 0.720, that were previously reported from the same area by Evans *et al.* (2010), in this area (Johnson 2018). $^{87}Sr/^{86}Sr$ values 0.716–0.718 in enamel could, therefore, on the grounds of biosphere data alone, be attributable to this area. Although a considerable amount of biosphere data is now available across Britain (*e.g.* J.A. Evans 2018), one other area of lithology for which coverage has, until now, been limited is granite on Dartmoor in SW England. Plants growing in an area of granite here have also recorded comparable values (Gundula Müldner, *pers. comm.*).

On the basis of the present biosphere evidence, the value of 0.717 that the individual 74.23H/9.2.3/P23 at Penywyrlod exhibits therefore suggests that they obtained their childhood diet a significant distance from where they were buried. As noted above, on the grounds of current biosphere data alone, both Dartmoor in south-west England and Scotland might perhaps be potential source areas for biosphere values of 0.717. However, there may be difficulty in attributing the values exhibited by this particular individual to these areas due to current dating of the onset of the Neolithic in both regions. Previous modelling of radiocarbon dates suggests that Neolithic material culture and practices began to appear in the south-west peninsula of England and north-eastern Scotland in the decades around 3800 cal BC (Bayliss *et al.* 2011, 736, 822–4, 835–40). Reappraisal of dating models for the start of the Neolithic in these regions is currently underway (see Chapter 12), but currently published estimates suggest that Neolithic practices had only just become established in these regions at the time Penywyrlod long cairn was being constructed, probably in the 38th century cal BC, in *3770–3710 cal BC* (*68% probability construct_Penywyrlod*; *or 3780–3680 cal BC*, *95% probability*; Chapter 4).

As described in Chapter 4 (this volume), the most recent modelling of radiocarbon dates shows that individual 74.23H/9.2.3/P23 dates to very shortly after the first appearance of Neolithic material culture and practices in south Wales and the Marches, which most probably appeared in this region in *3840–3770 cal BC* (*68% probability*; *start_early_Neolithic_south_Wales_and_Marches*; *3880–3740 cal BC*; *95% probability*). The burial of this individual occurred shortly after evidence for occupation in the region, it being *90% probable* that occupation evidence proceeds construction of monuments (Chapter 4). The burial post-dates evidence for the earliest pre-cairn activities at the site, which most probably began in *3860–3760 cal BC* (*68% probability*; *start_Penywyrlod*; *3940–3730 cal BC 95% probability*; Chapter 4 this volume), although it is axiomatic perhaps that evidence for the activities of a living population, such as use of domestic cereals and other forms of portable material culture should necessarily proceed death and burial activity.

Importantly, the strontium isotope results rule out an origin for the value (0.717) from south-eastern England, where present modelling suggest that Neolithic material culture and practices were established earlier than other regions of Britain, in the 41st and 40th centuries BC (Whittle *et al.* 2011, 833; see also Whittle *et al.* 2022; Whittle *et al.* in press). All present evidence suggests that individual 74.23H/9.2.3/P23 at Penywyrlod could not have obtained the value of 0.717 from south-eastern or south-central England. Biosphere data also rule out an origin for this value on the immediately adjacent European mainland in that direction, in areas such as north-eastern France or the Netherlands (Kootker *et al.* 2016; Willmes *et al.* 2018).

The early Neolithic individual who is buried at Penywyrlod is not alone in exhibiting values that exceed 0.716. Multiple individuals within the burial group at Whitwell cairn, in central England, have also been found to have values between 0.717–0.721 (Neil *et al.* 2020; Fig. 7.2). As at Penywyrlod (Chapter 4, this volume), Bayesian modelling of radiocarbon dates suggests that Whitwell was also probably constructed during the 38th century BC (Griffiths 2011; Vyner and Wall 2011). Whilst the value of 0.717 found at Penywyrlod could, on the grounds of biosphere data alone, be attributable to a restricted number of areas within Britain (see above), based on detailed study of the biosphere evidence Johnson (2018, 266) suggests that it is not plausible to attribute $^{87}Sr/^{86}Sr$ values that are higher than 0.720 to the biosphere of Britain. In the case of Whitwell this is particularly problematic, as several individuals in this group have values of 0.720–0.721.

Other regions on the European mainland record biosphere $^{87}Sr/^{86}Sr$ values of 0.717 and above, including the Massif Central in France (Willmes *et al.* 2018), Portugal (James *et al.* 2022), Norway and Sweden (*e.g.* Price *et al.* 2015; Blank *et al.* 2018) and the Alps (*e.g.* Müller *et al.* 2003).

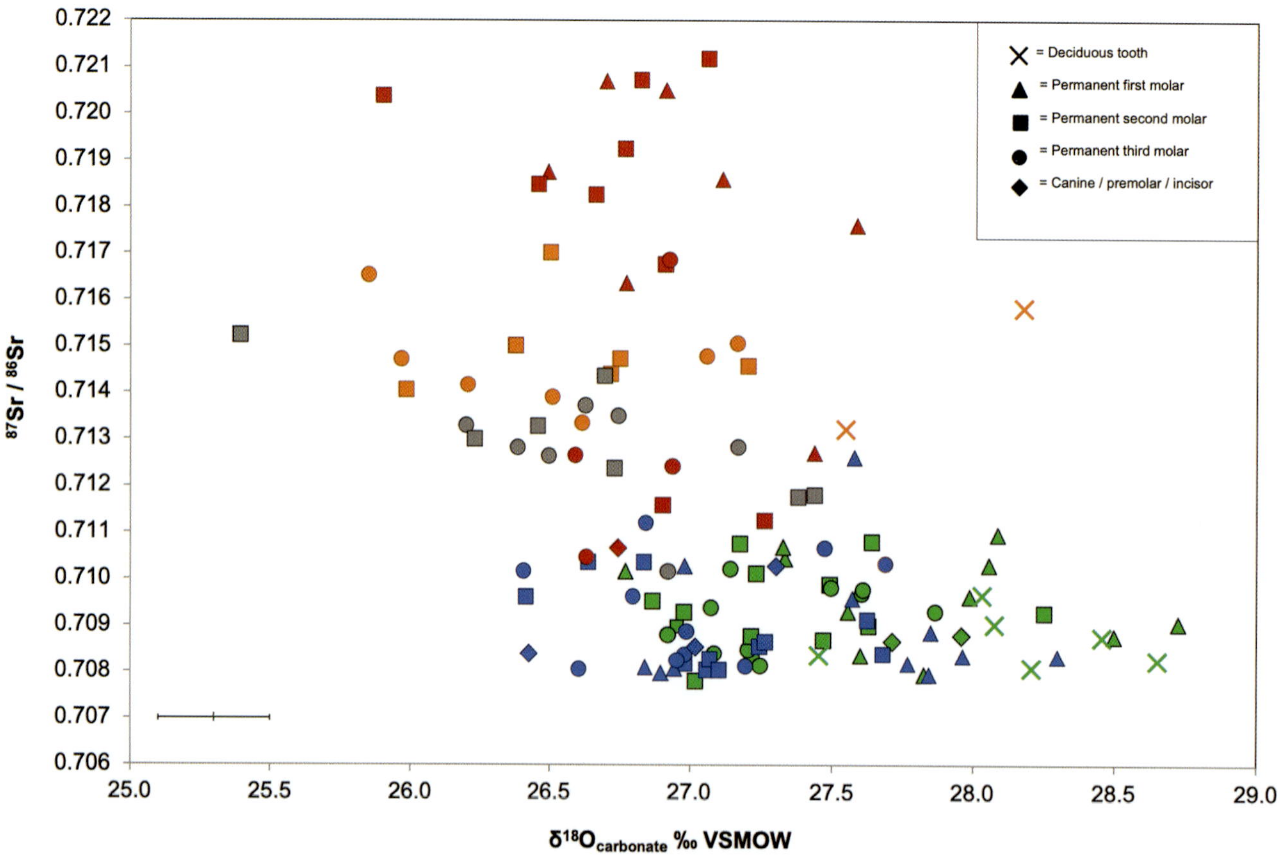

Fig. 7.2. Comparison of $^{87}Sr/^{86}Sr$ values versus measured $\delta^{18}O_{carbonate}$ VSMOW values in enamel from other early Neolithic burial groups excavated in England. ***Blue symbols*** *= Hazleton North long cairn (Gloucestershire, England, Neil* et al. *2016).* ***Green symbols*** *= Hambledon Hill (Dorset, England, Neil* et al. *2018).* ***Red symbols*** *= Whitwell cairn (Derbyshire, England, Neil* et al. *2020).* ***Grey symbols*** *= Ty Isaf.* ***Orange symbols*** *= Penywyrlod (Neil* et al. *2017; this chapter).*

However, these regions are not known to have Neolithic material culture similar to that found in Britain during the early 4th millennium cal BC. Oxygen isotope ratios values recorded at both Penywyrlod and Whitwell also contrast with those found in human burial populations in regions of cooler climate in Europe (*e.g.* Scandinavia: Chenery *et al.* 2014; Montgomery *et al.* 2014; Price and Naumann 2015; and the Alps: Müller *et al.* 2003). Here much lower values can be recorded ($\delta^{18}O_{carbonate}$ below approximately 24.5‰; $\delta^{18}O_{phosphate}$ below approximately 15.5‰).

Biosphere $^{87}Sr/^{86}Sr$ values comparable to those seen at Penywyrlod and Whitwell have been recorded in plants growing on the Armorican Massif within Lower Normandy and Brittany, in north-western France (Négrel and Pauwels 2004; Willmes *et al.* 2013; 2018). Connections between this particular region of the European mainland and Britain have been proposed on archaeological grounds (among others, see Sheridan 2010; Rowley-Conwy 2011; Pioffet 2015). This context is further discussed briefly in Chapter 12.

Radiocarbon dating indicates that the first few centuries of the 4th millennium cal BC were associated with the rapid spread of traditions and practices not previously present in Britain (Whittle *et al.* 2011). All these traditions and practices originate from the European mainland, including burial customs, construction of monuments, pottery manufacturing, material culture and new species of both animals and plants. Recent ancient DNA evidence demonstrates there was population movement from the European mainland to Britain during the early Neolithic (Brace *et al.* 2019). In the context of the range of other evidence for a high degree of mobility during the early Neolithic, strontium isotope results from both Penywyrlod and Whitwell that are higher than 0.717 appear to support arguments for movement of people over considerable distances during the first few centuries of the Neolithic. They may be interpreted to provide evidence for migration, the movement of people over long distances between different areas, during this period and the implications of this are followed further in Chapter 12. As always, however, the interpretation of $^{87}Sr/^{86}Sr$ results is based on the state of current evidence. It may in future be refined or altered, with production of further chronological and biosphere data.

8

Isotope evidence of human diets at four Neolithic chambered tombs in south Wales

Michael Richards

Introduction

Here the results are presented of dietary isotope analysis (carbon, nitrogen and sulphur) of bone collagen extracted from humans from four Neolithic tombs in south Wales. These sites are Penywyrlod and Ty Isaf in the Black Mountains, Heston Brake on the Severn, and Tinkinswood, close to present-day Cardiff in the Vale of Glamorgan. Also included are new isotope results from previously measured and published individuals from the Parc le Breos Cwm tomb on the Gower peninsula (Whittle *et al.* 1998).

These samples were taken from femurs from these tombs, as due to the very mixed contexts this was the best way to ensure that different individuals were sampled. These samples were first prepared and measured in 2000 using an older method that did not employ the use of ultrafiltration (Richards and Hedges 1999). Therefore, here we were able to re-process the extracted collagen to ultrafilter it (Brown *et al.* 1988), and then re-measure the isotope values of the ultrafiltered collagen using more accurate methods (namely the use of a 2-point calibration (Carter and Fry 2013)). We were also able to produce sulphur isotope measurements on the collagen using a new method and mass spectrometer equipment that allows simultaneous C, N and S measurements of relatively small amounts (1.5mg) of extracted collagen (Sayle *et al.* 2019). We were also able to measure, for the first time, sulphur isotope values from the previously published Parc le Breos Cwm samples.

Materials and methods

Isotope samples were collected from the four tombs at the National Museum and Galleries of Wales in 1999. Due to the nature of the burial practices, involving communal burials, and also the relative antiquity of some of the archaeological excavations, femurs were chosen as the best bone element to sample. This was to ensure that each sample represented a distinct individual, as only all left or all right femurs were sampled from each tomb, or in the cases where the femurs were clearly of different sizes and so from different individuals, both left and right femurs were sampled. The samples were taken as whole bone pieces, of approximately 500mg in size. Only previously damaged and broken femurs were sampled from the proximal or distal ends, and intact complete femurs were not sampled. Samples were selected with the guidance and advice of Michael Wysocki.

Samples were prepared at the Research Laboratory for Archaeology and the History of Art (RLAHA) at the University of Oxford. Extraction methods followed those outlined in Richards and Hedges (1999) where whole bone was demineralised in 0.5M HCl at 5°C, then gelatinised, filtered and freeze-dried. In 2021 we were able, where collagen remained, to re-hydrate the collagen and then ultrafilter it using 30 kDa filters (Brown *et al.* 1988).

The isotope values of the collagen were first measured at the RLAHA using a Europa 20/20 mass spectrometer with a Europa ANCA Roboprep elemental analyser. These samples of approximately 3mg in size were measured alongside a known-value secondary solid standard (a nylon standard), which was used to calibrate the data. Errors on these measurements are ±0.3‰ for carbon and ±0.4‰ for nitrogen.

In 2021 the collagen (where enough remained) was ultrafiltered and freeze-dried and then the isotope values of carbon, nitrogen and sulphur were measured at the Archaeology Isotope Laboratory at the Department of Archaeology, Simon Fraser University, Canada. The measurements were made using a Thermo Flash IRMS coupled to a Thermo Delta V gas isotope ratio mass spectrometer and the samples were calibrated using 2-point calibration and secondary and primary standards. Using the methods outlined in Sayle *et al.* (2019), we routinely simultaneously measure the carbon, nitrogen and sulphur isotope values of 1.5mg collagen samples. The errors on these measurements are ±0.1‰ for carbon, ±0.2‰ for nitrogen and ±0.5‰ for sulphur.

The use of bulk collagen carbon and nitrogen isotope values as palaeodietary indictors is a well-established method (Makarewicz and Sealy 2015; Britton 2017; Richards 2020). The collagen carbon and nitrogen isotope values are linked to the carbon and nitrogen isotope values of protein consumed over a number of years, and so present a long-term average of the sources of dietary protein, whereas the consumption of high calorie macronutrients such as fats and carbohydrates (from alcohol, for example) are unlikely to influence the bulk collagen isotope values. Further refinements of this method (compound-specific isotope analysis (Choy *et al.* 2010; Styring *et al.* 2010; Honch *et al.* 2012) use isotope measurements of single amino acids as a way to have a better idea of total diet and more refined trophic level determination, but for this study we only used bulk values that are indicators of dietary protein sources. The collagen carbon isotope values can distinguish between the consumption of marine and terrestrial proteins, and the nitrogen isotope values are used to determine the trophic position of humans (*i.e.* closer to herbivores or carnivores, therefore the relative amount of animal vs. plant protein in diets). The use of collagen nitrogen isotopes as a trophic level indicator does rely on the production of a local and contemporary isotope baseline using nitrogen isotope values of faunal remains. This is because the nitrogen values can vary between different regions, especially between arid and temperate environments. So, it is not usually possible to determine trophic position with only human isotope values and not having faunal values with which to compare them.

Sulphur isotope values in bone collagen are used as an indicator of the ecological and geographical source of the main proteins in diets (Nehlich 2015). The sulphur values can then be a dietary indicator (in concert with carbon and nitrogen isotope values), as freshwater and marine foods often have much different sulphur isotope values than terrestrial foods. Different geographical regions also have different baseline sulphur isotope values (analogous to strontium isotope values) so if the baseline sulphur values of a region are known, it may be possible to find 'migrants' in an area if some humans have very different sulphur isotope values compared to the local sulphur baseline values.

Results

The isotope data from the extracted bone collagen are presented in Table 8.1. Both the carbon and nitrogen measurements on non-ultrafiltered collagen from 2000 and the new carbon, nitrogen and sulphur isotope values from the same collagen extracts but ultrafiltered and re-measured in 2021 are presented.

On average the carbon isotope values differ between the 2000 and 2021 measurements by 0.4‰, and the nitrogen isotope values differ by an average of 0.6‰. So, although these differences are not substantial, especially considering the larger measurement errors on the 2000 measurements, only the new 2021 values measured on ultrafiltered collagen and with a two-point correction should be used going forward. It is worth noting, however, that both the 2000 and 2021 measurements do not have values indicating any significant amount of marine protein in diets (as will be discussed in more detail below). And all of the measured values (2000 and 2021) had collagen with C:N ratios in the acceptable range of 2.9 to 3.6 (Guiry and Szpak 2020).

The 2021 ultrafiltered carbon and nitrogen collagen values are shown in Figure 8.1, the carbon and sulphur values are plotted in Figure 8.2, and the nitrogen and sulphur values in Figure 8.3.

Discussion

The carbon isotope values show that all the humans studied had diets that were terrestrial in nature, and despite the relatively close proximity to the sea of three of the tombs (Heston Brake, Tinkinswood and Parc le Breos Cwm), there was no evidence of any measurable amounts of marine food consumption in any of the human isotope values. As collagen carbon isotope measurements indicate the main sources of dietary *protein* over many years, any fats or carbohydrates that may have originated from marine sources would not be detected. However, it would be unlikely that Neolithic humans would have processed marine foods to a large extent only for fats and not consumed marine protein (*i.e.* flesh) at the same time.

As we did not measure any animal samples from these tombs themselves, we were unable to produce a faunal nitrogen isotope baseline from these same sites for interpreting the human nitrogen isotope values. However, we can compare these human results to those of animals from other UK sites at this time. In a large-scale study of herbivore (cattle, horse, deer) isotope values in Holocene and late Pleistocene UK and north-western Europe, Richards and Hedges (2003) found that in middle Holocene UK herbivores had an average δ^{15}N value of approximately 6±1‰. Herbivores (red deer, sheep/goat, cattle) from Mesolithic and Neolithic contexts in Wales had an average δ^{15}N value of 4.9‰ (Schulting and Richards 2002). Using these average values for fauna we can see that the humans from all of our sites have much higher δ^{15}N values and using an offset of 3 to 5‰ between diet and bone collagen δ^{15}N (the 'trophic-level effect'), we can conclude that animal protein was an important part of Neolithic diets, from either meat or milk products. Indeed, there is evidence from pottery residue studies (Copley *et al.*

Table 8.1. Human bone collagen carbon, nitrogen and isotope data from various Neolithic long cairns in south Wales.

S-SFU	Sample number	$\delta^{13}C$ (2000)	$\delta^{15}N$ (2000)	NEW $\delta^{13}C$	NEW $\delta^{15}N$	NEW $\delta^{34}S$	NEW %C	NEW %N	NEW %S	NEW C:N	NEW C:S	Collagen yield %
Penywyrlod												
2653	P-1	-21.3	7.8	-21.3	8.4	16.4	41.9	15.0	0.2	3.3	701.2	4.9
2654	P-2	-20.9	8.1	-20.9	8.8	14.5	40.3	15.1	0.1	3.1	800.4	8.0
2655	P-3	-20.9	7.7	-21.3	8.4	15.8	31.0	11.9	0.1	3.0	652.3	9.5
2656	P-4	-21.3	8.9	-21.4	9.7	15.5	34.9	13.0	0.1	3.1	676.7	7.6
2657	P-5	-21.3	9.2	-21.3	9.9	15.8	31.1	11.9	0.1	3.1	753.6	8.6
2658	P-6	-20.7	7.9	-20.9	8.7	14.4	39.1	14.7	0.2	3.1	649.6	8.4
2659	P-7	-20.9	7.5	-20.9	8.1	15.7	41.9	15.4	0.2	3.2	653.8	12.3
Tinkinswood												
2660	Ti-1	-20.9	7.4	-20.7	8.1	13.7	43.2	15.7	0.2	3.2	692.8	13.8
2661	Ti-2	-20.8	8.1	-20.7	8.8	11.5	41.1	15.2	0.2	3.2	710.3	16.0
2662	Ti-3	-20.5	8.9	-20.7	9.6	12.4	35.3	13.2	0.2	3.1	552.8	6.3
2663	Ti-4	-20.8	8.8	-20.8	9.6	14.1	39.1	14.2	0.1	3.2	699.8	5.2
2664	Ti-5	-20.9	9.2	-21.0	9.8	16.3	44.2	16.0	0.1	3.2	860.9	18.6
2665	Ti-6	-20.8	8.2	-20.7	9.1	13.9	45.8	16.3	0.2	3.3	689.1	10.0
2666	Ti-7	-20.9	9.1	-20.7	9.7	13.9	45.5	16.4	0.2	3.2	775.6	20.4
2667	Ti-8	-20.8	8.7	-20.7	9.4	14.1	41.6	15.1	0.2	3.2	707.9	14.6
Ty Isaf												
2668	TY-1	-21.7	9.0	–	–	–	–	–	–	–	–	6.0
2669	TY-2	-20.7	8.0	–	–	–	–	–	–	–	–	3.0
2670	TY-3	-21.0	9.3	-20.8	9.9	13.9	43.6	15.3	0.2	3.3	669.7	8.6
2671	TY-4	-21.5	9.1	-21.8	10.0	14.3	38.7	14.9	0.2	3.0	501.1	17.5
2672	TY-5	-21.0	7.9	-22.2	8.6	16.4	44.2	15.0	0.2	3.4	668.3	7.4
2673	TY-6	-21.3	8.9	-22.5	9.5	13.7	42.4	15.2	0.2	3.2	736.9	11.5
2674	TY-7	-20.8	8.2	–	–	–	–	–	–	–	–	7.7
2675	TY-8	-21.4	9.2	–	–	–	–	–	–	–	–	3.0
2676	TY-9	-20.9	8.0	-22.0	8.6	16.5	43.7	15.4	0.2	3.3	729.7	11.2
Heston Brake												
2677	H-1	-20.3	9.8	–	–	–	–	–	–	–	–	6.3
2678	H-2	-20.3	10.4	-20.9	11.2	14.9	46.2	15.0	0.2	3.6	756.8	3.3
2679	H-3	-20.7	10.2	-21.2	11.0	14.1	22.6	8.6	0.1	3.1	443.1	12.9
2680	H-4	-20.9	10.1	-21.5	10.9	13.7	21.3	8.0	0.1	3.1	526.2	7.1
Parc le Breos Cwm												
2681	PA7922	-19.5	10.0	–	–	–	–	–	–	–	–	–
2682	PA7924	-19.7	9.8	–	–	–	–	–	–	–	–	–
2683	PA7925	-21.1	9.6	-21.1	9.7	17.7	27.6	10.5	0.1	3.1	714.0	–
2684	PA7926	-19.6	10.4	-21.5	10.1	12.7	24.3	9.8	0.1	2.9	490.3	–
2685	PA7927	-20.5	9.2	–	–	–	–	–	–	–	–	–
2686	PA7928	-21.6	8.9	-22.0	8.9	11.2	15.1	5.9	0.1	3.0	390.8	–
2687	PA7930	-22.1	9.7	–	–	–	–	–	–	–	–	–
2688	PA7932	-19.5	9.8	-21.9	9.8	13.2	22.8	9.1	0.1	2.9	478.6	–

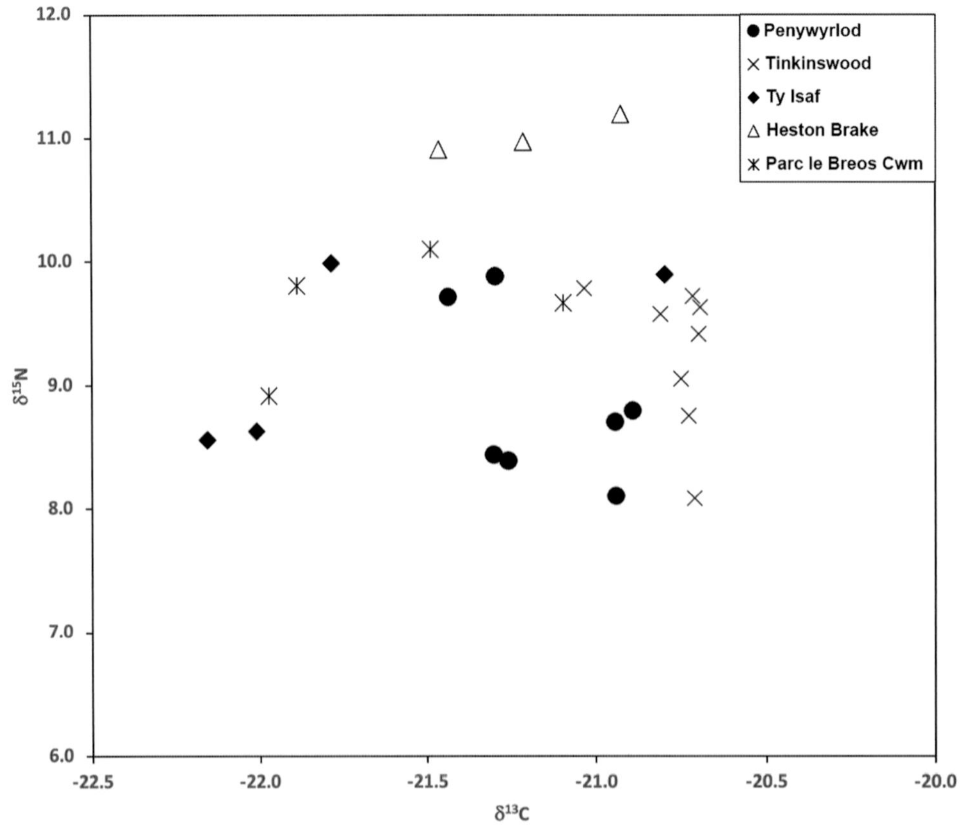

Fig. 8.1. Carbon and nitrogen isotope values from ultrafiltered human bone collagen from various early Neolithic long cairns in south Wales.

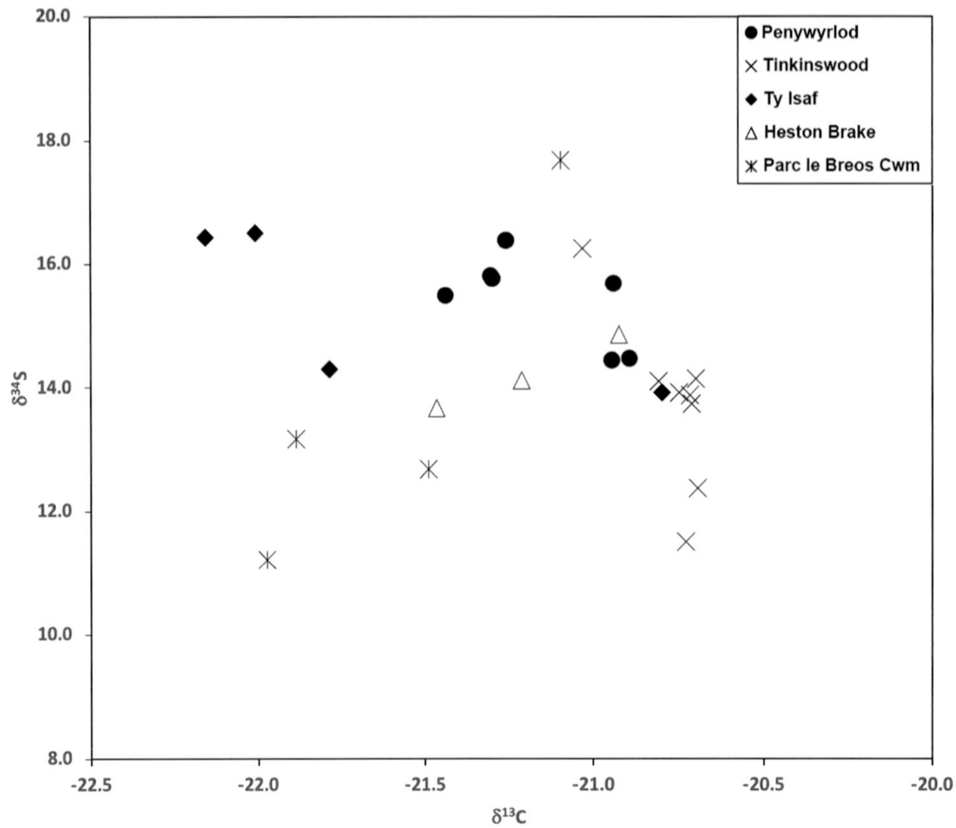

Fig. 8.2. Carbon and sulphur isotope values from ultrafiltered human bone collagen from various early Neolithic long cairns in south Wales.

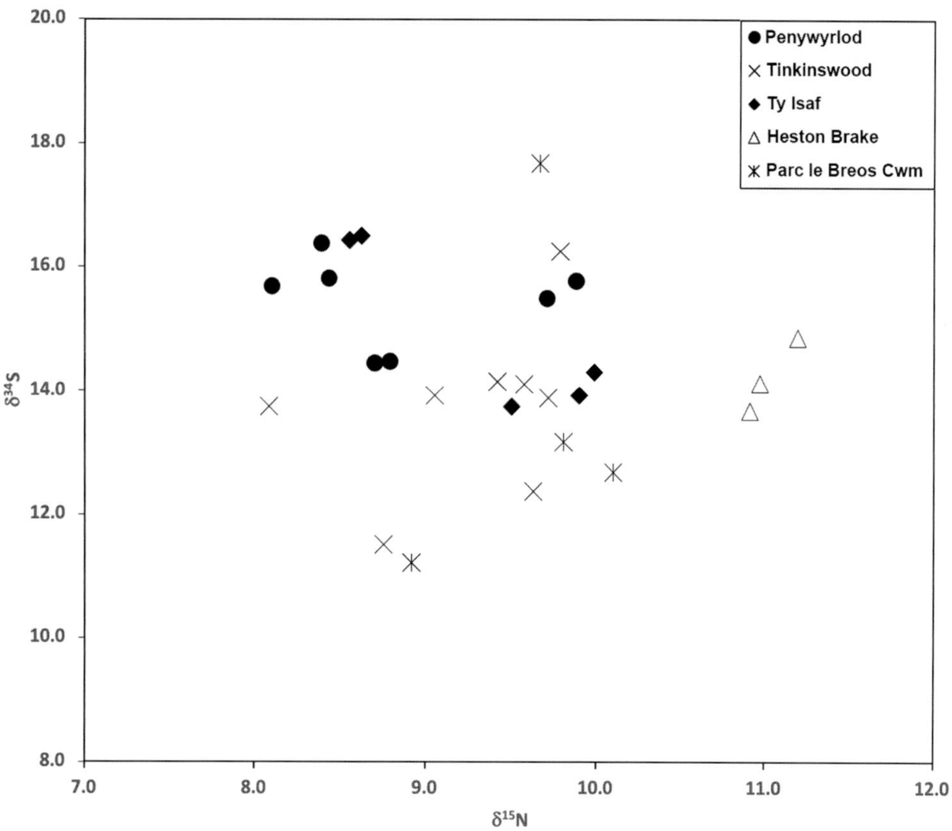

Fig. 8.3. Nitrogen and sulphur isotope values from ultrafiltered human bone collagen from various early Neolithic long cairns in south Wales.

2003; Cramp *et al.* 2014) for dairying at this time period, and the isotope evidence would support the importance of milk proteins in Neolithic diets. The residue analysis (compound-specific analysis of carbon in lipids) of pottery from the pre-cairn assemblage at the nearby site of Gwernvale by Isabel Wiltshire and Lucy Cramp (Chapter 11) found that they were used to store and process dairy products. Although Gwernvale dates to slightly later than the four tombs discussed here, the important results from the pottery residue analysis shows that dairy foods were present and likely an important part of the Neolithic economy. The human bone collagen isotope values could be interpreted as indicating a diet high in dairy products, although as noted a high amount of animal protein intake from meat would also produce similar isotope values.

Of note are the $\delta^{15}N$ values from Heston Brake which are higher than those of the other sites. Rather than this being due to a dietary difference it is likely that there is a baseline difference in $\delta^{15}N$ values between the area of this site and that of the others, due to the location of Heston Brake along the Severn. It has been noted that animals grazing in estuarine environments, and specifically salt marshes along the Severn, can have elevated $\delta^{15}N$ values compared to fauna from non-estuarine/non-salt marsh contexts (Britton *et al.* 2008). It is likely that this is the cause of the relatively elevated human $\delta^{15}N$ values at Heston Brake, with the humans buried here having consumed meat and/or milk from animals grazed in the surrounding estuarine salt marsh environment.

The Neolithic dietary isotope results presented here fit into a larger pattern of diets in the Neolithic across the UK, where there is little, if any, isotope evidence for the significant consumption of marine proteins in the Neolithic, in contrast to the frequent dominance of marine protein in coastal late Mesolithic sites (Richards *et al.* 2003; Schulting 2018). This is a pattern also seen in Wales itself (Schulting and Richards 2002; Schulting 2020). This points to the importance of terrestrial foods, most likely domesticated plants (Treasure *et al.* 2019) and animals, as being the dominant food sources in Neolithic diets in south Wales.

The sulphur isotope values can also be used as dietary indicators. For the dietary analysis, sulphur can be used with carbon and nitrogen to detect, for example, significant human consumption of freshwater foods (*i.e.* at the Iron Gates Gorge region of south-eastern Europe in the Mesolithic and Neolithic periods (Nehlich *et al.* 2010)). The sulphur data here do not show any measurable amounts of freshwater protein in the diets, especially when we compare the carbon and nitrogen values to the sulphur values (Figs 8.2 and 8.3). If, for example, the Heston Brake humans had higher nitrogen isotope values compared to the other humans because of the consumption of freshwater fish, we should see a difference in the sulphur isotope values, as freshwater contexts mainly have different baseline $\delta^{34}S$ values than surrounding terrestrial environments.

Sulphur isotope values can also be used to identify potential migrants to a region. As with the nitrogen values (and analogous to strontium isotope analysis), it is important to produce baseline sulphur values for each region of interest using faunal remains, but this was not possible here. If we look at the geographical location of the tombs, the humans from the Black Mountains region (Penywyrlod and Ty Isaf) all have similar values and this is likely within the 'local' sulphur isotope range for this region. Further south at Tinkinswood, Heston Brake and Parc le Breos Cwm most of the humans have lower sulphur values than the Black Mountain humans, with a few exceptions such as one individual from Parc le Breos who has the highest sulphur value of all (S-SFU 2683, $d^{34}S$=17.7‰).

It is unfortunate that only femurs were sampled for this isotope study, and not crania or mandibles with teeth, as then we could have compared the sulphur values with the strontium and oxygen isotope values for Penywyrlod and Ty Isaf presented in Neil *et al.* (2017; and see Chapter 7). Due to the commingled nature of the remains we cannot link the femurs with the same individuals' crania or mandibles, so we cannot present sulphur and strontium/oxygen data for the same individuals studied by Neil *et al.* (2017). Neil *et al.* (2017; and Chapter 7 here) found one individual at Penywyrold (74.23H/9.2.3/P23) with a relatively high strontium isotope value indicating a childhood location from outside of this region. The sulphur values presented here from Penywyrlod and Ty Isaf are all relatively similar to each other (within a 3‰ range), so there is no evidence of recent migrants from a region with differing sulphur isotope values. Again, however, the different periods of life that these elements are measuring should be noted, with the sulphur values indicating the source of foods in the last decade or so of life, whereas enamel strontium and oxygen indicate childhood location.

Neil *et al.* (2017) found that the Penywyrlod individuals whom they measured did not source their childhood diets locally, but those from the later site of Ty Isaf did. This interpretation has been revised in this volume (Chapter 7) as there are new environmental strontium data available for this region. The newer conclusion is that at both sites, childhood diets could have been sourced in the region, although there remains a difference in the strontium values between Penywyrold and Ty-Isaf that could indicate the use of different landscapes (*i.e.* woodland or more open areas). The dietary isotope data presented here did not show any differences in the isotope values between these two sites, but it should be noted that the isotope values are from adult femurs, which record adult diets over the last decade of life, so childhood diets would not be represented in the collagen carbon, nitrogen and sulphur values. The implications of these findings are discussed further in Chapter 12.

Conclusions

Collagen carbon, nitrogen and sulphur isotope values were presented for humans from five Neolithic tombs from south Wales. The isotope values were relatively similar within and between all sites and indicate diets where the main protein sources were coming from terrestrial foods, mainly animal products (meat and milk) and plants. The lack of marine foods in the diets is consistent with what has been previously found for most of the Neolithic in the UK, and contrasts with the largely marine-based diets of coastal humans in the late Mesolithic period. The sulphur isotope analysis did not identify any clear migrants in any of the tombs, but this method requires the future production of more regional baseline sulphur values to better interpret them as geographical indicators. It is hoped that in the future these studies will be a starting point for more detailed dietary studies using compound-specific isotope analysis, and also for mobility studies using sulphur, especially when these can be measured in the same individuals where enamel strontium and oxygen isotopes are also measured.

Acknowledgements

Rebecca MacDonald, Megan Wong and Helene le Cordier are thanked for their assistance with sample preparation and measurements. Thanks also to Alasdair Whittle and Michael Wysocki for support and help with this project.

9

Gwernvale: a review of some of the lithic artefacts

Elizabeth A. Walker

Introduction

Excavations at the Gwernvale Neolithic Severn-Cotswold tomb between 1977 and 1978 recovered over 2,000 knapped pieces of stone and an additional 12,000 plus chips and spalls representative of knapping activities from an intensive programme of sieving (Healey and Green 1984, 114). This substantive assemblage was analysed by Elizabeth Healey and Stephen Green who identified a range of tools diagnostic of late Upper Palaeolithic to the early Bronze Age dates (Healey and Green 1984).

It is not the purpose of this review to offer a comprehensive and full report of the assemblage, as the detailed analysis provided in 1984 largely still stands and does not require repeating. Instead, I will take the original work further by examining elements of it in more detail and will address new questions that have arisen in the years since its preparation and publication. The new analysis will look in detail at all the tools originally identified in the 1984 report and also at specific contexts in some detail. I have not re-examined all the chips, spalls or the general knapping debitage.

Focus of the reassessment

This report looks at some of the pre-cairn assemblage, focusing on a reassessment of those lithic artefacts originally deemed to be Upper Palaeolithic in age. It also takes the Mesolithic lithic component identified by Healey and Green and provides a new review of these artefacts. Some classes of tool are examined in detail, namely the abruptly backed blades, microliths, burins and scrapers, with a view to establishing whether any more nuanced comments may be offered about the dating of these particular tools. This reassessment ties to the reassessment of pre-cairn Neolithic activity in Chapter 3 and work undertaken on the plant remains of Mesolithic and Neolithic date from buried soils by Astrid Caseldine in Chapter 5. Comparisons are also drawn with the pre-cairn assemblages from a number of other key Neolithic Cotswold-Severn tombs where pre-cairn Mesolithic activity is also present, to determine whether the pattern represented by the assemblage and dating of Gwernvale is unique or not. The review concludes with a brief exploration of the concept of persistence, looking at the persistent places theories that have been developed since the mid-1990s around sites and monuments in the British landscape. Implications are followed further in Chapter 12.

Contexts

The artefacts that were reassessed in this review came primarily from buried soils below the Gwernvale cairn (contexts 28, 30, 92) and in the area of the forecourt (contexts 95, 202). With few exceptions (contexts 223, 26, 227, 286), material from pre-cairn features was not generally re-examined.

For the sake of consistency, the distributions of tool types and debitage shown in Figures 9.7–9.9 are restricted to the areas of sieved buried soils (context 30) below the cairn and in the forecourt (contexts 95, 202). The buried soils in these areas were excavated in a series of spits on the basis of a $1m^2$ grid. The total volume of soils was wet-sieved and residues sorted for the recovery of finds as well as charred plant remains.

The soil layer below the cairn (context 30) was up to 130mm thick. A lower soil layer in the forecourt (context 202), up to about 70mm thick, appeared to be continuous with the buried soil below the cairn. A darker upper soil layer (context 95) in the forecourt of the tomb was between about 60–100mm thick, though it is unresolved whether this represents a deposit that accumulated within the forecourt or in a Neolithic timber structure pre-dating the tomb. No stratification was observed in buried soils below the tomb and both these and the soils in the forecourt had evidently been thoroughly disturbed in antiquity at least in part by the digging of shallow pits and scoops in addition to the structural features belonging to the timber structure with, in some instances, diagnostic early Mesolithic, late Mesolithic and Neolithic tool types occurring in the same spits. (As noted in Chapter 3, we use a bipartite periodisation of the Mesolithic, simpler than the scheme proposed by Conneller (2022).) Consequently, there is no means of separating out the different assemblages on stratigraphic grounds and most of the lithic waste knapping debitage cannot be assigned to a particular period. Likewise, no particular foci of activity at different periods have been identified.

An Upper Palaeolithic presence at Gwernvale?

Healey and Green's review of the Gwernvale lithic assemblage recorded seven Upper Palaeolithic abruptly backed blades and suggested that all the flakes and blades of chalcedonic chert and some burins, scrapers and ground-edged pieces potentially might also belong to the same Palaeolithic industry (Healey and Green 1984, 129).

The attribution of the abruptly backed blades to the Upper Palaeolithic was later questioned by Alan Saville in his review of the Gwernvale publication (Saville 1985, 343). He doubted the presence of Upper Palaeolithic material at Gwernvale, suggesting that the seven tools could reasonably be considered to be Mesolithic and would sit comfortably in an assemblage of such date (Saville 1985, 343). Since these questions were raised a further review was undertaken by the author (E. Walker 2015). This work only examined the seven abruptly backed points, without considering the rest of the assemblage. The conclusions were left open, suggesting that an Upper Palaeolithic date for them was possible (E. Walker 2015, 118). It is therefore timely for a fuller review to consider the question of whether or not any of these finds really are Upper Palaeolithic. To achieve this, the wider assemblage has now been examined, rather than relying on scrutiny of just the handful of abruptly backed tools previously attributed an Upper Palaeolithic date by Healey and Green.

In the original report, the seven abruptly backed blades were described as backed tools of indiscernible type, with the exception of one piece that was classified as a penknife point (Fig. 9.1, no. 18) (context 202, find no. 2657; NMW acc. no. 79.54H/2.5; Healey and Green 1984, 121). This was classified using John Campbell's typology as type AC23; an oblique truncation with continual, or nearly continual, convex backing on the opposite edge forming a point at both ends (J. Campbell 1977, vol. 2, 4). The possible penknife point was described as having straight backing on one edge and a small area of retouch along the otherwise unmodified edge towards a point of the tool (Healey and Green 1984, 121). The location of the retouch on this tool makes it possible that this is a penknife point. There are, however, other potential explanations for it. It could be an area of steep leading-edge retouch on a microlith. Alternatively, it could be a fragment of an awl or piercing tool. A scan of any publication with sufficient illustrations of early Mesolithic microliths will depict forms with retouch along one edge and an oblique truncation. It is inevitable that microliths, as indeed other tools, may not necessarily always conform to the perfect form or shape that are illustrated in key publications as typical or standard for that tool. There may be a need to trim the point of the tool, particularly so if the original blade it is made on has any irregularities, or if the knapper has chosen to work the proximal, rather than the distal end of the blade. Parallels can be found for this particular shaped tool that are Mesolithic in date at Iping, Surrey (Reynier 2005, 14) or amongst the rhomboid forms from Thatcham III, Berkshire (Reynier 2005, 55). In Wales parallels can be found amongst the assemblage from Trwyn Du, Anglesey (R. White 1978, 38), and at Valley Field, Caldey Island, Pembrokeshire (E. Walker 2016, 29). Scrutiny of classic penknife points and comparisons with those recorded from Wales at Priory Farm Cave, Pembrokeshire, Nanna's Cave and Potter's Cave, Caldey Island, Pembrokeshire, all show that these tend to be broader in width than the Gwernvale example (E. Walker 2016, 14–16). The dimensions of the Gwernvale tool are therefore slightly smaller than penknife points from other Welsh sites. Direct comparison is hampered, however, by the fact that the Gwernvale tool is a short mesial fragment which is 12.6mm wide, and just 18.4mm long, but on balance there is a case to be made that this tool could well be of early Mesolithic age.

Tool, Figure 9.1, no. 19 (context 92, find no. 1142; NMW acc. no. 79.54H/2.1054; Healey and Green 1984, 118) was earlier reclassified as a fragment of an obliquely blunted point form of microlith and not Upper Palaeolithic in age (E. Walker 2015, 118). It is burnt and is made on the distal end of a blade. The tool is 9.6mm wide and is of certain early Mesolithic age. Tool, Figure 9.1, no. 20 (context 28, find. no. 1580; NMW acc. no. 79.54H/2.4; Healey and Green 1984, 118) is also a burnt mesial fragment of a tool with abrupt backing. It has an angled back on one edge, and is very small in size, just 19mm long and 9.8mm wide. There is a striking similarity between this tool and Figure 9.1, no. 36 (context 223, find no. 3127; NMW acc. no. 79.54H/2.858) which Healey and Green published as a broad-blade microlith. Why these two near identical tools were classified so differently is unclear, a fact that could support Saville's observation that to attribute any of these tools to an Upper Palaeolithic age can be called into question (Saville 1985, 343). Neither of these tools is sufficiently complete to be deemed an Upper Palaeolithic abruptly backed blade, rather

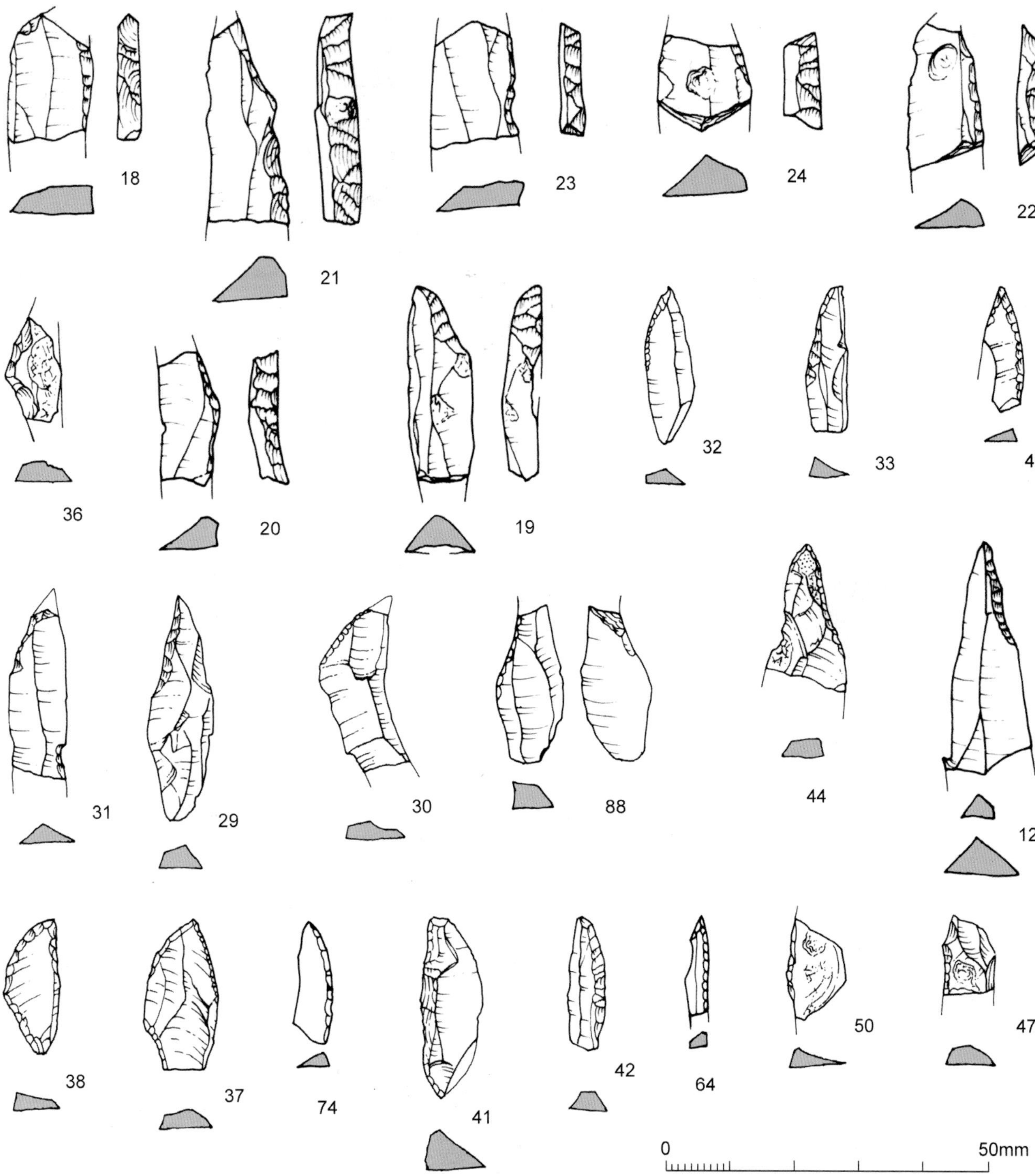

Fig. 9.1. Gwernvale: early Mesolithic microliths (numbering after Healey and Green 1984).

than a Mesolithic microlith fragment. If Mesolithic, as is suggested here, then both tools would sit well within the class of geometric microliths, such as isosceles or scalene triangle forms (for examples, see illustrations in David and Walker 2004, 304–305).

Figure 9.1, no. 21 (context 202, find no. 3073; NMW acc. no. 79.54H/2.6; Healey and Green 1984, 118) is also published as a mesial fragment of an abruptly backed blade. This piece has a 'shoulder' which gives it the appearance of having a deliberate angle knapped along one edge. On close examination it would seem that this was not intentional as heavy trimming around its edge suggests attempts to remove it. If this angle was unintentional then the tool can be classified as an early Mesolithic obliquely blunted point fragment. Both the ends are missing and the fragment that survives is 30mm long and 11.7mm wide, placing it within the range considered acceptable for an early Mesolithic age (Stanton 1984, 50). Three further small, burnt, mesial fragments have also been considered to be Upper Palaeolithic, however, these may also be considered as Mesolithic mid-sections of microliths with abruptly backed edges (Fig. 9.1 no. 23; context 95, find no. 1649, NMW acc. no. 79.54H/2.7; Fig. 9.1 no. 22; context 28, find no. 796, NMW 79.54H/2.853; and Fig. 9.1 no. 24; context 28, find no. 855 NMW 79.54H/2.855). All three tools could comfortably fall within the ranges for either a late Upper Palaeolithic or early Mesolithic age, but given that all of these pieces are such small fragments, it is not easy to say definitively one way or the other.

The seven tools classified as abruptly backed points by Healey and Green have average widths of 11.3mm whilst for those they classed as obliquely blunted points this is 8.3mm. These seven tools have apparently been separated in part, because of their greater width (Healey and Green 1984, 129). However, it is very difficult to resolve such matters on dimensions alone as we remain unable to determine exactly what amount of variation is acceptable within the size ranges of Mesolithic tool typologies within site assemblages (E. Walker 2015, 118). Healey and Green's analysis is based on the sample present in the assemblage and is reliant on their original identifications of the pieces, some of which this re-analysis has changed; this suggests that some of the tools are of different types or ages. This lends further doubt to the validity of this method of assessment. It therefore becomes necessary to turn attention to examine other tool types, in particular the burins and the scrapers, to establish whether or not the variation within these tools may make it possible to say whether or not any other tools in the assemblage are Upper Palaeolithic in age or not.

Burins (Fig. 9.2)

Burins are mostly found in Upper Palaeolithic and Mesolithic assemblages, but have been recorded in some Neolithic assemblages, such as Hurst Fen (Clark 1960, 223–224) and at Mynydd Rhiw (Houlder 1961, 132). The distinction between the different burin forms can be difficult to determine typologically and it remains tricky to identify any clear definitions for burins for each age. The literature all too often relies upon context for the separation of burins of Upper Palaeolithic and Mesolithic ages. Indeed, it becomes hard to locate assemblages that are mixed between periods with analysts tending to allocate tools to one period or the other. What is clear is that the burin is a ubiquitous tool in and amongst Late Glacial assemblages such as Hengistbury Head (Barton 1992) and their use continues on into the Mesolithic, where sites such as Nab Head and Star Carr contain a range of burin forms (David 2007, 101–104; Milner *et al.* 2018). Their presence in some, but not all, Mesolithic assemblages appears to depend on the nature of the assemblage.

Analysis of the Gwernvale burins suggests that a number of forms are present in the assemblage. Classification of these here loosely follows John Campbell's definitions with enhancements adopted from the definitions used by Nick Barton (J. Campbell 1977; Barton 1992). The resulting list is as follows:

Single angle burin on a prepared truncation	3
Dihedral asymmetrical burin	1
Dihedral symmetrical burin	2
Double angle burin on a break	3
Single angle burin	2
Possible burin fragments	4

Some other pieces previously classified in the original publication as burins have been reclassified in this analysis as general debitage. This is usually because they are too fragmentary and show ambiguities from the standard forms of burins.

The distinction between Late Glacial, early or late Mesolithic burins makes their separation difficult, and almost impossible, in the absence of any other dating or contextual evidence that can pin-point individual tools to phasing in ways that has been achieved for other sites, such as Hengistbury Head (Barton 1992), Star Carr (Milner *et al.* 2018) or Nab Head (David 2007). The possibility of separating the burins chronologically is therefore deemed to be impossible here and there is as much probability that they should be considered Mesolithic as of any other age.

Scrapers (Fig. 9.3)

Attempts to separate the scrapers chronologically by typology are often frustrated by the fact that, like the burins, there are many scraper forms which change little over time. The Gwernvale scrapers are quite varied in their forms, making it possible to create some distinctions, but there are forms represented that continue to be made from the Upper Palaeolithic into the Mesolithic. This new analysis of the scrapers from Gwernvale has identified a number of classic end-scrapers. These are traditionally found on both Upper Palaeolithic and Mesolithic sites. The general distinction that is often made is that Upper Palaeolithic assemblages tend to be dominated by a blade technology with scrapers often made on the end of blades, whereas Mesolithic groups may utilise flakes as well as blades for their scrapers. However, the presence of an end-scraper on a blade is not necessarily an indication of an Upper Palaeolithic age, as may be attested by the quantity of end-scrapers found at early Mesolithic sites including Nab Head, Daylight Rock and Palmerston Farm in Pembrokeshire (David 2007, 64, 78, 102). The Gwernvale assemblage has already been noted

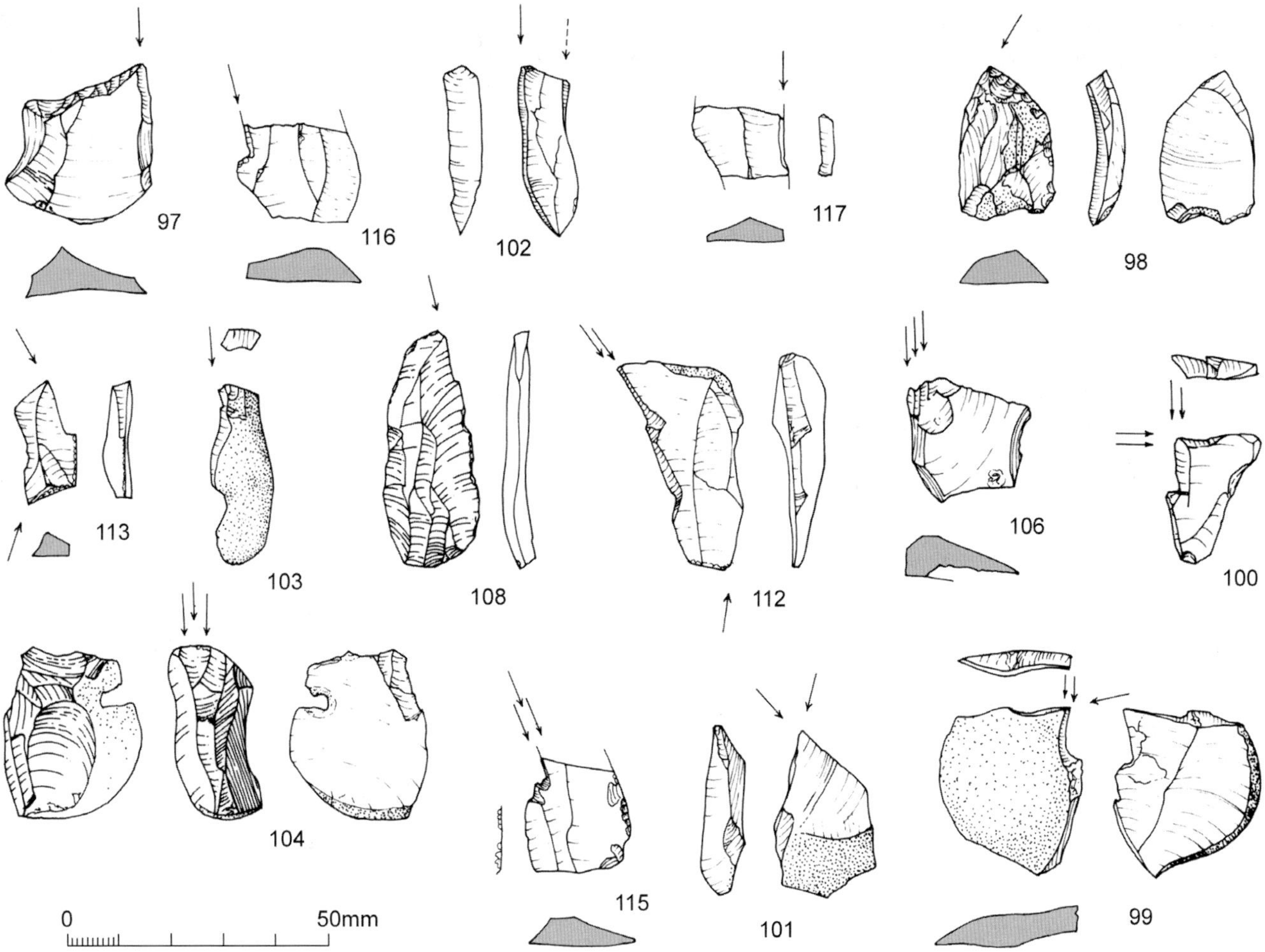

Fig. 9.2. Gwernvale: burins (numbering after Healey and Green 1984).

as being more flake- than blade-based (Healey and Green 1984, 118). This is also the case with some other Mesolithic sites, including Goldcliff, Monmouthshire, where the late Mesolithic assemblage is entirely dominated by flakes (Barton 2007, 109).

Amongst the Gwernvale assemblage some of the scrapers are made on flakes, whilst there are others made on blades. This analysis has looked at some of the characteristics of the scrapers, in particular identifying those that have a radial form of retouch at the distal end of a blade or flake with the retouch confined to a small area. This form of end-scraper is characteristic to both Upper Palaeolithic and Mesolithic scrapers and amongst the Gwernvale assemblage has been identified on 14 examples. Consequently, the distinction between the Upper Palaeolithic and the early Mesolithic scrapers is very much harder to separate. The review of the assemblage undertaken would suggest that there are no certain Upper Palaeolithic scrapers amongst the assemblage, but potentially these 14 examples could date to either of these periods.

It is necessary to draw the evidence together to address the question of whether or not there is a late Upper Palaeolithic assemblage represented at Gwernvale. There are no pieces amongst the assemblage that can only be attributed to an Upper Palaeolithic date. This leaves some uncertainty about whether or not there is any actual activity of such date evident at the site. The seven abruptly backed blade fragments previously postulated as Upper Palaeolithic would not sit out of place amongst a Mesolithic assemblage. The burins, scrapers and edge-ground pieces were left in limbo by Healey and Green in their analysis as they did not provide detail in the report by listing exactly which pieces they considered to be of each period. The new analysis, conducted for this report, demonstrates that there are no tools within this assemblage that could not equally sit comfortably amongst a Mesolithic or an Upper Palaeolithic assemblage.

The distinction drawn by Healey and Green in the 1984 report concerning raw material usage can also be deemed to be somewhat subjective. The grey chert used for these five pieces is not particularly unusual amongst Mesolithic assemblages, such as Nab Head, Pembrokeshire; Pen Pant Farm, Solva, Pembrokeshire; Rhuddlan, Denbighshire; Burry Holms, Gower, Swansea and Trwyn Du, Anglesey. All these are sites of Mesolithic date where a proportion of

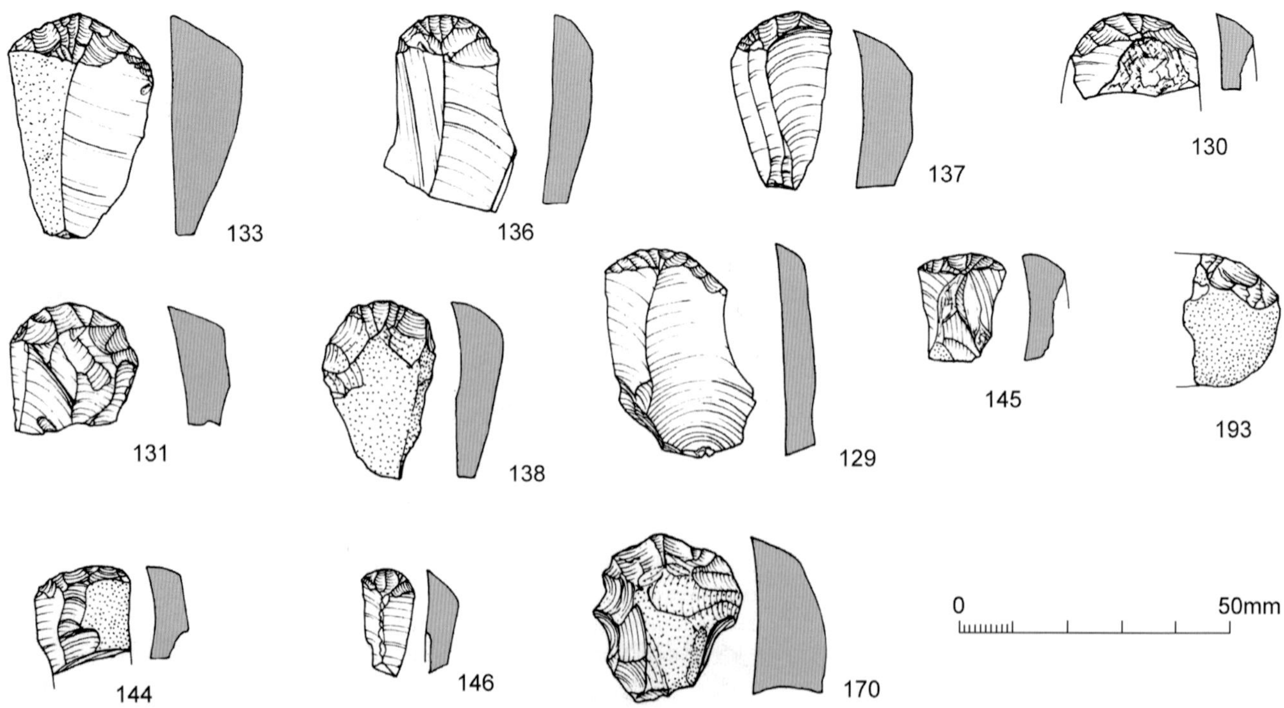

Fig. 9.3. Gwernvale: scrapers (numbering after Healey and Green 1984).

the raw materials used are not flint (R. White 1978; Berridge 1994; David and Walker 2004; David 2007; Walker and Davis 2021). The idea that one slightly out of the ordinary material equates with long-distance transport and then equates to be Upper Palaeolithic is somewhat unrealistic. Raw material transport is widespread sometimes over considerable distances during both the Upper Palaeolithic and the Mesolithic (Evans *et al.* 2010; Pettitt *et al.* 2012). The presence of these chert flakes and blades may therefore be nothing more than evidence for expeditious use of another raw material, rather than anything out of the ordinary, or indicative of a Palaeolithic presence. Furthermore, the blades and flakes would, in their forms, be more characteristic of a Mesolithic, or even a Neolithic, assemblage. Indeed, Healey and Green (1984, 114) cite sites of both Upper Palaeolithic age (Nanna's Cave, Caldey Island, Pembrokeshire and Cathole Cave, Gower, Swansea) where this chert has been used for the manufacture of Palaeolithic tools as well as sites (Barry, Welsh St Donats, Vale of Glamorgan; Frainslake, Pembrokeshire and Craig-y-Llyn, Rhondda) where this material has been utilised for Mesolithic tool making. This is further evidence that chert does not equate necessarily with Palaeolithic use.

To conclude, the balance of probability that there is a Palaeolithic assemblage at Gwernvale has diminished and in the absence of any certain evidence to corroborate a Late Glacial human presence on this site the assemblage can be deemed to most probably be of early Mesolithic, post-glacial age in the discussions that follow.

The Mesolithic assemblage at Gwernvale

Microliths are ubiquitous tools amongst Mesolithic assemblages and have been classified in different ways over the years. The main accepted distinction in Wales is that early Mesolithic forms tend to be 'broad-blade' and late Mesolithic forms 'narrow-blade'. Further chronological differences can be observed in the amount of backing retouch there is around pieces of different ages and forms. 'Broad-blade' forms are commonly made on blades worked to a point by oblique retouch along part of one end. Other variations include forms retouched along one entire edge; either straight or with a shoulder (Clark 1932, 23–24). In contrast 'narrow-blade', or geometric industries, are characterised by small, often minute scalene triangles and narrow-rods or including other forms such as micro-trapezoids, crescents and ultra-narrow tranchets (Radley and Mellars 1964, 13). Graham Clark suggested that the distinction between the two industries is chronological; with broad-blade forms being made earlier than the narrow-blade forms, although with some regional distinctions (Clark 1932, 50). Roger Jacobi's work also endorsed the thinking that microliths are part of a separation between an early and a late Mesolithic (Jacobi 1976, 67).

In Wales, Geoffrey Wainwright (1963) was first to analyse the available evidence for the Mesolithic and published his interpretation of the microlithic industries of Wales. His work focused on the location and distribution of sites around Wales rather than on chronology, hampered as he was, by a lack of solid dating evidence at that time. Jacobi (1980) picked up his work in his review of the Welsh Mesolithic, applying his own techno-criteria to the available evidence. This work has been developed further by Andrew David (1989; 1990). A further assessment of the chronological sequence of microliths has resulted in reviews of assemblages from across Wales by David and the author (David and Walker 2004; David 2007). The review of the Welsh Mesolithic undertaken in both publications reinforces the observation that a broad-blade microlith industry decreases in size over time. David's analysis of tools recovered from Prestatyn, Denbighshire, suggests that this reduction may have been an interim stage, and therefore not be as abrupt a change as earlier commentators suggest (David and Walker 2004, 317; David 2007, 116–18). This thinking can be applied to the interpretation of microliths amongst the Gwernvale assemblage. However, at Gwernvale detailed analysis is hampered by the facts that much of the assemblage is fragmentary or burnt and that some microliths are also unfinished.

Early Mesolithic assemblages have often been separated according to whether they are of Star Carr type or Deepcar type. The general trend, as observed and recorded by Michael Reynier, is that Star Carr type assemblages are dominated by geometric microlith forms, short end-scrapers, some burins and piercers, truncated pieces and core tools, such as axes. Deepcar type assemblages contain partially backed microlith forms, obliquely blunted points, scrapers of short-end form, but with some long end-scrapers, and fewer burins which, when present, tend to be of '*corbiac*' form, or pseudo-burins. Core tools, piercers, microdenticulates and truncated pieces are also present in varying numbers (Reynier 2005). Whilst this thinking may now be less clear-cut across parts of England, study of Welsh assemblages by the author and Andrew David has highlighted that this pattern may be clearly observed between early Mesolithic tool assemblages from different Welsh sites. The burin features far more frequently amongst assemblages such as Nab Head and Daylight Rock, Pembrokeshire, where the microlith assemblage is dominated by geometric forms of microlith, including large triangular forms and few obliquely blunted forms (David and Walker 2004, 303). In contrast, sites including Trwyn Du, Anglesey, Rhuddlan, Denbighshire, and Burry Holms, Gower, Swansea, all have assemblages dominated by microliths of obliquely blunted form, microdenticulates and with fewer burins. Taking the burin as an example, 64 are recorded from the Nab Head and 10 from Daylight Rock (amongst a smaller assemblage) in contrast with four from Burry Holms and two each from Trwyn Du and Rhuddlan. The 15 burins from Gwernvale might place the assemblage in either of the groupings.

The Gwernvale microliths have all been examined as part of this re-analysis of the Mesolithic assemblage. This review has re-classified all the microliths according to type and form, and then a knowledge of Welsh assemblages has been applied to determine whether or not they are early or late Mesolithic. This has highlighted that many of these tools are fragmentary and burnt and tools are generally small in size. There is, however, a useful distinction to be made between those pieces that may be considered to be early or late Mesolithic. The early Mesolithic assemblage includes a quantity of obliquely blunted points and the possibility of some that are of angled- or straight-backed forms (Fig. 9.1). Table 9.1 shows the representation of the various certain microlith forms at Gwernvale, but excludes the six pieces considered as possible abruptly backed pieces. If the abruptly backed points are included there would be a further six possible early Mesolithic tools. There are also a further 13 unclassifiable microlith fragments that may, or may not, be either early or late in date. The analysis of Gwernvale's early Mesolithic microliths shows that it displays characteristics of a Deepcar type assemblage, being dominated by obliquely blunted points.

Turning to the Mesolithic scrapers represented in the assemblage, it becomes more complex to determine what is, and what is not, early or late Mesolithic in age. Scrapers at Gwernvale take many forms, and whilst there has been some classification that has enabled some separation between those that are Mesolithic and the Neolithic forms, there remain many fragments that may, or may not, be from scrapers that are left unclassified. More caution has been exercised in this review than in the original publication, with just 20 now considered Mesolithic and fewer of the fragments being classified as scrapers. Indeed, there are also a number of flakes that might be scraper blanks, but which show no evidence for actual retouch, which have been reclassified in this analysis as flakes, rather than scrapers, as they were originally published. The Mesolithic scrapers from Gwernvale are generally end-scrapers made on flakes or blades, often with their proximal ends removed. There are also two highly cortical scrapers, where a scraping edge has been retouched into the distal end of a primary cortical flake

Table 9.1. Gwernvale: numbers of microliths by form and age.

	Early Mesolithic	*Late Mesolithic*	*Mesolithic*
Obliquely blunted points	14 (+1 unfinished)	1 (+1 unfinished)	–
Scalene triangles	–	8	–
Isosceles triangles	–	1	–
Convex-backed	2 (+1 unfinished)	7	–
Straight-backed	5	2	–
Lanceolate	–	1	–
Crescent	–	1	–
Rhomboid	–	1	–
Unclassified pieces	–	–	13
Totals	23	23	13

or blade. Such forms are commonly found on Welsh Mesolithic sites, possibly due to much of the raw material that is used during the Mesolithic in Wales being of poor-quality, locally available flint that has been transported either by ice or water and collected from coastal locations. A quick simple scraper made on a primary, cortical flake therefore makes use of an important and limited resource.

There are 13 notched blades and microburins in the Gwernvale assemblage (Fig. 9.4). Some of the eight notches can be considered to be mis-snapped microburins and these and the five true snapped microburins indicate microlith manufacture at the site. Other notched blades may have held a further function, but it is not possible to separate out those that may be early from those that may be late Mesolithic in age.

A late Mesolithic is also represented amongst the Gwernvale assemblage with microliths, scrapers and denticulated scrapers. The dominant forms of microliths at Gwernvale are small scalene triangle and small convex-backed forms (Fig. 9.5). Some of the scrapers are likely to be late Mesolithic in age and there is one denticulated scraper in the assemblage. This tool (Fig. 9.3, no. 170; context 95, find no. 2403; NMW acc. no. 79.54H/2.1015) is typical of late Mesolithic assemblages and it would not be out of character if it had been found in Pembrokeshire or Gower amongst a late Mesolithic assemblage (Healey and Green 1984, fig. 52, no. 170). Denticulated scrapers have been recorded by Andrew David at many late Mesolithic Pembrokeshire sites and increasingly they are now being recorded from Gower fields through the recording being undertaken by the author on finds reported through the Portable Antiquities Scheme. Traditionally these tools have been dated to the late Mesolithic, and they appear to be especially common in Pembrokeshire where David has recorded many from Nab Head Site II (David 2007, 140).

Burins, asymmetrical 'becs' or retouched points on flakes or bladelets also generally complete the typical late Mesolithic assemblage (David and Walker 2004, 323), and some of the Gwernvale burins might be of such date. Six truncated blades are also representative of a likely late Mesolithic age for a further class of tool (Fig. 9.6). Late Mesolithic assemblages, and frequently Welsh early Mesolithic Deepcar type assemblages, do not contain core tools. These are also absent from amongst the Mesolithic component of the Gwernvale assemblage. There are also no pebble tools amongst this assemblage. This is of interest, for so many of the classic late Mesolithic assemblages tend to come from coastal locations (E. Walker 2016, 41). So the absence of such implements, suggests that such tools may have had a function for processing marine resources so generally do not appear on inland sites.

The lithic assemblage from the forecourt of the tomb: context 95

A total of 262 lithic artefacts were recovered from context 95, which is the forecourt assemblage associated with the potential use of the cairn. A list of the finds in Table 9.2 from this context demonstrates that a number of periods feature amongst this assemblage. The early Mesolithic is represented by a mesial fragment of one of the abruptly backed blade fragments and also one burnt fragment of an obliquely blunted point. Also present are one complete and two fragments of late Mesolithic microliths of scalene triangle form and the denticulated scraper. Other pieces are categorised more generally as Mesolithic, including two end-scrapers, a notched blade, a burin fragment and a possible burin spall (Fig. 9.7). There are a number of Neolithic pieces including three flakes from Neolithic axeheads and two leaf-shaped arrowheads (Fig. 9.8). The rest of the assemblage is classed here as general knapping debitage, comprising flakes, blades, spalls and core working; and fragments which are evidence for knapping but for which no easy dating can be made. These have not been examined in detail for this chapter and so are listed as general prehistoric in Table 9.2. This supposed Neolithic layer does, apparently, contain 13 Mesolithic finds and it is realistic to assume that some of the debitage is also earlier in date than the context would suggest. The distributions suggest fewer finds of Mesolithic age were recovered from this area of the

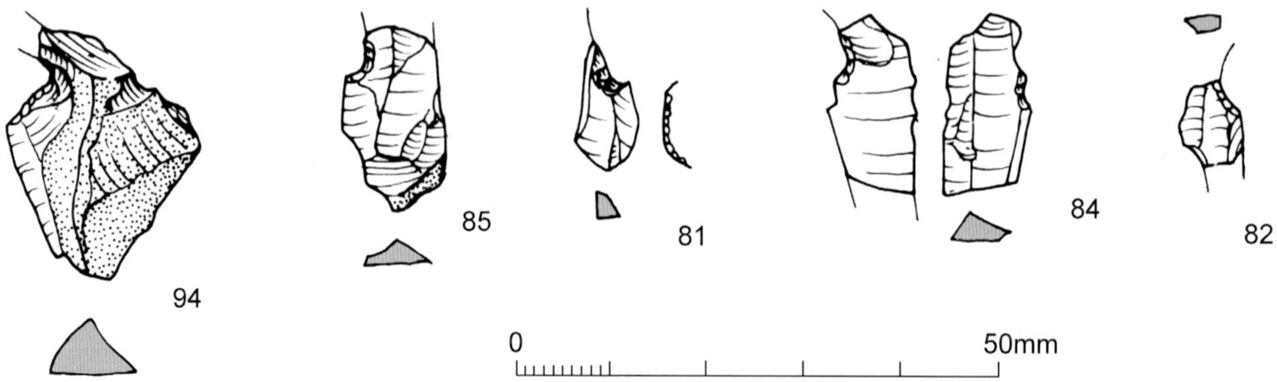

Fig. 9.4. Gwernvale: microburins (numbering after Healey and Green 1984).

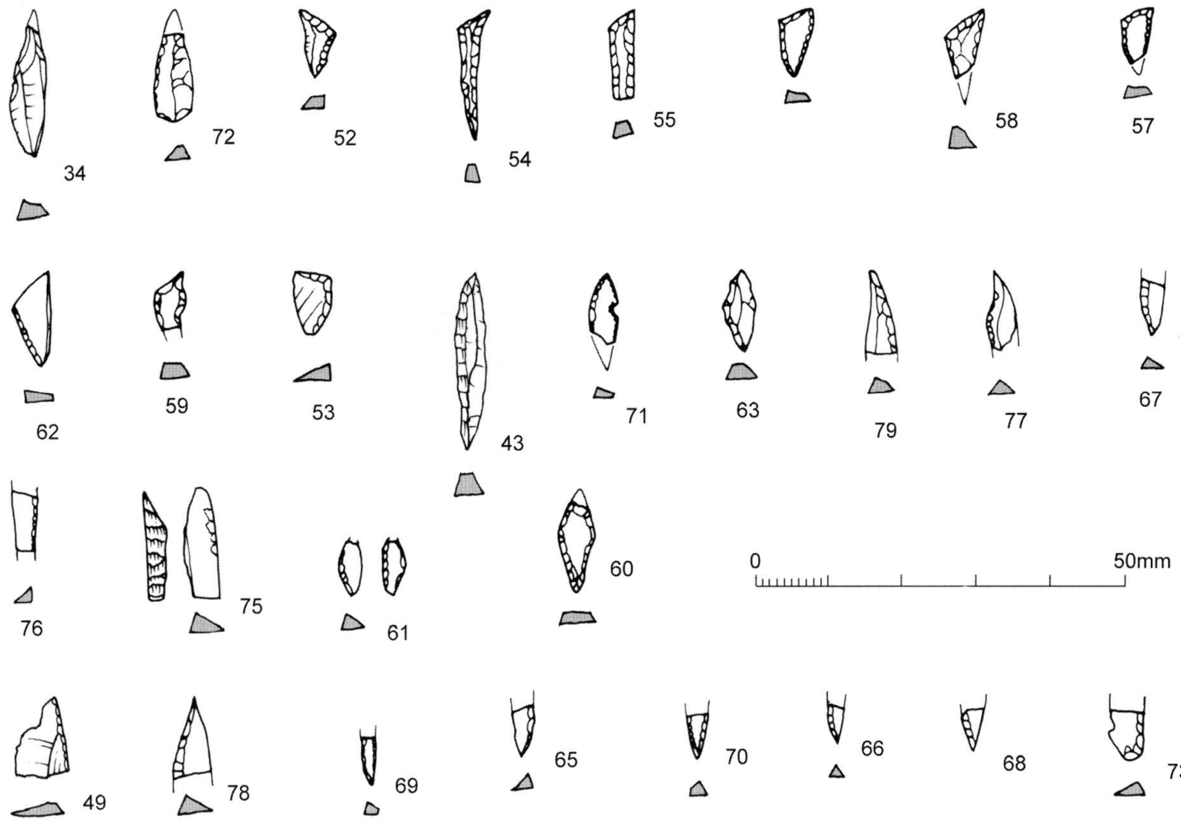

Fig. 9.5. Gwernvale: late Mesolithic microliths – with unclassified microlith fragments on bottom line (numbering after Healey and Green 1984).

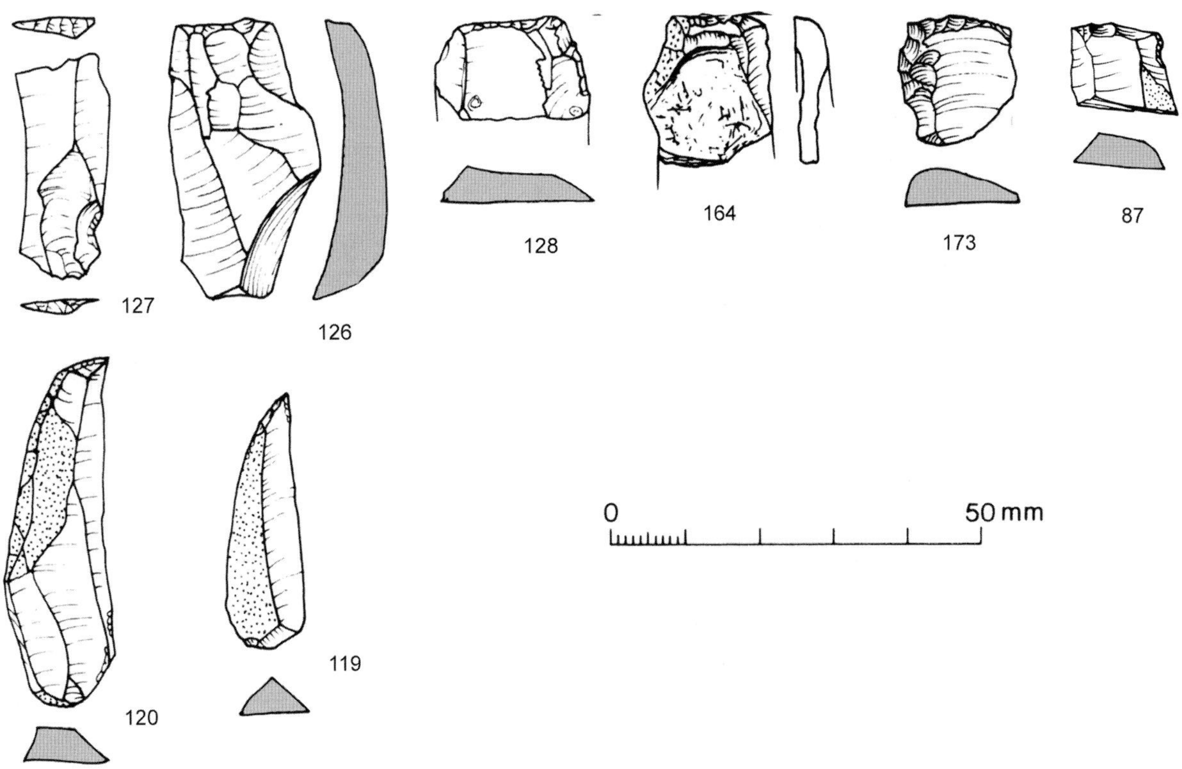

Fig. 9.6. Gwernvale: truncated blades (numbering after Healey and Green 1984).

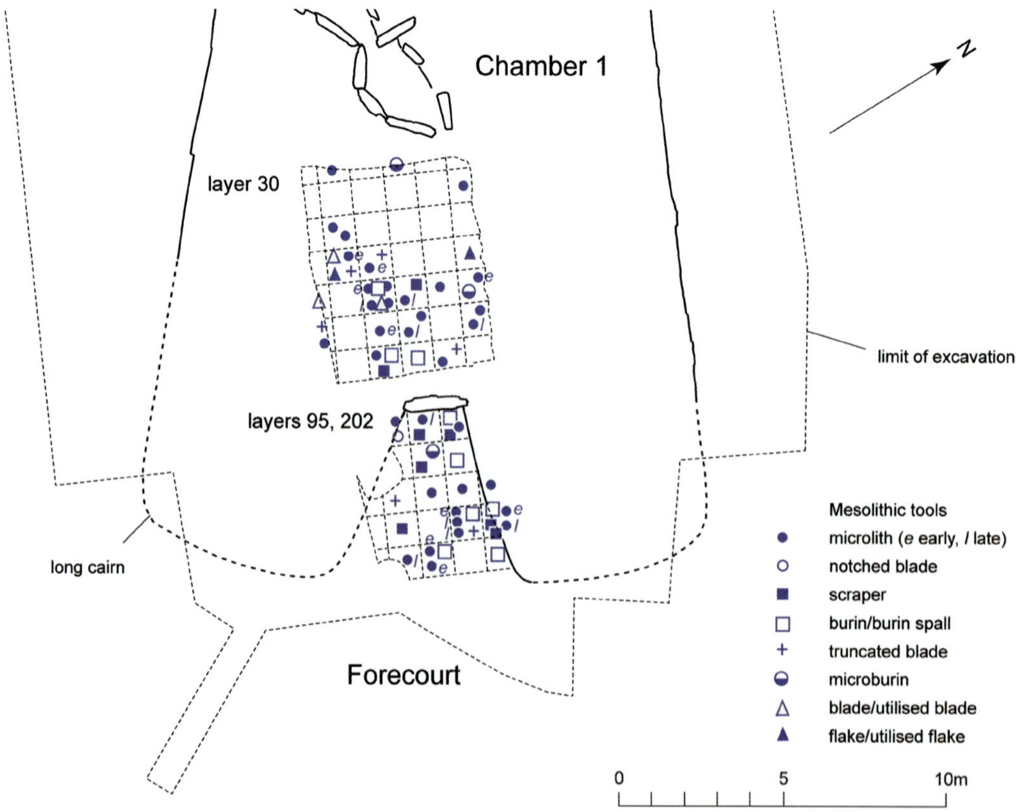

Fig. 9.7. Gwernvale: Mesolithic tools from sieved context 30 below the long cairn and contexts 95 and 202 in the forecourt area.

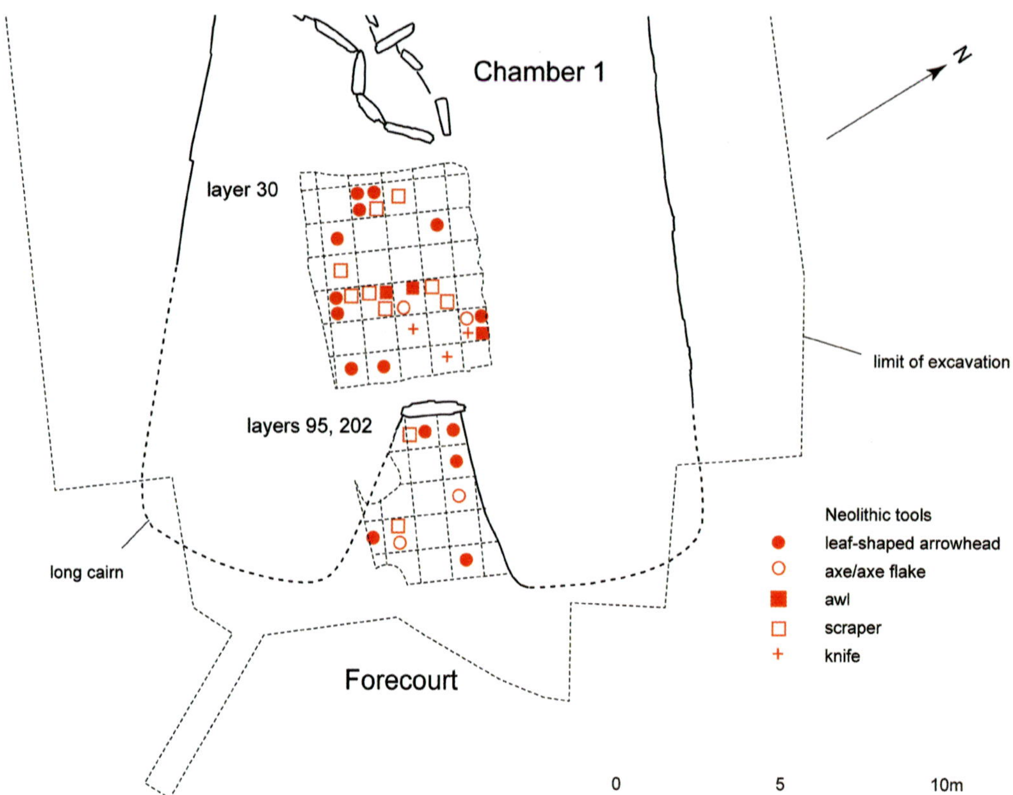

Fig. 9.8. Gwernvale: Neolithic tools from sieved context 30 below the long cairn and contexts 95 and 202 in the forecourt area.

Table 9.2. Gwernvale: lithic assemblage from the upper soil layer (95) in the forecourt area.

Period	Tool Form	Quantity
Early Mesolithic	Abruptly backed blade fragment	1
	Microlith – obliquely-blunted point	1
Late Mesolithic	Microlith – scalene triangle	3
	Denticulated scraper	1
Mesolithic general	End-scraper on a blade	2
	Notched blade	1
	Burin fragment	1
	Burin spall?	1
	Truncated blades	2
Neolithic	Leaf-shaped arrowhead	2
	Stone quern fragment	1
	Flakes from polished axeheads	3
	Natural quartz	51
Prehistoric general	Flint flakes and flake fragments	81
	Chert flakes and flake fragments	24
	Flint blades and blade fragments	4
	Retouched flakes	6
	Utilised flakes	3
	Utilised blades	1
	Core rejuvenation flake	1
	General flint knapping debitage	52
	General chert knapping debitage	20
Total		262

Table 9.3. Gwernvale: lithic assemblage from the buried soil (30) below the long cairn.

Period	Tool Form	Quantity
Early Mesolithic	Microlith – obliquely-blunted point of chert	1
	Microlith – straight-backed fragment	1
	Microlith – convex-backed	1
	Microlith – unclassified	4
Late Mesolithic	Microlith – convex-backed	4
	Microlith – straight-backed	1
	Microlith – obliquely-blunted point	1
Mesolithic general	Microlith – unclassified forms	5
	Truncated blades	4
	Scrapers	3
	Scraper blanks	1
	Burin	1
	Burin spall	2
	Microburin	2
	Ground-edged pieces	1
Late Mesolithic/ Neolithic	Awl	1
	End-side scraper	1
Neolithic	Scrapers	9
	Leaf-shaped arrowheads	7
	Awls	2
	Knives	4
	Axeheads	2
	Querns	2
Neolithic/Bronze Age	Arrowheads	3
	Possible arrowheads	2
Prehistoric general	Retouched flakes and flake fragments	18
	Retouched blades and blade fragments	4
	Utilised flakes and blades	14
	Blades	16
	Flint flakes	173
	Chert flakes	1
	Spalls	1
	Cores	9
	Core rejuvenation pieces	37
	General flint knapping debitage	147
	Split pebbles	3
	Unidentified tools	5
Totals		493

site and it is undetermined whether these are of early or late Mesolithic age (Fig. 9.7). The Neolithic finds are also few, as may be expected from the forecourt area of a Neolithic monument (Fig. 9.8).

The lithic assemblage from below the tomb: context 30

There is a broad range of material represented amongst the 493 pieces that have been recovered from the pre-cairn monument assemblage with tools dating from the early Mesolithic through to the Neolithic (Table 9.3). Distributions show a mix of early and late Mesolithic finds in this area, predominantly towards the eastern edge of the trench (Figs 9.7 and 9.9), whereas the Neolithic distribution shows fewer Neolithic finds, as may be expected, from this pre-tomb context (Fig. 9.8). But general trends show that there are a range of microlith forms of both early and late Mesolithic age, including a number of unclassifiable fragments in the assemblage. The substantive nature of the Mesolithic assemblage generally adds credence to the thinking that this was a site of some significance throughout the Mesolithic in the times prior to the construction of the monument. A range of Neolithic tool forms are also represented. Some are classic early forms, including some of the arrowheads where there is a dominance of leaf-shaped forms present. Other tools, including some evidence for axeheads, scrapers, awls and knives, are perhaps harder to pinpoint chronologically to give a sense of whether these are genuinely pre-cairn in age. The knapping debitage could support a suggestion that this area includes clearance and a midden deposit given the concentration of tools of Mesolithic and/or Neolithic age alongside a substantial concentration of cores and knapping debitage in this area of the site (Fig. 9.9).

Discussion

This review of some aspects of the lithic assemblage from Gwernvale demonstrates that the previous attribution of tools to the Late Glacial period can now be questioned. The seven abruptly backed pieces, burins, scrapers and

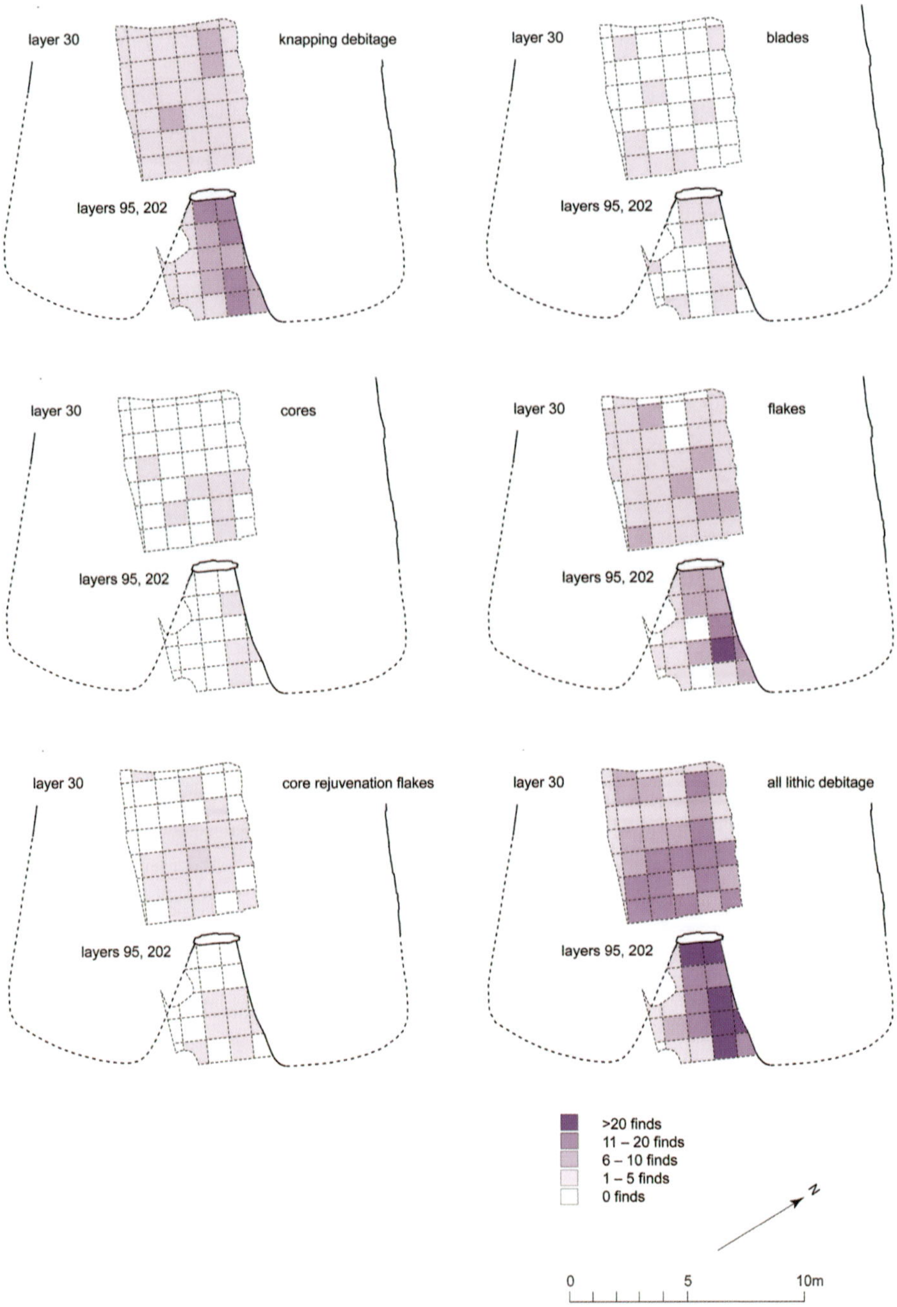

Fig. 9.9. Gwernvale: Mesolithic/Neolithic tools from sieved context 30 below the long cairn and contexts 95 and 202 in the forecourt area.

chalcedonic chert flakes and blades, previously considered to be of Upper Palaeolithic age can be adequately paralleled by tools of early or late Mesolithic date at other Welsh sites. The absence of any other complete tool forms of certain Upper Palaeolithic age that might conceivably be attributed to the Late Glacial and the absence of any environmental data could further support their Mesolithic age. However, the fact that the possible penknife point recovered from Gwernvale would indicate that were these tools to be Upper Palaeolithic in age, then it is a time right at the very end of the Late Glacial period that is represented. Penknife points have traditionally been dated to the *Federmesser-gruppen* techno-complex or the Final Palaeolithic (Barton and Roberts 1996, 252). This period is the later, warmest, part of the Late Glacial interstadial or Allerød chronosome and lies immediately before the start of the Younger Dryas stadial, when it is believed that all people moved out from Britain for warmer climates on mainland Europe (Jacobi and Higham 2011, 233). A gap in human presence of around 1,000 years is then believed to have occurred before people recolonised Britain during the early Holocene, or early Mesolithic, period.

The Mesolithic is represented at Gwernvale by tools that may be attributed to both the early Mesolithic as well as late Mesolithic age. An 8th-millennium date for a hazelnut shell from the buried soil below the cairn (SUERC-85563; Table 4.1) may lend support for an early Mesolithic dating for the early pre-cairn activity at Gwernvale. Parallels for the Gwernvale assemblage may be drawn with those from other similar sites, at Hazleton North, Gloucestershire, for example, where Saville identified both an early and a late Mesolithic amongst the assemblage (Saville 1990, 164). Here the early Mesolithic component is small, just three microliths, with far fewer forms than are present at Gwernvale. These tools are dismissed in the general synthesis and discussion, and indeed Saville has taken the view that the Mesolithic industry is, in general, essentially late Mesolithic on the basis that some broader-blade microliths could have been made throughout the Mesolithic (Saville 1990, 164). This contrasts with Ascot-under-Wychwood, where an early Mesolithic assemblage dominates and where fewer late Mesolithic tool forms are recorded (Cramp 2007, 294). At Eton Rowing Course, early Mesolithic flintwork is represented along with material of later date.

All four sites therefore have similarities in that all their early Mesolithic microlith assemblages include large obliquely blunted points. At Eton Rowing Course the early Mesolithic site is discrete and is located separately from areas of the site of later age. The late Mesolithic finds come from a number of areas. At Gwernvale the late Mesolithic presence, represented by narrow-blade microliths, is apparently mainly found in Neolithic contexts. This is an interesting observation for at Eton Rowing Course the suggestion is made that late Mesolithic forms are deposited in pits and in tree-throw holes. In particular, evidence from tree-throw hole 566 produced evidence for rod microlith manufacture (Anderson-Whymark 2013b, 521). The interpretation given is that the early Neolithic practice of deposition in tree-throw holes had its origins in the Mesolithic, which Anderson-Whymark interprets as indicating a shift in the Mesolithic economy towards the exploitation of resources associated with small clearances created by tree-fall (Anderson-Whymark 2013b, 521). The similarity of this with pit or hearth 308 at Gwernvale (see location on Fig. 3.22) with a 6th-millennium date (CAR-118; Table 4.1) is intriguing. At Gwernvale the feature is devoid of artefacts which might support such a date (Britnell 1984b, 136). Similar tree-throw holes at Ascott-under-Wychwood also suggest Mesolithic use, although here Kate Cramp suggests there are two phases, an early and a later one, separated by the fact that there appears to be some continuity of use of these sites, a point she further emphasises with another tree-throw hole (F11) where 5th millennium cal BC flintwork in its upper fill suggests a continuation of use beyond the Mesolithic and into the Neolithic (McFadyen *et al.* 2007, 26).

A further possible similarity and parallel between several of these Severn-Cotswold tombs is the presence of what has been interpreted as a midden. These possibly date to the early Neolithic and underlie several of these structures. Such deposits contain a range of flintwork of Mesolithic and Neolithic age. The suggestion is that the Mesolithic material has become mixed and incorporated into early Neolithic contexts with continuity of use of these landscapes. Key to this is evidence for the clearance of areas and the possible construction of timber structures at Ascott-under-Wychwood which, despite generating some later 5th millennium cal BC dates, had cut through tree-throw features (McFadyen 2007, 27). At Hazleton North an early linear structure may also be considered to be of similar age. This is associated with early Neolithic flintwork (Saville 1990, 240). At Eton Rowing Course, an early Neolithic midden was excavated but with a considerably larger lithic artefact assemblage than at any of the other sites (Cramp 2013). Such evidence, along with midden deposits, suggest similarities between these sites.

There certainly appears to be a continuity of use at all these sites. The dating, from early Mesolithic through to the construction of the large stone monuments suggests some significant special places. As Chris Tilley has suggested, there is cause for us to reconsider the Mesolithic-Neolithic transition as one that suggests complementary use of places through time, rather more than earlier theories of exclusive use of a place (Tilley 1994, 87). The importance of landscape is something that Tilley and other writers suggest leads to the continuity of places through space and time. Indeed, the term Mesolithic is perhaps too arbitrary a term to use to describe these cultures. It was a convenience adopted to mark the very end of the Last Glacial, until the climate and landscape stabilised and became more or less as today.

The continuity of aspects of technology that span the period from the Final Upper Palaeolithic, pretty much into the early Neolithic is seemingly therefore more of a continuum than is acknowledged, despite the short break in human presence in Britain during the Younger Dryas. Final Palaeolithic tools, such as abruptly backed blades and penknife points, burins and awls or piercing tools all have parallels that may be found in later assemblages. The fact that with the sole exception of hunting armatures and hunting equipment there is no easy way without good archaeological context to distinguish a burin, a scraper, an awl, or a serrated knife from one period into the other makes the separation of the Final Palaeolithic, early Mesolithic, late Mesolithic and early Neolithic somewhat arbitrary.

Without the microliths might we not have considered this a continuum of space and time? The assemblage from Gwernvale contains elements that can be separated and whilst it may be reasonable to consider that some tools might be Upper Palaeolithic, others are certainly either early or late Mesolithic, with a scatter of tools that might be of any of these periods, indeed even early Neolithic. Plotting distributions, obtaining radiocarbon dates and looking at the other material culture evidence and environmental data can help, to be reinforced by observations based on significant places – using Barton's 'persistent places' theory (Barton *et al.* 1995) – or places of memory, evidence of movement, and the phenomenology of landscape. This unpicking and categorisation may only provide a limited and narrow glimpse and thin interpretation for what were once complex societies, living at many varied places at different times, undertaking a range of activities over place and time that we can only start to glimpse before people began to construct their impressive monuments and place their dead within them as their final resting places. Further implications of a long occupation of place are followed in Chapter 12.

10

The Neolithic pottery from Gwernvale: an update and review

Alistair J. Barclay

The scope of this study

For its size, contextual associations and composition, the pre-cairn Carinated and Plain Bowl pottery assemblage from Gwernvale (Fig. 10.1) remains one of the more important not just from south Wales but for western Britain as a whole. The assemblage was comprehensively characterised and placed in its wider context by Frances Lynch in the original report (F. Lynch 1984), which provides the foundation for this review of the early Neolithic pottery. By contrast, only a handful of sherds of pottery have been recovered from Penywyrlod, including a single hemispherical bowl rim. The original Gwernvale report also included a study of the pottery fabrics by Tim Darvill (1984), which Lynch also considered as part of her wider discussion (1984). However, the review presented here focuses on differences in vessel forms, although the intention is not to diminish the importance of such work on fabrics, which would perhaps be better considered alongside a detailed regional review of lipid analysis (see Chapter 11). The Gwernvale assemblage also includes a number of Peterborough vessels, which appear to be contemporary with the use or closure of the tomb, and are briefly commented on below. Since 1984 our understanding of the precise radiocarbon chronology of the Peterborough (or Impressed) style has been transformed (Gibson and Kinnes 1997; Marshall *et al.* 2009; Ard and Darvill 2015; Roberts and Marshall 2020, fig. 7).

Early Neolithic pottery studies 40 years on

What has changed since the publication of Gwernvale in 1984? First, Herne (1988) published his seminal work defining Carinated Bowl, and then the early Neolithic pottery of Wales was the subject of a detailed study by Peterson (2003), and its wider context in Britain and Ireland was critiqued by Sheridan (2007; 2010) and Julian Thomas (2013). New assemblages from the Black Mountains and the Welsh Marches have been added and include the important material from Dorstone Hill, Herefordshire (which I will report on in due course as part of the site publication) and the South Wales Gas Pipeline (Darvill *et al.* 2020). In addition, there are the non-Carinated Bowl assemblages from the A477 road scheme, Carmarthenshire (Barber *et al.* 2019), Wellington Quarry, Herefordshire (Jackson and Miller 2011), and the Caerau, Cardiff, causewayed enclosure (Davis and Sharples 2017), none of which appear to date much before the 37th century cal BC.

Apart from a growing number of new assemblages, one major development is the paradigm shift in how we construct radiocarbon frameworks by employing a Bayesian approach (Whittle *et al.* 2011 and see Griffiths, Chapter 4), with a move away from the old periodisation frameworks to a more fluid, site-focused, and sympathetic approach to how we measure time and construct chronologies. The latter has allowed us to focus in on time and temporality. Where it was once considered adequate to place material and practices into broad periods, we are now challenged to look for sequence and change over a significantly more nuanced timeframe (Whittle *et al.* 2011; Whittle 2018). Since Herne published his paper (1988), there has been a simple tendency to split the pottery sequence at about 3800 cal BC, a division that is generally taken to separate Carinated Bowl or rather those assemblages in which this style of vessel is a dominating element, into an initial or classic phase followed by that of a developed or modified phase (Cleal 2004; Barclay and Case 2007; Sheridan 2007; J. Thomas 2013). However, the old periodisation nomenclature lingers and the straitjacket of such labels as 'Carinated Bowl' and 'Plain Bowl' is often retained to the detriment of

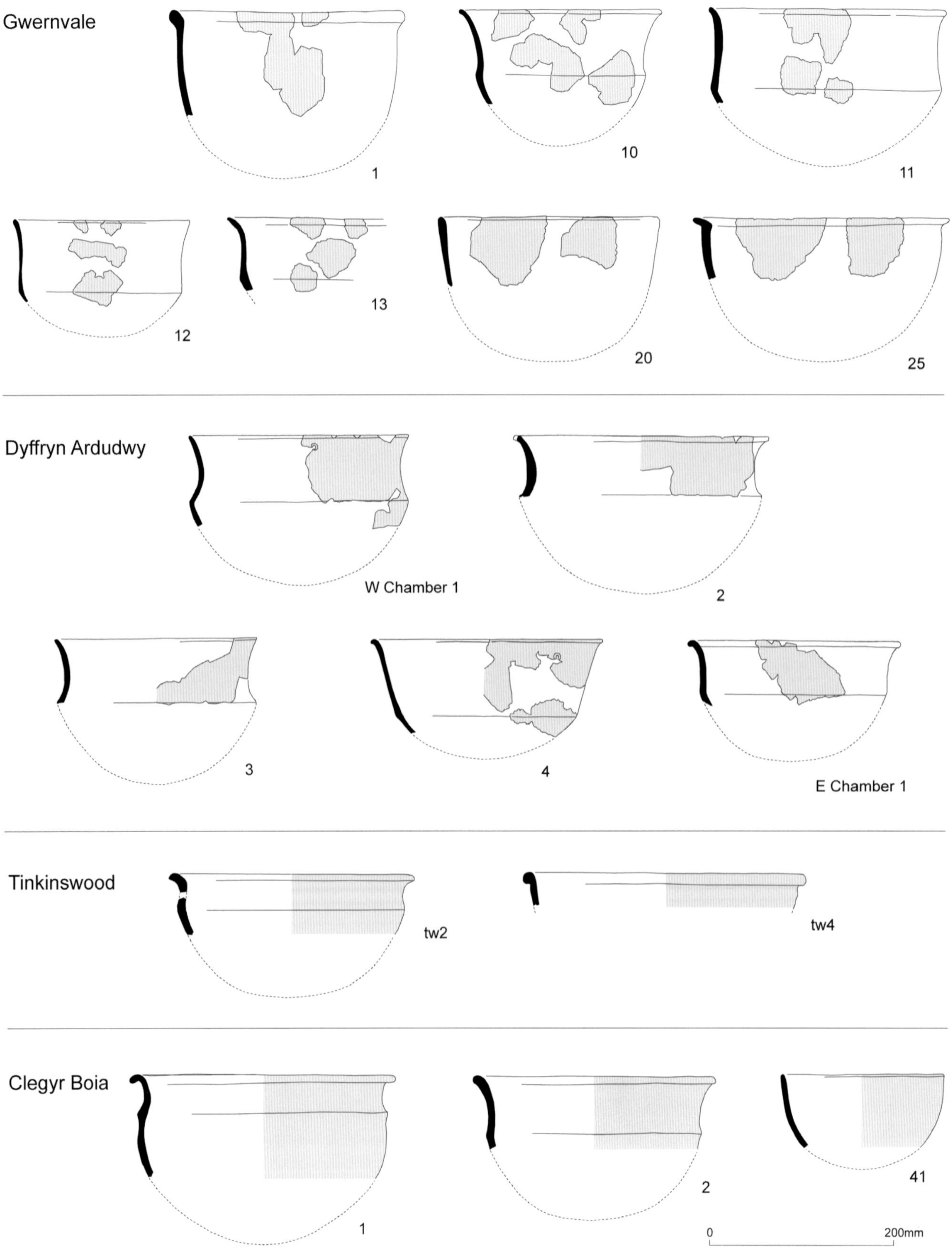

Fig. 10.1. Selected early Neolithic pottery from Gwernvale (after Britnell 1984b), Dyffryn Ardudwy (after Powell 1973), Tinkinswood (after Peterson 2003), and Clegyr Boia (after A. Williams 1953). Vessels numbered as in cited publications.

closer examination. Herne's work was useful in separating out an early 'Carinated Bowl' phase from the more general term of 'Plain Bowl'. However, what has now become apparent is that there was a period of transformation that occurs between what can be definitively labelled 'Carinated Bowl' (those assemblages that contain a very high number of carinated bowls) and 'Plain Bowl' (in which carinated bowls are rare), or between those assemblages that coincide with the first Neolithic during and before the 39th century cal BC and those that emerged by the 37th century cal BC. The gap in between is variously labelled as 'developed' or 'modified', which works at a broad and relative level but not with our desire to strive towards a new understanding of the Neolithic that the better use of radiocarbon provides. Another problem is the temporal distribution of sites across this period. We know more about some centuries than others, which can be helped by the appearance and construction histories of informative monuments and buildings, such as the more complex long cairns and the earlier deposits they cover, enclosure ditches and timber buildings. All present opportunities of useful shorter or longer sequences for relative dating and Bayesian modelling.

Although the term Carinated Bowl is useful, it can thus also mask the complexity of early Neolithic pottery both regionally and in terms of development, as Cleal has noted (2004), and its application can lead to some confusion. Its usefulness when describing the very earliest Neolithic pottery across Britain and Ireland is beyond doubt and the more so when applied to those assemblages of precisely known 40th and 39th century cal BC date (*e.g.* Ascott-under-Wychwood, Oxon: Barclay and Case 2007; Hazleton North, Gloucestershire: Smith and Darvill 1990; and Rowden, Dorset: Davies *et al.* 1991; Barclay *et al.* 2018). The terminology becomes less clear when applied to those assemblages of the 38th and early 37th centuries cal BC. A recent study of key assemblages from Wessex, mostly from pit groups (Barclay *et al.* 2018), incorporated a new dating programme and Bayesian models, and tested whether well-documented differences represented the development of forms or the co-existence of different styles (*e.g.* the Coneybury Anomaly: Barclay 2014). That study found that some of the differences were chronological, whilst some of the noted complexity of assemblage composition remains. Importantly, it also highlighted the possibility of charting the appearance and duration of certain vessel types.

The challenge is to unpack the composition of each assemblage over the 40th to 37th centuries despite the hindrance of limited knowledge of sequence, the fragmentary character and brokenness of each assemblage, a relatively low number of vessel profiles, and the restricted opportunities to provide good-quality, directly associated radiocarbon dates. In the absence of the latter, greater use can perhaps be made of typological parallels where more precise dates have been obtained (*e.g.* Barclay *et al.* 2018), although with the caveat that the Neolithic probably spread in time and space from one or more connecting strands (see Chapter 12 below).

There is a wide consensus that the Carinated Bowl style, what was previously known as Grimston/Lyles Hill style (I. Smith 1976, and incorporating 'Irish Sea Ware'), in its primary form belongs to the horizon at which Neolithisation first appeared, a time period that mostly pre-dates 3800 cal BC but may only have become more widespread during the 38th century onwards (see Whittle *et al.* 2011, and Chapter 12 below). The very earliest assemblages are dominated by carinated forms in which non-carinated bowls are all but absent. In the context of Wales only the stratigraphically early pit group from Dyffryn Ardudwy (Powell 1973; Fig. 10.1) stands out as a possible early group, leaving aside that from the pre-cairn deposits at Gwernvale, which is discussed in more detail below. There are of course a small number of individual vessels, in many cases only represented by rim or shoulder fragments, that could also be seen as typologically early but without direct dating these can add little to this discussion (see Peterson 2003; the Dorstone assemblage may contribute to this discussion in due course).

Perhaps from the decades around the end of the 39th and start of the 38th centuries cal BC ceramic assemblages began to show far greater variation with modifications made to the original carinated forms often culminating in heavier and coarser vessels and the addition of non-carinated forms. It is a moot point as to when hemispherical bowls, open shallow bowls or sinuous S-profiled bowls first appeared, but all could represent secondary developments during the 38th century cal BC. Thus, the very large assemblage from the pre-hilltop enclosure deposits at Clegyr Boia (A. Williams 1953) is not a primary Carinated Bowl assemblage (Fig. 10.1) but one that is Carinated Bowl-derived, although its exact chronological position relies solely on inter-regional comparison rather than direct dating (see below).

It is noteworthy that the very earliest assemblages from areas of southern England that securely pre-date 3800 cal BC contain a near-absence of non-carinated forms. This is certainly true of the pre-cairn assemblages from Ascott-under-Wychwood and Hazleton North in the Cotswolds (Barclay and Case 2007; Smith and Darvill 1990) and from Rowden near the south coast (Davies *et al.* 1991; Barclay *et al.* 2018). These assemblages all contain similar forms but there are also some important differences. Whilst there are close similarities between Rowden and Ascott, the former contained an example of a deep bowl (Barclay *et al.* 2018, fig. 5.7 after Woodward 1991) and the latter, as well as Hazleton, produced a number of cups (Barclay and Case 2007, fig. 10.2; Smith and Darvill 1990, 150). Both produced more open vessels with straight flaring necks, and in contrast Hazleton contained a vessel with a heavier rim (Smith and Darvill 1990, fig. 156.7). The pottery associated with the Sweet Track contains both classic carinated forms, modified carinated forms and non-carinated forms, as Barclay *et al.* (2018), Cleal (2004), Isobel Smith (1976) and Kinnes (1979) have all noted. The trackway was constructed in 3807/6 BC, was in use for less than a generation, and provides a useful snapshot of the range of vessels that were in use over a decade or so.

Whilst south Wales may have had a different developmental history to the Somerset Levels and the Cotswold Hills, it does none the less illustrate that the adoption of non-carinated vessels was underway in adjacent regions at some point after the pre-cairn activity at both Ascott and Hazleton and by the time the Sweet Track was constructed and in use. The pit group at Rowden is also earlier than the Sweet Track but possibly later than the two pre-cairn assemblages (Barclay *et al.* 2018, table 9, using the OxCal order function), and is also dominated by carinated forms as re-examination of the material has found. What is notable is that none of these assemblages appear to contain the uncarinated bowl forms that are found at Gwernvale in the pre-cairn and later contexts. This could be an indicator of the date range, coherence and contemporaneity of the component elements at Gwernvale.

The Gwernvale pottery assemblage revisited

Early Neolithic

In the reassessment of early phases of activity at Gwernvale presented in Chapter 3, it is argued that the pre-cairn assemblage of pottery was associated with a midden which appears to have been at least in part contemporary with a timber house whose remains may still have been visible when the long cairn was built. Modelling by Seren Griffiths in Chapter 4 of radiocarbon dates from the early phases at the site associated with this pre-cairn activity suggests that this pre-cairn activity began in the 39th to 37th centuries cal BC and continued for a period of 120–420 years, until possibly as late as the 36th or 35th century cal BC, when the long-cairn was constructed. Analysis of organic residues from a number of carinated vessels by Isabel Wiltshire and Lucy Cook in Chapter 11 indicates that at least some were associated with dairying activities.

As Frances Lynch recognised (1984, 106), the Gwernvale pre-cairn assemblage consists of two groups of vessels – one with relatively low-set shoulders or carinations and the other of simple unshouldered form. Starting with what can be termed 'carinated bowls', closer inspection indicates some subtle variation in profile (noting the caveat of original specialist interpretation given the illustrated incompleteness of most vessels). Of the four vessels (10, 11, 12 and 13) perhaps vessel 10 fits the template of a classic 'Carinated Bowl' of open form with a concave neck ending in a simple rim and a low-set carination. In contrast, vessels 11 and 12 are interpreted as having markedly straighter necks with again low-set carinations and are illustrated as neutral forms, while vessel 13 has an upright neck but with an out-curved rim and can possibly be seen as a carinated precursor to an S-profiled bowl. Lynch (1984, 106) draws attention to the pit group from Dyffryn Ardudwy, which again is often taken to typify Carinated Bowl in Wales or at least on its north-western seaboard. Where three vessels (Powell 1973, fig. 8: 1–3) are of neutral form and have concave necks and sharp carinations, a fourth, open bowl (Powell 1973, fig. 8.4) has a long straighter albeit splayed neck similar to vessels 11 and 12 from Gwernvale. There is a further important vessel from Dyffryn Ardudwy that comes from the forecourt of the east chamber. This vessel has a straight neck and low-set carination and a markedly out-curved and rolled rim (Powell 1973, fig. 9:1). Notwithstanding its carination, it can also be seen as a precursor to the so-called S-profiled bowls. Vessel 9 from Gwernvale consists of a small number of non-joining sherds and includes an everted rim, neck and shoulder sherds that could make a profile similar to either vessel 10 or 11 as suggested in the original report (Britnell 1984b, 99). At present there are no direct dates for the pottery or the Dyffryn Ardudwy site in general; the pottery with signs of repair could fall either before or after 3800 cal BC, whilst simple dolmen tombs could also have a similar uncertain date (see Chapter 12 below).

There is also a non-carinated bowl (vessel 1) from the pre-cairn assemblage at Gwernvale, although further rims (2, 7 and 8) indicate that others could have been present. Such vessels are generally missing from early carinated bowl assemblages, for example, Dyffryn Ardudwy and much further east at Ascott-under-Wychwood and Hazleton North. At Gwernvale the association between these heavy-rimmed hemispherical bowls of neutral form and the carinated component is ambiguous. However, the finding of much of bowl 1 within part of the bedding trench of the pre-cairn structure suggests that it was almost certainly in existence during construction and certainly its use. Of the remaining three rims (2, 7, and 8), it is unclear what form these took. Unfortunately, it is simply unknown how long the material from the midden and structure took to accumulate and whether this represents a single phase of activity or different subphases. The pre-cairn activity, which may have started in the 39th century cal BC (see Chapter 4), could have lasted for *120–420 years* (*95% probability, span_Gwernvale_premonument_neolithic*; *parameter not shown*). This long phase of activity perhaps leaves open the question of whether all the pottery was contemporary or actually belonged to one or more phases. Unfortunately, the evidence from Gwernvale is ambiguous and the current radiocarbon model is under-constrained as noted in Chapter 4. Two interpretations remain possible:

- The pre-cairn assemblage is broadly contemporary and includes both the carinated and hemispherical elements, and this is supported by the distribution of the vessel sherds and the association of the 'midden' material with the foundations of the structure. Differences in forms and fabrics would simply represent the use of different facets of material culture, something that is perhaps more common at enclosure sites; or

- That the pre-cairn assemblage represents two distinct phases of activity, an earlier one that resulted in an accumulation of midden-like material incorporating carinated vessels that was then disturbed by the construction of a building associated with an assemblage of non-carinated vessels. That this was the case could be supported by the discrete use of different fabrics as noted by Lynch (1984, 106). That both types of pottery occurred in the bedding trenches (vessels 1, 2, 9, 11 and 13) could simply reflect the accidental inclusion of residual material and the deliberate packing of old material, along with what was in use during construction and use. Vessel 13 stands out as a potentially developed form as noted by Lynch.

Since the original publication of Gwernvale several assemblages associated with timber buildings have been excavated or published including the two structures near Bangor in north-west Wales at Llandygai I (Lynch and Musson 2001, 27–36; Fig. 10.2) and Llandygai II (Parc Bryn Cegin) (Kenney 2008, 14–27; Fig. 10.2), and also the building at Parc Cybi, Holy Island, Anglesey (Kenney 2021; Fig. 10.2). These sites are all some distance from the Black Mountains but do provide a close comparison with the structure beneath Gwernvale and its associated pottery. All three structures produced assemblages of pottery and radiocarbon dates. Of the four dates associated with the Llandygai I house at least two, and possibly a third, are on oak, of which two could be mature wood rather than sapwood. They could all have age offsets, whilst the fourth (GrA-20012) on a charred hazelnut shell could be closer in date to the use of the building and is considerably younger in age. This latter result would place the building in the 37th century cal BC (see Lynch and Musson 2001, 117–18 and Appendix 1). Modelled dates for the Llandygai II house suggest that the use of the building began in the 38th century cal BC and continued into the 37th century cal BC (Kenney 2008, 26–7). A series of modelled dates were produced for the Parc Cybi house (Kenney 2021, 46, table 1 and fig. 28) on charred short-lived plant remains with suggested construction and use firmly within the 37th century cal BC.

The pottery associated with these buildings is characterised by a near-absence of fine carinated bowls (Lynch and Musson 2001, fig. 12 and Kenney 2008; 2021, fig. 27). and where more complete vessels occur these have the character of heavy and derived forms (e.g. Llandygai II/Parc Cybi vessel 1545/1559 and Llandygai I vessel B98; Fig. 10.2). Notable are a number of rims that are either heavy, semi-rolled or out-turned and forms that are either simple and straight-sided or sinuous. Of more interest are the date and pottery associated with Llandygai II, which includes a large hemispherical bowl with heavy out-turned rim (vessel SF167; Fig. 10.2) and sherds from a fine carinated bowl (SF77/84; Fig. 10.2). Of interest are the relatively smaller rim fragments (SF130) and a carinated bowl shoulder and base (SF134/149) from a patch of old ground surface. Collectively closer similarity occurs between this material and that from Gwernvale and this is supported by the earlier construction date for Llandygai II that appears to fall in the later 38th century cal BC (Kenney 2008, 26–7). The latter site could be an indicator that at least part if not all of the Gwernvale pre-cairn Neolithic activity belongs not before 3800 cal BC but potentially later in the 38th century cal BC.

Returning to the non-shouldered vessels, as Frances Lynch noted these can be closely paralleled with the vessels recorded from the tombs of Ty Isaf, Tinkinswood, Parc le Breos Cwm and Llanelwedd (F. Lynch 1984, 108; and see Peterson 2003, figs 7.10, 8.7 and 8.11). Whilst Gwernvale could represent the earliest recorded occurrence of such a vessel, the evidence from elsewhere would equally indicate a much later date (see Chapters 4 and 12). There are two further non-shouldered vessels from the use and blocking of the Gwernvale tomb. One is a simple plain bowl and the other is hemispherical with an out-turned rim (F. Lynch 1984, figs 40 and 41.20 and 25). The simple plain bowl (pot 20), found within the blocking of Chamber 2, is a form rare in other assemblages of this date but as Lynch (1984, 109) noted can be paralleled within those assemblages including Clegyr Boia that have similarities with the Hembury style of the south-west peninsula (and see F. Lynch 1969, 169). Vessel 25 is a simple hemispherical bowl with out-turned rim and can also be closely paralleled at this site.

The two vessels from the chamber deposits at Tinkinswood (Petersen 2003, 118 and fig. 8.11; Fig. 10.1) include a possible developed carinated bowl (tw2) and a heavier-rimmed neutral bowl (tw4). Both find parallels in the house assemblages discussed above and are probably of a similar date (see Chapter 4). In comparison, the pottery from Ty Isaf (Fig. 10.2) contains no carinated vessels, which is not surprising given its probably late date (see Chapter 4). Very little pottery was recovered from Parc le Breos Cwm (Petersen 2003; Whittle and Wysocki 1998) with the only diagnostic sherds being a small number of heavy rims that almost certainly came from simple bowl forms (Zienkiewicz 1998, 168–70, fig. 28.5–7). However, despite the fact that two of these vessels are from the surface and pre-date the tomb, this adds little to the argument of a possible early date for Gwernvale vessel 1.

The date of the simple bowl from Carreg Samson (Fig. 10.2) would on balance appear to be no earlier than some of the house and burial sites discussed above and certainly a close parallel for this vessel occurs from the house at Parc Cybi (vessel 1196) (Kenney 2021, fig. 27). This could

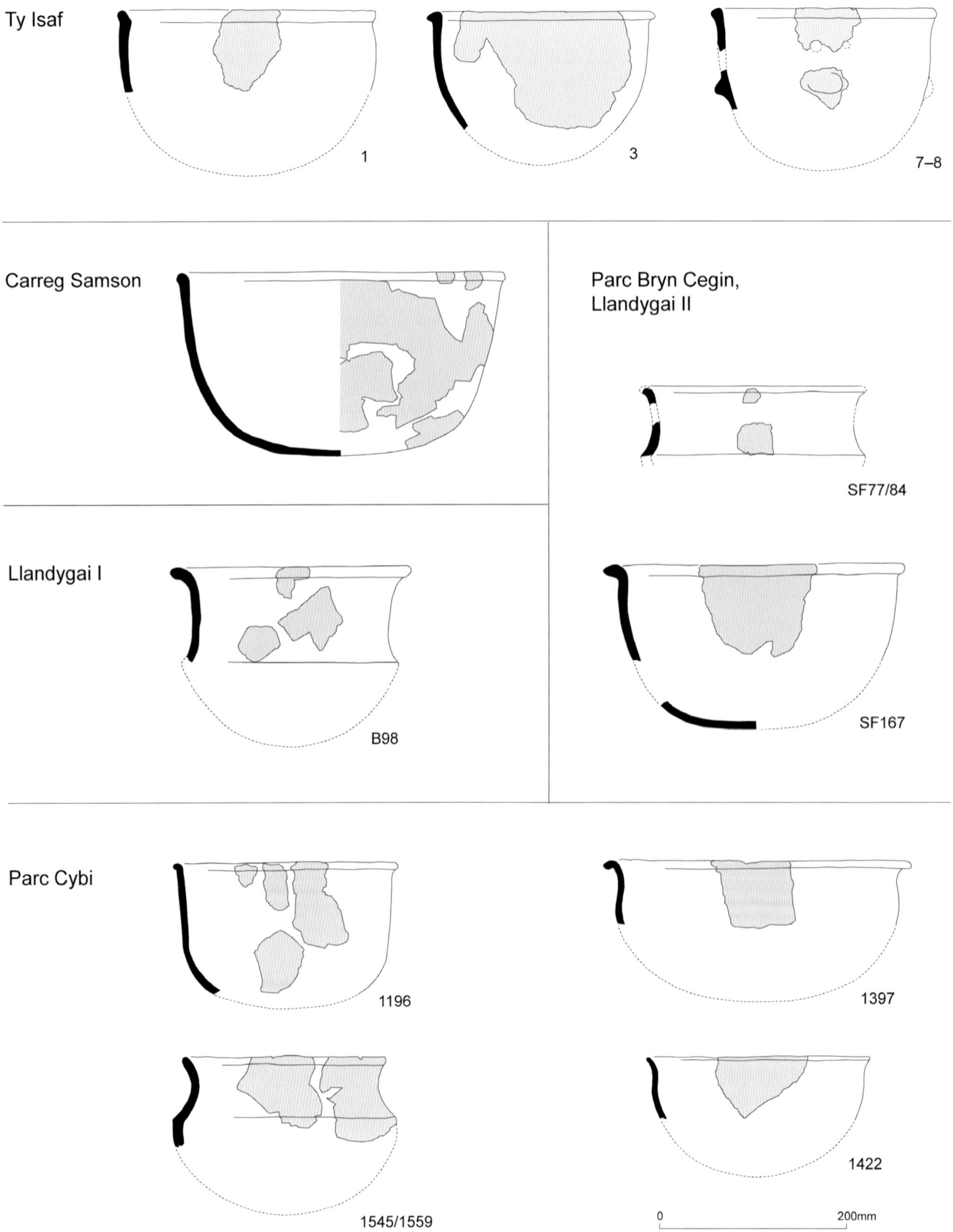

Fig. 10.2. Selected early Neolithic pottery from Ty Isaf (after Grimes 1939 and Peterson 2003), Carreg Samson (after F. Lynch 1975), Llandygai I (after Lynch and Musson 2001), Parc Bryn Cegin/Llandygai II (after Kenney 2008), and Parc Cybi (after Kenney 2008).

potentially place this monument in the later 38th century cal BC or even the 37th. There is certainly little evidence to support a much earlier date for this vessel and by association the construction of this simple monument. Again there is no direct dating and therefore no present reason to use this site to support an early occurrence of hemispherical bowls. The suggestion that this vessel may fit within the middle Neolithic assemblages of Normandy and is distinct from the earliest Carinated Bowl from Wales and Western England only works if an early pre-38th century date is attached to the tomb. As this is a vessel of simple form and without distinctive features the point is difficult to prove and there seem no compelling grounds for thinking that this was a vessel from Normandy (*contra* Sheridan 2010, 92).

It is unfortunate that the material from the South Wales Gas Pipeline, that runs from the edge of Gloucestershire, across Herefordshire, and along the edge of the Black Mountains as far as Milford Haven, is so fragmented with an absence of re-constructable vessel profiles (see Gibson 2013). No good groups were identified and from the 24 sites radiocarbon dates generally point to nothing earlier than the 38th century cal BC (Darvill 2020, 37–44) with much of the pottery being identified as 'Developed' Carinated Bowl and falling after 3800 cal BC (Gibson 2013).

The complex of early Neolithic monuments at Dorstone Hill, Herefordshire (Overton *et al.* 2022), which also includes a large timber building, is important and significant given its location. The site is still in the process of analysis but the pottery from the causewayed enclosure can be characterised as including carinated and S-profiled bowls, whilst heavy-rimmed vessels of simple bowl form (*e.g.* Gwernvale vessel 1) are notably absent (from my observations so far). The early modelled date for the construction of the Dorstone enclosure falls within the late 38th or early 37th century cal BC and would certainly fit with the presence of some carinated bowls within the associated pottery assemblage in contrast to the material from Caerau (Cardiff), which is dominated by rounded and possible baggy bowls, some with lugs and restricted use of decoration (Deacon 2017, 11 and fig. 7), and appears to belong to the 35th century cal BC (see Chapter 4 below). One last point is that the out-turned everted rim from Gwernvale vessel 25, would not be out of place within the latter assemblage (*e.g.* Deacon 2017, fig. 7.1 and 3).

The very large assemblage from the midden, posthole structures and possible hilltop enclosure at Clegyr Boia (A. Williams 1953) has no direct radiocarbon dating (dismissing the BM dates BM-1109 and 1110 as much later than their respective contexts: see Peterson 2003, 124) and typologically could belong to either the late 38th century cal BC or the early part of the 37th. As noted above, this assemblage contains carinated forms but only as a minor element alongside at least five other bowl forms and perhaps more (see Petersen 2003, 126–8). As Lynch (1969) notes, there is similarity with the South-Western or Hembury style, and its association with post-built structures, middens and a later hill-top enclosure of uncertain Neolithic date only strengthens this link. Its carinated vessels are of derived form and the rim forms are out-curved ('hooked') and semi-rolled. Cupped lugs and occasional use of slight decoration all point towards a later date.

Middle Neolithic

The latest Neolithic pottery from Gwernvale includes two vessels that were originally classified as Ebbsfleet (vessel 28) and Mortlake (vessel 26) (F. Lynch 1984, 110). Vessel 28, as Lynch concluded, is typical of the Ebbsfleet style and there is little that can be added to her original typological discussion other than the clarification of the likely date of this style following the redating and Bayesian modelling of such sites as the West Kennet long barrow (Bayliss *et al.* 2007d) and the Windmill Hill causewayed enclosure (Whittle *et al.* 2011, 778; see also Gibson and Kinnes 1997; Marshall *et al.* 2009; Ard and Darvill 2015). Vessel 26 with its much heavier overhanging rim and shoulder position marked with a decorated cordon has closer affinities with the Mortlake style but its bowl form is reminiscent of certain Decorated Bowl forms as Lynch notes, referencing the Abingdon style in particular (Whittle *et al.* 2011, 110). It must also be noted that whilst some of the Peterborough or Impressed style in Wales, like other regions of Britain, can be quite similar inter-regionally there are other examples where the opposite is true, with vessels perhaps reflecting regional development (see Gibson 1995). This would certainly be true of vessel 26.

There is little doubt that both these styles had their origins in the third quarter of the 4th millennium cal BC and that their stylistic affinities lie within the final Bowl assemblages. Their contextual association with the final use, blocking and post-blocking use (closure) of various tombs and their occurrence with new types of monument is well-understood and can be seen at Gwernvale. As noted in Chapter 4, the date for the construction of the long cairn as derived from the model is not as precisely determined as it could be due to a lack of samples. Its relatively late date for the start of construction could reflect this. The key pottery vessels (20, 25, 26 and 28) from the use and blocking would certainly support this interpretation of the modelled results and date. The recovery of parts of vessel 20 within Chamber 2 and parts of vessel 25 from below the blocking would not contradict the construction date if this was seen more as a *terminus ante quem*, whilst the use of the Ebbsfleet style bowl could be close to the date range for construction (3575–3130 cal BC (*95% probability*; or *3530–3330 cal BC 68% probability*; *construct_Gwernvale_monument*; Fig. 4.4; see Chapter 4). Vessel 26 fits well with the late 4th millennium cal BC dates obtained for Peterborough Ware activity at Gwernvale (see Chapter 4). Our understanding of the chronological position and sequence of Ebbsfleet Ware would certainly benefit from the direct dating of absorbed lipids as this would remove any contextual ambiguity from material recovered from less secure contexts, such as the blocking of tombs and the later ditch fills of monuments.

Conclusion: mind the gap

Gwernvale may still have the earliest pottery from Wales but along with the pit group from Dyffryn Ardudwy its precise rather than relative date remains uncertain. There seems little doubt that both assemblages could belong to the decades before or after 3800 BC cal BC, and to part of the period of contact, widespread cultural transmission and innovation that Thomas (2022) refers to as Neolithisation (see also Sheridan 2010). However, without direct dating (*e.g.* direct lipid radiocarbon dates or food residue dates), this will remain a matter for interpretation. That some of the material could be much later in date based on more securely radiocarbon dated groups seems plausible and that there could be a gap between the two groups appears possible. In the light of new sites and a more critical use of radiocarbon dating, we can certainly bring greater clarity to the understanding of the chronological development of early Neolithic pottery of the 39th to 37th centuries cal BC, which potentially has a fluid and complex history with regional drift from the original style (see Sheridan 2016). It is generally acknowledged that the earliest pottery is uniform and restricted in style but as Herne (1988) and others have noted appeared as a fully developed style and an imported technology and craft. With the more widespread onset of Neolithic practices and lifeways the more unified and conservative Carinated Bowl forms gave way to a more diverse range of vessels and the development of modified forms. This included sinuous open forms with more elaborate rims and in which the carination was less important and not always retained. Perhaps increasingly carinated vessels became less important, although they still form a high percentage, but perhaps no more than 50 percent, of the assemblages. If pottery innovation occurred during the 38th century cal BC with the development of new forms, it then begs the question of what drove this change in the well-established motor habits of the earliest communities and the decision for their potters to adapt their craft. By the 38th century cal BC societies were several generations into a Neolithic lifestyle (well beyond initial contact) and were beginning to develop monuments and visibly transform their world. Beyond the stone-built tombs and structures, were also the timber buildings: the larger hall-like structures, the smaller dwellings, and other shelters. Whatever their purpose such constructions provided new arenas for social gatherings and interaction in which pottery played an important part in the preparation, cooking and sharing of food, but also somewhere to make, safely store, display, use, repurpose, and discard pottery. It is into this different and changing world that new forms of pottery were developed and used. The possible sequence at Gwernvale from carinated to simpler forms reflects these chronological trends.

The likely cultural origins and influence of the Gwernvale pottery point to widespread connections between adjacent regions such as the Black Mountains and the associated river valleys and south Wales generally, the river valley of the Severn and the distant upland areas of the Cotswold Hills. There are certainly strong stylistic links with the similar carinated forms found at Dyffryn Ardudwy but also towards the east and the earlier assemblages from the Cotswolds and to the south such as the Sweet Track. Culturally some of the pottery appears to have its earliest links with the ubiquitous Carinated Bowl that appears to have derived from contact made along the south-east coast and spread both inland and along the British coast as suggested by Whittle *et al.* (2011, 849–53), with the earlier sites falling near the coast or in the south-east. It remains the case that no significant pottery group of pre-3800 cal BC has been securely dated leaving aside both Gwernvale and Dyffryn Ardudwy and beyond these two sites there could be little else before the later decades of the 38th century. This in itself may present a strong indicator of the nature, scale and frequency of the uptake of early Neolithic practices before 3700 cal BC, and of possible directions of cultural influence (see J. Thomas 2022; Sheridan 2010; and Chapter 12 below).

The pottery from the use and blocking of the Gwernvale long cairn can now be placed more precisely in a wider chronological framework with several new sites, enclosures and pits, where larger radiocarbon data sets have been obtained and have been subjected to Bayesian modelling (see above and Chapter 4). As noted in the original study this pottery is more limited and typologically different, belonging to the Plain Bowl (use and pre-blocking) and Peterborough Ware (blocking and pits) traditions that can now be more securely dated to the later centuries of the 4th millennium cal BC.

11

Organic residue analysis of early Neolithic pottery from Gwernvale

Isabel L. Wiltshire and Lucy J.E. Cramp

Introduction and methodology

Commodities that were processed and stored in unglazed ceramic vessels can be characterised using the presence, distribution and stable isotope analysis of preserved lipid components. These are extracted from the porous matrix of the pot and survive thanks to their hydrophobicity and physical protection from microbial decay. The extraction and analysis of the lipid residues can be used to identify surviving traces of terrestrial animal fats, marine animal fats, plant oils and waxes, beeswax and other organic products, giving diagnostic information on the original contents and use of the vessels (for examples see Roffet-Salque *et al.* 2017). Degraded animal fats, the most commonly characterised residue recovered from archaeological cooking pots, are characterised by high abundances of saturated fatty acids, specifically palmitic ($C_{16:0}$) and stearic ($C_{18:0}$) fatty acids. The stable carbon isotope composition of these fatty acids allows for the further distinction between ruminant (*e.g.* cow, sheep, goat, deer) and non-ruminant (*e.g.* porcine, aquatic) carcass fats. Dairy fats can also be distinguished from carcass fats for ruminant species, as the $C_{18:0}$ fatty acid from milk fats exhibits more depleted $\delta^{13}C$ values than adipose fats (Dudd and Evershed 1998; Evershed *et al.* 2002). Calculating $\Delta^{13}C$ values ($\delta^{13}C_{18:0}$ - $\delta^{13}C_{16:0}$) and plotting them against the $\delta^{13}C$ value of the $C_{16:0}$ fatty acid can remove variations arising from C_3 versus C_4 diets of the animals or other local variations, emphasising biosynthetic and metabolic characteristics of the fat source (Copley *et al.* 2003).

Ten sherds of early Neolithic pottery belonging to five vessels from pre-cairn contexts at Gwernvale were selected for the extraction and characterisation of absorbed lipid residues (Table 11.1) out of a minimum number of 17 pre-cairn vessels which were defined subjectively on their visual appearance with greater or lesser degrees of certainty. Although the early Neolithic assemblage at Gwernvale contained both Carinated Bowl (which has also been called Irish Sea ware) and heavy-rimmed unshouldered bowls (F. Lynch 1984), the five vessels (9–13) that were suitable for sampling

Table 11.1. Gwernvale: sherds of early Neolithic pottery selected for the extraction and characterisation of absorbed lipid residues.

ID	*Context*	*Site number*	*Museum accession number*	*Vessel number*	*Notes*
GWE_001	Pre-cairn soil	GV30/1780	79.54H/1.494	9	body
GWE_002	F149 (irregular trench)	GV149/2147	79.54H/1.216	10	body
GWE_003	Pre-cairn soil	GV30/1063	79.54H/2.225	10	body
GWE_004	Pre-cairn soil	GV31/2828	79.54H/1.231	11	shoulder
GWE_005	Pre-cairn soil	GV31/1324	79.54H/1.243	11	body
GWE_006	Pre-cairn soil	GV49/827	79.54H/1.382	12	body
GWE_007	Pre-cairn soil	GV30/1938	79.54H/1.386	12	body
GWE_008	Pre-cairn soil	GV31/1211	79.54H/1.492	13	body
GWE_009	F68 (pre-cairn pit)	GV68/1102	79.54H/1.532	13	body
GWE_010	Pre-cairn soil	GV30/2030	79.54H/1.535	13	body

were all classed in the original report as Carinated Bowls (four fine and one coarse). The sampled sherds (Fig. 11.1) all come from the area of either the pre-cairn midden or timber structure discussed in Chapter 3. The pre-cairn phase of activity as a whole has modelled dates of between *3840–3720 cal BC* (*68% probability*) and *3500–3240 cal BC* (*68% probablility*).

Total lipid extracts were obtained from these sherds, following Correa-Ascencio and Evershed (2014). These were screened and quantified using gas chromatography and where lipids were present, these were identified using gas chromatography-mass spectrometry. Stable carbon isotope analysis of individual fatty acids from residues identified as degraded animal fats was performed to further classify these fats, namely the separation of marine and non-ruminant (*e.g.* porcine, aquatic) fats from ruminants and, within the latter, dairy from carcass fats. Full details of the methodology can be found in the technical appendix below.

Results and interpretation

Lipids were well preserved in six of the 10 of sherds, representing all five vessels (Table 11.2). This is similar to the lipid recovery rates from early Neolithic pottery from southern England (57%; Copley *et al.* 2003), Scotland and northern Britain (54%; Cramp *et al.* 2014) and Ireland (60%; Smyth and Evershed 2016). The mean lipid concentration of the Gwernvale sherds containing lipids was 2.3 mg.g^{-1}, with a maximum lipid concentration of 5.5 mg.g^{-1}. This is very high and demonstrates good preservation, likely indicating that these vessels were subjected to sustained use in the processing of high lipid-yielding

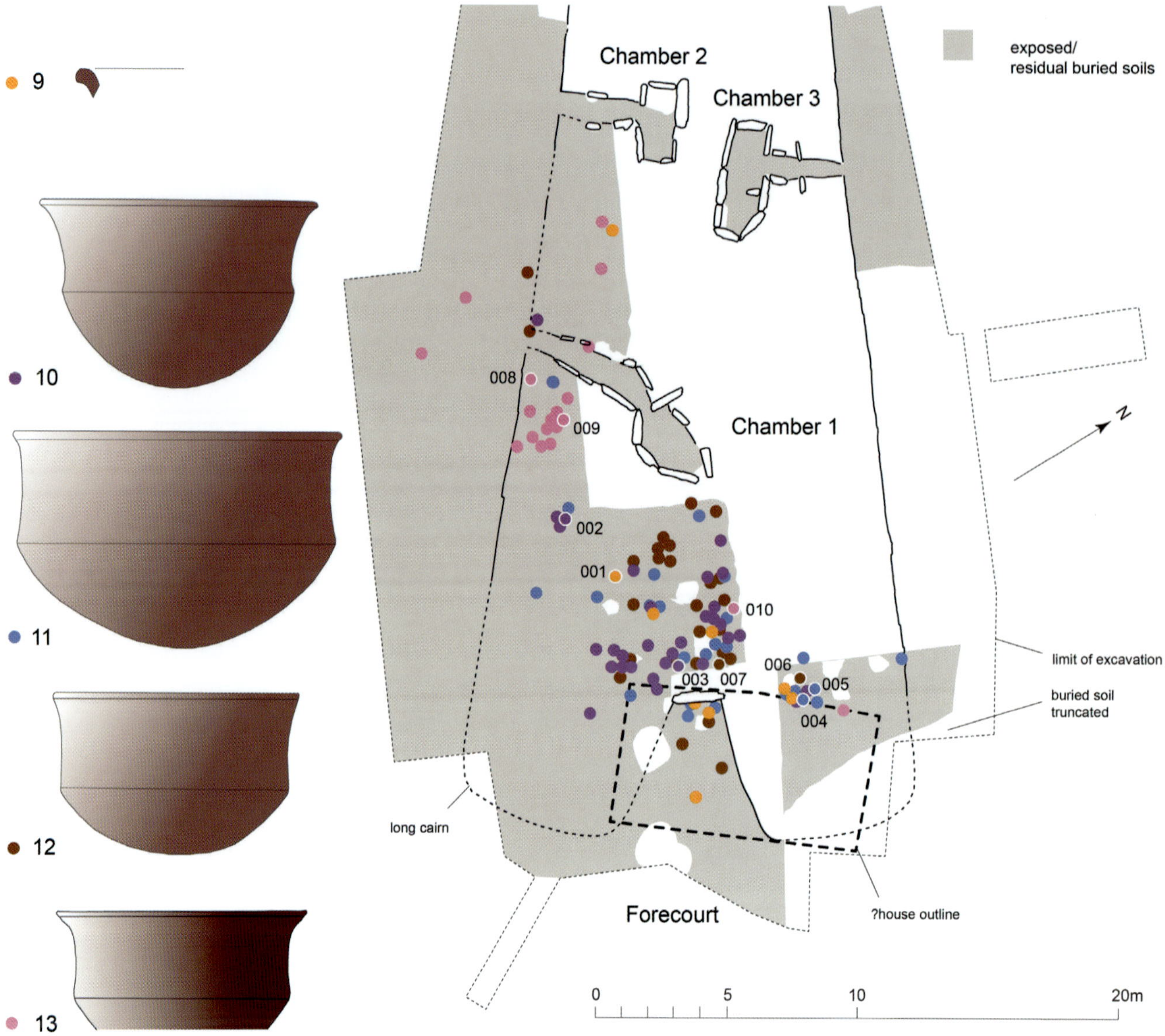

Fig. 11.1. Gwernvale: distribution of sherds sampled for organic residue analysis (ID nos GWE-001 –010) attributed to vessels 9–13 (reconstructed vessel forms).

commodities. For comparison, the mean lipid concentration from early Neolithic pottery from southern England was 0.14 mg.g^{-1}, with a maximum lipid concentration of 1.47 mg.g^{-1} (Copley *et al*. 2005). The lipid extracts all contained a distribution of saturated free fatty acids, predominantly palmitic ($C_{16:0}$) and stearic ($C_{18:0}$) fatty acids, indicative of the presence of degraded animal fats surviving in these vessels (Fig. 11.2).

Table 11.2. Gwernvale: summary of the results of the organic residue analyses.

ID	*Lipid concentration (μg.g^{-1})*	*Total lipid in extract (μg)*	*$\delta^{13}C_{16:0}$ ‰*	*$\delta^{13}C_{18:0}$ ‰*	*$\Delta^{13}C$ ‰*	*Lipid composition (FFAs – free fatty acids OCN – odd carbon number)*	*Attribution*
GWE_001	784	309	-29.9	-34.7	-4.8	FFAs (C14 – C18; inc. OCN)	Ruminant dairy fats
GWE_002	286	164	-29.5	-33.9	-4.3	FFAs (C14 – C18; inc. OCN, C18:1)	Ruminant dairy fats
GWE_003	76	42	–	–	–	–	–
GWE_004	4276	2775	-30.8	-35.4	-4.5	FFAs (C14 – C24; inc. OCN)	Ruminant dairy fats
GWE_005	5500	4412	-30.2	-35.1	-4.9	FFAs (C14 – C24; inc. OCN)	Ruminant dairy fats
GWE_006	2726	1170	-29.9	-35.3	-5.4	FFAs (C14 – C26; inc. OCN, C18:1)	Ruminant dairy fats
GWE_007	84	57	–	–	–	–	–
GWE_008	128	143	-29.4	-34.4	-5.1	FFAs (C14 – C24; inc. OCN)	Ruminant dairy fats
GWE_009	76	49	–	–	–	–	–
GWE_010	60	47	–	–	–	–	–

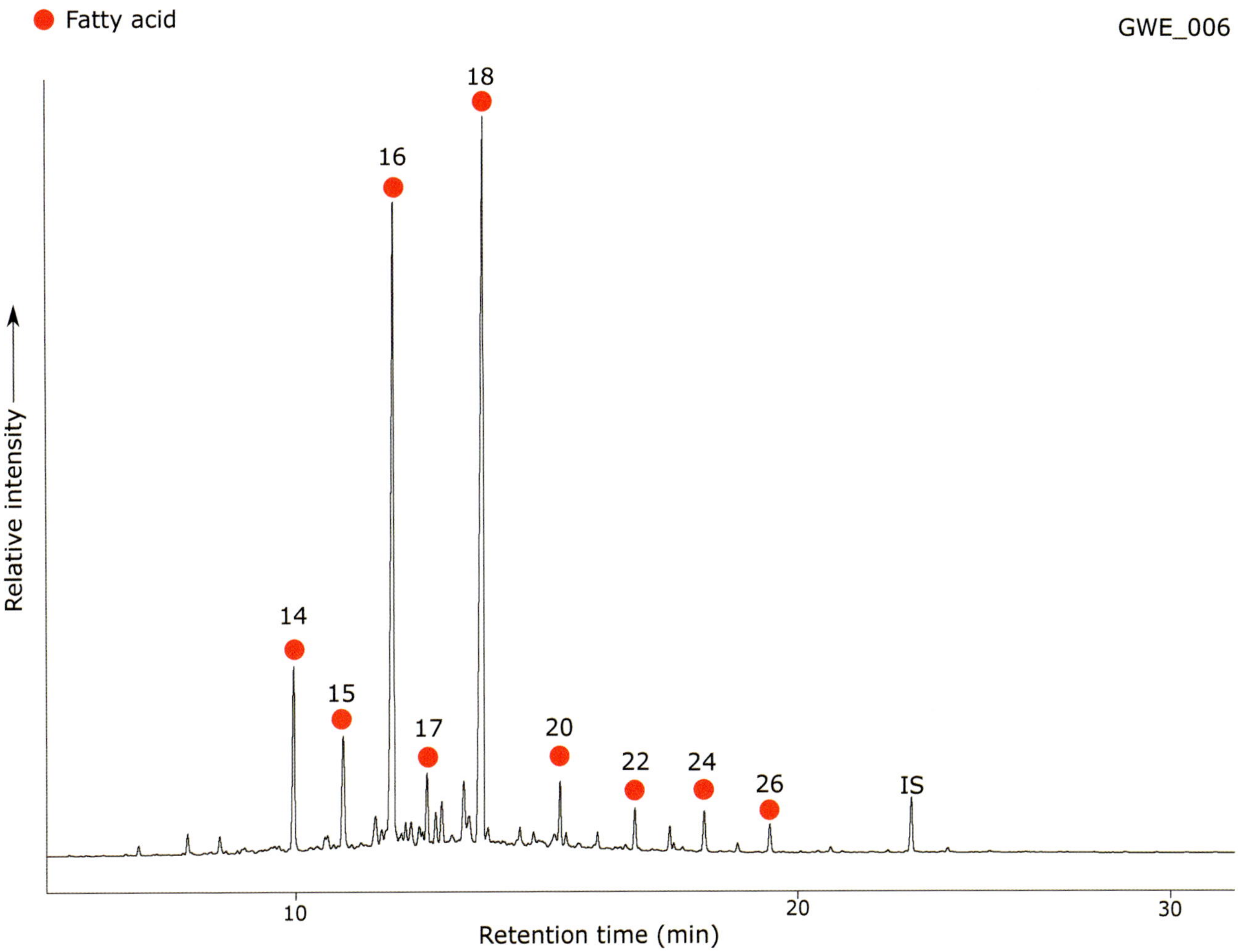

Fig. 11.2. Gas chromatogram of trimethylsilylated FAMEs from Gwernvale early Neolithic pottery extract of GWE_006 (sherd no. 1.382). Circles, n-*alkanoic acids (fatty acids, FA); IS, internal standard, C_{34}* n-*tetratriacontane.*

Variability in lipid contents was identified within individual vessels. For instance, multiple sherds from the same pot assigned to vessels 10, 12 and 13 contained lipid concentrations that ranged from negligible through to several hundred micrograms of lipid per gram of sherd. As most of the sherds analysed were featureless body sherds, it was not possible confirm where on the vessel they would have originated, meaning it cannot be determined whether the distribution patterns derive from the original use of the vessel.

Single compound stable carbon isotope values were determined for $C_{16:0}$ and $C_{18:0}$ fatty acids extracted from all six sherds that contained residues resembling degraded animal fats to ascertain the source of the lipids extracted. The $\delta^{13}C$ values of the $C_{16:0}$ and $C_{18:0}$ fatty acids from the lipid profiles are plotted on to a scatter plot, shown against reference animal fat ellipses obtained from the measurement of modern UK species of the major domesticates during the British Neolithic (cows, sheep, goat and pigs) raised on known C_3 diets (Copley *et al.* 2003) (Fig. 11.3a). If products of different origins have been processed in the vessel, contemporaneously or during its lifetime, extracted lipids will plot between the end points of those commodities; calculated theoretical mixing curves are also shown on the graph (Evershed *et al.* 2002; Mukherjee *et al.* 2005).

To remove local environmental effects on absolute fatty acid $\delta^{13}C$ values, the $\Delta^{13}C$ ($\delta^{13}C_{18:0} - \delta^{13}C_{16:0}$) values can be plotted against $\delta^{13}C_{16:0}$ values (Fig. 11.3b). Ruminant dairy fats are differentiated from ruminant adipose fats when they display $\Delta^{13}C$ values of less than −3.1 ‰ (Dunne *et al.* 2012; Salque *et al.* 2013). The lipid residues from the six extracts analysed all plot within, or just on the border of, the dairy reference fat ellipsis and have $\Delta^{13}C$ values below −3.1 ‰ indicating these vessels were all used to process dairy products such as milk, butter or cheese.

Although only five (29%) of the minimum of 17 vessels identified from pre-cairn contexts at Gwernvale were sampled, it is interesting to note that all of them were used for processing dairy products. This is high, even for early Neolithic pottery. Previous studies have shown the presence of dairy fats in 80% of early Neolithic vessels in Scotland and northern Britain (Cramp *et al.* 2014), and 89% in Ireland (Smyth and Evershed 2016). Lipids from Carinated Bowls from two sites in southern Britain were also predominantly of dairying origin (Eton Rowing Lake (78%; Copley *et al.* 2003) and Ascott-under-Wychwood (91%; Copley and Evershed 2007).

Although dairy lipids dominate in early Neolithic pottery from Britain and Ireland, it is relatively unusual for pots to have been exclusively used for the processing of dairy products. It is interesting to note, however, that the vast majority of the sampled vessels associated with the early Neolithic timber buildings at Parc Cybi and Parc Bryn Cegin were also solely associated with dairy products (Dunne and Evershed 2020a, 98; 2020b, 106; Kenney 2021). The presence of dairy lipids could be partly due to the use of milk as a waterproofing agent; however, the high lipid concentrations indicate the sustained use of the vessels for processing dairy products, comparable to the vessels at Parc Cybi, which also showed the presence of ketones (Kenney 2021, 41). Subsequent use of a vessel waterproofed with milk for other products would also be expected to result in an integrated lipid signature reflecting these multiple origins. The analysis of surface residues from pottery from the Carreg Coetan Arthur chambered tomb showed the processing of probable animal products in one vessel, but the source of the lipids was not investigated (Stern 2012).

To investigate whether this was a genuine phenomenon at Gwernvale or the result of random sampling, the probability P(N|Z) that N vessels would contain dairy lipids, given that five sampled vessels did, was calculated using Bayes Theorem (Fig. 11.4; see caption for details on calculation). N was defined as an integer between 5 and 17. It was assumed sampling was random and that all vessels contained lipids. The probability that all 17 vessels would contain dairy lipids, following these assumptions, was 5%. The scenario with the highest probability was for 15 of the 17 vessels (88%) to contain dairy lipids, which is consistent with previous studies. That is to say, the pottery at Gwernvale was probably used predominantly, but not exclusively, for the processing of dairy products. That is consistent with the pattern suggested by dietary isotope analysis of human remains from Penywyrlod, Ty Isaf, Tinskinswood and Heston Brake, presented in Chapter 8.

Conclusion

Ten early Neolithic pottery sherds, representing five vessels, from Gwernvale were selected for the extraction and characterisation of absorbed lipid residues. The recovery rate was good, with 60% of sherds yielding interpretable lipid profiles, although there was significant variation in the concentrations of lipids within vessels. Sherds containing lipids showed high concentrations, indicating that these vessels were probably subjected to sustained use processing high lipid-yielding commodities. All the vessels analysed showed evidence of dairy processing (100%).

This compares well to previously published data of the lipid analysis of early Neolithic pottery from Britain, where recovery rates are between 53% and 60%, and the proportion of dairy lipids in an assemblage are generally higher than 70% (Copley *et al.* 2003; Copley and Evershed 2007; Cramp *et al.* 2014; Smyth and Evershed 2016).

As noted above, the probability that all vessels from Gwernvale would have been used to process dairy was shown to be unlikely on statistical grounds. The early

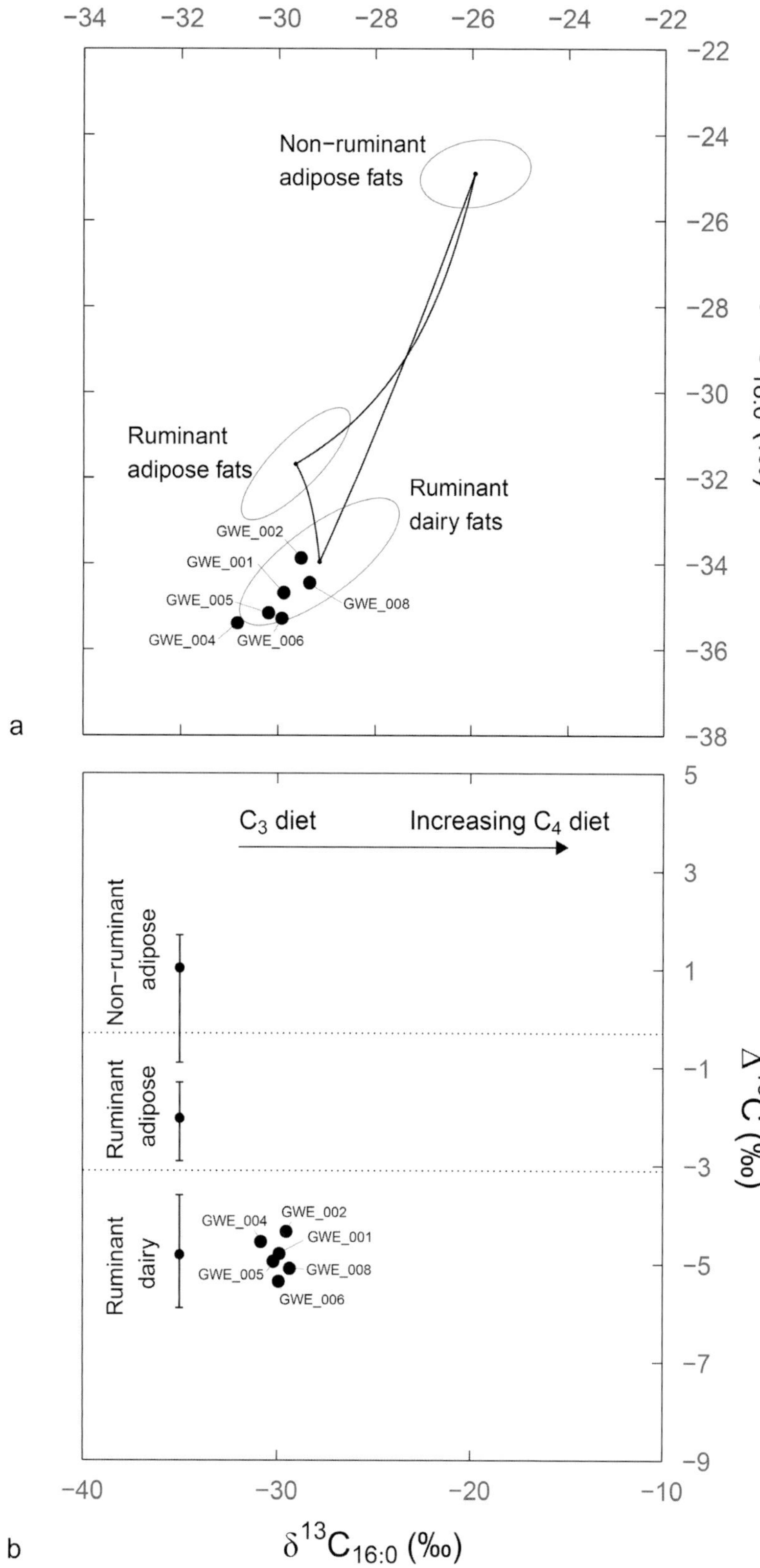

Fig. 11.3. Graphs showing: a) $\delta^{13}C$ values for the $C_{16:0}$ against $C_{18:0}$ fatty acids for archaeological fats extracted from Gwernvale early Neolithic ceramics. The three fields correspond to the P = 0.684 confidence ellipses for animals raised on a strict C_3 diet in Britain (Copley et al. *2003). Each data point represents an individual vessel. b) the $\Delta^{13}C$ ($\delta^{13}C_{18:0} - \delta^{13}C_{16:0}$) values plotted against $\delta^{13}C_{16:0}$ values from the same potsherds. The ranges shown here represent the mean ± 1 s.d. of the $\Delta^{13}C$ values for a global database comprising published modern reference animals from Europe, Africa and the Near East (Dunne* et al. *2012).*

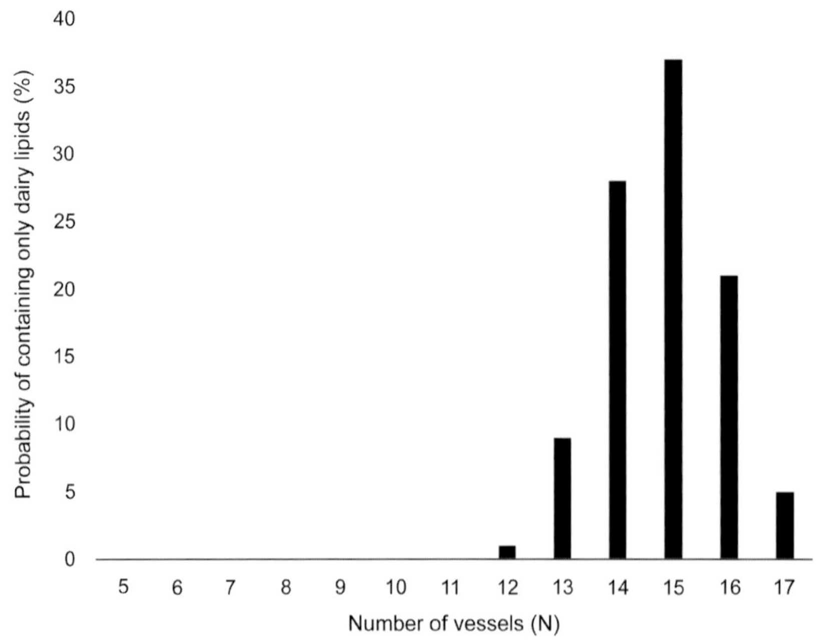

$$P(N|Z) = \frac{P(N) * P(Z|N)}{P(Z)} = \text{Bayes Theorem formula}$$

$P(N|Z)$ = probability that N vessels contain dairy lipids given 5 vessels did

$P(N)$ = probability that N vessels would contain dairy lipids generally

$$P(Z|N) = \frac{\binom{N}{5}}{\binom{17}{5}} = \text{probability of 5 vessels containing lipids given that N vessels did}$$

$$P(Z) = \sum_{N=5}^{17} P(Z|N) * P(N) = \text{probability that 5 vessels would contain dairy lipids generally}$$

Fig. 11.4. Bayes Theorem formula was used to calculate the probability that N vessels would contain dairy lipids, given that five sampled vessels did. This was plotted (top) as a percentage against N, which was defined as an integer between 5 and 17. It was assumed sampling was random and that all vessels contained lipids. The probability that N vessels would contain dairy lipids generally was obtained by generating a normal distribution around mean proportion of dairy lipids obtained from previous studies (Copley et al. *2003; Copley and Evershed 2007; Cramp* et al. *2014; Smyth and Evershed 2015).*

Neolithic vessels from Gwernvale were instead probably used predominantly, but not exclusively, for the processing of dairy products.

It has been shown that dairying was an important component of agricultural practices in most of Britain and Ireland from the early Neolithic onwards (*e.g.* Copley *et al.* 2005; Cramp *et al.* 2014; Smyth and Evershed 2015). The evidence from Gwernvale therefore fits well into this wider pattern of dairy exploitation and the processing of dairy products in pottery during the early Neolithic in Britain, which are discussed more fully in Chapter 12.

Acknowledgements

We thank Jody Deacon and the Museum of Wales for permission to use their collections and NERC (Reference: CC010) and NEIF (www.isotopesuk.org) for funding and maintenance of the GC-C-IRMS instrument used for this work; and Dr Sam Passmore for his help with the statistical analysis.

Technical appendix

Lipid extraction and analysis were carried out using established protocols described in detail in earlier publications (Correa-Ascencio and Evershed 2014). Each sherd was photographed before sampling. A modelling drill was used to clean the external surfaces of an area of sherd to be sampled. The cleaned area was sampled using a chisel and hammer before being ground to a fine powder with a glass mortar and pestle. The cleaned and ground sample was weighed, transferred to culture tube I along with 20 μL of internal standard (IS; *n*-tetratriacontane, 1 mg.ml^{-1}) then extracted with a solution of H_2SO_4/MeOH (5ml, 4% *v/v*,

70°C, 1 hour). Following this, the supernatant was centrifuged (2500 rpm, 10 min) and transferred to culture tube II, along with 2 mL of double-distilled water. The lipids were extracted using *n*-hexane (2 × 3mL, 2 × 2mL) and blown down to dryness under a gentle nitrogen stream at 40°C in a 3.5 mL vial. Solvents and reagents were HPLC grade. To avoid contamination, all disposable glassware was furnaced and reusable glassware was solvent-washed and furnaced. An analytical blank was run alongside all samples to monitor contamination in the laboratory.

Aliquots of the total lipid extract (TLE) was taken, blown down under N_2 and treated with 20 μL of BSTFA (N,O-bis(trimethylsilyl)trifluoroacetamide, 70°C, 1 hour) prior to screening using high temperature gas chromatography (HTGC). Aliquots from selected sherds were then trimethylsilylated (as above) for the structural identification of components using GC/mass spectrometry (GC/MS) and the determination of the stable carbon isotopic composition of the methylated fatty acids using GC-combustion-isotope ratio MS (GC/C/IRMS). The $\delta^{13}C$ values were derived according to the following expression and are relative to the international standard vPDB: $\delta^{13}C$ ‰ = $((R_{sample} - R_{standard})/R_{standard}) \times 1000$ where $R = {}^{13}C/{}^{12}C$. The $\delta^{13}C$ values were corrected for the carbon atoms added during methylation using a mass balance equation (Rieley 1994).

12

The first stones: taking and keeping the land

Alasdair Whittle, William Britnell and Seren Griffiths

Beyond the important individual details that recent research on the Penywyrlod and Gwernvale long cairns has added to our understanding of the early Neolithic in the Black Mountains, our main argument is that a distinctive set of practices can be seen in the history of this regional group of monuments in inland south-east Wales. That has been variously asserted before (Daniel 1950, 65; F. Lynch 2000, 69; Wysocki and Whittle 2000, 600), with much previous emphasis on perceived eccentricity, diversity and idiosyncrasy, but the wider case for distinctiveness can now be set out in greater depth within the framework of more detailed narratives for the local, regional and national contexts. The story can be seen as one of Neolithic land-taking, effected by the establishment of distinctive regional identities through attachment to place, tomb architecture and mortuary practices, and a play on regional connections and possible affiliations, and in due course of land-keeping and adherence to old ways as the world around changed. We try to break with the ingrained habit of offering generalised and often somewhat timeless accounts of Cotswold-Severn monuments, in an effort to get at more individual circumstances. This attempt will also underline what we still do not understand about the Black Mountains tombs and their setting, and thus help to frame further research in the future, both here and elsewhere.

Mesolithic occupation of south-east Wales

Our commentary is arranged chronologically, and we begin with the Mesolithic period. The first contribution of this volume has been to remove plausible support for a late Palaeolithic presence at Gwernvale, following the arguments set out by Elizabeth Walker in Chapter 9 about the character of the lithic assemblage. That frees us to concentrate on the Mesolithic occupation of inland south-east Wales, as seen around the fringes of the Black Mountains. The evidence from Gwernvale shows both an early and a late Mesolithic presence (note that we follow a simpler periodisation than Conneller (2022)). The situation at Penywyrlod was completely different, as we emphasise below.

The Gwernvale Mesolithic evidence, particularly the lithic assemblage rather than the minimal features recorded, is compatible with some kind of camp, rather than a specialised hunting stand or extraction site. The relatively small size and composition of the lithic assemblage seem best interpreted as small-scale, episodic settlement activity of short duration with a toolkit for hunting and processing (Healey and Green 1984, 129–30). The microliths, reviewed in Chapter 9, suggest both an early and a late Mesolithic presence.

There are few if any specific indicators of seasonality or duration of occupation, but given the timespans involved it is plausible that this was a place visited from time to time and probably seasonally. Mesolithic presences are widely documented, from the coast to far inland (Stanton 1984; Olding 2000; E. Walker 2004; Bell 2007; Conneller 2022); in another inland setting, at Waun Fignen Felen, further west (Fig. 12.1), there is evidence to suggest that repeated visits of short duration were made for hunting around the shore of an upland lake (Barton *et al.* 1995, 92, 105, 109). This was probably a progressively wooded environment, indicated regionally for example by pollen analysis of peats of the valley-bottom lake at Llangorse, just to the west of the Black Mountains, at a height of 160m. In the Mesolithic period the local vegetation around the lake was predominantly deciduous woodland dominated by hazel with some oak and birch, but with grasses, plantains and nettles suggesting cleared ground (Walker *et al.* 1993; Pardoe 2019).

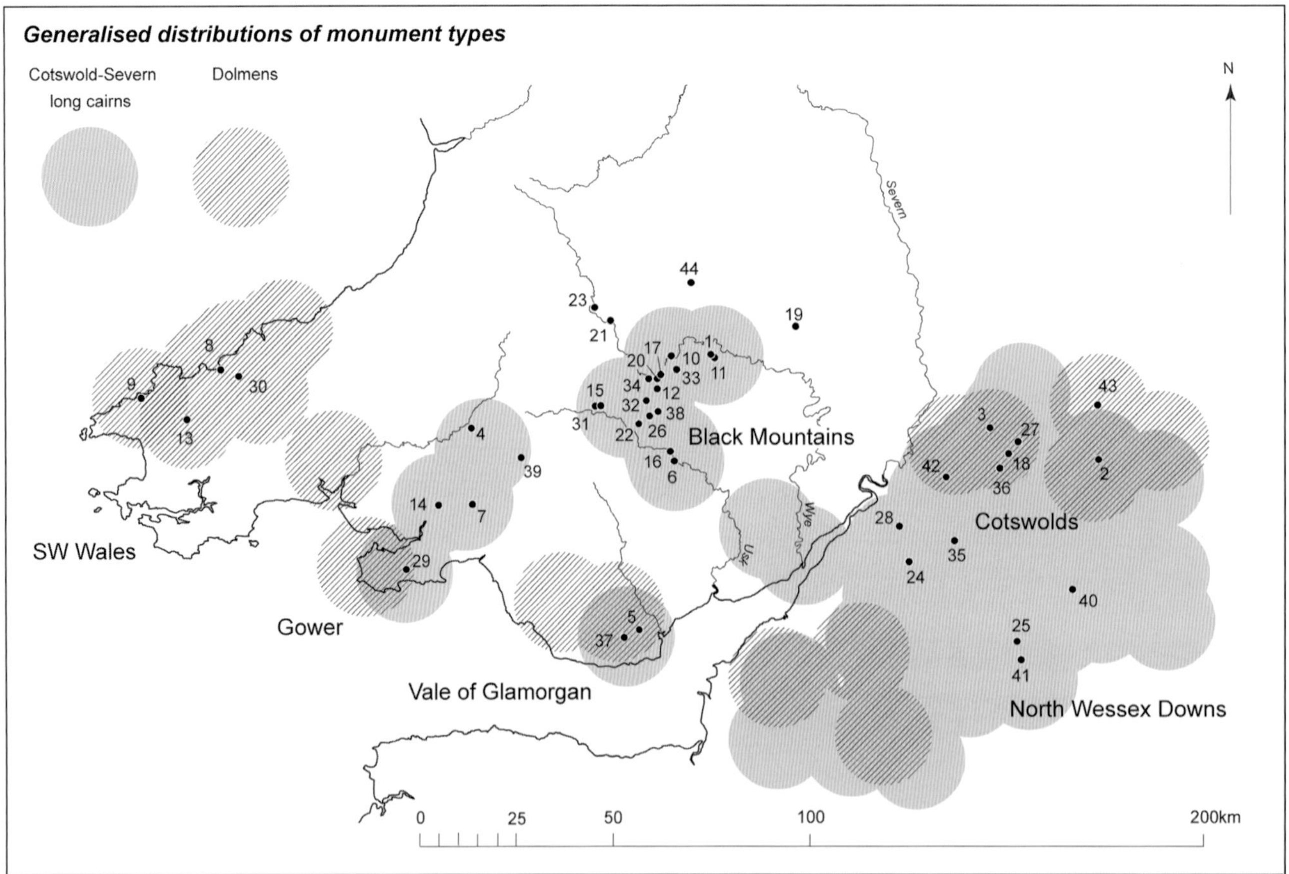

1 Arthur's Stone
2 Ascott-under-Wychwood
3 Belas Knap
4 Cae'r Ganfa
5 Caerau
6 Carn Goch
7 Carn Llechart
8 Carreg Coetan Arthur
9 Carreg Samson
10 Court Farm
11 Dorstone
12 Ffostyll North and South
13 Garn Turne
14 Graig Fawr
15 Gwenfrwyd
16 Gwernvale
17 Gwernyfed Park
18 Hazleton North and South
19 Hill Croft Field
20 Little Lodge
21 Llanelwedd
22 Llangorse
23 Llyn Mire
24 Luckington
25 Millbarrow
26 Mynydd Troed
27 Notgrove
28 Nympsfield
29 Parc le Breos Cwm
30 Pentre Ifan
31 Pen-y-Crug
32 Penywyrlod
33 Penywyrlod (Llanigon)
34 Pipton
35 Rodmarton
36 Sale's Lot
37 Tinkinswood
38 Ty Isaf
39 Waun Fignen Felen
40 Wayland's Smithy
41 West Kennet
42 West Tump
43 Whispering Knights
44 Womaston

Fig. 12.1. Map showing places in south Wales and the Cotswolds and adjacent areas mentioned in Chapter 12. (Generalised distributions of monument types after Darvill 2004 and F. Lynch 2011.)

The density of the Mesolithic presence regionally may have varied. Using just microliths as a diagnostic indicator, relatively few finds are known from the valleys around the Black Mountains; there may well be masking due to alluviation and modern land use (Myers 2007, 33), but the density of finds remains low even in excavated settings like Llangorse crannog (E. Walker 2019) or along the course of the South Wales Gas Pipeline (though some concentrations of finds have been made, for example around Dorstone Hill (Myers 2007, fig. 3.2; Ray 2016, 26). Plausibly, river valleys may have been routeways, and Gwernvale may have been one spot among many used in seasonal and other movements. From this perspective it is perhaps no coincidence that at the rather different, higher-lying, location of Penywyrlod there was minimal Mesolithic presence.

Likewise, although inland groups in inland south-east Wales were plausibly linked to the coast by seasonal and other movement (at Waun Fignen Felen both beach flint and mudstone beads were transported significant distances inland: Barton *et al.* 1995), nothing indicates that they were part of much wider, if probably rather sporadic, connections in the late Mesolithic period of the 5th millennium cal BC, as suggested variously, for example, by the evidence from Ferriter's Cove in western Ireland, the Scillies or Bexhill, Kent (Woodman *et al.* 1999; Garrow *et al.* 2017; Conneller 2022; Lawrence *et al.* in press). The decorated oak from near Maerdy, Glamorgan, has been compared to decorated stones in Breton monuments of probable 5th millennium cal BC date (J. Thomas 2022), but a direct connection is open to question.

Early Neolithic land-taking

At Gwernvale, early Neolithic occupation of the pre-cairn surface followed the Mesolithic use of the site, but there is no evidence for direct continuity. Here the first evidence for early Neolithic occupation, prior to the construction of the cairn, most probably dates to the 39th century cal BC, as set out in Chapter 4 (*3890–3790 cal BC, 60% probability*, or *3745–3715 cal BC 8% probability*; *start_Gwernvale_pre_cairn*; Fig. 4.4). So now the focus shifts to Penywyrlod and Dorstone. As set out in Chapters 2 and 4, their first Neolithic use probably goes back to the late 39th and 38th centuries cal BC. It will be for future analysis to determine which of these two locations was in operation first, or whether they were broadly contemporary. Although obviously there are other monuments in the Black Mountains distribution which have not been well dated or dated at all so far (Fig. 12.2), we assert here that Penywyrlod was early in the local sequence of early Neolithic development, following the preferred model set out in Chapter 4; the remaining chronological uncertainties must be fully acknowledged. In this chronological model, Penywyrlod was a signal part of the establishment of a Neolithic presence in inland south-east Wales, and we argue that this was effected in a striking and distinctive fashion.

There are several strands in the evidence for such a process of establishment. First, both pollen analysis and local and regional settlement evidence may suggest an initially low human impact, though the dating of possible trends leaves much to be desired.

There is in fact only limited evidence of the palaeoenvironmental contexts in which the Black Mountains tombs were constructed. No pollen evidence is directly associated with either Penywyrlod or Gwernvale, which are sited at heights of about 250m and 80m respectively. Pollen evidence from buried soil below the Mynydd Troed long barrow, at a height of about 370m, however, suggests that this tomb (of whatever date) was built on heathland dominated by plants of the heath or heather family in open woodland with some oak, ash and alder (Crampton and Webley 1966, 74). What is described as the 'pollen of cultivated grasses' was identified beneath a long mound at Llanelwedd above the Wye valley but the claim that this represents 'the first evidence of cereal-growing by Neolithic peoples in Wales' is now considered questionable, in view of the undoubted post-medieval date of the mound, despite the proximity of early Neolithic activity at the site (Caseldine 1990, 44; Britnell 2013, 210).

The palaeoenvironmental evidence in direct association with the Black Mountains tombs themselves is also limited. Various contexts within chambers and passages at Pipton produced samples of oak, Rosaceae, probably *Crataegus* (hawthorn), and hazel charcoal (Hyde 1956, 48) and these same species together with ash occur in undated contexts in the buried soil below the long cairn at Mynydd Troed (Crampton and Webley 1966, 74). Hazel and oak charcoal are present in the buried soil beneath Penywyrlod, and Maloideae charcoal (hawthorn, apple and whitebeams) and hazel charcoal are recorded from a burnt area below cairn collapse outside the entrance to Chamber NE I (see Chapter 2; Fig. 2.16). The hazel charcoal from these contexts dates to the first half of the 4th millennium cal BC (Table 4.3, SUERC-67741, -69931, -69932), with the first estimate for pre-cairn activity at Penywyrlod most probably also occurring in the 39th or 38th centuries cal BC (*3920–3720 cal BC, 95% probability*, or *3845–3760 cal BC, 68% probability*; *first_Penywyrlod_pre_cairn*; Fig. 4.12). As noted in Chapters 3 and 5, while there are suggestions that the main structural components of the pre-cairn timber structure at Gwernvale may have been built of oak, the presence of other species, including ash, hazel, blackthorn, and Maloideae, suggests the presence of more shrubby vegetation in the vicinity.

A preliminary model of a mainly wooded setting for early Neolithic activity, with low impacts from initial clearance, can therefore somewhat tentatively be proposed (cf. Cummings and Whittle 2004, 4; Rackham 2020, 154–5). Clearly, refinement of that picture should be an important goal for future research. In such a putative setting, there is scattered evidence for dispersed and small-scale early Neolithic settlement. Adding to existing knowledge (*e.g.* Olding 2000), the South Wales Gas Pipeline in particular has produced further sites, but has also served to underline the picture of generally small occupations. For example, a group of pits near Pen-y-Crug, Ysgir, in the Usk valley about 23km to the NW, contained featureless body sherds of probable early Neolithic date based on fabric (Gibson 2013, 25), flintwork, cereals and hazelnuts, with dates of the 37th and 36th centuries cal BC (Darvill *et al.* 2020, 43; see also Chapter 4); there is also evidence for a possible rectilinear timber building of modest proportions, but the structure is not directly dated (Darvill *et al.* 2020, fig. 4.5, B; Cotswold Archaeology 2014, 11). It is suggested that this and a second site at Gwenfrwyd, Llandefaelog, which also has traces of early Neolithic activity, might represent distant settlement associated with the Black Mountains tombs (Darvill *et al.* 2020, 43). Small undated assemblages of early Neolithic pottery possibly from domestic contexts are also known from the Wye valley at Gwernyfed Park, Aberllynfi (Lloyd and Savory 1958, 66) and from near Llanelwedd in a semi-upland location above the Wye valley (Britnell 2013, 214–16; Lynch and Darvill 2013).

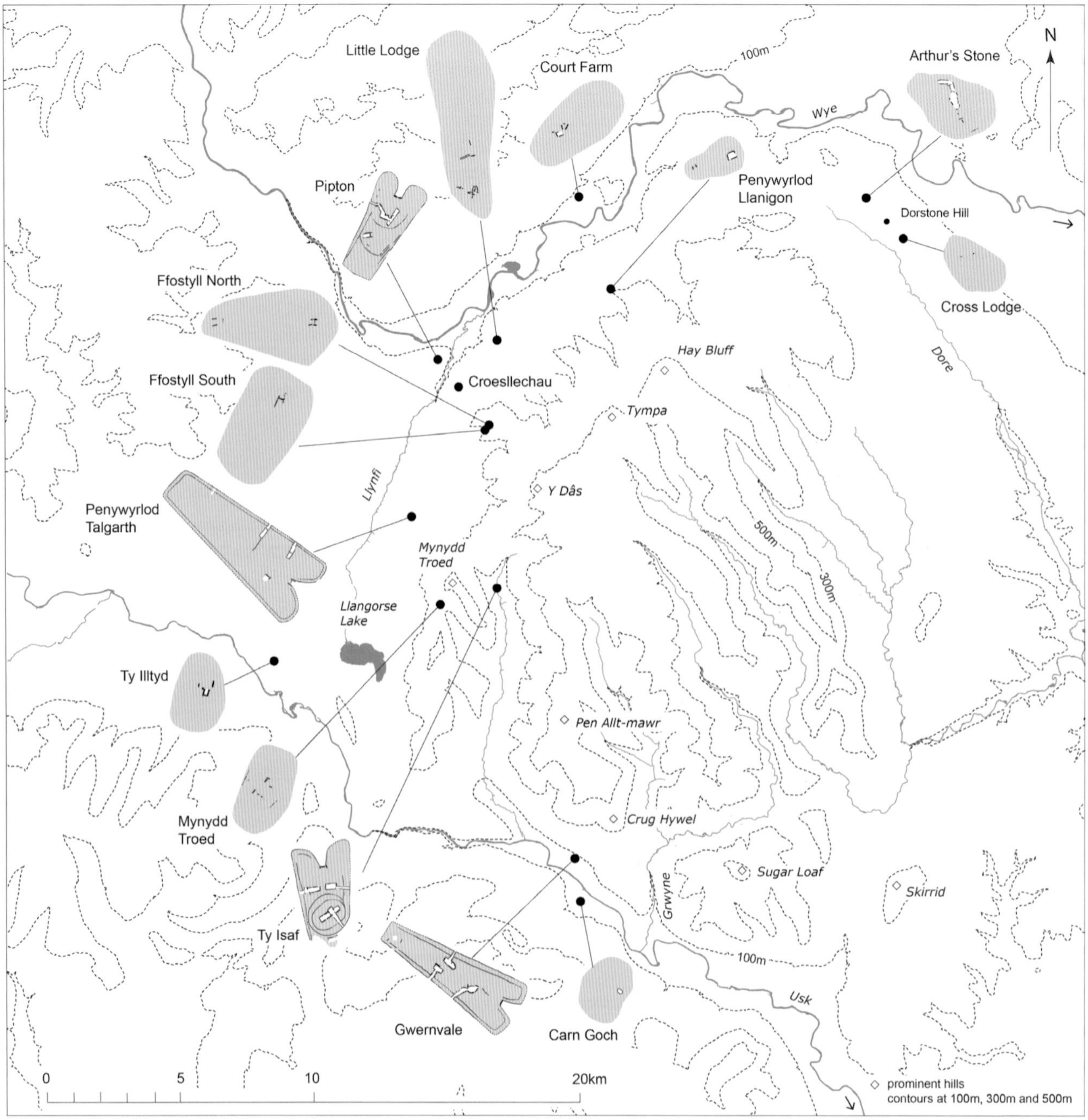

Fig. 12.2. The distribution of long cairns around the Black Mountains. All the sites are still extant, with the exception of Croesllechau which is known only from antiquarian accounts.

Some of this evidence, as also discussed in Chapter 4, is broadly dated to the first half and middle centuries of the 4th millennium cal BC. This spread of dates strongly indicates that there is little or no sign of any concentration of settlement activity very early in the regional sequence, and there is no sign yet in most of the region, apart from the evidence so far available from Dorstone (Fig. 12.3), of the large timber halls which have been taken elsewhere to mark founding or otherwise prominent early lineages (Ray and Thomas 2018). In a way this is a rather inconclusive picture – which should be another goal for sustained future research – but it does serve to suggest strongly that Penywyrlod as a construction early in the regional sequence would have been notable and prominent not only in its own monumental right but also by comparison to the relative lack of neighbours.

If Penywyrlod was constructed in the second half of 38th century cal BC, that invites a brief review of early

Fig. 12.3. The western mound at Dorstone Hill during excavation in July 2015.

Neolithic settlement in other parts of western Britain, from Cumbria down to Cornwall. Penywyrlod fits into a wider context of early Neolithic sites appearing up and down the west side of the country. In the south of Wales and the Marches, burial monuments most probably begin in the 39th or 38th centuries cal BC (*3830–3740 cal* BC, *95% probability*, or *3800–3760 cal BC, 68% probability*; *first_south_Wales_and_Marches_Neolithic_burial_monument*; Fig. 4.15).

This is not the place for detailed presentation of all the evidence. Initial modelling suggested a timelag in the appearance of the first Neolithic 'things and practices' in the south-west of England and then in south Wales and the Marches, compared with south-east and then south-central England, with start dates probably in the 39th and 38th centuries cal BC respectively (Whittle *et al.* 2011); a comparable picture for north Wales and north-west England was also available from other initial modelling (Griffiths 2011). Further modelling (Griffiths 2021), exploiting the availability of more dates, has produced slightly earlier estimates for the start of early Neolithic activity in north-west England, probably in *3940–3810 cal BC* (*95% probability*, or *3910–3825 cal BC, 68% probability*; *first_north_west_neolithic*; Griffiths 2021, 36).

In turn, revision is currently under way for the regional estimates for the start of Neolithic activity across England and Wales as a whole, initially presented in *Gathering Time* (Whittle *et al.* 2011, originally excluding north Wales, the Midlands and northern England; see also Whittle *et al.* 2022; in press). That will probably reinforce the picture for regional start dates given by Griffiths (2014; 2021). There is now an important rollcall of significant early Neolithic sites, too numerous to enumerate fully, but ranging from the Barrow peninsula (H. Evans 2018; Robinson *et al.* 2020), Stainton West (F. Brown 2021), the Bay Gateway (Bradley and Howard-Davis 2018) and now Windy Harbour on the Fylde peninsula (Oxford Archaeology 2020; Fraser Brown, *pers. comm.*) in north-west England, to Llandygai (Kenney 2008), Parc Cybi, Holyhead (Kenney 2021) and Llanfaethlu, Holyhead (Rees and Jones 2016; 2017), in north-west Wales, to Garn Turne, Pembrokeshire (Cummings and Richards 2021) and South Wales Gas Pipeline sites in Pembrokeshire in south-west Wales and other sites along its route to the east (Darvill 2020; and see Chapter 4), and to finally a slew of sites in the south-west of England, including in Cornwall along the North Cornwall Pipeline (Jones and Quinnell 2014), the South-West Reinforcement Pipeline (Mudd and Joyce 2014), Tregurra Valley (Taylor forthcoming), Penhale (Nowakowski and Johns 2015), Tregunnel Hill (Brindle forthcoming) and Cardinham North (Jones and Lawson-Jones 2018).

Even thus selected, this is quite a list. Nonetheless, these sites and others serve to define the broader early Neolithic context probably of the 40th to 39th and into the 38th centuries cal BC within which the construction of Penywyrlod and the first, arguably gradual establishment of Neolithic settlement in inland south-east Wales seems to have taken place. From this perspective, and without going into further details of inter-regional variation, in advance of further modelling for the revision of *Gathering Time*, Penywyrlod appears to fit in very well to this broader picture. It is already clearly not one of the very first sites of the wider early Neolithic phenomenon, but takes its place within the trend of Neolithisation up and down the western side of Britain. In south Wales and the Marches, this probably begins in the 39th or 38th centuries cal BC. The start of pre-cairn activity at Penywyrlod represents some of the earliest Neolithic activity in the region, most probably in the 39th or 38th centuries cal BC (Fig. 4.15). Further research will surely throw up more complexities in the story of the early Neolithic in the west of Britain, including the pace of adoption of cereal cultivation, as discussed in Chapter 4 (and see Griffiths 2018; 2021). There are also other considerations, and the whole picture remains complex.

First, the results of recent aDNA analysis (Brace *et al.* 2019; Brace forthcoming) must now be incorporated. These seem firmly to indicate that the process of Neolithisation was principally driven by the arrival of new people in both Britain and Ireland (see also Cassidy *et al.* 2016; 2020; Rivollat *et al.* 2020; Thomas 2022). Where those people came from has still to be determined with greater precision. There are indications from the sample available so far – widely spread across the country but still relatively small, and with gaps (Brace *et al.* 2019, fig. 1) – of variation which could suggest at least two sources of migration (Brace *et al.* 2019, 767). It has also been claimed that British populations were also of ultimately Iberian genetic descent, though mediated by changes in and through France (Brace *et al.* 2019, 766–7); given the absence of any obvious material connections between Iberia and Britain (or Ireland) at this date, it is far more likely that the Iberian dimension is a reflection of potentially complex population movements in France, perhaps variously connected with the development of the early Neolithic in north-west France and the Chasséen and Michelsberg cultures in northern France (Sheridan and Whittle forthcoming; cf. Rivollat *et al.* 2020, 7). A specifically Atlantic connection, however, has yet to be demonstrated.

Alison Sheridan (2010; 2021; see also Sheridan and Schulting 2020) has consistently argued for different strands of Neolithic movement into Britain, and the recent aDNA results certainly appear to support the general picture she has painted, of sustained colonisation at various scales and from different possible sources. In more detail, however, previously stated reservations about her vision of very early colonisation of western Britain from Brittany, the Breton component of her multi-strand model, largely still stand (Whittle *et al.* 2011, chapter 15). The issues are complex, and might seem to have little to do with the Black Mountains of inland south-east Wales, but the wider context of Neolithisation in western Britain is important, so that it is useful briefly to spell out some of the arguments again.

The range of sites in western Britain, from Cornwall to Cumbria, noted above, do not appear to be producing dates for early Neolithic activity as far back as the late 5th millennium cal BC, as initially proposed for the Breton strand. A more recent formulation (Sheridan and Schulting 2020), however, has shifted the chronological emphasis to the first part of the 4th millennium cal BC, compatible with the lower end of date estimates for Late Castellic pottery. The monument at Achnacreebeag, Argyll, with its decorated pot of claimed Late Castellic style, remains undated, and we are not confident that a diagnostically Breton style can be identified in simple monuments scattered up and down the west of Britain, from Carreg Samson, Pembrokeshire, to Achnacreebeag itself (F. Lynch 1975; Sheridan 2010; Sheridan and Schulting 2020). Nor are any of those other monuments, as far as we are aware, associated with Late Castellic-style pottery. A further difficulty may be that the simple, polygonal-chambered monuments in Brittany could date from very early in the sequence there, whereas by the turn of the 5th millennium they may have been replaced by passage graves (Boujot and Cassen 1993; Schulz Paulsson 2017). The Achnacreebeag pot itself does not, in our opinion, have to be seen as ancestral to others in its regional context in western Scotland and northern Ireland which appear to be a little more securely dated, such as from Blasthill, Kintyre, perhaps from the 37th century cal BC and later (but note some spread of dates: Cummings and Robinson 2015, 9, and table I; Thompson *et al.* 2015); the fabric of the Achnacreebeag pot also fits directly into the regional spectrum (Thompson *et al.* 2015, 137). On the other hand, given what we now know about population transfers and movements thanks to aDNA research, it may be wise to keep an open mind. There is at least one possible example of the wider dispersal (or imitation) of Late Castellic pottery, from Dombate, Galicia, in north-west Spain, and sherds from other sites are also mentioned (Cassen *et al.* 2012, 979, and fig. 36; Callaghan and Scarre 2017, 358), and pottery from Vierville in the Channel Islands can also be cited (Sheridan 2010, fig. 9.3, 5), so perhaps some element of movement from Brittany by users of Late Castellic pottery is possible after all, though not necessarily on the scale envisaged by Sheridan, and perhaps connected in part with the movement of variscite from Iberian sources. It is worth noting that among the jadeitite axes in Britain, specifically Breton types ('haches carnacéennes') are very rare; the only example of

Tumiac type was found in uncertain context at High Peak, Sidmouth, Devon (inv. JADE 2008_66) (Sheridan and Pailler 2012, 1053; see also Callaghan and Scarre 2017, 356). A plausibly later link with southern Brittany, not discussed by Sheridan, is explored below in connection with monuments with transepted chambers.

Another important proposal has been of further movement into western Britain as a 'Trans-Manche-Ouest' strand of colonisation, with claimed connections to Normandy and north-west France, most visible from the 38th century cal BC, and seen in pottery and monuments including simple passage graves and rotundas (Sheridan *et al.* 2008; Sheridan 2010; 2011; Sheridan and Schulting 2020). This too could be part of the Neolithisation of western Britain in the 40th, 39th and 38th centuries cal BC, but the scale and direction of putative movement of this kind remain very unclear. Perhaps only Broadsands, Devon (Sheridan *et al.* 2008), can be seen as a convincing simple passage grave, and even here the characterisation of the monument is open to question, since it has also been seen as having a long rather than a round mound (Scarre 2015). Rotundas seem to be confined, in quite small numbers, to the Cotswolds, rather than being found widely across the south-west (and see further discussion below), and their possible French inspirations as free-standing constructions are not found only in Normandy; the example further south at Prissé-la-Charrière, Deux-Sèvres (Fig. 12.11), is a good case in point (Scarre *et al.* 2003; Laporte *et al.* 2021). The origins and inspirations of South-Western pottery are also open to question and review. Again, it may be unwise to exclude connections with Normandy, as Sheridan has proposed; it was also the view of Hélène Pioffet (2015; 2017) that there are similarities in ceramic technology between Normandy and Brittany on the one hand and western Britain on the other. Another factor to take into account, however, is variation within the Carinated Bowl tradition and its distribution (see Sheridan 2021, 181). This is not the place to set out all the ceramic associations in detail, or the nuances and complexities of style, but plenty of the western sites in question appear to have varieties of Carinated Bowl pottery (and see again Chapter 10). Once again, the situation may be much more complex than has been modelled so far.

Julian Thomas (2022) has reasserted an alternative view of Neolithisation, which allows for greater indigenous input into early Neolithic genetic signatures in Britain than on the adjacent continent, and proposes a more gradual process which involved initial small-scale movements followed by continuing and larger-scale migration streams. The possibility of lasting migration streams is certainly raised by the isotopic evidence from Penywyrlod and Whitwell, Derbyshire, as discussed by Samantha Neil in Chapter 7. However, the scale of possible indigenous contribution to the composition of early Neolithic populations is not really quantified, and the overall shift in the evidence in support of colonisation is not challenged.

Given all this recent evidence, and while noting ongoing debate, it therefore seems to us at this stage of research most likely that the early Neolithic intake of inland south-east Wales was the work of new arrivals or perhaps more probably their descendants, potentially from a variety of points of origin and by no means necessarily confined to a single event. The dominant strand in the Neolithisation of Britain appears to be connected with Carinated Bowl, but we cannot be sure that this was a unified phenomenon, far less a single event. This was a world with demonstrable long-range movement by sea (witnessed in variscite and jadeitite) so we do not totally exclude the possibility of very small-scale contributions by people from north-west France, though the strands from that source look far slighter than so far proposed. The strontium evidence presented by Samantha Neil in Chapter 7 suggests that, as individuals have values that exceed the measured biosphere range around Penywyrlod, the majority of those analysed were not local to where they were buried and had obtained their diet from elsewhere. Biosphere $^{87}Sr/^{86}Sr$ values of 0.714 have been recorded in regions that lie relatively close by, in the Welsh Borderlands and Malvern Hills. However, derivation of $^{87}Sr/^{86}Sr$ values of 0.714 from regions further afield cannot be ruled out. Based on all available current evidence the individual in the group who exhibits an $^{87}Sr/^{86}Sr$ value of 0.717 did not obtain their diet locally. They could have moved to the area, either from elsewhere in Britain or from further afield. The isotope results from Penywyrlod could perhaps indicate that individuals moved to the area from more than one location and, as noted also by Julian Thomas (2022), could therefore suggest continuing migration streams rather than a single migration event. Unfortunately, preservation of aDNA in human bone from the Black Mountains monuments themselves was too poor for successful analysis (Tom Booth, *pers. comm.*), but a sample from Tinkinswood in the Vale of Glamorgan did give a result which firmly fits the wider picture (Brace *et al.* 2019), and further analysis there is planned (Sophy Charlton, *pers. comm.*).

Our general argument focuses on the specific history of one region, but it is worth considering how many other smaller regions could now profitably be investigated from that perspective. Most if not all models of Neolithisation tend to work with a broad brush and a high level of generalisation. The time is surely ripe for more detailed and particularising narratives. The discussion below will seek to investigate both differences and possible affiliations among monument builders to the west and the east of the Black Mountains, and other potentially striking regional sequences can be noted within the wider process of Neolithic land-taking. The lack of Neolithic monuments in the region to the north of the Black Mountains was remarked upon in Chapter 1, for example, and research in the Walton basin has underscored a rather different sequence there, arguably beginning with a later intake represented by the Womaston causewayed enclosure, probably dating to the 36th or 35th century cal BC (N. Jones 2009; Whittle *et al.* 2022, fig. 13.3). This kind of more regional perspective could be extended in many other areas, including in the Cotswolds themselves.

The recent aDNA results have also indicated a probably low contribution by indigenous hunter-gatherer people to the genetic signatures of the early Neolithic population (Brace *et al.* 2019, 768; *pace* J. Thomas 2022), and further analysis may serve to reduce that input even further (Brace forthcoming). There are signs of variation from south to north, with potentially more (though still low) indigenous input in Scotland, so we cannot be sure of the situation in a region such as inland south-east Wales which will perforce remain uninvestigated. Nonetheless, it is important to keep an open mind on how best to translate the raw figures into more nuanced narratives of practice and interaction. We will stress again below the setting of Penywyrlod and its melding with the local landscape, and speculate whether the 'wrapping' involved could have been inspired in part by indigenous belief. On that note, and referring back to the early Neolithic sites in the west of Britain listed above, an interesting picture is beginning to emerge. Sites with Mesolithic evidence such as Stainton West (Brown 2021; see also Sheridan 2021) and Windy Harbour (Oxford Archaeology 2020) show evidence for subsequent Neolithic activity. This superficial superimposition belies different processes. At Stainton West, the minimum interval of several hundred years between these signatures (and much longer back to the main phase of Mesolithic activity) makes any form of continuity unlikely – this location seems better understood as an expedient place to occupy. The picture at Windy Harbour, and on the Barrow Peninsula at Roose Quarry and Holbeck Park (Evans *et al.* 2021; Griffiths 2021), shows much closer timing and patterns of activity between latest Mesolithic evidence and earliest Neolithic material culture and practices.

The first stones: building and using Penywyrlod

Within the broader context as sketched above of the Neolithic colonisation of western Britain and the plausible intake of inland south-east Wales by descendants of new arrivals, we can now emphasise the distinctive character of the 'first stones' – as seen in building and using the Penywyrlod long cairn. The challenge is to try to put the construction and start of the use of Penywyrlod into its probably 39th or 38th century cal BC context (see again Chapter 4), thinking away from the often over-generalised accounts of Cotswold-Severn or Severn-Cotswold tombs. From a more particularising perspective, Penywyrlod emerges as striking, helping to initiate a distinctive regional tradition. That has been noted before, for example by Wysocki and Whittle (2000, 600), who wrote that the Black Mountains group as a whole could represent 'a network of semi-autonomous communities, engaged in both maintaining individual identities or social boundaries and a series of wider interactions'. With the information now available, the development of such a regional character can be fleshed out in more detail.

Penywyrlod was constructed in a place that had seen some of the earliest Neolithic activity in south Wales and the Marches. The nature of this pre-cairn activity is unclear but included the presence of charred cereal remains, and isolated pottery and lithic finds. In addition, a possible microlith and fragment of human skull were recovered. This activity therefore does not appear to represent midden deposits (see Allen *et al.* 2013; Edwards *et al.* submitted), but it does suggest an early Neolithic presence for between *1–130 years* (*95% probability*, or *1–60 years, 68% probability*; *duration_Penywyrlod_pre_cairn*; Fig. 4.4) prior to the construction of the monument, which might have represented small-scale and perhaps transient occupation. The very different situation by the time Gwernvale came to be constructed, and in turn the circumstances under Hazleton North (hereafter mainly referred to as Hazleton) and Ascott-under-Wychwood long cairns in the Cotswolds, are discussed below. Those monuments could be seen as to do with consolidating a hold on already occupied Neolithic locations, with a further overlay of older memories going back into the Mesolithic. Penywyrlod, by contrast, can be argued to be to do with taking new land, as part of the changes that occurred after the earliest Neolithic. The setting is important too, perhaps linked to the process of land-taking. The monument was constructed away from and above the river valleys which may have been a particular focus of Mesolithic occupation and movement. From its positioning, Penywyrlod has wide-ranging views (whatever the state of the immediate woodland cover; cf. Cummings and Whittle 2003) over a broad swathe of land, taking in hills local and distant, upland slopes, part of the Wye valley and the country beyond. If there were substantial timber halls at Dorstone at a similar or broadly comparable date (see again Chapter 4), it is noticeable how there too the location has extensive and wide-ranging views.

Within such a setting at Penywyrlod, as already emphasised in Chapter 2, a particular connection with the striking local hill, Mynydd Troed, seems to have been asserted, through the wrapping (cf. Cummings and Richards 2017) of the monument with distinctively coloured outer walling probably derived from the upper slopes. The monument also looks towards that hill, given the orientation of its long axis and the position of the forecourt. Building drew this part of the local landscape into the very fabric of the construction, and once the construction of the outer walling was in place, the means were provided by which access to the passages and chambers could be controlled; drawing in the local landscape was fundamental to commissioning the active use of the monument. A further possible symbolic relationship between tomb and hill can be suggested by the outer walling and blocked chamber entrances at Penywyrlod which have the appearance of mimicking or replicating the jointed and finely bedded strata visible in outcrops on Mynydd Troed from which the building stone appears to have been obtained (Fig. 2.1). The eventual erosion the outer wall face would also in time match the scree slopes which lie below these outcrops. It is noticeable that Mynydd Troed, which dominates the skyline to the SE, and even the more distant peaks of the Brecon Beacons to the SW, disappear from view a matter of only tens of metres further north or west (Cummings and Whittle 2004, 78). Christopher Tilley (1994, 136), amongst others, has even suggested that Penywyrlod's own profile actually mirrored that of Mynydd Troed, which is higher and broader at its NW summit (see Fig. 12.4).

Now, these kinds of referencing and re-arrangements of things went on to be part of local – and indeed wider – practice in subsequent times, one element in the distinctive character of the Black Mountains tombs as a group. We next briefly note some of those more general characteristics, before returning to the central point here of the creation of this practice in the first place, at the start of the regional tradition.

The landscape setting of the Black Mountains tombs has inspired a lively debate about their orientation, grouping, pairing, intervisibility, sidedness, and visual relationships with prominent hills and escarpments, mountain passes, rivers and streams (Tilley 1994; Nash 1997; Fleming 1999; 2005; Children and Nash 2001; Cummings *et al.* 2002; Cummings and Whittle 2004). Visual associations appear to be particularly significant and might help to explain the absence of tombs on the SE side of the hills, where the landscape is fragmented by the valleys of the Grwyne and Monnow and their tributaries and is visually less dramatic (Fig. 1.5). This seems to underline an association between the distribution of the tombs and the 'visually spectacular escarpment' of the northern, western and south-western flanks of the Black Mountains (Cummings and Whittle 2004, 84–6) and might emphasise a distinction to be drawn between early Neolithic tombs which *referenced* distinctive landforms and early Neolithic enclosures which *occupied* them (cf. Davis and Sharples 2017, 23).

Other tombs in the Black Mountains cluster appear to reference other similarly conspicuous peaks in the Black Mountains, such as Twmpa (Lord Hereford's Knob) and Y Dâs on the northern escarpment of the Black Mountains (Fig. 12.5, 2–3), Pen allt-mawr in the Rhiangoll valley (Fig. 12.5, 5), and Crug Hywel in the Usk Valley (Fig. 12.5, 6), almost all of which are intervisible with one or more of the Black Mountains long cairns (Cummings 2004, 186–99). It is, of course, impossible at this stage of research to know the dating of all these monuments relative to Penywyrlod, since we lack a comprehensive chronological sequence, but it seems likely that many are later. In time, a powerful

Fig. 12.4. View of Mynydd Troed on the skyline from several kilometres away to the NE. Christopher Tilley in A phenomenology of landscape *(1994) noted the similarity in visual form between Mynydd Troed and the possible original shapes of long cairns such as Penywyrlod.*

association may have arisen between the multiple possible symbolic dimensions of these tombs and the dramatic, arguably mythologised landscape around the northern escarpment of the Black Mountains. Recent work at the Arthur's Stone chambered tomb suggests that it may have had a quite different structural history, preceded by a turf and timber mound and avenue of posts. It is perhaps therefore not unsurprising that its topographical references appear to be quite different to other tombs in the Black Mountains group, and include the unparalleled early Neolithic ceremonial complex on Dorstone Hill of which it forms a part as well as views of the distant, pointed peak of Skirrid/Ysgryd Fawr (Fig. 12.5, 8), lying southwards down the Golden Valley (Manchester University 2021).

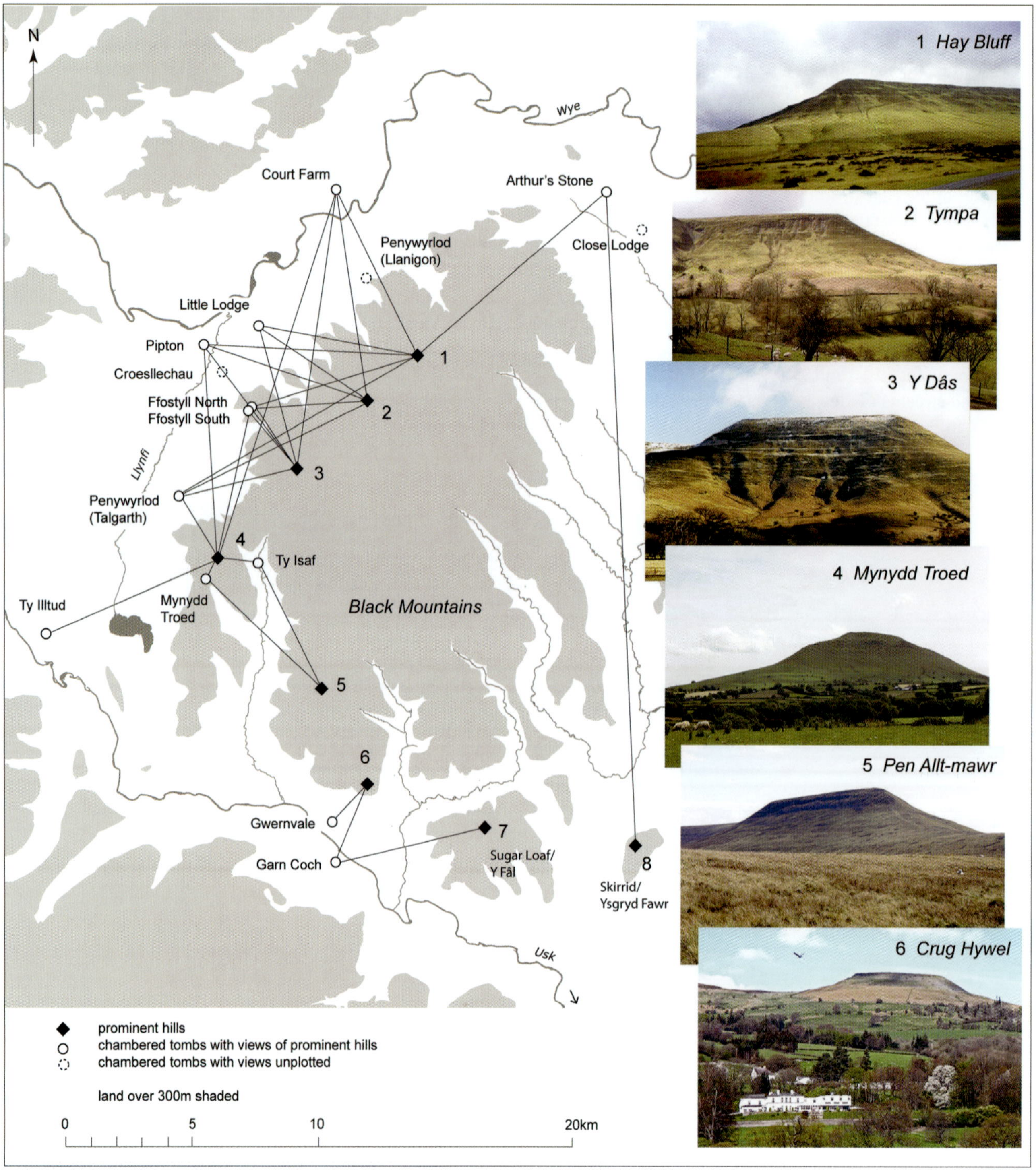

Fig. 12.5. Visual associations between chambered tombs looking inwards to distinctive peaks in the Black Mountains (based on Cummings 2004).

At the time of the construction of Penywyrlod most probably in the 38th century cal BC, this plausible assertion of a link between local land and landform and the emergent, novel monuments would have been even more striking. It is for ongoing discussion whether this should be seen as a connection to the beliefs of the indigenous population or a signal of the reactions of incomers to new territory, landscapes and geologies, as Vicki Cummings and Colin Richards (2021) have argued in their recent discussion of dolmens further west as objects of wonder and awe.

In the 38th century cal BC, such novelty was further underscored by the very size of the construction. Penywyrlod was a very large monument (as detailed in Chapter 2). If anything, its appearance of size was probably further enhanced by the natural slope of the ground which may have exaggerated the apparent height of the tomb as well as consciously integrating it within its landscape. As there is no evidence for subsequent major additions or alterations (see Chapter 2), presumably it was the conscious intention of the builders to create at an eye-catching scale, in a new location within the wooded and probably sparsely settled landscape.

The resulting outcome was distinctive. It combined several elements, from the great bulk of the cairn, the fine outer walling or skin, and the forecourt and portal stones to the multiple compartments concealed within. Given that there is no evidence for major phases of addition or rebuilding, presumably the sheer size of the construction, reinforced by the scale of the portal stones at the focal point of a generously spaced forecourt (discussed in Chapter 2), was a very deliberate intention of the builders from the outset of the project. As well as the symbolism of the outer skin, seemingly drawing in and mimicking the hilltop of Mynydd Troed (Fig. 12.6), the walling created was of high quality, with blockings of entrances to chambers skilfully done, on repeated occasions (as also discussed in Chapter 2).

Inside this creation, there were probably several chambers, as set out in Chapter 2. That is not without comparanda within the total range of Cotswold-Severn tombs, but unfortunately we do not yet know the detailed chronology of sites such as Belas Knap (Darvill 2004, 256; Whittle *et al.* 2011, 470; but see now below), and in the early context of the 38th century cal BC this kind of assemblage of multiple compartments may well have been unprecedented in a southern British context as a whole. Evidently there was variation in the scale of the chambers, one substantial one being balanced as it were by three rather smaller ones (from the visible sample). All were united in being concealed from the outside. There is also considerable diversity in the nature of the deposits of human bone inserted into these chambers, or parts of them. There are strong differences in the composition of the human bone assemblages in the three adjacent chambers investigated so far: NE I with virtually nothing (was it emptied at some point?), NE II with an emphasis on young adult males, and NE III with adults of both sexes and children (Fig. 12.7). There seems to be evidence for repeat visits, and possibly removal of bones. Numbers of individuals per chamber vary (as set out in important detail in Chapter 6), as well as completeness and perhaps the extent of articulation; even NE III does not have a large assemblage (though disturbance and damage may have removed some original contents). It has to be remembered that the radiocarbon dates (as set out in Chapter 4) indicate a long span of use, probably at intervals, of the Penywyrlod chambers, so divining what the original or first depositions might have been like is difficult if not impossible. The overall impression at this site may be one of diversity, selection and tokenism. Certainly the chronological evidence gives an impression of a monument that was returned to repeatedly throughout the 4th millennium cal BC, with the use of the chambers representing individuals who died over *190–505 years* (*95% probability*, or *320–445 years, 68% probability*; *span_primary_Penywyrlod*; Fig. 4.4). This duration of interment gives the impression of Penywyrlod as a place where traditions were reworked and reinterpreted, and the sequence of pre-cairn activity followed by repeated

Fig. 12.6. Mimicking nature? Left: Blocking in the entrance to the passage of Penywyrlod Chamber NE I. Right: Strata and natural fissures in outcrops on the NE face of the summit of Mynydd Troed overlooking Penywyrlod.

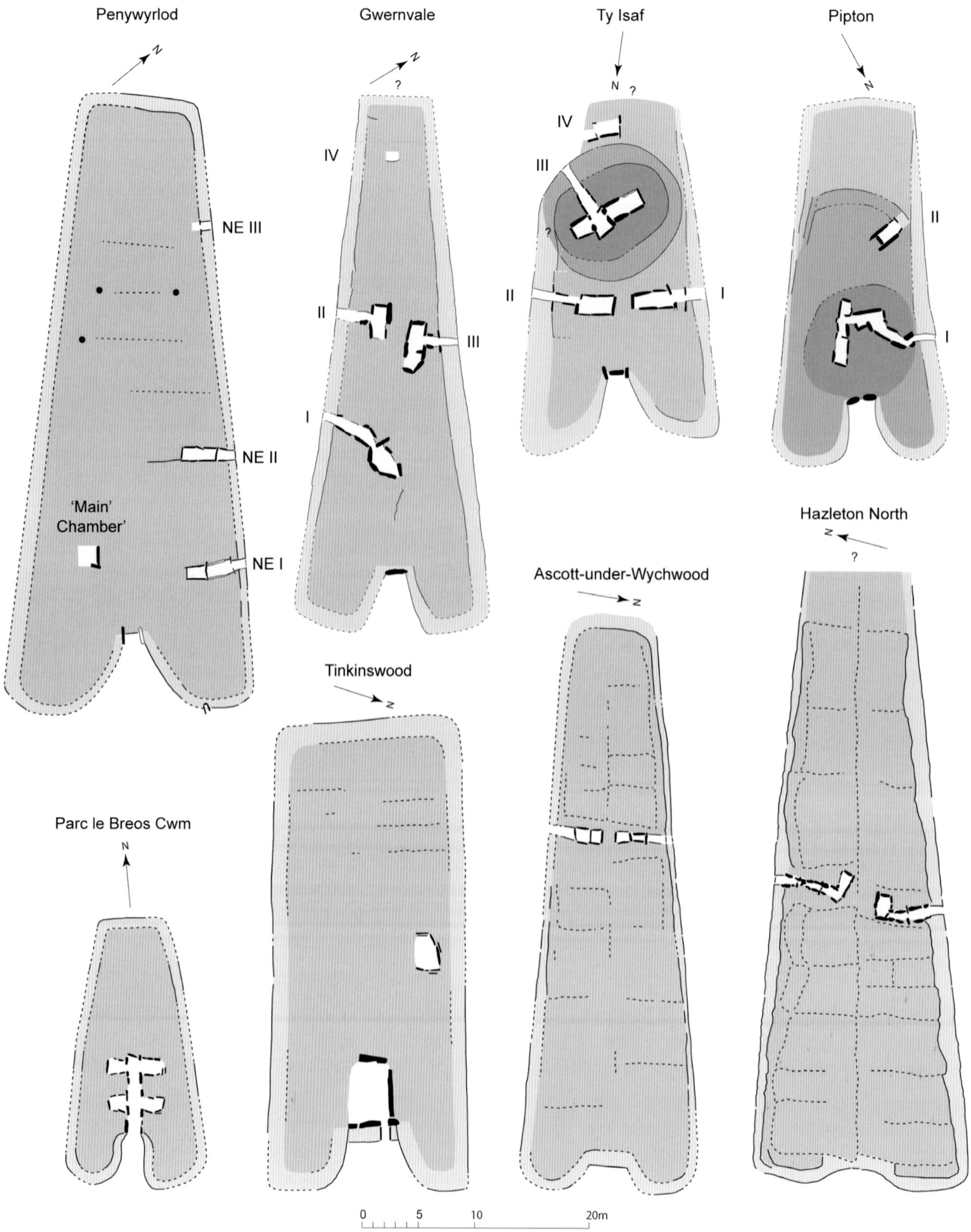

Fig. 12.7. Interpretative plans of some excavated Severn-Cotswold tombs in south-east Wales and in the Cotswolds (Ty Isaf after Grimes 1939; Pipton after Savory 1956; Parc le Breos Cwm after Whittle and Wysocki 1998; Tinkinswood after Ward 1915; Ascott-under-Wychwood after Benson and Whittle 2007; Hazleton North after Saville 1990). The presence of inner revetment walls at Tinkinswood, as shown here, is hinted at on Ward's published plan (Ward 1915, fig. 10) but these are not explicitly mentioned in his account of the excavations.

interments and revisiting is reminiscent of the pattern from Ascott-under-Wychwood (Bayliss *et al.* 2007a; 2007b). The picture appears in contrast to other sites where a much shorter-lived pattern of deposition appears to have occurred.

If that is so, what might be the wider significance of this combination of things: the eye-catching bulk of the cairn, its distinctive trapezoidal plan, the multiple but concealed chambers within, protected and unified by the outer skin of the monument which drew in a notable feature of the local landscape, and the perhaps fractured representation of human social groupings and relationships? Now it has been argued that in the early Neolithic context in Britain both large timber halls and tombs could have been the work of founding or leading lineages (Ray and Thomas 2018, 113, 171). The recent stunning demonstration through aDNA analysis at Hazleton of a dominant patriline operating over five generations, with evidence also of maternal sublineages, female exogamy and adoption into the dominant male line (as well as the presence of some unrelated others) (Fowler *et al.* 2021), certainly reinforces the likely reality of lineage-like arrangements. Those can also be suspected in other comparable southern British tombs like Ascott-under-Wychwood (Benson and Whittle 2007), and perhaps widely elsewhere (Sánchez-Quinto *et al.* 2019; Fowler 2022). The importance of dominant lineages in other contexts has also been asserted, for example in the early spread of the LBK across central and western Europe (Frirdich 2005). Whether this applies to a context like that of Penywyrlod in the 38th century cal BC, however, as inland south-east Wales was putatively being colonised and settled by newcomers, is open to question. Perhaps in this setting there was considerable fragmentation among a scattered and wide-ranging population (as the isotope evidence set out in Chapter 7 suggests), and perhaps there were varied social groupings and relationships (see also Fowler 2022). Though they are not precisely dated, there are up to three instances of inter-personal violence in the human remains from Penywyrlod: the embedded arrowhead, the depressed parietal, and the closely associated arrowhead (all detailed in Chapter 6). Whether or not these show more than low-level, endemic bickering and skirmishes, they certainly illustrate here, as elsewhere (Schulting and Wysocki 2005), the potential for conflict. Taking all this into account, one major role of the Penywyrlod monument therefore could have been to create a sense of unity and unification, among people and their immediate forebears on the one hand and with the landscape and thus the local past on the other. These could be some of the combinations of aspects of social organisation and philosophical-religious beliefs (Carr 1995) discussed in Chapter 1, and also specific manifestations of the general suggestions made by Frances Lynch (2000; see also Darvill 2004, 132), also set out in Chapter 1.

Speculatively, lineages as seen at Hazleton by the first half of the 37th century cal BC (Meadows *et al.* 2007; Fowler *et al.* 2021; Fowler 2022) might have been a development *subsequent* to the initial establishment of early Neolithic settlement, if there was a dynamic of gradually and steadily increasing social competition, which in turn helped to foster and encourage the adoption and elaboration of enclosures (Whittle *et al.* 2011, chapter 15; 2022). The lineages that have been identified at Hazleton post-date the construction of the monument in the 37th century cal BC (*3695–3650 cal BC, 95% probability*, or *3690–3660, 68% probability*; *construction finished*; Meadows *et al.* 2007). This was a difference of some *300–490 years* (*95% probability*, or *325–410 years, 68% probability*; figure not shown) between the estimate for the construction of Hazleton and the earliest evidence that we have for Neolithic practices or things in Britain (in *4235–3985 cal BC, 95% probability*, or *4115–4010 cal BC, 68% probability*; *start Neolithisation*; Whittle *et al.* 2011, 740). The establishment of lineages that were buried in these monuments – and there may be pathological evidence from Coldrum (one of the earliest burial monuments in the UK; Wysocki *et al.* 2007) that here too some people were selected for burial because of social identities that included close biological relationships – occurred sometime after the earliest Neolithic presence. Burial in monuments represents a fundamentally new practice, a novel way of representing relationships and relating to place that occurred in the 39th and 38th centuries.

Locally, the possible process of tighter definition and bounding of social groupings might be seen in the subsequent difference between the bone deposits and numbers of remains at Pipton and Ty Isaf respectively. That possibility is followed further below.

A last important dimension to examine is the pattern of connections and affiliations suggested by the Penywyrlod monument. The first point to stress once more is the chronological context of its construction. Over and over again the literature has offered generalised comparisons, within the totality of Cotswold-Severn practice. Informative though that process can be, it does not necessarily catch what was distinctive about the 38th century cal BC and the local context, which is why our discussion throughout has been ambivalent about the best terminology to employ (that is, Cotswold-Severn or Severn-Cotswold). Multiple connections and affiliations might have been displayed and projected by Penywyrlod, and we will try to unpick some of these.

To begin with the dominant visual aspect of the finished Penywyrlod cairn, its plan – and profile – could have evoked a very large series of memories and links, though it is hard to choose a single inspiration among these. Inscribed in the bulk and the trapezoidal form of the cairn there could, for example, have been a long-lasting social memory of the form of earlier timber longhouses in areas of central and western Europe, but these could also be argued to refer to early timber halls in the British context itself (Whittle

2019; cf. Savory 1977, 163–7; 1984, 31; Darvill 2004, 130). Once again, the further elucidation and dating of the early stages of Dorstone (Overton *et al.* 2022) will be important in following this possible thread. There is also rather obviously a multitude of long mounds and cairns on the adjacent continent, some going well back into the 5th millennium, from which the idea of a large trapezoidal cairn might have been derived, by some form of social memory. The list could conceivably go as far back as Passy-style monuments in the Paris basin, including in Normandy (Rivollat *et al.* 2022), and certainly also a range of long cairns and mounds in Brittany and Normandy, and beyond (Laporte *et al.* 2002a; 2002b; Joussaume and Laporte 2006; Scarre 2011; 2015). This range includes trapezoidal cairns, as at Colombiers-sur-Seulles in Normandy (Scarre 2015, fig. 6.4). If Penywyrlod was constructed in the 38th century cal BC, it is obvious there could have been considerable intervals between it and many of these possible sources of inspiration, memory or copying.

Other Cotswold-Severn laterally chambered monuments are the next obvious point of comparison, distinct from constructions with terminal chambers, having either simple or transepted compartments (Daniel 1950; Corcoran 1969; Darvill 2004). Including Pipton in this category (though a case for its hybrid character can also be made: Britnell 1984a, 4) as well as Penywyrlod, it is worth remembering the inland distribution of laterally chambered tombs stressed by Glyn Daniel (1950, 155). There is a range of examples in the Cotswolds themselves, including Belas Knap, Rodmarton, Luckington, both Hazleton North and South, and Ascott-under-Wychwood (Corcoran 1969; Darvill 2004, fig. 39). These in turn range from those with symmetrically paired and opposed single sets of chambers or cists, like Hazleton and Ascott-under-Wychwood, to the multiple arrangements of Belas Knap, Rodmarton, Luckington, West Tump and others (Darvill 2004 and references). The dating evidence for these is varied. Ascott-under-Wychwood probably belongs to the second half of the 38th century cal BC (Bayliss *et al.* 2007b; Benson and Whittle 2007; Whittle *et al.* 2011, 466) and so its construction could overlap with that of Penywyrlod, but it does not appear to be definitively earlier, apart from being simpler in plan. Hazleton probably dates to the first half of the 37th century cal BC (Meadows *et al.* 2007; Whittle *et al.* 2011, 466; Fowler *et al.* 2021) and as well as, like Ascott, being simpler in layout, appears a definitely later construction than Penywyrlod (on the model followed in this chapter). What date are other laterally chambered Cotswold monuments with multiple chambers? It is not clear that *any* of these are necessarily as early as Penywyrlod itself (Darvill 2004; Smith and Brickley 2006; Whittle *et al.* 2011). Belas Knap in the central Cotswolds (Hemp 1929; Berry 1930), at the head of the Coln – but not that far from the Severn and potentially looking westwards towards Wales – previously undated (as referenced above) now has dates on skulls (shared by Rick Schulting as this volume was in proofs), suggesting deposition from the 37th century cal BC onwards. It is conceivable that a construction like Belas Knap could have served as a model for the building of Penywyrlod, but it is also now more likely that the relationship should be reversed. To underscore the uncertainties over such relationships, however, we should also highlight the early dates from Burn Ground in the Cotswolds, probably going back to the 40th or 39th centuries cal BC (Whittle *et al.* 2011, 469, fig. 9.25; Brace *et al.* 2019, supplementary material). Burn Ground has a combination of transepted terminal chambers and a lateral passage, set in a long cairn (Grimes 1960).

It is also possible that *all* of these constructions, potentially early in their respective regional sequences, could have owed their inspiration to monuments elsewhere. In that case, parallels and resemblances might be sought instead in Normandy, Brittany and western France, as explored long ago by Hubert Savory (1977; 1980a; 1984) (see Fig. 12.11) and reinforced in Alison Sheridan's concept of a 'Trans-Manche Ouest' migration stream or strand coming into western Britain at a slightly later start date than that of the Carinated Bowl complex (Sheridan 2010; 2011; see also Laporte and Tinévez 2004; Scarre 2015). As with the Black Mountains group of tombs, it will go on being important to try to unpick the presumably complex history of the development of Cotswold tombs (remodelling of the Cotswold early Neolithic is underway as part of the revision of *Gathering Time* for England and Wales). We consider transepted chambers further below.

Given continuing uncertainties on dating, this dimension of relationships and possible inspiration remains far from clear, but a good case can be made that in one or other of these ways Penywyrlod had connections, connotations or affiliations that linked it to the east and potentially even further away to the south across the Channel. It may be that similar connections to the east will also be found in the early material and features uncovered at Dorstone including Carinated Bowl pottery and substantial timber halls (Ray and Thomas 2018; Overton *et al.* 2022; and see Chapter 10), but that awaits further analysis.

Contrasts with emergent practices in the Black Mountains can also now start to be discussed in more detail, thanks on the one hand to further dating of monumental constructions further west and on the other in part to greater awareness of regional differences (Brophy and Barclay 2009; Graeber and Wengrow 2021). Severn-Cotswold – or Cotswold-Severn – monumental architecture appears to have a finite distribution. The most westerly examples seem to occur only a little further west than the Black Mountains themselves, represented by Cae'r Ganfa on the western edge of the Brecon Beacons, Graig Fawr and Carn Llechart to its south, and Parc le Breos Cwm on the Gower (F. Lynch 2011, fig. 2; see also Fig. 12.1). There are possible echoes

Fig. 12.8. The dolmen at Pentre Ifan, Pembrokeshire, seen from a local outcrop, of the kind used for capstones. Photograph: Vicki Cummings and Colin Richards.

of Cotswold-Severn architectural practice in various monuments in north Wales (F. Lynch 2011, fig. 2), but there is a big gap in between across mid-Wales, and the connections up there seem generally weak. By contrast, what has now been suggested as a general tradition or practice of dolmen construction dominates in south-west (see Fig. 12.8) and to a large extent in north-west Wales, as well as elsewhere in western Britain and Ireland (F. Lynch 2011, fig. 2; Cummings and Richards 2021). (We follow Cummings and Richards (2021) in referring to dolmens in general rather than specifically portal dolmens or portal tombs.)

The respective distributions of dolmen and Severn-Cotswold architecture appear to some extent interleaved. Tinkinswood in the Vale of Glamorgan, for example, can be seen as an original dolmen construction later converted into a Severn-Cotswold cairn (Cummings and Richards 2021, fig. 6.15), and the Whispering Knights in the Cotswolds themselves is often cited as the most easterly example of a dolmen (Darvill 2004, 268–9 and references). The portal stones at Penywyrlod itself have already been noted above as potentially referring to the more westerly dolmen tradition, and interestingly a prominent so-called false portal with possibly the same kind of connotations is found at Belas Knap (Fig. 12.9) in the Cotswolds (Darvill 2004, fig. 101; Cummings and Richards 2021, fig. 6.17).

We still know rather little about the detailed chronology of dolmen construction. In south-west Wales, Carreg Coetan Arthur (Rees 2012) appears to be no earlier than the mid-4th millennium cal BC, but the construction of the main dolmen at Garn Turne in Pembrokeshire, with its massive, collapsed capstone, may date to the 38th century cal BC (Cummings and Richards 2021, 218, fig. 7.40), although the presence of 3rd and 1st millennium cal BC material makes the chronological sequence difficult to interpret. Further afield, it appears that Poulnabrone in western Ireland was constructed around the turn of the 39th and 38th centuries cal BC (A. Lynch 2014; Schulting 2014). We could wish for more dated sites, but on the basis of those two examples it appears that dolmens were being constructed in the same times as Penywyrlod in the Black Mountains.

That being so, and with enhanced awareness of regional variation and the deliberate creation of difference (recently dubbed 'schismogenesis', reviving an older anthropological concept: Graeber and Wengrow 2021, 56–8), the essence of dolmen architecture can be seen to evoke a series of contrasts with Severn-Cotswold architecture. Vicki Cummings

Fig. 12.9. Forecourt and false portal at Belas Knap Cotswold-Severn long cairn, Gloucestershire.

and Colin Richards (2021) emphasise the performance and display involved in the lifting of great capstones (cf. Whittle 2004), the enchanting technology employed and the emotional affects created, the management of concealment and revelation, the animating effects of the addition of human bodies, and in general the sense of wonder and awe engendered by dolmen monuments. Some elements may have been shared with Severn-Cotswold practice; emotional responses can hardly be confined to dolmens alone, and human bodies could also be thought of as animating Severn-Cotswold tombs with their substances and vitality. Overall, however, there seem to be a series of contrasts: different kinds of size or bulk, display versus concealment, and differing uses of human remains. We can also note, as a further strand of diversity (see also Cummings and Whittle 2004, chapter 1) the mainly coastal cave burials of the earlier 4th millennium cal BC (Schulting 2020). It is probably dangerous to use mortuary and monumental practice and architecture alone as proxies for complex issues of identity (see again Fowler 2022), but perhaps as the timing and sequence of constructions begin to be better understood, these contrasting emergent practices could stand for different strands within the Neolithisation process in Britain. Can such differences relate, at least in part, to the suggested double strands of origin as suggested by the aDNA evidence (Brace *et al.* 2019; Brace forthcoming)?

Whatever the answer to that difficult question, the contrasts which we have highlighted serve further to underline the distinctiveness of the setting, circumstances and creation of Penywyrlod in inland south-east Wales probably in the 38th century cal BC. We go on now to follow possible subsequent developments.

Pipton and Ty Isaf: infill and consolidation

An earlier account had suggested that the Black Mountains tombs 'appear to incorporate repeated concepts or common themes not seen elsewhere: symmetrically laid out chambers, angled passages, hidden cists. As a group they might be seen to share an inner dynamic which suggests points of contact and agreements of ideas, borrowed here and modified there, between various local tomb-building communities, yet with each monument maintaining its own individual identity. Similarly, treatment of ancestral remains, particularly at Penywyrlod and Pipton, suggests a consensus of ideas about ways of doing things, which are not seen east of the Severn. Geographically most of the group is concentrated in a small area and isolated from the other southern Welsh and Cotswold concentrations. A picture may be suggested of a network of semi-autonomous communities, engaged in both maintaining individual identities or social boundaries and a series of wider interactions' (Wysocki and Whittle 2000, 600). With the suggestion now of an outline chronology, set out in Chapter 4, this proposed distinctiveness can begin to be examined in a little more detail against an improving understanding of timeframes.

The chronological evidence that we have presented in Chapter 4 suggests that the construction of Penywyrlod was followed by the construction and beginnings of use of Pipton (Savory 1956) in *3940–3635 cal BC (95% probability*, or *3760–3650 cal BC, 68% probability*; *start_Pipton*; Fig. 4.15) and then Ty Isaf (Grimes 1939) in *3970–3520 cal BC (95% probability*, or *3740–3560 cal BC 68% probable*; *start_Ty_Isaf*; Fig. 4.15). The three mounds at Dorstone, also to the east of this region like Penywyrlod, were most probably constructed in the 38th century cal BC (Ray *et al.* 2022). With Penywyrlod and the Dorstone mounds among the first, foundational burial monuments in the region, the locations of both Pipton and Ty Isaf as successors look significant. Pipton overlooks the Wye valley to its N, and the hills beyond in that direction, while 'there are clear views of the Black Mountains scarp and Hay Bluff and Twmpa are particularly prominent. Mynydd Troed is just visible…' (Cummings and Whittle 2004, 193) (Fig. 12.5). Ty Isaf sits within a bowl inside the northern portion of the Black Mountains, with much more restricted views than is the case at Penywyrlod or Pipton. Mynydd Troed is visible to the SW, closest to the monument, and then Castell Dinas to the NW and the Black Mountains themselves including Pen Trumau almost directly E (Cummings and Whittle 2004, 190).

It does not seem fanciful, given the proposed outline chronology, that these locations represent a process of the expansion and infilling of settlement. With other, neighbouring tombs undated – Little Lodge 2km to the NE and the Ffostyll pair 3km to the SE of Pipton, and the Mynydd Troed monument only 2km away from Ty Isaf but on the other side of Mynydd Troed itself (Cummings and Whittle 2004, 190, 193) – it is harder to follow this process in more detail; slightly further afield, the Lower Luggy long barrow may date to the 37th–36th centuries cal BC (see Chapter 4). There is some evidence for pre-monument activity at both Pipton and Ty Isaf, but this is limited (and certainly does not seem to compare with the situation at Gwernvale), and it is possible that both monuments were part of making a mark on largely fresh ground. At Pipton, there were sherds and evidence of burning (Savory 1956, 15), and there was a cattle horncore within the forecourt, though that cannot be placed precisely within the site sequence (Savory 1956, 33). It was thought that the ground surface had been deliberately levelled and some evidence of a layer of stone chippings was thought to be associated with construction (Savory 1956, 15), but that need not relate to activity any earlier than construction. At Ty Isaf, likewise, Grimes hints at the possibility of some artificial levelling (Grimes 1939, 124).

It is worth remembering that the evidence suggests the continuing, probably episodic, use of Penywyrlod. The intervisibility of Black Mountains tombs has been the subject of some discussion, particularly with regard to Penywyrlod, the two tombs at Ffostyll, Little Lodge and Pipton (*e.g.* Tilley 1994; 127; Fleming 1992, 122). Viewshed analysis has been used to explore this and other issues in relation to the siting of a number of the tombs, notably at Little Lodge and at Ty Isaf (Cummings and Whittle 2004, figs 6.9, 7.7). A new viewshed centred on Penywyrlod (Fig. 12.10) suggests that the tombs at Court Farm, Pipton and Ffostyll might just have been visible, though it does not suggest that ensuring intervisibility with neighbouring tombs was a primary concern to the builders of the monuments. Perhaps with Pipton and Ty Isaf, it was more a matter of staking out claim to or control over further portions of the local landscape. Settlements identified and dated in the pipeline investigations also appear to belong broadly to this kind of period (Darvill *et al.* 2020; and see Chapter 4). And the combined isotopic evidence for both lifetime movement and diet, set out in Chapters 7 and 8, suggests the possibility of less wide-ranging lifestyles than may have been the case at Penywyrlod. Finally, to the east, the construction of the Dorstone causewayed enclosure appears to fall in the earlier part of the 37th cal BC (Whittle *et al.* 2022, fig. 13.2; Ray *et al.* 2022). This said, the limited available samples from the earliest fills within this monument (because of the highly variable preservation conditions on the site) mean that the chronology of this monument may never be as robustly understood as other causewayed enclosure sites (Ray *et al.* 2022).

Both Pipton and Ty Isaf were monuments of some bulk, each around 25m long, but both were approximately half the size of Penywyrlod, some 10 km away. Perhaps that also speaks to some fragmentation of social groupings and cohesion in a putative process of infill, though of course it may be dangerous to interpret monument size too simplistically in this regard (Fowler 2022). When completed, both may have presented a rather inscrutable exterior, finished with fine walling, like Penywyrlod. (It is evident from published photographs that the thin slabs used for the outer walling were quite distinct from what is assumed to be more locally derived material used for the construction of the body of the cairns but the possible sources of this stone have not been identified in either instance.) That is to set aside the view of Grimes (1960, 93–4), subsequent to the publication of the original excavation report, that outer passages at Ty Isaf had been unroofed and had been accessed in a similar manner to that suggested by Clifford and Daniel at Rodmarton, via a 'shallow shaft' entered from the surface of the cairn behind the outer cairn wall. This interpretation, however, was based upon the assumption that 'extra revetment' material outside the cairn formed part of the original structure of the monument, though this is now generally considered to represent later collapse.

Within, both monuments offer quite unusual internal arrangements, part of the evidence for the distinctiveness of the Black Mountains tombs overall. Before going into the detail and the many uncertainties involved, it is worth noting that in both there are fewer chambers or compartments overall than at Penywyrlod, and perhaps this also can speak to the scale or nature of the social groupings involved.

Both Pipton and Ty Isaf were investigated long ago, and there are many uncertainties about their sequences, despite the experience and field skills of both excavators. Pipton presents a closed cist, Chamber II, on a different alignment to the axis of the long cairn as a whole; there is also curving double walling to the S (Fig. 2.30). Savory (1956, 23) noted that the heaped stonework on the W side of the chamber resembled 'the blocking of an entrance'. The possible 'blocking' appears to have overlain the basal courses of the outer revetment wall of the 'rotunda' encircling one side of the chamber (Savory 1956, 29), which could suggest that before the long cairn was extended the chamber was

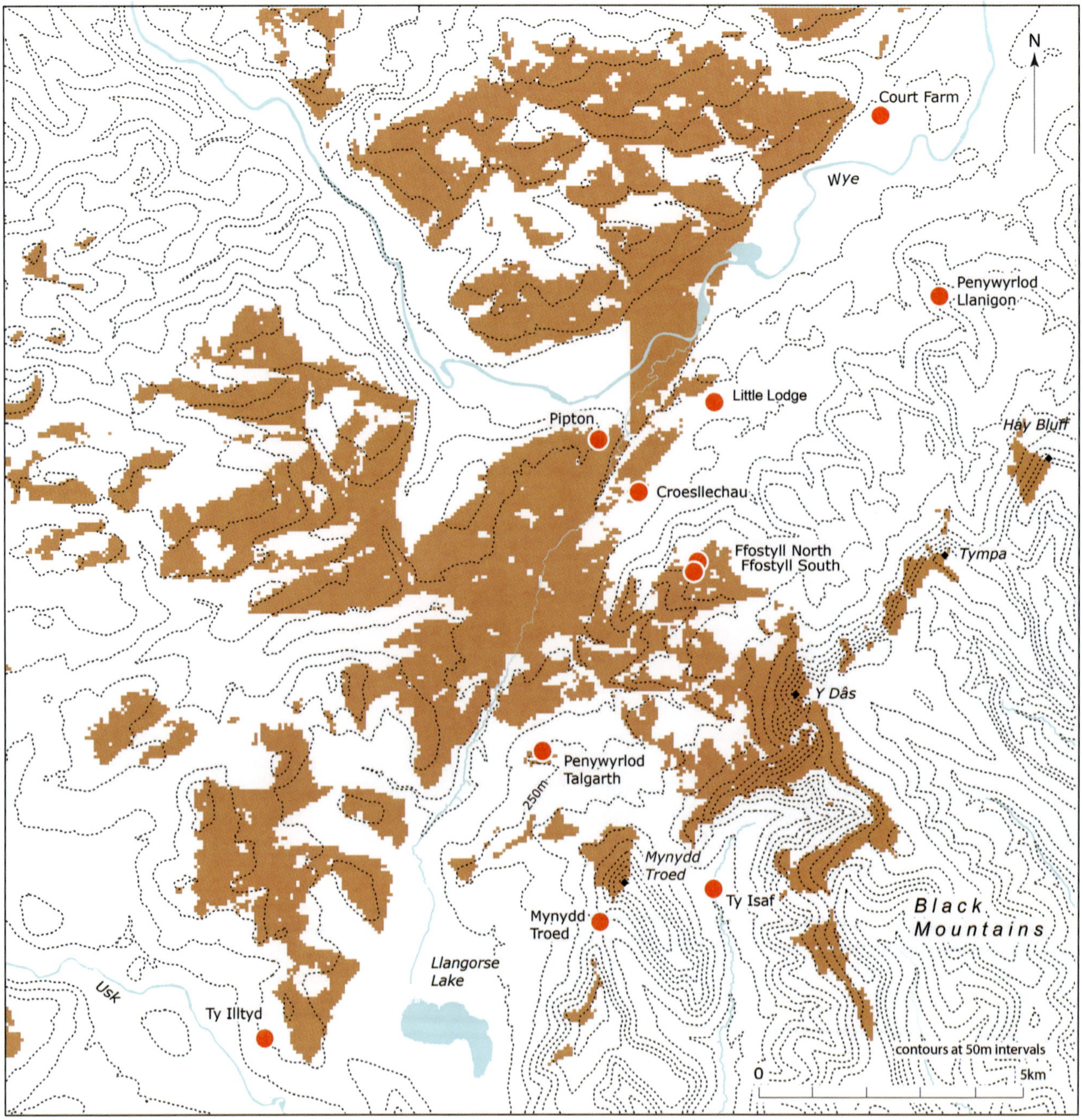

Fig. 12.10. Penywyrlod: viewshed from the Penywyrlod (Talgarth) long cairn, showing intervisibility with other neighbouring chambered tombs in the Black Mountains group and distinctive peaks along the NW escarpment of the Black Mountains. There are much more distant views from the site in an arc clockwise from the SW to the NE. (Viewshed by Nigel Jones, CPAT, based on Ordnance Survey 10m contour data.)

functional and had an entrance passage which extended to the outside of a cairn with a rounded end. Chamber III at Ty Isaf, transepted and approached by a substantial passage, is also surrounded by double walling, oval in plan. Both have been seen as akin to rotundas (e.g. Savory 1984, 24, for Pipton; Grimes 1939, 128 for Ty Isaf), better known elsewhere in various tombs in the Cotswolds (Darvill 2004, 61–71); we will review this classification below. However they might best be labelled (and to keep a distinction, we use inverted commas for those in the Black Mountains), it is important, first, to stress that both excavators (Savory 1956, 29, 37–9; Grimes 1939, 136–40) were firmly convinced that these structures marked stages in construction rather than earlier features which had been free-standing for any length of time. This interpretation was challenged by Corcoran who reinterpreted both Ty Isaf and Pipton and some other Cotswold-Severn tombs as multi-period constructions, partly on the presence of the 'rotundas' and partly on the angled alignment of the chamber passages such as Ty Isaf Chamber III and Pipton Chamber I (Corcoran 1969, 86–7). He also advanced a similar argument in the case of the so far undated Penywyrlod (Llanigon) whose plan suggested to him a rounded mound with a central cist to which a tail had been added (Fig. 2.30; Corcoran 1972, 61 and fig. 2, b), though this is as yet unsupported by structural evidence (cf. RCAHMW 1997, 62). He passed no judgment, however, on the similar-sized rounded mound enclosing a cist or chamber at Carn Goch (RCAHMW 1997, fig. 41), just south of Gwernvale, where Grimes had detected faint traces of a tail (Grimes 1936, 282).

Since Corcoran it has become something of an orthodoxy that rotundas represent an earlier phenomenon in the Cotswold-Severn region (Darvill 2004, 61–6, 68–71) and that they form part of the repertoire of monumental architectural styles and construction techniques indicating cross-Channel contacts in the early 4th millennium cal BC (Pailler and Sheridan 2009, 37–8; Sheridan 2010, 99–100). The assimilation of circular mounds within long trapezoidal mounds seemingly paralleled much earlier, 5th-millennium sequences recognised in parts of northern, western, and west-central France (Joussaume and Laporte 2006, 335; Cousseau 2015, 39), both round and long forms having been thought to symbolise ancestral domestic structures (Laporte and Tinévez 2004). Rotundas have been shown to be stratigraphically early within the Cotswold-Severn long cairns in which they have been found but there is some doubt about whether they were necessarily a particularly early monumental form within the region (Bayliss *et al.* 2007b, 43; Whittle *et al.* 2011, 469, fig. 9.30).

The structural sequences at both Ty Isaf and Pipton are quite complex, however, and will probably not be fully understood without further excavation – the sequence at Ty Isaf being particularly difficult to follow (Fig. 12.7). There was even uncertainty in Corcoran's mind about whether the Ty Isaf 'rotunda' was a primary or secondary structure (Corcoran 1969, 84–6; 1972, 61). The radiocarbon dating programmes undertaken at Pipton and Ty Isaf are relatively modest but provide no evidence that earlier free-standing structures existed at either site for any significant period of time. Chronological modelling of the dates from Pipton (see Chapter 4) does suggest that those from Chamber II are earlier than those from Chamber I, with there being *25–235 years* (*95% probability*, or *135–205 years, 65% probability*, or *60–70 years, 3% probability*) difference between the earliest burial evidence from Chamber I, and the latest burial evidence from Chamber I. To complicate matters further, another possible circular structure surrounds and encloses Chamber I (Fig. 2.30). Modelling the available dates from Ty Isaf suggests that the earliest burials from Chamber III within the 'rotunda' are no earlier than those within the two other lateral chambers, Chambers I–II, with the first burials from Chamber I, Chamber II and the 'rotunda' each most probably occurring in the 35th century cal BC. (The angled alignment of Gwernvale Chamber 1 (Fig. 12.7), which is thought to be essentially a single-period construction, suggests that the orientation of Ty Isaf Chamber III and Pipton Chamber I may likewise not have a chronological significance.)

An alternative possibility is that neither structure in question at Pipton and Ty Isaf need have anything to do directly with rotundas identified in the Cotswolds, for example at Notgrove, where there was a possibly closed central cist with a corbelled roof and finely built outer walling (Clifford 1937, 125–5). Other circular features surrounding chamber areas, for example the single, roughly built revetment wall around the transepted terminal chamber at Nympsfield (Clifford 1938, 199), may look more like a phase or technique of construction rather than a free-standing structure. In turn, Chamber III at Ty Isaf combined with the 'rotunda' around it have more the appearance of a passage grave or something similar. Sale's Lot in the Cotswolds could be another comparable case: O'Neil 1966, 15–17; cf. Darvill and Grinsell 1989; Smith and Brickley 2006, 351). The free-standing monument at Broadsands, Devon, probably dated to the 38th century cal BC or possibly the 39th (Sheridan *et al.* 2008; Whittle *et al.* 2011, 516, fig. 10.30), might also serve as a pre-existing exemplar of this kind of construction.

Whatever their precise constructional sequences may have been, both Pipton and Ty Isaf show, like Penywyrlod, access and repeat visits, possibly over substantial periods of time. Little mention is made in the published report on Pipton about the arrangements at the entrance to the passage of Chamber I (Fig. 12.7), though photographs show the basal course of the outer revetment wall running part-way across the opening (Savory 1956, pl. vi, 2). This suggests that like the entrance to Penywyrlod Chamber NE I the entrance passage had been entered by removing walling along the line of the outer revetment wall which here survived to a height of 0.76m. Savory (1956, 18, 21) suggested that the passage had probably originally been roofed with corbelling. The inner part of the entrance passage survived to a height of at least 1m but was only about 0.45m wide. The chamber, whose entrance was again constricted to about 0.4m, was up to about 1.4m high, parts of which are still roofed with capstones.

Grimes's original report on Ty Isaf focused on the morphology and sequence of construction of the tomb and little mention is made of the manner in which the chambers and chamber passages may have been accessed. Photographic evidence, however, suggests that the entrances to the passages to lateral Chamber II and the 'rotunda' around Chamber III (Fig. 2.30) had both, like Penywyrlod Chamber

NE I, been closed by blocking walls more or less down to ground level (Grimes 1939, pl. xiv, 3 and pl. xv, 1). The entrance passage to Ty Isaf Chamber I had been much more disturbed and only the bottom courses survived (Grimes 1939, pl. xiv, 2). Although there is no evidence that the outer revetment walling had been broken through to gain access to this passage and chamber, this may not preclude the possibility that they had been entered following completion of the tomb. A single capstone survived above one of the orthostats of Ty Isaf Chamber II but otherwise there is no evidence of how other chambers and their entrance passages may have been roofed. The chamber entrances at Ty Isaf are severely constricted, all probably being less than 0.45m across. Though some of the chambers had later filled with stone, none appear to have been deliberately filled before abandonment.

In terms of accessibility, it is worth noting, finally, Beaker pottery in the disturbed upper fill of Chamber I at Ty Isaf, fragments of an urn from Chamber IV which are possibly associated with cremated bone (Grimes 1939, 135–6; Savory 1980b, 138), and a child's tooth outside Chamber II, dated to the earlier 2nd millennium cal BC (see Chapter 4; Fig. 4.15). Late Neolithic dates (see also Chapter 4; Fig. 4.15) have also been obtained from human remains from upper contexts within the central element of Ty Isaf Chamber III and a cow's tooth from Ty Isaf Chamber I is dated to *2635–2465 cal BC* (*93% probability*; *SUERC-57788*; Fig. 4.15). We comment on endings below.

As for the contents of the various chambers at Pipton and Ty Isaf, there are many signs (set out again in detail in Chapter 6) of a continuation of the same kind of selective deposits as seen at Penywyrlod. Pipton Chamber II (Fig. 12.7) contained a deposit of mixed, grouped and disarticulated human remains similar in many respects to the assemblage within Penywyrlod Chamber NE III (see Chapter 6). Savory considered that it represented a single, closed deposit of material made during the construction of the monument but as noted above there is some evidence to suggest that the chamber may have been accessed via an entrance passage during an earlier phase in the life of the monument. For all its size and architectural elaboration, Pipton Chamber I had very little material.

Chapter 6 has also set out the detail for the contents of Ty Isaf. Individual deposits are quite modest, and articulated or articulating remains are scarce. Some cremations are present. Cumulatively the number of people represented at Ty Isaf appears to be greater than in the excavated chambers of Penywyrlod, though there are obvious issues of comparability. It is possible, as noted above, that the situation could reflect a locally more established community or communities, but the dangers of such an interpretation are obvious. Though the sites in question are not dated, it is worth noting with regard to distinctive local tradition a similar predominance of partial, disarticulated and fragmented human remains elsewhere in the Black Mountains, as suggested by earlier reports on excavations at Ffostyll South (Vulliamy 1921, 303–5; 1922, 151–2), Ffostyll North (Vulliamy 1923, 321–2), Penywyrlod (Llanigon) (Keith 1921–23), and Little Lodge (Vulliamy 1929, 35–6; RCAHMW 1997, 53).

Finally, the connections and affiliations potentially signalled by the architecture of Pipton and Ty Isaf point mainly eastwards, and possibly even further afield in the case of Ty Isaf. The earlier cist at Pipton (Chamber II) and Chamber III and 'rotunda' at Ty Isaf have been discussed above, and could have points of reference both to the east and south. The finished form of both cairns seems to evoke a wider tradition by this time of Severn-Cotswold tombs, there being by now more tombs in the Cotswolds (Whittle *et al.* 2011, chapter 9). The trapezoidal cairns with fine exterior walling and the forecourts with false portals would have been a familiar architectural vocabulary across this area. As discussed with reference to Penywyrlod, the portals, impressively constructed (two substantial if slightly uneven stones at Pipton set at right-angles to the axis of the cairn and an H-shaped arrangement of three stones at Ty Isaf) might nod still in the direction of dolmens further west, but by this date were also part of established Severn-Cotswold building grammar. All this, however, was here in a local tradition, with the hills firmly as the framing landscape. Slightly further afield in south Wales both Tinkinswood (perhaps after an initial phase with an enclosed cist) and Parc le Breos Cwm on the Gower also evoked at this sort of time (see Chapter 4: probably 38th–37th centuries cal BC onwards for the former and the 37th century cal BC for the latter) the Cotswold connection (Thompson 2019; Whittle and Wysocki 1998). Whether the T-shaped arrangement of Chamber I at Pipton might have anything to do with chamber form further afield, for example angled passage graves in Brittany (Scarre 2011, 137–45) or in western France more generally (cf. Savory 1980a; 1984), is open to discussion.

It is also useful to remind ourselves that Savory (1977; 1980a; 1984) stressed on more than one occasion the potential parallels and inspirations in western France also for transepted chambers, another obvious element of Cotswold practice, also found of course in south Wales, at Ty Isaf as just discussed and at Parc le Breos Cwm on the Gower (Whittle and Wysocki 1998). Before him, of course, Daniel (1939; 1941; 1950, 158–9; see again Chapter 1 here) had also looked closely at similar possible connections in transepted tomb architecture with his notion of a Retz group in southern Brittany. This was then made more specific by Stuart Piggott (1962) with his proposal of a Pornic-Notgrove group; details of transepted chambers in southern Brittany have been updated also by Laporte and Tinévez (2004, 223–5). Piggott's map (1962, fig. 20) highlights a striking distribution, on the one hand of tombs in southern Brittany as far as the far side of the mouth of the Loire, and on the other in south-east Wales and central-southern England. In line with the thinking of his day, Piggott (1962, 61) was inclined to construct a narrative of very specific connections ('the material expression of close contacts in funerary ritual between the two areas') and a story of events (a presumed first 'landing' in south-east Wales and a second landing in the Severn, with 'subsequent penetration' of the chalk downland), though he did recognise and somewhat struggle to reconcile (Piggott 1962, 63–4) the differing forms of cairns and barrows in which transepted chambers were set in western France and southern Britain. With more knowledge of French sites (see Fig. 12.11), detailed differences between the two regions in how transepted chambers were set in their cairns and mounds can be emphasised (Laporte and Tinévez 2004, 224), and a probable difference in date also emerges (Laporte and Tinévez 2004, 225), with the French examples perhaps (as at Quélarn, Finistère: Laporte and Tinévez 2004, fig. 4A, 4) earlier than the southern British ones, probably no earlier than the 37th century cal BC (summarised in Whittle *et al.* 2011; but note again Burn Ground). In the case of Ty Isaf, we could just refer to established or developing practice in the Cotswolds, or more locally on the Gower, and leave things at that, but the wider possible link remains intriguing. It is easy to dismiss Stuart Piggott's narrative as culture-historical over-interpretation, but does it, like some of Hubert Savory's speculations about distant sources, in fact speak to possibilities of continued connections and ongoing strands of human contact and movement, even at a date substantially later than the start of the Neolithic in Britain?

If Pipton, Ty Isaf and other monuments can be seen to evoke some kind of process of infill and consolidation, it is worth reflecting that we are beginning to accumulate more evidence for the conditions of existence in these centuries of established settlement. The human bones themselves strongly indicate a wide range of types of activity and activity-regimes (Chapter 6). The strontium isotope analysis may suggest a slightly more restricted scale of lifetime movement in the samples from Ty Isaf, compared to those from Penywyrlod, consistent with a shift from pioneering conditions to those of perhaps more established settlement (Chapter 7). The pre-cairn evidence from Gwernvale shows cereal cultivation (Chapter 5) which could date to the second half of the 39th or 38th centuries cal BC. There is also pre-cairn evidence from Gwernvale for the presence of domesticated stock. On that simple basis, a mixed economy could be asserted, but the dietary isotopic evidence and the lipid analysis set out in Chapter 8 and 11 strongly suggest an emphasis on dairy products and therefore the animal side of the economy.

As noted in Chapter 11, the association between early Neolithic ceramics with dairy products is now widespread throughout Britain and Ireland. As at Gwernvale, a high proportion of the sampled early Neolithic vessels associated with the timber buildings at Parc Cybi and Parc Bryn Cegin may have been used almost exclusively for dairy products. The importance of cattle in early Neolithic society has long been recognised in economic and cultural terms as well as for their potential impact upon settlement strategies (Ray and Thomas 2003). Other work on lipids and herd structure indicated by osteological evidence (Legge 2005) highlights the importance of dairying in early Neolithic farming strategies. Indeed, it can be argued that dairying was crucial for the earliest expansion of farming systems into central and western Europe in presenting an efficient mechanism for substantially increasing the yields of animal husbandry in comparison to meat consumption (Ethier *et al.* 2017). It also allows for the preservation of foodstuffs in a form which can be transported (Charlton *et al.* 2019, 6191) and need not therefore imply permanence of settlement. Potential parallels might be made with the widespread but often poorly documented practice of transhumant dairying in historic times in Europe, typically undertaken by a particular subset of a population group, whether based upon gender or age (Costello and Svensson 2018, 7).

It remains an open question (as discussed in Chapter 5) whether the latest pre-cairn cereal evidence at Gwernvale might reflect wider claimed trends towards a decline in cereal production and use (Steven and Fuller 2012; cf. Bishop 2015).

Other aspects of the human bone, finally, illuminate some of the other dimensions of life at this time (Chapter 6), from habitual activities such as repeated chewing and squatting, to the hazards of tooth loss. Alongside the events of monument construction, funerals and other mortuary rituals, there was plenty of routine.

The last stones, in an old place: monumentalising at Gwernvale

The Mesolithic and then early Neolithic use of the Gwernvale site was discussed earlier in this chapter. Well on into the early Neolithic, a tomb was also constructed here, probably in the 36th–35th centuries cal BC (as set out in Chapters 3 and 4). The principal features of the Gwernvale monument were by now familiar in many ways, and that is one reason why it is so easy to carry on with generalised accounts of the Severn-Cotswold architectural tradition. A substantial, symmetrical, trapezoidal cairn, a forecourt with a single large false portal stone, four chambers, fine exterior walling, use of the chambers for deposition of human remains (even if the evidence for that is sparse: Britnell 1984b, fig. 18, i), and repeated blockings and unblockings, are all features which can easily be paralleled elsewhere across the Severn-Cotswold architectural distribution.

In more detail on one of these features, it is possible that the passage entrances of all four chambers had been accessed by the removal and reinstatement of blocking walls set along the line of the outer revetment wall, which in the case of Chambers 2–3 may have been repeated on at least

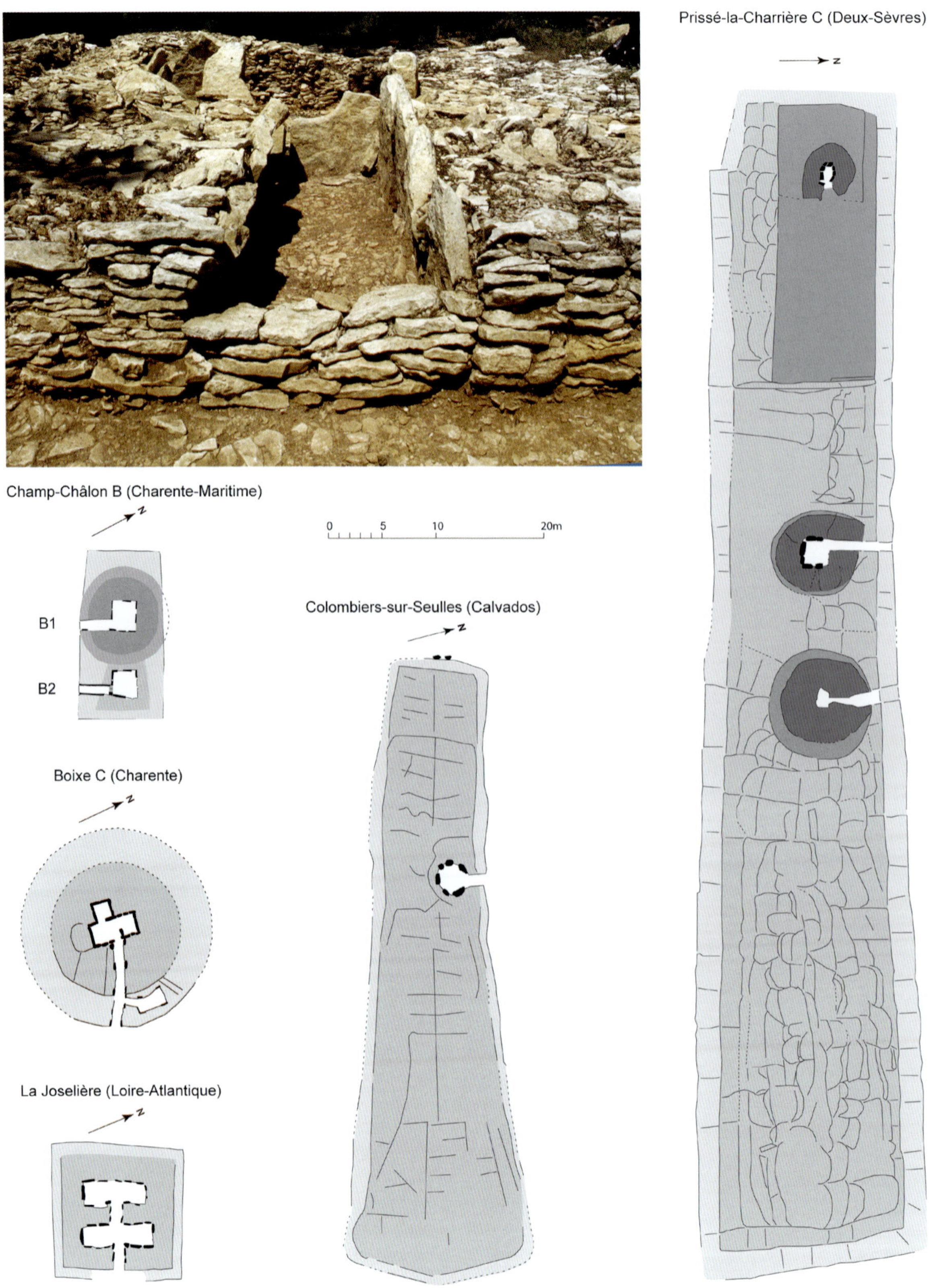

Fig. 12.11. Selected parallels and resemblances in the form, sequence of construction and manner of usage of Cotswold-Severn tombs in W and NW France. Top left: Blocked entrance to lateral chamber B2 at Champ-Châlon Tumulus B. A pair of stones at the inner end of the passage are shaped to form a 'porthole entrance'. Photograph: Frances Lynch. Below: Interpretative plans of Champ-Châlon (after Joussaume 2006), Boixe C (after Joussaume and Laporte 2006), La Joselière (after L'Helgouach et al. *1989), Colombiers-sur-Seulles (after Joussaume and Laporte 2006) and Prissé-la-Charrière (after Laporte 2015).*

two or three occasions (Britnell 1984b, 143–9). Unlike the chamber itself, the outer entrance passage to Chamber 3 was packed with stone between the line of the inner cairn wall to the outer face of the cairn, possibly as a final act of closure (Britnell 1984b, 82–3). It was largely because of this that it was suggested in the original report that the outer passage, between the inner and outer revetment walls, had been unroofed and that the chamber would only have been accessible by the removal of this stonework. However, on the basis of the evidence from Hazleton and Penywyrlod, it now seems more likely that the outer passage was roofed with corbelling and capping stones and that the stonework in the passage represents a final act of sealing the tomb. Concentrations of large, pitched slabs immediately outside the entrances to Gwernvale Chambers 2 and 3, which were formerly interpreted as external blocking structures (Britnell 1984b, fig. 20, iv and fig. 23, v; cf. Darvill 1982), might again in retrospect represent the outward collapse of passage roofing.

Distinctive local practice can be seen to be maintained in the building of an angled passage for Chamber 1, in the use of fine stone for the exterior walling (as described in Chapter 3), and in the plausible referencing by the monument of the prominent local hill, Crug Hywel. Issues about the orientations of the Black Mountains tombs have been much debated. One suggestion is that the monuments orient themselves along river valleys or point towards prominent hills (Tilley 1994, 125; Cummings and Whittle 2004, 61). In the case of Gwernvale, the orientation of both the underlying building and the tomb eastwards along the valley seems the most meaningful, but it also seems significant that the long axis (40° E of OS grid north) of the building points directly towards the prominent hilltop of Crug Hywel to the NE (Fig. 12.5, 6). More widely, visual associations appear to be particularly significant (*pace* Fleming 1999; 2005) and might help to explain the absence of tombs on the SE side of the mountains where the landscape is fragmented by the valleys of the Grwyne and Monnow and their tributaries and is visually less dramatic (Fig. 1.5). This seems to underline an association between the distribution of the tombs and the 'visually spectacular escarpment' of the northern, western and south-western flanks of the Black Mountains (Cummings and Whittle 2004, 84–6).

It is of course difficult to draw any firm conclusions from the plan of the monument alone as to what sort of social grouping or groupings may have conceived of and used the tomb. It is striking that Chambers 2 and 3 are nearly symmetrically opposed, and could invite comparisons with the layouts of both Hazleton and Ascott-under-Wychwood, the former now with the aDNA evidence noted above for a male-dominated lineage over five generations. Chambers 1 and 4 add diversity, however, and we simply have to admit that this social dimension is not open to us here. Perhaps a contrast with Penywyrlod at least might be suggested, and with enclosures of this sort of date in the wider region (see below), and a set of smaller groupings might be proposed.

So far, so familiar. What the studies represented in this volume may further suggest, however, is the distinctiveness of this late construction. Gwernvale can be seen as both subtly different and archaic in its local and wider contexts, drawing on a history of local place not seen (on the basis of research so far) in other Black Mountains tombs, and elaborating some of its symbolism through that history. This may in those senses have been a story of land-keeping, or even of specific family or local community history, at a time of change.

By the time Gwernvale was constructed, many generations of tomb building across the overall distribution of Severn-Cotswold architecture had passed. There is no sign of earlier features being incorporated, as at Pipton and Ty Isaf. The wider world around Gwernvale was by now changing. More enclosures appear to have been constructed in south Wales and the Marches from around the start of the 36th century cal BC, including Caerau outside Cardiff and Womaston in the Walton basin (N. Jones 2009; Davis and Sharples 2017; Whittle *et al.* 2022, fig. 13.2) (Fig. 12.12); we should note, however, the possibility of an earlier date estimate for the simple enclosure at Hill Croft Field, as set out in Chapter 4. Further afield, the first passage tombs had been built in Ireland (Hensey 2015), though whether those on Anglesey are this early is open to question. The middle of the 4th millennium cal BC appears to have been a time of change and considerable diversity. A range of 'diverse and small' mortuary structures were constructed in southern Britain (Whittle *et al.* 2011, 724, fig. 14.43), and the first, successive individual burials at Duggleby Howe on the Yorkshire Wolds go back to the 36th or 35th centuries cal BC (Gibson and Bayliss 2009). Gwernvale does not stand alone as a late example of traditional long cairn or long barrow construction. We can cite Millbarrow in Wiltshire, just north of Windmill Hill (Whittle 1994), probably from the 34th or 33rd centuries cal BC (Whittle *et al.* 2011, 105, fig. 3.30), and Wayland's Smithy II on the downland scarp above the Vale of the White Horse (Whittle 1991), probably from the 35th or 34th centuries cal BC (Whittle *et al.* 2007). The latter is very similar in plan to the West Kennet long barrow, built two or three centuries earlier (Bayliss *et al.* 2007d).

There might be an argument that there was simply a degree of timelag or conservatism in south Wales and the Marches, as witnessed by the predominance of later enclosures, noted above. More plausibly, we suggest a deliberate and conscious maintenance of tradition – even a defiance of forces of change operating elsewhere – through the construction of Gwernvale at this time. Old ways of doing things could still be powerful (and it is worth noting the general dearth of subsequent, 3rd-millennium monuments including henges in the region: Tim Darvill, *pers. comm.*).

Fig. 12.12. Butt-end of one of the inner causewayed ditches at the Womaston causewayed enclosure in the Walton basin, Radnorshire, during excavation in 2008. Photograph, Nigel Jones, Clwyd-Powys Archaeological Trust.

There are plausibly three further dimensions of that in the case of Gwernvale.

First, the Gwernvale monument memorialised an old place in ways not seen locally in the case of earlier Black Mountains tombs. It was placed above the traces of Mesolithic and then early Neolithic occupation. The latter perhaps suggests something small-scale, though there are both a midden and a wooden building. There is evidence for a range of domestic animals including cattle, pig and sheep (O'Connor 1984), which comes mostly from the area of the midden in the area between Chamber 1 and the forecourt (Fig. 3.19). (Although the assemblage is very small the predominance of cattle remains (65%) is characteristic of larger early Neolithic midden assemblages elsewhere, as at Ascott-under-Wychwood (Mulville and Grigson 2007) and Eton Rowing Lake (G. Jones 2013).) There are fragments of a single red deer tooth, the undomesticated animal certainly represented. There are equally quite abundant cereal remains, as reported in significant detail in Chapter 5 (and see Griffiths 2018), but the overall picture from both dietary isotope analyses and the lipid analysis from the Gwernvale pre-cairn pottery assemblage (Chapters 8 and 11 respectively) seems to suggest a predominance of dairying and animal use. Is that just the local picture, appropriate to subsistence in and around the uplands of the Black Mountains, or does that too presage a probable wider reduction in or abandonment of cereal production in the latter part of the early Neolithic (Stevens and Fuller 2012; but see also Bishop 2015)? Is this possible trend another sign of a changing world?

Secondly, the Gwernvale monument elaborates an older symbolism of the transformation of house into tomb – the detail for which has been presented in Chapter 3 – and may play on notions of doorways into other worlds (cf. C. Richards 1992). That too is novel in the local context, from the sample of excavated constructions which we have so far, since these aspects are missing from Penywyrlod, Pipton and Ty Isaf as far as we know; perhaps ongoing excavations at Arthur's Stone, noted above (and Fig. 12.13), will complicate that picture.

Fig. 12.13. Arthur's Stone, Dorstone, Herefordshire. Wikipedia Commons CC-BY-SA-3.0.

It is as though the construction of the Gwernvale monument on its own was not sufficient for the purposes of the builders. Land-keeping and the maintenance of old ways were bolstered by enlisting a venerably old place and by multiplying the layers of symbolic significance. Finally, the uncanny similarity of the successions of occupations, middens, structures and tombs at Ascott-under-Wychwood, Hazleton and Gwernvale has often been commented on (*e.g.* Darvill 1982; 2004; Saville 1990; Benson and Whittle 2007), and it is hard to think that these sequences are not in some way or ways connected. It is now possible, however, to begin to contextualise them better according to time and place. The situations at Ascott-under-Wychwood and Hazleton can now be seen to be significantly older than that at Gwernvale, since Ascott was probably constructed in the second half of the 38th century cal BC and Hazleton in the first half of the 37th century cal BC. If we believe that the situation at Gwernvale mirrors these two older contexts, then a memory of some kind must have been preserved over both the temporal and spatial intervals between them. Whether that was a general understanding across the Cotswold-Severn distribution, or special, periodically transmitted ritual knowledge not open to everyone (cf. Barth 1987), is open to discussion. In either case, to the memorialisation of local place and the elaboration of symbolisms of transformation, was added, finally, a sense of venerated and remembered old practice from relatively far away. If the first stones were placed when a new world was young to link builders to place, to take the land and to begin to create a distinctive regional identity, then the last stones, we could say, were ancient, used to keep the land by evoking memories from older pasts and connections to far away.

Afterlives

We have argued that the initiation of both Penywyrlod and Gwernvale can be related to circumstances of significant change; in their differing ways, the emergence of both can be seen as dramatic. In contrast, their endings were much more restrained. As an endnote, we should register that our knowledge of what followed the construction of the Gwernvale monument is very patchy, since poor representation of bones in the chambers precludes dates and any estimate of duration of use, and this and the late history of the Black Mountains tombs in general are an obvious target for further research in general. We do know, however, that there was a quiet afterlife of sorts at Gwernvale, Penywyrlod and Ty Isaf.

At Gwernvale itself, Middle to Late Neolithic pottery was deposited in pits outside the entrance to Chambers 2 and 3 (Britnell 1984b, 104–5), which chronological modelling suggests occurred between *3320–2545 cal BC* (*95% probability*, or *3270–2880 cal BC, 68% probability*; *last_Gwernvale_post_cairn*; see Chapter 4, Fig. 4.5). Similar activity involving the deposition of sherds of Peterborough Ware has been noted at Cotswold-Severn tombs elsewhere (Darvill 2004, 182–5) as well as other types of early Neolithic site which may have retained a possibly ancestral significance, suggesting a means of reconnecting with the past (Whittle *et al.* 1999, 380; Ard and Darvill 2015, 27). Similar activity has even been noted at a number of early Neolithic timber houses, suggesting that even less prominent sites may have remained recognisable within the landscape by some means or another for many centuries after abandonment, which has possible significance for the sequence from house to tomb observed at Gwernvale, Hazleton and Ascott. The early Neolithic houses at Parc Bryn Cegin (Kenney 2008, 42), Llanfaethlu (Rees and Jones 2017) and White Horse Stone and Pilgrims Way (Garwood 2011, 71, 96–8), for example, are each associated with otherwise unexplained Middle and/or Late Neolithic ceramics in secondary contexts, often deposited within pits.

Evidence of continued activity at Cotswold-Severn tombs from the later 3rd millennium onwards is less usual but has been noted at a number of sites in the Black Mountains and elsewhere (Darvill 2004, 215–16). The cist inserted into the walling of the S horn at Penywyrlod is undated but might be late 3rd or 2nd millennium in date. Burials in pits had begun to appear in Wales in the Middle Neolithic but cist burials appear to be otherwise unrecorded prior to the Chalcolithic (Tellier 2018, 20–5). The only other evidence of prehistoric activity in the vicinity of Penywyrlod is a single round barrow to the S identified by recent fieldwork and a possible, undated, sub-rectangular ditched enclosure identified by geophysical survey (Fig. 2.12, no. 3).

Later finds at Ty Isaf include Beaker pottery in the disturbed upper fill of Chamber I, fragments of an urn from Chamber IV which are possibly associated with cremated bone (Grimes 1939, 135–6; Savory 1980b, 138), and a child burial outside Chamber II, with a 2nd millennium date (see again Tables 4.1, 4.2 and Neil *et al.* 2017, 18). Late Neolithic dates have also been obtained from human remains from upper and lower contexts within the central element of Ty Isaf Chamber III and from a cow's tooth in Ty Isaf Chamber I (see Tables 4.1, 4.2).

Small fragments of Beaker and Food Vessel are also recorded from Penywyrlod (Llanigon), some at least from the E chamber (Savory 1980b, 136; Roese 1979–80, 45). Unprovenanced fragments of Food Vessel and Collared Urn are said to come from Ffostyll South (Roese 1979–90, 43) though the excavator himself stated that no pottery had been found (Vulliamy 1921, 305). Again in south Wales, Beaker pottery is known from Tinkinswood (Savory 1980b, 136). The remains of several individuals of Late Neolithic to Early Bronze Age date allegedly from the passage of the Parc le Breos Cwm tomb (Whittle and Wysocki 1998, 147–9; Chapter 4, Table 4.2) are in fact probably from the nearby Cat Hole cave (Wysocki *et al.* in press).

As history moved on, these were muted endings, as monuments previously of prime significance gradually faded away.

Appendix: Monument conservation at Penywyrlod

William Britnell

Many hundreds of tonnes of stone had been quarried from the Penywyrlod tomb in the 1970s to create a platform for the erection of steel-framed farm buildings (SO 15312 31830) next to Penyrwyrlodd Farm before its archaeological significance was appreciated. This left a quarry about 20m by 12m across and up to about 2m deep on the NE side, a small quarry on the summit of the cairn, together with scarping along the NW side and a lowering of its tail (see Figs 2.4 and 2.7).

Following its discovery the tomb was designated a Scheduled Ancient Monument (Br175) and in the 1980s it eventually became a Guardianship Monument in the care of the then Ancient Monuments Branch of the Welsh Office – subsequently Cadw, the Welsh Government's historic environment service. Following its acquisition by the state the former hedge-line which crossed the SW side of the mound was removed (see Fig. 2.7) and a new fenced enclosure was erected around the visible extent of the monument.

Fig. App 1. Penywyrlod: on-site meeting in August 2015 by members of staff of Cadw – Welsh Government and Mann Williams, Consulting Civil and Structural Engineers to consider options for the long-term conservation of the monument. Note the eroding edges of the quarry dug into the broader end of the long cairn in the 1970s and the splitting of the remaining upright of the portal structure.

Conservation issues

The relatively shallow trenches excavated in the 1970s were backfilled but the sections cut into the cairn by quarrying remained exposed. By the beginning of the new millennium some vegetation had begun to take hold and the monument had acquired something of the air of a picturesque ruin (Fig. 1.8), cherished as a teaching aid by various archaeological groups and university departments.

Continuing deterioration became a matter of growing concern as exposed sections of the cairn continued to gradually erode. A further issue was that some of the exposed orthostats, such as those of Chamber NE II and the one portal stone still standing (Fig. App 1), are composed of a flaggy sandstone which readily splits upon weathering. Even some structural elements of the chambers, such as the outer capstone of Chamber NE III, had collapsed.

Various options for the conservation and display of the monument were considered, taking into account its archaeological and aesthetic values and the fact that, despite the damage suffered in the 1970s, it is still the best preserved of the tombs in the Black Mountains area. A number of schemes were considered that would involve display and interpretation but after some debate the decision was made to adopt a scheme that would involve the introduction of a landscaped batter, which would provide protection for the eroding quarry face on the NW side of the mound and the exposed and weathering orthostats of the portal structure and Chambers NE I and NE II. Similar issues arose at Belas Knap, for example, after it had been taken into Guardianship in the 1920s. There, it was eventually decided to reconstruct and display the stonework revealed by excavation even though this was a departure from the normal practice of HM Office of Works (see Hemp 1929, 264). The principal considerations at Penywyrlod were that such a scheme should provide continued protection for the monument, involve a minimum of disturbance, be reversible and require low maintenance.

Conservation work undertaken at Penywyrlod

A conservation scheme devised by Mann Williams, Consulting Civil and Structural Engineers, was eventually adopted. This involved first the covering of the exposed faces of the long cairn, the portal structure and the visible remains of Chambers NE I and II in sheets of geotextile (Multitrak 1000 geotextile) held in place where necessary with wooden pegs. Against this were placed hessian sacks filled with a light-weight aggregate (Leca LWA-10-20-R) of a kind extensively used in civil engineering and structural applications. Around the quarry face this required up to about 20 layers of sacks, laid horizontally and stacked up to three deep and battered at an angle of approximately 20 degrees from the vertical and reinforced with sheets of a stiff polymer mesh (Tensar TriAx Geogrid) about every four courses (Figs App 3–4). These were covered by a single layer of geotextile sacks (FlexMSE) filled with a sand and soil mixture, held in place by interlocking polypropylene plates, the bottom courses being covered in wire netting to deter burrowing animals. Finally, a slurry of a mixture of wild plants, grasses and mulch (hydroseeding) was sprayed on to the surface of the landscaping to encourage vegetation to become established (Fig. App 5). Of the stonework only part of the fallen portal stone and lintel and the displaced outer capstone of Chamber NE III remain visible.

Conservation work was undertaken by Taliesin Conservation between March and May 2016. The conservation work required almost 100m^3 of material weighing about 50 tonnes. Since this needed to be transported over a distance of almost 0.5km across wet ground during the early months of the year it was air-lifted by helicopter (Fig. App 2) from a dropping-off point on the public road.

Fig. App 2. Penywyrlod: helicopter air lift of conservation materials to the site in March 2016.

Fig. App 3. Penywyrlod: hessian sacks filled with a light-weight aggregate being put in place to consolidate the surviving remains of Chamber NE I in March 2016.

Fig. App 4. Penywyrlod: hessian sacks filled with a light-weight aggregate and a single outer layer of geotextile sacks filled with a sand and soil mixture being put in place in March 2016 to consolidate the eroding edges of the quarry dug into the long cairn in the 1970s. A slurry of a mixture or wild plants, grasses and mulch was later sprayed on to the surface of the sacks to encourage vegetation to become established.

Fig. App 5. Penywyrlod: the same view in September 2016 showing vegetation starting to become established on the consolidated sides of the NE area of the long cairn quarried for stone in the 1970s.

Sites to visit

A number of the long cairns in the Black Mountains group are on private land and can only be visited with the permission of landowners though others are accessible by foot. Penywyrlod near Talgarth (SO 1505 3156), in the care of Cadw, is accessible from several public footpaths including ones beginning near Penywyrlodd to the NE and from near Neuadd-fach to the SE. Gwernvale (SO 2110 1920) lies on the northern verge of the A40 road, just to the W of Crickhowell. Carn Goch (SO 2123 1771) lies in a public recreation area at Llangattock. Mynydd Troed (SO 1615 2843) lies on open-access land on the S side of Mynydd Troed. Ty Isaf (SO 1819 2906) and Penywyrlod near Llanigon (SO 2248 3987) both lie on or close to public footpaths. Arthur's Stone, Dorstone (SO 3180 4313), is in the care of English Heritage.

Bibliography

Aldhouse-Green, S. 2000. Palaeolithic and Mesolithic Wales. In F. Lynch, S. Aldhouse-Green and J.L. Davies, *Prehistoric Wales*, 1–41. Stroud: Sutton.

Allen, J.R.L. 1974. The Devonian rocks of Wales and the Welsh borderland. In T.R. Owen (ed.), *The Upper Palaeozoic and post-Palaeozoic rocks of Wales*, 47–84. Cardiff: University of Wales Press.

Allen, M. and Gardiner, J. 2002. A sense of time: cultural markers in the Mesolithic of southern England? In B. David and M. Wilson (eds), *Inscribed landscapes: marking and making place*, 139–53. Honolulu: University of Hawaii Press.

Allen, T., Barclay, A., Cromarty, A.M., Anderson-Whymark, H., Parker, A., Robinson, M. and Jones, G. 2013. *Opening the wood, making the land. The Eton College rowing course project and the Maidenhead, Windsor and Eton flood alleviation scheme. Volume 1: Mesolithic to early Bronze Age*. Oxford: Oxford Archaeology.

AlQahtani, S.J., Hector, M. and Liversidge, H.M. 2010. The London atlas of human tooth development and eruption. *American Journal of Physical Anthropology* 142, 481–90.

Anderberg, A. 1994. *Atlas of seeds. Part 4 Resedaceae-Umbelliferae*. Stockholm: Swedish Museum of Natural History.

Anderson-Whymark, H. 2013a. The struck flint from Area 6. In T. Allen, A. Barclay, A.M. Cromarty, H. Anderson-Whymark, A. Parker, M. Robinson and G. Jones, *Opening the wood, making the land: the archaeology of a Middle Thames landscape. The Eton College rowing course project and the Maidenhead, Windsor and Eton flood alleviation scheme. Volume 1: Mesolithic to early Bronze Age*, 148–78. Oxford: Oxford Archaeology.

Anderson-Whymark, H. 2013b. Appendix 2 – Struck flint: methodology and overview. In T. Allen, A. Barclay, A.M. Cromarty, H. Anderson-Whymark, A. Parker, M. Robinson and G. Jones, *Opening the wood, making the land: the archaeology of a Middle Thames landscape. The Eton College rowing course project and the Maidenhead, Windsor and Eton flood alleviation scheme. Volume 1: Mesolithic to early Bronze Age*, 513–26. Oxford: Oxford Archaeology.

Angel, J.L. 1966. Porotic hyperostosis, anemias, malarias and marshes in the prehistoric eastern Mediterranean. *Science* 153, 760–3.

Archaeological Services Durham University 2013. 2011 Excavation Borras Quarry, Wrexham. Palaeoenvironmental analysis. Archaeological Services Durham University. Unpublished Report 2988.

Ard, V. and Darvill, T. 2015. Revisiting old friends: the production, distribution and use of Peterborough Ware in Britain. *Oxford Journal of Archaeology* 18, 356–75.

Ashbee, P. 1966. The Fussell's Lodge long barrow: excavations 1957. *Archaeologia* 100, 1–80.

Ashbee, P., Smith, I.F. and Evans, J.G. 1979. Excavation of three long barrows near Avebury, Wiltshire. *Proceedings of the Prehistoric Society* 45, 207–300.

Aufderheide, A.C. and Rodriguez-Martin, C. 1998. *The Cambridge encyclopedia of human paleopathology*. Cambridge: Cambridge University Press.

Austin, P. 2000. The emperor's new garden: woodland, trees and people in the Neolithic of southern Britain. In A. Fairbairn (ed.), *Plants in Neolithic Britain and beyond*, 63–78. Oxford: Oxbow Books.

Bakker, J.A. 1992. *The Dutch hunebedden: megalithic tombs of the Funnel Beaker culture*. Michigan: Ann Arbor.

Bapty, I. 2007. *Lower Lugg archaeology and aggregates resource assessment*. Herefordshire Archaeology Report 226. Document prepared for English Heritage. Hereford: Herefordshire Archaeology.

Barber, A., Hardy, A. and Mudd, A. 2019. *The prehistoric archaeology of the A477 St Clears to Red Roses Road Improvement Scheme 2012*. Cotswold Archaeology Monograph 12. Cirencester: Cotswold Archaeology.

Barber, A. and Hart, J. 2014a. South Wales gas pipeline project. Site 503. Land east of Vaynor Farm, Llanddowror, Carmarthenshire. Archaeological Excavation. Cotswold Archaeology. Unpublished Report 13328.

Barber, A. and Hart, J. 2014b. South Wales gas pipeline project. Site 511/514. Land South-East of Upper Neeston, Herbrandston, Pembrokeshire. Archaeological Excavation. Cotswold Archaeology. Unpublished Report 13254.

Barclay, A. 2007. Connections and networks: a wider world and other places. In D. Benson and A. Whittle (eds), *Building memories: the Neolithic Cotswold long barrow at Ascott-under-Wychwood, Oxfordshire*, 331–44. Oxford: Oxbow Books.

Barclay, A. 2013. Early Neolithic pottery from Area 6. In T. Allen, A. Barclay, A.M. Cromarty, H. Anderson-Whymark, A. Parker, M. Robinson and G. Jones, *Opening the wood, making the land. The Eton College rowing course project and the Maidenhead, Windsor and Eton flood alleviation scheme. Volume 1: Mesolithic to early Bronze Age*, 106–48. Oxford: Oxford Archaeology.

Barclay, A.J. 2014. Re-dating the Coneybury Anomaly and its implications for understanding the earliest Neolithic pottery from southern England. *PAST* 77, 11–13.

Barclay, A. and Bayliss, A. 1999. Cursus monuments and the radiocarbon problem. In A. Barclay and J. Harding (eds), *Pathways and ceremonies: the cursus monuments of Britain and Ireland*, 11–29. Oxford: Oxbow Books.

Barclay, A.J., Bayliss, A., Bronk Ramsey, C., Cleal, R., Cook, G., Healy, F., Higbee, L., Marshall, P., Pelling, P. and Stevens, C.J. 2018. *Dating the earliest Neolithic ceramics of Wessex*. Historic England: Research Report Series 63-2018 (online).

Barclay, A. and Case, H. 2007. The early Neolithic pottery and fired clay. In D. Benson and A. Whittle (eds), *Building memories: the Neolithic Cotswold long barrow at Ascott-under-Wychwood, Oxfordshire*, 263–81. Oxford: Oxbow Books.

Barclay, A., Chaffey, G. and Manning, A. 2012. A possible second Neolithic house and an unusual Mortlake bowl from Kingsmead Quarry, Horton, Berkshire. *Past* 71, 1–2.

Barclay, A., Field, D. and Leary, J. (eds) 2020. *Houses of the dead?* Oxford: Oxbow Books.

Barclay, A.J. and Harris, O.J.T. 2017. Community building: houses and people in Neolithic Britain. In P. Bickle, V. Cummings, D. Hofmann and J. Pollard (eds), *The Neolithic of Europe: papers in honour of Alasdair Whittle*, 222–34. Oxford: Oxbow Books.

Barclay, W.J. and Wilby, P.R. 2003. *Geology of the Talgarth district – a brief explanation of the geological map. Sheet Explanation of the British Geological Survey. 1:50 000 Sheet 214 Talgarth (England and Wales)*. Keyworth: British Geological Survey.

Barfield, L. 2007. Later lithics in the West Midlands counties. In P. Garwood (ed.), *The undiscovered country: the earlier prehistory of the West Midlands*, 97–108. Oxford: Oxbow Books.

Barrett, J.C. 2021. *Archaeology and its discontents: why archaeology matters*. Abingdon: Routledge.

Barth, F. 1987. *Cosmologies in the making: a generative approach to cultural variation in inner New Guinea*. Cambridge: Cambridge University Press.

Barton, R.N.E. 1992. *Hengistbury Head, Dorset, volume 2: the Late Upper Palaeolithic and early Mesolithic sites*. Oxford: Oxford University Committee for Archaeology.

Barton, R.N.E. 2007. Goldcliff lithic artefacts. In M. Bell, *Prehistoric coastal communities: the Mesolithic in western Britain*, 103–24. York: Council for British Archaeology.

Barton, R.N.E., Berridge, P.J., Walker, M.J.C. and Bevins, R.E. 1995. Persistent places in the Mesolithic landscape: an example from the Black Mountain uplands of South Wales. *Proceedings of the Prehistoric Society* 61, 81–116.

Barton, R.N.E. and Roberts, A.J. 1996. Reviewing the British Late Upper Palaeolithic: new evidence for chronological patterning in the Late Glacial record. *Oxford Journal of Archaeology* 15, 245–65.

Bass, W.M. 1992. *Human osteology: a laboratory and field manual* (third edition). Columbia: Missouri Archaeological Society.

Bayliss, A. 2015. Quality in Bayesian chronological models in archaeology. *World Archaeology* 47, 677–700.

Bayliss, A., Benson, D., Bronk Ramsay, C., Galer, D., McFadyen, L., van der Plicht, J. and Whittle, A. 2007a. Interpreting chronology: the radiocarbon dating programme. In D. Benson and A. Whittle (eds), *Building memories: the Neolithic Cotswold long barrow at Ascott-under-Wychwood, Oxfordshire*, 221–36. Oxford: Oxbow Books.

Bayliss, A., Benson, D., Galer, D., Humphrey, L., McFadyen, L. and Whittle, A. 2007b. One thing after another: the date of the Ascott-under-Wychwood long barrow. *Cambridge Archaeological Journal* 17.1, supplement, 29–44.

Bayliss, A., Bronk Ramsey, C., van der Plicht, J. and Whittle, A. 2007c. Bradshaw and Bayes: towards a timetable for the Neolithic. *Cambridge Archaeological Journal* 17.1, supplement, 1–28.

Bayliss, A. and Whittle, A. (eds) 2007. Histories of the dead: building chronologies for five southern British long barrows. *Cambridge Archaeological Journal* 17.1, supplement.

Bayliss, A., Whittle, A., Healy, F., Ray, K., Dorling, P., Lewis, R., Darvill, T., Wainwright, G. and Wysocki, M. 2011a. The Marches, south Wales and the Isle of Man. In A. Whittle, F. Healy and A. Bayliss, *Gathering time: dating the early Neolithic enclosures of southern Britain and Ireland*, 521–61. Oxford: Oxbow Books.

Bayliss, A., Healy, F., Whittle, A. and Cooney, G.. 2011b. Neolithic narratives: British and Irish enclosures in their timescapes. In A. Whittle, F. Healy and A. Bayliss, *Gathering time: dating the early Neolithic enclosures of southern Britain and Ireland*, 682–847. Oxford: Oxbow Books.

Bayliss, A., Whittle, A. and Wysocki, M. 2007d. Talking about my generation: the date of the West Kennet long barrow. *Cambridge Archaeological Journal* 17.1, supplement, 85–101.

Beamish, M. 2009. Island visits: Neolithic and Bronze Age activity on the Trent valley floor. Excavations at Egginton and Willington, Derbyshire, 1998–1999. *Derbyshire Archaeological Journal* 129, 17–172.

Behrensmeyer, A.K. 1978. Taphonomic and ecologic information from bone weathering. *Paleobiology* 4, 1150–62.

Bell, M. 2007. Prehistoric coastal communities: the Mesolithic in western Britain. York: Council for British Archaeology.

Bell, M. 2020. *Making one's way in the world*. Oxford: Oxbow Books.

Bennett, F.J. 1913. Coldrum monument and exploration 1910. *Journal of the Royal Anthropological Institute* 43, 76–85.

Benson, D. and Whittle, A. (eds) 2007. *Building memories: the Neolithic Cotswold long barrow at Ascott-under-Wychwood, Oxfordshire*. Oxford: Oxbow Books.

Bentley, R.A. 2006. Strontium isotopes from the earth to the archaeological skeleton: a review. *Journal of Archaeological Method and Theory* 13, 135–87.

Berggren, G. 1969. *Atlas of seeds and small fruits of Northwest-European plant species with morphological descriptions. Part 2. Cyperaceae*. Stockholm: Swedish Museum of Natural History.

Berggren, G. 1981. *Atlas of seeds and small fruits of Northwest-European plant species with morphological descriptions. Part 3. Salicaceae-Cruciferae*. Stockholm: Swedish Natural Science Research Council.

Berridge, P. 1994. General discussion of the Mesolithic at Rhuddlan. In H. Quinnell, M.P. Blockley, and P. Berridge,

Excavations at Rhuddlan, Clwyd 1969–73 Mesolithic to Medieval, 126–31. York: Council for British Archaeology.

Berrizbeitia, E.L. 1989. Sex determination with the head of the radius. *Journal of Forensic Sciences* 34, 1206–13.

Berry, J. 1930. Belas Knap long barrow, Gloucestershire; report on the excavations of 1930. *Transactions of the Bristol and Gloucestershire Archaeological Society* 52, 123–50.

BGS 2004. *England & Wales Sheet 214. Talgarth. Solid & Drift*. Keyworth: British Geological Survey.

Bishop, R.R. 2015a. Did Late Neolithic farming fail or flourish? A Scottish perspective on the evidence for Late Neolithic arable cultivation in the British Isles. *World Archaeology* 47, 834–55.

Bishop, R.R. 2015b. Summed radiocarbon probability distributions from cereal grains: arable cultivation proxy or the 'archaeology of us'? (a reply to Stevens and Fuller 2015). *World Archaeology* 47, 876–81.

Bishop, R.R. 2019. Experiments on the effects of charring on hazelnuts and their representation in the archaeological record. *Journal of Archaeological Science: Reports* 26, 101839.

Bishop, R.R., Church, M.J. and Rowley-Conwy, P.A. 2009. Cereals, fruits and nuts in the Scottish Neolithic. *Proceedings of the Society of Antiquaries of Scotland* 135, 47–103.

Bishop, R.R., Church, M.J. and Rowley-Conwy, P.A. 2013. Seeds, fruits and nuts in the Scottish Mesolithic. *Proceedings of the Society of Antiquaries of Scotland* 143, 9–71.

Bishop, R.R., Church, M.J. and Rowley-Conwy, P.A. 2015. Firewood, food and human niche construction: the potential role of Mesolithic hunter-gatherers in activity structuring Scotland's woodlands. *Quaternary Science Reviews* 108, 51–75.

Black, T.K. 1978. A new method for assessing the sex of fragmentary skeletal remains: femoral shaft circumference. *American Journal of Physical Anthropology* 48, 227–32.

Blank, M., Sjögren, K.-G., Knipper, C., Frei, K.M. and Storå, J. 2018. Isotope values of the bioavailable strontium in inland southwestern Sweden – a baseline for mobility studies. *PLoS One 13*(10), p.e0204649.

Blinkhorn, E. 2012. The Mesolithic and the planning process in England. Unpublished PhD thesis, University of York.

Blinkhorn, E. and Little, A. 2018. Being ritual in Mesolithic Britain and Ireland: identifying ritual behaviour within an ephemeral material record. *Journal of World Prehistory* 31, 403–20.

Bogaard, A. 2005. 'Garden agriculture' and the nature of early farming in Europe and the Near East. *World Archaeology* 37, 177–96.

Bogaard, A., Fraser, R., Heaton, T.H.E. Wallace, M. Vaiglova, P., Charles, M., Jones, G., Evershed, R.P., Styring, A.K., Andersen, N.H. and Arbogast, R.M., Bartosiewicz, L., Gardeisen, A., Kanstrup, M., Maier, U., Marinova, E., Ninov, L., Schäfer, M. and Stephen, E. 2013. Crop manuring and intensive land management by Europe's first farmers. *Proceedings of the National Academy of Sciences of the United States of America* 110, 12589–94.

Bogaard, A. and Jones, G. 2007. Neolithic farming in Britain and central Europe: contrast or continuity? In A. Whittle and V. Cummings (eds), *Going over: the Mesolithic-Neolithic Transition in north-west Europe*, 357–76. Oxford: Proceedings of the British Academy 144.

Boujot, C. and Cassen, S. 1993. A pattern of evolution for the Neolithic funerary structures of the west of France. *Antiquity* 67, 477–91.

Brace, S. forthcoming. A tale of two transitions, Part Two: The Early Neolithic in Britain. In A. Whittle, J. Pollard and S. Greaney (eds), *Ancient DNA and the Neolithic: relations and descent*. Oxford: Oxbow Books.

Brace, S., Diekmann, Y., Booth, T.J., van Dorp, L., Faltyskova, Z., Rohland, N., Mallick, S., Olalde, I., Ferry, M., Michel, M., Oppenheimer, J., Broomandkhoshbacht, N., Stewardson, K., Martiniano, R., Walsh, S., Kayser, M., Charlton, S., Hellenthal, G., Armit, I., Schulting, R., Craig, O.E., Sheridan, A., Parker Pearson, M., Stringer, C., Reich, D., Thomas, M.G. and Barnes, I. 2019. Ancient genomes indicate population replacement in Early Neolithic Britain. *Nature Ecology and Evolution* 3, 765–71.

Bradley, J. and Howard-Davis, C. 2018. *From Mesolithic encampment to medieval estate: the archaeology of the Bay Gateway*. Lancaster Imprints 24. Lancaster: Oxford Archaeology North.

Bradley, R. 1993. *Altering the earth; the origins of monuments in Britain and continental Europe*. Edinburgh: Society of Antiquaries of Scotland.

Bradley, R. 1996. Long houses, long mounds and Neolithic enclosures. *Journal of Material Culture* 1, 239–56.

Bradley, R. 1998. *The significance of monuments: on the shaping of human experience in Neolithic and Bronze Age Europe*. London: Routledge.

Bradley, R. 2001. Orientations and origins: a symbolic dimension to the long house in Neolithic Europe. *Antiquity* 75, 50–6.

Bradley, R. 2019. *The prehistory of Britain and Ireland* (second edition). Cambridge: Cambridge University Press.

Bradley, R., Over, L., Startin, D.W.A. and Weng, R. 1976. The excavation of a Neolithic site at Cannon Hill, Maidenhead, Berkshire 1974–75. *Berkshire Archaeological Journal* 68, 5–20.

Brannlund, L. 2013. South Wales gas pipeline project. Site 286. Land West of Lower Scoveston, Milford Haven, Pembrokeshire. Archaeological Watching Brief. Cotswold Archaeology. Unpublished Report 13216

Brannlund, L. 2014. South Wales Gas Pipeline Project: Sites 52.01 to 52.05, Land South of Llandefaelog, Yscir, Powys, 25–36. Cotswold Archaeology Report 13333.

Brettell, R., Evans, J.A., Marzinzik, S., Lamb, A. and Montgomery, J. 2012a. 'Impious Easterners': can oxygen and strontium isotopes serve as indicators of provenance in Early Medieval European cemetery populations? *European Journal of Archaeology* 15, 117–45.

Brettell, R., Montgomery, J. and Evans, J. 2012b. Brewing and stewing: The effect of culturally mediated behaviour on the oxygen isotope composition of ingested fluids and the implications for human provenance studies. *Journal of Analytical Atomic Spectrometry* 27, 778–85.

Brickley, M.B. 2018. Cribra orbitalia and porotic hyperostosis: a biological approach to diagnosis. *American Journal of Physical Anthropology*, 167, 896–902.

Bridges, P.S. 1989. Changes in activities with the shift to agriculture in the Southeastern United States. *Current Anthropology* 30, 385–94.

Briggs, S. 1984. Gwernvale in antiquarian history. In W.J. Britnell and H.N. Savory, *Gwernvale and Penywyrlod: two Neolithic long cairns in the Black Mountains of Brecknock*, 45–8. Cardiff: Cambrian Archaeological Association.

Brightman, J. 2009. Mercia Marina, Findern Lane, Willington, Derbyshire. Unpublished report on an archaeological excavation. Bakewell: Archaeological Research Services Ltd.

Brindle, T. forthcoming. A multi-period prehistoric landscape at Tregunnel Hill, Newquay: excavations in 2012. Online Publication Report. CA report 18441. Cirencester: Cotswold Archaeology.

Britnell, W.J. 1984a. Neolithic long cairns in the Black Mountains. In W.J. Britnell and H.N. Savory, *Gwernvale and Penywyrlod: two Neolithic long cairns in the Black Mountains of Brecknock*, 3–9. Cardiff: Cambrian Archaeological Association.

Britnell, W.J. 1984b. The Gwernvale long cairn, Crickhowell, Brecknock. In W.J. Britnell and H.N. Savory, *Gwernvale and Penywyrlod: two Neolithic long cairns in the Black Mountains of Brecknock*, 41–154. Cardiff: Cambrian Archaeological Association.

Britnell, W.J. 1992. Penywyrlod long cairn, Talgarth, Powys: survey and recommendations. Unpublished report. Clwyd-Powys Archaeological Trust Report No. 19.

Britnell, W.J. 2013. Cairns, coneys and commoners on Llanelwedd Rocks, Radnorshire. *Archaeologia Cambrensis* 162, 142–273.

Britnell, W.J. 2015a. Penywyrlod long cairn: archaeological excavation. Unpublished report. Clwyd-Powys Archaeological Trust Report No. 1369.

Britnell, W.J. 2015b. Talgarth, Penywyrlod long cairn. *Archaeology in Wales* 55, 48–9.

Britnell, W.J. 2016. Penywyrlod long cairn: further excavation and recording. Unpublished report. Clwyd-Powys Archaeological Trust Report No. 1408.

Britnell, W. and Jones, N. 2018. The Dyffryn Lane and Hindwell Neolithic cursuses and other cursus monuments in Wales revisited. *Archaeologia Cambrensis* 167, 19-67.

Britnell, W.J. and Savory, H.N. 1984. *Gwernvale and Penywyrlod: two Neolithic long cairns in the Black Mountains of Brecknock*. Cardiff: Cambrian Archaeological Association.

Britton, K. 2017. A stable relationship: isotopes and bioarchaeology are in it for the long haul. *Antiquity* 91, 853–64.

Britton, K. 2020. Isotope analysis for mobility and climate studies. In K. Britton and M.P. Richards (eds), *Archaeological science: an introduction*, 99–124. Cambridge: Cambridge University Press.

Britton, K., Fuller, B.T., Tütken, T., Mays, S. and Richards, M.P. 2015. Oxygen isotope analysis of human bone phosphate evidences weaning age in archaeological populations. *American Journal of Physical Anthropology* 157, 226–41.

Britton, K., Müldner, G. and Bell, M. 2008. Stable isotope evidence for salt-marsh grazing in the Bronze Age Severn Estuary, UK: implications for palaeodietary analysis at coastal sites. *Journal of Archaeological Science* 35, 2111–18.

Brophy, K. and Barclay, G. (eds) 2009. *Defining a regional Neolithic: the evidence from Britain and Ireland*. Oxford: Oxbow Books.

Bronk Ramsey, C. 1995. Radiocarbon calibration and analysis of stratigraphy: the OxCal program. *Radiocarbon* 37, 425–30.

Bronk Ramsey, C. 2009. Bayesian analysis of radiocarbon dates. *Radiocarbon* 51, 337–60.

Bronk Ramsey, C., Higham, T.F., Bowles, A. and Hedges, R.E.M. 2004. Improvements to the pre-treatment of bone at Oxford. *Radiocarbon* 46, 155–63.

Brown, A. 2007. Mesolithic to Neolithic human activity and impact at the Severn Estuary wetland edge: studies at Llandevenney, Oldbury Flats, Hill Flats and Woolaston. In M. Bell (ed.), *Prehistoric coastal communities: the Mesolithic in western Britain*, 249–62. York: Council for British Archaeology.

Brown, F. 2021. Stainton West: a late Mesolithic and early Neolithic site on the banks of the River Eden. In G. Hey and P. Frodsham (eds), *New light on the Neolithic of northern England*, 17–30. Oxford: Oxbow Books.

Brown, T.A., Nelson, D.E., Vogel, J.S. and Southon, J.R. 1988. Improved collagen extraction by modified Longin method. *Radiocarbon* 30, 171–7.

Buck, C., Kenworthy, J., Litton, C. and Smith, A. 1991. Combining archaeological and radiocarbon information: a Bayesian approach to calibration. *Antiquity* 65, 808–21.

Buck, C., Litton, C. and Smith, A. 1992. Calibration of radiocarbon results pertaining to related archaeological events. *Journal of Archaeological Science*, 19, 487–512.

Buck, C., Cavanagh, W. and Litton, C. 1996. *Bayesian approach to interpreting archaeological data.* Chichester: John Wiley and Sons.

Budd, P., Montgomery, J., Barreiro, R.G. and Thomas, R.G. 2000. Differential diagenesis of strontium in archaeological human dental tissues. *Applied Geochemistry* 15, 687–94.

Buikstra, J.E. and Ubelaker, D. 1994. *Standards for data collection from human skeletal remains*. Fayetteville: Arkansas Archaeological Survey Research Series No. 44.

Bunch, B. and Fell, C.I. 1949. A stone axe-factory at Pike of Stickle, Great Langdale, Westmorland. *Proceedings of the Prehistoric Society* 15, 1–20.

Burrow, S. 2003. *Catalogue of the Mesolithic and Neolithic collections in the National Museums and Galleries of Wales*. Cardiff: National Museum of Wales.

Burrow, S. 2006. *The tomb builders in Wales 4000–3000 BC*. Cardiff: National Museum Wales Books.

Burrow, S. 2009. The magic flute. Available online at http://www.museumwales.ac.uk/blog/2009-07-29/The-magic-flute/.

Burrow, S. 2010. The face of a 6,000-year-old man. Available online at https://museum.wales/articles/2010-01-22/The-face-of-a-6000-year-old-man/.

Burrow, S. 2020. Pre-Iron Age domestic buildings in Wales. *Archaeologia Cambrensis* 169, 71–103.

Busby, P. 2013. South Wales Gas Pipeline Project: Site 51.02 Land at Pysgodlyn Farm, Yscir, Powys. Archaeological watching brief. Cotswold Archaeology Report 13330.

Callaghan, R. and Scarre, C. 2017. Biscay and beyond? Prehistoric voyaging between the two Finisterres. *Oxford Journal of Archaeology* 36, 355–73.

Cameron, J. 1934. *The skeleton of British Neolithic man*. London: Williams and Northgate.

Campbell, G. 2000. Plant utilization; the evidence from charred plant remains. In B. Cunliffe, *The Danebury Environs Programme: the prehistory of a Wessex landscape. Vol I:*

Introduction, 45–59. London: English Heritage and Oxford University Committee for Archaeology.

Campbell, J.B. 1977. *The Upper Palaeolithic of Britain: a study of man and nature in the Late Ice Age*. Oxford: Clarendon Press.

Capasso, L., Kennedy, K.A.R. and Wilczak, C.A. 1999. *Atlas of occupational markers on human remains*. Journal of Paleontology, Monographic Publication 3. Teramo: Edigrafital S.p.A.

Capo, R.C., Stewart, B.W. and Chadwick, O.A. 1998. Strontium isotopes as tracers of ecosystem processes: theory and methods. *Geoderma* 82, 197–225.

Cappers, R.T.J., Bekker, R.M. and Jans, J.E.A. 2006. *Digital seed atlas of the Netherlands*. Groningen Archaeological Studies 4. Eelde: Barkhuis Publishing.

Carr, C. 1995. Mortuary practices: their social, philosophical-religious, circumstantial, and physical determinants. *Journal of Archaeological Method and Theory* 2, 105–200.

Carruthers, W. 2019. Charred waterlogged and mineralised remains. In J. Rady and J. Holman (eds), *Beneath the seamark: 6000 years of an island's history. Archaeological investigations at 'Thanet Earth', Kent 2007–12. Volume 2: Specialist reports*, 1087–1135. Canterbury: Canterbury Archaeological Trust.

Carter, J.F. and Fry, B. 2013. Ensuring the reliability of stable isotope ratio data – beyond the principle of identical treatment. *Analytical and Bioanalytical Chemistry* 405, 2799–814.

Caseldine, A. 1990. *Environmental archaeology in Wales*. Lampeter: Department of Archaeology, St David's University College.

Caseldine, A.E. 1992. The Neolithic carbonized plant remains from pit 206. In K. Murphy, 'Plas Gogerddan, Dyfed: a multi-period burial and ritual site'. *The Archaeological Journal* 149, 24–6.

Caseldine, A. and Griffiths, C.J. 2005. The charred plant remains. In K. Murphy and R.T.J. Evans, Excavation of three ring-ditches and a prehistoric palisaded enclosure at Cwm Meudwy, Llandysul, Ceredigion, 2003, 15. Unpublished report. Llandeilo: Cambria Archaeological Trust.

Caseldine, A.E. and Griffiths, C.J. 2006. The charred plant remains. In K. Murphy and R.T.J. Evans, 'Excavation of Neolithic pits, three ring-ditches and a palisade enclosure at Cwm Meudwy, Llandysul, Ceredigion, 2003'. *Archaeologia Cambrensis* 155, 42–3.

Caseldine, A.E., Griffiths, C.J. and Peck, I. 2014. Charred plant remains. In G. Smith, 'A Late Bronze Age/Early Iron Age hill-top enclosure with evidence for Early and Middle Neolithic and Early Medieval settlement at Carrog, Llanbadrig, Anglesey', *Studia Celtica* 48, 76–81.

Cassen, S., Boujot, C., Domínguez-Bella, S., Guiavarc'h, M., Le Pennec, C., Pilar Prieto Martínez, M., Querré, G., Santrot, M.-H. and Vigier, E. 2012. Dépots bretons, tumulus carnacéens et circulations à longue distance. In P. Pétrequin, S. Cassen, M. Errera, L. Klassen, A. Sheridan and A.-M. Pétrequin (eds), *Jade. Grandes haches alpines du Néolithique européen. Ve et IVe millénaires av. J.-C.*, 918–95. Besançon: Presses Universitaires de Franche-Comté; Gray: Centre de Recherche Archéologique de la Vallée de l'Ain.

Cassidy, L.M., Martiniano, R., Murphy, E.M., Teasdale, M.D., Mallory, J., Hartwell, B. and Bradley, D.G. 2016. Neolithic and Bronze Age migration to Ireland and establishment of the insular Atlantic genome. *Proceedings of the National Academy of Sciences of the United States* 113, 368–73.

Cassidy, L.M., Ó Maoldúin, R., Kador, T., Lynch, A., Jones, C., Woodman, P.C., Murphy, E., Ramsey, G., Dowd, M., Noonan, A., Campbell, C., Jones, E.R., Mattiangeli, V. and Bradley, D.G. 2020. A dynastic elite in monumental Neolithic society. *Nature* 582, 384–8.

Chaffey, G. and Brook, E. 2011. Domesticity in the Neolithic: excavations at Kingsmead Quarry, Horton, Berkshire. In H. Anderson-Whymark and J. Thomas (eds), *Regional perspectives on Neolithic pit disposition: beyond the mundane*, 200–15. Oxford: Oxbow Books.

Challinor, D. 2015. Charcoal. In A. Barber and J. Hart, *South Wales Gas Pipeline Site 509 Land West of Middle Bastleford Rosemarket*, 28–9. Cotswold Archaeology Report 13252.

Challinor, D. 2017. Charcoal analysis. In A. Gibson, 'Excavation of a Neolithic house at Yarnbury, near Grassington, North Yorkshire'. *Proceedings of the Prehistoric Society* 83, 199–201.

Chambers, F. 1983. Three radiocarbon-dated pollen diagrams from upland peats north-west of Merthyr Tydfil, south Wales. *Journal of Ecology* 71, 475–87.

Chapman, R.W. 1981. Archaeological theory and communal burial in prehistoric Europe. In I. Hodder, G. Isaac and N. Hammond (eds), *Pattern of the past: studies in honour of David L. Clarke*, 387–411. Cambridge: Cambridge University Press.

Chapman, R.W. and Randsborg, K. 1981. Perspectives on the archaeology of death. In R.W. Chapman and K. Randsborg (eds), *The archaeology of death*, 1–24. Cambridge: Cambridge University Press.

Charlton, S., Ramsøe, A., Collins, M., Craig, O.E., Fischer, R., Alexander, M. and Speller, C.F. 2019. New insights into Neolithic milk consumption through proteomic analysis of dental calculus. *Archaeological and Anthropological Sciences* 11, 6183–96.

Chatterton, R. 2006. Ritual. In C. Conneller and G. Warren (eds), *Mesolithic Britain and Ireland: new approaches*, 101–20. Stroud: Tempus.

Chenery, C., Mueldner, G., Evans, J., Eckardt, H. and Lewis, M. 2010. Strontium and stable isotope evidence for diet and mobility in Roman Gloucester, UK. *Journal of Archaeological Science* 37, 150–63.

Chenery, C.A., Pashley, V., Lamb, A.L., Sloane, H.J. and Evans, J.A. 2012. The oxygen isotope relationship between the phosphate and structural carbonate fractions of human bioapatite. *Rapid Communications in Mass Spectrometry* 26, 309–19.

Chenery, C.A., Evans, J.A., Score, D., Boyle, A. and Chenery, S.R. 2014. A boat load of Vikings? *Journal of the North Atlantic* 7, 43–53.

Childe, V.G. 1939. *The dawn of European civilization* (third edition). London: Kegan Paul, Trench, Trubner & Co.

Children, G.C. and Nash, G.H. 2001. *Monuments in the landscape: the prehistory of Breconshire*. Hereford: Logaston Press.

Choy, K., Smith, C.I., Fuller, B.T. and Richards, M.P. 2010. Investigation of amino acid $\delta^{13}C$ signatures in bone collagen to reconstruct human palaeodiets using liquid chromatography–isotope ratio mass spectrometry. *Geochimica et Cosmochimica Acta* 74, 6093–111.

Clark, J.G.D. 1932. *The Mesolithic Age in Britain*. Cambridge: The University Press.

Clark, J.G.D. 1960. Excavations at the Neolithic site at Hurst Fen, Mildenhall, Suffolk (1954, 1987 and 1958). *Proceedings of the Prehistoric Society* 26, 202–45.

Cleal, R.M.J. 2004. The dating and diversity of the earliest ceramics of Wessex and south-west England. In R. Cleal and J. Pollard (eds), *Monuments and material culture: papers in honour of an Avebury archaeologist: Isobel Smith*, 164–92. Salisbury: Hobnob Press.

Clifford, E.M. 1937. Notgrove long barrow, Gloucestershire. *Archaeologia* 86, 119–61.

Clifford, E.M. 1938. The excavation of Nympsfield long barrow, Gloucestershire. *Proceedings of the Prehistoric Society* 4, 188–213.

Clifford, E.M. and Daniel, G. E. 1940. The Rodmarton and Avening portholes. *Proceedings of the Prehistoric Society* 6, 133–65.

Cobain, S. 2019. Plant macrofossils and charcoal. In A. Barber, A. Hardy and A. Mudd, *The prehistoric archaeology of the A477 St Clears to Red Roses Road Improvement Scheme 2012*, 89–107. Cotswold Archaeology Monograph 12. Cirencester: Cotswold Archaeology.

Coles, J.M. and Orme, B.J. 1976. The Sweet Track, Railway site. *Somerset Levels Papers* 2, 34–65.

Coles, J.M. and Orme, B.J. 1984. Ten excavations along the Sweet Track (3200 bc). *Somerset Levels Papers* 10, 5–45.

Colledge, S. and Conolly, J. 2014. Wild plant use in European Neolithic subsistence economies: a formal assessment of preservation bias in archaeobotanical assemblages and the implications for understanding changes in plant diet breadth. *Quaternary Science Reviews* 101, 193–206.

Colledge, S., Conolly, J. and Shennan, S. 2005. The evolution of Neolithic farming from SW Asian origins to NW European limits. *European Journal of Archaeology* 8, 137–56.

Collins, T. 2009. Hermitage, Ireland: life and death on the western edge of Europe. In S. McCartan, R. Schulting, G. Warren, and P. Woodman (eds), *Mesolithic horizons: papers presented at the seventh international conference on the Mesolithic in Europe, Belfast 2005*, 876–9. Oxford: Oxbow Books.

Conneller, C. 2022. *The Mesolithic in Britain: landscape and society in times of change*. Abingdon: Routledge.

Copley, M.S., Berstan, R., Dudd, S.N., Docherty, G., Mukherjee, A.J., Straker, V., Payne, S. and Evershed, R.P. 2003. Direct chemical evidence for widespread dairying in prehistoric Britain. *Proceedings of the National Academy of Sciences* 100, 1524–9.

Copley, M.S., Berstan, R., Mukherjee, A.J., Dudd, S.N., Straker, V., Payne, S. and Evershed, R.P. 2005. Dairying in antiquity. III. Evidence from absorbed lipid residues dating to the British Neolithic. *Journal of Archaeological Science* 32, 523–46.

Copley, M.S. and Evershed, R.P. 2007. Organic residue analysis. In D. Benson and A. Whittle (eds), *Building memories: The Neolithic Cotswold long barrow at Ascott-under-Wychwood, Oxfordshire*, 283–8. Oxford: Oxbow Books.

Corcoran, J.X.W.P. 1969. The Cotswold-Severn group. In T.G.E. Powell, J.X.W.P. Corcoran, F.M. Lynch and J.G. Scott (eds), *Megalithic enquiries in the west of Britain*, 13–104. Liverpool: Liverpool University Press.

Corcoran, J.X.W.P. 1970. The Giant's Caves, Luckington (Wil 2). *Wiltshire Archaeological and Natural History Magazine* 65B, 39–63.

Corcoran, J.X.W.P. 1972. Multi-period construction and the origins of the chambered long cairn in western Britain and Ireland. In F. Lynch and C. Burgess (eds), *Prehistoric man in Wales and the West*, 31–63. Bath: Adams and Dart.

Correa-Ascencio, M. and Evershed, R.P. 2014. High throughput screening of organic residues in archaeological potsherds using direct acidified methanol extraction. *Analytical Methods* 6, 1330–40.

Costello, E. and Svensson, E. 2018. Transhumant pastoralism in historic landscapes: beginning a European perspective. In E. Costello and E. Svensson (eds), *Historical archaeologies of transhumance across Europe*, 1–13. Abingdon: Routledge.

Cotswold Archaeology 2014. South Wales Gas Pipeline Project Site 51.07. Unpublished report, Cotswold Archaeology Report 13220.

Cousseau, F. 2015. Megalithic constructional techniques in north-west France: cairn III at Prissé-la-Charrière. In L. Laporte and C. Scarre (eds), *The megalithic architectures of Europe*, 39–48. Oxford: Oxbow Books.

Cowley, L.F. 1939. Report on the osseous remains from Ty-isaf, Breconshire, 1938. In W.F. Grimes, 'The excavation of Ty-isaf long cairn, Brecknockshire'. *Proceedings of the Prehistoric Society* 5, 141–2.

Cramp, L.J.E., Jones, J., Sheridan, A., Smyth, J., Whelton, H., Mulville, J., Sharples, N. and Evershed, R.P. 2014. Immediate replacement of fishing with dairying by the earliest farmers of the northeast Atlantic archipelagos. *Proceedings of the Royal Society B: Biological Sciences* 281, 20132372.

Cramp, K. 2007. The flint. In D. Benson and A. Whittle (eds), *Building memories: the Neolithic Cotswold long barrow at Ascott-under-Wychwood, Oxfordshire*, 289–314. Oxford: Oxbow Books.

Crampton, C.B. 1967. Analysis of pollen in a soil buried beneath a pillow mound at Llanelwedd, S. Radnorshire. *Bulletin of the Board of Celtic Studies* 22, 273–4.

Crampton, C.B. and Webley, D. 1966. A section through the Mynydd Troed long barrow, Brecknock. *Bulletin of the Board of Celtic Studies* 22, 71–7.

Crawford, O.G.S. 1925. *The long barrows of the Cotswolds*. Gloucester: John Bellows.

Cummings, V. 2004. Inventory. In V. Cummings and A. Whittle, *Places of special virtue: megaliths in the Neolithic landscapes of Wales*, 102–99. Oxford: Oxbow Books.

Cummings, V. 2008. The architecture of monuments. In J. Pollard (ed.), *Prehistoric Britain*, 135–59. Oxford: Blackwell.

Cummings, V. 2012. What lies beneath: thinking about the qualities and essences of stone and wood in the chambered tomb architecture of Neolithic Britain and Ireland. *Journal of Social Archaeology* 12, 29–50.

Cummings, V. 2017. *The Neolithic of Britain and Ireland*. Abingdon: Routledge.

Cummings, V., Jones, A. and Watson, A. 2002. In between places: axial asymmetry and divided space in the monuments of the Black Mountains, south-east Wales. *Cambridge Archaeological Journal* 12, 57–70.

Cummings, V. and Richards, C. 2014. How to build a dolmen: exploring Neolithic construction at Garn Turne. *Current Archaeology* 286, 32–5.

Cummings, V. and Richards, C. 2016. A monumental task: building the dolmens of Britain and Ireland. In L. Laporte and C. Scarre (eds), *The megalithic architectures of Europe*, 49–58. Oxford: Oxbow Books.

Cummings, V. and Richards, C. 2017. Passage graves as material technologies of wrapping. In P. Bickle, V. Cummings, D. Hofmann and J. Pollard (eds), *The Neolithic of Europe*, 235–48. Oxford: Oxbow Books.

Cummings, V. and Richards, C. 2021. *Monuments in the making: raising the great dolmens in early Neolithic northern Europe*. Oxford: Windgather Press.

Cummings, V. and Robinson, G. 2015. The life and times of a chambered tomb: the results of survey and excavation at Blasthill chambered tomb, Kintyre, western Scotland. *Archaeological Journal* 172, 1–29.

Cummings, V. and Whittle, A. 2003. Tombs with a view: landscape, monuments and trees. *Antiquity* 77, 255–66.

Cummings, V. and Whittle, A. 2004. *Places of special virtue: megaliths in the Neolithic landscapes of Wales*. Oxford: Oxbow Books.

Cunningham, S.L., Kirkland, S.A. and Ross, A.H. 2011. Bone weathering of juvenile-sized remains in the North Carolina Piedmont. In A.H. Ross and S.M. Abel (eds), *The juvenile skeleton in forensic abuse investigations*, 180–96. New York: Springer Science+Business Media.

Cuttler, R., Davidson, A. and Hughes, G. 2012. *A corridor through time: the archaeology of the A55 Anglesey Road Scheme*. Oxford: Oxbow Books.

Daniel, G. 1937. The chambered barrow in Parc le Breos Cwm, south Wales. *Proceedings of the Prehistoric Society* 3, 71–86.

Daniel, G.E. 1939. The transepted gallery graves of western France. *Proceedings of the Prehistoric Society* 5, 143–65.

Daniel, G.E. 1941. The dual nature of the megalithic colonization of prehistoric Europe. *Proceedings of the Prehistoric Society* 7, 1–49.

Daniel, G.E. 1950. *The prehistoric chamber tombs of England and Wales*. Cambridge: Cambridge University Press.

Daniel, G. 1958. *The megalith builders of western Europe*. London: Hutchinson.

Dark, P. 2007. Plant communities and human activity in the lower submerged forest and on Mesolithic occupation sites. In M. Bell (ed.), *Prehistoric coastal communities: the Mesolithic in western Britain*, 169–87. York: Council for British Archaeology.

Darling, W.G., Bath, A.H. and Talbot, J.C. 2003. The O and H stable isotopic composition of fresh waters in the British Isles: 2, surface waters and groundwater. *Hydrology and Earth* System Sciences 7, 183–95.

Darvill, T.C. 1982. *The megalithic chambered tombs of the Cotswold-Severn region*. Highworth: Vorda.

Darvill, T.C. 1984. A study of the Neolithic pottery fabrics from Gwernvale. In W.J. Britnell and H.N. Savory, *Gwernvale and Penywyrlod: two Neolithic long cairns in the Black Mountains of Brecknock*, 110–13. Cardiff: Cambrian Archaeological Association.

Darvill, T.C. 1996. Neolithic buildings in England, Wales and the Isle of Man. In T. Darvill and J. Thomas (eds), *Neolithic houses in northwest Europe and beyond*, 77–112. Oxford: Oxbow Books.

Darvill, T. 2002. White on blonde: quartz pebbles and the use of quartz at Neolithic monuments in the Isle of Man and beyond. In A. Jones and G. MacGregor (eds), *Colouring the past: the significance of colour in archaeological research*, 73–92. Oxford: Berg.

Darvill, T. 2004. *Long barrows of the Cotswolds and surrounding areas*. Stroud: Tempus.

Darvill, T. 2010. Megaliths, monuments, and materiality. *Journal of Neolithic Archaeology*, available at: http://www.jna.uni-kiel.de/index.php/jna/article/view/32, accessed: 07 Oct. 2019. doi: https://doi.org/10.12766/jna.2010.32.

Darvill, T., David, A., Griffiths, S., Hart, J., James, H., Murphy, K. and Rackham, J. 2020. *Timeline: the archaeology of the South Wales Gas Pipeline*. Cirencester: Cotswold Archaeology.

Darvill, T. and Grinsell, L.V. 1989. Gloucestershire barrows: supplement 1961–88. *Transactions of the Bristol and Gloucestershire Archaeological Society* 107, 39–105.

Daux, V., Lécuyer, C., Héran, M.A., Amiot, R., Simon, L., Fourel, F., Martineau, F., Lynnerup, N., Reychler, H. and Escarguel, G. 2008. Oxygen isotope fractionation between human phosphate and water revisited. *Journal of Human Evolution* 55, 1138–47.

David, A. 1989. Some aspects of the human presence in west Wales during the Mesolithic. In C. Bonsall (ed.), *The Mesolithic in Europe*, 241–53. Edinburgh: John Donald.

David, A.E.U. 1990. Palaeolithic and Mesolithic settlement in Wales with special reference to Dyfed. Unpublished PhD thesis, University of Lancaster.

David, A. 2007. *Palaeolithic and Mesolithic settlement in Wales with special reference to Dyfed*. Oxford: British Archaeological Reports.

David, A. 2020. Hunter gatherers: Upper Palaeolithic and Mesolithic discoveries: 12,600–4000 BC. In T. Darvill, A. David, S. Griffiths, J. Hart, H. James, K. Murphy and J. Rackham, *Timeline: the archaeology of the South Wales Gas Pipeline*, 22–31. Cirencester: Cotswold Archaeology.

David, A. and Painter, T. 2014. Hunter-gatherers in the Western Cleddau valley, Pembrokeshire, west Wales. *Archaeologia Cambrensis* 163, 43–98.

David, A. and Walker, E.A. 2004. Wales during the Mesolithic period. In A. Saville (ed.), *Mesolithic Scotland and its neighbours*, 299–337. Edinburgh: Society of Antiquaries of Scotland.

Davies, S.M., Woodward, P.J. and Ellison, A.B. 1991. The pottery. In P.J. Woodward, *The South Dorset ridgeway: survey and excavations 1977–84*, 96–101. Dorchester: Dorset Natural History and Archaeological Society.

Davies, S.R. 2009. Location, location, location: a landscape based study of early Neolithic longhouses in Britain. *Rosetta Journal* 7, 57–101.

Davis, O. and Sharples, N. 2017. Early Neolithic enclosures in Wales: a review of the evidence in the light of recent discoveries at Caerau, Cardiff. *Antiquaries Journal* 97, 1–26.

Deacon, J. 2017. The Caerau pottery. In O. Davis and N. Sharples, 'Early Neolithic enclosures in Wales: a review of the evidence in the light of recent discoveries at Caerau, Cardiff'. *Antiquaries Journal* 97, 9–11.

Dee, M. and Ramsey, C. 2014. High-precision Bayesian modeling of samples susceptible to inbuilt age. *Radiocarbon* 56, 83–94.

DiBennardo, R. and Taylor, J.V. 1979. Sex assessment of the femur: a test of a new method. *American Journal of Physical Anthropology* 50, 635–7.

Dicken, A. 2005. *Radiogenic isotope geology* (second edition). Cambridge: Cambridge University Press.

Dittrick, J. and Suchey, J.M. 1986. Sex determination of prehistoric central California skeletal remains using discriminant analysis of the femur and humerus. *American Journal of Physical Anthropology* 70, 3–9.

Donovan, D.T. 1977. Stony Littleton long barrow. *Antiquity* 51, 236–7.

Dorshorst, T. 2019. *Archery's lasting mark: a biomechanical analysis of archery*. University of Massachusetts Amherst: Master's Thesis 827. https://scholarworks.umass.edu/masters_theses_2/827.

Dresser, Q. 1984. Radiocarbon dating. In W.J. Britnell and H.N. Savory, *Gwernvale and Penywyrlod: two Neolithic long cairns in the Black Mountains of Brecknock*, 152. Cardiff: Cambrian Archaeological Association.

Dresser, Q. 1985. University College Cardiff radiocarbon dates I. *Radiocarbon* 27, 338–85.

Dudd, S.N. and Evershed, R.P. 1998. Direct demonstration of milk as an element of archaeological economies. *Science* 282, 1478–81.

Dunne, J., Evershed, R.P., Salque, M., Cramp, L., Bruni, S., Ryan, K., Biagetti, S. and di Lernia, S. 2012. First dairying in green Saharan Africa in the fifth millennium BC. *Nature* 486, 390–4.

Dunne, J. and Evershed, R.P. 2020a. Organic Residue Analysis of Neolithic and Bronze Age Pottery from Parc Cybi. In Parc Cybi, Holyhead. Final Report on Excavations. Volume 3: Specialist Reports, 96–103. Unpublished report, Gwynedd Archaeological Trust Report 1512.

Dunne, J. and Evershed, R.P. 2020b. Organic residue analysis of Early Neolithic pottery from Parc Bryn Cegin, Llandygai, near Bangor, Wales. In Parc Cybi, Holyhead. Final Report on Excavations. Volume 3: Specialist Reports, 104–9. Unpublished report, Gwynedd Archaeological Trust Report 1512.

Dupras, T.L., Schulz, J.J., Wheeler, S.M. and Williams, L.J. 2011. *Forensic recovery of human remains: archaeological approaches* (second edition). Boca Raton: CRC Press.

Edwards, B., Miket, R., Griffiths, S., Kabuku C. and Millson, D. submitted. The excavation of an enclosed Neolithic farmstead at Threefords, Milfield, Northumberland. Manchester: MCPHH Research Reports.

Entwistle, R. and Grant, A. 1989. The evidence for cereal cultivation and animal husbandry in the southern British Neolithic and Bronze Age. In A. Milles, D. Williams and N. Gardner (eds), *The beginnings of agriculture*, 203–15. Oxford: British Archaeological Reports.

Ericson, J.E. 1985. Strontium isotope characterization in the study of prehistoric human ecology. *Journal of Human Evolution* 14, 503–14.

Ethier, J., Bánffy, E., Vuković, J., Leshtakov, K., Bacvarov, K., Roffet-Salque, M., Evershed, R.P. and Ivanova, M. 2017. Earliest expansion of animal husbandry beyond the Mediterranean zone in the sixth millennium BC. *Scientific Reports* 7, 7146. https://doi.org/10.1038/s41598-017-07427-x

Evans, A.A., Langer, J.L., Donahue, R.E., Wolframm, Y.B. and Lovis, W.A. 2010. Lithic raw material sourcing and the assessment of Mesolithic landscape organization and mobility strategies in northern England. *The Holocene*. doi.org/10.1177/0959683610369500.

Evans, C., Pollard, J. and Knight, K. 1999. Life in woods: tree-throws, 'settlement' and forest cognition. *Oxford Journal of Archaeology* 18, 241–54.

Evans J.A. 2018. Biosphere Isotope Domain Map GB (V1): strontium isotope data. (Online resource) DOI 10.5285/ba36de6f-5a20-476b-965d-48182166114a.

Evans, J.A., Chenery, C.A. and Montgomery, J. 2012. A summary of strontium and oxygen isotope variation in archaeological human tooth enamel excavated from Britain. *Journal of Analytical Atomic Spectrometry* 27, 754–64.

Evans, J.A., Montgomery, J., Wildman, G. and Boulton, N. 2010. Spatial variations in biosphere $^{87}Sr/^{86}Sr$ in Britain. *Journal of the Geological Society* 167, 1–4.

Evans, J.G. and Smith, I.F. 1983. Excavations at Cherhill, north Wiltshire, 1967. *Proceedings of the Prehistoric Society* 49, 43–117.

Evans, H. 2018. An early Neolithic assemblage from Holbeck Park Avenue, Barrow-in-Furness. *Transactions of the Cumberland and Westmorland Antiquarian and Archaeological Society* 18, 1–22.

Evans, H., Dickson, A. and Druce, D. 2021. Recent work on the Neolithic landscapes of Cumbria and North Lancashire. In G. Hey and P. Frodsham (eds), *New light on the Neolithic of northern England*, 111–24. Oxford: Oxbow Books.

Evershed, R.P., Dudd, S., Copley, M.S. and Mutherjee, A. 2002. Identification of animal fats via compound specific $\delta^{13}C$ values of individual fatty acids: assessments of results for reference fats and lipid extracts of archaeological pottery vessels. *Documenta Praehistorica* 29, 73–96.

Faccia, K., Waters-Rist, A., Lieverse, A.R., Bazaliiskii, V.I., Stock, J.T. and Katzenberg, M.A. 2016. Diffuse idiopathic skeletal hyperostosis (DISH) in a middle Holocene forager from Lake Baikal, Russia: potential causes and the effect on quality of life. *Quaternary International* 405, 66–79.

Fairweather, A.D. and Ralston, I.B.M. 1993. Neolithic plant macrofossils from the Balbridie Timber Hall, Grampian Region, Scotland: a preliminary note. *Antiquity* 67, 313–23.

Faure, G. 1986. *Principles of isotope geology*. New York: John Wiley & Sons.

Faure, G. and Mensing, T.M. 2005. *Isotopes: principles and applications* (third edition). Hoboken, New Jersey: John Wiley and Sons.

Fisher Jr., J.W. 1995. Bone surface modifications in zooarchaeology. *Journal of Archaeological Method and Theory* 2, 7–68.

Fleming, A. 1999. Phenomenology and the megaliths of Wales: a dreaming too far? *Oxford Journal of Archaeology* 18, 119–25.

Fleming, A. 2005. Megaliths and post-modernism: the case of Wales. *Antiquity* 79, 921–32.

Formicola, V. and Franceschi, M. 1996. Regression equations for estimating stature from long bones of early Holocene European samples. *American Journal of Physical Anthropology* 100, 83–8.

Fowler, C. 2022. Social arrangements. Kinship, descent and affinity in the mortuary architecture of Early Neolithic Britain and Ireland. *Archaeological Dialogues*, 1–22. doi:10.1017/S1380203821000210.

Fowler, C., Olalde, I., Cummings, V., Armit, I., Büster, L., Cuthbert, S., Rohland, N., Cheronet, O., Pinhasi, R. and Reich, D. 2021. A high-resolution picture of kinship practices in an Early Neolithic tomb. *Nature*. https://doi.org/10.1038/s41586-021-04241-4.

French, C., Lewis, H., Allen, M.J., Green, M., Scaife, R. and Gardiner, J. 2007. *Prehistoric landscape development and human impact in the upper Allen valley, Cranborne Chase, Dorset*. Cambridge: McDonald Institute for Archaeological Research.

Frirdich, C. 2005. Struktur und Dynamik der bandkeramischen Landnahme. In J. Lüning, C. Frirdich and A. Zimmermann (eds), *Die Bandkeramik im 21. Jahrhundert. Symposium in der Abtei Brauweiler bei Köln vom 16.9.–19.9.2002*, 81–109. Rahden: Marie Leidorf.

Gale, R. 2002. The charcoal. In N. Page, A477(T) Sageston-Redberth bypass: excavation of a Neolithic occupation site 2001, 31–5. Unpublished report. Llandeilo: Cambria Archaeological Trust.

Gale, R. and Cutler, D.F. 2000. *Plants in archaeology: identification manual of artefacts of plant origin from Europe and the Mediterranean*. Otley: Westbury and Royal Botanic Gardens Kew.

Gardiner, P. 2003. Caught in the act – where is the transition? In L. Bevan and J. Moore (eds), *Peopling the Mesolithic in a northern environment*, 103–12. Oxford: British Archaeological Reports.

Garrow, D. 2006. *Pits, settlement and deposition during the Neolithic and Early Bronze Age in East Anglia*. Oxford: British Archaeological Reports.

Garrow, D., Griffiths, S., Anderson-Whymark, H. and Sturt, F. 2017. Stepping stones to the Neolithic? Radiocarbon dating the early Neolithic on islands within the 'western seaways' of Britain. *Proceedings of the Prehistoric Society* 83, 97–135.

Garton, D. 1991. Neolithic settlement in the Peak District: perspective and prospects. In R. Hodges and K. Smith (eds), *Recent developments in the archaeology of the Peak District*, 13–21. Sheffield: J.R. Collis Publications.

Garwood, P. (ed.) 2007. *The undiscovered country: the earlier prehistory of the West Midlands*. Oxford: Oxbow Books.

Garwood, P. 2011. Early prehistory. In P. Booth, T. Champion, S. Foreman, P. Garwood, H. Glass, J. Munby and A. Reynolds, *On track: the archaeology of High Speed I Section I in Kent*, 37–150. Oxford and Salisbury: Oxford Wessex Archaeology.

Gat, J.R. 2010. *Isotope hydrology: a study of the water cycle*. London: Imperial College Press.

Gejvall, N.G. 1969. Cremations. In D. Brothwell and E. Higgs (eds), *Science in archaeology* (second edition), 468–79. New York: Praeger.

Gibson, A. 1994. Excavations at the Sarn-y-Bryn-Caled cursus complex, Welshpool, Powys, and the timber circles of Great Britain and Ireland. *Proceedings of the Prehistoric Society* 60, 143–223.

Gibson, A. 1995. First impressions: a review of Peterborough Ware in Wales. In I. Kinnes and G. Varndell (eds), *Unbaked urns of rudely shape: essays on British and Irish pottery for Ian Longworth*, 23–39. Oxford: Oxbow Books.

Gibson, A. 2000. Survey and trial excavation at a newly discovered long barrow at Lower Luggy, Berriew, Powys. *Studia Celtica* 34, 1–16.

Gibson, A. 2001. Appendix 6. Assessment of the prehistoric pottery. In A. Boucher (ed.), *Causeway Farm, Hereford. A report on an archaeological evaluation*. Unpublished report. Hereford: Archaeological Investigations Ltd.

Gibson, A. 2003. A newly discovered Neolithic enclosure at Lower Luggy, Berriew, Powys. *PAST* 45, 1–2.

Gibson, A. 2006. Excavations at a Neolithic enclosure at Lower Luggy, near Welshpool, Powys, Wales. *Proceedings of the Prehistoric Society* 72, 163–91.

Gibson, A. 2013. Milford Haven to Aberdulais and Felindre to Brecon Gas Pipeline: the Neolithic and Bronze Age pottery from the archaeological investigations. Report No. 121v2. 2nd August 2013. Report prepared for Cotswold Archaeology.

Gibson, A. 2017. Excavation of a Neolithic house at Yarnbury, near Grassington, North Yorkshire. *Proceedings of the Prehistoric Society* 83, 189–212.

Gibson, A. and Bayliss, A. 2009. Recent research at Duggleby Howe, north Yorkshire. *Antiquaries Journal* 166, 39–78.

Gibson, A. and Kinnes, I. 1997. On the urns of a dilemma: radiocarbon and the Peterborough problem. *Oxford Journal of Archaeology* 16, 65–72.

Gowen, M. and Tarbett, C. 1989. Tankardstown South. Neolithic/Bronze Age. In I. Bennett (ed.), *Excavations 1988: summary accounts of archaeological excavations in Ireland*, 24–6. Dublin: Wordwell.

Gowen, M. and Tarbett, C. 1990. Tankardstown South. Neolithic house sites. In I. Bennett (ed.), *Excavations 1989: summary accounts of archaeological excavations in Ireland*, 38–9. Dublin: Wordwell.

Graeber, D. and Wengrow, D. 2021. *The dawn of everything: a new history of humanity*. London: Allen Lane.

Graf, J.C. 2012. *Windows into the past: an investigation into prior activity at Neolithic monuments in Britain*. Durham theses, Durham University. Available at Durham E-Theses Online: http://etheses.dur.ac.uk/3510/.

Graustein, W.C. 1989. $^{87}Sr/^{86}Sr$ ratios measure the sources and flow of strontium in terrestrial ecosystems. In P.W. Rundel, J.R. Ehleringer and K.A. Nagy (eds), *Stable isotopes in ecological research*, 491–512. New York: Springer.

Gregg, M.W., Banning, E.B., Gibbs, K. and Slater, G.F. 2009. Subsistence practices and pottery use in Neolithic Jordan: molecular and isotopic evidence. *Journal of Archaeological Science* 36, 937–46.

Greig, J.R.A. 1991. The British Isles. In W. van Zeist, K. Wasylikowa and K.-E. Behre (eds), *Progress in Old World palaeoethnobotany*, 299–334. Rotterdam: Balkema.

Griffiths, S. 2011. Chronological modelling of the mesolithic-neolithic transition in the midlands and north of England. Unpublished PhD thesis, Cardiff University.

Griffiths, S. 2014. Points in time: the chronology of rod microliths. *Oxford Journal of Archaeology* 33, 221–43.

Griffiths, S. 2018. A cereal problem? What the current chronology of early cereal domesticates might tell us about changes in late fifth and early fourth millennium cal BC Ireland and Britain. *Environmental Archaeology*, doi: 10.1080/14614103.2018.1529945

Griffiths, S. 2019. *Bayesian modelling and radiocarbon results*. Unpublished report on the Caerau enclosure.

Griffiths, S. (ed.) 2022. *Scientific dating in archaeology*. Oxford: Oxbow Books.

Griffiths, S. 2021. The last hunters of a wise race. In G. Hey and P. Frodsham (eds), *New light on the Neolithic of northern England*, 31–51. Oxford: Oxbow Books.

Grimes, W.F. 1936. The long cairns of the Brecknockshire Black Mountains. *Archaeologia Cambrensis* 91, 259–82.

Grimes, W.F. 1939. The excavation of Ty-isaf long cairn, Brecknockshire. *Proceedings of the Prehistoric Society* 5, 119–40.

Grimes, W.F. 1960. *Excavations on defence sites, 1939–1945. I: mainly Neolithic–Bronze Age*. London: HMSO.

Guiry, E.J. and Szpak, P. 2020. Quality control for modern bone collagen stable carbon and nitrogen isotope measurements, *Methods in Ecology and Evolution* 11, 1049–60.

Guttman, E.B. 2005. Midden cultivation in prehistoric Britain: arable crops in gardens. *World Archaeology* 37, 224–39.

Haglund, W.D. and Sorg, M.H. (eds) 1997. *Forensic taphonomy: the postmortem fate of human remains*. Boca Raton: CRC Press.

Haglund, W.D. and Sorg, M.H. (eds) 2001. *Advances in forensic taphonomy: method, theory, and archaeological perspectives*. Boca Raton: CRC Press.

Halstead, P. 2018. Forest clearance and land use by early farmers in Europe: insight from north Greek oral history. *Quaternary International* 496, 42–50. http://dx.doi.org/10.1016/j.quaint.2017.04.010.

Harman, M., Molleson, T.I. and Price, J.L. 1981. Burials, bodies, and beheadings in Romano-British and Anglo-Saxon cemeteries. *Bulletin of the British Museum of Natural History* 35, 145–88.

Harris, O.J.T. 2021. *Assembling past worlds: materials, bodies and architecture in Neolithic Britain*. Abingdon: Routledge.

Hart, J. 2013. South Wales Gas Pipeline Project Sites 24.06 and 24.07. Land North-East of Gurrey Cottage, Llandeilo, Carmarthenshire. Archaeological excavation. Cotswold Archaeology. Unpublished Report 13274.

Hart, J. 2014. South Wales gas pipeline project: 26.05. Land west of Cwmifor, Manordeilo and Salem, Carmarthenshire. Cotswold Archaeology Report 13308.

Hart, J. and Busby, P. 2014. South Wales gas pipeline project: sites 245 and 253. Land south of Wiston, Pembrokeshire, 17–21. Cotswold Archaeology Report 13201.

Hart, J. and Leonard, C. 2014 South Wales gas pipeline project: site 51.07. Land north-west of Pen-y-Crug, Yscir, Powys. 29–62. Cotswold Archaeology Report 13220.

Hastie, M. 2011. Charred plant remains. In M. Kirby, 'Lockerbie Academy: Neolithic and Early Historic timber halls, a Bronze Age cemetery, an undated enclosure and a post-medieval corn-drying kiln in south-west Scotland'. *Scottish Archaeological Internet Report* 46, 20–3.

Hawkes, J. 1934. Aspects of the Neolithic and Chalcolithic periods in western Europe. *Antiquity* 7, 24–42.

Hawkey, D.E. and Merbs, C.F. 1995. Activity-induced musculoskeletal stress markers (MSM) and subsistence strategy changes among ancient Hudson Bay Eskimos. *International Journal of Osteoarchaeology* 5, 324–38.

Headland Archaeology 2011. Arthur's Stone, Dorstone (Neolithic burial chamber), Dorstone, Herefordshire. Archaeological excavation & survey. Hereford: Headland Archaeology.

Healey, E. and Green, H.S. 1984. The lithic industries. In W.J. Britnell and H.N. Savory, *Gwernvale and Penywyrlod: two Neolithic long cairns in the Black Mountains of Brecknock*, 113–32. Cardiff: Cambrian Archaeological Association.

Hedges, R.E.M. and Millard, A.R. 1995. Bones and groundwater: towards the modelling of diagenetic processes. *Journal of Archaeological Science* 22, 155–64.

Helbaek, H. 1953. Early crops in southern England. *Proceedings of the Prehistoric Society* 18, 194–233.

Hemp, W.J. 1929. Belas Knap long barrow, Gloucestershire. *Transactions of the Bristol and Gloucestershire Archaeological Society* 51, 261–72.

Hemp, W.J. 1935. Arthur's Stone, Dorstone, Herefordshire. *Archaeologia Cambrensis* 90, 288–92.

Hensey, R. 2015. *First light: the origins of Newgrange*. Oxford: Oxbow Books.

Herne, A. 1988. A time and a place for the Grimston bowl. In J.C. Barrett and I.A. Kinnes (eds), *The archaeology of context in the Neolithic and Bronze Age: recent trends*, 9–29. Sheffield: Department of Archaeology and Prehistory, University of Sheffield.

Hey, G. and Robinson, M. 2011. Neolithic communities in the Thames Valley: the creation of new worlds. In T. Morigi, D. Schreve, M. White, G. Hey, M. Robinson, A. Barclay and P. Bradley, *The Thames through time: the archaeology of the gravel terraces of the Upper and Middle Thames, early prehistory: to 1500 BC*, 221–60. Oxford: Oxford Archaeology.

Hey, G., Bell, C., Dennis, C. and Robinson, M. 2016. *Yarnton: Neolithic and Bronze Age settlement and landscape*. Oxford: Oxford Archaeology.

Hillman, G. 1981. Reconstructing crop husbandry practices from charred remains of crops. In R. Mercer (ed.), *Farming practices in British prehistory*, 123–62. Edinburgh: Edinburgh University Press.

Hillson, S. 1986. *Teeth*. Cambridge: Cambridge University Press.

Hillson, S. 1996. *Dental anthropology*. Cambridge: Cambridge University Press.

Hodder, I. 1994. Architecture and meaning: the example of Neolithic houses and tombs. In M. Parker Pearson and C. Richards (eds), *Architecture and order: approaches to social space*, 73–86. London: Routledge.

Holland, T.D. 1991. Sex assessment using the proximal tibia. *American Journal of Physical Anthropology*, 85, 221–7.

Honch, N.V., McCullagh, J.S.O. and Hedges, R.E.M. 2012. Variation of bone collagen amino acid $\delta^{13}C$ values in archaeological humans and fauna with different dietary regimes: developing frameworks of dietary discrimination. *American Journal of Physical Anthropology* 148, 495–511.

Houlder, C.H. 1961. The excavation of a Neolithic stone implement factory on Mynydd Rhiw in Caernarvonshire. *Proceedings of the Prehistoric Society* 27, 108–43.

Hugh-Jones, C. 1996. Houses in the Neolithic imagination: an Amazonian example. In T. Darvill and J. Thomas (eds), *Neolithic houses in northwest Europe and beyond*, 185–93. Oxford: Oxbow Books.

Humpage, A.J. 1992. The Late Quaternary glacial history of part of the middle and lower Usk valley. Unpublished BSc dissertation, University of Liverpool.

Humpage, A.J. 2016. Geological assessment of the Penywyrlod long cairn. In W.J. Britnell, Penywyrlod long cairn: further excavation and recording, 12–20. Unpublished report, Clwyd-Powys Archaeological Trust Report No. 1408.

Hyde, H.A. 1956. Report on plant remains from Pipton long cairn (Breckn.). In H.N. Savory, 'The excavation of the Pipton long cairn, Brecknockshire'. *Archaeologia Cambrensis* 105, 48.

Işcan, M.Y., Loth, S.R. and Wright, R.K. 1984. Metamorphosis at the sternal rib end: a new method to estimate age at death in white males. *American Journal of Physical Anthropology* 66, 147–56.

Işcan, M.Y. and Miller-Shaivitz, P. 1984. Determination of sex from the tibia. *American Journal of Physical Anthropology* 64, 53–7.

Jackson, R. and Miller, D. 2011. *Wellington Quarry, Herefordshire (1986–96): investigations of a landscape in the Lower Lugg Valley*. Oxford: Oxbow Books.

Jacobi, R.M. 1976. Britain inside and outside Mesolithic Europe. *Proceedings of the Prehistoric Society* 42, 67–84.

Jacobi, R.M. 1980. The early Holocene settlement of Wales. In J.A. Taylor (ed.), *Culture and environment in prehistoric Wales*, 131–206. Oxford: British Archaeological Reports.

Jacobi, R. and Higham, T. 2011. The Later Upper Palaeolithic recolonisation of Britain: new results from AMS radiocarbon dating. In N.M. Ashton, S.G. Lewis and C.B. Stringer (eds), *The ancient human occupation of Britain*, 223–47. Amsterdam: Elsevier.

Jacomet, S. 2006. *Identification of cereal remains from archaeological sites*. Basel: Archaeobotany Lab, IPAS, Basel University.

James, H.F., Adams, S., Willmes, M., Mathison, K., Ulrichsen, A., Wood, R., Valera, A.C., Frieman, C.J. and Grün, R. 2022. A large-scale environmental strontium isotope baseline map of Portugal for archaeological and paleoecological provenance studies. *Journal of Archaeological Science* 142, 1055–95.

Johnson, L.J. 2018. Finding radiogenic Sr-isotope biospheres: can a home in Britain be found for people with high $^{87}Sr/^{86}Sr$? Unpublished PhD thesis, Durham University.

Johnson, L., Evans, J., Montgomery, J. and Chenery, C. 2022. The forest effect: biosphere $^{87}Sr/^{86}Sr$ shifts due to changing land use and the implications for migration studies. *Science of the Total Environment*, 156083.

Jones, A.M. and Lawson-Jones, A. 2018. Pits and flints: archaeological recording along the A30 Temple to Higher Carblake road scheme, Cornwall. *Cornish Archaeology* 57, 1–31.

Jones, A.M. and Quinnell, H. 2014. *Lines of archaeological investigation along the north Cornish coast*. Oxford: British Archaeological Reports.

Jones, G. 2000. Evaluating the importance of cultivation and collecting in Neolithic Britain. In A.S. Fairbairn (ed.), *Plants in Neolithic Britain and beyond*, 79–84. Oxford: Oxbow Books.

Jones, G. 2005. Garden cultivation of staple crops and its implications for settlement location and continuity. *World Archaeology* 37, 164–76.

Jones, G. 2013. Early Neolithic animal bone from Area 5. In T. Allen, A. Barclay, A.M. Cromarty, H. Anderson-Whymark, A. Parker, M. Robinson and G. Jones, *Opening the wood, making the land: the archaeology of a Middle Thames landscape. The Eton College rowing course project and the Maidenhead, Windsor and Eton flood alleviation scheme. Volume 1: Mesolithic to early Bronze Age*, 183–98. Oxford: Oxford Archaeology.

Jones, G.E. and Bogaard, A. 2017. Integration of cereal cultivation and animal husbandry in the British Neolithic: the evidence of charred plant remains from timber buildings at Lismore Fields. In P. Rowley-Conwy, D. Serjeantson and P. Halstead (eds), *Economic zooarchaeology: studies in hunting, herding and early agriculture*, 221–6. Oxford: Oxbow Books.

Jones, G. and Rowley-Conwy, P.A. 2007. On the importance of cereal cultivation in the British Neolithic. In S. Colledge and J. Conolly (eds), *The origins and spread of domestic plants in southwest Asia and Europe,* 391–420. California: Walnut Creek.

Jones, N. 2009. Womaston Neolithic causewayed enclosure, Powys: survey and excavation 2008. *Archaeologia Cambrensis* 158, 19–42.

Joussaume, R. 2006. *Les tumulus de Champ-Châlon à Benon (Charente-Maritime)*. Groupe Vendéen d'Études Préhistorique 42.

Joussaume, R. and Laporte, L. 2006. Monments funéraires néolithiques dans l'ouest de la France. In R. Joussaume, L. Laporte and C. Scarre (eds), *Origine et développement du mégalithisme de l'ouest de l'Europe,* vol. 1, 319–43. Bougon: Musée des Tumulus de Bougon.

Kacki, S., Velemínský, P., Lynnerup, N., Kaupová, S., Jeanson, A.L., Povýšil, C., Horák, M., Kučera, J., Rasmussen, K.L., Podliska, J., Dragoun, Z., Smolík, J., Vellev, J. and Brůžek, J. 2018. Rich table but short life: diffuse idiopathic skeletal hyperostosis in Danish astronomer Tycho Brahe (1546–1601) and its possible consequences. *Plos One*, https://doi.org/10.1371/journal.pone.0195920

Keeley, H.C.M. 1978. Interim soil report for the site of Gwernvale chambered tomb, Crickhowell, Powys. Ancient Monuments Laboratory Report 2670.

Keeley, H.C.M. 1980. Soils associated with Gwernvale chambered tomb, Crickhowell, Powys. Ancient Monuments Laboratory Report 3105.

Keiller, A. and Piggott, S. 1938. Excavation of an untouched chamber in the Lanhill long barrow. *Proceedings of the Prehistoric Society* 4, 122–50.

Keiller, A., Piggott, S., Passmore, A.D. and Cave, A.J.E. 1938. Excavation of an untouched chamber in the Lanhill long barrow. *Proceedings of the Prehistoric Society* 4, 122–50.

Keith, A. 1921–23. Report No. 1. On the bones. In W.E.T. Morgan and G. Marshall, Report on the excavation of a long barrow at Llanigon, co. Brecon, *Transactions of the Woolhope Club*, 1921–3, 36–8.

Kendall, C., Høier Eriksen, A-M., Kontopoulos, I., Collins, M. J. and Turner-Walker, G. 2018. Diagenesis of archaeological bone and tooth. *Palaeogeography, Palaeoclimatology, Palaeoecology* 491, 21–37.

Kenney, J. 2008. Rescue excavations at Parc Bryn Cegin, Llandygai, near Bangor, north Wales. *Archaeologia Cambrensis* 157, 9–142.

Kenney, J. 2020. A dialogue with the dead? The relationship between an early Neolithic rectangular timber building and a chambered tomb on Holy Island, Anglesey, north-west Wales. In A. Barclay, D. Field, and J. Leary (eds), *Houses of the dead?*, 135–44. Oxford: Oxbow Books.

Kenney, J. (ed.) 2021. *A Welsh landscape through time: excavations at Parc Cybi, Holy Island, Anglesey*. Oxford: Oxbow Books.

Kenney, J., McGuinness, N., Cooke, R., Rees, C., and Davidson, A. 2011. Parc Cybi, Holyhead: post excavation assessment of potential report volume 1, unpublished report, Gwynedd Archaeological Trust Report 954.

Kerney, M.P. and Cameron, R.A.D. 1979. *A field guide to the land snails of Britain and north-west Europe*. London: Collins.

Kinnes, I.A. 1979. Description of the Neolithic bowl. In J.M. Coles and B.J. Orme, 'The Sweet Track: Drove site'. *Somerset Levels Papers* 5, 52–4.

Klippel, W.E. and Synstelien, J.A. 2007. Rodents as taphonomic agents: bone gnawing by brown rats and gray squirrels. *Journal of Forensic Sciences* 53, 765–73.

Knüsel, C. 2007. The arrowhead injury to Individual B2. In D. Benson and A. Whittle (eds), *Building memories: the Neolithic Cotswold long barrow at Ascott-under-Wychwood, Oxfordshire*, 218–20. Oxford: Oxbow Books.

Knusel, C.J. and Robb, J. 2016. Funerary taphonomy: an overview of goals and methods. *Journal of Archaeological Science Reports* 10, 655–73.

Kootker, L.M., van Lanen, R.J., Kars, H. and Davies, G.R. 2016. Strontium isoscapes in The Netherlands. Spatial variations in $^{87}Sr/^{86}Sr$ as a proxy for palaeomobility. *Journal of Archaeological Science: Reports* 6, 1–13.

Kreuz, A. and Schäfer, E. 2011. Weed finds as indicators for the cultivation regime of the early Neolithic Bandkeramik culture? *Vegetation History and Archaeobotany* 20, 333–48.

Lamdin-Whymark, H. 2008. *The residue of ritualized action: Neolithic deposition practices in the Middle Thames Valley*. Oxford: British Archaeological Reports.

Lane, A. and Redknap, M. 2019. *Llangorse crannog: the excavation of an early medieval royal site in the kingdom of Brycheiniog*. Oxford: Oxbow Books.

Laporte, L. 2015. Structural functions and architectural projects within the long monuments of western France. In L. Laporte and C. Scarre (eds), *The megalithic architectures of Europe*, 17–30. Oxford: Oxbow Books.

Laporte, L., Cousseau, F., Scarre, C. and Soler, L. 2021. Vingt ans de fouilles sur le tumulus C de Péré à Prissé-la-Charrière (Deux-Sèvres): bilan, état des recherches et perspectives. In V. Ard, E. Mens and M. Gandelin (eds), *Mégalithismes et monumentalismes funéraires: passé, présent, futur*, 29–48. Leiden: Sidestone Press.

Laporte, L., Joussaume, R. and Scarre, C. 2002a. The perception of space and geometry. Megalithic monuments of west-central France in their relationship to the landscape. In C. Scarre (ed.), *Monumentality and landscape in Atlantic Europe*, 73–83. London: Routledge.

Laporte, L., Joussaume, R. and Scarre, C. 2002b. Le tumulus C de Péré à Prissé-la-Charrière (Deux-Sèvres). *Gallia Préhistoire* 44, 167–214.

Laporte, L. and Tinévez, J.-Y. 2004. Neolithic houses and chambered tombs of western France. *Cambridge Archaeological Journal* 14, 217–34.

Lawrence, T., Donnelly, M., Kennard, L., Souday, C. and Grant, R. in press. Britain in or out of Europe during the late Mesolithic? A new perspective of the Mesolithic-Neolithic transition. In T. Perrin, B. Marquebielle, S. Philibert and N. Valdeyron (eds), *Proceedings of the Mesolithic in Europe 2020 Conference*. Berlin: Open Archaeology.

Legge, T. 2005. Milk use in prehistory: the osteological evidence. In J. Mulville and A.K Outram. (eds), *The zooarchaeology of fats, oils, milk dairying – 9th ICAZ Conference*, 8–13. Oxford: Oxbow Books.

Leonard, C. 2014a. South Wales gas pipeline project: sites 01.24–01.26, Land east of Pant-y-ffin, Mawr, Swansea, 14–17. Cotswold Archaeology Report 13284.

Leonard, C. 2014b. South Wales gas pipeline project. Site 50.5. Land west of Aberyscir Court, Yscir, Powys. Archaeological excavation. Cotswold Archaeology. Unpublished Report 13256.

Levinson, A.A., Luz, B. and Kolodny, Y. 1987. Variations in oxygen isotopic compositions of human teeth and urinary stones. *Applied Geochemisty* 2, 367–71.

Levitan, B. 1990. The non-human vertebrate remains. In A. Saville, *Hazleton North: the excavation of a Neolithic long cairn of the Cotswold-Severn group*, 199–214. London: English Heritage.

L'Helgouach, Le Gouestre, D. and Poulain, H. 1989. Le monument mégalithique transepté de la Joselière (ou du Pissot) au Clion-sur-Mer (Loire Atlantique). *Revue Archéologique de l'Ouest* 6, 31–50.

Lightfoot, E. and O'Connell, T.C. 2016. On the use of biomineral oxygen isotope data to identify human migrants in the archaeological record: intra-sample variation, statistical methods and geographical considerations. *PLoS One* 11, e0153850.

Little, A., Van Gijn, A., Collins, T., Cooney, G., Elliott, B., Gilhooly, B., Charlton, S. and Warren, G. 2017. Stone dead: uncovering Early Mesolithic mortuary rites, Hermitage, Ireland. *Cambridge Archaeological Journal* 27, 223–43.

Lloyd, C. and Savory, H.N. 1958. Excavations at an Early Iron Age hillfort and a Romano-British iron-smelting place at Gwernyfed Park, Aberllynfi, in 1951. *Brycheiniog* 4, 1–52.

Longinelli, A. 1984. Oxygen isotopes in mammal bone phosphate: a new tool for paleohydrological and paleoclimatological research? *Geochimica et Cosmochimica Acta* 48, 385–90.

Loveday, R. 2012. Aston on Trent 1: excavation of a round barrow and protected cursus land surface. *Derbyshire Archaeological Journal* 132, 80–128.

Lovejoy, C.O. 1985. Dental wear in the Libben population: its functional pattern and role in the determination of adult skeletal age at death. *American Journal of Physical Anthropology* 68, 47–56.

Luff, R.M., Brothwell, D.R. and O'Connor, T.P. 1984. The human and animal remains. In W.J. Britnell and H.N. Savory, *Gwernvale and Penywyrlod: two Neolithic long cairns in the Black Mountains of Brecknock*, 36–9. Cardiff: Cambrian Archaeological Association.

Luz, B. and Kolodny, Y. 1985. Oxygen isotope variations in phosphate of biogenic apatites, IV. Mammal teeth and bones. *Earth and Planetary Science Letters* 75, 29–36.

Luz, B., Kolodny, Y. and Horowitz, M. 1984. Fractionation of oxygen isotopes between mammalian bone-phosphate and environmental drinking water. *Geochimica et Cosmochimica Acta* 48, 1689–93.

Lynch, A. 2014. *Poulnabrone: an early Neolithic portal tomb in Ireland*. Dublin: Stationery Office.

Lynch, F. 1969. The megalithic tombs of North Wales. In T.G.E. Powell, J.X.W.P. Corcoran, F.M. Lynch and J.G. Scott (eds), *Megalithic enquiries in the west of Britain*, 107–48. Liverpool: Liverpool University Press.

Lynch, F. 1972. Portal dolmens in the Nevern Valley, Pembrokeshire. In F. Lynch and C. Burgess (eds), *Prehistoric man in Wales and the West*, 67–84. Bath: Adams and Dart.

Lynch, F. 1975. Excavations at Carreg Samson, Mathry, Pembrokeshire. *Archaeologia Cambrensis* 124, 15–35.

Lynch, F.M. 1984. The Neolithic pottery: discussion. In W.J. Britnell and H.N. Savory, *Gwernvale and Penywyrlod: two Neolithic long cairns in the Black Mountains of Brecknock*, 106–10. Cardiff: The Cambrian Archaeological Association.

Lynch, F. 2000. The earlier Neolithic. In F. Lynch, S. Aldhouse-Green and J.L. Davies, *Prehistoric Wales*, 42–78. Stroud: Sutton.

Lynch, F. 2011. Megalithic studies in Wales. *Archaeology in Wales* 50, 3–12.

Lynch, F., Aldhouse-Green, S. and Davies, J.L. 2000. *Prehistoric Wales*. Stroud: Sutton.

Lynch, F. and Darvill, T. 2013. Neolithic pottery from below Llanelwedd pillow mound 1. In W.J. Britnell, 'Cairns, coneys and commoners on Llanelwedd Rocks, Radnorshire'. *Archaeologia Cambrensis* 162, 232–5.

Lynch, F. and Musson, C. 2001. A prehistoric and early medieval complex at Llandegai, near Bangor, North Wales. *Archaeologia Cambrensis* 150, 17–142.

MacLaughlin, S.M. and Bruce, M.F. 1985. A simple univariate technique for determining sex from fragmentary femora: its application to a Scottish short cist population. *American Journal of Physical Anthropology* 67, 413–17.

Macphail, R.I. 1990. The soils. In A. Saville (ed.), *Hazleton North, Gloucestershire, 1979–82: the excavation of a Neolithic long cairn of the Cotswold-Severn group*, 223–6. London: English Heritage.

Makarewicz, C.A. and Sealy, J. 2015. Dietary reconstruction, mobility, and the analysis of ancient skeletal tissues: expanding the prospects of stable isotope research in archaeology. *Journal of Archaeological Science* 56, 146–58.

Manby, T.G. 1976. The excavation of the Kilham long barrow, East Riding of Yorkshire. *Proceedings of the Prehistoric Society* 42, 111–60.

Marshall, P., Hamilton, W.D., van der Plicht, J., Bronk Ramsey, C., Cook, G. and Goslar, T. 2009. Scientific dating. In M.G. Beamish, 'Island visits: Neolithic and Bronze Age activity on the Trent Valley floor. Excavations at Egginton and Willington, Derbyshire, 1998–1999'. *Derbyshire Archaeological Journal* 129, 62–81.

McClatchie, M., Bogaard, A., College, S., Whitehouse, N.J., Schulting, R.J., Barratt, P. and McLaughlin, T.R. 2014. Neolithic farming in north-western Europe: archaeobotanical evidence from Ireland. *Journal of Archaeological Science* 51, 206–15.

McClatchie, M., Bogaard, A., Colledge, S., Whitehouse, N., Schulting, R.J., Barratt, P. and McLaughlin, T.R. 2016. Farming and foraging in Neolithic Ireland: an archaeobotanical perspective. *Antiquity* 90, 302–18.

McFadyen, L. 2003. A revision of the materiality of architecture: the significance of Neolithic long mound and chambered monument building practice, with particular reference to the Cotswold-Severn Group. Unpublished PhD thesis, University of Wales College, Newport.

McFadyen, L. 2007. Making architecture. In D. Benson and A. Whittle (eds), *Building memories: the Neolithic Cotswold long barrow at Ascott-under-Wychwood, Oxfordshire*, 348–54. Oxford: Oxbow Books.

McFadyen, L., Benson, D. and Whittle, A. 2007. The pre-barrow contexts. In D. Benson and A. Whittle (eds), *Building memories: the Neolithic Cotswold long barrow at Ascott-under-Wychwood, Oxfordshire*, 23–54. Oxford: Oxbow Books.

McKinley, J. 2000. The analysis of cremated bone. In M. Cox and S. Mays (eds), *Human osteology in archaeology and forensic science*, 403–21. London: Greenwich Medical Media.

Meadows, J., Barclay, A. and Bayliss, A. 2007. A short passage of time: the dating of the Hazleton long cairn revisited. *Cambridge Archaeological Journal* 17.1, supplement, 45–64.

Megaw, J.V.S. 1984. The bone ?flute. In W.J. Britnell and H.N. Savory, *Gwernvale and Penywyrlod: two Neolithic long cairns in the Black Mountains of Brecknock*, 27–8. Cardiff: Cambrian Archaeological Association.

Mein, A. G. 1992. Excavations at Trostrey Castle, Usk, Gwent. *Archaeology in Wales* 32, 11–14.

Mein, A.G. 1994. Trostrey Castle, Trostrey. *Archaeology in Wales* 36, 48–50.

Mein, A.G. 1996. Trostrey Castle, Trostrey. *Archaeology in Wales* 36, 64–6.

Mein, A.G. 2002. Trostrey Castle, Trostrey. *Archaeology in Wales* 42, 107–10.

Mein, A.G. 2003. Neolithic mortuary ritual at Trostrey, Monmouthshire [and] Trostrey Castle, Trostrey. *Archaeology in Wales* 43, 65–9, 107–10.

Millard, A.R. 2004. Conventions for reporting radiocarbon determinations. *Radiocarbon* 56, 555.

Milner, N., Conneller, C. and Taylor, B. 2018. *Star Carr. Volume 2: studies in technology, subsistence and environment*. York: White Rose Universities Press.

Milner, N. and Craig, O. 2009. Mysteries of the middens: change and continuity across the Mesolithic-Neolithic transition. In M. Allen, N. Sharples and T. O'Connor (eds), *Land and people: papers in honour of John G. Evans*, 169–80. Oxford: Oxbow Books.

Moffett, L., Robinson, M.A. and Straker, V. 1989. Cereals, fruits and nuts: charred plant remains from Neolithic sites in England and Wales and the Neolithic economy. In A. Milles, D. Williams and N. Gardner (eds), *The beginnings of agriculture*, 243–61. Oxford: British Archaeological Reports.

Molleson, T. and Cox, M. 1993. *The Spitalfields Project. Volume 2: The anthropology – the middling sort*. York: CBA Research Report No. 86.

Monckton, A. 2001. Appendix 2. Assessment of charred plant remains from Hereford, Asda site 2001 (ASD.01). In D. Rouse, Causeway Farm, Hereford: a report of an archaeological evaluation. Archaeological Investigations Ltd. Unpublished report.

Monk, M.A. 1988. Appendix 3: archaeobotanical study of plant remains from pipeline sites. In M. Gowen (ed.), *Three Irish gas pipelines: new archaeological evidence in Munster*, 185–91. Dublin: Wordwell.

Monk, M.A. 2000. Seeds and soils of discontent: an environmental archaeological contribution to the nature of the Early Neolithic. In A. Desmond, G. Johnson, M. McCarthy, J. Sheehan and E. Shee Twohig (eds), *New agendas in Irish prehistory: papers in commemoration of Liz Anderson,* 67–8. Bray: Wordwell.

Montgomery, J. 2002. Lead and strontium isotope compositions of human dental tissues as an indicator of ancient exposure and population dynamics: the application of isotope source-tracing methods to identify migrants among British archaeological burials and a consideration of ante-mortem uptake, tissue stability and post-mortem diagenesis. Unpublished PhD thesis, University of Bradford.

Montgomery, J. 2010. Passports from the past: investigating human dispersals using strontium isotope analysis of tooth enamel. *Annals of Human Biology* 37, 325–46.

Montgomery, J., Grimes, V., Buckberry, J., Evans, J.A., Richards, M.P. and Barrett, J.H. 2014. Finding Vikings with isotope analysis: the view from wet and windy islands. *Journal of the North Atlantic* 7, 54–70.

Mook, W. G. 2005. *Introduction to isotope hydrology: stable and radioactive isotopes of hydrogen, carbon, and oxygen*. Leiden: Taylor & Francis.

Moore, P.D. 1978. Studies in vegetational history of mid-Wales. V. Stratigraphy and pollen analysis of Llyn Mire in the Wye Valley. *New Phytologist* 80, 281–302.

Morgan, F. de M. 1959. The excavation of a long barrow at Nutbane, Hants. *Proceedings of the Prehistoric Society* 25, 15–51.

Morris, I. 1991. The archaeology of ancestors: the Saxe-Goldstein hypothesis revisited. *Cambridge Archaeological Journal* 1, 147–69.

Mudd, A. and Joyce, S. 2014. *The archaeology of the South-West Reinforcement Gas Pipeline, Devon: investigations in 2005–2007*. Cirencester: Cotswold Archaeology.

Mukherjee, A.J., Copley, M.S., Berstan, R., Clark, K.A. and Evershed, R.P. 2005. Interpretation of $\delta^{13}C$ values of fatty acids in relation to animal husbandry, food processing and consumption in prehistory. In J. Mulville and A.K. Outram (eds), *The zooarchaeology of fats, oils, milk dairying – 9th ICAZ Conference*, 77–93. Oxford: Oxbow Books.

Müller, W., Fricke, F., Halliday, A.N., McCulloch, M.T. and Wartho, J.-A. 2003. Origin and migration of the Alpine Iceman. *Science* 302, 862–66.

Mulville, J. and Grigson, C. 2007. The animal bones. In D. Benson and A. Whittle (eds), *Building memories: the Neolithic Cotswold long barrow at Ascott-under-Wychwood, Oxfordshire*, 237–53. Oxford: Oxbow Books.

Mulville, J. and Outram, A.K. (eds) 2005. *The zooarchaeology of fats, oils, milk dairying – 9th ICAZ Conference*. Oxford: Oxbow Books.

Murphy, K. 1992. Plas Gogerddan, Dyfed: a multi-period burial and ritual site. *Archaeological Journal* 149, 1–38.

Murphy, K. 2003. Cwm Meudwy, Llandysul (SN 405 419). *Archaeology in Wales* 43, 92–4.

Murphy, K. and Evans, R. 2007. Excavation of Neolithic pits, three ring-ditches and a palisaded enclosure at Cwm Meudwy, Llandysul, Ceredigion, 2003. *Archaeologia Cambrensis* 155, 23–48.

Murphy, P.L. 2012. Charred plant remains and palaeoeconomy. In T.J. Wilkinson, P.L. Murphy, N. Brown and E.M. Heppell, *The archaeology of the Essex coast, Volume II: excavations at the prehistoric site of The Stumble*, 71–91. Chelmsford: East Anglian Archaeology Report 144.

Myers, A. 2007. The Upper Palaeolithic and Mesolithic archaeology of the West Midlands. In P. Garwood (ed.), *The undiscovered country: the earlier prehistory of the West Midlands*, 23–50. Oxford: Oxbow Books.

Nash, G.H. 1997. Monumentality and the landscape: the possible symbolic and political distribution of long chambered tombs around the Black Mountains, central Wales. In G.H. Nash (ed.), *Semiotics of landscape: archaeology of the mind*, 17–30. Oxford: British Archaeological Reports.

Neef, R., Capperes, R.T.J. and Bekker, R.M. 2012. *Digital atlas of economic plants in archaeology*. Eelde: Barkhuis Publishing. http://depa.eldoc.ub.rug.nl.

Négrel, P. and Pauwels, H. 2004. Interaction between different groundwaters in Brittany catchments (France): characterizing multiple sources through strontium and sulphur isotope tracing. *Water, Air, and Soil Pollution* 151, 261–85.

Nehlich, O. 2015. The application of sulphur isotope analyses in archaeological research: a review. *Earth-Science Reviews* 142, 1–17.

Nehlich, O., Borić, D., Stefanović, S. and Richards, M.P. 2010. Sulphur isotope evidence for freshwater fish consumption: a case study from the Danube Gorges, SE Europe. *Journal of Archaeological Science* 37, 1131–9.

Neil, S., Evans, J., Montgomery, J. and Scarre, C. 2016. Isotopic evidence for residential mobility of farming communities during the transition to agriculture in Britain. *Royal Society Open Science 3*(1), 150522.

Neil, S., Evans, J., Montgomery, J. and Scarre, C. 2018. Isotopic evidence for landscape use and the role of causewayed enclosures during the earlier Neolithic in southern Britain. *Proceedings of the Prehistoric Society* 84, 185–205.

Neil, S., Evans, J., Montgomery, J. and Scarre, C. 2020. Isotopic evidence for human movement into central England during the Early Neolithic. *European Journal of Archaeology* 2020, 1–18.

Neil, S., Montgomery, J., Evans, J., Cook, G.T. and Scarre, C. 2017. Land use and mobility during the Neolithic in Wales explored using isotope analysis of tooth enamel. *American Journal of Physical Anthropology* 164, 371–93.

Nielsen-Marsh, C., Gernaey, A., Turner-Walker, G., Hedges, R., Pike, A.W.G. and Collins, M. 2000.The chemical degradation of bone. In M. Cox and S. Mays (eds), *Human osteology in archaeology and forensic science*, 439–54. London: Greenwich Medical Media.

Noble, G. 2017. *Woodland in the Neolithic of northern Europe: the forest as ancestor*. Cambridge: Cambridge University Press.

Nowakowski, J.A. and Johns, C. 2015. *Bypassing Indian Queens. Archaeological excavations 1992–1994. Investigating prehistoric and Romano-British settlement and landscapes in Cornwall*. Truro: Cornwall Archaeological Unit.

O'Brien, C. 2016. Penywyrlod long cairn, Wales. Plant macrofossil and pollen assessment. Unpublished report, Archaeological Services Durham University Report 4024.

O'Connor, T. 1984. The human and animal bone remains. In W.J. Britnell and H.N. Savory, *Gwernvale and Penywyrlod: two Neolithic long cairns in the Black Mountains of Brecknock*, 153–4. Cardiff: Cambrian Archaeological Association.

Olalde, I., Brace, S., Morten E. Allentoft, M.E., Ian Armit, I., Kristiansen, K., Rohland, N., Mallick, S., Booth, T., Szécsényi-Nagy, A., Mittnik, A., Altena, E., Lipson, M., Lazaridis, I., Patterson, N., Broomandkhoshbacht, N., Diekmann, Y., Faltyskova, Z., Fernandes, D., Ferry, M., Harney, E., de Knijff, P., Michel, M., Oppenheimer, J., Stewardson, K., Barclay, A., Alt,

K.W., Avilés Fernández, A., Eszter Bánffy, E., Bernabò-Brea, M., Billoin, D., Blasco, C., Bonsall, C., Bonsall, L., Allen, T., Büster, L., Carver, S., Castells Navarro, L., Craig, O.E., Cook, G.T., Cunliffe, B., Denaire, A., Egging Dinwiddy, K., Dodwell, N., Ernée, M., Evans, C., Kuchařík, M., Farré, J.F., Fokkens, H., Fowler, C., Gazenbeek, M., Garrido Pena, R., Haber-Uriarte, M., Haduch, E., Hey, G., Jowett, N., Knowles, T., Massy, K., Pfrengle, S., Lefranc, P., Lemercier, O., Lefebvre, A., Maurandi, J.L., Majó, T., McKinley, J.I., McSweeney, K., Balázs Gusztáv, M., Modi, A., Kulcsár, G., Kiss, V., Czene, A., Patay, R., Endrődi, A., Köhler, K., Hajdu, T., Cardoso, J.L., Liesau, C., Parker Pearson, M., Włodarczak, P., Price, T.D., Prieto, P., Rey, P.-J., Ríos, P., Risch, R., Rojo Guerra, M.A., Schmitt, A., Serralongue, J., Silva, A.M., Smrčka, V., Vergnaud, L., Zilhão, J., Caramelli, D., Higham, T., Heyd, V., Sheridan, A., Sjögren, K.-G., Thomas, M.G., Stockhammer, P.W., Pinhasi, R., Krause, J., Haak, W., Barnes, I., Lalueza-Fox, C. and Reich, D. 2018. The Beaker phenomenon and the genomic transformation of northwest Europe. *Nature* 555, 190–6.

Olding, F. 2000. *The prehistoric landscapes of the eastern Black Mountains*. Oxford: Archaeopress.

O'Neil, H. 1966. Sale's Lot long barrow, Withington, Gloucestershire. *Transactions of the Bristol and Gloucestershire Archaeological Society* 85, 5–35.

Ó Nualláin, S. 1972. A Neolithic house at Ballyglass near Ballycastle, Co. Mayo. *Journal of the Royal Society of Antiquaries of Ireland* 102, 49–57.

Ó Nualláin, S. 1983. Irish portal tombs: topography, siting and distribution. *Journal of the Royal Society of Antiquaries of Ireland* 113, 75–105.

Ortner, D.J. 2003. *Identification of pathological conditions in human skeletal remains* (second edition). London: Academic Press.

Outram, A.K., Stear, N.A., Bendrey, R., Olsen, S., Kasparov, A., Zaibert, V., Thorpe, N. and Evershed, R.P. 2009. The earliest horse harnessing and milking. *Science* 323, 1332–5.

Overton, N., Ray, K. and Thomas, J. 2022. Structural and sequential complexity in causewayed enclosures: implications from Dorstone Hill, Herefordshire. In J. Last (ed.), *Marking place: new perspectives on Early Neolithic enclosures*, 43–60. Oxford: Oxbow Books.

Oxford Archaeology 2020. A585 Windy Harbour to Skippool Improvement Scheme, Lancashire, archaeological evaluation report. Unpublished report no. 2020/2099. Lancaster: Oxford Archaeology North.

Pailler, Y. and Sheridan, A. 2009. Everything you wanted to know about ... la néolithisation de la Grande-Bretagne et de l'Irelande. *Bulletin de la Société Préhistorique Française* 106, 25–56.

Page, N. 2001. A477 Sageston-Redberth bypass (SN 082 038). *Archaeology in Wales* 41, 124.

Page, N. 2002. A477(T) Sageston-Redberth bypass. Excavation of a Neolithic occupation site 2001. Unpublished client report. Llandeilo: Cambria Archaeological Trust.

Pardoe, H.S. 2019. The pollen and earliest environmental data. In A. Lane and M. Redknap, *Llangorse crannog*, 152–8. Oxford: Oxbow Books.

Parker Pearson, M. 1999. *The archaeology of death and burial.* Stroud: Sutton.

Parker Pearson, M., Pollard, J., Richards, C., Welham, K., Casswell, C., Schlee, D., Shaw, D., Simmons, E., Stanford, A., Bevins, R. and Ixer, I. 2019. Megalith quarries for Stonehenge's bluestones. *Antiquity* 93, 45–62.

Pelling, R. and Campbell, G. 2013. Plant resources. In M. Canti, G. Campbell and S. Greaney (eds), *Stonehenge World Heritage Site synthesis: prehistoric landscape, environment and economy*, 37–60. Swindon: English Heritage Research Department Report Series.

Pelling, R., Campbell, G., Carruthers, W., Hunter, K. and Marshall, P. 2015. Exploring contamination (intrusion and residuality) in the archaeobotanical record: case studies from central and southern England. *Vegetation History and Archaeobotany* 24, 85–99.

Peterson, R.G. 1999. The construction and use of categories of Neolithic pottery from Wales. Unpublished PhD thesis, University of Southampton.

Peterson, R.G. 2003. *Neolithic pottery from Wales: traditions of construction and use*. Oxford: Archaeopress.

Peterson, R. 2019. *Neolithic cave burials: agency, structure and environment.* Manchester: Manchester University Press.

Pettitt, P., Rockman, M. and Chenery, S. 2012. The British Final Magdalenian: society, settlement and raw material movements revealed through LA-ICP-MS trace element analysis of diagnostic artefacts. *Quaternary International* 272–273, 275–287.

Piggott, S. 1937. The long barrow in Brittany. *Antiquity* 11, 441–55.

Piggott, S. 1962. *The West Kennet long barrow: excavations 1955–56*. London: Her Majesty's Stationery Office.

Pioffet, H. 2015. Sociétés et identités du premier Néolithique de Grande-Bretagne et d'Irlande dans leur contexte ouest européen: caractérisation et analyses comparatives des productions céramiques entre Manche, Mer d'Irlande et Mer du Nord. PhD thesis: Durham University and Université de Rennes 1.

Pioffet, H. 2017. Societies and identities during the Early Neolithic of Britain and Ireland in their west European context: characterisation and comparative analyses of pottery production between Channel, Irish Sea and North Sea. *Past* 87, 5–7.

Plomp, E., von Holstein, I.C., Kootker, L.M., Verdegaal-Warmerdam, S.J., Forouzanfar, T. and Davies, G.R. 2020. Strontium, oxygen, and carbon isotope variation in modern human dental enamel. *American Journal of Physical Anthropology* 172, 586–604.

Pollard, J. 2017. Substantial and significant pits in the Mesolithic of Britain and adjacent regions. *Hunter Gatherer Research* 3, 165–84.

Powell, T.G.E. 1973. Excavation of the megalithic chambered cairn at Dyffryn Ardudwy, Merioneth, Wales. *Archaeologia* 104, 1–50.

Price, M.D.R. 1981. Palynological studies on the Black Mountains, south Wales. Unpublished PhD thesis, University of London.

Price, M.D.R. and Moore, P.D. 1984. Pollen dispersion in the hills of Wales: a pollen shed hypothesis. *Pollen et Spores* 26, 127–36.

Price, T.D., Frei, K.M. and Naumann, E. 2015. Isotopic baselines in the North Atlantic region. *Journal of the North Atlantic* 7, 103–36.

Price, T.D. and Naumann, E. 2015. The peopling of the North Atlantic: isotopic results from Norway. *Journal of the North Atlantic* 7, 88–102.

Purcell, A. 2002. Excavation of three Neolithic houses at Corbally, Kilcullen, Co. Kildare. *Journal of Irish Archaeology* 11, 31–75.

Rackham, J. 2020. Environment and economy: the evidence from plant remains recovered along the pipeline. In T. Darvill, D.A. David, S. Griffiths, J. Hart, H. James, K. Murphy, and J. Rackham, *Timeline: The archaeology of the South Wales Gas Pipeline*, 148–73. Cirencester: Cotswold Archaeology.

Radley, J. and Mellars, P. 1964. A Mesolithic structure at Deepcar, Yorkshire, England, and the affinities of its associated flint industries. *Proceedings of the Prehistoric Society* 30, 1–24.

Ray, K. 2016. *The archaeology of Herefordshire: an exploration*. Little Logaston: Logaston Press.

Ray, K. and Thomas, J. 2003. In the kinship of cows: the social centrality of cattle in the earlier Neolithic of southern Britain. In M. Parker Pearson (ed.), *Food, culture and identity in the Neolithic and Early Bronze Age*, 37–44. Oxford: British Archaeological Reports.

Ray, K. and Thomas, J. 2018. *Neolithic Britain: the transformation of social worlds*. Oxford: Oxford University Press.

Ray, K. and Thomas, J. 2020. Houses foundational: gathering histories at Dorstone Hill, Herefordshire. In A. Barclay, J. Leary and D. Field (eds), *Houses of the dead?*, 107–19. Oxford: Oxbow Books.

Ray, K., Thomas, J., Overton, N., Griffiths, S., Hoverd, T., Allen, M.J., Barclay, A., Birchenall, J., Challinor, D., French, C., Healey, E., Ixer, R., Roseveare, A., Roseveare, M., Garcia Rovira, I., Stanford, A. and Wiltshire, I. 2022. Dorstone Hill: a Neolithic timescape. Unpublished manuscript.

Reaney, D. 1968. Beaker burials in south Derbyshire. *Derbyshire Archaeological Journal,* 88, 67–81.

Rees, C. and Jones, M. 2015. Neolithic houses from Llanfaethlu, Anglesey. *PAST* 81, 1–3.

Rees, C. and Jones, M. 2016. Neolithic houses on Anglesey. *British Archaeology* 147 (March–April 2016), 46–51.

Rees, C. and Jones, M. 2017. Wales' earliest village? *Current Archaeology* 332, 18–26.

Rees, S. 2012. Excavations at Carreg Coetan Arthur chambered tomb, Pembrokeshire. *Archaeologia Cambrensis* 161, 51–163.

Reimer, P., Austin, W., Bard, E., Bayliss, A., Blackwell, P., Bronk Ramsey, C., Butzin, M., Cheng, H., Wdwards R., Friedrich, M., Grootes, P., Guilderson, T., Hajdas, I., Heaton, T., Hogg, A., Hughen, K., Kromer, B., Manning, S., Richards, D., Scott, M., Southon, J., Turney, C., Waker, L., Adolphi, F., Büntgen, U., Capano, M., Fahrni, S., Fogtmann-Schulz, A., Friedrich, R., Köhler, P., Kudsk, S., Miyake, F., Olsen, J., Reinig, F., Sakamoto, M., Sookdeo, A. and Talamo, S. 2020. The IntCal20 northern hemisphere radiocarbon age calibration curve (0–55 cal kBP). *Radiocarbon,* 1–33. doi:10.1017/RDC.2020.41.

Redknap, M. 2002. *Re-creations: visualizing our past*. Cardiff: National Museum Wales.

Renfrew, C. 1973. Monuments, mobilization and social organization in Neolithic Wessex. In C. Renfrew (ed.), *The explanation of culture change: models in prehistory*, 539–58. London: Duckworth.

Renfrew, C. 1976. Megaliths, territories and populations. In S.J. de Laet (ed.), *Acculturation and continuity in Atlantic Europe*, 198–220. Brugge: de Tempel.

Resnick, D. and Niwayama, G. 1988. *Diagnosis of bone and joint disorders* (second edition). Philadelphia, PA: W.B. Saunders.

Reynier, M. 2005. *Early Mesolithic Britain: origins, development and directions*. Oxford: Archaeopress.

Richards, C. 1992. Doorways to another world: the Orkney-Cromarty chambered tombs. In N. Sharples and A. Sheridan (eds), *Vessels for the ancestors: essays on the Neolithic of Britain and Ireland in honour of Audrey Henshall*, 62–76. Edinburgh: Edinburgh University Press.

Richards, M.P. 2020. Isotope analysis for diet studies. In M.P. Richards and K. Britton (eds), *Archaeological science: an introduction*, 125–43. Cambridge: Cambridge University Press.

Richards, M.P. and Hedges, R.E.M. 1999. Stable isotope evidence for similarities in the types of marine foods used by late Mesolithic humans at sites along the Atlantic coast of Europe. *Journal of Archaeological Science* 26, 717–22.

Richards, M.P. and Hedges, R.E.M. 2003. Variations in bone collagen $\delta^{13}C$ and $\delta^{15}N$ values of fauna from northwest Europe over the last 40,000 years. *Palaeogeography, Palaeoclimatology, Palaeoecology* 193, 261–7.

Richards, M.P., Schulting, R.J. and Hedges, R.E.M. 2003. Archaeology: sharp shift in diet at onset of Neolithic. *Nature* 425, 366.

Rieley, G. 1994. Derivatization of organic compounds prior to gas chromatographic–combustion–isotope ratio mass spectrometric analysis: identification of isotope fractionation processes. *Analyst* 119, 915–19.

Ritchie, A. 1983. Excavations of a Neolithic farmstead at Knap of Howar, Papa Westray, Orkney. *Proceedings of the Society of Antiquaries of Scotland* 113, 40–122.

Rivera, F. and Lahr, M. 2017. New evidence suggesting a dissociated etiology for cribra orbitalia and porotic hyperostosis. *American Journal of Physical Anthropology*. 164, 76–96.

Rivollat, M., Jeong, C., Schiffels, S., Küçükkalıpçı, İ, Pemonge, M.-H., Rohrlach, A.B., Alt, K.W., Binder, D., Friederich, S., Ghesquière, E., Gronenborn, D., Laporte, L., Lefranc, P., Meller, H., Réveillas, H., Rosenstock, E., Rottier, S., Scarre, C., Soler, L., Wahl, J., Krause, J., Deguilloux, M.-F., Haak, W. 2020. Ancient genome-wide DNA from France highlights the complexity of interactions between Mesolithic hunter-gatherers and Neolithic farmers. *Science Advances* 6, eaaz5344, 29 May 2020.

Rivollat, M., Thomas, A., Ghesquière, E., Rohrlach, A.B., Späth, E., Pemonge, M.-H., Haak, W., Chambon, P. and Deguilloux, M.-F. 2022. Ancient DNA gives new insights into a Norman Neolithic monumental cemetery dedicated to male elites. *Proceedings of the National Academy of Sciences*, 119 (18) e2120786119.

Roberts, C. and Manchester, K. 1997. *The archaeology of disease* (second edition). Stroud: Sutton Publishing.

Roberts, D. and Marshall, P. 2020. Pit digging and lifeways in Neolithic Wiltshire. *Wiltshire Archaeological and Natural History Society* 113, 16–34.

Roberts, S.B., Coward, W.A. and Ewing, G. 1988. Effect of weaning on accuracy of doubly labelled water method in infants. *American Journal of Physiology: Regulatory, Integrative and Comparative Physiology* 254, R622–R627.

Robinson, D.E. 2007. Exploitation of plant resources in the Mesolithic and Neolithic of southern Scandinavia: from gathering to harvesting. In S. Colledge and J. Conolly (eds), *The origins and spread of domestic plants in southwest Asia and Europe*, 359–74. California: Walnut Creek.

Robinson, G., Town, M., Ballin, T.B., Clarke, A., Dunne, J., Evershed, R.P., Gardiner, L.F., Gibson, A. and Russ, H. 2020. Furness's first farmers: evidence of early Neolithic settlement and dairying in Cumbria. *Proceedings of the Prehistoric Society* 86, 165–98.

Robinson, M. 2000. Further consideration of Neolithic charred cereals, fruits and nuts. In A.S. Fairbairn (ed.), *Plants in Neolithic Britain and beyond*, 85–90. Oxford: Oxbow Books.

Robinson, M. 2013. Charred plant remains from the early Neolithic midden deposit in Area 6. In T. Allen, A. Barclay, A.M. Cromarty, H. Anderson-Whymark, A. Parker, M. Robinson and G. Jones, *Opening the wood, making the land: the archaeology of a Middle Thames landscape. The Eton College rowing course project and the Maidenhead, Windsor and Eton flood alleviation scheme. Volume 1: Mesolithic to early Bronze Age*, 198–201. Oxford: Oxford Archaeology.

Roe, F. 2007a. Geology of stone used in construction. In D. Benson and A. Whittle (eds), *Building memories: the Neolithic Cotswold long barrow at Ascott-under-Wychwood, Oxfordshire*, 80–1. Oxford: Oxbow Books.

Roe, F. 2007b. The worked stone objects. In D. Benson and A. Whittle (eds), *Building memories: the Neolithic Cotswold long barrow at Ascott-under-Wychwood, Oxfordshire*, 315–18. Oxford: Oxbow Books.

Roese, H.E. 1978–79. Some unpublished objects from excavated Neolithic and Bronze Age sites in Breconshire. *Brycheiniog* 18, 31–46.

Roffet-Salque, M., Dunne, J., Altoft, D.T., Casanova, E., Cramp, L.J., Smyth, J., Whelton, H.L. and Evershed, R.P. 2017. From the inside out: upscaling organic residue analyses of archaeological ceramics. *Journal of Archaeological Science Reports* 16, 627–40.

Rogers, J. and Waldron, T. 2001. DISH and the monastic way of life. *International Journal of Osteoarchaeology* 11, 357–65.

Rösch, M., Kleinmann, A., Lechterbeck, J. and Wick, L. 2014. Botanical off-site and on-site data as indicators of different land use systems: a discussion with examples from southwest Germany. *Vegetation History and Archaeobotany* 23, 121–33.

Roseveare, M.J. and Lewis, D. 2015. Penywyrlod long cairn environs, Talgarth, Powys. Unpublished report, Archaeophysica PLC151.

Roseveare, M.J. and Roseveare, A.C.K. 2015. Penywyrlod long cairn, Powys. Geophysical survey report. Unpublished report, ArchaeoPhysica PLC141.

Rowley-Conwy, P. 2011. Westward Ho! The spread of agriculture from central Europe to the Atlantic. *Current Anthropology* 52, S431–51.

Rowley-Conwy, P., Gron, K.J., Bishop, R., Dunne, J., Evershed, R., Longford, C., Schulting, R. and Treasure, E. 2020. The earliest farming in Britain: towards a new synthesis. In K.J. Gron, L. Sørensen and P. Rowley-Conwy (eds), *Farmers at the frontier: a pan-European perspective on Neolithisation*, 401–24. Oxford: Oxbow Books.

Royal Commission on the Ancient and Historical Monuments of Wales 1997. *An inventory of the ancient monuments of Brecknock (Brycheiniog). The prehistoric and Roman monuments. Part 1. Late prehistoric monuments and unenclosed settlements to 1000 A.D.* Aberystwyth: RCAHWM.

Salque, M., Bogucki, P.I., Pyzel, J., Sobkowiak-Tabaka, I., Grygiel, R., Szmyt, M. and Evershed, R.P. 2013. Earliest evidence for cheese making in the sixth millennium BC in northern Europe. *Nature* 493, 522–5.

Sánchez-Quinto, F., Malmström, H., Fraser, M., Girdland-Flink, L., Svensson, E.M., Simões, L.G., George, R., Hollfelder, N., Burenhult, G., Noble, G., Brittong, K., Talamo, S., Curtis, N., Brzobohata, H., Sumberova, R., Götherström, A., Storå, J. and Jakobsson, M. 2019. Megalithic tombs in western and northern Neolithic Europe were linked to a kindred society. *Proceedings of the National Academy of Sciences* doi/10.1073/pnas.1818037116.

Saržinski, D. 2009. Forensic analysis of skeletal trauma and bilateral asymmetry in a Romano-British cemetery at Driffield Terrace, York. MSc Dissertation, University of Central Lancashire.

Sausins, D. 2013. South Wales gas pipeline project: site 238. Land south-west of Gelli-Wern-Isaf. Archaeological watching brief. Cotswold Archaeology Report 13218.

Saville, A. 1985. Review of Gwernvale and Penywyrlod: two Neolithic long cairns in the Black Mountains of Brecknock by W.J. Britnell and H.N. Savory. *Proceedings of the Prehistoric Society* 51, 342–44.

Saville, A. 1990. *Hazleton North, Gloucestershire, 1979–82: the excavation of a Neolithic long cairn of the Cotswold-Severn group*. London: English Heritage.

Savory, H.N. 1956. The excavation of the Pipton long cairn, Brecknockshire. *Archaeologia Cambrensis* 105, 7–48.

Savory, H.N. 1973. Pen-y-wyrlod: a new Welsh long cairn. *Antiquity* 47, 187–92.

Savory, H.N. 1977. The role of Iberian communal tombs in Mediterranean and Atlantic prehistory. In V. Markotić (ed.), *Atlantic Europe and the Mediterranean*, 161–80. Warminster: Aris and Phillips.

Savory, H. 1980a. The Neolithic in Wales. In J.A. Taylor (ed.), *Culture and environment in prehistoric Wales*, 207–32. Oxford: British Archaeological Reports.

Savory, H.N. 1980b. *Guide catalogue of the Bronze Age collections*. Cardiff: National Museum of Wales.

Savory, H.N. 1984. The Penywyrlod long cairn, Talgarth, Brecknock. In W.J. Britnell and H.N. Savory, *Gwernvale and Penywyrlod: two Neolithic long cairns in the Black Mountains of Brecknock*, 11–39. Cardiff: Cambrian Archaeological Association.

Sayle, K.L, Brodie, C.R., Cook, G.T. and Hamilton, W.D. 2019. Sequential measurement of $\delta^{15}N$, $\delta^{13}C$ and $\delta^{34}S$ values in archaeological bone collagen at the Scottish Universities Environmental Research Centre (SUERC): a new analytical frontier. *Rapid Communications in Mass Spectrometry* 33, 1258–66.

Scarre, C. 2011. *Landscapes of Neolithic Brittany*. Oxford: Oxford University Press.

Scarre, C. 2015. Parallel lives? Neolithic funerary monuments and the Channel divide. In H. Anderson-Whymark, D. Garrow and F. Sturt (eds), *Continental connections: exploring cross-Channel relationships from the Mesolithic to the Iron Age*, 78–98. Oxford: Oxbow Books.

Scarre, C. 2016. Dolmens without mounds in Britain, France and Ireland. In P. Eriksen and N. Andersen (eds), *Dolmens in Denmark: architecture and function*, 217–33. Aarhus: Aarhus University Press.

Scarre, C. 2018. Megalithic people, megalithic missionaries: the history of an idea. *Estudos Arqueológicos de Oeiras* 2018, 161–74.

Scarre, C., Laporte, L. and Joussaume, R. 2003. Long mounds and megalithic origins in western France: recent excavations at Prissé-la-Charrière. *Proceedings of the Prehistoric Society* 69, 235–51.

Scarre, C. and Oosterbeek, L. 2019. *Megalithic tombs in western Iberia: excavations at the Anta de Lajinha*. Oxford: Oxbow Books.

Scheirs, S., Malgosa, M., Sanchez-Molina, D., Ortega-Sanchez, M., Velazquez-Ameijde, J., Arregui-Dalmases, C., Medallo-Muniz, J. and Galtes, I. 2017. New insights in the analysis of blunt force trauma in human bones: preliminary results. *International Journal of Legal Medicine* 131, 867–76.

Scheuer, L. and Black, S. 2000. *Developmental juvenile osteology*. London: Academic Press.

Schmidl, A., Carrott, J. and Jacques, D. 2008. Appendix XIV: the biological remains. In J. Kenney, *Recent Excavations at Llandygai, near Bangor, north Wales. Volume III: appendices*, 122–82. Gwynedd Archaeological Trust Unpublished Report 764.

Schoch, W.H., Pawlik, B. and Schweingruber, F.H. 1988. *Botanical macro-remains*. Bern and Stuttgart: Paul Haupt.

Schoch, W., Heller, I., Schweingruber, F.H. and Kienst, F. 2004. *Wood anatomy of central European species*. Online version: www.woodanatomy.ch.

Schofield, D.I., Millar, I.L., Wilby, P.R. and Evans, J.A. 2010. A new, high-precision U/Pb date from the oldest known rocks in southern Britain. *Geological Magazine* 147, 145–50.

Schofield, D.I., Potter, J., Barr, S.M., Horák, J.M., Millar, I.L. and Longstaffe, F.J. 2016. Reappraising the Neoproterozoic 'East Avalonian' terranes of southern Great Britain. *Gondwana Research* 35, 257–71.

Schulting, R.J. 2014. The dating of Poulnabrone. In A. Lynch, *Poulnabrone: an early Neolithic portal tomb in Ireland*, 93–113. Dublin: Stationery Office.

Schulting, R.J. 2018. Dietary shifts at the Mesolithic–Neolithic transition in Europe: an overview of the stable isotope data. In J. Lee-Thorp and A. Katzenberg (eds), *The Oxford handbook of the archaeology of diet*. Oxford: Oxford University Press. doi: 10.1093/oxfordhb/9780199694013.013.35.

Schulting, R.J. 2020. Claddedigaethau mewn ogofâu: prehistoric human remains (mainly) from the caves of Wales, *Proceedings of the University of Bristol Spelaeological Society* 28, 185–219.

Schulting, R., Fibiger, L., Macphail, R., McLaughlin, R., Murray, E., Price, C., and Walker, E. 2013. Mesolithic and Neolithic human remains from Foxhole Cave, Gower, South Wales. *Antiquaries Journal* 93, 1–23.

Schulting, R.J. and Richards, M.P. 2002. Finding the coastal Mesolithic in southwest Britain: AMS dates and stable isotope results on human remains from Caldey Island, south Wales. *Antiquity* 76, 1011–25.

Schulting, R. and Wysocki, M. 2005. 'In this chamber tumulus were found cleft skulls ...': an assessment of the evidence for cranial trauma in the British Neolithic. *Proceedings of the Prehistoric Society* 71, 107–38.

Schulz Paulsson, B. 2017. *Time and stone: the emergence and development of megaliths and megalithic societies in Europe*. Oxford: Archaeopress.

Schweingruber, F.H. 1978. *Microscopic wood anatomy*. Birmensdorf: Swiss Federal Institute of Forestry Research.

Shennan, S. 2018. *The first farmers of Europe: an evolutionary perspective*. Cambridge: Cambridge University Press.

Sheridan, A. 2007. From Picardie to Pickering and Pencraig Hill? New information on the 'Carinated Bowl Neolithic' in northern Britain. In A. Whittle and V. Cummings (eds), *Going over: the Mesolithic-Neolithic transition in north-west Europe*, 441–92. Oxford: Oxford University Press for The British Academy.

Sheridan, A. 2010. The Neolithization of Britain and Ireland: the 'big picture'. In B. Finlayson and G. Warren (eds), *Landscapes in transition*, 89–105. Oxford: Oxbow Books.

Sheridan, A. 2011. The Early Neolithic of south-west England: new insights and new questions. In S. Pearce (ed.), *Recent archaeological work in south western Britain: papers in honour of Henrietta Quinnell*, 21–40. Oxford: Archaeopress.

Sheridan, J.A. 2016. Scottish Neolithic pottery in 2016: the big picture and some details of the narrative. In F.J. Hunter and J.A. Sheridan (eds), *Ancient lives: object, people and place in early Scotland. Essays for David V Clarke on his 70th birthday*, 189–212. Leiden: Sidestone Press.

Sheridan, A. 2021. A view from north of the border. In G. Hey and P. Frodsham (eds), *New light on the Neolithic of northern England*, 177–88. Oxford: Oxbow Books.

Sheridan, A. and Pailler, Y. 2012. Les haches alpines et leurs imitations en Grande Bretagne, Irlande et dans les Iles anglo-normandes. In P. Pétrequin, S. Cassen, M. Errera, L. Klassen, A. Sheridan and A.-M. Pétrequin (eds), *Jade. Grandes haches alpines du Néolithique européen. Ve et IVe millénaires av. J.-C.*, 1046–87. Besançon: Presses Universitaires de Franche-Comté; Gray: Centre de Recherche Archéologique de la Vallée de l'Ain.

Sheridan, A. and Schulting, R. 2020. Making sense of Scottish Neolithic funerary monuments: tracing trajectories and understanding their rationale. In A.B. Gebauer, L. Sørensen, A. Teather and A.C. Valera, *Monumentalising life in the Neolithic: narratives of change and continuity*, 195–215. Oxford: Oxbow Books.

Sheridan, A., Schulting, R., Quinnell, H. and Taylor, R. 2008. Revisiting a small passage tomb at Broadsands, Devon. *Proceedings of the Devon Archaeological Society* 66, 1–26.

Sheridan, A. and Whittle, A. forthcoming. aDNA and modelling the Mesolithic-Neolithic transition in Britain and Ireland. In A. Whittle, J. Pollard and S. Greaney (eds), *Ancient DNA and the Neolithic*. Oxford: Oxbow Books.

Simpson, D. 1996. The Ballygalley houses, Co. Antrim, Ireland. In T. Darvill and J. Thomas (eds), *Neolithic houses in northwest Europe and beyond*, 123–32. Oxford: Oxbow Books.

Slovak, N.M. and Paytan, A. 2011. Application of Sr isotopes in archaeology. In M. Baskaran (ed.), *Handbook of environmental isotope geochemistry*, 743–68. Berlin: Springer.

Smith, C.A. 1987. The excavation of the Trefignath burial chambers – 1977 to 1979. In C.A. Smith and F.M. Lynch, *Trefignath and*

Din Dryfol: the excavation of two megalithic tombs in Anglesey, 1–88. Cardiff: Cambrian Archaeological Association.

Smith, I.F. 1976. The pottery. In J.M. Coles and B.J. Orme, 'The Sweet Track: railway site'. *Somerset Levels Papers* 2, 63–4.

Smith, I.F. 1983. Pottery. In J.G. Evans and I.F. Smith, 'Excavations at Cherhill, north Wiltshire, 1967. *Proceedings of the Prehistoric Society* 49, 84–92.

Smith, I.F. and Darvill, T.C. 1990. The prehistoric pottery. In A. Saville, *Hazleton North, Gloucestershire, 1979–82: the excavation of a Neolithic long cairn of the Cotswold-Severn group*, 141–52. London: Historic Buildings and Monuments Commission for England.

Smith, M. and Brickley, M. 2006. The date and sequence of use of Neolithic funerary monuments: new AMS dating evidence from the Cotswold-Severn region. *Oxford Journal of Archaeology* 25, 335–55.

Smith, M.J., Brickley, M.B. and Leach, S.L. 2007. Experimental evidence for lithic projectile injuries: improving identification of an under-recognised phenomenon. *Journal of Archaeological Science* 34, 540–53.

Smyth, J. 2014. *Settlement in the Irish Neolithic: new discoveries at the edge of Europe*. Oxford: Oxbow Books.

Smyth, J. 2020. House of the living, house of the dead: an open and shut case from Ballyglass, Co. Mayo. In A. Barclay, J. Leary and D. Field (eds), *Houses of the dead?*, 145–57. Oxford: Oxbow Books.

Smyth, J. and Evershed, R.P. 2015. The molecules of meals: new insight into Neolithic foodways. *Proceedings of the Royal Irish Academy Section C* 115, 27–46.

Smyth, J. and Evershed, R.P. 2016. Milking the megafauna: using organic residue analysis to understand early farming practice. *Environmental Archaeology* 21, 214–29.

Smyth, J., McClatchie, M. and Warren, G. 2020. Exploring the 'somewhere' and 'someone' else: an integrated approach to Ireland's earliest farming practice. In K.J. Gron, L. Sørensen and P. Rowley-Conwy (eds), *Farmers at the frontier: a pan-European perspective on Neolithisation*, 425–41. Oxford: Oxbow Books.

Spangenberg, J.E., Jacomet, S. and Schibler, J. 2006. Chemical analyses of organic residues in archaeological pottery from Arbon Bleiche 3, Switzerland – evidence for dairying in the late Neolithic. *Journal of Archaeological Science* 33, 1–13.

Spencer, R. 2009. Stable isotope analysis of DISH and diet. In S. Baker, A. Gray, K. Lakin, R. Madgwick, K. Poole and M. Sandias (eds), *Food and drink in archaeology 2: University of Nottingham Postgraduate Conference 2008*, 90–9. Totnes: Prospect Books.

Stanton, Y.C. 1984. The Mesolithic period: early post-glacial hunter-gatherer communities in Glamorgan. In H.N. Savory (ed.), *Glamorgan County History Volume II: early Glamorgan*, 33–121. Cardiff: Glamorgan County History Trust Limited.

Stanford, S.C. 1982. Bromfield, Shropshire – Neolithic, Beaker and Bronze Age sites, 1966–70. *Proceedings of the Prehistoric Society* 48, 279–320.

Steele, D.G. and Bramblett, C.A. 1988. *The anatomy and biology of the human skeleton*. College Station: Texas A&M University Press.

Stern, B. 2012. Analysis of organic residues on the Neolithic pottery. In S. Rees, 'Excavations at Carreg Coetan Arthur chambered tomb, Pembrokeshire'. *Archaeologia Cambrensis* 161, 121–3.

Stevens, C. 2007. Reconsidering the evidence: towards an understanding of the social contexts of subsistence production in Neolithic Britain. In S. College and J. Conolly (eds), *The origins and spread of domestic plants in southwest Asia and Europe*, 375–90. Walnut Creek: Left Coast Press.

Stevens, C. and Fuller, D. 2012. Did farming fail? The case for a Bronze Age agricultural revolution in the British Isles. *Antiquity* 86, 707–22.

Stevens, C.J. and Fuller, D.Q. 2015. Alternative strategies to agriculture: the evidence for climatic shocks and cereal declines during the British Neolithic and Bronze Age (a reply to Bishop). *World Archaeology* 47, 856–75.

Stewart, T.D. 1979. *Essentials of forensic anthropology especially as developed in the United States*. Springfield, Ill.: Charles C. Thomas.

Straker, V. 1990. Carbonised plant macrofossils. In A. Saville, *Hazleton North, Gloucestershire, 1979–82: the excavation of a Neolithic long cairn of the Cotswold-Severn group*, 214–18. London: English Heritage.

Stroud, G. 1993. The human bones. In G. Stroud and R.L. Kemp, *The archaeology of York Vol. 12: the medieval cemeteries. Fasc. 2: cemeteries of the Church and Priory of St. Andrew, Fishergate*, 160–241. York: Council for British Archaeology.

Stuart-Macadam, P. 1987. Porotic hyperostosis: new evidence to support the anaemia theory. *American Journal of Physical Anthropology* 74, 521–6.

Stuiver, M. and Reimer, P. 1993. Extended ^{14}C data base and revised CALIB 3.0 ^{14}C age calibration program. *Radiocarbon* 35, 215–30.

Styring, A.K, Sealy, J.C. and Evershed, R.P. 2010. Resolving the bulk δ^{15}N values of ancient human and animal bone collagen via compound-specific nitrogen isotope analysis of constituent amino acids. *Geochimica et Cosmochimica Acta* 74, 241–51.

Suggett, R. 2005. *Houses and history in the March of Wales: Radnorshire 1400–1800*. Aberystwyth: Royal Commission on the Ancient and Historical Monuments of Wales.

Taylor, S.R. forthcoming. *Down the bright stream: the prehistory of Woodcock Corner and the Tregurra Valley*. Oxford: Archaeopress.

Tellier, G. 2018. *Neolithic and Bronze Age funerary and ritual practices in Wales, 3600–1200 BC*. Oxford: British Archaeological Reports.

TerraDat 2010. Geophysical survey report. Geophysical survey to characterise a long cairn. Unpublished report, TerraDat UK Ltd.

Thomas, A. 2014. Bioarchaeology of the middle Neolithic: evidence for archery among early European farmers. *American Journal of Physical Anthropology* 154, 279–90.

Thomas, G.S.P. and Humpage, A.J. 2007. The glacial morphology of the lower and middle Usk. In S.J. Carr, C.G. Coleman, A.J. Humpage and R.A. Shakesby (eds), *The Quaternary of the Brecon Beacons*, 161–73. London: Quaternary Research Association.

Thomas, J. 1986. Relations of power: the Neolithic of central south-west England. Unpublished PhD thesis, University of Sheffield.

Thomas, J. 1988. The social significance of Cotswold-Severn burial practices. *Man* 23, 540–59.

Thomas, J. 1999. *Understanding the Neolithic*. London: Routledge.

Thomas, J. 2013. *The birth of Neolithic Britain: an interpretive account*. Oxford: Oxford University Press.

Thomas, J. 2022. Neolithization and population replacement in Britain: an alternative view. *Cambridge Archaeological Journal* 32, doi:10.1017/S0959774321000639.

Thomas, R. and McFadyen, L. 2010. Animals and Cotswold-Severn long-barrows: a re-examination. *Proceedings of the Prehistoric Society* 76, 95–113.

Thompson, C.W. and Floyd, R.T. 1994. *Manual of structural kinesiology* (12th edition). St. Louis: Mosby-Yearbook Inc.

Thompson, E., Cummings, V. and Peterson, R. 2015. The biography of early Neolithic pottery assemblages from chambered tombs in western Scotland and eastern Ireland. In V. Cummings and G. Robinson, *The Southern Kintyre project: exploring interactions across the Irish Sea from the Mesolithic to the Bronze Age*, 113–37. Oxford: BAR Publishing.

Thompson, J.E. 2019. Tinkering with the dead: taphonomic analysis of human remains from Tinkinswood chambered tomb, Wales. *Archaeologia Cambrensis* 168, 35–57.

Tilley, C. 1994. *A phenomenology of landscape: places, paths and monuments*. Oxford: Berg.

Tilley, C. 1996. The power of the rocks: topography and monument construction on Bodmin Moor. *World Archaeology* 28, 161–76.

Timberlake, S. 1990. Review of the historical evidence for the use of firesetting. In P. Crew and S. Crew (eds), *Early mining in the British Isles*, 49–52. Porthmadog: Snowdonia Press.

Titmus, G.L. and Woods, J.C. 1986. An experimental study of projectile point fracture patterns. *Journal of California and Great Basin Anthropology* 8, 37–49.

Treasure, E.R., Gröcke, D.R., Caseldine, A.E. and Church, M.J. 2019. Neolithic farming and wild plant exploitation in western Britain: archaeobotanical and crop stable isotope evidence from Wales (*c*. 4000–2200 cal BC). *Proceedings of the Prehistoric Society* 85, 193–222.

Trickett, M.A., Budd, P., Montgomery, J. and Evans, J. 2003. An assessment of solubility profiling as a decontamination procedure for the $^{87}Sr/^{86}Sr$ analysis of archaeological human skeletal tissue. *Applied Geochemistry* 18, 653–58.

University of Manchester 2021. Archaeologists reveal origins of famous Stone Age monument, 10 August 2021, available at https://www.manchester.ac.uk/discover/news/archaeologists-reveal-origins-of-famous-stone-age-monument/, accessed 1 December 2021.

Villa, P. and Mahieu, E. 1991. Breakage patterns of human long bones. *Journal of Human Evolution* 21, 27–48.

Vondrovský, V. 2018. Let the sunshine in: the issue of Neolithic longhouse orientation. *European Journal of Archaeology* 21, 528–49.

Vulliamy, C.E. 1921. The excavation of a megalithic tomb in Breconshire. *Archaeologia Cambrensis* 76, 300–5.

Vulliamy, C.E. 1922. Excavation of a long barrow in Breconshire. *Man* 22, 150–2.

Vulliamy, C.E. 1923. Further excavations in the long barrows at Ffostill. *Archaeologia Cambrensis* 78, 320–4.

Vulliamy, C.E. 1929. Excavation of an unrecorded long barrow in Wales. *Man* 29, 34–6.

Vyner, B.E. 1984. The excavation of a Neolithic cairn at Street House, Loftus, Cleveland. *Proceedings of the Prehistoric Society* 50, 151–96.

Vyner, B. and Wall, I. (eds) 2011. A Neolithic cairn at Whitwell, Derbyshire. *Derbyshire Archaeological Journal* 131, 1–131.

Wainwright, G.J. 1963. A reinterpretation of the microlithic industries of Wales. *Proceedings of the Prehistoric Society* 29, 99–132.

Wainwright, G.J. 1967. *Coygan Camp: a prehistoric, Romano-British and Dark Age settlement in Carmarthenshire*. Cardiff: Cambrian Archaeological Association.

Walker, E.A. 2004. The Mesolithic period: the final hunter-gatherer-fishers of south eastern Wales. In M. Aldhouse-Green and R. Howell (eds), *The Gwent County History Volume I*, 29–55. Cardiff: University of Wales Press.

Walker, E.A. 2015. Scratching the surface: new Late Glacial lithic artefacts from south-east Wales. In N. Ashton and C. Harris (eds), *No stone unturned: papers in honour of Roger Jacobi*, 113–25. London: Lithic Studies Society.

Walker, E.A. 2016. The Palaeolithic and Mesolithic periods in Pembrokeshire. In H. James, M. John, K. Murphy and G. Wainwright (eds), *The Pembrokeshire County History Volume I: Prehistoric, Roman and Early Medieval Pembrokeshire*, 1–54. Haverfordwest: The Pembrokeshire County History Trust.

Walker, E.A. 2019. The prehistoric lithic artefacts. In A. Lane and M. Redknap, *Llangorse crannog: the excavation of an early medieval royal site in the kingdom of Brycheiniog*, 194–204. Oxford: Oxbow Books.

Walker, E.A. and Davis, O. 2021. Burry Holms, Gower, Wales, UK: the prehistory of an island. *Archaeological Journal*. doi: 10.1080/00665983.2021.1936754.

Walker, M.J.C. 1982. Early and mid-Flandrian environmental history of the Brecon Beacons, S. Wales. *New Phytologist* 91, 147–65.

Walker, M.J.C., Buckley, S. and Caseldine, A.E. 2001. Landscape change and human impact in west Wales during the Late glacial and Flandrian. In M.J.C. Walker and D. McCarroll (eds), *The Quaternary of west Wales: field guide*, 17–29. London: Quaternary Research Association.

Walker, M.J.C., Griffiths, H.I., Ringwood, V. and Evans, J.G. 1993. An early Holocene pollen, mollusc and ostracod sequence from lake marl at Llangorse Lake, south Wales. *The Holocene* 3, 138–49.

Walker, P.L, Bathurst, R.R, Richman, R., Gjerdrum, T. and Andrushko, V.A. 2009. The causes of porotic hyperostosis and cribra orbitalia: a reappraisal of the iron-deficiency-anemia hypothesis. *American Journal of Physical Anthropology* 139, 109–25.

Ward, G. and Wilson, S. 1978. Procedures for comparing and combining radiocarbon age determinations: a critique. *Archaeometry* 20, 19–31.

Ward, J. 1915. The St Nicholas chambered tumulus, Glamorgan. *Archaeologia Cambrensis* 15, 253–320.

Ward, J. 1916. The St. Nicholas chambered tumulus, Glamorgan. *Archaeologia Cambrensis* 16, 239–67.

Warham, J.O. 2011. Mapping biosphere strontium isotope ratios across major lithological boundaries. A systematic investigation of the major influences on geographic variation in the $^{87}Sr/^{86}Sr$ composition of bioavailable strontium above the Cretaceous and

Jurassic rocks of England. Unpublished PhD thesis. University of Bradford.

Warren, G., Davis, S., McClatchie, M. and Sands, R. 2014. The potential role of humans in structuring the wooded landscape of Mesolithic Ireland: a review of data and discussion of approaches. *Vegetation History and Archaeobotany* 23, 629–46.

Waterbolk, H. 1971. Working with radiocarbon dates. *Proceedings of the Prehistoric Society* 37(2), 15–33.

West, C.M. 1956. Report on bones from Pipton long cairn. In H.N. Savory, 'The excavation of the Pipton long cairn, Brecknockshire'. *Archaeologia Cambrensis* 105, 47.

White, R.B. 1978. Excavations at Trwyn Du, Anglesey, 1974. *Archaeologia Cambrensis*, 127, 16–39.

White, T.D. 1991. *Human osteology*. London: Academic Press.

Whitley, J. 2002. Too many ancestors. *Antiquity* 76, 119–26.

Whittle, A. 1988. *Problems in Neolithic archaeology*. Cambridge: Cambridge University Press.

Whittle, A. 1991. Wayland's Smithy, Oxfordshire: excavations at the Neolithic tomb in 1962–63 by R.J.C. Atkinson and S. Piggott. *Proceedings of the Prehistoric Society* 57, 61–101.

Whittle, A. 1993. The Neolithic of the Avebury area: sequence, environment, settlement and monuments. *Oxford Journal of Archaeology* 12, 29–53.

Whittle, A. 1994. Excavations at Millbarrow Neolithic chambered tomb, Winterbourne Monkton, North Wiltshire. *Wiltshire Archaeological and Natural History Magazine* 87, 1–53.

Whittle, A. 2003. *The archaeology of people: dimensions of Neolithic life*. London: Routledge.

Whittle, A. 2004. Stones that float to the sky: portal dolmens and their landscapes of memory and myth. In V. Cummings and C. Fowler (eds), *The Neolithic of the Irish Sea: materiality and traditions of practice*, 81–90. Oxford: Oxbow Books.

Whittle, A. 2007a. Uses and continuity of place: Mesolithic into Neolithic. In D. Benson and A. Whittle (eds), *Building memories: the Neolithic Cotswold long barrow at Ascott-under-Wychwood, Oxfordshire*, 344–48. Oxford: Oxbow Books.

Whittle, A. 2007b. The temporality of transformation: dating the early development of the southern British Neolithic. In A. Whittle and V. Cummings (eds), *Going over: the Mesolithic-Neolithic transition in north-west Europe*, 377–98. Oxford: Oxford University Press for the British Academy.

Whittle, A. 2011. Grand narratives and shorter stories. In A. Hadjikoumis, E. Robinson and S. Viner (eds), *The dynamics of Neolithisation in Europe: studies in honour of Andrew Sherratt*, 10–24. Oxford: Oxbow Books.

Whittle, A. 2019. The long and short of it: memory and practice in the Early Neolithic of Britain and Ireland. In A. Barclay, D. Field and J. Leary (eds), *Houses of the dead?*, 79–90. Oxford: Oxbow Books.

Whittle, A., Barclay, A., Bayliss, A., McFadyen, L., Schulting, R. and Wysocki, M. 2007. Building for the dead: events, processes and changing worldviews from the thirty-eighth to the thirty-fourth centuries cal. BC in southern Britain. *Cambridge Archaeological Journal* 17.1, supplement, 123–47.

Whittle, A., Bayliss, A. and Healy, F. 2022. A decade on: revised timings for causewayed enclosures in southern Britain. In J. Last (ed.), *Marking place: new perspectives on Early Neolithic enclosures*, 203–22. Oxford: Oxbow Books.

Whittle, A., Galer, D. and Benson, D. 2007. The layout, composition and sequence of the human bone deposits. In D. Benson and A. Whittle (eds), *Building memories: the Neolithic Cotswold long barrow at Ascott-under-Wychwood*, 137–88. *Oxfordshire*. Oxford: Oxbow Books.

Whittle, A., Bayliss, A. and Wysocki, M. 2007. Once in a lifetime: the date of the Wayland's Smithy long barrow. *Cambridge Archaeological Journal* 17.1, supplement, 103–21.

Whittle, A., Healy, F. and Bayliss, A. 2011. *Gathering time: dating the Early Neolithic enclosures of southern Britain and Ireland*. Oxford: Oxbow Books.

Whittle, A., Marshall, P., Bayliss, A. and Healy, F. in press. Time re-gathered: a fresh look at the development of causewayed enclosures in southern Britain. In P. Lefranc (ed.), *Le phénomène des enceintes dans le Néolithique du nord-ouest de l'Europe. Actes du 33e colloque interrégional sur le Néolithique, Saint-Dié-des-Vosges, 8–9 novembre 2019, Supplément à la Revue Archéologique de l'Est*.

Whittle, A., Pollard, J., and Grigson, C. 1999. *The harmony of symbols: the Windmill Hill causewayed enclosure, Wiltshire*. Oxford: Oxbow Books.

Whittle, A. and Wysocki, M. 1998. Parc le Breos Cwm transepted long cairn, Gower, west Glamorgan: date, contents and context. *Proceedings of the Prehistoric Society* 64, 139–82.

Wieberg, D.A.M. and Wescot, D.J. 2008. Estimating the time of long bone fractures: correlation between postmortem interval, bone moisture content and blunt force trauma fracture characteristics. *Journal of Forensic Sciences* 53, 1028–34.

Wilkinson, C. 2010. Facial reconstruction – anatomical art or artistic anatomy? *Journal of Anatomy* 216, 235–50.

Williams, A. 1953. Clegyr Boia, St. David's (Pemb.): excavation in 1943. *Archaeologia Cambrensis* 102, 20–47.

Williams, D. 1999. Plant macrofossils. In S.J. White and G. Smith, 'A funerary and ceremonial centre at Capel Eithin, Gaerwen, Anglesey: excavations of Neolithic, Bronze Age, Roman and early medieval features in 1980 and 1981'. *Transactions of the Anglesey Antiquarian Society* 1999, 109–12.

Williams, G.J. 1968. Contributions to the Pleistocene geomorphology of the middle and lower Usk. Unpublished PhD thesis, University of Wales.

Willis, C.C. 2019. *Stonehenge and Middle to Late Neolithic cremation rites in mainland Britain (c.3500–2500 BC)*. PhD thesis, Institute of Archaeology, University College London. https://discovery.ucl.ac.uk/id/eprint/10094088/.

Willis, C. 2021. *Stonehenge and Middle to Late Neolithic cremation rites in mainland Britain (c. 3500–2500 BC)*. Oxford: BAR Publishing.

Willmes, M., Bataille, C.P., James, H.F., Moffat, I., McMorrow, L., Kinsley, L., Armstrong, R.A., Eggins, S. and Grün, R. 2018. Mapping of bioavailable strontium isotope ratios in France for archaeological provenance studies. *Applied Geochemistry* 90, 75–86.

Witts, G.B. 1880–81. Description of the long barrow called 'West Tump', in the parish of Brimsfield, Gloucestershire. *Transactions of the Bristol and Gloucestershire Archaeological Society* 5, 201–11.

Woodman, P., Anderson, E. and Finlay, N. 1999. *Excavations at Ferriter's Cove, 1983–95: last foragers, first farmers on the Dingle Peninsula*. Bray: Wordwell.

Woodward, P.J. 1991. *The South Dorset Ridgeway: survey and excavations 1977–84*. Dorchester: Dorset Natural History and Archaeological Society.

Worssam, B. 1990. Geological aspects of the excavation. In A. Saville, *Hazleton North: the excavation of a Neolithic long cairn of the Cotswold-Severn group,* 228–31. London: English Heritage.

Wright, L.E. and Schwarcz, H.P. 1998. Stable carbon and oxygen isotopes in human tooth enamel: identifying breastfeeding and weaning in prehistory. *American Journal of Physical Anthropology* 106, 1–18.

Wyatt, S. 2009. Soul music: instruments in an animistic age. In S. Banfield (ed.), *The sounds of Stonehenge*, 11–16. Oxford: Archaeopress.

Wysocki, M. 1998. Penywyrlod, Talgarth. Unpublished osteological report.

Wysocki, M., Bayliss, A. and Whittle, A. 2007. Serious mortality: the date of the Fussell's Lodge long barrow. *Cambridge Archaeological Journal* 17.1, supplement, 65–84.

Wysocki, M., Griffiths, S., Hedges, R., Bayliss, A., Higham, T., Fernandez-Jalvo, Y. and Whittle, A. 2013. Dates, diet, and dismemberment: evidence from the Coldrum megalithic monument, Kent. *Proceedings of the Prehistoric Society* 79, 61–90.

Wysocki, M., Walker, E.A., Jacobi, R. and Whittle, A. in press. Skeletal remains from Parc le Breos Cwm and Cat Hole Cave: a case of mistaken identity. *Archaeologia Cambrensis* 171 (2022), 21–8.

Wysocki, M. and Whittle, A. 2000. Diversity, lifestyles and rites: new biological and archaeological evidence from British earlier Neolithic mortuary assemblages. *Antiquity* 74, 591–601.

Zienkiewicz, L. 1998. Pottery. In A. Whittle and M. Wysocki, 'Parc le Breos Cwm transepted long cairn, Gower, west Glamorgan: date, contents and context'. *Proceedings of the Prehistoric Society* 64, 168–70.

Zuckerman, M.K., Garofalo, E.M., Frohlich, B. and Ortner, D.J. 2014. Anemia or scurvy: a pilot study on differential diagnosis of porous and hyperostotic lesions using differential vault thickness in subadult humans. *International Journal of Paleopathology* 5, 27–33.

Zvelebil, M. 1994. Plant use in the Mesolithic and its role in the transition to farming. *Proceedings of the Prehistoric Society* 60, 35–74.